HERITAGE
AND
HOOP SKIRTS

HERITAGE AND HOOP SKIRTS

How Natchez Created the Old South

PAUL HARDIN KAPP

University Press of Mississippi / Jackson

Publication of this work was supported in part by the Campus Research Board of the University of Illinois at Urbana-Champaign.

The University Press of Mississippi is the scholarly publishing agency of the Mississippi Institutions of Higher Learning: Alcorn State University, Delta State University, Jackson State University, Mississippi State University, Mississippi University for Women, Mississippi Valley State University, University of Mississippi, and University of Southern Mississippi.

www.upress.state.ms.us

The University Press of Mississippi is a member of the Association of University Presses.

Copyright © 2022 by University Press of Mississippi
All rights reserved
Manufactured in the United States of America

First printing 2022

∞

Library of Congress Cataloging-in-Publication Data

Names: Kapp, Paul Hardin, author.
Title: Heritage and hoop skirts : how Natchez created the Old South / Paul Hardin Kapp.
Description: Jackson : University Press of Mississippi, [2022] | Includes bibliographical references and index.
Identifiers: LCCN 2022014500 (print) | LCCN 2022014501 (ebook) | ISBN 9781496838780 (hardback) | ISBN 9781496838797 (epub) | ISBN 9781496838803 (epub) | ISBN 9781496838810 (pdf) | ISBN 9781496838827 (pdf)
Subjects: LCSH: Natchez Garden Club. | Pilgrimage Garden Club of Natchez. | Heritage tourism—Mississippi—Natchez. | Historic preservation—Mississippi—Natchez. | Architecture, Domestic—Mississippi—Natchez. | Natchez (Miss.)—History. | Natchez (Miss.)—Social life and customs. | Natchez (Miss.)—Description and travel. | Natchez (Miss.)—Buildings, structures, etc.
Classification: LCC F349.N2 K37 2022 (print) | LCC F349.N2 (ebook) | DDC 976.2/26—dc23/eng/20220414
LC record available at https://lccn.loc.gov/2022014500
LC ebook record available at https://lccn.loc.gov/2022014501

British Library Cataloging-in-Publication Data available

CONTENTS

Introduction ~ 3

Chapter 1 ~ 25
A PLACE CALLED NATCHEZ

Chapter 2 ~ 63
THE EVOLVING NARRATIVE

Chapter 3 ~ 135
THE MAKING OF THE PILGRIMAGE AND
THE INVENTION OF CONNELLY'S TAVERN

Chapter 4 ~ 201
DISTRICT 17

Chapter 5 ~ 285
CREATING THE NATCHEZ TRACE PARKWAY

Chapter 6 ~ 341
FEUDING AND BRANDING

Chapter 7 ~ 393
AFTERMATH

Author's Note and Acknowledgments ~ 429
Appendix: Biographical Notes ~ 433
Notes ~ 439
Selected Bibliography ~ 487
Index ~ 503

HERITAGE AND HOOP SKIRTS

Figure 0.1: Postcard depicting southern belles at D'Evereux during the Natchez Spring Pilgrimage of Antebellum Homes in 1952, Natchez, Mississippi. (Courtesy of the Archives and Records Services Division, Mississippi Department of Archives and History)

INTRODUCTION

> Gone with the Wind—the golden age of Natchez when mansions bloomed like cotton bolls in a sunny field. But the vanished era lives again as costumed belles conduct tours of some 30 houses for the spring Natchez Pilgrimage, retelling old legends in accents soft as a southern breeze. Union cavalry clattered into the checkerboard foyer of Monteigne; at iron-gated Dunlieth [sic], a ghost walks at dusk. Palatial Stanton Hall, built as "an ornament to the town" in 1857, cost the owner only $82,362.23. The original French mirror reflect [sic] the spacious ballroom.[1]

Today, the passage above seems as much a *Gone with the Wind* period piece as the scene it describes: mansions blooming like cotton bolls; costumed belles with soft, southern-breeze accents retelling stories of some gallant gentlepeople. We might assume it is from a travel magazine or a vacation brochure, probably published in the early twentieth century. This is not the case. It is a caption from the National Geographic Society's *Visiting Our Past: America's Historylands*, published in 1977, whose lead editor, Daniel J. Boorstin, was an award-winning American historian and the twelfth librarian of Congress. In this lavish book, given pride of place on coffee tables across America, the history lesson about Natchez, Mississippi, begins with the struggle for the conquest of North America, when "many flags had flown" over Natchez. Founded by the French, Natchez "grew up" Anglo-Saxon, but the town also strongly identified with other ethnic and cultural traditions, from the open, exotic bazaars in "creole-fashion" to the stuccoed houses with iron balconies that line the streets laid out by the Spanish in the eighteenth century. *Visiting Our Past*'s readers are invited to imagine how, in the colonial days, Natchez was a cosmopolitan place; its early residences—Hope Farm, Airlie, Linden—"knew the tread of Spanish boots."

Below the bluffs, where the grand mansions presided, was the river port, known as "Natchez Under-the-Hill." Readers learn that here were the roughened and rowdy denizens of the American underbelly: "Below the bluffs, the river men, gamblers, prostitutes, and the rude backwoodsmen who traveled the Natchez Trace frolicked in the taverns and brothels."[2] During its heyday, this was the "worst hell-hole on earth," but the editors reassuringly inform us that nothing remained of it in 1977 except a single saloon and a few boarded-up shacks.

But up on the town's tranquil heights, civility and grace were the order of the bygone days of Natchez. The book recounts how ambitious northern men came here, got rich on cotton, and built opulent mansions. So many stately homes were built that one Chicago newspaper writer exclaimed in an article, "Stop multiplying the abortive temples with which the land groans!"[3] King's Tavern and Connelly's Tavern vied for affluent people's dollars. Boarding at Connelly's Tavern, where Aaron Burr conspired to build for himself a western empire out of Texas and Mexico, you were expected to obey the rules: "No more than five to sleep in one bed and organ grinders to sleep in the Wash House."[4] The quirky, wood-framed house, set from the steep grade of Ellicott's Hill—where George Washington's handpicked emissary, Andrew Ellicott, defiantly hoisted the American flag in front of Spanish Fort Rosalie—winched up its wooden drawbridges every night and was the terminus of the fabled Natchez Trace.

Natchez, Mississippi: a town "swarmed with millionaires," a place of the chivalric gentry, who enjoyed their mint juleps in urbane lavishness and their backs facing away from their working plantations where enslaved African Americans toiled and died raising cotton; a town whose halcyon days ended in 1863, when the Civil War abruptly came to its outskirts and its mayor valiantly surrendered it to the Union Army. This is what we are led to believe in *Visiting Our Past* as the chapter on Natchez, one of America's "historylands," draws to a conclusion.

It is, by and large, untrue.

Nineteenth-century Natchez was not only "swarmed with millionaires"; there were also tradespeople and professionals who lived in the city. Free Black people and middle-class white storekeepers, lawyers, doctors, and artisans (who were both Black and white) lived there as well, and all within its compact, gridiron town design. And while there are a significant number of white-columned mansions, one can hardly say it is overwhelmed by "the abortive temples with which the land groans."

In 1974, three years before *Visiting Our Past: America's Historylands* was published, an independent researcher determined that the late eighteenth-century Connelly's Tavern was never a tavern at all, merely a residence that may have been built in 1798. It was never owned by Patrick Connelly, although he did own an inn on Jefferson Street near the structure.[5] A simple property deed search, not an extensive architectural or archaeological analysis, debunked its venerated history. Frontiersmen did not sleep five to a bed on its lower level, and organ grinders did not sleep in its washhouse, which never existed. And Aaron Burr did not

Figure 0.2: Postcard depicting Connelly's Tavern, 1937. (Roane Fleming Byrnes Collection [MUM00057], Department of Archives and Special Collections, J. D. Williams Library, The University of Mississippi)

commit treason in it. "Certainly, it is a shock to find this error, and it's hard to stop thinking of our headquarters as 'Connelly's Tavern,'" replied Margaret Moss, at the time the immediate past president of the Natchez Garden Club that still owns the building.[6] She stated elsewhere: "The truth, however, is always more fascinating than fiction and we believe that a very positive step in the right direction has been taken by our club in tracking down the actual facts and correcting the misconceptions.... Our club has always tried to be open and above-board. I hope we will never fail to accept the challenge of new discoveries which have been carefully researched."[7]

Other members, like Mrs. Rawdon Blankenstein, understood that heritage tourism had become based more on history than heritage. She noted, "The American tourist is better informed about history and historic preservation than ever before. He wants facts, not fairy tales. Now known as 'the House on Ellicott's Hill,' the Natchez Garden Club presents it as a late eighteenth century building to tourists still fascinated by historic places" (figure 0.2).[8]

Were all these stories about Natchez intentionally misleading? Yes and no. Anyone seeking a disinterested, discerning, and authoritative knowledge of past places, people, and events, *the crucial underpinning of the field of history*, will not find it in the presentation of Natchez. Its heritage, developed during the 1930s in the depths of the Great Depression by middle-class women of Natchez, popular writers, and professional architects and landscape architects, is how we commonly understand this "historyland," and it was the motivating force that preserved it throughout the twentieth century. Heritage theorist David Lowenthal distinguishes history and heritage in saying, "History explores and explains the past grown ever more opaque over time; heritage clarifies pasts so as to infuse them with present purposes"; so these clarifications provide individuals and groups a sense of identity.[9] In Natchez during the 1930s, heritage was put to specific purposes: to develop a sense of identity and to use that identity to make money.

As a historic preservationist, I work at the intersection of heritage and history, story and place. Indeed, these elements of past and present are always entangled; perhaps nowhere is this more evident than in Natchez, Mississippi, a place long synonymous with the romanticized and mythic "Old South." In 1934, Natchez even adopted the motto "Where the Old South Still Lives."[10] Its architecture made Natchez a cultural tourism destination. But what we associate with the built patrimony of the city dates not to the antebellum era but to the New Deal programs that were capitalized on by its enterprising residents. We know from history that Natchez was at one time a wealthy town, famed for the gracious homes of elite cotton planters. But its story did not end with the outbreak of the Civil War. For the fifty years following the Civil War, many of the historic Natchez homes had fallen into disrepair.

And yet, a mere five years later, Natchez was established as a tourist destination, known for its grand Greek Revival architecture and its annual cultural and social event, the Natchez Spring Pilgrimage of Antebellum Homes. It was the women of the Natchez Garden Club (NGC) who so remarkably transformed the economic fortunes of this city through their enterprising and creative work within their primary social organization, the NGC, and later in rivalry and then in conjunction with the Pilgrimage Garden Club (figure 0.3). A profitable industry emerged in this small city, one without smokestacks or cotton factories—an industry we know today as cultural tourism. But the transformation of the nineteenth-century mansions of Natchez into its romanticized and highly marketable patrimony in the 1930s came at a social, economic, and racial cost. Not only is Natchez paradigmatic of the "Old South," but the story of its transformation is archetypical of that idea's complexity and controversial long-term consequences. As is the case with the other "historylands" featured in the National Geographic book, Natchez is a place where architecture and scenery are embedded with narratives that are loosely grounded in history, steeped in lore, and activated by

Figure 0.3: Two women walking down Main Street of Natchez, Mississippi, 1938, Ben Shahn, Photographer. (Library of Congress, Prints & Photographs Division, Farm Security Administration/Office of War Information Photograph Collection, LC-DIG-fsa-8a16478)

tradition. The narrative became the city's heritage, which motivated its townspeople to preserve and renovate it and then profit from it by making it a cultural tourism destination during the twentieth century. For nearly the last thirty years, Natchez has been downplaying the glorification of its southern heritage while also acknowledging the unsavory aspects of that heritage. Since its founding in 1979, the Historic Natchez Foundation has focused on African American history and continues to do so. The two garden clubs are now racially integrated, and the clubs integrate African American experiences into their interpretations.

As a concept, "historyland" is uncannily like Disneyland. Invented by the Swedish ethnographer Artur Hazelius at Skansen, near Stockholm, in 1891, the open-air museum, or living museum concept, was conceived to preserve folk life against modernity and reinforce national identity through the displaying of relics: buildings, landscapes, tools, and implements. At these large museum complexes, national customs were perpetuated through educational demonstrations, and the museum complex conveyed an earlier lifestyle.[11] As is the case at Disneyland and Disney World, fantastical or nostalgic buildings are erected or restored for the

TYPE OF OLD AMERICAN TOWN HALL, DEARBORN, MICH.

Figure 0.4: The Old American Town Hall, Greenfield Village, Dearborn, Michigan, 1935. (Library of Congress, Prints & Photographs Division, LC-DIG-det-4a27695)

Figure 0.5: View of Prentis Store, 214 Duke of Gloucester Street after its restoration, Williamsburg, Virginia, circa 1938. (Library of Congress, Prints & Photographs Division, Historic American Buildings Survey, HABS VA,48-WIL,48-)

sole purpose of entertainment. In the US during the early twentieth century, when both nationalism and industrialism ran rampant, the open-air museum became the living history museum. These constructs were a means to familiarize Americans with their national heritage, but above all, visiting these historical attractions was intended to be entertaining and relaxing. Often, visiting them, even if only briefly, was a means of escape from an otherwise oppressive industrial world. Experiencing "historyland" was considered an indulgence, which was enjoyed by the family, perhaps as the highlight of the annual vacation or as a weekend getaway. Until the 1980s and '90s, most Americans perceived the past as a prologue to a progressive future, and for these people, to engage in the past for a prolonged period while escaping the trials and burdens of the modern world was an undeniably romantic extravagance.

By the 1930s, as John Jakle noted, "history tended to be packaged as contrived attractions."[12] Henry Ford opened Greenfield Village in 1928 in Dearborn, Michigan, to display his collection of nearly one hundred relocated historic buildings, arranged in a "village" setting (similar in concept to Skansen) (figure 0.4). Greenfield Village's historic buildings include Noah Webster's Connecticut Home; the Wright Brothers' Bicycle Shop from Ohio; and the Logan County, Illinois, courthouse where Abraham Lincoln tried law cases. These buildings were meticulously restored but will always remain curiously disjointed from each other, which was Ford's intent—to create "a pocket edition of America."[13] In the same year, John D. Rockefeller Jr. funded the construction of Colonial Williamsburg. Through the tireless advocacy of the rector of Bruton Parish Church, William A. R. Goodwin, the former colonial Virginia capital was transformed from its sleepy Victorian state into the architectural vision of colonial life. The Capitol, Governor's Palace, Old Gaol, and its taverns—Shields, Chowning's, Raleigh, and Christiana Campbell's—were all re-created. Unlike Greenfield Village, all the buildings were part of an ensemble, which provided an idyllic and patriotic idea of early America (figure 0.5).

Creating "historylands" across the country in the 1930s, from Santa Fe, New Mexico, to Old Sturbridge, Massachusetts, was a direct response to the birth of modern tourism in the US, which was centered around the automobile. With improved roads, automobiles, and wages, middle-class Americans now had the opportunity to experience places and entertainment that were beyond their means in their everyday lives. Sightseeing became not only accessible but also experiential. It provided a familiar and genteel way to escape from the uncertain industrialized and modernized world of Depression-era America.[14] Encountering America's past was vital to them. Boorstin explained how they wanted

Figure 0.6: Natchez, Mississippi, 1940, Marion Post Wolcott, Photographer. (Library of Congress, Prints & Photographs Division, Farm Security Administration/Office of War Information Photograph Collection, LC-DIG-fsa-8a42673)

to learn from the landscape as much as from the written page of history, and more importantly, Americans wanted to be entertained by history.[15]

These early automobile-driving tourists loved to learn what their historic buildings and sites could say to them. But were the historic monuments speaking to them? Do they speak to us now? The answer to both questions is obviously no. We apply an idea of significance to them, often based on our appreciation of tradition, which was assigned to a monument by the politically powerful ruling elite of the place at a specific time. Historic shrines like George Washington's Mount Vernon in Virginia and Lincoln's home in Illinois have values and meanings applied to them by the original generation that sought to preserve them or erect them. Later, subsequent generations add different meanings and ideas of significance. We continue to assign meanings to tangible monuments today, often through a political lens and decided by individuals who wield political power. But after a while, we overlook and even forget the motives for the heritage narrative on a historic monument by the original preservationists who saved these monuments. This is the case in examining the built patrimony in Natchez.[16]

During the early twentieth century, images and ideas were projected upon older buildings and landscapes. In the West, in places like Santa Fe, the city was transformed into the environment it should have been and what it never was—a contrived conjecture of a lost Pueblo culture. In the South, where economic depression persisted long after the Civil War, landscapes and many towns were "frozen in time," ideal objects on which to project a narrative of what the past should have been, by both their owners and the tourists who sought them out (figure 0.6). Early twentieth-century tourists sought the familiar in historic sites and

Figure 0.7: Elms Court, Natchez, Mississippi, 1938. Journalist Ernie Pyle described how the overgrown vines were destroying the grand house's cast-iron portico. Frances Benjamin Johnston, Photographer. (Frances Benjamin Johnston Photograph Collection, Library of Congress, Prints & Photographs Division, LC-DIG-ppmsca-32354)

Figure 0.8: The near-ruinous condition of the main parlor at Propinquity, 1938. Before the Spring Pilgrimage, most owners faced great difficulty maintaining their opulent antebellum homes. Frances Benjamin Johnston, Photographer. (Frances Benjamin Johnston Photograph Collection, Library of Congress, Prints & Photographs Division, LC-DIG-ppmsca-23955)

attached a romance to them that the contemporary and industrial landscape could not warrant. And for them, there was nothing more familiar and sentimental than the Civil War and, most especially, the antebellum era that preceded it, what Robert Penn Warren referred to as "our felt history." In it they could, as David Blight notes, forget the facts that were painful, and look beyond the legacy of it—that is, the primary reason why it was fought, slavery, and its legacy, institutionalized racial discrimination. They could visit the Civil War-era sites and imagine a life of Victorian heroism and Victorian feminine virtue, albeit for a short time. Blight reminds us of William Dean Howells's remark, "What the American public always wants is a tragedy with a happy ending."[17]

In the 1930s, American tourists found this familiar and sentimental narrative in the old houses of Natchez. Depression-era Natchez was the ideal place to imagine "what might have been." *Raleigh News and Observer* editor Jonathan Daniels wrote, "Poverty is a wonderful preservative of the past. It may let restoration wait as it ought not to wait, but it will keep old things as they are because it cannot afford to change them in accordance with style and preferences. In Natchez, the living occupy the past."[18] Beginning with the first Spring Pilgrimage, held in the last week of March 1932, tourists were fascinated to venture and peer into aging mansions, many of which were, quite frankly, shabby and broken down. Journalist Ernie Pyle remarked after visiting Elms Court, "The house is cold and dark. The rugs are frayed. The fantastic grillwork around the porch has crumbled in sections. Many of the rooms are mere storehouses. In all its 1850 richness, it is not a place the average person would want to live in" (figure 0.7).[19] But tourists found all of it captivating. They dressed up as if they were paying a social call to the important homeowner of the grand mansion and were "received" by the daughters of the home, who were wearing antebellum hoopskirt costumes and passing out camellia blossoms to their out-of-town guests. The grace and manners of the white southern gentlepeople; the chipped paint, faded wallpaper, and frayed rugs were all a reminder of the defeated but gallant Confederacy. This is what the women of the NGC sold at the early pilgrimage (figure 0.8).

Not everyone enjoyed this antebellum vision of Natchez. Like other ethnic groups throughout the US, the African American citizens of Natchez first became marginalized and then victimized by the commodification of the historic place's contrived heritage. As the pilgrimages grew more and more successful, the images that it created took

Figure 0.9: Children playing with their "mammy" outside of The Elms, circa 1930. African Americans played a subservient role in the depiction of the mythic "Old South" culture in Natchez. (From *Natchez of Long Ago and the Pilgrimage* by Katherine Grafton Miller [Natchez, MS: Relimak Publishing Co., 1938])

Figure 0.10: Linden was one of the original homes showcased in the first Spring Pilgrimages. Frances Benjamin Johnston, Photographer. (Frances Benjamin Johnston Photograph Collection, Library of Congress, Prints & Photographs Division, LC-DIG-ppmsca-23948)

on a force of their own, beyond the romantic and the commercial and into the political. The denigration of Natchez African Americans first began as an idea, then a narrative, and finally an accepted image of how things have been and ought to continue to be (figure 0.9). Natchez, by implementing the "Old South" ideal, implicitly degraded the very African Americans who helped make it unique. The racial fallout from the commodification of heritage was not unique to Natchez; African Americans suffered humiliation in being relegated to submissive roles in historic southern cities, while Pueblo and Hispanic cultures were trivialized in places like Santa Fe, New Mexico, and Santa Barbara, California.[20] But in Natchez, systematic racism—specifically, the Black race serving the elite white one—was real, not simply contrived (as was the case in Santa Fe), and it was implicit in the tourist experience of the city.

Unlike cities such as Santa Fe and Williamsburg, Natchez did not create an illusion of authenticity.[21] Architecturally and spatially, today's Natchez is not much different from its Depression-era version. Tourists still experience the town in single vignettes, arriving by automobile from one historic home to the next (figure 0.10). The NGC women innately understood the intrusion of modernity into their city.[22] They urged their visitors to use their imagination and "put themselves under the spell of the place,"[23] and be willing to enter the historic houses with zest and "into the mood of 'Let's pretend' that is a part of the passport necessary to really enjoy the life of this town of 'long ago.'"[24]

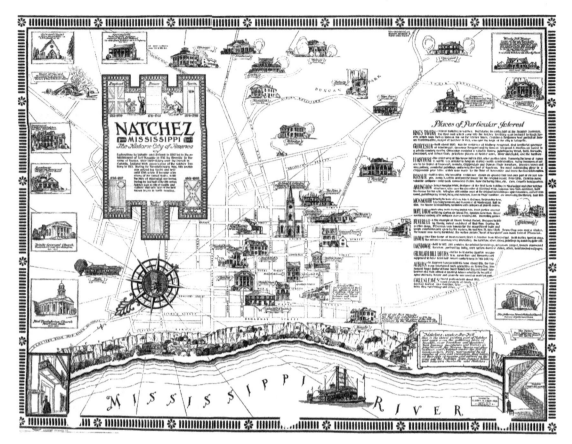

Figure 0.11: Map depicting the historic homes in Natchez, Mississippi, 1936, Harry Weir, delineator. This map was produced by one of the architects involved in the Historic American Buildings Survey of Mississippi during the Great Depression. (Mississippi Department of Archives and History)

What makes Natchez a unique historyland is how it was created by the NGC women in the 1930s as a cultural tourist attraction. Two maps demonstrate my point. One is a map delineated by J. T. Liddle Jr. and Harry E. Weir, two young architects working for the Historic American Buildings Survey in 1936 (figure 0.11). In it, we see beautifully drawn vignettes of the historic architecture, scattered all around the map of the city. The steep bluffs are carefully detailed, and a steamboat rolls down the Mississippi River. The entry of Monmouth, with a southern belle at the front door, is placed on the lower left-hand corner, while a comparable drawing of the spectacular winding stairway in Auburn adorns the right-hand one. The title of the map prominently features the flags that had dominion over the city: British, French, Spanish, thirteen-star early American, Confederate, and contemporary American. There is a flamboyantly delineated "North" arrow, which radiates diagonally across the city map grid, and displays the head of a proud Natchez Indian. The map is visually exciting and well crafted but completely useless as a wayfind-

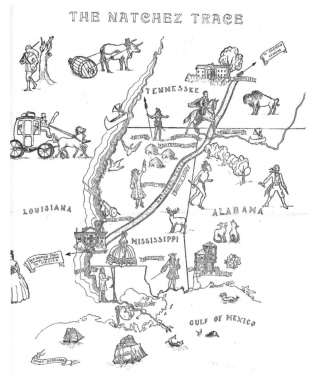

Figure 0.12: Cartoon map of the Natchez Trace Parkway, 1936, Louise Hernandez, delineator. This map depicts the romantic notions of the history of the Natchez Trace and how it became part of the "Old Spanish Trail," which led to Mexico City. (Roane Fleming Byrnes Collection [MUM00057], Department of Archives and Special Collections, J. D. Williams Library, The University of Mississippi)

ing tool. The second map is similarly dominated by drawn icons (figure 0.12). It was drawn by NGC member Louise Hernandez, also in 1936, and it features the proposed Natchez Trace Parkway, cutting diagonally across the state of Mississippi, beginning in Natchez and culminating in Nashville, Tennessee. Little can be learned about the distance of the roadway or the topography it crosses; important cities, including Mississippi's capital city of Jackson, are omitted. But what it shows us are the people (Native American, Spanish, French, and American), the heroes like Andrew Jackson, and the places, caricatures of southern mansions and wood stockade forts, that made the historic ancient road and Natchez unique to the nation's history and culture. The two maps do not present us with the physical geography of Natchez, or even of Mississippi and Alabama or Tennessee. Instead, they are documents conveying the geography of imagination—more specifically, the imagination of the NGC women who preserved the city and then transformed it in a way that conformed to the narrative they created. Through their willingness to use their imagination to sell Natchez to the outside world, the women of the NGC created a historyland unlike any other in the US.

The two maps also present how the NGC women spatially delineated this heritage. Instead of a created environment like Greenfield Village or Colonial Williamsburg, they presented the historic homes as individual objects, separated by geography, accessed by the automobile, and

Figure 0.13: Children playing at Melrose. Visitors were "received" by belles into the historic homes in 1934. (Courtesy of the Archives and Records Services Division, Mississippi Department of Archives and History)

tied together by an imaginative narrative. To experience Natchez during the pilgrimage of the 1930s (and today as well), you drove from home to home. When you arrived at the mansion, you were greeted by an African American who was playing the role of a servant; you presented your ticket at the front door, and then you were "received" by a southern belle (figure 0.13). Each home on the pilgrimage tour was unique, and the belles described them in elaborate detail. They presented to their inquiring pilgrims the architectural details, the rare John James Audubon prints, the imported antiques, and the chandeliers. The tourists enjoyed the distinctive architectural features like the spiral staircase in Auburn and the "Great Punkah" in the dining room at Melrose. During the first Spring Pilgrimage, the tourists could ramble freely throughout the interiors of the mansions, but that soon changed when homeowners discovered that some of the tourists were stealing their belongings. Soon after the first two years of the annual event, the interiors of the mansions were roped off.[25]

Of the several ways that the women presented their homes and marketed their southern narrative of the place, none were as successful or as innovative as the "tableaux." Originally a type of entertainment, meaning "living picture" in French and popular during the Victorian era, tableau productions were widely performed in Natchez, particularly during Mardi Gras festivities. They were a series of dramatic scenes using costumes, dance, and music, but did not have any spoken parts. For the Spring Pilgrimage, they were conceived to re-create scenes from

Natchez's conjured past that the Natchez Garden Club knew would be well received by tourists. There were twelve tableaux presented during the Pilgrimage Week. The most elaborate one, originally called the Confederate Ball and then known as the Confederate Pageant, showcased the annual pilgrimage king and queen and their royal court. The sons and daughters of the town's upper and middle classes donned the Confederate officer uniforms and hoop skirts that their grandparents had worn. The pageant has not been performed since 2015. Other tableaux included a "reenactment" of the eighteenth-century king of Spain visiting his colony of West Florida and Natchez, a foxhunt at Melrose, and a Ball of a Thousand Candles at Elms Court.

"Heaven Bound," an African American folk drama that portrayed the struggles of pilgrims striving to reach the gates of heaven, was the only singing or speaking performance presented during the Spring Pilgrimage. Zion Chapel A.M.E. Church members Julie Harrison and Cornelia Dumas wrote the performance and recruited African Americans from other churches and students from Natchez Junior College, a historically Black college, to join the choir for the performance.[26]

None of these tableaux had historical precedent; they were designed to steep tourists more deeply in the romanticized antebellum era and its environs. Obviously, there was no "king or queen" of the Confederacy. Foxhunting was never a Deep South pastime. King Charles IV of Spain never visited Natchez or even North America.[27] What truly made the tableaux unique and compelling were the settings in which they were performed: the mansions. On special occasions, such as James A. FitzPatrick's *Traveltalks* and Dave Garroway's television show, the setting became the main character: homes like Melrose, Dunleith, Green Leaves, The Elms, and The Briars came to life for the tourists, and their stories were intertwined with the pilgrimage.[28]

A mere three years after the first pilgrimage of 1932, the NGC women experienced success beyond their wildest dreams. Fifteen hundred pilgrims came to Natchez for the first pilgrimage; the tourist visitation increased tenfold by 1935. The following year, 1936, was the pivotal year in the history of preserving Natchez and establishing the town as a prominent cultural destination. Leading national newspapers, including the *New York Times*, the *Christian Science Monitor*, the *Chicago Tribune*, and the *Los Angeles Times*, began regularly writing feature articles on the town and its preservation; these newspapers would continue to do so throughout the twentieth century. Tales of salacious acts by sadistic land pirates in Natchez and on the Natchez Trace, described by Robert Coates in *The Outlaw Years: The History of the Land Pirates of the Natchez Trace* (published in 1930), ignited the imagination of Americans engrossed

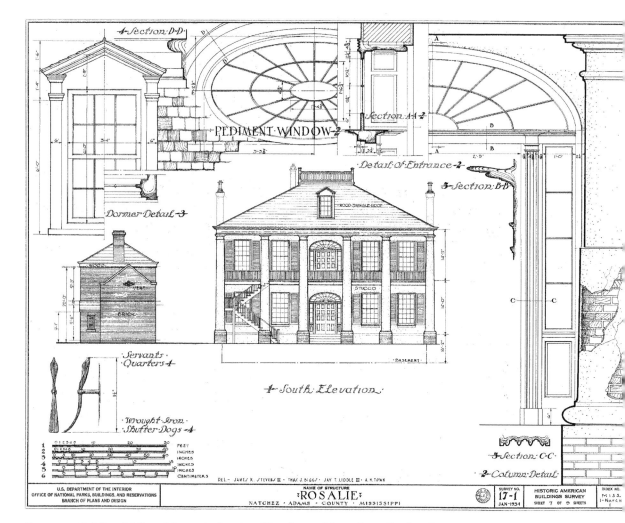

Figure 0.14: Building details and the south elevation of Rosalie, 100 Orleans Street, Natchez, Mississippi, James R. Stevens, Thomas S. Biggs, and Jay T. Liddle, delineators, 1934. Rosalie was one of the first buildings measured and documented by District 17 of the Historic American Buildings Survey. (Library of Congress, Prints & Photographs Division, Historic American Buildings Survey, HABS MISS,1-NATCH,1- [sheet 7 of 9])

by the idea of the "anti-hero" of the American frontier and the mystical haunts they inhabited. *So Red the Rose* (published in 1934) by Stark Young, which was set in Natchez, and *Gone with the Wind* (published in 1936) by Margaret Mitchell were published in the 1930s. Eudora Welty combined the romantic and gallant ideal of the Natchez gentlepeople with the tawdry Natchez Trace bandit archetype in her American frontier version of a Grimm fairytale novella, *The Robber Bridegroom*, published in 1942. Suddenly, the romance of the lost cause of the Confederacy became all the rage in American popular culture. Four years of marketing by the NGC women on a national scale paid off as attendance at the pilgrimage increased substantially. The state of Mississippi created a tourism commission, which featured Natchez and the Mississippi Gulf Coast as the state's primary tourist attractions. The Works Progress Administration (WPA) programs the WPA Writers' Project and the Historic American Buildings Survey (HABS) were underway in Natchez in 1936. Through the Writers' Project, the historic architecture of Natchez was identified, and formerly enslaved persons were interviewed for the Writers' Project Slave Narrative Collection. Architects from Jackson and New Orleans measured and documented historic buildings in the town (figure 0.14). In an editorial for the *Chicago Daily News*, Lloyd Lewis proposed that the town of Natchez follow the precedents set in European and Mexican cities and pass ordinances to preserve its historic architecture.[29] *Chicago Tribune* travel writer Edith Weigle commended the Natchez Garden Club women's amazing work and how Stark Young's book "put it on our present-day map," but she also called for "another Rockefeller" to step up and completely restore the historic town.[30]

In 1936, the NGC women began to ambitiously plan on making Natchez an even more successful tourist destination. Using some of their profits from the previous pilgrimages, they started to restore the old Gilreath Hill house into "Connelly's Tavern." They also resurrected an idea from an earlier generation of Natchez women, the Natchez Chapter of the Daughters of the American Revolution, to rebuild the ancient Native American path and frontier road known as the Natchez Trace from Nashville, Tennessee, to Natchez. By obtaining federal funding, the Natchez Trace Parkway became one of the most successful projects undertaken by the WPA. And the women were not finished. Even before the Natchez Trace Parkway was begun, they aspired to continue rebuilding the ancient road from Natchez to Mexico City, thereby making it an *international* historical parkway with Natchez as its centerpiece. In wooing support for their audacious road project, they entertained governors, newspaper editors, prominent representatives of Franklin Roosevelt's administration, and even the ambassador and the interior minister of Mexico.[31]

Most of what the NGC women set out to do they accomplished, but by the end of 1936, their more far-reaching ideas were dashed. Internal and external strife quashed their work. Petty jealousy and greed among these women nearly destroyed the pilgrimage idea. A group of Natchez homeowners, who were not happy about receiving only one-third of the pilgrimage profits and who disapproved of the idea to use pilgrimage proceeds to restore what they considered eyesore buildings, threatened to split from the NGC. The next year, these dissenters established the Pilgrimage Garden Club and competed with the NGC for tourist dollars during the spring. What became known as the "War of the Hoop Skirts" and "The Big Split" reached a climax in 1941, when the two warring women's clubs went to court and sought an injunction against each other.[32] External forces outside of Natchez stunted the development of the cultural tourist idea as well. As the economy recovered from the Great Depression, architects in Mississippi sought more lucrative work than documenting Natchez's built patrimony for HABS. Thus, the architectural documentation of the town languished. Federal appropriations to build the Natchez Trace Parkway came in fits and starts throughout the twentieth century. The last planned northern section of it was completed in Alabama, and the southern terminus was completed at Liberty Road, three miles from the bluffs along the Mississippi River. Both road sections were completed in 2005.

America entered World War II at the end of 1941, and both the automobile-based tourism in the country and historic preservation in Natchez ceased. After the war, in 1946, the Natchez Garden Club and the Pilgrimage Garden Club came to an agreement to work with each other in conducting the pilgrimage, and the "War of the Hoop Skirts" came to an end.[33] Today, Natchez (and numerous historic homes across the South) still remains the historyland experienced mainly by automobile. Henry Ford, Eleanor Roosevelt, General Douglas MacArthur, actress Elizabeth Taylor, and, as recently as 2016, rocker Mick Jagger, all have enjoyed the Natchez story and the place.[34]

This is a story of how the narrative of place was developed and the struggles that occurred in making it on many levels—local, statewide, national, intellectual, architectural, and cultural—during the first half of the twentieth century in the US. What Blight notes about the making of memory at the end of the nineteenth century, that "American cultural romance triumphed over reality, sentimental remembrance won over ideological memory," was even more so by the 1930s in America.[35] Moreover, as Jakle points out, with the advent of automobile-based tourism, history was packaged into contrived attractions. The result was more than Lowenthal's notable quip, "the past became the past"—history became heritage.[36]

It is important to emphasize that what the women created in Natchez was not a myth; it was a narrative based on a myth. Architecture, public ceremony, literature, and even dress already existed in Natchez, and all of this was manifested in the tradition of the place, which all Natchezians took for granted until they realized that their traditional way of experiencing the place was not only desirable to the outside world but also potentially profitable. Anthropologist Edward Shils said it best: "Their past legitimated their future."[37]

Natchez has long been more than a regional story with only regional consequences and impacts. The story of its preservation and its celebra-

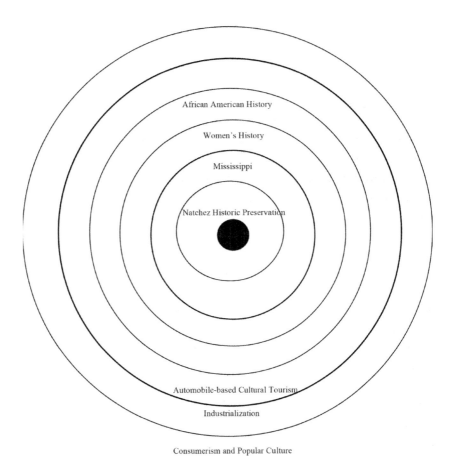

Figure 0.15: Diagram describing how historic preservation in Natchez has influenced modern American history in the fields of women's history and African American history. (Diagram by the author)

tion fascinated the entire nation, and for most of the twentieth century, it was examined by scholars and social scientists. Public historian Jack Davis noted that, in the 1930s, when Harvard anthropologist W. Lloyd Warner was searching for a southern community to serve as a research subject, he selected Natchez and rationalized his decision by saying, "We felt that the tradition of the 'Old South' had carried on [in Natchez] much better and with far greater security than [in] any other place we could find in the deep south."[38] Scholars in women's history, including Drew Gilpin Faust and Anne Firor Scott, have also examined the Natchez Garden Club's accomplishments in transforming their town. *Heritage and Hoop Skirts* examines how the "Old South" idea was created not only through both race and gender motives, but also using the tangible and most prominent actors in the story—the historic houses and mansions of Natchez. It is through the architecture of the place that the NGC women seized control of the community's cultural identity and influenced popular American culture. The ramifications of their work continue to be felt today (figure 0.15).

Figure 0.16: Mammy's Cupboard, Natchez, Mississippi. (Photograph by the author)

Figure 0.17: Katherine Grafton Miller and young Natchez belles picking daffodils at Hope Farm in Natchez, Mississippi. No woman in Natchez personified the southern belle myth more than the middle-class-raised Katherine Miller. (From *Natchez and the Pilgrimage* by Georgie Wilson Newell and Charles Cromartie Compton [Kingsport: Southern Publishers, 1935])

This book not only explains how the "Old South" myth was fabricated in Depression-era Natchez but also explores the struggle of making the narrative, on multiple levels. Through archival documentation, the story is described from the viewpoints of the protagonists. First, we encounter the Natchez women who with guile and tenacity first invent the "Old South" and then later market it to the world.

Second, we learn how the creation of the Natchez narrative affected the development of American architectural history through the Historic American Buildings Survey. Readers will be introduced to the WPA policymakers who developed the HABS program.

Third, I present how the NGC women enlisted the support of men in the South to expand the influence of Natchez through the creation of another conjured narrative, the Natchez Trace. We learn the struggle between the National Park Service men in restoring and preserving the built patrimony and the desire of these Natchez women to promote their "Old South" idea.

Fourth, I present how the romantic Natchez narrative is presented in literature—Stark Young's *So Red the Rose*, Harnett Kane's *Natchez on the Mississippi*, and Eudora Welty's *The Robber Bridegroom*. And I also discuss how the women influenced lurid versions of their narrative, most notably, Robert Coates's *The Outlaw Years*. We see how Natchez was marketed through Hollywood and how it influenced the most celebrated movie of the 1930s, *Gone with the Wind*. Finally, I discuss how the Natchez narrative is marketed in consumer products and how it attracted kitsch—from Mammy's (now known as Mammy's Cupboard Restaurant) to the ca. 1940 Fort Rosalie Visitor Center (figure 0.16).

I conclude the book with my reflections on the legacy of commodified heritage of the twentieth century and how it influences the way we look at our built patrimony today—from Charlottesville, Virginia, to Santa Fe, New Mexico. I challenge the reader, after learning about Natchez, to consider how meanings of historic buildings evolved over time and did so because of many motives. I remind readers that the NGC women never initially set out to make a southern heritage, but by reacting to the whims of the tourism market in the 1930s, they eventually made one. If we are to understand how to preserve and manage or even extricate the built heritage that we may perceive as insulting, inappropriate, or anachronistic, we must first understand how the meanings and values were placed on them. To understand the complicated heritage of the South, we must first go to Natchez, "Where the Old South Still Lives" (figure 0.17).

Figure 1.1: Aerial view of Natchez, Mississippi, and the Mississippi River, 1860. (Historic Natchez Foundation)

· Chapter 1 ·

A PLACE CALLED NATCHEZ

Although Natchez was founded as a French settlement in 1716 with the establishment of Fort Rosalie, its greatest colonial legacy—its urban design—comes from its Spanish rule. The first city plan was abandoned, and a new city plan was surveyed by John Girault in 1790–91 on behalf of Spanish colonial governor Manuel Gayoso de Lemos, who directed that a public green be laid out on the edge of the bluff. The green, or esplanade, originally extended from Canal Street to the edge of the bluff (figure 1.1).[1]

The esplanade, now known as Bluff Park, provided a natural amenity to the city. It can be said that it is the earliest established tourist attraction in the city.[2] During his travels through the American South in 1852, landscape architect Frederick Law Olmsted was very taken by the esplanade bluff. It was here, after strolling through an otherwise unbroken forest, that he first saw the Mississippi River—which translates from the Algonquin as "Father of Waters"—its ends "lost in the vast obscurity of the Great West."[3] The esplanade in Natchez still exists. Bluff Park, as it is now called, remains one of the most unique places in the US to enjoy the Mississippi River. Preservation has always been at the center of Natchez's development, and the women who preserved its architecture in the 1930s, '40s, and '50s innately understood preservation's value.

During the 1930s, cities throughout the American South—Williamsburg, Virginia, Charleston, South Carolina, Savannah, Georgia, St. Augustine, Florida, and New Orleans, Louisiana—attempted to commodify and market their built heritage for the emerging automobile-based cultural tourism economy, but it was here in Natchez where the antebellum and southern heritage was showcased for financial gain for the local economy and to preserve the city's history and architecture. Nowhere is this more evident than in Natchez.

Tourists have always come to Natchez to be entertained, not necessarily to be taught actual history. The seminal month-long springtime event that showcases the architecture of this historic city, the Natchez Spring Pilgrimage of Antebellum Homes, has been the traditional way that tourists come and celebrate the architecture, decorative arts, and culture of this "historyland." Historically, it has been an opportunity for Americans to escape the dreariness of winter and indulge in the supposedly graceful world of "Old South civility." Presenters, almost all the club women, dress in the latest fashion of 1850, hoop skirts and antebellum ball gowns, and receive their "guests"—they are not considered "tourists"—in the grand opulent villas and some more humble historic buildings. It is an intimate and personal presentation, much more so than one experiences in a historical museum or what can be found on an app on your phone. It is a presentation that changes as the times change, and it varies for a specific audience. The women's presentations are theatrical, improvised, individualized, and loosely scripted. They go into "character," whether in an actual period moment or as a native modern-day Natchezian. Entertainment is the pilgrimage's objective, and it is irrelevant whether the performer is presenting a rehearsed interpretation or merely ad-libbing it. You will not hear the same thing twice, but you will always learn about the history and architecture of the city. They have been doing it this way since 1932. Despite the current-day challenges of presenting a controversial, racially conflicted heritage, women belonging to the Natchez Garden Club and the Pilgrimage Garden Club continue today to showcase the antebellum architecture as they have been for over eighty-five years.

During the Spring Pilgrimage, held in mid-March through mid-April, and also the abbreviated Fall Pilgrimage, held in late September to early October, your $45-per-tour-package ticket gets you a choreographed architectural and cultural experience, touring twenty-four to thirty historic buildings.[4] At these two special times of the year, Natchez opens its doors for tourists from around the country and the world. It is a festive event, centered around relaxation and enjoyment of antiquarian objects. During the pilgrimage's first decades, the women of the Natchez Garden Club (NGC) and later the rival splinter group, the Pilgrimage Garden Club (PGC), staged the event, but it is now managed by a private tour operator, Natchez Pilgrimage Tours, jointly owned by the two previously competing women's clubs. During the month-long event, you can discover publicly owned and privately owned antebellum homes and experience interactive historical presentations. In the morning, you can take a tour of three perhaps-private residences, and in the afternoon a different set of residences. In the evening, there is entertainment that celebrates the essence of Natchez through costumed performances known as "tableaux." There are concerts and special dining experiences to revel in as well.[5] The pilgrimage has been a considerable revenue generator for this historic city and continues to determine social status within the white established families—particularly the women—of the city. Proceeds from the profits of the pilgrimages help maintain more than thirty individually owned and club-owned historic residences and buildings. And since 1932, owning one of these houses has always enhanced one's social status in Natchez. New owners have purchased several of the mansions during the past twenty years. Natchez has a large LGBTQ+ population, many of whom have purchased the historic homes and joined one of the two garden clubs.[6]

One must consider the actual landscape and the architecture, along with the narrative used to celebrate both of them, if one is to understand Natchez. The city bluffs and the Mississippi River are dominant features that determined how the city was built and cannot be ignored. So are the rolling hills and stands of live oak trees, covered with moss, all along the Natchez Trace Parkway, which many tourists drive on their way to the pilgrimage. During the antebellum period, Natchez developed in a suburban manner, with large and small estates scattered around it, and this has played a significant role in the city's preservation since it can be best described as a loose ensemble of historic houses scattered throughout the city and not necessarily being an intact historic district or urban quarter. What has tied all these buildings together as a "historyland" is a common narrative. Without its narrative, the tourist may find Natchez too confusing to comprehend, and it may appear no different from the numerous comparable towns and cities built along the Mississippi River and in the Deep South during the early part of the nineteenth century. The pilgrimage, the journey by tourists to pay homage to the city's architecture, the homes' antique collections, and the region's heritage, is the primary way to learn about this city and its preservation, and it happens twice a year. However, important houses such as Stanton Hall, Longwood, Rosalie, Melrose, and Auburn are open year-round for tours. Visitors also can learn about Natchez historic preservation at the Natchez Visitor Center.

So how do you experience this city when the pilgrimages are not going on? Does one experience the "Old South" ambience by simply driving through it and walking down its streets? Perhaps. In this chapter, I introduce the reader to the actual Natchez, the Natchez anyone can see and judge on its tangible, visual merits, without paying $45 (or more) for the pilgrimage tours. It is a city not frozen in time; it has grown and evolved like any other comparably sized city, either in the Deep South or in the Midwest. Along with the narrative created by the garden club women of the 1930s, who lived in Natchez, there are additional narratives applied to it that are more current and reflect the ideas emerging within the modern twenty-first-century state of Mississippi. The Mississippi River was the driving force in creating Natchez, and how the city was planned

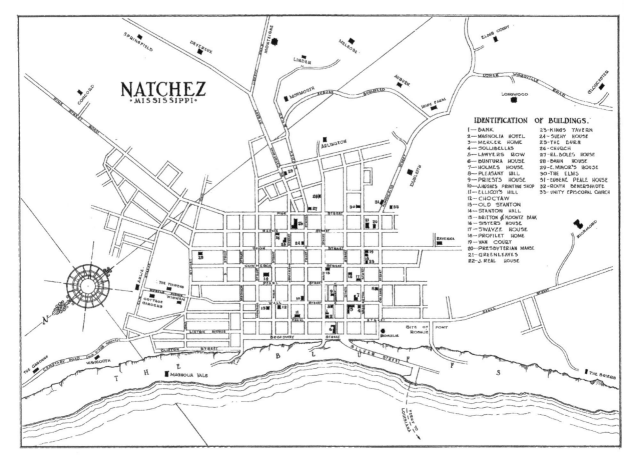

Figure 1.2: Map of Natchez, Mississippi, depicting locations of the historic homes in Natchez. This map shows the majority of the opulent villas are located away from the center of the city. (Library of Congress, Prints & Photographs Division, Historic American Buildings Survey, HABS MISS,1-NATCH)

around the river helped define its antebellum age and its tourism economy. And although it has branded itself as the quintessential place for Federal and Greek Revival architecture, another hallmark of its cultural tourism economy, there are numerous other cities throughout the country that rival it. After all, Greek Revival architecture was considered the national form of built expression between 1820 and 1860. What makes Natchez unique is how, through the pilgrimage, its inhabitants combined the intangible heritage of storytelling with the tangible heritage of an intact architecture in a well-planned narrative, most notably for pleasure-seeking.

Along with an introduction to the geography and architecture of Natchez, I will explain how the tools used for communicating the narrative—theatrical performance and extemporaneous acts—were developed and how these accoutrements remain practically unchanged today. Performing the narrative is more than just an act; it is a way to bring the city's inhabitants, Black and white, privileged and working class, to work together to reaffirm the city's identity. Even today, both African Americans and whites in Natchez partake in the pilgrimage. The narrative is attached to the historic buildings and monuments through the pageants, balls, and tableaux, all held in the grand houses, the African American churches, and the early twentieth-century-built city auditorium. This intangible heritage defines how we understand and value this built history, and it also influences how it is preserved. Unlike the tangible heritage (i.e., the buildings and monuments), it is both fluid and evolving. In this chapter's conclusion, I present the reader with a brief summary of how, in today's Natchez, tourism has evolved to encompass more than the "Old South." The narrative has evolved over the decades, and it will continue to progress, but it is indisputable that since the Great Depression, past and progress have always been intermingled in Natchez (figure 1.2).

NATCHEZ NOW

Natchez has always wanted to be a forward-looking and progressive city; it became one during the first decades of the twentieth century by relying on its past—or at least what its leaders wanted to convey as its past to the rest of the world. And in the process of using their past to shape their future, the NGC women created what we now know as cultural tourism. While cultural tourism has flourished for centuries in Europe, this industry happened first in Natchez, to profit from its Confederate history past. The Natchez Garden Club introduced it to the regional economy in 1932. Cultural tourism became the means through which the locally acknowledged white elites generated some new, and much needed, income. More importantly, they buttressed the all-important perception of their gentility within their communities and throughout the nation. Cultural tourism also created jobs for lower- and middle-class whites and African Americans. Street vendors, retailers, hotel clerks and support staff, restaurant waitstaff, and day laborers, both Black and white, benefited from this new economy, which, by its very nature, is not industrially based.[7]

Historically, Natchez has showcased its exceptional architecture, which is comprised of a loose ensemble of villas, townhouses, public buildings, and private buildings. The villas were built in the English tradition that John Ruskin defined as detached large and small residences set in what we consider now a suburban setting, attempting to compositionally work in harmony with nature. The architecture of these residences reflects Victorian English character and ideals. The Victorian English embraced the value of hard work, Christianity, frugality, ingenuity, family, and home. Americans embraced these ideals throughout the nineteenth century. The English villa epitomized these ideals. As Ruskin noted, the English-inspired villa architecture can "be beautiful, or graceful, or dignified, and equally unable to be absurd"; most importantly, he added, there is a proud independence about it.[8]

Townhouses such as the Commercial Bank and Banker's House, Cherokee, Choctaw, Greenlea, Green Leaves, the House on Ellicott Hill, Magnolia Hall, and Stanton Hall were built during the city's heyday as well. Natchezians built impressive public buildings like the Commercial Bank, the Agricultural Bank, Memorial Hall; they built antebellum churches like First Presbyterian Church, Trinity Episcopal Church, and St. Mary Basilica. And there are several notable plantation residences near Natchez, such as Brandon Hall, Lansdowne, Selma, Mount Repose, Edgewood, and Mistletoe. The significant amount of noteworthy pre–Civil War architecture, all accessible by automobile, makes Natchez a distinctive historic town.

Builders of the villas were nineteenth-century planters—some of whom came to Mississippi from the mid-Atlantic and Northeast to make a fast fortune on land speculation and cotton, while others were Mississippi natives. While some of them built villas within the street blocks of the small gridiron town, most built outside of the town boundaries on multi-acre parcels.[9] Most planters owned and managed multiple estates in Mississippi (and even in Louisiana), and the suburban villa became an accepted way for domestic living in Natchez and other Mississippi towns, such as Vicksburg and Columbus, for the cotton elite. The villa complex typically consisted of the stand-alone villa for the family, kitchen and food preparation buildings, stables and carriage houses, and slave and servant cabins for the enslaved workers who served the planter and his family. The villa in Natchez was almost an independent entity, set in a suburban setting, but with each villa complimenting the other within the social structure and geography of Natchez.

During Natchez's antebellum heyday beginning in 1800, planters built ever more opulent villas in order to outdo each other. By the 1850s and until the beginning of the Civil War, they built villas farther away from the center of town in more elaborate fashions. These planters built their complexes and bestowed them with romantic names: Airlie, Green Leaves, Lansdowne, Magnolia Vale, etc. Some of them hired accomplished master builders/architects from the East and from Europe who had moved to Natchez, such as Jacob Byers, the builder of Melrose, or Levi Weeks, the builder of Auburn; the Scottish-born builders James Hardie and Andrew Brown; and the English-born Thomas Rose. But there were other planters who hired the most notable professional

Figure 1.3: Longwood, Samuel Sloan, Architect, 1860. (Library of Congress, Prints & Photographs Division, Historic American Buildings Survey, HABS MISS, 1-NATCH.V,3-1)

architects of their day. The culmination of this competition in opulence before the Civil War was when Haller Nutt hired Philadelphia architect Samuel Sloan to design Longwood—the largest octagonal-shaped residence in the US, which is essentially an Italianate house with exotic Moorish and Byzantine influences in its detailing (figure 1.3). Although never completed (due to the onset of the Civil War), Longwood is truly an independent villa, set on a gentle rising knoll with a full accompaniment of supporting outbuildings. It was so ornate that Ruskin may have regarded it as "absurd" had he seen it.

Natchez developed more as a suburban enclave of villas and less as an urban entity, and this provided the spatial structure experienced by twentieth-century tourists and enabled its preservation individually, one building at a time. This practice also allowed the garden club women to package its history into contrived attractions that became popular for automobile-driven tourists during the 1920s and '30s. The original layout of the villas, scattered throughout the city, allowed these historic places to coexist with the contemporary scene. Natchez's coexistence of old and new contrasts with other comparable historic cities, where progress made the existence of the past incompatible.[10] In Natchez, newness has its place, and the built heritage has its place. Leaving down the gravel driveway at Longwood, you experience this juxtaposition of old and new as you gaze through the historic site's grove of trees and see the big box retail store looming in the distance.

Despite efforts to broaden heritage tourism in Natchez, one must still enter the mood of "Let's pretend"—an inclination to look beyond the contemporary landscape and appreciate the historical one—that is a passport necessary to really enjoy the life of this town of "the long ago." Natchez is a Mississippi River town, port town, and a scenic place along the east banks of the river. It is the county seat of Adams County, and it is located in the southwest corner of the state of Mississippi. It is ninety miles southwest of Mississippi's state capital, Jackson, and eighty-five miles due east of Louisiana's state capital, Baton Rouge, with a total population of nearly sixteen thousand people (as of the 2010 US Census).[11] It has a predominantly poor population (the median income for a family is approximately $29,000), and like most of rural and small-town America, the population has decreased since 2000. This is due to increased suburbanization brought about by the development of residential subdivisions and a golf course neighborhood built outside the city limits.

ARRIVING IN NATCHEZ

Natchez is accessible only by automobile. Passenger rail service, which was inefficient during the first half of the twentieth century there, no longer exists.[12] The garden club women's greatest legacy, the Natchez Trace Parkway, is the most enjoyable and most romantic way to arrive in the city. The more than four-hundred-mile parkway begins near the southwest corner of Nashville, Tennessee, clips the northwest corner of Alabama, enters Mississippi, and passes Tupelo, where the National Park Service maintains the parkway's administration offices. It swings around the western edge of Mississippi's state capital, Jackson, and its last eighty miles leads you to Natchez. Driving along the parkway and entering Natchez from the northeast, you experience this masterpiece in both landscape design and narrative. The parkway is how the garden club women created Natchez's anecdotal and physical association with the rest of Mississippi, the South, and the nation. As you drive, approaches are framed by your car windshield—these are carefully planned vignettes along the parkway: rolling topography, landscaped with live oaks and hanging Spanish moss (figure 1.4). The immediate right-of-way is carefully mowed, even sculpted, to provide a designed landscape. You see roadside markers and staged sites like the "Old Agency" near Jackson—the place where Silas Dinsmoor represented the US to the Choctaw Indians until the Treaty of Doak's Stand in 1820.[13] But this is not the real Natchez Trace, originally an ancient footpath created by Native Americans, bison, and deer, following a prehistoric geologic ridge line; it is a modern parkway. The 1930s National Park Service planners never intended to reproduce the trace, only *memorialize* it.[14] As it was stated

Figure 1.4: View of the Natchez Trace Parkway, 1960. (Library of Congress, Prints & Photographs Division, photograph by Carol M. Highsmith, LC-DIG-highsm-04810)

by Congress, the parkway is the roadway, which "provides a recreational parkway from Nashville, Tennessee, to Natchez, Mississippi, following the Old Natchez Trace."[15] The parkway exits onto another roadway, which bypasses downtown Natchez, but is also embedded with cultural meaning: US Highway 61.

Highway 61 runs north and south, skirting east of Natchez as it connects New Orleans, Louisiana, to Wyoming, Minnesota. It is known as the "Blues Highway." It is at the intersection of US 61 and US 49, in Clarksdale, Mississippi, 216 miles north of Natchez that Robert Johnson purportedly sold his soul to the devil in exchange for mastery of the blues. There are other legends and myths associated with Highway 61 and the blues. Blues singer Bessie Smith died in an automobile accident in 1937 on it in the state's delta country.[16] Songs and legends lament her death. And it is on Highway 61 that Bob Dylan sings about God telling Abraham to "kill me a son." Abe replies, "Where do you want this killin' done?" God says, "out on Highway 61."[17]

The Highway 61 you drive on today does not immediately conjure up black and white images of Robert Johnson, Bessie Smith, or Bob Dylan. It is a modern four-lane highway featuring all the convenience stores, gas stations, fast food restaurants, billboards, and suburban sprawl one typically experiences driving through today's America. The flamboyant "Crossroads" sign, with its guitars and cartoon-like highway number signs, may confuse you if you do not know the story behind the monument (figure 1.5). The landscape of the blues has changed. The impoverished world of Black sharecroppers hand-picking cotton gave way to

Figure 1.5: "The Crossroads Sign," intersection of Highway 61 and Highway 49, Clarksdale, Mississippi. This is the legendary spot where Robert Johnson sold his soul to the Devil in order to master the blues. (Photograph by the author)

industrialized farming decades ago. The simple two-lane road is now a four-lane highway, placed east of the Mississippi River. You must first know and then appreciate the legend and lore of Robert Johnson, Bessie Smith, and Highway 61 if you seek to understand its narrative associated with monuments like "Crossroads."[18] Today's Highway 61 is no different from any other US highway you drive along in middle America; but in Mississippi, where the past and present coexist but are juxtaposed, progress alters place, and stories become wayfinding tools into the past.

The Mississippi River is the most important geographical feature of the city, even though its role in the everyday lives of the city's inhabitants has waned over the decades. It was the reason why Natchez was founded over three hundred years ago. With its high bluffs, the city's site is clearly the best one suited to build a city in southwest Mississippi and eastern Louisiana. Like most river towns, the city acknowledges the river through its urban design. After all, it was the primary means for transportation and commerce throughout most of the nineteenth century for all of the towns built along its banks. Quite simply, the river was the primary reason Natchez was built in the first place. Once, Natchez had a thriving river port, but over the course of a century, the Mississippi River has eroded the land where the infamous "Natchez Under-the-Hill" once stood; still, there remains a significant row of historic buildings on the east side of Silver Street. There are now more prosperous ports,

Figure 1.6: View of Natchez Under-the-Hill in 1972 when most of the buildings were abandoned. Today, only the row of buildings beneath the bluffs remains. (Library of Congress, Prints & Photographs Division, Historic American Buildings Survey, HABS MISS,1-NATCH,30-10)

like Baton Rouge to the south and Memphis to the north. Riverboats full of tourists stop below the Natchez bluffs and briefly experience the city; visitors are transported by large buses to the "Top-of-the-Hill," the downtown, and the villas.

Today, the river is engineered and managed by the US Corps of Engineers to prevent flooding of low-lying river towns and developments; it also manages the river as a navigable waterway for freight and goods from the Midwest, terminating at the Port of New Orleans and then shipped to the broader world. In the upper Midwest, the Mississippi River now behaves more like a lake than a major river, but seasonal flooding along the river occurs in Louisiana and Mississippi (figure 1.6).[19]

US 425/65/84 is where you cross the Mississippi River in Natchez and enter the smaller and more modern Vidalia, Louisiana. The Natchez-Vidalia Bridge is currently the tallest bridge in the state of Mississippi, consisting of two twin cantilever bridges: the westbound two-lane bridge was built in 1940, and the eastbound two-lane bridge was built in 1988. Citizens in Natchez lobbied long and hard for the funding for the original bridge throughout the 1930s. In 1936, the Works Progress Administration originally rejected this request, but then, at the urging of Senator Pat Harrison of Mississippi, reconsidered the proposal and jointly funded the bridge with Natchez and Vidalia. By providing a direct link to Louisiana, the bridge brought about tremendous change to the two small cities on each side of the river.[20] On the Louisiana side, flood control systems, first built after the Great Mississippi Flood of 1927, reassured Vidalia's developers enough that they built a primary care medical office building and a couple of hotels where large expanses of cotton fields once were. Driving along John R. Junkin Drive (US 425) in Natchez, you turn onto Canal Street, which features restaurants, two hotels, and a small casino.

With the Natchez Trace Parkway cutting diagonally across the entire state and terminating at the border of Natchez's historic district, it can be said that culturally Mississippi may belong to Natchez, but Natchez does not necessarily belong to Mississippi. As the parkway was completed, Natchez became more and more the state's premier "historyland." But from its beginning, this river city has been more attuned to New Orleans and Louisiana than to its home state. As it became the state's unofficial "historyland," the rest of Mississippi, especially cities like Jackson, pursued a progressive agenda of modernism in urban and regional development.[21]

As a tourist town, Natchez surprisingly does not have an abundance of choices for hotel accommodation. Comparable cultural tourism cities—Savannah, Charleston, and Williamsburg—have a much greater array of choices for short-term lodging. In the downtown area, the Natchez Grand Hotel, designed in a neo-Georgian style, resembles a college dormitory more than a luxury hotel. It is located near the recently built neoclassical Natchez Convention Center. The once grand mid-rise Eola Hotel, which Ernie Pyle admired and favorably compared to sophisticated New York hotels, sits abandoned and decaying. A development company is now planning to transform it into a luxury hotel.[22] Approximately one hundred historic villas, plantations, commercial buildings, and cottages are now used as "boutique" hotels or bed and breakfasts.[23]

Driving into the downtown, coming in from the east and crossing Highway 61 on Liberty Road as it intersects Melrose Avenue, you encounter Monmouth as the first villa, or "old house" as they are popularly known. The mansion fronts onto Quitman Parkway and Melrose Avenue and is currently functioning as a bed and breakfast inn. This villa has a storied history. Mexican-American War hero, Mississippi governor, and militant secessionist John A. Quitman made it his home in 1826 and hired James McClure to build the Grecian portico and the rear wing.[24] Five years later, he died there, rumored to have been poisoned; but some scholars theorized that he may have fallen ill to National Hotel Disease, which became later known as Legionnaire's Disease, at President James Buchanan's inauguration. Stark Young prominently featured the villa and Quitman's wife, Eliza, in his novel *So Red the Rose*. Set away from Liberty Road and fronting a large lawn, this grand house, with its colossal tetrastyle portico with four square brick Doric pillars and painted brick stucco exterior, was the inspiration for the design of the fictional Tara in the movie *Gone with the Wind* (figure 1.7).

Figure 1.7: View of Monmouth, at the corner of East Franklin Street and Melrose Avenue in Natchez. With its four colossal piers and grand portico, this grand house was the inspiration for Tara in the movie *Gone with the Wind*. (Library of Congress, Prints & Photographs Division, Historic American Buildings Survey, HABS MISS,1-NATCH,29-)

Liberty Road flows into Main Street and St. Catherine Street. Rolling hills and narrow ravines, which are locally referred to as "bayous," give you hints that you are approaching the city's bluffs and the Mississippi River. As the city developed, many of the bayous were filled and hills were leveled. Today, the downtown gently slopes toward the west and the river, often between steep banks with buildings set on top. The bayous and hills, which still exist, form natural boundaries between the historic down-

Figure 1.8: Arlington in ruins, Main Street in Natchez, after a disastrous fire destroyed the main section of this National Historic Landmark on September 17, 2002. The Historic Natchez Foundation funded a new roof to stabilize it. Because the absentee owner neglected it, vandals destroyed or defaced most of its architectural elements. The Natchez Preservation Commission sued the absentee owner in Mississippi Superior Court; the owner was fined after being convicted of demolition by neglect. (Photograph by ∧ \/\/ ∧ from Jackson, Mississippi, USA, CC BY-SA 2.0)

Figure 1.9: Natchez, under the hill. Photograph by William Henry Jackson, c. 1885. (Library of Congress, Prints & Photographs Division, LC-DIG-ds-13542)

town and the more modern suburbs.[25] Privately owned small houses—some from the late nineteenth century, some from the early twentieth century, but most of them built during the 1950s, '60s, and '70s—face the street. Behind a growth of trees and adjacent to the Duncan Park Public Golf Course is Auburn, which was donated as a public park by its owner. A mile from the public golf course is Arlington, once considered one of the grandest of the old villas in the city but now in a state of ruin after being ravaged by fire in 2002 (figure 1.8).[26]

Downtown Natchez is mostly comprised of altered mid-nineteenth-century buildings, several Greek Revival landmark buildings, a small number of early to mid-nineteenth-century buildings, and a few early twentieth-century storefront buildings. Its historical architecture is similar in architectural detailing to most commercial buildings found in Mississippi towns or cities. Most of the streets were renamed after the city enacted an ordinance to rename them in 1834. Prior to that, the streets were all identified by only direction and/or number. There are also alleys—Arrighi, Cotton, Parker, Bank, Locust, Sycamore, and Rose—that serve an important role in the functionality of the downtown, providing places for deliveries and garbage removal.[27]

Natchez "On-Top-of-the-Hill" is organized around the Spanish esplanade, Bluff Park; it is a unique feature for a Mississippi River town. Most river towns were established after the War of 1812, when Congress paid veterans in land for their military service, and were built by Americans who were developing the landscape for the Industrial Revolution. Amer-

Figure 1.10: An aerial view of Quincy, Illinois, 1859. (Courtesy of the Historical Society of Quincy and Adams County)

Figure 1.11: View of Natchez Bluffs by John James Audubon. (Historic Natchez Foundation)

icans built these river cities with a compact street gridiron; a town square or park at the town center, typically where the courthouse sat; and a riverfront complex, dedicated to industrial production. Following the European way of town-making that the Spaniards implemented along the Mississippi River, the French designed and developed New Orleans and Baton Rouge in Louisiana and St. Louis and Cape Girardeau in Missouri (figures 1.9, 1.10, and 1.11).

Figure 1.12: First Presbyterian Church on South Pearl Street. This Greek Revival church, renovated by James Hardie in 1851, is one of the finest Federal/Greek Revival church buildings in the American South. (Thomas H. and Joan W. Gandy Photograph Collection, Mss. 3778, Louisiana and Lower Mississippi Valley Collections, LSU Libraries, Baton Rouge, Louisiana)

Figure 1.13: View from the roof of the Eola Hotel in downtown Natchez. The US courthouse and the city hall are in the foreground; the city's numerous churches and the Temple B'nai Israel can be seen in the background. (Library of Congress, Prints & Photographs Division, photograph by Carol M. Highsmith, LC-DIG-highsm-03663)

Today's Natchez has a complete and intact downtown defined by churches and commercial buildings and has several surface parking lots. Most of the churches were built during the city's antebellum heyday. Trinity Episcopal Church, which was organized in 1822 and first occupied the building in 1823 on South Commerce Street, is the oldest church in the city. Originally built in the Federal style, a tetrastyle Doric two-story portico was later added, and stucco, with scored mortar courses that imitate ashlar stone, was applied to its exterior between 1838 and 1840.[28] The Jefferson Street Methodist Church features a Romanesque Revival interior. The 1842 Gothic masterpiece, St. Mary Basilica, was granted the status of "minor basilica" by Pope John Paul II in 1998, as a recognition of its historic and architectural importance.[29] The First Presbyterian Church, located on South Pearl Street, is a Federal-style church building with later Greek Revival-style features, including the 1851 pulpit, in the interior as well as Italianate detailed windows, added in 1859, on the exterior (figure 1.12).[30] Zion Chapel African Methodist Episcopal (A.M.E.) Church is another Greek Revival Doric tetrastyle temple. Originally built as the Second Presbyterian Church in 1858 by J. Edwards Smith, it was sold to the A.M.E. congregation in 1866, who raised the money to purchase it from its enslaved and free congregants.[31] Built in 1904 in the American Beaux Arts style for the city's burgeoning Jewish community, Temple B'nai Israel on Commerce Street completes the ensemble of historic religious structures in the city (figure 1.13).[32]

At the corner of Main and Canal Streets, there is one of the city's most iconic Greek Revival buildings, the Commercial Bank and Banker's House. Perhaps owner Levin R. Marshall instructed builder Andrew Brown to build the temple-like bank on Main Street and connect it to a free-standing residence at its rear, which faces Canal Street.[33] The elegant Ionic temple, with its gray marble and stuccoed brick exterior, is the only antebellum building in Mississippi with a facade of finished ashlar stone.[34] Behind the temple is the connected but visually distinct banker's house. The residence is also stuccoed and features an elegantly designed Greek Doric stone porch. The banker's residence remains a private residence; over the decades, the bank has been adapted for different uses but currently is vacant (figure 1.14).[35]

Figure 1.14: The front façade of the Commercial Bank on Main Street in Natchez, Mississippi. (Library of Congress, Prints & Photographs Division, Historic American Buildings Survey, HABS MISS,1-NATCH,26-)

Figure 1.15: Choctaw in 1938. (Frances Benjamin Johnston Photograph Collection, Library of Congress, Prints & Photographs Division, LC-DIG-ppmsca-23941)

Figure 1.16: Cherokee in 2006. (Library of Congress, Prints & Photographs Division, Historic American Buildings Survey, HABS MS-275)

There are numerous grand houses in the historic downtown. Two townhouses grace Wall and High Streets: Choctaw and Cherokee. Joseph Neibert built Choctaw, which stylistically dates to the mid-1830s. Its form is Federal in style, with its colossal tetrastyle Ionic columns based on Roman orders. Also built in 1836, the story-and-a-half Cherokee has a distinctive Greek Doric columned portico, recessed and set in antis.[36] These two residences convey a greater sense of grandeur than their actual size (figures 1.15 and 1.16).[37]

When one says "Natchez," the image of the resplendent Stanton Hall readily comes to mind. It is the grandest residence in downtown Natchez. It is located between Pearl and Commerce Streets. English master builder Thomas Rose built it for a native Irishman and prominent cotton broker named Frederick Stanton in 1857. With its flamboyant portico Corinthian columns, based on the ones found in Minard Lafever's *The Beauties of Modern Architecture*,[38] its cast-iron and wrought iron railings and ornamentation, and its Carrara marble mantelpieces, bronze chandeliers, and gold-framed mirrors, the building was more a showplace than a home. The death of Frederick Stanton's widow in 1893

Figure 1.17: Stanton Hall, 1857, Thomas Rose, Builder/Architect. Stanton Hall was built as a showplace by cotton merchant Frederick Stanton. After the Civil War, his descendants could not maintain it, and it became the Stanton College for Young Ladies. Today, it is the headquarters of the Pilgrimage Garden Club. (Library of Congress, Prints & Photographs Division, Historic American Buildings Survey, HABS MISS, 1-NATCH, 21-)

prompted the sale of the house and division of its furnishings (many of which have been returned to it). It then housed the Stanton College for Young Ladies and later returned to being a private residence. Today, it is a house museum and the headquarters of the Pilgrimage Garden Club (figure 1.17).[39]

There are other landmarks you can drive to in Natchez. Forks of the Road, at the intersection of St. Catherine Street with D'Evereux Drive (once called the Road to Washington) and Liberty Road, was the site of the second largest slave market in the Deep South. A roadside marker reminds us that this place was once where the leading slave-trading firm of Isaac Franklin and John Armfield of Alexandria, Virginia, sold African Americans who had walked from Virginia and Maryland (where the plantation economy declined after the land was devastated due to overcultivation of tobacco) along the Natchez Trace to further bondage and hard labor in Mississippi and Louisiana.[40] The former American Beaux Arts post office, built in 1904 on Main Street, is now home of the Natchez Museum of African American History and Culture, where the Natchez African American experience is explained to tourists.

There are more historic buildings to explore and enjoy. You walk by the eighteenth-century King's Tavern on Jefferson Street; walk by the House on Ellicott's Hill and Lawyers' Lodge on North Canal Street; drive by the Federal-style Rosalie on Orleans Street; and read signs that briefly describe Texada on South Wall Street and Magnolia Hall on South Pearl Street. Many houses, too many to mention, feature signs that state their historical importance.

You do feel a sense of history and see beautiful architecture walking and driving around Natchez, but there are also grand antebellum homes located all along the Mississippi River, found in river towns and in rural settings nearby. Are all of the great Natchez landmarks any more extraordinary than comparable ones found in neighboring river cities or other places in the Deep South or in any other part of the country? That is debatable. For example, the Society of Architectural Historians and the American Institute of Architects consider the John Wood House in Quincy, Illinois, one of the most iconic Greek Revival residences in the country. Built in 1835 for John Wood, a successful land developer in Adams County, governor of Illinois, and confidant of Abraham Lincoln, it is an opulent masterpiece, with Doric tetrastyle portico, elaborate mantelpieces, ornamental plaster and wood trim, and even an elaborate bathroom with an oversized bathtub, all of which rival any of the Natchez villas in both opulence and exquisite detail (figures 1.18 and 1.19).[41] The Bank of Louisville (1837), with its iconic acroterion, ashlar limestone façade, and Ionic columns set in antis, is a masterpiece in commercial

Figure 1.18: The John Wood Mansion, Quincy, Illinois, John Cleaveland, Builder/Architect, 1835. Located on 12th Street near downtown Quincy, the John Wood Mansion is considered one of the finest Greek Revival buildings in the Midwest. Since 1906, it has been a historic house museum that is owned and managed by the Historical Society of Quincy and Adams County. (Library of Congress, Prints & Photographs Division, Historic American Buildings Survey, HABS ILL,1-QUI,2-)

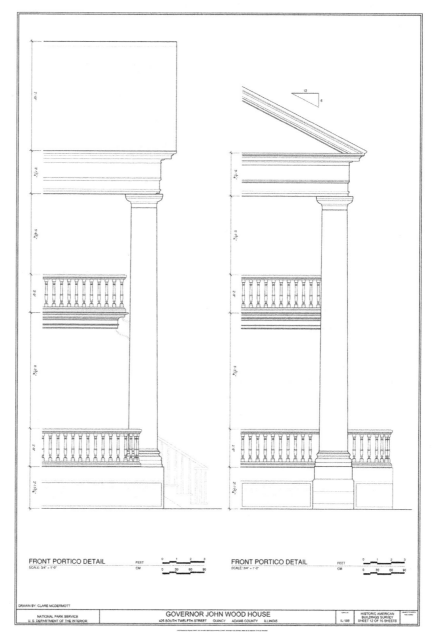

Figure 1.19: Portico details of the John Wood Mansion, Quincy, Illinois, delineated by Claire McDermott. The Doric tetrastyle portico adheres to the detail and proportion prescribed by Asher Benjamin. (Library of Congress, Prints & Photographs Division, Historic American Buildings Survey, HABS ILL,1-QUI,2-)

Figure 1.20: The Bank of Louisville, 1837, Louisville, Kentucky, by James Dakin, completed by Gideon Shyrock. (Library of Congress, Prints & Photographs Division, Historic American Buildings Survey, HABS KY,56-LOUVI,1-)

Figure 1.21: Government Street Presbyterian Church, 1837, Mobile, Alabama, James Gallier and Charles Dakin, Architects. (Library of Congress, Prints & Photographs Division, Historic American Buildings Survey, HABS ALA,49-MOBI,1-)

Figure 1.22: Shamrock, 1850, Vicksburg, Mississippi, William Nichols, Architect. (Library of Congress, Prints & Photographs Division, Historic American Buildings Survey, HABS MISS,75-VICK,1-)

Greek Revival architecture, not only in the South, Midwest, and along the great rivers (Ohio, Missouri, or Mississippi), but in the United States as a whole. James Dakin designed the building, and it was completed by Gideon Shyrock, another accomplished Greek Revival architect. Dakin did not stay very long in Kentucky; he moved on to New Orleans and designed several important Greek Revival buildings with James and Charles Gallier in New Orleans and the Gothic Revival masterpiece Louisiana State Capitol in Baton Rouge (figure 1.20).[42] Charles Dakin and James Gallier's Government Street Presbyterian Church in Mobile, Alabama, can be considered perhaps the most complete Greek Revival church ever built (figure 1.21).[43] San Francisco, Oak Alley Plantation, and Houmas, all stately plantation homes along Louisiana's River Road, are considered outstanding examples of nineteenth-century architecture. I could argue that these buildings, and many others, are more "southern" than any building in Natchez (figure 1.22).

Excellent Federal, Greek Revival, and Gothic Revival architecture, comparable to the architecture in Natchez, can be found in cities and towns not only throughout the South but also all along the Mississippi River. Natchez shares features with other Mississippi River towns of the nineteenth century such as Quincy and the Mormon-built Nauvoo in Illinois.[44] Moreover, Natchez, with its ensemble of suburban villas, became the American response to Ruskin's ideal of freestanding villas for the rising upper class.

Natchez became the historyland, "Where the Old South Still Lives," through the preserving and restoring of its antebellum architecture in a way that reinforced the "Old South" myth that developed during the early twentieth century. From the 1930s until the end of the twentieth century, historic preservation in Natchez shaped the southern narrative of the city, and consequently the narrative determined what was preserved and what

Figure 1.23: The bas relief sculpture of the Natchez Indian, commemorating the ancient American Indians, perhaps of Aztec descent, who originally populated southwestern Mississippi. This is part of a monument located on the corner of Main Street and Commerce Street. The Natchez tribe killed the earliest French settlers at Fort Rosalie in 1729. The French massacred the entire tribe in an act of revenge. (From *Natchez: Symbol of the Old South* by Nola Nance Oliver [New York: Hastings House, 1940])

was abandoned or demolished. And it was the narrative by which the garden club women revealed (or created), through performances relating to the architecture and its antebellum past, how uniquely "southern" Natchez was. Through historic preservation and cultural tourism, two activities that were developed (but had yet to be defined as such) during the 1930s, Natchez discovered that past can be profitable.

You must first learn this narrative, which is both conflicted and exaggerated, to understand and appreciate this city. Without knowing anything about the legend and lore of the place, you may find it visually impressive but perhaps not compelling. And you might not understand the importance of landmarks that you encounter, such as the Natchez Indian Monument, located at the corner of Main Street and Commerce Street (figure 1.23). But as important as the narrative is to the city, how it is presented to the tourist, through dramatic performance, is equally as important; performance determines a building's preservation.

PERFORMING THE NARRATIVE

In his chapter for the edited volume *Southern Heritage on Display*, Steven Hoelscher captures the essence of a typical tour given during the Natchez Spring Pilgrimage. It is a warm afternoon in March 2000, and Hoelscher is with an elderly woman, Alma Cassell Kellogg Carpenter, at her home, The Elms. Earlier that year, Hoelscher, a cultural geographer and professor of American studies at the University of Texas at Austin, met with "Miss Alma," as she liked to be called, in the "new wing" (built in 1855) of her house and learned about her interest in local archaeology, history, politics, preservation, and the internet. Miss Alma was well educated for a Natchez woman of her generation, earning a bachelor's degree from Hollins College in Virginia and a master's degree from the University of Mississippi. This was the educational path for a young and affluent Natchez woman during the first half of the twentieth century.[45]

Miss Alma grew up with the pilgrimage, her family home, and historic preservation in Natchez. Her mother, Alma Stratton Cassell Kellogg, was the treasurer of the Natchez Garden Club during the 1930s. As a little girl, Miss Alma danced around the Maypole in a tableau during the first pilgrimage. As a young woman, with blonde hair and striking looks, she was the queen of the pilgrimage in 1946. During a time when divorce was considered taboo, she was married and divorced twice. When she married her second husband, Nathaniel Leslie Carpenter, she moved to the grand villa, Dunleith on Homochitto Street, where she raised three children, restored the house, and showcased it at pilgrimages through-

Figure 1.24: The Elms photographed in 2007 when it was undergoing an extensive renovation. (Courtesy of the Archives and Records Services Division, Mississippi Department of Archives and History)

out the 1950s, '60s, and '70s. When she divorced Carpenter in the 1970s, she returned to The Elms and restored it as well, using her own savings and the money earned from the pilgrimage. During her later years, she published in scholarly journals, served on important historical and archival boards in both Louisiana and Mississippi, and received numerous historic preservation awards for her work in Natchez. When she died in 2005, she was extolled as the "Doyenne of Natchez History."[46]

But on this warm March day in 2000, Miss Alma is not thinking about her lifetime accomplishments. Wearing a hoop skirt and a crisply pressed blouse, she waits for the next busload of tourists coming to experience The Elms. She glances at her rambling home with its two-story porches, primitive balustrade, and exterior stairs. Judging by the photographs taken in 2007 by the Mississippi Department of Archives and History, I can presume that she was preoccupied with the thoughts of maintaining her family home. In these pictures, I can see that the exterior stucco needs to be restored. The metal standing-seam porch roof is rusting and needs to be replaced. Inside, the paint on the architectural trim is chipped, and the cast-iron staircase in the main hall needs the rust brushed off and to be repainted (figure 1.24). She knows that her share of the profits earned by the Pilgrimage Garden Club for this spring's pilgrimage will help pay for some of these repairs, but the list of items needing renovation at The Elms seems endless.[47] Living in, and owning, an old house museum is not for the faint of heart.[48]

Standing aside as an onlooker, Hoelscher watches Miss Alma light a cigarette. I can only assume that she thinks about all of this as she watches the next round of tourists exit the large coach and gather at her front gate. She extinguishes her smoke, but being a child of the Great Depression, she does not discard it. Instead, she gracefully conceals the half-burned cigarette behind her back, tucking it into the waistband of her hoop skirt. She will relight it at a later time. Elderly but most definitely not decrepit, she prepares herself for the tourists. Alma Carpenter is about to perform. She "receives" her guests: "I'm Alma Carpenter and welcome to my home, The Elms. My family has lived here since 1878, so I guess that's long enough to call it home." She then points out the "old" wing and then the "new" wing. Both wings were built in the nineteenth century, in 1805 and 1855, respectively. She explains how the cast-iron interior staircase was once outside but was relocated during the 1855 renovation. She vividly talks about its first builder, John Henderson, the author of the first published book in Mississippi and the first postmaster in the Mississippi territory. She responds to questions about her dress and others from a couple from Iowa about what happened in Natchez during what she called the "War between the States." She lets a little girl hold her pilgrimage queen tiara and scepter. She concludes her introduction with a pleasant-sounding, lyrical delivery, completely invoking southern propriety: "Now if you have any more questions, don't hesitate to ask—don't be shy now, you hear." And as the coach drives away after another successful tour, Miss Alma enjoys the rest of her half-smoked cigarette and waits for the next group to arrive, when she will perform her narrative of The Elms, Natchez, and the pilgrimage all over again.[49]

Other women have been doing this performance here since 1932.

These individually owned large homes placed a significant financial burden on their owners throughout the second half of the nineteenth century and into the twentieth century. Until 1932, there was little, if any, revenue brought into the city to preserve them. Cotton, the cash crop that brought wealth to their grandparents and great-grandparents, had been all but obliterated, first by the abolition of slavery and then the infestation of the boll weevil in the early 1900s. The economic calamity of the Great Depression only made matters worse. Cultural tourism, through the celebration of exceptional late eighteenth- and nineteenth-century architecture, provided the means by which the historic homes were preserved. Improvisational performance, pertaining to showcasing antebellum heritage and historic architecture that fulfilled the perceptions and expectations of the northern tourists, made it successful.

Improvisation in giving tours of southern plantation houses or Natchez villas is a predominant aspect of southern cultural tourism. But in Natchez, almost all of the improvisations are centered around a common theme: "Where the Old South Still Lives." The presenters rarely adhere to a script describing the history and heritage of a historic place.[50] Pre-

Figure 1.25: D'Evereux photographed in 1934. (Library of Congress, Prints & Photographs Division, Historic American Buildings Survey, HABS MISS,1-NATCH.V,2-)

senting the narrative of the place in Natchez, and in nearly everywhere else in the South, has been, and continues to be, an extemporization, a theatrical expression that reflects the presenter's personality, her personal outlook on the world, and her reaction to the specific physical traits and queries of the audience. Place and entertainment are the only constants within the experience for the audience.[51] The narrative enabled the women in the Natchez Garden Club to enliven the historic architecture, as well as present it in a manner suitable for the individual audience experiencing it for the first time. This made, and continues to make, the tour more nuanced and complex, especially as the pilgrimage becomes ever more racially diverse for both presenters and tourists. More importantly, the individualized narrative enables them to do what they initially intended to do with the tourists: "pretend" (figure 1.25).[52]

There has never been one singular heritage narrative in Natchez. Since the beginning, tourists have laughed about getting a different story every time they visited a historic home. However, each narrative or presentation relates to the common theme of the city.[53] There are three ways in which the narrative works in making Natchez a historyland: the place—the historic buildings, the collection of nineteenth-century American architecture in this southern town that makes Natchez unique; the presenters—docents and guides who provide an intimate experience to each tourist; and the performance—the individual presentation and the tableaux—presenting the women's personalized and subjective image of their town and its heritage.

Place is the primary feature in the Natchez experience. Unlike Savannah, Charleston, New Orleans, or Williamsburg, which are perceived more as intact urban complexes by tourists, Natchez presents itself in a fresh and fluid manner during the pilgrimages. The villas are distinct from one another, yet each one contributes to the collective experience through their geographical proximity, the period in which they were first built, and their shared history. And they do juxtapose with each other: the sublime and resplendent Melrose, Stanton Hall, and Dunleith; the incomplete and tragic Longwood and Arlington; and the plain, ordinary, and quirky—Hope Farm and the House on Ellicott Hill. The pilgrimage was designed to be experienced via automobile, and motorized transportation has always been provided but at an added cost to the tourist. The garden club women explicitly stated that guides are not necessary: arrows and signs, designed as silhouettes of southern belles, provide all the directions needed for the tourists.[54] The physical experience is that of touring houses individually, thereby viewing them as individual vignettes. Tourists appreciate the city's collective heritage through the common thread of a loosely scripted narrative, which is conveyed from one historic home to another and through staged performances. With approximately eighteen to twenty-four of the forty historic homes featured during any given pilgrimage, and only a few of the most well-known ones opened to the public annually, the presenters evolve the nuances of the narrative to best suit the house's architecture. The fluid nature of the Natchez narrative runs counter to the prevailing scholarly perceptions of plantation tours (or pilgrimage tours).[55] Most literature about southern cultural tourism in heritage management and anthropology focuses on performance and script, and it is often preoccupied with functional categorization and representation of the place's original inhabitants, for example, "master and slave" (by Eichstedt and Small)[56] or "affective inequality" (by Modlin).[57] Little, if any, of the literature explores the role of the ever-enduring and historically preserved place—the "big house" or mansion and its supporting structures: slave cabin, kitchen building, and stable, which can be found at both the plantation and the Natchez villa. In their examinations of cultural tourism in the South, public historians and anthropologists typically focus on the interpersonal relations between white master and enslaved African Americans, the region's intangible heritage. But pilgrimage tourism is more than the intangible. The architecture of these places is distinct and, in most cases, exceptional. How the architecture shaped the culture, specifically, the intangible heritage,

Figure 1.26: Mrs. William T. Martin of Philadelphia, Pennsylvania (formerly Miss Eliza Couner of Natchez). Many of Natchez's belles married northerners and moved to the Northeast and the Midwest. They returned to Natchez and volunteered their time as docents for the early pilgrimages. (From *Natchez and the Pilgrimage* by Georgie Wilson Newell and Charles Cromartie Compton [Kingsport: Southern Publishers, 1935])

is hardly ever discussed, but it is the place that enables the tourist to ponder racial relations in the nineteenth-century South. The perception of the place changes through time, and the meaning of it varies from the person experiencing it. However, the house, or monument, remains static and preserved. While some forms of cultural tourism—music and food—may not completely be tied to place, plantation tourism and "Old South" tourism is most definitely entwined with place. The Natchez villas and the plantation homes adjacent to them are powerful symbols of the region, and they are architectural and cultural monuments that attract tourists. In summary: no Natchez villas, no Natchez tourism.

The presenters of the narrative, through the place, play the second most important role in how the narrative sustains and preserves the "historyland." The presenters' objective has always been to entertain their tourists and entice them to eagerly tour the next historic home. "Romance lurks in every corner of Natchez, almost every structure has its own legend," wrote Bette Barber Hammer for *Holland's Magazine* in 1955.[58] The presenters' point of view, background, and characteristics—economic, social, and racial—influence it. The presenters are most often women, but men do guide tourists around the villas. They can be professionals, like the National Park Service rangers at Melrose, but most often they are either volunteers or paid part-time staff.

Social class plays a role in how the narrative is conveyed. There are two types of presenters: docents and guides. Docents are owners of the villa (like Miss Alma), women associated with the owners of the house, or personal friends and relatives who take part in the pilgrimage as a confirmation of their social status within the city. Ownership of one of the historic homes or volunteerism (active membership in either the Natchez Garden Club or the Pilgrimage Garden Club) are the ways in which a Natchez woman climbs the social ladder or maintains her position on it. Most of these women have been receiving their tourist guests for decades. Dressed in the period hoop skirts, bonnets, and bangles, surrounded by the opulent antiques and house furnishings, these Natchez women portray a nineteenth-century stereotype of the "southern lady" that idealized passivity and male protection. The "lady of the house" is first a docent and, in the case of Miss Alma, through her extensive knowledge of Natchez history, eventually becomes a "doyenne" of the city's narrative (figure 1.26).[59]

For her article "'She Goes into Character as the Lady of the House': Tour Guides, Performance, and the Southern Plantation," published in the *Journal of Heritage Tourism*, Amy Potter interviewed twenty-eight docents and guides at four River Road plantations in Louisiana, located approximately 121 miles south of Natchez in White Castle, Louisiana, in order to understand the demographics of these women, the skills needed to be a guide, and the ways they addressed racially charged issues, namely slavery.[60] In one of her interviews, a female tour guide explains how class plays a role in this work:

> I guess the irony is that we're actually not docents. Docents are rich-born women. [laughter] Um, we're just straight guides. We're workers. . . . For eight hours, [we] have to be bright and sunny. We sometimes deal with deaths in the family, with things happening with our families, with being out in this heat in costumes, with dealing with people who are not always kind to us because they see us as nothing more than service workers, and we do it anyway. We get up. We drink coffee. We deal with whatever craziness . . . life is throwing at us and when we step out on a tour, we're like jazz hands, spirit fingers.[61]

The guides vary in age, race, and education, but they all have one thing in common: they mostly enjoy performing the Natchez narrative for tourists.[62] Younger women are often high school or college students who work during the pilgrimage or on weekends or give tours of the historic houses during the summer. Older women often are volunteers. They all bring specific skill sets to the job.[63] Every docent or guide understands that they are entertainers, and their audience does not wish to listen to a script; visitors want to experience the place and perhaps escape from the contemporary world for only a short while. "I don't just offer a tour," explained one guide, "I give them the experience to let them know how the Southern people lived in the seventeen and eighteen hundreds."[64] Through a cultural performance with a historical landscape, which reaffirms a perception of a place from a visiting group of people, and by enacting a cultural ritual, which reaffirms the place's social hierarchy, docents and guides perpetuate a tradition based on heritage and lore. "The past is not simply there in memory," noted cultural anthropologist Andreas Huyssen, "but it must be *articulated* to become a memory."[65]

Performance is the final component that enables the narrative to work with the place and makes a fulfilling tourist experience during the pilgrimage and other times of the year. Until 2016, there were two types of performances: the house tour and the tableaux, which will no longer exist in the future.[66] These performances made the thirty or so individual historic buildings a coherent "historyland" experience. Hoelscher describes these acts as cultural performances, which are non-ordinary, framed public events that require participation by a sizable group, emphasizing that they are "reflexive instruments of cultural expression in which a specific group of people reaffirm their identity by simply telling a story about itself."[67] Social anthropologist and memory studies scholar Paul Connerton states that "performance is the chief way in which societies remember."[68] In tying performance to cultural identity, Hoelscher reaffirms Shils's ideas of tradition and how society uses it, what Lowenthal refers to as heritage, and what British heritage management expert Mike Robinson defines as "intangible heritage."[69] But Hoelscher does not acknowledge the most important and obvious aspect of the "non-ordinary cultural performance" that occurs in Natchez or at any southern historic plantation—that is, place.[70] Without the historic homes and landmark buildings scattered throughout the city, the narrative would have no meaning or relevance. Place and performance are integral to each other. The garden club women innately understood that their place was different—even exotic to the outside world—and grew up performing and romanticizing about it.[71] To them, the performances, *relating to place*, were the obvious means to make the city interesting for tourists.

The house tour is a multifaceted performance, which is based partly on scripted elements and a large measure of spontaneity. It has to be more than simply reciting a part in a play. A guide or docent must be a group leader, information giver, and entertainer.[72] Partly due to the sense of monotony and partly due to the expectations of a particular audience, no two performances are the same. The performances in the house are ephemeral, but over time they build up to be the cultural tourism experience.

As the demographics of tourists have changed over the years, so has the house tour performance. Potter notes this and, as an example, points out how docents and guides depict slavery in the South and in Natchez. She contends that the guides are prone to change their narrative from audience to audience, concluding that these changes are mainly driven by differing viewpoints between the generations and that the guides perceive these viewpoints through their experiences of presenting their narratives. She quotes an African American female guide:

> I mean, I'll admit, you can tell who's looking for what. Elderly white southerners tend to want the *Gone with the Wind* view. Younger people, they tend to want the view that's more balanced. African Americans, they tend to want a more Afro-centric view. African Americans from the West Coast, then tend to perceive it as all the slaves were beaten to death and they're angry.

Potter also quotes a white female guide:

> So, if the audience is full of say 40-something African Americans, there is something they want to hear about slavery and to hear that slaves had it really good could be offensive. They don't necessarily want to hear that it was 100 percent horrible. . . . For many people coming out here, validation of their own family history and a way of life is what they're looking for and especially African Americans who come here, seeking something. Some kind of evidence of where they came from because it's difficult to trace their family roots. So as an educator you know you throw out those "do you have any questions?" or you throw out those phrases to get someone to ask you a question.[73]

Potter demonstrates the fluid nature of any given house tour. She also shows how it varies from one demographic to another. But what is important to remember about it is that it is done for entertainment, both on Louisiana's River Road and in Natchez. And while the audience expects to learn from it, they nevertheless want to be entertained. They enjoy watching and participating in pretending. Docents and guides do more than perform; they pretend to be the lady of the house or an enslaved African American or servant, or what an outsider perceives as a "southerner" or a "Natchezian." The original pilgrimage women understood what the paying audience wanted, and through their ability to perform "non-ordinary performances," they delivered a heritage experience that reaffirmed the audience's ideal of the southern past. At first,

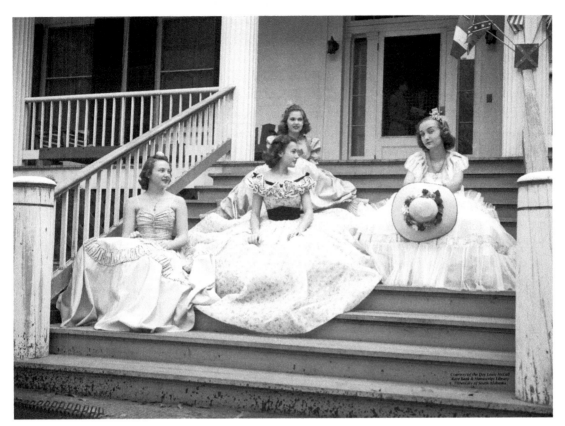

Figure 1.27: Four girls in period dresses, 1940. (S. Blake McNeely Collection, Doy McCall Rare Book and Manuscript Library, University of South Alabama)

they wanted to show them what they loved about Natchez—its Spanish colonial heritage. But soon after the first pilgrimage, they gave them what they wanted: antebellum southern heritage. The docent and guide improvisations are personalized entertainment, wrapped up in a milieu of history, which is heritage (figure 1.27).

The second type of performance is a clever dramatic device, invented in the eighteenth century, that women and men may have originally enjoyed when they were children growing up in the late nineteenth century. It is commonly known as the tableau, but it has also been called the "tableau vivant." According to Natchez Pilgrimage Tours, "a tableau is a living picture; a representation of a scene by a person or group without moving. Before the age of modern technology, this was a popular form of entertainment in private homes, theaters, and schools and continued into the twentieth century."[74] The tableau was a recreational experience, typically performed in upper-class parlors during the nineteenth century, in which a group of people, mostly women, pose for a striking scene.[75] The relaxed atmosphere of the parlor, away from public rudeness, provided the refuge to socialize (i.e., gossiping and entertaining) through drama, even if there were no speaking parts in it. The tableau vivant was a parlor game.[76]

Tableaux were popular in antebellum Natchez, but they became very popular there during the latter part of the nineteenth century. Guidebooks published by the Daughters of the American Revolution and other women's organizations recommended allegorical tableaux to represent abstract virtues of the South and the nation. These performances provided nineteenth- and early twentieth-century women the opportunity to take part in national celebrations that expressed their strong sense of patriotism and social interaction.[77] Natchez women were no different. In 1887, 150 local amateur male and female actors performed a *kirmess*, which included a tableau, featuring actors representing the nations of the world during a Fourth of July celebration in the city. Tableaux were typically performed during the city's Mardi Gras celebration and at Christmas.[78] Women who would later create the Spring Pilgrimage grew up performing tableaux, and for most of them, it became an outlet for their creative dramatic expression and a means for their fantasies to be expressed about their homes and city in a way that portrayed their families' and their homes' history. In 1921, founding Natchez Garden Club member Anna Metcalfe Fleming wrote and performed her own tableaux for her friends' enjoyment and later as a fundraising activity for her church. One of them, her "Garden of Dreams," contained no dialogue, only allegorical scenes depicting old age, youth, and childhood; the women performing it wore elaborate dresses, and Anna used her antebellum home, Ravenna, as the backdrop for her drama.[79]

During the late nineteenth and early twentieth centuries, transforming local history into plays and pageant dramas was a trend occurring throughout the US. The outdoor drama movement, which originated in North Carolina with the successful production of "The Lost Colony" in 1937, drew thousands of tourists to the state's northeast coast to watch the ill-fated adventures of John White's 1587 colony. Paul Green's "The Common Glory" for Williamsburg, Virginia, and "Cross and Sword" for St. Augustine, Florida, are other examples of plays developed for cultural tourism at the same time the Natchez pilgrimage developed. But those events were intentionally created as scripted dramatic productions.[80] By keeping the Natchez pilgrimage performance simple, in tableau form, women were able to enlist their family and friends into the event and provide room for improvisation, which became a popular attraction during the pilgrimage (figure 1.28).[81]

From the beginning of the pilgrimage, race has always played a significant part in the Natchez heritage experience. The NGC women saw

Figure 1.28: "Ballet Tableau" in 1934. (From *Natchez and the Pilgrimage* by Georgie Wilson Newell and Charles Cromartie Compton [Kingsport: Southern Publishers, 1935])

this as an opportunity to bring the financial prosperity of the city's cultural tourism to whites and African Americans, but some of them were also uncomfortable exploiting African Americans living with them in the city.[82] Since the beginning of the pilgrimage in the 1930s, the tableau performances occurred in the evenings, while the tours were done during the day. In planning the tableau offerings during the pilgrimage, these women interspersed Confederate and southern gentility-themed tableaux with separate African American gospel spirituals. In their churches, African Americans presented their own performances that reaffirmed their cultural identity in Jim Crow-era Natchez. Most of the garden club women were not only comfortable including the African American experience in their pilgrimages; they were fascinated with the kind of entertainment the African American churches offered in their performance of gospel singing and their tableaux that evolved from their African, Caribbean, and Creole roots.[83] In the early years of the pilgrimages, respect and allotted time were given to the African Americans in Natchez through their churches. The Greek Revival temple Zion Chapel, Rose Hill Missionary Baptist Church, and Beulah Missionary Baptist Church received proceeds equal to the antebellum homeowners for the produced performances of "Heaven Bound."

It would only be later, as the pilgrimage became more commercially successful and nationally renowned, that the role of race changed from a place of segregated but equal mutual respect to a more submissive one: of white master and enslaved Black person. While it cannot be denied that racial prejudice during the first half of twentieth century and the reaffirmation of white elite superiority played a significant role in making this transition happen, economic, marketing, and commercial demand by tourists, who came to Natchez expecting to experience a place of antebellum slavery, also played one as well. In 1932, in the depths of the Great Depression, poverty did not recognize the difference between white and Black in Natchez or the rest of Mississippi. In a state that was first devastated by the boll weevil, which nearly obliterated its primary cash crop, cotton, and then suffered through the banking and investment calamity that was the Great Depression, poverty became a shared condition among everyone. In an interview at the end of her life, Roane Fleming Byrnes summarized the general sentiment of both Black and white residents regarding the dire economic situation created by the Great Depression:

> Look, we are considered the poorest state in the Union. We have nothing but pride and interest, it is a different kind of poor. These people have their historical societies, they're interested in music, a wonderful band out there. It is nothing in the world like the poverty you are thinking of. They are people with pride and interest in things. You are talking about really trash, but when you are talking about these people, you are talking about people with pride.[84]

Today, cultural tourism in Natchez attempts to strike a balance between the city's white and African American heritage. The infamous slave market, Forks of the Road, a site belonging to the city of Natchez and private property owners, is recognized by a Mississippi Department of Archives and History roadside plaque and slave chains laid into the concrete.[85] The Rhythm Club Fire, also known as the Natchez Dance Hall Holocaust, when 209 African Americans were killed in what is now ranked as the fourth deadliest assembly and night club fire in US history, is also presented to tourists.[86] Through the leadership of the Historic Natchez Foundation, African American landmark such as the all-Black Brumfield School, have been listed on the National Register of Historic Places.[87] The Natchez Museum of African American History and Culture attempts to fill the history and heritage gap in the Natchez African American story between slavery and Martin Luther King Jr.[88] There are also more modern narratives that are presented to tourists in Natchez. Historian Karen L. Cox's book *Goat Castle: A True Story of Murder, Race, and the Gothic South* recounts the grisly story of how two of Natchez's most eccentric white citizens, Richard Dana and Octavia Dockery, solicited African American George Pearls to rob their reclusive neighbor, Jennie Merrill. During the mishap, Merrill was shot and killed. Today, the 1932 scandal has become part of the updated Natchez narrative.[89]

Figure 1.29: A white girl in period dress with an elderly African American woman depicting the role of a house servant sitting in front of the cooking fireplace in Arlington, circa 1975, Natchez, Mississippi. Even the utilitarian architectural elements play a prominent role in depicting the narrative of antebellum Natchez. (Courtesy of the Archives and Records Services Division, Mississippi Department of Archives and History)

How Natchez perceives its position within the state, region, and nation influences its "sense of place." David Glassberg writes that local residents determine their sense of place through their historical consciousness and their place consciousness. Historical consciousness evolves from history or folklore that is attached to the locality. It is a web of memory sites and social interactions constructed by a place's inhabitants. Place consciousness is formed through the way inhabitants relate their environment to the broader world. Glassberg further states that history attached to a particular place communicates political ideology, group identity, and revenue gain. Perception of place is the result of historical consciousness: combining the remembrance of the past, through history, ballads, yarns, and legends, and place consciousness forged by social and political forces, both within and beyond the community, which are inextricably intertwined.[90] Through this viewpoint, residents transform their everyday environments into "storied places," which have a specific historical character that is embraced by the prevailing political elite and conveyed to tourists. Henry Glassie describes the final outcome of this ritualistic act, in which history becomes more than a crucial part of the environment, by stating, "history is the essence of the idea of place."[91] It becomes a novelty to the "storied" landscape, and it helps make the place a different one for tourists to compare with their homeland.[92] History also becomes the catalyst for preserving and maintaining the place. Few municipalities embrace their historical and place consciousness and attempt to commodify them—but Natchez certainly did.

The commodification of their history into their heritage influenced how Natchezians, and others outside of Mississippi, preserved their built patrimony. This became the narrative. It is a heritage story, which celebrates what is noteworthy about the city's history, both white and Black; gives meaning to its built patrimony; and is the driver of how historic preservation works in Natchez. Like most everything you experience in this city, it is not exactly what you expect (figure 1.29).

Chapter 2

THE EVOLVING NARRATIVE

The mythic "Old South" Natchez we know today was preserved and then showcased by the women of the Natchez Garden Club and later with the Pilgrimage Garden Club, all of whom were middle-aged and middle class to upper class, with great energy, enthusiasm, and imagination. They sought to improve Natchez by leveraging their place in the town's hierarchy as southern ladies, a social position that they had inherited from their mothers and grandmothers. They used their natural base of power, their homes, as the primary means to generate revenue through the built environment of Natchez. From their vantage point, a new economy was evident—one based on tourism, not industrial production. As they became increasingly successful, their narrative evolved and expanded. Beginning in 1932, it included both white and African American history and lore. As the romanticized narrative of the "Old South" gained popularity, authors, architects, newspaper reporters, and even movie producers capitalized on it—incorporating the women's narrative into stories, novels, and motion pictures, culminating with the release of the motion picture *Gone with the Wind* in 1939. As is the case in any historical place, history becomes more accurate and refined, and cultural values change, over time. New narratives that teach about the African American experience in this city have emerged. The Natchez narrative, which made it a compelling place to visit and experience during the early and mid-twentieth century, continues to evolve.

Opulent antebellum mansions, riverboat travel on the lazy Mississippi River, and gracious southern belles—all of this conjures up images perpetuated by eight decades of popular culture that we identify as the "Old South." But "old" and "south" are relative terms. Early generations regarded Natchez as part of the "Old Southwest," and the Civil War was once not an "old" event. Our perceptions of pastness change, especially as pastness is marketed for popular consumption.

The "Old South" that the garden club women wanted to originally celebrate in Natchez was a lot older than the "Old South" we know in Natchez today. In its 1932 mission statement, the Natchez Garden Club (NGC) stated its original objective for the pilgrimage: "To perpetuate the history, traditions and architecture of the Southern Colonial period in Natchez, to heighten civic interest in the town's rich inheritance from the past, and to make Natchez a mecca for students of America's early life and development and thus bring improvement and increased prosperity to the whole community."[1]

The "Southern Colonial" period they referred to was the period between 1779 and 1797, when Natchez was part of the Spanish colony of West Florida.[2] To the NGC members, this was when Natchez was at its most exotic, most enlightened, and most romantic. But no sooner did the pilgrimages began than the women encountered a significant problem: early twentieth-century Natchez could not be characteristically or architecturally described as "Spanish." It had been an American town for a very long time. Unlike places like Old Sturbridge Village in Massachusetts, which Diane Barthel labeled a "staged symbolic community," Natchez is a working city, beset by real problems, and its inhabitants were not, and are not, predominantly Hispanic or Spanish.[3]

Through the invention of the Spring Pilgrimage, which Katherine Grafton Miller claimed to have invented and was inspired by the Virginia Garden Club's Garden Week, these Natchez women attempted what Kevin Lynch observed in heritage places and urban centers: "Choose a past to construct their future."[4] Specifically, they sought to communicate the past and control the present in order to shape the social identity of places and people in their city.[5] The women first evaluated Natchez's historic architecture through their own nostalgia and patriotism, then marketed it for commercial purposes. At first, their initial objective—to celebrate their colonial past through the ritual piety of the pilgrimage—failed to satisfy the demands of the commercial tourism that was attracted to Natchez. The paying tourist audience did not connect with the stories of Spanish history; that narrative was not something that they could see and experience, nor had they learned much about it in school. What they could see, however, was the built patrimony of Natchez: architecture that was tied to antebellum Natchez. The garden club women cannily revised the pilgrimage narrative, shifting the historical era from Spanish colonial Natchez to antebellum Natchez—"Where the Old South Still Lives."[6]

THE USES OF COLLECTIVE MEMORY

Between 1932 and 1942, these Natchez women created a way to commercialize and market their historic city through a loosely configured narrative. Unlike the Spanish colonial narrative, their antebellum narrative was based on their collective memory and their female tradi-

Figure 2.1: The surviving veterans of "Natchez Rifles of 1861," 1910. (Thomas H. and Joan W. Gandy Photograph Collection, Mss. 3778, Louisiana and Lower Mississippi Valley Collections, LSU Libraries, Baton Rouge, Louisiana)

Figure 2.2: Governor Holmes House (Conti House) in 1936, James Butters, Photographer. The stucco on the house was removed during the 1960s to make it resemble American Federal-style architecture typically found in Virginia and Maryland. (Library of Congress, Prints & Photographs Division, Historic American Buildings Survey, HABS MISS,1-NATCH,11-)

tions. French philosopher and sociologist Maurice Halbwachs defined collective memory as the shared pooled of knowledge of the memories of a social group.[7] Further, collective memory is the way a social group acquires, recalls, recognizes, and localizes its identities through memory. In this context, collective memory is related to images and places, events and people. It does not recall the real past; instead, it is a facsimile, based on constructions meant to create an idea of a place that is greater than the place itself. Collective memory and history are distinct. History seeks to be unbiased—a systematic account of acts, ideas, or events of a place and a group of people. Collective memory constructs the past for the present, especially in relation to a social group or a specific audience. There can be different and competing collective memories; this occurs in Natchez with the African American and white collective memories.[8] But what is important to consider is that a collective memory is constructed out of the past as a *narrative*, with a beginning, middle, and a satisfactory, even happy, ending.[9]

These Natchez women constructed the narrative of their city from their collective memory, their self-identity, and their "pastness." Pastness derives from a social group's desired relationship to the past through material things. Pastness does not address how something is; instead, it is a cultural construct of the present, or, in the case of Natchez, of a past the women wanted to convey for commercial consumption, with an aspirational future. It is the result of a particular perception or experience; it is firmly entrenched in a given cultural context. Pastness is related to history, but it is also related to tradition. What matters most are the perceptions of pastness—specifically, the past of an audience's imagination (figures 2.1 and 2.2).[10]

We cannot fully account for the "Old South" Natchez narrative without understanding its connection to pastness. Doing so requires that we understand the lives and experiences of its originators: the NGC women in the 1930s. These women's self-image became intertwined with the narrative they constructed, so much so that the women themselves are part of the Natchez narrative today.

THE GARDEN CLUB WOMEN OF NATCHEZ

The Natchez women who created the pilgrimage were born in the late nineteenth and early twentieth centuries. Their mothers and grandmothers experienced the Civil War and its aftermath; those memories were still vivid—the NGC members themselves had experienced the decline of Natchez and the attempt to industrialize a backwater town. And they suffered through the financial hardships that were the Great Depression. As southern women, they inherited their mothers' sense of duty to protect and perpetuate their region's culture and morals, along with their mothers' strong sense of patriotism and regional pride. But they were also modern women: they were educated, ambitious, and understood the hard reality facing them in early twentieth-century Natchez and Mississippi.

These women's perception of themselves influenced the "Old South" narrative. It also compelled them to create it. These Natchez women inherited and embraced the concept of the "southern lady." Anne Firor Scott explains that the southern lady was a social construct developed in the early nineteenth century, and she defines it as follows:

> This marvelous creation was described as a submissive wife whose reason for being was to love, honor, obey, and occasionally amuse her husband, to bring up his children and manage his household. Physically weak, and "formed for the less laborious occupations," she depended upon male protection. To secure this protection she was endowed with the capacity to "create a magic spell" over any man in her vicinity. She was timid and modest, beautiful and graceful, "the most fascinating being in creation . . . the delight and charm of every circle she moves in."[11]

The southern lady was first the southern belle, who flitted and flirted her way through parties and balls, dreamed of her handsome and gallant ideal beau, and hoped to marry him as soon as she could. These nineteenth-century women first learned the ideal as young girls from their mothers. Later, it was reinforced in finishing or boarding schools, which emphasized Christian virtue and useful skills, such as knitting and sewing.[12] During the nineteenth century, these girls felt considerable pressure to live up to the southern belle persona. An excerpt from a diary of a young Natchez girl suggest the onus on them: "I long to die because I cannot find a husband. I know I would make a faithful and dutiful wife, loving with all my heart, yielding entire trust in my husband."[13]

As married women, they made heroic efforts to live up to the southern lady ideal. They were loyal and submissive to their husbands, but, most importantly, they sought to be devoted mothers of their children, stewards of Christian and southern morals, and protectors of their culture.[14] Their home was their base of power. The southern lady was expected not to be hampered by household chores like cooking, cleaning, and raising a vegetable garden—she only oversaw her servants, who were given these menial tasks. But in reality, the southern lady actively worked in keeping up the home, raising her children, and managing the family's expenses. Along with these expectations, she was expected to engage in society and work to better her community.[15]

The grandmothers of the Natchez Garden Club women had endured the Civil War, which left them a legacy of an aspirational but conflicting archetype. Drew Gilpin Faust describes the inherent tension "of wanting to be useful, patriotic, willing to sacrifice for a greater cause," but at the same time "challenging the assumptions and norms explicitly stated

Figure 2.3: The women of the Executive Board of the Natchez Garden Club, ca. 1934. First row: Sophie Junkin, Margaret Marshall, Olivia Ullman, Kate Doniphan Brandon, Lallie Adams. Second row: Bessie Rose Pritchartt, Katherine Grafton Miller, Emma Marks, Ruth Audley Beltzhoover. Third row: Alma Kellogg, Harriet Dixon. Fifth row: Harriet Ratcliff. (Historic Natchez Foundation)

by their men."[16] Faust contends that, through their experiences and at the end of their lives, southern women of the antebellum and postbellum periods "sought to invent new foundations for self-determination and self-worth."[17] The NGC women combined this nineteenth-century ideal with the emerging modern woman ideal of the early twentieth century—independent, politically active, entrepreneurial, and worldly. They were both the southern woman of propriety, virtue, and patriotism and the enterprising and politically engaged modern American woman (figure 2.3).

As was the case throughout the South, industrialization did arrive in Natchez during the first decades of the twentieth century, albeit meekly. And with it came greater opportunities in business and professions for women (figure 2.4). As Scott states, "the Southern woman could remain single and become a professional worker, she could marry and enliven her life with volunteer work, she could marry and still hold a job, or she could marry and fit into the traditional pattern of domesticity."[18] Mainly due to cultural pressures, women of the elite white class in Natchez predominantly chose to marry their Natchez beaux and enrich their lives

Figure 2.4: Natchez Cotton Mill, circa 1910. (Library of Congress, Prints & Photographs Division, LC-D43-T01-1566)

with volunteer work. But unlike their grandmothers, the expectation of being a fruitful mother had waned. Most of the prominent women of the Natchez Garden Club either were childless or had fewer children than their mothers had. By the time they started the club in 1929, their children had reached young adulthood, and most of the women were middle-aged. Two idealized images from the postbellum period endured of their mothers and were accepted by the elite class of early twentieth-century white Natchez women: one, the southern lady as saintly mother, and two, the southern lady as pious queen of the Confederacy. Scott quotes suffragist Lucian Lamar Knight's introduction to the 1920 *Biographies of Representative Women of the South* in defining the perception of the archetype in the early twentieth century:

> The Confederate Woman. Imagination cannot dwell too tenderly upon a theme so inspiring. Reverence cannot linger too fondly at so pure an altar. The historian's pen, which tells of a Rome and of a Sparta—aye the pen of inspiration which tells of an Israel—has not portrayed her superior, if, indeed, her equal; nor may we expect to find it in all the hidden future. It took the civilization of an Old South to produce her—a civilization whose exquisite but fallen fabric now belongs to the Dust of dreams. But we have not lost the blood royal of the ancient line; and in the veins of an infant Southland still ripples the heroic strain. The Confederate woman, in her silent influence, in her external vigil, still abides. Her gentle spirit is the priceless heritage of her daughters. The old queen passes, but the young queen lives; and radiant, like the morning, on her brow, is Dixie's diadem.[19]

Knight's paean to the southern lady was the cultural patrimony the Natchez women inherited and attempted to embody. It was expected of them to not concern themselves with the prosaic business world of their husbands; they were to be submissive to their husbands, no matter how poorly these men treated their wives. They were also not to endure the mundane work of housekeeping; the servants did the chores. Once their motherly duties were behind them or if they were childless, their calling was to better their culture and protect it from foreign interference. And through their volunteer commitments, they could socialize, enjoying parties and cotillions.

But behind this façade, these women knew very well the difficult and impoverished circumstances of Depression-era Natchez. Throughout the last decades of the nineteenth century, entrepreneurship came to Natchez, much like many towns and cities across the South after the Civil War. Natchez entrepreneurs developed railroad lines, cotton mills and gins, a street railway, a water works, gas works, and a modern hotel. Natchez promoters in 1892 touted its promise: "The manufacturing spirit of the people of Natchez, together with its facilities for carrying on industries of all kinds, points to the conclusion that it will become one of the most important of southern manufacturing cities."[20] However, the infestation of the boll weevil in Adams County beginning in 1907 crippled the local economy. Wealthy planters Alfred Stone and Julian Fort stated in their report of their observations to the First National Bank of Greenville, Mississippi, that the boll weevil had created "panic and demoralization" among the cotton planters in the Natchez District.[21] Economic conditions continued to deteriorate, and by 1920 Natchez was run down. Economic conditions were already dire there before the collapse of 1929. Commercial buildings were dilapidated, and only a few modern buildings were built (figures 2.5 and 2.6).[22]

Poverty was pervasive and only grew worse during the Great Depression. Letters written in 1932 from George Malin Davis Kelly, owner of the grand villa Melrose and considered one of the richest men in town, to his wife, Ethel Moore Kelly, describe the financial uncertainties during the bleak early period of the Great Depression. He constantly worried if checks he has written for his daughter Marion's New York City wedding will clear the bank.[23] He petitioned the city to lower his property taxes because he worried that he may not have the money on hand to pay them.[24] He lamented that old friends had committed suicide, no longer capable of facing financial ruin. He shared with her that their other acquaintances talked bitterly and openly about Communism.[25] Stock dividends, which many of the elite families had come to rely on for their well-being, were cut in half.[26] In 1933, he informed Ethel that the US

Figure 2.5: View of Main Street in Natchez, Mississippi, circa 1925. (Thomas H. and Joan W. Gandy Photograph Collection, Mss. 3778, Louisiana and Lower Mississippi Valley Collections, LSU Libraries, Baton Rouge, Louisiana)

Figure 2.6: Sam Anzalone's service station, Natchez, Mississippi, circa 1930. (Thomas H. and Joan W. Gandy Photograph Collection, Mss. 3778, Louisiana and Lower Mississippi Valley Collections, LSU Libraries, Baton Rouge, Louisiana)

Post Office laid off 15 percent of its employees that year. A year earlier, it had laid off 9 percent of its employees. Many poor African Americans became unemployed as the surrounding farms grew increasingly financially unstable (figures 2.7 and 2.8).[27]

Despite these women's intentions to continue to live up to the southern lady ideal, they realized one grim certainty: they were far from being wealthy. In fact, most of them constantly worried about their financial well-being. Their husbands, originally the "ideal beaux" of their youth,

Figure 2.7: Natchez street scene, 1938, Ben Shahn, Photographer. (Library of Congress, Prints & Photographs Division, Farm Security Administration/Office of War Information Photograph Collection, LC-DIG-fsa-8a16489)

Figure 2.8: Natchez residential scene, 1938, Ben Shahn, Photographer. (Library of Congress, Prints & Photographs Division, Farm Security Administration/Office of War Information Photograph Collection, LC-DIG-fsa-8a16407)

were either incapable of withstanding financial hardships or were in denial. To make matters worse, their homes, the resplendent villas of nineteenth-century planter class Natchez, which were originally built for opulence and large families, were in a state of ruin and expensive to maintain (figure 2.9). Although these stately villas were the base of these women's political and social power, they were nevertheless a financial albatross. Unable to actively engage in the business world and largely ignored by their husbands and the businessmen of the town, they turned to their volunteer work—civic improvement and patriotic pride—to change their fortunes.

Figure 2.9: Hope Farm (Villa), 1938, Frances Benjamin Johnston, Photographer. (Library of Congress, Prints & Photographs Division, Historic American Buildings Survey, HABS MISS,1-NATCH.V,7-)

Their mothers and grandmothers had laid the foundation to transform their built patrimony into a lucrative industry. Natchez began memorializing its Confederate veterans in 1887. Initially, men of the Adams Light Infantry and the Natchez Light Rifles founded the Confederate Memorial Association (CMA), but at their first meeting, the men elected thirty-five women as honorary members. The CMA women took a more directed approach in memorializing the "Lost Cause of the Confederacy," initially maintaining and decorating Confederate soldiers' graves in the Natchez City Cemetery and later raising funds for a monument to the city's fallen Confederate soldiers and still-living Confederate veterans, placed near Saint Mary's Cathedral in the city's Memorial Park. By 1890, women took leadership roles in the CMA. Melanie Frank served as the CMA's vice president, assisted by Laura Montieth, Ellen Henderson, and Livie J. Baker. Female membership in the CMA soon outgrew male membership; 160 members were women, while sixty were male, all veterans of the Adams Light Infantry. As the Civil War generation began to age out and then pass away, the next generation of women transformed this civic activity in Natchez. Inspired by memories of the Civil War, passed down by their family members and a sweeping wave of patriotism that began in the mid-nineteenth century, these women founded the Mississippi State Society of the Daughters of the American Revolution (DAR) in 1897 and helped transform the CMA into the United Daughters of the Confederacy (UDC) in 1900. By 1923, with most of the Civil War generation passing, the United Confederate Veterans (an outgrowth of the CMA) merged with the UDC, thereby assigning the mission of preserving Confederate monuments to these women of Natchez (figure 2.10).[28]

Figure 2.10: The Natchez confederate monument placed in the St. Mary's Basilica Cemetery. (Photograph by the author)

Figure 2.11: The Natchez Trace monument near Tupelo, Mississippi, presented by the Daughters of the American Revolution in 1914. (Library of Congress, Prints & Photographs Division, Historic American Engineering Record, HAER MS-15)

During the first decades of the twentieth century, patriotic commemoration through the erection of monuments had become a primary motive for civic-minded women throughout the nation. In 1906, Elizabeth Jones of Holly Springs, in north Mississippi, and a founder of the Mississippi State Society of the DAR, proposed marking the old Natchez Trace with stone monuments. Her intent was to memorialize the trace for patriotic reasons. Soon, DAR women along the old trace from Nashville to Natchez funded granite and bronze markers to commemorate the famous trail (figure 2.11).

Mourning and memorialization may have been these women's original motives for preserving historic monuments, but so was preserving the home values, family ties, and regional identity the monuments represented. For American white upper-class women, the act of stewarding the historical landscape became another way to safeguard the ideal of home and exercise moral authority in society through virtue, refinement, and patriotism. Today, preservationists, public historians, and cultural geographers describe those women's approach as "personalism," and it was the foundation of the historic preservation movement in America. Historic preservation traces its beginnings to Ann Pamela Cunningham, who established the Mount Vernon Ladies Association of the Union, which led and financed the restoration of George Washington's Mount Vernon in 1853. James Lindgren defines personalism as "the feminine-based historic preservation that is based on an individual's or society's intimate bond with human settlements that connected the living with the dead." Personalism focuses on the interconnectedness of spirit, body, and nature; it places greater importance on an artifact's ties to values of individual character, love of family, respect for community, personal intimacy, and humility before God. Lindgren summarizes, "personalism stressed the material and immaterial bonds that made people human."[29] Because it is rooted in the connection of intangible to tangible heritage, personalism in the built patrimony can only be communicated by tradition. And the means for tradition to communicate, to anyone, is through narrative.

Personalism also allowed these women to develop a collective memory, which was based on their intrinsic beliefs and the way they attributed memories to the tangible monuments around them. It also provided them the excuse to meet, discuss the affairs of their meeting clubs, socialize, and gossip. Historical places became the forum where family memories were repurposed for modern purposes. Rituals, meetings, social occasions, and ceremonies reinforced these women's sense of purpose and also enabled them to participate in the public sphere. Throughout the country in the nineteenth century, women were forbidden to publicly speak about civic affairs. In 1890 Natchez, women of the CMA sat silent as the men spoke about the efforts to erect a Confederate monument, which these women had predominantly raised the funds to build. Most men expected women of the late nineteenth and early twentieth centuries to follow the advice of Saint Paul: "Oh let the women keep silent all." But through personalism, which compelled them to preserve, and gave them a purpose and an excuse to socialize, these turn-of-the-century women saved old and decaying historical monuments from demolition. From Concord, Massachusetts, to Jamestown, Virginia, women like the ones in Natchez, through personalism, preserved historical monuments in order to promote those values and be the means by which they expressed the meanings and values of their collective memory.[30]

Personalism provided them an agenda to improve their society, along with allowing them to display the noble attributes of motherhood (even if some were childless). And while organizations like the UDC and the DAR continued to flourish in Natchez and continued to preserve landmarks throughout Natchez and Mississippi, new women's organizations catering to the needs of modern upper and middle-class women emerged. None did so more successfully than the Garden Club of America.[31]

Societal and recreational pursuits were the initial objectives of the garden club movement, which swept across the country during the 1910s and 1920s. Garden clubs attracted white middle- and upper-middle-class women to organize, socialize, and improve their communities. But through the organizations, particularly in the Natchez Garden Club, these women became more engaged in the political and economic spheres. In examining how women's associations evolved, Jean Gould Bryant notes that "it was soon evident that male critics of the various female associations had been correct: membership in such organizations did cause women to question their limited sphere; it did make them more independent and assertive, and it did cause them to invade the public arena."[32] Unlike in the DAR and the UDC, traveling to various towns and cities to tour gardens and learn about ornamental flowers and enjoy lavish gardens became the primary motives for meeting in regional and state garden clubs.[33]

Personalism and historical sites soon became part of the mission of garden clubs throughout the South. Recording and preserving historic American ornamental gardens were prominent activities in eastern garden clubs throughout the 1920s and early 1930s. Alice G. B. Lockwood's *Gardens of Colony and State* (published between 1931 and 1934) compiled the research that these amateur horticulturists and preservationists produced during this time. Lockwood's publication was a massive

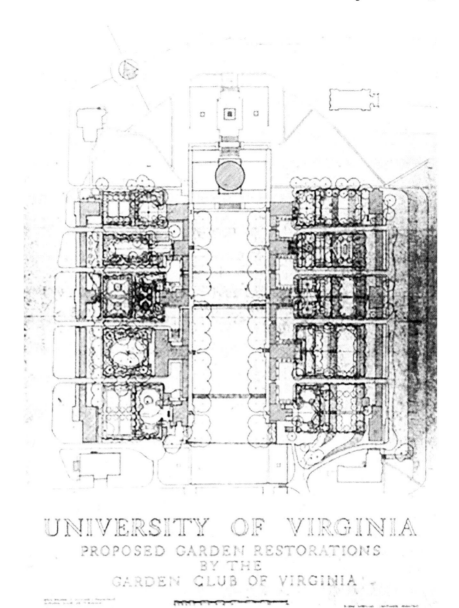

Figure 2.12: The lawn of the University of Virginia by the Garden Club of Virginia, 1930. (Library of Congress, Prints & Photographs Division, Historic American Buildings Survey, HABS VA, 2-CHAR,1B-)

two-volume work. Its publication marked the first time that gardens were recognized to have landmark value in the US. Lockwood not only catalogued historic gardens in the Northeast but also historic gardens in Virginia and the Carolinas. For these women, historic gardens, or at the least the memory of them, had personal meaning, and they projected American feminine virtues onto them.[34] Through this publication, along with publicly enjoying gardens, the southern lady ideal was reintroduced to many women in the South, but it now merged with the new modern woman ideal. Garden club women also embraced historic preservation through personalism. In the South, the most pioneering garden club was the Garden Club of Virginia (GCV); from its founding in 1913, the GCV began restoring historic gardens in the state—most notably, Monticello, the East Lawn of the University of Virginia, the Adam Thoroughgood House, and Bacon's Castle. In 1929, the GCV conducted the first tour of the historic gardens. Virginia's Historic Garden Week became instantly popular; it spurred the establishment of other garden clubs throughout the South (figure 2.12).[35]

In 1929, the State Garden Club of Mississippi was founded. That same year, the Natchez Women's Club established the Natchez Garden Club as an outgrowth of the Natchez Women's Club's city beautification program.[36] The way the NGC was established is an important point. Unlike with the UDC and DAR, historical memorialization was not the NGC's original intent. This social club was established by a new generation of white Natchez women who first adhered to the southern lady ideal. But these were also predominantly middle-class modern women. The NGC provided a means for socializing, a place to work together to engage in civic improvement, and lastly, a way to reinforce the social order of their families within Natchez. Most notably, these women based their power structure on their tangible and intangible power base—the historic villa and home—and their traditional role, as described by Faust, as the manager of it (figure 2.13). Although initially based on the national model for civic improvement, garden restoration, in reality, was merely an aspirational objective for the NGC. Few of its members had the means to return their gardens to their nineteenth-century magnificence. Yet as a

Figure 2.13: Virginia Roane Beltzhoover on horseback in front of Green Leaves, 1922. (Thomas H. and Joan W. Gandy Photograph Collection, Mss. 3778, Louisiana and Lower Mississippi Valley Collections, LSU Libraries, Baton Rouge, Louisiana)

Figure 2.14: The Spanish Market, Canal Street, Natchez, Mississippi, 1927. (Thomas H. and Joan W. Gandy Photograph Collection, Mss. 3778, Louisiana and Lower Mississippi Valley Collections, LSU Libraries, Baton Rouge, Louisiana)

new forum for promoting values of the collective memory of these Natchez women, the NGC allowed them to balance the southern lady ideal with the aspirational one of the modern woman.

The NGC women were different from their mothers' generation. Although they continued to project the impression of being submissive to their husbands and uninterested in business affairs, they were highly aware of financial matters and "real world" business. They remained quiet at times, but they did not the heed the advice of Saint Paul. Their first effort to preserve historic buildings in Natchez was a disappointment: they failed to save the Old Spanish Market from demolition in 1924.[37] The campaign to save the Spanish Market says a lot about these women's interest in their city's heritage. Unlike the personalism ideas of their mothers, who had spent the past thirty years memorializing the Civil War and the Confederacy, this generation of Natchez women found colonial Natchez more appealing than the Confederate one. To them, the old Spanish Market was one of the primary landmarks of that heritage. It symbolized the exotic nature of what they thought Natchez should have been during the eighteenth century, when it was ruled by the Spanish crown (figure 2.14).[38]

It was through their involvement in the preservation of historic Natchez that these women found their voice and purpose in society. Particularly notable were Katherine Grafton Miller, Roane Fleming Byrnes, Edith Wyatt Moore, Ruth Audley Beltzhoover, Harriet Shields Dixon, Ethel Moore Kelly, Alma Cassell Kellogg, and Mary Louise Kendall Goodrich Shields. At the beginning of the pilgrimage enterprise, these women mainly supported their husbands and aspired to conform to the southern lady persona. By the end of their lives, they were leaders of Natchez and had earned the respect of not only Mississippi, but the nation. They restored important and not-so-important buildings in their city, they built and marketed a commercial empire, and they helped build an iconic parkway. They saw the country and the world, and they worked with and persuaded the country's most powerful, influential politicians and policymakers to help fund their initiatives.

From the 1930s until the late 1970s, Katherine Miller and Roane Byrnes played instrumental roles in preserving Natchez. Their influence defined and shaped the "Old South" in Natchez; the legacy of their successes—for Natchez, Mississippi, and the South—is both impressive and conflicted. No one, especially not them, could have ever expected what they would accomplish when they first helped organize the Spring Pilgrimage in 1932. Byrnes was four years older than Miller, and they knew each other quite well. They both came from old, established families and shared the same friends throughout their youth and early adulthood. In the beginning, they worked together, but soon pursued their separate passions. For Miller, it was the development of the pilgrimage; for Byrnes, it was the building of the Natchez Trace Parkway. Through the Pilgrimage Garden Club, Miller led the efforts to preserve Stanton Hall, Longwood, and King's Tavern. Through the Natchez Garden Club, Byrnes preserved Connelly's Tavern (The House on Ellicott's Hill) and the Priest's House (James Andrews's house). Neither woman had children, but throughout their lives they strived to live up to the motherly ideals of the southern lady. Miller urged her friends' children to call her "Play Mama,"[39] while Byrnes loved for children to call her "Sweet Auntie."[40] Both women indulged in their wild and romantic imaginations, which centered around Natchez and were first perceived, by some, as mere immaturity. But by using personalism, they helped form the collective memory of the town, and they turned the stories that they created out of it into the compelling part of a profitable narrative, which launched a cultural tourism industry in Natchez.

Both women were enthusiastic, possessed great energy, and were eternally optimistic and very charming, even flirtatious. They enjoyed the company of women, especially their fellow garden club members, but they also enjoyed working with men, some of whom were leaders not only in America but in Mexico. Throughout their lives, Katherine Miller

Figure 2.15: Katherine Grafton Miller in 1936. This photograph was featured in the Clarksdale (Mississippi) *Press Register*. (Roane Fleming Byrnes Collection [MUM00057], Department of Archives and Special Collections, J. D. Williams Library, The University of Mississippi)

Figure 2.16: Portrait of Katherine Grafton Miller, located in Stanton Hall. Miller is glamorized. (Photograph by the author)

and Roane Byrnes believed that they could "create a magic spell" over any man. Miller enjoyed wearing antebellum-style costumes and performing as the southern lady across the country throughout her career. Byrnes did as well at first, but in her later years she chose to present herself as a modern woman in very "ladylike" fashion—stylish hats and a feminine umbrella by her side became her hallmark. Miller could be charming but insincere in conveying her true intentions; acquaintances of hers in Natchez said that about her.[41] Byrnes, on the other hand, projected a childlike carefree spirit and optimism, which her friends and colleagues found beguiling.[42] But underneath the southern lady image that they projected were two determined and entrepreneurial modern women who were never vanquished and who eventually got what they wanted.

Katherine Miller was the most colorful, dominant, and powerful of these Natchez women. Statuesque with sharp features, dark hair, and brown eyes, she was described as more stylish than beautiful. Like most Natchezians, she was of Scots Irish descent. Throughout her life, she sought to present herself as the ultimate southern lady. She was vivacious, flamboyant, theatrical, and even bombastic in nature; she could display her short temper and curtness to people who displeased her in an instant. Among her more outlandish acts, she took sole credit for creating the Natchez Spring Pilgrimage of Antebellum Homes (figures 2.15 and 2.16).[43]

Born into a well-established but fortune-declining family, Katherine understood firsthand the hardships felt in Natchez during the early twentieth century. Her family settled in and around Natchez around 1800, having relocated there from South Carolina.[44] After arriving in Adams County, the Graftons soon began acquiring land and enslaved African Americans and became prominent planters. By 1860, they had acquired hundreds of acres of land and seventy-one enslaved persons. During the antebellum era, their fortunes ascended, and they became part of the planter class elite. Katherine's paternal grandfather, Thomas Grafton, was an important Natchez leader. He served in the Mississippi House of Representatives and commanded a Confederate regiment during the Civil War. After the war, he was elected Adams County treasurer and then served the remaining years of his life as an editor of the *Natchez Democrat*, a justice of the peace, and a notary public. Although he most likely endured declining economic fortunes after the war, he was a respected member of Natchez society.[45]

Perhaps Katherine Miller's love of the architecture of Natchez also came through her reverence for her maternal and paternal ancestors' heritage. Her maternal great grandfather, Thomas Rose, was one of the most prolific builders of antebellum Natchez. As a master builder and architect, he helped build Auburn, the first home in Natchez built using an architectural plan. He also built The Elms, Elms Court, Edgewood, and, most notably, Stanton Hall.[46]

At the time Katherine was born, the Graftons were still considered among the Natchez elite. Her father, Kirby W. Grafton, worked as a clerk, and her mother, Elodie Rose, was a schoolteacher. Her unmarried aunts, Molly and Jennie Grafton, were seamstresses after the Civil War. Reflecting on her girlhood, Katherine described herself as a daydreamer whose "head was in the clouds most of the time." As a young woman, she faced financial uncertainty due to the decline of the Graftons' financial and social status. But she was a born saleswoman and even sold automobiles in town. She also briefly operated a dance studio in Natchez and worked for a few months as a stenographer. She was in her mid-thirties when the NGC established the Spring Pilgrimage.[47]

As a young woman, Katherine was determined to enhance her social standing in Natchez. She married Joseph Balfour Miller in 1917, when she was twenty-two. Balfour, as he was known, was from several old Natchez families; he was descended from David Hunt's daughter, Catherine, who had married William Balfour. They built Homewood, the largest mansion ever built in Natchez, which burned in 1940. Catherine's sister married George Marshall, who owned Lansdowne. Like Katherine, Balfour was a born salesman and became a somewhat successful real estate agent. Although his colleagues found Balfour charming, they were also suspicious of him and wary of any business opportunity he presented to them. Some people described him as a "grasping swindler."[48] Throughout his marriage, he was also known as a philanderer, a character trait that Katherine largely chose to ignore.[49]

Katherine Miller understood that, to secure her power base in Natchez, she would have to own a Natchez villa. In 1927, she persuaded Balfour to purchase Hope Farm on Homochitto Street from the once wealthy but now impoverished Montgomery sisters. Built around 1789, Hope Farm, which was also called Hope Villa, was one of Natchez's oldest houses; but by the early twentieth century, it was in a state of ruin. Katherine and Balfour devoted the next twenty years to restoring it, along with its garden. Restoring it (among other expenses) put a continuous squeeze on their finances.[50]

Katherine Miller was one of the founding members of the Natchez Garden Club. In 1931, she was elected president of the NGC. In a moment of false modesty, a common trait for the southern lady persona, she later wrote, "I had never belonged to any organization, civic or otherwise. I was inexperienced in club work, but the Garden Club idea appealed to me strongly and soon I was putting my heart and soul into the work of beautifying Natchez. A new venue was thereby opened to me, and since that time it seems that my feet have trod in a garden of lovely experience."[51] While she may have considered beautifying Natchez a noble calling when she joined and soon after led the NGC, she no doubt considered this new venue a way for her to become the elite southern lady of her aspirations. For her, the NGC and the pilgrimage allowed her to transform herself into a flamboyant promoter and performer through her duties as the club's publicity chair. "I at last had found that which I had been seeking all my life," she later recalled, "a worthwhile interest, in which I could turn a seemingly fantastic imagination to good account."[52] Miller devoted her life to Natchez and the pilgrimage; she recognized the potential of heritage-based tourism for Natchez more than anybody and continued to improve on the pilgrimage idea through marketing and preservation of the city's most iconic landmarks.

Her efforts in promoting the pilgrimage began as a civic obligation but soon became her mission. She first began writing earnest letters to newspaper editors to promote the pilgrimage week, but later she gave countless presentations to garden clubs and women's organizations in over seventy cities. She sold the pilgrimage and Natchez with passion and cunning. She audaciously called the town's antebellum houses "lordly structures" and explained that the pilgrimage was more than a mere garden tour; it was a moving *experience*. She frequently boasted that Natchez was able to draw tourists from all parts of the country, who were eager to see the great houses that are "typical of halcyon days of romance and beauty."[53] Writing for the *Chicago Tribune*, Norma Lee Browning described Miller as "a dreamer, an enthusiast, completely charming in the best deep south tradition, and as compelling in full swing as a Kansas cyclone."[54] Author Harnett Kane described her as a "dark-eyed brunette young matron with something of the pent-up energy of a buzz-bomb . . . a combination of Miss Nelly of N'Oleans and Tallulah Bankhead, with a slight dash of P. T. Barnum."[55] And while she always projected herself as the southern lady, Miller also possessed the aggressiveness and audacity of the modern American woman. Journalist Ernie Pyle noted these traits in her: "Mrs. Miller is dynamic and sophisticated, a natural-born-doer-of-things. They say she has fifteen ideas a minute and that thirteen of them are terrible but the other two are knockouts. She is a southerner from generations back, yet she gives you the feeling of a New Yorker, in sporty dress, doing big things in a big way."[56]

In selling the pilgrimage, Katherine Miller dressed the part, attired as a belle of the South, according to historian Karen Cox, "with black lace mitts and heavy gold bracelets," charming Depression-era audiences.[57] One columnist Cox quotes described how "from the moment that Mrs. Miller appears, clad in the picturesque and becoming dress of the [nineteenth] century, we, of the audience, find ourselves living in the past, the romantic past of the South." Harnett Kane, also quoted in Cox's article, attributed Katherine's success to her ability "to outtalk most people she met." As one Atlanta woman remarked, according to Cox, "Mrs. Miller is young and very good to look at, and has one of the most beautiful speaking voices I have ever heard." Kane summarized her as "Woman met Career."

If Katherine Miller could not charm people to get her way, she would then try to intimidate them. A colleague of hers, physician and preservationist Dr. Thomas Gandy, described her as "sweet at times, but domineering as Hell."[58] Even when she was not an elected officer of the NGC and later the Pilgrimage Garden Club, she wanted to forcefully control meetings and ideas. Fellow garden club women recall, according to Falck, that it was "'yes,' Katherine, or 'no,' Katherine." If she liked you, there was nothing she would not do for you; but if she didn't like you, she would stop at nothing to hurt your reputation.

Figure 2.17: Roane Fleming Byrnes in 1936. This photograph was featured in the Clarksdale (Mississippi) *Press Register*. (Roane Fleming Byrnes Collection [MUM00057], Department of Archives and Special Collections, J. D. Williams Library, The University of Mississippi)

Figure 2.18: Roane Fleming Byrnes, 1968, in her parlor at Ravennaside, Natchez, Mississippi. (Roane Fleming Byrnes Collection [MUM00057], Department of Archives and Special Collections, J. D. Williams Library, The University of Mississippi)

For Roane Fleming Byrnes, the transformation from kept housewife and gentlewoman of southern aristocracy to the visionary who would help transform Natchez and Mississippi was more gradual than it was for Miller (figures 2.17 and 2.18). Initially, Byrnes was unsure about taking on the challenges of remaking Natchez, but once she committed her efforts to the NGC, her impact was dramatic. Like Miller, she was vivacious and gregarious. She had always found herself in the middle of the social circles in the city. In her youth, she was an attractive young woman, dark-haired and petite. Her friends later recalled how she enjoyed her "mad career of social whirl."[59] She was regarded as the best waltzer in town, with handsome suitors always flocking to her. Although a good student at Stanton College for Girls in Natchez, she was not a stellar one. She grew up at Ravenna in Natchez, which was built in 1835–36 as the residence of William Harris.[60] She lived with her grandfather, her parents, a bachelor uncle, a distant widowed cousin, her mother's sister, Tildy, and their two children.[61] In her unpublished autobiography, she recalled her childhood as a time that was "unruffled, faintly melancholy satisfaction."[62] During their teenage days, Roane and her sister, Lalie, were regarded as the most popular young belles in Natchez. In adulthood, Lalie would be Roane's steadfast confidante, especially during Roane's NGC and Natchez Trace adventures.[63]

When she was a young woman, Roane yearned to be an accomplished writer and was inspired by familial stories and her surroundings at Ravenna. With its deep, pillared double galleries, grand staircase, and large parlors filled with family heirlooms, the villa stirred Roane's imagination. She was also fascinated by the home's surroundings, the two large formal flower gardens, and, most notably, a large ravine that fronted the home. Family lore also was a source of inspiration to her. A favorite story centered around her strong-willed grandmother, Zuleika Lyons Metcalfe, who hid food and ammunition beneath her hoop skirts and used the ravine to smuggle them to the Confederate soldiers defending Natchez during the Civil War. After arresting Zuleika, Union troops removed her and her family from Ravenna. Zuleika and her children spent the remaining years of the war in a house nearby, but this did not discourage her from routinely confronting Union soldiers and insulting them. Another family legend that Roane relished was about her great-grandfather, Dr. John Coates Cox, an Irishman who lived in the late eighteenth and early nineteenth centuries and served in the British navy. According to the story, he was captured as a young man by African warriors in the kingdom of Timbuktu. During his imprisonment, the African tribe suffered through an epidemic. Dr. Cox saved the life of Crown Prince Abduhl Ibrahim Rahahman, and in a show of gratitude, the African king freed the young doctor, who then returned to England. The story culminates with an older Dr. Cox, who had recently immigrated to Natchez from England, encountering Rahahman, now enslaved, on the street. John bought Rahahman's freedom[64] and paid for his voyage back to Africa, so the prince returned home to his kingdom.[65] This family story was based on the true story of an enslaved African named Abd Rahman Ibrahima, who was the son of King Sori of Futa Jalon ("the land of the Fulbe and Jalunke").[66]

At twenty-three, amidst the whirl of her society engagements, courtships, and family activities, Roane found the time to write a silent movie screenplay called "The Temple of the Sun," based on a legend about the Natchez Indians. Full of adventure and romance, but with an awkward and naive plot, the script was promptly rejected by a Santa Monica movie studio.[67] Undeterred, she wrote five more movie scripts: "The Derelict," "The Countess of the Steerage," "Thru the Ages," "The Serenade," and "For She's a Jolly Good Fellow," which was a joint project with her friends Lallie Lawrence and Mary Mounger. All were rejected by movie studios and publishers.[68] Realizing that scripts were not her calling, Roane moved on to writing romance and gothic short stories. Sentimental and lacking any plot development, these were all rejected by publishers as well. Undaunted, she returned to her childhood love of fairy tales and began writing children's stories. Finally, acknowledging that she might benefit from some guidance, she applied to a home study course from Columbia University in juvenile story writing. She was accepted into the program, and Dr. Mable Robinson was assigned as her instructor. Robinson encouraged her to write about the world she understood and to "see things concretely."[69] Since few good children's stories had been written with the local color of the South, Robinson suggested to Roane that she could fill this niche. In 1927, Roane's short story depicting life in Natchez, "The Secret of the Wild Cherry Tree," was published in *Child Life*. She was thirty-seven years of age, and for all of her hard work she earned forty dollars. For the next two years, Roane continued writing short stories for children, with meager success. By 1930, she had abandoned writing. Later in her life, she recalled that she never viewed her attempts at being a writer as a failure; rather, she discovered her true talent—as a storyteller of places. Her talent would play a crucial part in the creation of Natchez as a heritage construct that defined the idea of the "Old South."

The year of the first pilgrimage, 1932, proved to be a difficult one for Roane Byrnes. On January 17, her father, James Stockman Fleming Sr., died. She was devastated, and her friends recollected that she had often commented, "I worship my dad" (figure 2.19).[70]

Figure 2.19: Britton and Koontz National Bank Building, Natchez, Mississippi. (Thomas H. and Joan W. Gandy Photograph Collection, Mss. 3778, Louisiana and Lower Mississippi Valley Collections, LSU Libraries, Baton Rouge, Louisiana)

Roane's husband, Charles Ferriday Byrnes, known as Ferriday, was a man described in polite southern society as a "good man," their euphemism for a man who was not particularly successful or well liked—a "louse" and a "good-for-nothing."[71] Ferriday and Roane were the same age and grew up together in Natchez society. While Roane enjoyed being courted by numerous admirers, Ferriday seethed with jealousy. Eventually, the two became engaged. Leaving his fiancée in Natchez, Ferriday earned a bachelor's degree at Southwestern Presbyterian University in Memphis (now Rhodes College), and later he earned a law degree at the University of Mississippi and served in the army during World War I. Ferriday had never wanted to return to Natchez and always believed that his life would have been more fulfilling somewhere else. He was an alcoholic, and each day after work, he would immediately retire to their bedroom and drink heavily. By 1930, he was drinking in his office during the day; as time passed, people would see him wandering around downtown Natchez, inebriated.[72] While Roane was disillusioned and sad whenever Ferriday drank, she never complained. As was typical with and expected of most southern women at this time, she tolerated his bad behavior and his alcoholism, and stood by him for the rest of his life.[73]

Ironically, the woman who would later be called the "Queen of the Natchez Trace Parkway" never learned how to drive an automobile, although she tried multiple times to master it when she was young.[74]

Roane's upbringing and young adulthood conformed to the southern belle persona. Friends recollect that she "never washed a cup or saucer in her life, never fried an egg, never lighted a stove, never did anything that would classify her as a housewife." She preferred playing bridge and Mahjong and working in religious and civic organizations. She also enjoyed horseback riding, swimming in the local creek holes, and bird watching, especially with her mother.[75]

Unlike Katherine Miller, relentless ambition did not motivate Roane Byrnes. Although she was childless like Miller, Byrnes seemed to truly enjoy children; she never lost her childlike wonderment of the world. And even though she had come to the realization that she was never going to be an accomplished writer, she enjoyed spinning a story. Friends and acquaintances recalled how, as one friend remembered, one could "give her just an idea and before it was over, you have a complete and maybe totally different slant on the whole event."[76] Whereas Miller found the pilgrimage an opportunity to pursue her true natural calling, Byrnes enjoyed the adventure that it presented to her. Extroverted by nature, she was a perfect hostess and used this attribute to become a sophisticated lobbyist for what became her passion, the Natchez Trace Parkway. And although she projected a carefree and playful image like Miller, she was tenacious and had high expectations for what she could accomplish.

Edith Wyatt Moore was different from most of her fellow NGC members. Moore became the southern but modern woman who was both married and held a job (figure 2.20). She was also not a native of Natchez; she and her husband, Frank Jefferson Moore, were from Georgia, and her daughters were born in Georgia in 1906 and 1910. Moore had a professional writing career as a correspondent for a newspaper in Chattanooga, Tennessee, and she moved with her family to Natchez in 1919.[77] By 1930, she was a widow. Unlike Byrnes and Miller, she had children. After her two daughters graduated from high school, she became actively involved in the NGC and began researching and writing about the city. She and Byrnes served as the NGC publicists. Moore brought to the club an attitude of learned earnestness and a cerebral approach to the pilgrimage and the showcasing of Natchez. Early on, she wrote historical sketches of pilgrimage homes, which appeared in special "Pink Editions" of the *Natchez Democrat* during the pilgrimage season. Eventually, her status as a historian became accepted by her fellow club members and citizens, so much so that she was hired as a historian for the WPA Writers' Project in 1934. She documented what she considered all of the historic homes and buildings in the city on typed index cards, as stipulated by the WPA. Like Miller and Byrnes, she indulged in making

Figure 2.20: Edith Wyatt Moore in 1937 at Connelly's Tavern. Moore, dressed in antebellum attire, presented her version of the history of Natchez to women's clubs throughout the Midwest. (Roane Fleming Byrnes Collection [MUM00057], Department of Archives and Special Collections, J. D. Williams Library, The University of Mississippi)

the women's collective memory of the place the Natchez narrative; however, as the self-proclaimed historian of Natchez, she went further and legitimized the narrative as accepted fact. As the outgoing president of the club in 1934, Moore impressed on its members her opinion that Natchez history should be showcased as the primary facet of the pilgrimage.

Moore embellished the city's history, but she did not intentionally fabricate it. She was actually accurate about many of the properties she wrote about, and through her work she advocated for historic preservation in Natchez. Her work for the WPA Writers' Project has recently drawn criticism. Historian Ellen Hampton argues that local historians like Moore intimidated and manipulated elderly enslaved persons into saying that they had been happy in slavery.[78] But we cannot prove that her intention was malicious. Norman Yetman points out that the interviews during the WPA project are nuanced.[79]

Like other NGC members, Edith Moore enjoyed dressing up in nineteenth-century hoop skirts, touring the country, and presenting slide shows to promote the history of Natchez. Her calm, level-headed demeanor provided the right counterbalance to Katherine Miller's and Roane Byrnes's exuberance. In the 1950s, she published *Natchez Under-the-Hill* (1957).

Figure 2.21: Dixon Hardware Store, circa 1920. (Thomas H. and Joan W. Gandy Photograph Collection, Mss. 3778, Louisiana and Lower Mississippi Valley Collections, LSU Libraries, Baton Rouge, Louisiana)

Other women fulfilled key roles in developing the Natchez narrative and the pilgrimage business venture. Some of them did not quite fit into the southern lady mold. NGC women like Harriet Shields Dixon were middle-class, wives of downtown retailers, and did not own a historic Natchez villa. Dixon was competent and reliable and attempted to facilitate differences between club members. She was president of the NGC during the organization's two most critical years, 1937 and 1941. Her Shields family was once one of the wealthiest planter families in Natchez, but by the early twentieth century, due to the declining value of their plantations, they were deemed middle class. She married Joseph F. Dixon, who owned the local paint and hardware store, which she helped manage (figure 2.21). Using her retail background, she and Lillie Vidal Boatner later helped market the imagery of "Old South" Natchez to oil companies, furniture companies, toiletry manufacturers, fine cutlery makers, fine china makers, and even Hollywood.[80]

Figure 2.22: Concord, circa 1790, 305 Gayoso Street. Spanish governor Don Manuel Gayoso de Lemos, or possibly his predecessor, Carlos de Grand Pré, built the original residence. Natchez builder Levi Weeks built the classical portico for Stephen ("Don Estevan") Minor between 1812 and 1819. (Thomas H. and Joan W. Gandy Photograph Collection, Mss. 3778, Louisiana and Lower Mississippi Valley Collections, LSU Libraries, Baton Rouge, Louisiana)

Figure 2.23: Concord ruins, 1936. Fire destroyed the historic villa in 1901. (Library of Congress, Prints & Photographs Division, Historic American Buildings Survey, HABS MISS,1-NATCH.V,10-)

Other NGC women were recognized as being wealthy, primarily because their families owned the most lavish villas, but in actuality had limited finances. Ethel Moore Kelly and her husband owned the opulent and grand Melrose. She cannot be considered completely a southern lady for a number of reasons. First, she was born in Manhattan and, in 1901, married George Malin Davis Kelly, whose family was originally from Natchez but relocated to New York after the Civil War. George's family, his grandparents, George Malin and Elizabeth Davis, and then his mother, Julia Davis Kelly, managed to retain their Natchez property after the Civil

War. George Malin Davis also owned the eighteenth-century former Spanish governor Manuel Gayoso de Lemos's residence, Concord (figures 2.22 and 2.23), and two of the most elegant townhouses in Natchez, Choctaw and Cherokee, along with several plantations in Louisiana.

Ethel Kelly's mother-in-law, Julia Davis, had married Stephen Kelly in 1873. Julia died in January 1883, and her father, George Malin Davis, died in October 1883, at which time six-year-old George Malin Davis Kelly inherited the property. Distraught after the death of his wife, Stephen Kelly moved with his son to New York in 1883 and became president of the Fifth National Bank in New York, which his father, Richard Kelly, had founded (figure 2.24).[81] Young George Malin Davis Kelly grew up in New York, was raised by his paternal grandmother, and graduated from Columbia University, where he pursued his passion for singing and acting. A year after their marriage, George took Ethel on an extended honeymoon tour. When they were in Pensacola, Florida, he suggested to her that they visit Natchez and see the villas that he owned (figure 2.25). He toured Ethel through Concord, Choctaw, and Cherokee before leaving for the outskirts of town and Melrose.[82] When they arrived, they were greeted by two Davis servants, Alice Sims and Jane Johnson, who'd been formerly enslaved (figure 2.26). After they were freed, the two African American women joined their former mistress, Julia Davis, at Melrose and continued to work there for many years. Although a local white property agent managed Melrose in Stephen Kelly's absence, it was actually Sims and Johnson who led other free African Americans on the estate and maintained and preserved the iconic villa as it was in 1865. After both women were freed in 1863 with the arrival of the Union Army, Jane Johnson initially left the service of the Davis family but eventually returned (figure 2.27). They even resisted attempts by local residents to steal the villa's fine decorative arts and furnishings. The Kellys were fortunate that Sims and Johnson had protected the villa's contents from plunderers (figures 2.28 and 2.29). With Sims and Johnson, the Kellys continued to preserve Melrose as an antebellum Natchez villa, and after the birth of their only child, daughter Marian in 1909, it became their permanent home. The sisters are today considered two of the earliest preservationists in Natchez. They lived on the estate with the Kellys until they were quite old and later returned for frequent visits until their deaths. Sims died in the 1930s, and Johnson died in 1946 at the age of 103 (figure 2.30).[83]

Ethel Kelly was an active and engaged leader in the NGC and considered Roane Byrnes and Alma Kellogg two of her closest friends; she merely tolerated Katherine Miller. She was very close to her husband,

Figure 2.24: Stephen Kelly in front of Melrose. This photograph was taken before he and his son, George Malin Davis Kelly, relocated from Natchez to New York. (Thomas H. and Joan W. Gandy Photograph Collection, Mss. 3778, Louisiana and Lower Mississippi Valley Collections, LSU Libraries, Baton Rouge, Louisiana)

Figure 2.25: Ethel Moore Kelly and George Malin Davis Kelly at Melrose. The couple relocated from New York to Natchez and began restoring Melrose to its antebellum appearance. (Natchez National Park)

Figure 2.26: Jane Johnson, circa 1900. Jane Johnson and Alice Sims, two formerly enslaved women at Melrose, remained there after the Civil War and preserved the villa for the young absentee owner, George Malin Davis Kelly. Together with George and Ethel Kelly, they continued to preserve it. Both women died and were buried in Natchez in the 1940s. (Historic Natchez Foundation)

Figure 2.27: Melrose, circa 1900. This picture was taken approximately when George and Ethel Kelly returned to Natchez and made it their permanent home. (Historic Natchez Foundation)

Figure 2.28: Servants at Melrose, circa 1910. (Historic Natchez Foundation)

George. They had a warm and loving marriage. To escape the excessive spring and summer heat, she spent several months of the year in Manhattan and New England, where she continued to keep close relationships with her family and friends. After her daughter, Marian Kelly, married Dexter Ferry of Detroit, Ethel spent time in Grosse Pointe, Michigan. During this time away, Ethel and George wrote each other letters every day. On some days, George wrote her twice. In these letters, he kept Ethel updated on the politics surrounding the garden club and in Natchez. He also wrote repeatedly about Ferriday's drunken exploits. Today, George Kelly's letters are owned by the Natchez National Historical Park.[84]

Although they were considered one of the wealthiest families in town, the Kellys worried about their finances—another challenge to her being

Figure 2.29: Dependency buildings at Melrose, circa 1910. (Historic Natchez Foundation)

Figure 2.30: Melrose during the 1933 pilgrimage. (Roane Fleming Byrnes Collection [MUM00057], Department of Archives and Special Collections, J. D. Williams Library, The University of Mississippi)

a southern lady. George complained bitterly to Ethel when his New York stockbroker raised his fee from 2 percent to 5 percent.[85] He managed his family's plantations in Louisiana and occasionally harvested the timber from them; more often than not, he was disappointed in the profits from his timber transactions. The couple were active in civic affairs in town, and they socialized with the other elite families there. Ethel was involved in the First Presbyterian Church and the NGC. George played golf with his friends and sang in several churches in town, as well as Temple B'nai Israel, to which he did not belong to but shared his singing talents. He

also sang in minstrel shows at Institute Hall.[86] Both George and Ethel Kelly made light of the stressful financial times that occurred during the Great Depression. However, in relying on his family's investments in New York, they were often uncertain of their finances. Once, during the pilgrimage, a tourist asked one of the guides showing Melrose, "How did George Kelly manage to survive the Depression with these fine things?" Later, he told the guide, with a sardonic smile, that she should have replied, "He didn't."[87]

Alma Cassell Kellogg, mother of Alma Carpenter (referred to in Chapter 1), was the longtime treasurer of the NGC and later the Pilgrimage Garden Club. She was born at The Elms; her father, Albert Gallatin Cassell, was a middle-class druggist and merchant. She returned to Natchez, inherited The Elms, and married Joseph Bentley Kellogg.[88] A natural-born accountant, Alma Kellogg took great pride in keeping accurate books of the garden clubs' finances throughout her life. She was friends with Katherine Miller, Roane Byrnes, Edith Moore, and Ethel Kelly.[89]

Theodora Britton Marshall was also a combined southern lady and modern career woman of the 1930s. She was born into the elite Marshall family, who owned the villa Richmond. Marshall graduated from the Natchez Institute and never married. She taught at the Oakridge School and worked in the Adams County Sheriff's office; later, she became the Deputy City Tax Assessor. Through her membership in the NGC, she became interested in historic preservation in Natchez. Using the wealth of information she gained working in the city tax office, she began writing tour books of Natchez, which were based on the narrative the women created for their city.[90] Capitalizing on the emerging tourism industry, she partnered with Catherine Dunbar Brown, a friend she met at the Natchez Institute, and established "Ye Olde Booke Shoppe" in the basement of Richmond. Catherine was a former teacher who went on to become a bank teller and insurance agent. In her forties, she married George Brown. Catherine Brown became more involved in the DAR than the NGC. Along with the book shop business, she also started one of the first antique shops in Natchez, capitalizing on the pilgrimage women's showcasing of furnishings and decorative arts in the city.[91]

The youngest of these women, and the longest living, was Mary Louise Netterville Kendall Goodrich Shields. Born in Louisiana, she first married William Kendall, whose family owned Monteigne. Unlike any of the other women, she was very active in politics. In 1936, at the age of twenty-nine, she was elected a Democratic National Committeewoman from Mississippi, a position she held for twelve years. The Kendalls were financially stable, owners of the Natchez Coca-Cola Bottling Company. After William Kendall died in 1961, she married Hunter Goodrich, William's roommate from Princeton, in 1964. She then divided her time between her home in New York and Monteigne. She would marry once again in 1995, at the age of eighty-nine, to Dunbar Shields.[92]

There were other women, like Kate Doniphan Brandon, Ruth Audley Beltzhoover, and Annie Green Barnum, who joined the NGC and worked their collective memory into the marketable Natchez narrative. Brandon stood up against the Natchez politicians and male power brokers whenever they hindered preservation in town or the pilgrimage. And there were other entrepreneurial women, like Lillie Vidal Boatner who relentlessly badgered Hollywood producers to feature Natchez in movie theaters and convinced corporations to include Natchez in their advertising campaigns.[93] Using their shared personalism and romantic imaginations, these women convinced tourists to look beyond the paved streets and modern hotels, as well as the electrically lit downtown street lamps that illuminated their run-down city and barely functioning factories and see instead "the glamorous aura of history and romance from which one does not easily escape."[94] In order to accomplish this, they needed to craft a narrative to evoke a certain atmosphere—the romance of a mythic "Old South."

INVENTING THE NARRATIVE

"Romance lurks in every corner of Natchez, almost every structure has its own legend!" So exclaimed Bette Barber Hammer in her book, *Natchez' First Ladies: Katherine Grafton Miller and the Pilgrimage*.[95] Partly based on fact and partly on lore, the Natchez narrative has always been the product of personalism, which was brought about by economic circumstances caused by the Great Depression. And it remains this way to this day. Throughout the decades, it has never been completely dismissed by Natchezians, only modified. It continues to be a living and evolving story of the place, influencing how Natchez is preserved.

Even the origin of the pilgrimage is part of the narrative and is a mixture of fact and lore. According to the story, in early 1931, the NGC accepted an offer to host the Mississippi Federation of Garden Clubs' state convention, scheduled to be held in March. Prior to this event, the NGC's only accomplishment was to distribute flowers to the African American community to urge them to clean up their yards.[96] With only fifty charter members, each paying one dollar a year in dues, the NGC women feverishly set out to raise money to host the convention and impress the other state garden clubs. Roane Byrnes recalled that the NGC used treasure hunts throughout town to raise money: "We thoroughly enjoyed the hunts of course, and if we cleared as much as five or ten dollars, we were more than satisfied."[97]

Legend has it that an early March freeze, which followed a warm February, killed all the blooms on the shrubbery and flowering trees in the Natchez gardens in 1931. The women were mortified at the prospect of not having any of the gardens presentable to the State Federation, but then, awakening from a flu-induced dream, Katherine Miller had an idea: "Why not show our homes?" All of the women loved her suggestion and hastily reorganized the convention program around showcasing their historic homes rather than the gardens of Natchez. Prior to this time, no one had thought their old and dilapidated homes were of any interest to anyone.[98] And so they designed a program for the convention that featured twenty of the historic Natchez residences. The gardens were shown to the visitors, but their curiosity compelled some of the owners to open the doors of their historic homes.[99] The convention was a tremendous success. Women from garden clubs throughout Mississippi were thrilled to tour the grand antebellum houses and view the rare and expensive family antiques, art, and silver that each of them held.

Like most narratives of historic places, the beginnings of the Natchez Pilgrimage are creatively fabricated.

The late frost legend, which inspired the women, out of desperate necessity, to open up their historic villas to the public, was perpetuated by the Natchez Garden Club throughout these women's lives, but the fact is that there was no freeze in Mississippi in March 1931. The Jackson *Clarion-Ledger* and the *Natchez Democrat* featured front-page articles stating that Mississippi had escaped a winter storm coming from Colorado and moving north and away from Natchez.[100] In a footnote in her book on the Natchez Pilgrimage, Katherine Miller blamed tour guides, not Garden Club members, for spreading the late freezing rumor.[101]

Miller also admitted that the idea of opening up the historic villas had been discussed throughout the early twentieth century. She noted that, in 1903, Eva Lowell, her Sunday School teacher, wrote a small booklet with the idea of attracting visitors to Natchez.[102]

During the 1920s, visitors had been coming to Natchez to tour the historic houses. Often, they were well-to-do antiquarians who sought out grand, high-style historic buildings, such as Melrose, Dunleith, Auburn, and D'Evereux (figure 2.31).[103] Hollywood movie producers made silent pictures at Dunleith (*A Gentleman from Mississippi*) and Melrose (*Heart of Maryland*), for which electricity was installed to the property line at the movie studio's expense and the Kellys paid to wire the property.[104] Katherine Miller noted that Charlie Compton, a female "Natchezian steeped in the history and lore of Natchez," often showed interested people the historic villas before the pilgrimage idea was ever proposed.[105] Noted architectural historians and antiquarians like Fiske Kimball and Talbot Hamilin traveled throughout the South, including Natchez, to tour historic homes during the 1920s. Fascination with early American architecture was not new among academics in the early twentieth century but with other Americans as well. What the Natchez women soon discovered was that middle-class Americans were fascinated by it as well.

The reality was that the Natchez Garden Club did not really have any gardens at all to showcase to the Mississippi Federation of Garden Clubs women. Katherine Miller, Roane Byrnes, and the other NGC women understood that the city's gardens were neglected and some

Figure 2.31: D'Evereux, 1934. (Library of Congress, Prints & Photographs Division, Historic American Buildings Survey, HABS MISS,1-NATCH.V,2-1)

outright forsaken. This reality compelled them to use their narrative of their city for the first time and suggest to tourists to look beyond the shabby reality of 1930s Natchez and, instead, imagine with them what it looked like in its antebellum glory. Miller summarized their approach in her welcome address at the first pilgrimage in 1932: "Take yourself back from the days of modern homes and gardens and go with us in imagination and memory to the glory and grandeur of the Old South as we re-create for you the atmosphere of the antebellum mansions and the beautiful gardens of Old Natchez."[106] During her stint as chair of the hostess committee, Byrnes went further in explaining the kind of pilgrimage the convention attendees were going to experience. In her article, published in the March 21, 1932, *Natchez Democrat*, she attempted to temper expectations:

> Today we begin our garden pilgrimages through town and countryside, and we of Natchez are glad to open our gates in welcome to the garden lovers of our neighboring cities.
>
> But before we start perhaps it would be well to give a word of explanation for those who may have formed too high an expectation of what they will see here. As a matter of fact, we now have very few gardens in the generally accepted sense of the word.
>
> In those far-off palmy days before the Civil War, Natchez was famous for her gardens. The wealthy cotton planters of the early 19th century brought skillful gardeners from Germany, France and the British Isles who in a short space of time transformed the plantations, just carved from the wilderness into country estates with formal gardens, beautifully clipped hedgerows and winding avenues. Rare plants were imported from Europe and Asia, and the rolling acres of Adams County burst into beautiful blooming. But of all this, little now remains.[107]

Byrnes went on to explain that, in the decades after the Civil War, insects ravaged the grand ornamental gardens, and although the NGC had been busy restoring the city's gardens to their former splendor, they had been harmed when "a warm February made them bud out and a frosty March nipped them back again." Katherine Miller went even further in persuading the visitors to look past Natchez's dilapidated state in saying, "With the disappearance of formal gardens, planned in many instances by famous European landscape architects, Natchez on its lofty bluffs and wooded hills above the Mississippi River has held her natural beauty and seems a garden—a Garden of Eden—untouched and lovely."[108]

Roane Byrnes knew that the architecture, not the landscape, was Natchez's appeal to visitors. In her newspaper piece, she shifted the focus from the gardens to the homes. She asks the visitors of 1932 to "use your imagination, to put yourselves under the spell of the place, and to visualize the homes as they used to be with ladies in hoop-skirts, girls in their pantalettes and tight bonnets, and dashing beaux of the sixties whispering good-byes to their sweethearts in the shade of an old summer house, before they rode off to the war which was to change the world for them."[109]

Did the rolling hills of Adams County full of exotic shrubbery from Asia and Europe blooming in fabulous glory in the 1860s still exist in 1932? No. Did it really matter to tourists experiencing the first pilgrimages in the 1930s? No. The NGC women used a small facet of Natchez history to weave a grander Natchez narrative, which eventually became its heritage. But what the women learned from the 1931 convention in preparing the 1932 pilgrimage was, first, that people were fascinated with the architecture and romance of the historic Natchez villas, and second, that those sites were within their sphere of influence. As southern ladies, their homes were their traditional base of political and cultural power in Natchez. And they also realized that 1930s America was ready to join them in their indulgence of "let's pretend." The grim reality of the Depression, along with improving roads and highways, inspired middle-class Americans to romantically look at the western and southern regions of the US.[110] This was the beginning of American middle-class automobile-based tourism, and Natchez was the first city in Mississippi to benefit from this new tourism trend. New Orleans, Savannah, and Charleston were also beneficiaries of this renewed interest. Americans were eager to indulge in history and readily accessible, seemingly exotic settings. Karen Cox points out that Americans in the 1930s had long been fascinated by the "Old South" concept. Beginning in the nineteenth century, the "Old South" was celebrated in the popular Stephen Foster songs "Swanee River," "My Old Kentucky Home," and "Old Black Joe" and made even more popular in the early twentieth century through Joel Chandler Harris's Uncle Remus tales. The mythic "Old South" became part of American culture—so much so that Aunt Jemima became an advertising icon in the twentieth century. By the end of the 1930s, midwesterners and northeasterners were so familiar with the demeaning stereotypes of African Americans that they wanted to see them and the fabricated "gracious" southern culture in person.[111] As Bette Barber Hammer noted, during the Great Depression, visitors were enthralled "experiencing balls and old-fashioned barbeque suppers—everywhere Negro mammies and butlers served in costumes long ago. Soft music of the minuet mingled with the throaty Negro spirituals [that] will take you back to yesteryear, to the Golden days of the South."[112]

Twenty-two villas were showcased to the state garden club convention women: King's Tavern, Hope Farm, The Elms, Clover Nook (which, according to Katherine Miller, was not a historic house but it contained "many interesting antiques"), Linden, Airlie, Gloucester, Green Leaves, Arlington, Elms Court, The Briars, Monmouth, Ravenna, Melrose, Magnolia Vale, D'Evereux, Elgin, Stanton Hall, Lansdowne, Monteigne, and Rosalie.[113] The convention attendees thoroughly enjoyed themselves, and everyone considered the event a great success.[114]

Through the 1931 state convention, the NGC women had discovered that their villas and their history could become a way to generate much-needed money in their forgotten town. Through neglect by the rest of the country, it had, as David Cohn of the *Atlantic Monthly* put it, "not for years been either of the world or of the country of which physically it is a part."[115] These women's tactic to fashion a story to sell their town to tourists worked. After the 1931 event, Natchez became known as a town that modernization forgot, where romance and nostalgia thrived. Holistically, this was not the case. Natchez had modern amenities, but by making the pilgrimage tour an experience, based on a series of singular vignettes, it became a cultural tourism place.[116] Soon after the convention, the NGC began planning for its (and the nation's) first commercial pilgrimage. Although the first pilgrimage of 1932 showcased nineteenth-century Greek Revival masterpieces like Melrose, lesser-known villas such as Airlie, built in the old Spanish style, and the simple wood-framed King's Tavern were prominently featured.[117]

On Thursday evening, April 7, 1932, Roane Byrnes was one of the hostesses for a minstrel show that performed Spanish-themed music aboard the steamer *Ouachita*. On the final day, she assisted in conducting tours at Richmond. She dressed as a Spanish senorita in an "exquisite costume of black lace, with the headgear of a black lace mantilla, woven with the huge Spanish comb" and entertained tourists with "weird and colorful stories" of the house's Spanish past.[118] Also during this time, Edith Moore began designating homes that had Spanish heritage lineage. She declared that houses near Natchez, such as Saragossa and Sunny Side, were of Spanish origin, with Spanish land grants from Gayoso de Lemos for the original owners, "who were associates of royalty."[119]

By 1935, the Spring Pilgrimage was well established as an annual event in Natchez, and the Natchez narrative was codified in guidebooks intended for tourists. Throughout the 1930s, '40s, and '50s, women in the NGC wrote and produced these guidebooks. The first was *Natchez and the Pilgrimage* by two sisters, Georgie Wilson Newell and Charles (Charlie) Cromartie Compton (Kingsport, TN: Southern Publishers, 1935). *Natchez: Symbol of the Old South* by Nola Nance Oliver (New

York: Hastings House, 1940) soon followed. Oliver published a sequel to her guidebook, *This Too Is Natchez* (New York: Hastings House, 1940). Other NGC women like Pearl Vivian Guyton published smaller guidebooks throughout the 1930s and 1940s. Katherine Miller published a guidebook, which was more or less her memoirs, in 1938.

The guidebooks legitimized the personalized narrative that the women created during their youth. *Natchez and the Pilgrimage* set the trend for Natchez guidebooks for the next fifty years. With lavish photographs by local photographer Earl Norman, whose family had been taking photographs of both Natchez and Natchezians for several decades, the guidebook first introduces the reader to the Natchez narrative and then rationalizes the state of Natchez in the Great Depression. In her foreword to the book, Ruth Faxon Macrare sets the tone. She informs the tourist that, in Natchez, "You will see, as in a dream, the picturesque life the manners and customs and very atmosphere, of the Old South reproduced for you: old interiors in their original setting; maidens in laces and jewels and hoopskirts; mellow candlelight from candelabra, and chandeliers sparkling though a thousand prisms; kindly negroes, descendants of old slaves, playing an important part. The picture is as clearly and sharply transfixed upon our minds as if projected upon a screen" (figure 2.32). She concludes the foreword and sets the tone of the

Figure 2.32: Interior hall at Elms Court, 1935. Authors Georgie Wilson Newell and Charles Cromartie Compton claimed that the large carved sideboard table was a gift to the original owners, the McKittrick family, by the Duke and Duchess of Devonshire. (From *Natchez and the Pilgrimage* by Georgie Wilson Newell and Charles Cromartie Compton [Kingsport: Southern Publishers, 1935])

Natchez narrative by saying, "Natchez is a shrine, filled to the brim with a priceless inheritance. It is indeed unique in possessing so much that makes the 'South before the War' stand out in history."[120]

The sisters begin their guidebook by turning the long-considered liability—that Natchez was a backwater and forgotten town—into a glorious attribute. In the sisters' minds, Natchez is now the southern version of the mythic Brigadoon, a priceless gem long hidden from the modern world. It is a city "that is a beautiful survival of an earlier period of our history." And the city "awaits the haggard and long-traveled tourist with the doors of its grand villas open and welcoming; the sweet air of the place is vibrant with mellowed associations" of the genteel southern life. But they reassure the wary northern tourists by saying that Natchez has all the comforts of the modern age: "paved streets, and smart hotels, electric light, indoor plumbing and heat, fine shops and modern factories"—the last item a must for any modern 1930s American city or town. But more importantly, the sisters declare, "Natchez has always been exclusive and wide-awake socially." In wanting to emphasize that the Natchez families are more than eager to welcome northern tourists, they exclaim, "Natchez has now awakened! And its inhabitants, descendants of aristocracy, await you [the tourist] with their hospitality."[121]

The sisters mention in their guidebook that it was a stroke of luck that the Civil War stopped construction in Natchez. The inhabitants now enjoy "the architectural perfection of the Greek influence," and they fortunately do not have to endure the architecture blemish of "pseudo-Gothic and Moorish monstrosities." In their book, there is no mention of the Moorish-revival Longwood. They even rationalize the way the NCG has commercialized the city, writing that, "Through the efforts of its Garden Club, The Pilgrimage has become an amazingly successful means to bring the world to Natchez. Could anything be more delightful than the way these women are going about the business of commercializing their town, since commercialized it must be, to move forward, lest some of its abandoned old homes and landmarks slip irrevocably into that state beyond reclaiming?"[122]

The sisters acknowledged that the NGC women were deliberately commercializing their heritage through their narrative. Commercialization was inevitable in Natchez, so why shouldn't these women use it to save their irreplaceable homes? And why should they deny the pilgrims from the North the enjoyment of experiencing them?

Katherine Miller was behind the book, and although she is not mentioned in it, she had a hand in selecting the architecture pictures that Norman photographed for it. During the 1930s and '40s, she was constantly bringing newspaper and magazine journalists, along with their photographers, into her friends' historic villas to produce articles on the architecture of what they considered the finest villas of the city. She often came to her friends' front doors unannounced. Indeed, her friends and contemporaries often remarked that Miller was relentless in barging into her friends' home with a photographer to capture the right moment in the parlor or the grand hall. As can be expected, this annoyed many of her friends and fellow NGC members; yet she persisted in getting photographs taken in the grandest Natchez interiors. And the exquisite images Earl Norman captured, which are showcased in the book, are the result of Miller's determination to present Natchez in its best light.[123]

The book presents the history that these Natchez women wanted to convey to the world. For them, everything that happened to Natchez, from its beginning up to 1935, was either intentional or blessed luck in making their city a place of beauty and pleasure. The sisters first state that its "history is interesting and colorful" and tell the reader/tourist that Natchez had been under six flags: French, Spanish, British, American, Confederate, and Native American (it is doubtful that the American Indians carried any flag). The French founded the city in 1716, only to have its Fort Rosalie destroyed by the Natchez Indians in 1729. The sisters neglect to mention that the French retaliated and obliterated the Natchez tribe. They emphasized the role the Spaniards played in creating the city, explaining, "the Spanish rule, lasting from 1779 to 1797, left its marks on Natchez in the architectural plane of the town and homes." They celebrate "Bluff Park," Gayoso's esplanade, noting that it played a special part in the social life of the city and was the place where artists and dreamers gazed upon the Mississippi River. Being two very patriotic women, the sisters gloss over the fact that during the American Revolution, Natchez was pro-British.[124] Instead, they celebrate its European flair and an ambivalence to Mississippi and the rest of the US. They quote another Natchez woman, Carolyn C. McDonnell, who glamorizes colonial Natchez: "Miles of forest hemmed Natchez in from other means of contact. Her associations were with the Old World, for her isolation had, at different climaxes in world history, attracted Royalists from France, turbulent grandees from Spain, and Tories from the Colonies. Natchez was as European as the blueblood of foreign nations could make her. It was utterly distinctive."[125] Interestingly, the sisters suggest that Natchez was not really part of the Civil War. They also contend that, during the decades preceding the war, it was noncommittal in its allegiance to either the Confederacy or the Union. Instead, because it had such a European flair, "it was never truly American until many years after the Civil War." Thus, its *savoir faire* attitude enabled it to have "a flavor spicy and unique, on this side of the Atlantic, and rich with romance." They do mention that during the war a defective shell from the federal gunboat *Essex* hit the downtown and killed a twelve-year-old girl, and during its occupation only a few houses were pillaged.[126] However, this part of the narrative allows the sisters to perpetuate a myth that became popular throughout the 1930s in the city and its environs: during the Civil War, Natchezians hastily buried chests of gold, silver, and jewelry all around the historic buildings. And they reassure the reader that while some of these treasure chests have been unearthed by the present generation, others remain untouched and unknown.[127]

Did the sisters believe that their city was being commercialized? Yes. Absolutely. But the fine women of the Natchez Garden Club were commercializing it in the best way imaginable. They had personalized their built patrimony and then marketed it, a trend that would continue nationally throughout the South. The NGC women created a "town gala" in which "expectancy is in the air; friendly cordiality awaits you. The strains of the negro orchestra, surprisingly good, serenades you at [the NGC] headquarters." The tourists who descend on Natchez during the pilgrimage are a "fashionable throng on a pleasure bent, and willing to enter with zest into the mood of 'Let's pretend' that is a part of the passport necessary to really enjoy the life of this town of the long ago." Continuing, they reassure the reader that "the commercialization of the town is forgotten, once you have registered, paying the nominal fee to the Garden Club for the privilege of seeing the old homes."[128]

The inherent racism of the place and times is also romanticized in *Natchez and the Pilgrimage*. The sisters describe how the tourist may first approach a historic home on the pilgrimage tour:

> Perhaps a grizzled, bent, old ex-slave stands to bow you in, or a strapping, courteous young negro will direct the parking of your car and reply if you question him, that he is of Natchez or Louisiana, as the case may be, and that his people have been here since "befo' de' War" in the service of the same family. At another place as you step up onto the gallery a little colored boy stoops and wipes your shoes lest you have the embarrassment of taking in unnoticed souvenirs of park and garden.[129]

The NGC women began the pilgrimage not intending that they would manipulate and demean African Americans in Natchez, but they soon changed their approach from showcasing African American tableau performance like the one at Zion Chapel. The women's attitude toward race was indicative of the mindset of white southern America at the time. They either were simply not aware that they were debasing their African American neighbors and employees, or they simply did not care.[130]

Figure 2.33: Natchez Train Station, circa 1900. Passenger rail service was never an efficient means to travel in or out of Natchez. It often took as long as four hours to travel eighty miles from Natchez to Jackson, Mississippi, on a passenger coach that was attached to a freight train. (Thomas H. and Joan W. Gandy Photograph Collection, Mss. 3778, Louisiana and Lower Mississippi Valley Collections, LSU Libraries, Baton Rouge, Louisiana)

And what about the difficulties in traveling to Natchez during the 1930s? At that time, one could only reach Natchez by train on a day coach, attached to a freight train, that took five or six hours to travel one hundred miles.[131] What about the dilapidated roads that connected Natchez to the rest of Mississippi? According to the sisters, the citizens of Natchez had always wanted it this way. Back in 1890 when the railroad made a request for a right of way to bring a main line of a large railroad into the city, "Natchezians said, No! Keep out!" (figure 2.33). And thus, the lovely town "let the world go by a few miles from its door."[132] But fortunately, they tell the reader that a newly paved Natchez Trace is underway, and it will enable tourists to travel in the same way the "landed gentry" of Natchez did as they headed east to the cooler climate of the mountains of Tennessee, Kentucky, and Virginia, where festive parties awaited them.[133]

The sisters also reminded the reader that famous men and their steadfast women enjoyed old Natchez. Varina Davis grew up in The Briars and married Jefferson Davis there. Andrew Jackson married his beloved Rachel Robards (Donelson) at Springfield (figure 2.34). And treacherous villains fraternized in this exotic city: Aaron Burr was tried for treason in conspiring to create an empire for himself out of Texas and Mexico. And in 1807, beneath the twin oaks fronting the military school, Jefferson

Figure 2.34: Exterior view of Springfield, 1935, Natchez vicinity, Adams County, Mississippi, where Andrew Jackson courted Rachel Donelson Robards. (From *Natchez: Symbol of the Old South* by Nola Nance Oliver [New York: Hastings House, 1940])

Figure 2.35: "Aaron Burr Oaks" in front of Jefferson College in Washington, Mississippi, north of Natchez. Under these oaks, Aaron Burr was first tried for treason against the United States in 1807. (From *Natchez: Symbol of the Old South* by Nola Nance Oliver [New York: Hastings House, 1940])

Figure 2.36: King's Tavern, circa 1939. (From *Natchez: Symbol of the Old South* by Nola Nance Oliver [New York: Hastings House, 1940])

Figure 2.37: Main parlor in Arlington, 1935. Expensive furniture and decorative arts were prominently featured during the pilgrimage tours. (From *Natchez and the Pilgrimage* by Georgie Wilson Newell and Charles Cromartie Compton [Kingsport: Southern Publishers, 1935])

Figure 2.38: View of the Old Natchez Trace, 1935, the picture of the trace near Natchez before the Natchez Trace Parkway was planned. (From *Natchez and the Pilgrimage* by Georgie Wilson Newell and Charles Cromartie Compton [Kingsport: Southern Publishers, 1935])

College, Burr was first tried for treason (figure 2.35). Down in "Natchez Under-the-Hill, along the Trace, and even in King's Tavern" (figure 2.36), cold murderous bandits lurked—the terrible Harpes, the warped and twisted Mason, and the genteel but sinister Murrell. Romance may have lurked around every corner in Natchez, but so did danger, which added spiciness to the Natchez narrative.[134]

An exotic and romantic town built on grounds inhabited by a noble tribe of Indians, descendants of the ancient Aztecs, and colonized by royalist French and Spanish aristocrats, who brought to the American wilderness old world sophistication, continental town planning, and romance. A place where the American planter elite built opulent villas, filled them with finest European furnishings and decoration, and planted exotic shrubbery from Europe and Asia, along with making manicured hedgerows (figure 2.37). A town where the descendants of the American planter elite lovingly sustained their families' legacy and even willfully refused modernity to enter it—except for all the amenities the modern tourist needed. A city of mystery and intrigue, where villains once roamed and hidden treasure may be buried beneath your feet (figure 2.38). This forgotten place in the South, which has now been awakened and ready to greet the world through the loving commercialization brought about by the women of the Natchez Garden Club, who "receive" you wearing hoop skirt gowns and jewelry of many neck chains, lockets, stomachers, bracelets, cameos, and miniatures (all heirlooms), and who use their big earnings from the pilgrimage to retain the city's treasures and reclaim its grand houses and gardens. These women, who put on the pilgrimage not because they want to make money, but because of their *noblesse oblige* to sacrifice their privacy for the greater good of all. A place where the formerly enslaved and their descendants continue to gleefully serve their white masters and entertain the tourists-guests.[135] The place "Where the Old South Still Lives" as a transplanted town from old Europe on the Mississippi, full of romance and festive hospitality, now open for the American tourist's delight and awe. All this was what the two sisters, Georgie Wilson Newell and Charles Cromartie Compton, presented in *Natchez and the Pilgrimage*. This book is the first codified version of the Natchez narrative, which invited tourists from across the country to do what Katherine Miller and Roane Byrnes wanted them to do: come to Natchez and pretend.

PUTTING THE NARRATIVE IN PRINT

In a span of eighteen years, the Natchez narrative, based completely on personalism of the place, had been commodified and revised through publication at least three times. It began by casting Natchez as a romantic, magical, and forgotten place, but it evolved into a narrative of commercial success through historic preservation by the NGC women. It is also a juxtaposition of the far away past and the present: of Spanish Natchez, antebellum Natchez, and also present-day Natchez, most notably, the NGC experiences and the Goat Castle Murder.

Although *Natchez and the Pilgrimage* was the first guidebook on Natchez and was considered a success, not everyone was pleased with it. These women continued to refine their guidebooks as their narrative changed. Each new guidebook was a reaction to comments they received from visitors and Natchezians. Melrose owner George Malin Davis Kelly complained about *Natchez and the Pilgrimage*. He felt that it did not sufficiently feature the historic villas. Although he appreciated Earl Norman's photograph of D'Evereux (figure 2.39), he told Ethel that there should have been more images of the Natchez villas like the ones of Rosalie (figure 2.40). He grumbled that there were too many pictures of doors—Jefferson College (figure 2.41), Linden (figure 2.42), and Auburn (figure 2.43). He expressed his frustration that the only picture of Melrose in the book was of the "Great Punkah"[136] in the dining room (figure 2.44). George Kelly concluded his criticism of the book by saying it that "it only has 19 illustrations, all by Norman, and the book is unbalanced and a little thin."[137]

Natchez and the Pilgrimage is an interesting starting point in examining the codified Natchez narrative. The sisters' intent was not to write solely on Natchez architecture; instead, they sought to convince the reader of the exotic and refined air of the place. Atmospheric pictures of Lake St. John (figure 2.45) and an ancient stretch of the Natchez Trace are juxtaposed against the precise photographs of the front doors of Jefferson College, Linden, and Auburn. Scattered throughout the book are images of blithe southern belles; Katherine Miller is front and center in the frontispiece photograph (figure 0.17). There is a photograph of a loving Black mammy (in reality, the authors' cook), taking care of two young girls at The Elms—Alma Kellogg Carpenter (later known as Miss Alma) is the little girl sitting on the settee by her mammy and playing with her friend, Sally Junkin (figure 0.9). Both of these girls would grow up and become southern ladies in Natchez. There are no pictures of downtown Natchez, no images of the "smart hotels" or the city's "progressive industry," and no images of any villa that counters the sisters' assertion that Natchez is graced only by noble Greek Revival architecture. The Gothic Revival St. Mary Basilica is not featured in this book. The sisters never intended for the book to actually guide tourists through Natchez; it is the narrative that is the creation and commercialization myth of Natchez.

Figure 2.39: View of D'Evereux, 1935. (From *Natchez and the Pilgrimage* by Georgie Wilson Newell and Charles Cromartie Compton [Kingsport: Southern Publishers, 1935])

Figure 2.40: View of Rosalie, 1935. (From *Natchez and the Pilgrimage* by Georgie Wilson Newell and Charles Cromartie Compton [Kingsport: Southern Publishers, 1935])

They wanted to lull you into visiting this city of enchantment, where you can experience romantic tales of long ago in complete harmony with the quiet beauty—"a respite from the rush of modern existence."[138]

The second guidebook, which built on the narrative introduced in *Natchez and the Pilgrimage*, was Nola Nance Oliver's *Natchez: Symbol of the Old South* (New York: Hastings House, 1940). A mere five years after publication of the first guidebook, Natchez had become part of the national consciousness, especially after the release of the movie *Gone with the Wind*. That Oliver's book was published by a national press, not a regional one as with *Natchez and the Pilgrimage*, reflects the city's

Figure 2.41: The front doors of Jefferson College, 1935. In *Natchez and the Pilgrimage*, Georgie Wilson Newell and Charles Cromartie Compton state that the front doors of Jefferson College are similar to the ones at Gloucester and may have been executed from the original designs of the Brothers Adam of England. (From *Natchez and the Pilgrimage* by Georgie Wilson Newell and Charles Cromartie Compton [Kingsport: Southern Publishers, 1935])

Figure 2.42: The front door of Linden, 1935. The intricate carvings along the frieze of the door are celebrated in *Natchez and the Pilgrimage*. (From *Natchez and the Pilgrimage* by Georgie Wilson Newell and Charles Cromartie Compton [Kingsport: Southern Publishers, 1935])

Figure 2.43: Interior door at Auburn, 1935. Newell and Compton claimed that all of the details of the grand villa were copied and reproduced in a house constructed in the 1930s in Nashville, Tennessee. (From *Natchez and the Pilgrimage* by Georgie Wilson Newell and Charles Cromartie Compton [Kingsport: Southern Publishers, 1935])

Figure 2.44: The "Great Punkah" in the dining room at Melrose, 1935. (From *Natchez and the Pilgrimage* by Georgie Wilson Newell and Charles Cromartie Compton [Kingsport: Southern Publishers, 1935])

Figure 2.45: Lake St. John, across the Mississippi River in Louisiana, 1935. Georgie Wilson Newell and Charles Cromartie Compton described Lake St. John as "the water playground of Natchez." In their book, they suggested that Ponce de León may have found his "fountain of youth" there. (From *Natchez and the Pilgrimage* by Georgie Wilson Newell and Charles Cromartie Compton [Kingsport: Southern Publishers, 1935])

new status as a cultural tourist destination. But unlike the sisters' book, the villas are the primary feature of Oliver's small book. Louise Learned Metcalfe and Mary Henderson Lambdin assisted and inspired Oliver to write the guidebook, and in *Natchez*, she truly embellishes Natchez's history. She reiterates that Natchez derived its name from the ancient, noble, and sun-worshipping Natchez tribe. She boldly states that it is the second oldest town in the United States; only St. Augustine is older. She neglects to acknowledge colonial-era cities: Boston, Providence, Philadelphia, Annapolis, Williamsburg, Charleston, and even Santa Fe, all of which were founded in the late seventeenth century. She expresses in *Natchez* the patriotic and regional sentiments that were prevalent by the end of the 1930s. Like the sisters, she celebrates that five different flags flew over the city and that the US flag first flew over the lower Mississippi valley in Natchez but also "another flag, which some call 'the conquered banner,' the beloved flag of the Confederate States of America, floated over Natchez, 1861–65."[139]

By 1940, as demonstrated in Oliver's book, the racial myth of the served elite white class and the serving African American class is embedded into the Natchez narrative. She celebrates as a charming part of Natchez life the prevalent poverty that persisted in Black Natchez during the

1930s. First, she mentions the African American performances held in churches like Zion Chapel: "Spirituals are sung in old-fashioned Negro churches where the 'pahson' is eager to greet 'our white friends.'" The nationally popular images of Uncle Remus and Aunt Jemima have now been woven into the Natchez narrative. Oliver used Black poverty as a marketing ploy in the pilgrimage and in the narrative with her description of "Penny Day":

> A custom which has long prevailed in Natchez is the placing of coins in a box for old darky beggars. On Saturdays every merchant observes "Penny Day." As it was called. It originated as a time saver, the box being placed in a convenient location to avoid interruption of the store's 'business. There are many regular "customers" for this feature and they are always welcome. "Penny Day" is a thoughtful, good natured gesture to the needy Negro from his "white folks."[140]

In the book, she pictures "Uncle Wash, A Regular Customer on Penny Day" (figure 2.46). Uncle Wash is haggard, old, but dignified in his pose, wearing his ragged hat and a dirty bandana for this studio picture. Was there an established "Penny Day" in the 1930s when the Natchez retailers provided the African American beggars of Natchez penny bargains on goods on Saturdays?[141] It seems very unlikely. Nola Oliver's comment about Uncle Wash in *Natchez* demonstrates a prevailing trait in racial relations during the Great Depression: racism enabled whites to express their superiority over African Americans through class distinctions and

Figure 2.46: Portrait of "Uncle Wash" featured in *Natchez and the Pilgrimage* (From *Natchez: Symbol of the Old South* by Nola Nance Oliver [New York: Hastings House, 1940])

Figure 2.47: Airlie, circa 1935. (Library of Congress, Prints & Photographs Division, Historic American Buildings Survey, HABS MISS,1-NATCH,15-)

poverty. Women in Natchez like Nola Oliver believed in this paternal view of poorer African Americans, and they also commercialized it, incorporated it into their narrative, and sold it to a white America, who were eager to soothe their own misfortunes with a false sense of racial superiority, which most African Americans resented.

Oliver's guidebook focuses on the villas and is intended to aid the tourist traveling by automobile from villa to villa during the pilgrimage. In describing villas such as Airlie (figure 2.47), she continues to extoll the Spanish Colonial heritage by describing the central portion "built on Old Spanish style, with beams and timbers held together with wooden pegs." But unlike Georgie Wilson Newell and Charles Cromartie Compton, she romanticizes its Civil War history, noting "during the War Between the States when conflicts at Airlie left blood stains on its floors and walls which are clearly visible today." In one way, this description compromised the "Old South" myth the women originally proposed; but by 1940, the lost cause of the Confederacy had also become part of the narrative. Romance, lost treasure, and now wartime bloodstains—these were things that enticed tourists to visit Natchez.

Nola Oliver only briefly describes the milieu of Natchez at the beginning of her book; instead, she lists the villas and describes their architecture. There is the spiral stairway at Auburn (figure 2.48), as well as the grand Ionic columned tetrastyle portico designed by Levi Weeks (figure

Figure 2.48: The spiral stairway rising to the grand hallway in Auburn. (From *Natchez and the Pilgrimage* by Georgie Wilson Newell and Charles Cromartie Compton [Kingsport: Southern Publishers, 1935])

Figure 2.49: Auburn, 1932. The *St. Louis Post-Dispatch* photographed Auburn for a feature story on the first pilgrimage. The image was used in several of the early Natchez guidebooks. (From *Natchez and the Pilgrimage* by Georgie Wilson Newell and Charles Cromartie Compton [Kingsport: Southern Publishers, 1935])

Figure 2.50: Brandon Hall, Natchez vicinity, Adams County, Mississippi. (Library of Congress, Prints & Photographs Division, Historic American Buildings Survey, HABS MISS,1-WASH.V,1-)

Figure 2.51: Main hall and stairway in Brandon Hall. (Library of Congress, Prints & Photographs Division, Historic American Buildings Survey, HABS MISS,1-WASH.V,1-)

Figure 2.52: Exterior view of The Briars. (From *Natchez: Symbol of the Old South* by Nola Nance Oliver [New York: Hastings House, 1940])

Figure 2.53: Mantel in the main parlor of The Briars. In 1845, in front of this mantel, Jefferson Davis married Varina Howell. The Briars became a shrine to the Confederate president and first lady in Natchez during the 1930s. (From *Natchez: Symbol of the Old South* by Nola Nance Oliver [New York: Hastings House, 1940])

Figure 2.54: Exterior side view of Cottage Gardens. (Frances Benjamin Johnston Photograph Collection, Library of Congress, Prints & Photographs Division, LC-DIG-ppmsca-32352)

Figure 2.55: Main hallway and stairway, Cottage Gardens. (Frances Benjamin Johnston Photograph Collection, Library of Congress, Prints & Photographs Division, LC-DIG-ppmsca-32353)

Figure 2.56: Don Jose Vidal grave monument at Cottage Gardens. (From *Natchez: Symbol of the Old South* by Nola Nance Oliver [New York: Hastings House, 1940])

2.49). She does reuse the previously mentioned Norman photograph from *Natchez and the Pilgrimage* of an interior door portal at Auburn, but in this guidebook the architecture now plays a more prominent role in the narrative and provides an armature for it. Villas like Brandon Hall (figure 2.50), which had no salacious story line, are featured because of their elegant Greek Revival interior architecture (figure 2.51), alongside villas that had important stories in the Natchez narrative such as The Briars (figure 2.52). With its Federal-style mantel (figure 2.53), The Briars embodies high architectural style in Natchez, but its significance is what happened in it: in front of that mantel was where Jefferson Davis married Varina Howell. Oliver states that it was built by William Burr Howell, a cousin of Aaron Burr. Later documentation shows that it was built about 1818 for John Perkins.[142] The Briars was the type of villa these Natchez women wanted to celebrate: one with both high-style architectural features and a romantic story.[143]

By 1940, the basic structure of the Natchez narrative had been established, becoming more specific and tied to numerous buildings. Nola Oliver does continue to celebrate the Spanish Colonial period with her insights about lesser-known cottages like Cottage Gardens (figure 2.54), but she balances the architectural significance such as its high-style Greek Revival stairway (figure 2.55) with its association with Spanish royalty. She states that its original owner, Don Jose Vidal, Spanish military governor, built a tomb for his wife, Donna Vidal, on a bluff overlooking the Mississippi River in order to see her as he went about his duties across the river in Louisiana (figure 2.56).[144]

Mixed in with romance there always had to be adventure. Oliver features in her book evidence of armed struggle in early Natchez. She shows bullet holes in the lower door at King's Tavern (figure 2.57), claims they came from a late eighteenth-century American Indian attack, and retells the ghost legend of the dilapidated structure. "At night," according to her, "when all's dark and quiet at King's Tavern, ghosts of American Indian warriors in the full dress of their tribes wander through the old Tap Room, lean against the old bar, peer out through small crevices, and then disappear through the heavy doors that lead onto the street."[145]

As success and notoriety grew in Natchez during the 1930s, Nola Oliver added contemporary stories to the city's narrative. In 1932, the same year as the first pilgrimage, two eccentrics of the declining elite class of Natchez, Richard Dana and Octavia Dockery, enlisted an African American man named George Pearls to rob their reclusive neighbor, Jennie Merrill. Something went wrong, and Jennie Merrill was shot and killed during the attempted robbery. The story became a national sensation, and the press labeled Richard Dana "Wild Man" and Octavia Dockery

Figure 2.57: Assumed bullet holes in the side door at King's Tavern. Legends about the violent and raucous days of frontier America were popular in places like Natchez during the 1930s. (From *Natchez: Symbol of the Old South* by Nola Nance Oliver [New York: Hastings House, 1940])

Figure 2.58: Glenwood, also known as Goat Castle, 1940. The ruinous villa was the home of Richard Danna and Octavia Dockery, who were acquitted of murdering Jennie Merrill. The couple lived an eccentric life afterward, and the house became a modern Depression-era tourist attraction in Natchez. (From *Natchez: Symbol of the Old South* by Nola Nance Oliver [New York: Hastings House, 1940])

"Goat Woman" because of their eccentric, erratic behavior and wild and disheveled appearance. The national media also enjoyed reporting that Dana and Dockery lived in squalor, allowing their decaying villa, Glenwood, to fall into utter decay, epitomizing the Gothic South stereotype. Goats roamed the grounds and romped inside the villa; chickens roosted in the primary bedroom. Dana and Dockery were acquitted of murdering Jennie Merrill, and an innocent African American woman, Emily

Burns, was convicted of the murder. The couple went on to profit from their weird celebrity status, charging tourists to see Richard play the piano and Octavia tell outlandish stories; all the while, goats rummaged through the "Goat Castle" (figure 2.58).[146]

Richard and Octavia were not the only ones to profit from the tourism generated by the "Goat Castle," also known as "Glenwood." Nola Oliver alluded to it in the pilgrimage, and she featured the decayed villa and its owners in *Natchez*. But even deranged eccentrics in Natchez are genteel and sophisticated. Oliver describes Richard—or Dick, as she calls him—as a "man of aristocratic breeding and birth." She describes Dick's live-in girlfriend as his stalwart guardian. But she rationalizes the terrible decay of Glenwood and accepts the way it has become a Natchez tourist attraction: "Conditions at Glenwood are not conducive to pride in the hearts of Natchez people, and yet it is doubtful if any tourist leaves Natchez without hearing, in some way, about this dilapidated old place. As all things good or bad by comparison, it may not be amiss when depicting the glory of Natchez to glimpse the other side."[147] She later adds, "A Northern tourist upon seeing Glenwood (known today as 'Goat Castle') said, 'Well, I don't know whether to cry or swear.'" Only in 1930s Natchez can decay, resulting in what present-day preservationists refer to as "demolition-by-neglect," be turned into a cultural tourism asset and selling point.

By 1940 and after five years of being featured in American popular culture, the "Old South" was the predominant theme in the Natchez narrative, and the city's antebellum architecture became the tangible expression of the Lost Cause. This is clearly evident by comparing Nola Oliver's descriptions of two earlier overlooked yet very grand villas, Longwood and Stanton Hall. She states that Longwood "is a monument to a dream that was interrupted by the tragedy of the War Between the States in 1861–65." She laments that because of the war the villa was never finished, and there are "huge sections of carved moulding, old paint buckets and brushes, tool boxes and carpenters' tools scattered about the upper floors—just as they were left almost 75 years ago." To this day, they remain scattered for tourists to see, a romantic lost dream, exactly as these Natchez women intended to present. On the other hand, Oliver merely mentioned Stanton Hall, a remarkable architectural expression of Minard Lafever's ideas of Greek Revival architecture, stating that "Stanton Hall is the most handsome old home, and probably the most expensive in the entire Natchez area. It is not of great historical value but represents the architectural grandeur of the Old South."[148]

Several years after World War II, Oliver published a sequel to *Natchez: Symbol of the Old South*: a similar small picture and narrative guidebook titled *This Too Is Natchez* (New York: Hastings House, 1953). Edith Moore influenced her to write it, which went beyond the villas that were only open and shown during the pilgrimage. In the foreword, Oliver explains what motivated her to write the second book:

> The annual spring pilgrimage, sponsored by the Natchez Garden Club and the Pilgrimage Garden Club, attracts thousands from every part of the country, who come to make a tour of thirty of the most outstanding homes of the town. But this list by no means includes all the interesting homes of the town. Indeed, Natchez boasts of a larger number of well-preserved ante-bellum houses than any other Southern community. It is not to be wondered at, therefore, that many tourists, in passing, exclaim, "Why, how lovely! Can't we see this one too?" Or: "What a charming cottage! Why don't we go in?" Or: "Where can we get information about this old mansion, with the grand, pillared portico?"
>
> This book is the answer. It contains pictures and sketches of the "forgotten," unpublicized houses, of old plantation architecture, of mansions in miniature, of many old homes still occupied by descendants of the original builders and owners, and it tells about our rich heritage of old public buildings. It also gives account of the fascinating legends which cling, like the Spanish moss on the mighty live oaks that shade many of them, around these ancient structures.
>
> Here you see Routhland, The Towers, Mistletoe, Holly Hedges, Magnolia, Sweet Auburn and many other ante-bellum houses not encountered on the Pilgrimage Tours. Twin Oaks is included, once forgotten and falling into neglect, but restored to its original lines since the publication of my first book on Natchez.[149]

Edith Moore's influence can be seen in *This Too Is Natchez*. Although romance and legend continue to be celebrated in this book—and by 1950, lore was deeply embedded into the Natchez narrative—historical facts are more prevalent in it than the previous one. More importantly, these Natchez women's reputation as pioneering preservationists is now an important part of the narrative. They are no longer enthusiastic and naive but enterprising women; by the 1950s, they are accomplished and successful historic preservationists. *This Too Is Natchez* celebrates the preservation successes of the city. In it, you will find early pictures of Natchez Under-the Hill juxtaposed with 1950s photographs. There is the Texaco Filling Station, which once was Lawyers Row on the corner of State and Wall Streets. Hearkening back to the Spanish Colonial period (as many of these Natchez women, especially Moore, were fond of doing), she features Texada Tavern, which was probably built by Manuel

Garcia de Texada, between 1798 and 1805. But she neglects to inform the reader that it was later purchased by Edward Turner in 1817.[150]

Thirteen years after Nola Oliver had said that a villa as grand and imposing as Stanton Hall had no great historical value, this same author now celebrates the nondescript Aunt Hill for no other reason except that "four sweet old aunts lived here." But she also appeals to the prospective preservationist of the time and displays houses that needed preservation and renovation. The Forsyth Spanish House, a raised cottage, is shown in need of desperate repair; she says it is her hope that the recent purchaser of it, Hugo Stallone, from Bessie Bailey Moore (a descendant of a proud Natchez family), will "undertake its restoration." Her passage about Sweet Auburn, near Washington, reads like a caption from a preservationist's real estate publication: "It is the hope of old Washington village that someone may take over Sweet Auburn and restore to its old glories." She celebrates the restoration of villas like Twin Oaks, which was restored by Homer Whittington. She gushes over Twin Oaks "as though some fairy godmother had waved a magic wand and restored it to all its original beauty and elegance."[151]

The first pilgrimage tourists' interest in Civil War history and the accompanying sanitized version of antebellum, racially based social structure drove the narrative away from what these Natchez women considered unique about their place—Spanish colonialism—and more toward the Confederate Natchez of their grandmothers and mothers. But in spite of hardened caricatures of slavery and African Americans in 1930s Natchez, there were heritage stories that both Black and white Natchez claimed as their own, none more so than the legend of Abdulrahman Ibrahim Ibn Sori, the "Prince among Slaves" in Natchez.

THE LINKED AFRICAN AMERICAN AND WHITE NARRATIVE IN NATCHEZ

In his essay "Where the South Still Lives: Displaying Heritage in Natchez, Mississippi," Steven Hoelscher describes the African American performance at Zion Chapel, which has been performed since the earliest pilgrimages, during the 2000 Spring Pilgrimage. The lights first dim, and the narrator of the performance emerges from the choir and explains what to expect to the audience of tourists:

> The songs, chants, moans, groans, and hymns that you are about to hear is the music that extends from the captivity of African Americans during the time of slavery to the present day. These songs are a testament to the ability of blacks in Natchez to create their own culture, to survive oppression.

African Americans sang in the field and in secret—wherever and whenever they could. Many of the songs have been adapted to present-day usage, but the power and dignity that they impart remain.

Then from behind the altar rail another man slowly walks down onto the main floor and stands behind one of the two microphones. He speaks:

> I am Ibrahima. I was born in 1762 near Timbuktu, Africa, and was a prince and a colonel in my father's army until 1788, when I was defeated in battle and sold into slavery. I was brought to Natchez and purchased by a wealthy planter named Thomas Foster. In 1807, an Irish doctor, whose life had been saved in Africa by my father, recognized me. Although the doctor was unable to secure my release, the publicity generated through his efforts made me a local and national celebrity. In the 1820s, I was finally freed and made the return voyage to my native Africa.[152]

The story of Abdulrahman Ibrahim Ibn Sori, also known as Ibrahima (figure 2.59), is a fascinating example of the linked Natchez narrative in white and African American Natchez. As mentioned earlier, Roane Byrnes claimed the Ibrahima story as part of her personal heritage; her great-great grandfather, John Coates Cox, was the Irish doctor mentioned in the Holy Family Catholic Church performance who generated the publicity to free the African prince. There are consistencies and discrepancies that come from the differing points of view, white and Black, in the legend of the "Prince among Slaves." Roane Byrnes's family legend depicts Cox as a doctor on an eighteenth-century English sailing vessel arriving on the African coast. After anchoring, the English crew went ashore, and Dr. Cox joined a hunting party of sailors. During the hunting expedition, he became lost and separated from his English companions, and they eventually left him behind and sailed away. Young Cox wandered in the African wilderness and ended up in the African kingdom of Timbuktu, where he was captured by African warriors. During his brief captivity, he came upon the young crown prince, Ibrahima, who was dying as result of an epidemic in the kingdom. The young Dr. Cox saved the young prince's life, and, in a gesture of gratitude, the king granted Cox's freedom and led him to the coast, where an English ship was waiting. From there, Cox returned to England; later he emigrated to America and made his way to Natchez and began his life there as a physician.

In the meantime, after Ibrahima recovered, he led his father's warriors in a victorious battle against a rebellious tribe; but upon his return to Timbuktu, he was ambushed, captured, and sold into slavery. He was then carried away on a slave ship that sailed to New Orleans.

Figure 2.59: Abdulrahman Ibrahim Ibn Sori, known as Ibrahima, "The Prince Among Slaves" (1762–1829). (University of Illinois Library, Urbana, Illinois)

There, Ibrahima was sold to Natchez planter Thomas Foster, lived as an enslaved man on Foster Fields Plantation, and toiled in the cotton fields for forty years. Around 1807, an older Dr. Cox encountered Ibrahima on the streets of Natchez. The two men immediately recognized each other. Dr. Cox worked tirelessly to free Ibrahima from slavery but was unable to accomplish his laudable goal and died as an old man later that year. His son, Rousseau Cox, took up Dr. Cox's cause.

But like so many stories and legends that make up the NGC women's narrative of Natchez, Ibrahima's is fraught with complexity and nuance. Roane Byrnes's family story is mistaken. Over the decades in Natchez, this true story was never forgotten, but it was changed. There are numerous discrepancies in her family legend. Ibrahima was a prince of the Muslim territory of Futa Jalon (now part of the Republic of Guinea), not Timbuktu. Cox's campaign, which began in 1807 in Natchez, became a rallying cause for the Society for the Colonization of Free People of Color of America, commonly known as the American Colonization Society (ACS), which supported the immigration of free African Americans to Africa during the 1820s. Neither Cox nor Cox's son purchased Ibrahima's freedom. Thomas Hopkins Gallaudet, a founder and first

Figure 2.60: Andrew Marschalk (1767–1838), publisher of the *Mississippi State Gazette* in Natchez from 1802 until 1838. Marschalk advocated for Ibrahima's freedom, often writing letters to President John Quincy Adams and Secretary of State Henry Clay. He was a prominent member of the African Colonization Society in the South. (Mississippi Department of Archives and History)

principal of the first institution for the education of individuals who are deaf, took up Ibrahima's cause and in 1828 published a statement in a fundraising pamphlet by the "Committee Appointed to Solicit Subscriptions to aid redeeming the Family from Slavery" and the ACS. In writing this appeal, Gallaudet stated Ibrahima's story. He had been purchased by Thomas Foster, but through the philanthropic efforts of the ACS he was able to obtain his freedom. Now freed, he was trying to buy the freedom of his wife and children. Gallaudet states that it was Cox who became ill in Africa and was nursed back to wellness by Ibrahima, whose father, in a gesture of generosity, gave him gold, ivory, and new clothes and had his warriors escort Cox to Sierra Leone. There, Cox found his old ship and safely returned to England. Gallaudet then states that Cox offered Foster one thousand dollars for Ibrahima's freedom, but he declined the offer, saying that Ibrahima was too valuable to sell.[153]

It was the editor and publisher of the *Mississippi State Gazette* of Natchez, Andrew Marschalk (figure 2.60), who initially took up Ibrahima's cause and raised the money in Natchez to buy his freedom. A Dutch immigrant who fought for the colonies during the American Revolution, Marschalk is credited with printing, in Natchez, the first newspaper in Mississippi. A local activist in the first decades of the nineteenth century, he and Natchez lawyer and publisher of the *Southern Galaxy*, Cyrus Griffin,[154] petitioned several prominent members of the ACS, including Secretary of State Henry Clay and later President John Quincy Adams, to pressure Foster to grant Ibrahima's freedom and grant him passage back to Africa. Clay and Adams intervened on Ibrahima's behalf, and with this political pressure, Foster begrudgingly accepted the money to free Ibrahima in 1828. Now freed, Ibrahima toured New York, Philadelphia, and New England and raised over three thousand dollars to buy his wife's and children's freedom. Foster also owned them and now demanded that he should also be paid to free them. Ibrahima eventually returned to Africa but unfortunately died before reaching his kingdom.[155]

With its national notoriety, the Ibrahima story endured in Black and white lore in Natchez during throughout the nineteenth and early twentieth centuries. For African Americans, it represented how enslaved Black people endured hardship and humiliation in antebellum Natchez with grace and strength. For white Natchezians, most notably women, it was an example that while slavery was inhumane, their ancestors often did the right thing and freed the enslaved who deserved it—a good deed that their ancestors did to reward a noble African who merited his freedom. African Americans also identified with the Ibrahima story as an example of how many of their ancestors had been members of royalty in Africa. As the Natchez narrative developed in a way that claimed practically everyone was aristocratic or associated with royalty, then why not include one who was enslaved?

Sentimental stories were published about Ibrahima during the late nineteenth century in Natchez, but it was not until prominent Duke University historian Charles S. Sydnor published Ibrahima's story in the *South Atlantic Quarterly* in 1937 that the story was first documented. He most likely stumbled upon the story during his research on early newspapers in Mississippi with Marschalk and Griffin. While factual, Sydnor's account failed to cite his sources, and the story continued to be part of the lore of the city.[156] Along with Roane Byrnes, other NGC women were aware of the story. Ada Foster, who was distantly related to Thomas Foster, was aware of it through oral and written accounts of her family history. NGC member Jennie Dixon Stewart, who was a descendant of Marschalk, also knew the story.[157]

In 1968, historian Terry Alford began chronicling Ibrahima's history when he was a graduate student at Mississippi State University. An African American Mississippian during the civil rights movement, Alford recalls going to Natchez while researching slavery in the Adams County Courthouse. To his astonishment, he came across an 1828 letter from

Figure 2.61: Marschalk Printing Office, built circa 1810, corner of Wall and Franklin Streets, Natchez, Mississippi, James Butters, Photographer. The building was demolished in 1960, and the site is now a parking lot. A roadside plaque commemorates the site as being where the first newspaper building in Mississippi once stood. (Library of Congress, Prints & Photographs Division, Historic American Buildings Survey, HABS MISS,1-NATCH,13-)

Henry Clay, then US secretary of state, concerning the freedom of an enslaved man who was said to be a Moorish prince. Later that day, he met Mary Elizabeth Postlethwaite, an eccentric Natchez antiquarian who told him the story. After spending seven years researching Ibrahima in Mississippi, New Orleans, Philadelphia, London, and Africa, Alford verified Postlethwaite's story and published *Prince Among Slaves* in 1977.[158]

Although Ibrahima is a story of African diaspora and white elitist story-making embellishment by the NGC women, there is little left of the tangible heritage associated with it. Fosters Fields, the plantation that Ibrahima toiled on for forty years, is now part of Natchez suburbia. The plantation was later sold to the Henderson family, and in the twentieth century, the manor house was demolished.[159] Foster's descendants now identify with Thomas Foster's brother's home, Foster's Mound. It is listed on the National Register of Historic Places, not so much for the modest Greek Revival house on top of the mound, but because of the prehistoric Indigenous artifacts that rest beneath it in the actual Native American burial mound. Marschalk's publishing office was documented by the Historic American Buildings Survey in 1936 (figure 2.61), not because of its association with Ibrahima but because it was the place where journalism began in Mississippi. In the 1960s, the early nineteenth-century

Figure 2.62: Miss Roane Adams, queen of the 1939 Confederate Ball in Natchez, Mississippi. (From *Natchez and the Pilgrimage* by Georgie Wilson Newell and Charles Cromartie Compton [Kingsport: Southern Publishers, 1935])

Figure 2.63: "The Confederate Ball," 1940, Natchez, Mississippi. (From *Natchez: Symbol of the Old South* by Nola Nance Oliver [New York: Hastings House, 1940])

publishing office, which was modeled after east coast shop-residences, was demolished. In its place is a parking lot.

In addition to Ibrahima's story being documented by Alford in his book, a 2006 documentary told his story (figure 2.62). Several more guidebooks were published throughout the twentieth century, which reflected the changes in the narrative from Spanish colonial Natchez to antebellum Natchez, but the core of it remains as best stated in the latest guidebook, first published in 1969, about the city, Steven Brooke's *The Majesty of Natchez* (figure 2.63):

Figure 2.64: The Gates of Dunleith featured in *Natchez: Symbol of the Old South*. (From *Natchez: Symbol of the Old South* by Nola Nance Oliver [New York: Hastings House, 1940])

Chivalry and romance, grandeur and wealth, adventure, and power—this is Natchez.

Listen for the echoes of Aaron Burr's whispered intrigues and the laughter and song of Lafayette's jubilant soirees. Discover the sunken roads upon which Andrew Jackson marched to battle or quietly strolled in courtship. Look through the early morning fog on a Vidalia sandbar for the ghosts of proud gentlemen, pistols in hand, risking their lives in defense of honor.

Walk the tree-lined streets of architectural treasures and be refreshed in the long shallows of great white pillars. Enjoy the legendary Southern cuisine and incomparable hospitality. Finally, gaze upon the mighty Mississippi River, so intimately tied to the fortunes of antebellum Natchez, a silent witness to the colorful history of this, its oldest settlement.

At every turn, Natchez will charm and delight you—and remain forever in your memory.[160]

What began in 1932 as a story of an exotic, enlightened-but-removed Spanish colonial historyland became the archetype of what 1930s America imagined the antebellum South was. Through the NGC women's perceptions of themselves, the city's historic architecture, and its tortured and cruel history of slavery and race, Natchez became the place "Where the Old South Still Lives." The Natchez narrative was a highly inventive way to preserve a built patrimony, but it was more than that—it was an incredible work of marketing. Edith Moore had contrived a history of Natchez, and Katherine Miller sold it, but Roane Byrnes captured its mythology.

Black and white and diaspora, fascination of the national media, and Hollywood's imagination helped develop this collective memory by a handful of white middle-aged women into a highly profitable commercial brand. But as Natchez's tourism fortunes were ascending, it was nearly halted by greed and conflict within the very group that invented the commercial venture—the Natchez Garden Club women (figure 2.64).

Chapter 3

THE MAKING OF THE PILGRIMAGE AND THE INVENTION OF CONNELLY'S TAVERN

TO PUT THEMSELVES UNDER THE SPELL OF THE PLACE

The women of the Natchez Garden Club (NGC) were feeling confident and proud during their year-end meeting in 1934. The last two Spring Pilgrimages had been successful beyond their imagination, and the club found itself with a $3,000 profit.[1] Other groups affiliated with the pilgrimages had profited as well. The African American Zion Chapel earned a thousand dollars[2] in ticket receipts for its spiritual concert, "Heaven Bound," and the profits were invested back into the old church building. Both Black and white residents had thronged the event; several of the NGC women would later recall how much they enjoyed the performance. Meanwhile, hotels were filled to capacity with tourists, and homeowners also benefited, renting out spare bedrooms, while local eateries enjoyed a spring bounce in business after the doldrums of winter. And some of the NGC women opened small restaurants in their homes for the tourists. Even more promising, representatives from Paramount Pictures and Universal Studios had come from Hollywood to observe the club members' activities and participate in the pilgrimages.

Any doubts about whether tourists would willingly come to Natchez to tour the old houses and buildings were put to rest. For the more visionary women of the club, the profits raised aspirational questions: How could they increase the scope of the pilgrimage? How could it improve their town in the long term? And how could they continue to find outlets for their awakened creativity?

The 1931 Mississippi Federation of Garden Clubs' annual convention was the catalyst that spawned the idea to hold pilgrimages and begin preserving the historic buildings in the city. Two hundred garden club women from all over the South arrived in Natchez in late March that year, and after registering for the convention at the Natchez Eola Hotel,

Figure 3.1: Ruth Audley Beltzhoover (left) and her daughter, Virginia Beltzhoover, in the drawing room of Green Leaves. Beltzhoover was a close friend of Katherine Grafton Miller and a fellow planner during the early pilgrimages in Natchez. (From *Natchez of Long Ago and the Pilgrimage* by Katherine Grafton Miller [Natchez: Relimak Publishing Co., 1938])

they were assigned to automobiles that were lined up along the street; the cars were provided by husbands of the NGC women. Once situated in their cars, the visitors began a parade down Main Street and off to see the gardens and historic homes. Although the visiting women were impressed with the landscape features, such as the fountains at Monteigne, they were more captivated by the villas. Later in her life, Ruth Audley Beltzhoover recalled that the out-of-town garden club women pleaded, "Oh, can't we go in the house? We'd love to go in the house."[3] Based on the accounts of events during the 1931 garden club meeting, the weather turned cold and blustery. Events, such as the tea at Monteigne, had to be moved indoors. Katherine Miller and Beltzhoover took matters into their own hands and approached the homeowners who had agreed to let the garden clubs tour the gardens and asked if they would open up their homes as well. The homeowners agreed to open their doors, even reclusive ones, like Monteigne's Amie Carpenter. The poor weather persisted during those two days, and so the Natchez women opened up other houses—Magnolia Vale, Dunleith, and Richmond. Beltzhoover summed up their realization: "So they loved houses, we discovered."[4]

The NGC women did not invent the idea of a Spring Pilgrimage featuring their historic homes to raise money for their civic projects; the

Garden Club of Virginia held the first event, "Historic Garden Week." But the women of Natchez were the first to commercialize this cultural tourism event in the US, and they did it to preserve the historic architecture of their town.[5] Ruth Beltzhoover recounted that it was her husband, Melchoir, not Katherine Miller, who came up with the pilgrimage idea. She remembered his saying, "Why don't you girls get busy and have a House Tour?," and she stated that even Miller acknowledged he suggested the idea, but not too often (figure 3.1).[6]

In 1931, the NGC members began planning their first pilgrimage with only $55 in their treasury. Dues were one dollar, and although Roane Byrnes fondly remembered scavenger hunts and other fundraising ploys throughout the year, she also acknowledged that those events may have raised only $10.[7] Most of the men in town derided the idea, convinced that no one would drive to Natchez and pay money to walk through dilapidated houses. Emboldened by the reaction they witnessed during the state garden club event, the women believed the pilgrimage was going to be successful. Katherine Miller approached Ethel Kelly to open up Melrose and Agnes Marshall to open up Lansdowne. Beltzhoover also agreed to open up Green Leaves for annual pilgrimages. Miller was always blunt in her demands and refused to accept a no when she approached her friends to open their houses for the pilgrimage tour, as one remembered:

> KATHERINE: Now Miss Agnes, we're going to come out to your house and bring some people.
> MISS AGNES [and probably others]: Indeed, you are not going to bring strange people into my house to see it like it is. Indeed, I am not about to do it!
> KATHERINE: We are going to be there.[8]

And like all the others, she relented and opened her house to Miller and tourists.

Mary Louise Kendall Goodrich Shields reiterated what everyone thought about Miller's idea: "Really, we all said that, 'Katherine is crazy.' Who wants to come to Natchez?" (figure 3.2).[9] And Miller, Beltzhoover, Byrnes, and Alma Kellogg not only approached the homeowners to open their homes for the pilgrimage tour; they also asked each homeowner to sign for a loan of $200[10] to finance the pilgrimage venture. The homeowners grudgingly agreed to sign for the loan, and the women were able to obtain an interest-free loan, thanks to Melchoir.[11]

Miller planned for the event in her usual enthusiastic and determined way. She purchased table linens, flower arrangements, food, and fes-

Figure 3.2: Mary Louise Kendall Goodrich Shields sits with her two daughters, Mary Lou (right) and Ann, at Montaigne in the 1930s. Shields was the youngest member of the Natchez Garden Club and the oldest surviving one when she died in 2015 at the age of 109. (Historic Natchez Foundation)

Figure 3.3: Downtown Natchez, Mississippi, 1940. (Library of Congress, Prints & Photographs Division, Farm Security Administration/Office of War Information, LC-DIG-fsa-8c30759)

tive decorations from downtown merchants. Beltzhoover remembered Miller would come into a retail store and say, "'Now we're ordering this and this,' and the retailer would say, 'Now who are we charging this to?' She always replied, 'The Natchez Garden Club.' The store proprietor then would look in astonishment, and then say to either Ruth Audley or Alma, the treasurer of the club, 'Would you sign it?' And they always did."[12] Miller later admitted that she had been impulsive and unorganized in planning the first pilgrimage.[13]

The women energetically planned the first pilgrimage, with each committee proposing an idea for it. All of them cost money, and treasurer Kellogg vetoed almost every one of them. As novices in planning a major

Figure 3.4: Miss Elise Brown, Natchez pilgrimage parade queen of 1932. For their first pilgrimage, the Natchez Garden Club women planned an elaborate parade for the event, which turned out to be too taxing for them, and it was not appreciated by the tourists. (Courtesy of the Archives and Records Services Division, Mississippi Department of Archives and History)

economic and tourist event, these women misjudged nearly everything that the tourists wanted and were completely overwhelmed with the logistics of the affair. The first pilgrimage was planned to last four days, March 28 to April 2; and they wanted it to be more of a festive event than merely a simple house tour. They rented some rooms to sell tickets in the Eola Hotel and proudly hung a banner proclaiming "Pilgrimage Headquarters" (figure 3.3).

Relying on their past experiences in planning festive events as southern ladies, they expended a lot of energy and time in planning a parade for the first pilgrimage. The parade was suggested and partly financed by the town merchants, who wanted it as a contingency event if the pilgrimage did not attract tourists.[14] The women labored on preparing the floats for the parade and neglected the planning for the house tours. They bickered among themselves over selecting a parade queen. Elise Brown eventually was selected as the Natchez Pilgrimage Parade Queen (figure 3.4); Roane Byrnes and Lallie Adams urged Adams's son, Bill, to be the parade's king, to which he reluctantly agreed. The parade did not have a theme, but there were Natchez-themed floats, and several members of the club rode in the parade in their horse-drawn surreys. Confederate imagery was not used in either the parade or the evening ball; the women were inspired more by Mardi Gras celebrations than the Confederacy. Club member Elizabeth Dunbar Murray revamped an older historical pageant called "Under Many Flags" and made it the theme of the pilgrimage. The girls in the court wore handmade dresses of tarlatan that cost no more than $7.50 to make. The women rented morning coats for the boys and asked them to wear gray flannel slacks. They wanted the boys and girls participating in the parade and balls to be called dukes and duchesses, another reference to Mardi Gras festivities, and this only confused the tourists experiencing the event.[15]

The parade haphazardly occurred on the first day of the pilgrimage. Margaret Marshall remembered riding in her family's surrey with her sister and their children. Their African American gardener drove the carriage wearing a paper top hat that Margaret made that morning.[16] That evening, they held a pilgrimage ball, featuring the town's teenagers dancing; Carolyn Davis Eidt and Hartman Moritz were the queen and king of the ball.

On the second day, the NGC members staged a daytime ballet tableau at Melrose. Local dance instructor Trebby Poole organized and trained both girls and boys to perform the ballet. She called her ballet "Audubon," and it celebrated the birds and flora of Natchez. Prior to the ballet was the tableau named "The Hunt," intended to depict the gentlemanly English fox-hunting tradition of nineteenth-century Natchez. It consisted of many of the women's husbands parading in front of Melrose, wearing English riding habit attire and walking their bird or coon dogs across the front lawn (figure 3.5). Rebecca Benoist recalled how the dogs were prone to having "accidents" when they were excited, so after "The Hunt" tableau, the women had to rush onto the lawn with brooms and pans to clean up after them before the ballet could start; the tourists were very amused.[17]

During the first pilgrimage, the NGC women were focused more on colonial Natchez than antebellum Natchez. For the second evening's entertainment, they put on a dance they called the "Bal Poudre." Held at the Natchez Hotel, the women and their husbands dressed in white colonial-era ball attire and powdered their hair white. The tourists watched them dance and were utterly confused. The women's fascination with their colonial past was incongruent with their nineteenth-century antebellum architecture.[18]

In planning the future pilgrimages, the NGC women corrected the problem and reworked their planned entertainment events, like the evening ball, to give their tourists what they wanted—the Confederate South—but on the women's terms. Ruth Beltzhoover suggested that the final ball be a tableau consisting of women wearing antebellum gowns

Figure 3.5: "The Hunt" tableau, 1934. Men from Natchez dressed in English riding attire and paraded their bird hunting and coon hunting dogs in front of Melrose during the pilgrimages. (Courtesy of the Archives and Records Services Division, Mississippi Department of Archives and History)

and young men in Confederate uniforms. She wanted the audience to imagine a magical Natchez and stated as much in the first pageant program.[19] The climax of the ball/tableau featured the king and queen and court of the ball entering Institute Hall to the tune of "Dixie" and led by the Confederate flag. And so the "Confederate Pageant" was born, a curious event that combined the women's ideas of their Confederate heritage with their traditional Mardi Gras festival.[20] By removing all political associations of the Confederacy and replacing these associations with European ideas—kings, queens, and royal courts—the women succeeded in making the days leading up to 1861 more mythical and ideal than they actually were. Katherine Miller boasted that the Confederate Ball was compared by many to "the vivid portrayals of the Oberammergau Passion Play."[21]

In 1932, the Natchez Garden Club women were quite simply overwhelmed by the planning and management of a major cultural tourism event like the pilgrimage. With Miller purchasing items for the event without any accountability, numerous complicated performances planned throughout the four-day event, and the effort that went into making more than twenty gardens and houses presentable to the tourists, it is a wonder that it even happened. But there were other issues confronting the women that they did not foresee. Estimates vary by the women who experienced it when they recollected the 1932 pilgrimage, but it appears that between five hundred and 750 people arrived in Nat-

Figure 3.6: View of the Eola Hotel in 1927. The Eola Hotel was the most modern and up-to-date hotel in Natchez during the first pilgrimages. (Thomas H. and Joan W. Gandy Photograph Collection, Mss. 3778, Louisiana and Lower Mississippi Valley Collections, LSU Libraries, Baton Rouge, Louisiana)

chez in late March to view the historic villas. Almost all of them arrived by automobile. Some of them drove themselves, while the wealthier tourists were chauffeur-driven, so housing for the African American drivers in racially segregated Natchez was a problem. Suddenly, the garden club had to manage congested traffic and contend with limited parking for automobiles in the historic town. The women pleaded for assistance from the police department to manage the increased automobile traffic. There were also tourists who arrived by train, and there was no one to drive them to their accommodations. The women and their husbands picked up those visitors in their automobiles and drove them to their hotels or private homes. The two hotels, the Natchez Hotel and the more modern Eola Hotel (figure 3.6), were filled to capacity with tourists. The women hastily secured spare bedrooms for the tourists to rent. And there were no sleeping accommodations for the African Americans in Natchez in 1932. Beltzhoover remembered how African American house servants in town provided rooms for the African American chauffeurs who drove the affluent tourists to Natchez. Dining was also a problem. The hotels and the town's most popular eatery, White's Restaurant, struggled to accommodate the tourists.

Managing the financial accounts for such a large event proved to be problematic for the NGC. Invoices for services and goods were lost, and no one actually knew how much money the club was earning during the four-day event. Confusion ensued, and the women begged for assistance from the Natchez Chamber of Commerce, which did provide them some bookkeeping services and advice for keeping up with their accounts.[22] Finally, the $1.50 ticket price to tour all of the homes was simply too low. The club lost money putting on the four-day event. The women all donated their time to the club and the pilgrimage; as with most volunteer groups, their work was inconsistent. Mary Louise Metcalf summed it up, "It was just sort of 'catch as catch can.'"[23]

Many people in Natchez, especially the male leaders, had scoffed at the pilgrimage idea, asking, "Who wants to come to Natchez?" But people in Natchez were also concerned about the effects of the Depression on their event. Did anyone have any money to spend traveling to Natchez? The 1932 pilgrimage answered those questions. Yes, people wanted to come to Natchez. And they had money to purchase tickets to tour the villas, purchase tickets to all of the tableaux, and pay for hotel and dining accommodations. The men may have laughed at the NGC women in late 1931, when they were planning the event, but by mid-April 1932, they were not laughing anymore.[24] The 1931 state garden club meeting convinced the women that they had something in Natchez that was unique—a tour of an assortment of high-style nineteenth-century villas set within a suburban landscape. The spatial arrangement of them made it convenient to tour and appreciate. Furthermore, their city was never built as a place of industry but one of leisure; this aspect of Natchez appealed to the Depression-era tourists who lived in industrialized cities that had long ago lost their agrarian charm. The planter class of Natchez left the Depression generation a valuable and marketable built patrimony. In her reminiscences about the early pilgrimages, Margaret Marshall remembered when she met Edith Bolling Wilson, the widow of President Woodrow Wilson, when she came to Natchez in 1931 with the Garden Club of Virginia and said to her: "'Mrs. Marshall, we have so many beautiful homes scattered all over Virginia, but they are forty or fifty miles apart. I never dreamed there was a small area in the United States that contained so many gorgeous antebellum mansions.' I thought if she was impressed, we had a good thing going!"[25]

If Katherine Miller did not solely invent the Natchez pilgrimage, she most definitely seized upon the idea. She saw the economic potential in showcasing the city's historic villas, but more importantly, she also saw the opportunity to use the pilgrimage as a means to preserve the historic city. As she stated in her book, *Natchez of Long Ago and the Pilgrimage*, she saw what Edith Wilson saw in Natchez's potential: "Here in Natchez we have one of the unique little cities in America, the only one with so many valuable old mansions within so small a radius—brain children of a vanished era."[26] Using her innate gift of salesmanship, she advocated to her fellow club members for the garden club to be a leader in the preservation of Natchez, saying, "We've got to do something to save Natchez. We have got to do something to interest the world in Natchez and to interest the Natchez people in saving what we have. So, let's invite the world to come to Natchez."[27]

Miller's impassioned pleas to her fellow garden club members motivated them to rethink their mission and commit their efforts to historic preservation in Natchez. As they witnessed historic houses, especially on corner lots, demolished and replaced with filling stations, they not only wanted to preserve the historic homes but to also promote Natchez as a historic city.[28]

In recalling the first pilgrimage, Miller made the case that the pilgrimage brought a different kind of economy to Natchez than the industrial-based one that the men aspired to build: "Now, with the opening of the Pilgrimage, we once more were taking our place among the other cities of the South, not as an industrial center but as a place unique from all others—a place for lovers of beauty, romance, and history to come, a place in which to forget the hubbub of the outside world: a place to dream."[29]

Emboldened by what they experienced in hosting the state garden club meeting and in the positive responses they heard from tourists during the first pilgrimage, the women set out to make the Natchez Garden Club's primary mission to preserve the built patrimony of the city. And now they knew how to do it—cultural tourism.

Armed with her self-confidence and enthusiasm and her version of the Natchez narrative, but possessing little money, Miller set out to market the next four pilgrimages. Her campaign started off modestly; she and Roane Byrnes first started writing articles about the historic architecture of Natchez for newspapers across the state. Miller then began planning a lecture, which she called "Natchez—Where the Old South Still Lives," to present to civic groups, first across the state and then across the country. She innately understood how powerful photographs could be in bringing a faraway place to life; she developed a slide presentation about Natchez that was based on the collective memory that she and the other NGC women believed about Natchez, which was embellished by her vivid imagination. She commissioned Earl Norman, the popular photographer in town, to take slides of staged scenes that she choreographed. The black and white slides were compelling, but Miller wanted to create a magical aura of Natchez for her audiences, and so she had the slides hand-colored by the leading photographic colorist in the country, the Edward van Altena firm in New York City. She built up the presentation slowly; she asked her fellow club members for financial contributions for her project—ten or perhaps fifteen dollars to purchase and color the slides. Ever resourceful, she routinely asked everyone if they were traveling to Memphis or New Orleans, and if they were, she continued, "Let me ride with you. I'll go and show my slides." She would then borrow a lantern from her church and off she went, often sleeping and dining at friends' houses in nearby towns and cities. She began her informal tour in Vicksburg, then Memphis, Jackson, Baton Rouge, and New Orleans. Later, she began traveling across the Midwest. She met garden club women in all of these places and cultivated relations with them. And by networking with them, she promoted Natchez mainly by word of mouth. Always audacious, she convinced garden club women in cities and towns throughout the Deep South and the Midwest to invite her to give her talk at their garden club meetings, and they always relented. She gave lectures to garden clubs in Chicago, Atlanta, Nashville, Kansas City, and Des Moines. Miller loved every moment of it. She was now the premiere "Southern Lady of Natchez."[30]

In promoting Natchez during the early 1930s, Miller was one of the pioneers in cultural tourism marketing. When others asked who wants to come to Natchez, she made sure that *a lot* of people wanted to come to Natchez. And they did. Each year after the first pilgrimage, the number of tourists attending grew significantly. She instinctively understood about Natchez what John Jakle noted: "oldness and historic places can be romanticized."[31] And by doing just that, she constructed a contrived attraction, developed for a specific market—white middle-aged, middle-class women of the Great Depression. Her slide presentation, along with her charisma, enabled Miller to project a visual story about the city that women living in industrialized cities could vicariously enjoy. The world that she presented was one of romance, gallantry, feminine morals, beauty, nature, adventure, and privilege. Through her three dozen slides, she made her audiences believe that Natchez was a time capsule, forgotten by progress. She persuaded her audiences, both men and women, to see it for themselves.

She first presented to her audiences the romance of Natchez, a place where beautiful belles lived in magnificent villas. In one slide, taken from D'Evereux's balcony, a young woman smiles beguilingly from below, while resting on the abutment of the portico. The composition is alluring: one wants to either sit next to this lovely young woman or be her. The splendid architecture is a world away from the industrial city. When tinted in vivid color, the image is all the more compelling (figure 3.7).

Figure 3.7: A view of a southern belle from the balcony of D'Evereux, Katherine Grafton Miller Slide Presentation, 1934. Miller tied the historic architecture of Natchez to the ideal of the "southern lady" in her Natchez promotional presentations. (Courtesy of the Archives and Records Services Division, Mississippi Department of Archives and History)

Figure 3.8: Belles and beaux at D'Evereux, Katherine Grafton Miller Slide Presentation, 1934. Romance and southern antebellum nostalgia were what Miller used as primary selling points for promoting Natchez in the Midwest. (Courtesy of the Archives and Records Services Division, Mississippi Department of Archives and History)

Making of the Pilgrimage and Invention of Connelly's Tavern   147

Figure 3.9: Katherine Grafton Miller in front of Hope Farm, Katherine Grafton Miller Slide Presentation, 1934. Miller linked the exotic Natchez gardens to her southern-focused narrative of the city. (Courtesy of the Archives and Records Services Division, Mississippi Department of Archives and History)

Miller cleverly utilized the city's historic buildings to bolster her pitch, making Natchez more romantic than it was in reality. By capitalizing on the planning of the city—array of individual villas, clustered in close proximity to each other—she was able to choreograph vignettes, which were similar to the tableaus. Each slide image presented a story, an intimate one that viewers could project themselves into; these were images full of romance and nostalgia. More importantly, by making the villas a protagonist in her scenes, she capitalized on how antiquity gave added value to the experience—an intangible value, which could not be added to a modern structure. Only this type of architecture, which was isolated and forgotten by progress, could obtain it (figure 3.8).[32]

Even though the Natchez Garden Club was broadening its mission to include historic preservation, Miller and others continued the gardening and nature component of their cause and existence. But Miller especially wanted to feature the early and warm springs that occurred in southwestern Mississippi to appeal to prospective tourists. The alluring warm and colorful spring, where exotic flowering shrubs bloomed and Spanish moss draped from evergreen live oaks, easily induced housewives, tired of cold winters, to drive to Natchez and enjoy a respite among the historic architecture and gardens. And there, in her slides, was Miller welcoming them to her garden at Hope Farm (figure 3.9).

Perhaps Miller was the first to present the southern lady ideal in popular culture in 1933. Stark Young's *So Red the Rose* was published in 1934, and Margaret Mitchell's *Gone with the Wind* was published in 1936. This supposed feminine ideal, which the NGC members embraced, had been

Figure 3.10: Katherine Grafton Miller sewing in her bedroom at Hope Farm, Katherine Grafton Miller Slide Presentation, 1934. Miller depicted herself as the ultimate southern lady, the archetype of motherhood, even though she was childless. (Courtesy of the Archives and Records Services Division, Mississippi Department of Archives and History)

firmly established for over a hundred years in the South. But what was once part of an isolated region was now being introduced to the broader nation and commercialized for the tourist economy. Unlike Young's heroine, Valette Bedford, or Mitchell's Scarlett O'Hara, Katherine Miller made herself the real southern lady. And she presented herself in her slides from her own base of feminine power, her antebellum home. In one of her slides, she features herself as the dutiful wife and lady of the house, wearing a hoop skirt and lace, darning socks in her well-kept bedroom with its modest but elegant four-poster bed and her Greek Revival chest of drawers with a vanity mirror on top. The slide is the embodiment of the myth of graceful, dutiful southern femininity—and a vision of what one could aspire to become (figure 3.10).

And even though Miller reaffirmed that a southern lady's virtues were still very much part of the Natchez world, she also reminded prospective tourists that Natchez had always been a place of leisure and opulence. As a youthful and vital place, its architecture and gardens were built for coquettish merriment. And Miller wanted the prospective tourists to know that the owners of the grand villas were eagerly waiting to welcome them into this world, albeit for a short while, and let them admire the splendors (figure 3.11). Here was where a middle-class housewife could leave her onerous and tedious house chores and be charmed by a dashing beau (figure 3.12).

Making of the Pilgrimage and Invention of Connelly's Tavern 149

Figure 3.11: A Natchez belle greets the viewer at the front gates of Stanton Hall. (Courtesy of the Archives and Records Services Division, Mississippi Department of Archives and History)

Figure 3.12: Beaux and belles, Katherine Grafton Miller Slide Presentation, 1934. Miller cleverly presented dashing beaux courting blushing belles in her presentations to suggest to her midwest audiences that romance awaited them in Natchez. (Courtesy of the Archives and Records Services Division, Mississippi Department of Archives and History)

Figure 3.13: The idealistic life in antebellum Natchez, Katherine Grafton Miller Slide Presentation, 1934. Miller skillfully choreographed her photographs to depict a focused message, one of lovely gardens and Victorian manners. (Courtesy of the Archives and Records Services Division, Mississippi Department of Archives and History)

In Miller's slides, the viewer was placed into the story. Whether it was the photographer Norman or Miller herself who designed each vignette, the foreground of the image is cleverly maximized. Through her verbal descriptions, she attempted to entice the viewer to cross the picture plane and enter the fantastical world. The scenes are intimate, and it is as if the viewer can be a part of the moment—but that is impossible, unless you first travel to Natchez (figure 3.13).

Miller prominently featured African American servitude in her slide presentations. The white ruling elite class is served by a caring and submissive African American servant class. There are scenes of Black chauffeurs, always wearing top hats and morning coats, driving surreys with elegant women to an opulent villa, where a gentle but privileged family awaits to greet them beneath the Spanish moss (figure 3.14). Later, in her book *Natchez of Long Ago and the Pilgrimage*, Miller depicted the African Americans in Natchez in a condescending way, describing a group of African American boys as "Natchez Pickaninnies." The term "pickaninny" was at the time used to describe African Americans in what was thought to be a neutral or perhaps affectionate manner as it derives from a Portuguese word meaning "little." But the word reveals her racist attitude toward African Americans, which was shared by most white middle-class southerners of her generation. As the pilgrimages became more popular, African Americans developed businesses to serve tourists, and the NGC women encouraged them to do so (figure 3.15). All the same, Miller conveyed to the nation the image of elite whites being served by the enslaved African Americans (figure 3.16).

Figure 3.14: African American driver driving a Natchez family to Linden, Katherine Grafton Miller Slide Presentation, 1934. Miller reinforced stereotypical images of African Americans serving gentlepeople of the antebellum South in her presentations during the 1930s. (Courtesy of the Archives and Records Services Division, Mississippi Department of Archives and History)

Figure 3.15: A photograph of "Natchez Pickaninnies" in Katherine Grafton Miller's book, *Natchez of Long Ago and the Pilgrimage*. Both the image and the caption reveal Miller's opinion about African Americans, which was a typical sentiment felt by most elite white southerners during the Great Depression. (Library of Congress, Prints & Photographs Division, LC-USZ62-38197)

Figure 3.16: A southern belle served by an African American woman servant, Katherine Grafton Miller Slide Presentation, 1934. Miller presented a world in which middle-class American women of the 1930s could project themselves as belles being served by African Americans in a life of glamour and romance; notice the magnolia flower arrangement in the foreground. (Courtesy of the Archives and Records Services Division, Mississippi Department of Archives and History)

Figure 3.17: The Confederate flag unfurled on the side porch of Green Leaves, Katherine Grafton Miller Slide Presentation, 1934. Miller presented the Confederacy as part of the romance and regional patriotism found in Natchez during the pilgrimage. (Courtesy of the Archives and Records Services Division, Mississippi Department of Archives and History)

Figure 3.18: Two boys dressed in Confederate uniforms standing next to the front door of Linden, Katherine Grafton Miller Slide Presentation, 1934. Miller promoted the supposed glory of the Confederacy in her presentation even though Natchez played a marginal role in the Civil War. (Courtesy of the Archives and Records Services Division, Mississippi Department of Archives and History)

Figure 3.19: A Confederate officer with two belles in the dining parlor at Green Leaves, Katherine Grafton Miller Slide Presentation, 1934. Miller skillfully combined romance with the historic architecture, the "southern lady" ideal, and the Confederacy in making Natchez the idealized personification of the mythic "Old South." (Courtesy of the Archives and Records Services Division, Mississippi Department of Archives and History)

Miller learned from the 1932 pilgrimage that Natchez's association with the Confederacy interested tourists. In her presentations, she linked the Confederate cause to the city's architecture. In one slide, she showed the Stars and Bars Confederate flag unfurled on the second-floor porch at Green Leaves (figure 3.17). In another slide, two young cadets flank the front door of Linden; one is holding the Confederate battle flag, while another, who is quite young, stands upright at attention next to the door (figure 3.18). In her presentation of Natchez and the Confederacy, she reaffirmed the southern sentiment at the time that the Confederate cause was a patriotic one. She glossed over the fact that it was actually a rebellion against the United States—an act of treason triggered by the desire to maintain slavery in perpetuity in North America.

But Miller went even further with the Confederate history in Natchez; through the imagery she conceived, she tied the historic architecture with the Confederacy and her ideas of romance to create "a tragedy with a happy ending," which the tourists enjoyed. There are scenes like the one she constructed in Monteigne's parlor of gallant Confederate officers dining with lovely belles. The scene conveys a melancholy foreboding of the wartime tragedy to come, and her audience can feel the drama in the scene (figure 3.19).

Figure 3.20: The "Polka" performed by Natchez teenagers at the Confederate Ball, Katherine Grafton Miller Slide Presentation, 1934. Miller presented the tableaux entertainment, which was featured during the evenings of the pilgrimage. This performance was held in the high school gymnasium and auditorium. In 1940, the tableaux moved to the newly built Natchez Auditorium. (Courtesy of the Archives and Records Services Division, Mississippi Department of Archives and History)

Figure 3.21: Young women in main garden of Green Leaves, Katherine Grafton Miller Slide Presentation, 1934. (Courtesy of the Archives and Records Services Division, Mississippi Department of Archives and History)

When it was complete, Miller's slide presentation communicated a picture of the 1930s Natchez narrative: not of what Natchez actually was in the 1930s, but for Miller and others like Roane Byrnes, Edith Moore, and Ruth Beltzhoover, what it should have been. She had reinvented her small and forgotten town into a "historyland." She made Natchez a contrived and commodified package for the tourist. This backwater

Figure 3.22: Miss Mimi Brown and a "Black mammy" in front of Linden. Many of the African Americans depicted in Katherine Miller's photographs were middle-class people; some of them were nurses, teachers, and tradesmen. (From *Natchez of Long Ago and the Pilgrimage* by Katherine Grafton Miller [Natchez: Relimak Publishing Co., 1938])

and long-overlooked town was the most unlikely place to become a tourist attraction, but Miller did it, and now an influx of outside money came into the town every spring. Natchez became "historic" rather than historically accurate, which signifies its importance in popular culture rather than its actual historical significance. She brilliantly wove the visual narrative of the Natchez tableau and its social life into her presentation. She presented herself and her friends as southern aristocracy, worthy of living in the grand villas that their ancestors built long ago. She showed her audiences young couples dancing the polka at the Confederate Ball along with the everyday activities of elite white Natchez women (figures 3.20 and 3.21).

What is truly remarkable about the presentation is that all of the men and women posing for her staged scenes were ordinary folk in Natchez, everyday middle-class people. Some of them, most notably the African Americans, were skilled tradesmen or nurses portraying servants of the nineteenth century (figure 3.22).[33]

Using her vivid imagination, Katherine Miller created the Natchez we know today: a Natchez that embodied the ideals of southern feminin-

Figure 3.23: Natchez Garden Club women wearing antebellum attire in the parlor at Hope Farm, Katherine Grafton Miller Slide Presentation, 1934. Miller presented her modest home, along with several other modest homes in Natchez, as opulent showplaces, where southern ladies demonstrated their manners and customs in Natchez. Miller is dressed in a dark gown and sitting at the right side of the mantel. (Courtesy of the Archives and Records Services Division, Mississippi Department of Archives and History)

Figure 3.24: Children playing at the front gates of Dunleith, Katherine Grafton Miller Slide Presentation, 1934. (Courtesy of the Archives and Records Services Division, Mississippi Department of Archives and History)

Figure 3.25: Natchez belle posing in front of a gilded full-length mirror, Katherine Grafton Miller Slide Presentation, 1934. (Courtesy of the Archives and Records Services Division, Mississippi Department of Archives and History)

ity, romance, family, patriotism, privilege, and the Confederate cause. It became a new place in the public eye because of its oldness (figure 3.23). She presented a place where elegance and the carefree days of childhood went hand and hand (figure 3.24), a place not encumbered by the grim reality of the Great Depression. But more importantly, she re-created Natchez as a glamorous place, one more accessible than Hollywood (figure 3.25).

THE BUSINESS OF THE PILGRIMAGES

The NGC women learned quite a lot from their initial pilgrimage in 1932. The next pilgrimage was going to be different: the NGC was determined to make a profit. The women focused on the logistics of accommodating a large number of tourists in 1933. By 1934, they were organized and focused, and at the end of the 1933 pilgrimage their venture became profitable, not only for the garden club but for merchants and restaurant and hotel proprietors as well.

For the 1933 pilgrimage, the first thing the NGC women did was to extend the event from four days to a week-long event. They also raised the price of the tickets from $1.50 for four tours to $2 per villa. The women worked out arrangements for renting spare bedrooms in people's homes to the tourists, and they worked with the Natchez Police Department to better manage the increased traffic during the event. During the 1932 pilgrimage, the women literally wore their grandmothers' or great-grandmothers' antebellum-era dresses, which often tore or fell apart during the event. For the 1933 pilgrimage, they decided to make new dresses for themselves (figure 3.26).[34] The women hired Ellen Starnes, the most popular seamstress in town, to make the dresses; she became so busy that she hired several African American seamstresses to assist her in making the costumes. They convinced the men in town participating in the pilgrimages to order their nineteenth-century costumes from Van Dorn's of New York (figure 3.27).[35]

The year 1933 was also when the NGC women began in earnest a historic preservation movement in Natchez. Mary Louise Metcalf recalled how she, Miller, Byrnes, and Beltzhoover spoke at various times to the Chamber of Commerce, urging them to preserve the historic downtown. Metcalf said that "most of the businessmen thought we were crazy" since business and civic leaders like Mayor Joseph Byrne wanted the downtown to look "modern" and "progressive." The women struggled to convince the business leaders to preserve their historic buildings, and like most preservation struggles, they succeeded in saving one old building

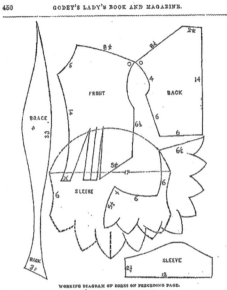

Figure 3.26: "Dress, November 1855" from *Godey's Lady Book and Magazine*. In 1933, the Natchez Garden Club women consulted this leading fashion book and magazine of the mid-nineteenth century and re-created new hoop skirts for the pilgrimage. (University of Vermont Library, Burlington, Vermont)

Figure 3.27: Family dressed in antebellum attire for the 1936 Natchez pilgrimage. The Natchez Garden Club women commissioned local seamstresses to sew new period clothing for men and women participating in the pilgrimages. (Courtesy of the Archives and Records Services Division, Mississippi Department of Archives and History)

but later watched as another was demolished. Metcalf later bemoaned, "We sold the world on Natchez, but we couldn't sell the Natchez business people on Natchez. It was a tragedy really."[36]

Concerned about the decayed state of the villas, Byrnes and Metcalf began a campaign to have the homeowners solicit the services of Richard Koch, the most respected preservation architect of New Orleans during the first half of the twentieth century.[37] The women knew him as "Dick," and they trusted his advice. He was lifelong friends of Roane and Ferriday Byrnes; he often stayed at Ravennaside when he was in town.[38]

Often Dick Koch examined the historic villas and wrote in letters to the owners his recommendations to remedy a specific problem. He understood that the women and the property owners often lacked the money to pay for a detailed design, and he adjusted his services and expectations in order to provide the consultation needed to preserve historic villas in the city. He traveled to Natchez periodically and performed inspections on several houses during a single visit. He was paid either by a group of owners or by the Natchez Garden Club; usually his services cost between $300 and $500. He understood the owners' apprehensions about hiring an architect. Some owners complained; one said, "I've lived in this house all my life. I'm not going to have a strange man come here and tell me what I can and can't do!"[39] But other owners listened to him, and his advice was straightforward: "Use your money on the roof. Then the foundation." He often said not to worry about the looks on the inside or outside until those two items had been addressed.[40] He later produced drawings for restoration of the House on Ellicott Hill and designed a new house at Magnolia Vale after a fire destroyed the historic house. Koch and Richard Wilson produced a design for the Ewald family at about the same time as the Magnolia Vale project.[41]

Bolstered by the success that they achieved, first with the state garden club convention and then with the first two pilgrimages, the NGC women became ever more entrepreneurial in planning the 1934 pilgrimage. The crowds grew larger, and it became difficult for the two or three restaurants to accommodate them. Beltzhoover's husband, Melchoir, came up with another idea: to start feeding them by opening a tea room. And she did. She arranged the back gallery at Green Leaves to seat a hundred people and placed tables under the trees in an area she called "The Patio of the Oaks." She then converted her washroom into a kitchen and rented stoves from a local restaurant supplier, along with china and silver. She charged seventy-five cents for lunch and a dollar for dinner; she and Melchoir served the meals, and her friend and fellow garden club member Kate Lewis took vacation days from the Wilson Box Company and worked in the kitchen. For lunch they served chicken gumbo, rice, cornbread, and pineapple salad, and for dinner, they served fried chicken, rice and gravy, and spoonbread for dessert. The "tea room" was so successful that the next year Ruth hired young African American men as waiters. Most of them were part of the great migration of African Americans from the Deep South to the North; they had moved to Chicago and returned to Natchez during the pilgrimage to visit family and make a little money. Ruth had them outfitted in white coats, and they ushered people from the front gates of Green Leaves to the villa and the makeshift restaurant. The young African American men even stopped traffic, inviting people to come into the restaurant.

Katherine Miller started a similar business venture with her mother in her parents' home on Washington Street, and they served fried chicken during lunch. And even the owner of Monteigne, Amie Carpenter, who had reluctantly opened her home to the state garden club women three years earlier, opened a small restaurant in her villa.

But not everyone was happy to see the NGC women develop supporting businesses for the pilgrimages. Seeing paying customers patronizing the temporary dining establishments, the restaurant and hotel owners in town, who were all men, complained about the women to the municipal officials. Ruth Beltzhoover remembered how she was reported to the Natchez Health Department:

> And the funniest thing happened: the other restaurants got upset about our restaurant, though I was paying for a license. So, they came down and said they would have to close the restaurant.
>
> The official [stated it was] because I didn't have the proper equipment to sterilize the dishes. I said, "What do you mean?" And the official said, "Well, you are supposed to have three different washes." So, I said, "Come look in my kitchen." And he nearly fainted. Here in the kitchen we have a huge big wash tub; in fact, we had three of them. Then he said, "Oh. When did you do that?" And I told him, "About 1910."
>
> So, the next thing they said was that I was serving margarine,[42] and a horrible man, who was here with the officials, said I would have to pay a thousand dollars or I'd go to jail. So, I immediately rang Mr. Laub and Mr. Engel,[43] and they said, "Well, I guess they've got you for serving margarine." So, I paid the thousand dollars. And Kate Lewis wrote to the President and told him about it, and we got our thousand dollars back. We weren't serving margarine on the plate—we were cooking with it. He didn't ask me, but I wouldn't have known if he'd asked me, because Kate was in charge.[44]

Miller used every social connection she had to market the pilgrimage, but perhaps no one helped her more than New Orleans *Times-Picayune*

Figure 3.28: Promotional poster for the 1932 Natchez pilgrimage by Henry Barrow, New Orleans *Times-Picayune*. As a personal favor to editor and Natchez native George Healy Jr., newspaper illustrator Henry Barrow designed and illustrated the first pilgrimage promotional poster. Healy invented the slogan on the spot: "Come to Natchez, Where the Old South Still Lives and Where Shaded Highways and Antebellum Homes Greet New and Old Friends." (From *Natchez of Long Ago and the Pilgrimage* by Katherine Grafton Miller [Natchez: Relimak Publishing Co., 1938])

editor George Healy Jr. in promoting it. In his autobiography, *A Lifetime on Deadline: Self-Portrait of a Southern Journalist,* Healy recalled his 1932 meeting with Miller at his office in New Orleans. She informed him that his hometown was in the "doldrums" and that the Natchez Garden Club had a plan for attracting visitors. Healy asked *Times-Picayune* artist Henry Barrow to sketch a poster for the pilgrimage event and have it engraved. He then came up with the slogan: "Come to Natchez, Where the Old South Still Lives and Where Shaded Highways and Antebellum Homes Greet New and Old Friends."[45] The slogan was used to promote the Spring Pilgrimage for the next forty years and now epitomizes the spirit of the event, often used in articles in the media to this day (figure 3.28).[46] Miller loved the sketch and declared it "drawn by a real artist who is now a member of the Associated Press art staff in New York City, whose pen and pencil portraits of the world's most famous men have been reproduced in thousands of newspapers."[47]

The 1933 pilgrimage was successful beyond anyone's imagination. In letters to his wife, Ethel, soon after the pilgrimage had ended, George Kelly stated that four thousand people toured Melrose and, even after the pilgrimage had officially ended, people from New Orleans continued to drive up and beg to tour the grand villa.[48] Tourists were impressed by the Natchez experience. Even a woman from Virginia acknowledged that "there was nothing else in the country like Natchez."[49] The *Clarion Ledger*, the *Times-Picayune*, and the *Commercial Appeal* featured favorable articles about the event.[50]

The 1933 pilgrimage earned $6,204.35,[51] double the amount the Natchez Garden Club earned from the preceding year's event. The NGC women were even more successful in 1934, earning $9,263.04. After expenses, mainly from making costumes and producing the ball and tableau, the NGC allocated $2,605.15 to the homeowners of the historic villas, which was an average of $90.10 per homeowner,[52] and added to its treasury $2,726.22. In 1934, they gave the homeowners $3,973.01, $177.02 per homeowner, and added $4,033.32 to the treasury. In 1932, the NGC had $38 in its treasury; two years later, it had accrued over $8,000.[53] Success continued for the next two years, but uncertainty followed.

In five years, the Natchez Garden Club had evolved from a social outlet to a significant statewide economic development organization. In staging the first two Spring Pilgrimages, the women of the club had found the vehicle for fulfilling their true avocational potential—tourism. The success of the pilgrimage was featured in the *New York Times*, the *Chicago Tribune*, and *Life*. The ambitions of the garden club women were sparked.

FROM GILREATH HILL TO CONNELLY'S TAVERN

Motivated by the success they experienced during the 1934 pilgrimage, the Natchez Garden Club women planned for an even larger crowd for the 1935 event, and their expectations were fulfilled. In fact, the 1934 pilgrimage was so financially rewarding that the club found itself with $3,000 in the bank at the conclusion of the tours. Countless arguments ensued among the women over how to spend the money. A long delay in reaching a decision appeared inevitable until members like Alma Kellogg heard rumors in town that the club may have to pay income taxes from its profits. The prospect of being liable for taxes motivated the women and hurried them into reaching a consensus on how to spend the profits.

The NGC women proposed numerous ideas. Some members argued for funding the construction of a new city auditorium, suitable for their tableau, ballet, and the Confederate Pageant. Other members urged the club to purchase antebellum period furnishings for the city-owned Auburn. Still others wanted to buy the dilapidated Britton Place[54] and renovate it. But Roane Byrnes wanted to use the money to promote the

Figure 3.29: Gilreath Hill, 1933. Abandoned after having been used as housing for mill workers, the old house was dismissed by most people as an eyesore, but Roane Fleming Byrnes was captivated by it and championed its restoration to the Natchez Garden Club in December 1934. (Library of Congress, Prints & Photographs Division, Historic American Buildings Survey, HABS MISS,1-NATCH,2-)

city's Spanish history. Captivated by her romantic ideas, she wanted the NGC to renovate and showcase the old house on Gilreath Hill. She reached out to Kellogg for assistance in developing a financial plan for its purchase and renovation. Together, they produced a financial plan and an argument to use the club's earnings to fund its primary mission—preserving the historic buildings of Natchez.[55] And even though historic preservation had become part of the club's understood mission, there were other members—homeowners—who were vehemently opposed to the idea. They wanted more of the profits from the pilgrimage. For most of these club members and homeowners, repairing their own homes was a more pressing concern. Moreover, homeowners incurred costs in opening up their homes and managing the tourists experiencing them. Since 1929, the idea of financing the restoration of historic Natchez, a laudable and civic-minded endeavor, was just an idea. But now, after two successful pilgrimages and the anticipation of even more profitable pilgrimages in the future, this charitable idea was reconsidered, and it eventually became a lightning rod among the women that caused lifelong animosities among friends and nearly ended the pilgrimage idea and historic preservation in Natchez before it started.

There were dozens of historic houses in Natchez in need of restoration projects, but Byrnes realized the potential in what was perhaps the town's oldest structure, on Canal Street between Jefferson and

Franklin Streets. At the December meeting that year, the club members debated how to spend their considerable profits, and Byrnes presented her idea: she wanted to restore the house on Gilreath Hill (figure 3.29).

The location and the structure were called at the time Gilreath Hill, where J. R. Gilreath's school had once been located. In the nineteenth century, it was remembered as the James Moore House, the home of a prominent early nineteenth-century merchant. Others referred to it as Gilreath's Hill Tavern or Ellicott's Inn. By the 1930s, hardly anyone paid any attention to the frame house, which, while in a near-ruinous state, was housing workers employed by a nearby cotton mill.

Architecturally, the house was not like any other historic building in Natchez, and this appealed to Byrnes's love for the exotic. It was built on the hill overlooking Canal Street and a block from Bluff Park. The first-story walls were made of brick and covered with stucco, while the second story was a timber-framed structure covered by weatherboard. Across its west-facing front was a two-story gallery, supported by a row of six square posts; the gallery had an exterior stairway at one end of it, parallel to the exterior wall. The house's most characteristic feature was its roofline. The central portion had a steep-pitched gable roof punctuated by chimneys on its north and south ends. Low-pitched shed roofs set off the central roof covering the west exterior gallery and side rooms on the north, east, and south. The building's interior lacked an interior hall; instead, there was a series of rooms that adjoined each other. On the house's east end, a dry moat separated the exterior wall from the brick retaining wall that supported the hill. At the second-floor level, there were three bridges spanning the dry moat that connected the second floor to the graded crest of the hill. Some referred to the old building as an example of buildings built in Natchez during the Spanish colonial period; others saw similarities to the early buildings of New Orleans and even of the West Indies. Everyone agreed that the old structure on Gilreath Hill was really old, but no one knew its story.[56]

Byrnes consulted Edith Moore, who had just started working for the WPA Writers' Project in Natchez. Moore had determined that Gilreath Hill was in fact important, not only to the history of Natchez but to the history of Mississippi and the nation. Her research led her to claim that the building had been built in the early 1790s by a skilled Spanish carpenter, perhaps a shipbuilder or ship's captain, from the cypress timbers of old ships. It was originally the residence of the Spanish governor and thus one of the few Spanish buildings still standing in Natchez. Moore determined that Patrick Connelly purchased it in 1796 and converted it into a tavern. For the first two decades of the nineteenth century, it served as an important inn at the termination of the Natchez Trace.

According to Moore, the most significant historical event associated with the building, which she determined should be known as "Connelly's Tavern," occurred in 1797, when, for the first time in the Mississippi Territory, the American flag was raised behind it atop the hill it straddled. In 1795, the United States and Spain signed the Treaty of San Lorenzo, also known as the Treaty of Madrid. This agreement established formal relations between the two nations, determined the boundaries of the Spanish colony of West Florida, and ceded the lands that included what is now southern Mississippi, which included Natchez, to the United States. In 1797, President George Washington appointed Andrew Ellicott, a Pennsylvania surveyor, to finalize the southwestern boundary of the US with Spain and also to establish formal relations between the federal government and the Spanish colonial governor. Ellicott arrived in Natchez in February 1796. He demanded that Governor Gayoso, who resided at Natchez's Fort Rosalie,[57] and his soldiers vacate Natchez and the newly designated American Mississippi territory at once. Gayoso delayed withdrawal from the area because he did not want to surrender the fertile land near the Mississippi River. In an act protesting Gayoso's tactics, Ellicott, who had pitched a tent behind Connelly's Tavern on the crest of the hill, unofficially raised the flag of the United States for all of the soldiers garrisoned at Fort Rosalie to see. Gayoso ordered him to take it down; Ellicott refused, stating that the flag would remain until it rotted on the pole. Ellicott then submitted a proclamation to the people of Natchez in which he stated: "When the civil and military representatives of the King of Spain make their formal evacuation they will be replaced at once by military and civil representatives of the United States, and the flag we are now raising will then mark your new citizenship and will give you promise of liberty and justice at home and protection from every foreign enemy." The following year, US Army Captain Issac Guion and his troops seized Fort Rosalie from the Spaniards, but prior to the capture, they officially raised the US flag behind Connelly's Tavern on the same hill where Ellicott first raised it.[58] Ellicott's bold patriotic gesture, soon followed by Guion's, was the first time the Stars and Stripes were flown in what was then referred to as the southwest region of the US.

Edith Moore's research also led her to declare that another important event in American history happened in Connelly's Tavern. While functioning as an inn on the Natchez Trace, Connelly's Tavern was the place where, in 1807, Aaron Burr and Harman Blennerhassett conspired and planned the treasonous plot to separate the American West from the US. She was convinced that they finalized their military expedition plans to conquer the Southwest in one of the rooms in Connelly's Tavern.

Spanish craftsmen constructing a building out of Spanish ships for a royal Spanish governor's residence; an elegant inn owned by Patrick Connelly at the terminus of the Natchez Trace; the scene of Andrew Ellicott's patriotic stand against royal tyranny; and the rooms where a clandestine plot was concocted by the infamous Aaron Burr—it all made for a compelling history for the abandoned and decayed building on Canal Street.[59] There is indeed a historical record for all of these facts: a Spanish royal governor did live in Natchez from 1787 until 1797; Patrick Connelly did establish a tavern; Andrew Ellicott did raise an American flag in Natchez;[60] and Aaron Burr did visit Mississippi in 1807. But none of these events are associated with the building on Gilreath Hill. If all of this historical significance was not enough, Moore elaborated on the building's history even more: Samuel Brooks of Exeter, New Hampshire, and a personal friend of President William Henry Harrison, when he was an army officer in Cincinnati, purchased the tavern from Connelly in 1810.[61] Moore attempted to associate the old structure with a US president, albeit very tangentially.

Gilreath Hill was not Connelly's Tavern, but Moore refused to admit this reality. Infused with enthusiasm for archival research and a conviction that Natchez was the scene of pivotal events in American history, Moore tied incongruent facts together to determine a history of a place, which eventually became the narrative for the building's heritage. We see this often when we travel through small towns and down country roads, past the road signs that claim that "Washington slept here" or "Lincoln slept here." In cities and towns across the country, pride of place often obfuscates the facts.

Roane Byrnes was enthralled with the history that Moore presented; it reinforced her conviction that Connelly's Tavern must be saved and restored. Yet Byrnes and Moore differed in their view of Natchez. For Moore, historic events happened *in* Natchez. It was a colonial capitol in what was then West Florida; Ellicott, representing Washington, did declare independence for Mississippi there; before the Civil War, it claimed more millionaires than New York or any other city in the US; and Ulysses Grant did occupy it during the Civil War. For Byrnes, however, the gracious architecture, the real and (and imagined) gardens, the winding Mississippi River, the narrow roads lined with mossy oak trees—along with the lure and legends of the town and its residents, including her own family—constituted something beyond place and history. It was heritage. Throughout her time researching and writing about Natchez, Moore was well respected for her work. It should be noted that she did not explicitly set out to write false histories of old Natchez houses. She was an amateur historian with no formal training in the field.

While Moore may have wanted to inflate Natchez's laudable place in American history, Byrnes wished to improve Natchez and return it to its romantic resplendence. But also ever practical, Byrnes understood that a romantic Natchez made money. She saw the potential in the old, broken-down building that none of the politicians, businessmen, and only a few of the women in town saw: the gateway to a more prosperous town.

In November 1934, rumors spread throughout the town that the Natchez Garden Club wanted to buy and restore the old building on Gilreath Hill. Most of the town was appalled and stupefied that anyone would want to do anything with the old building but burn it down. Some residents became convinced that the NGC knew something they didn't, and rumors circulated that there was treasure buried beneath the first floor of the building. Soon after, while Roane Byrnes and her friends were examining the old house, they found floorboards and brick pavers removed and the ground below the first floor dug up. Byrnes used the vandalism as a part of her narrative for Connelly's Tavern—the forlorn building *may* contain hidden treasure. Long after it was restored, the legend of its lost treasure was part of the story told to tourists.[62]

Byrnes convinced members of the executive committee of the club to let her investigate the feasibility of purchasing the building and then restoring it. An absentee landlord, Robert J. Sanders of Jackson, Mississippi, had owned the building for several years and did little to maintain it. Sanders was one of the leading industrialists in Mississippi.[63] Accompanied by incoming club president Alma Kellogg, Byrnes drove to Jackson to meet Sanders. Alma Kellogg's husband, Joe, was driving her to a statewide meeting of the Natchez Trace Association. Byrnes went along to the meeting to support her friend, who accompanied Byrnes as moral support in meeting Sanders. It was the first time Byrnes met with a man to negotiate a real estate transaction. Sanders had the reputation of being a hard-nosed, difficult-to-deal-with businessman.[64] Both Byrnes and Kellogg were terrified to meet with him. Years later in a talk to the club, Byrnes recalled how she and Kellogg faced Sanders:

When we got to his office we were so frightened we could hardly speak.

Alma poked me so I blurted out: "Mr. Sanders, we want to know if you will sell us 'Gilreath Hill?'"

"What do you want with it?" he asked.

We told him it was a very historic place, that the Natchez Garden Club wanted to restore it.

"All right," he said, "I'll sell it."

This was an encouraging start so we managed to quaver, "What would your price be?"

"How much money have you got?" was the reply.

We told him "three thousand dollars."

"Very well," he said: "I'll sell it to you for three thousand."

At this moment, we screwed up our courage and explained that we needed a thousand to put a new roof and prop up the left side of the building else it might fall down before the next Pilgrimage—our only source of revenue.

"All right," he agreed, "I'll let you have it for two thousand." [65]

With an agreement in hand from Sanders, Byrnes and Kellogg prepared a budget for the restoration of Connelly's Tavern. Byrnes consulted contractor William Stietenroth regarding what it would take to stabilize its sagging floors, crumbling walls, and flagging roof.[66] He reported that the cost for restoring it would be between three and four thousand dollars.[67]

Byrnes then made her pitch to the Natchez Garden Club to purchase Gilreath Hill and transform it into Connelly's Tavern. At the meeting, she began her appeal by saying, "I am going to worry you again about Gilreath Hill." Then she provided the club with the overall budget: $2,000 to purchase, an additional $3,000 to $4,000 for restoring, with a total cost between $5,000 and $6,000. In her plea to the garden club members, she claimed that "the little inn is still the cutest place in the world" and that "it was a house in [a] fairy story."[68]

After Byrnes's presentation at the December meeting, other women passionately presented their favorite ideas to the club of how to spend the money. But Byrnes succeeded in convincing the Natchez Garden Club to purchase and restore the building by a forty-seven to three vote.[69] The December 9, 1934, *Natchez Democrat* reported, "Restoration on Ellicott Hill Started by Club." It was now public knowledge that the garden club intended to make historic preservation a priority in its mission.[70]

Not everyone was happy with the outcome of the vote, especially Katherine Miller. From the NGC's founding in 1929, there was an understanding that there would be a split in the net profits from the pilgrimage between the owners of the historic homes and the garden club. The original intention was that the club was to use its share of the profits to expand and market the pilgrimage, to continue to beautify the city, and then, finally, to purchase and restore historic properties for future tours. The homeowners used their share of the profits to preserve their historic homes so they could continue to open to tourists during the pilgrimage season. Now that Byrnes had succeeded in persuading the club to restore a historic property and transform it into a tourist attraction, the final part of the club's mission now became a reality. But this new project troubled homeowners like Miller who viewed the restoration project as a clear threat to her share of the pilgrimage money. Miller's late eighteenth-century wood-framed house required a lot of upkeep, and while she was working extremely hard marketing the pilgrimage, her husband, Balfour Miller, was not earning enough through his business ventures and investments to take care of the home. In short, she needed more money.

Profits from the proceeds of the pilgrimage continued to grow.[71] The NGC women started new side businesses to support the pilgrimage and profit from it—from temporary makeshift restaurants to books and interior decoration boutiques. Established downtown businesses flourished, as well as the two main hotels during the event, and laborers as well as African American Natchezians returning from Chicago also benefited from the week-long event. But the tension between the club women over the Connelly's Tavern project increased over the months. Homeowners grew weary of supporting the pilgrimage, whether it involved managing traffic, cleaning up after the tourists, or purchasing additional theft insurance. "It certainly is expensive to take part in the Pilgrimage—wages, damage, etc.," George Kelly wrote to Ethel.[72] Resentment among the disgruntled homeowners continued to fester throughout the year, even when the event continued to be more successful, and Natchez became recognized across the country as a significant tourist attraction.

The 1935 pilgrimage started on March 31 and ended on April 7. By then, the NGC women had become more organized. Sophie Junkin was chair of the touring committee and devised silhouette signs of a southern belle as a clever tool for directing the tourists driving from one villa to the next one. But coordination between committees remained problematic. The touring committee told the homeowners that the tourists would arrive at 2 p.m. on the first day, but the printed program said the tours started in the morning.[73] This caused a considerable amount of confusion when long lines of cars awaited the opening of the gates and most of the young women were still busy getting dressed in their antebellum attire.[74] Soon after the 1935 pilgrimage ended, George Kelly reported to Ethel about the week-long event. One of the full-time Melrose tradesmen, who was parking automobiles during the event, informed George Kelly that 277 cars entered the grounds of Melrose, and he had heard that nearly as many cars were counted at D'Evereux, with license plates from states as far away as California and Connecticut.[75] The 1935 pilgrimage brought into the Natchez economy $19,000,[76] and it only cost the garden club $3,000 to produce. On the whole, tourists enjoyed the event, but some of them complained about the poor roads that led into Natchez.

Even though the garden club was spending its funds renovating Gilreath Hill, each homeowner received $300 ($5,500 in 2019 dollars) for taking part in the 1935 pilgrimage. While some of the homeowners pocketed the money, most of them used it to fix up their historic villas. Charlotte Feltus used her proceeds to repair the leaking roof and paint the exterior of her villa, Linden. Renovation work on the villas was expensive; painting the exterior of the grander villas cost a minimum of $300, and good tradesmen were in demand.[77] Other homeowners used their proceeds to embellish their villas and to aggrandize their social standing. Annie Barnum built a new grand gate to the entrance of Monmouth, finishing it just in time for the pilgrimage; in building the imposing gate to her grounds, she wanted to outdo the gates at Melrose.[78]

Roane Byrnes devoted most of 1935 to managing the renovation of Gilreath Hill and managing new preservation and economic development initiatives for Natchez, specifically the Natchez Trace Parkway project. Purchasing the building from Sanders took more time than she expected. But discussions about the project in the membership of the garden club were also time-consuming. What began as a deliberation on how to spend the club's profits soon turned into a conversation in the town on how to improve NGC management. By the end of the year, the Gilreath Hill project became the catalyst for splitting the garden club women into two feuding factions, and everyone in town was compelled to side with one faction or the other.[79]

SUCCESS AND STRIFE

Five years earlier, town merchants and hotel owners had laughed at the NGC women and taunted them by saying, "Who wants to come to Natchez?" They were not laughing any more, and now they wanted to influence how the pilgrimage was conducted.[80] The pilgrimage had become their primary means for making an annual profit. Clarence Eyrich, owner of the Natchez Hotel, informally suggested to the women that the club should consider running the pilgrimage longer than one week. He complained that all the people who came for the event could not be accommodated in a seven-day time span. Even hotels in nearby towns were unable to accommodate all the tourists coming to Natchez. George Kelly mentioned that a hotel clerk from Ferriday, Louisiana, told him that, at his hotel alone, thirty-two parties tried to make reservations, and the clerk could not accommodate all of them. "Even the little 2nd class Ferriday hotel felt the benefits of the Natchez Pilgrimage," Kelly exclaimed. In arguing for a longer pilgrimage, Eyrich told the women that "other hoteliers say that their big tourism events usually last one month." In 1935, it cost $4,000 annually to operate the Natchez Hotel; Eyrich argued that, if the pilgrimage lasted for an extra day, it would take in $1,000, which would help pay for the hotel overhead accommodating the pilgrimage. Eyrich summed up the sentiments of the Natchez business community in saying, "It seems as if, with the Pilgrimage growing larger each year, it must eventually come to be organized upon a money-making basis for all who take part."[81]

But some homeowners could not open their villas and manage the crowds for any longer than a week. Hordes of tourists required costly management during the event and damaged the buildings and grounds. Interiors required repair; ruts, caused by people driving their cars over the front yards, required regrading and replanting.[82] Tourists were also trying to cheat the garden club out of the fee for seeing the villas. Some of them offered twenty-five cents to see one of the historic houses and then leave town. When George Kelly brought this up with Katherine Miller, her response was "Whole tour or nothing, is the rule."[83] The pilgrimage idea needed to be reconsidered by the Natchez Garden Club, but in 1935, its members were preoccupied with arguing over how the profits were to be divided.

After the Gilreath Hill vote, a group of homeowners began a year-long quarrel to renegotiate the split in the profits between the NGC and the homeowners. Two factions emerged: the homeowners, led by Miller, Beltzhoover, and Barnum (all of whom were also members of the club); and the garden club group, led by Moore, Byrnes, and Harriet Dixon. Miller was proactive and impatient in making demands for the homeowners, while Dixon, who consulted with Byrnes and Moore, was more measured but equally strong in responding to the homeowners' demands. At first, the garden club faction was conciliatory and offered to change the original split of the pilgrimage revenue—the NGC keeping two-thirds of the net profits and the homeowners receiving one-third—to an even 50–50 split. Miller stated that it was not enough for the homeowners.

George Kelly's daily letters to Ethel Kelly, who was spending time in Grosse Pointe, Michigan, with her daughter (who was a new mother), give us unique insight into the political and personal intrigue of the disagreements.[84] As a loyal husband, George Kelly not only obliged in providing the news from the Natchez Garden Club, but he seemed to rather enjoy commenting on it as well.

From the beginning of the row, Katherine Miller allied herself with another discontented homeowner, club member and friend Annie Barnum. Together, they enlisted Alma Kellogg and Ruth Beltzhoover. During the January 1935 NGC meeting at which Byrnes made her pitch for the Gilreath Hill restoration, Miller demanded that the club give

75 percent of the net proceeds of the pilgrimage to the homeowners. Arguments ensued. Moore and Dixon sought to temper the situation by making a motion to table the issue until the next meeting. Dixon then began informally negotiating with Miller and Barnum about a more equitable split, which would provide more money to the homeowners and enough money for the NGC to fund historic preservation projects like Gilreath Hill, which she contended was a way that the club could improve the city.

The NGC women put aside their differences and focused on the pilgrimage during the winter months, but the success of the 1935 pilgrimage only emboldened the two warring factions. Byrnes, Moore, and Dixon were more convinced than ever that the pilgrimage's objective was to raise needed funding for civic improvement. But Miller, Barnum, and Beltzhoover were determined to use the pilgrimage funding to solely serve the homeowners, of which they were a part.

At first, Miller tried to charm the other faction into agreeing with her to give the profits to the homeowners. George Kelly remarked several times that she was very cordial to him whenever they met at social functions. This only raised his suspicions about her: what motivated Miller to be so tenacious about the profits? he mused.[85]

As planning proceeded for the renovation of Gilreath Hill during the autumn months, the crisis came to a head. The homeowners flatly refused to concede anything: they wanted 75 percent of the net profits. Representing the garden club contingent, Theodora Marshall plainly stated that was not going to happen. Then the homeowners threatened to do what had been considered unthinkable: if they could not have the cut they wanted, they would plan and conduct their own pilgrimage. The entire town was both shocked and captivated at the fight brewing within the Natchez Garden Club. Individuals, other civic groups, and even the town government were forced to pick a side in the scrap. George Kelly stated to Ethel, "they are killing the goose that laid the golden eggs."[86]

Since George Kelly was not a member of the Natchez Garden Club, he relied on Roane Byrnes and Lallie Adams for news of the quarrel behind the club's closed doors. By now, the strain of the pilgrimage and the feud was beginning to take a toll. Miller suffered a physical breakdown and was hospitalized to recover in nearby Magee, Mississippi. Byrnes not only was preoccupied with the Gilreath Hill renovation project but with personal problems at home—her father, Jim Fleming, resigned as vice president of the Britton and Koontz Bank in protest over questionable loans to borrowers in nearby Tensas Parish in Louisiana. This placed a strain on the Fleming-Byrnes family budget at Ravennaside. Ferriday Byrnes only made matters worse as his alcoholism increased.

The October 2, 1935, NGC meeting was the breaking point in the club. On behalf of the homeowners and her own interests, Katherine Miller presented the following demands. The homeowners wanted 70 percent of the gross profits of the pilgrimage, with 5 percent going solely to Miller. This amount, estimated at $800,[87] was to be her salary for marketing the pilgrimages. And if that was not enough, Miller demanded more: she wanted the power to appoint the club's executive committee—the club's secretary, treasurer, and vice president—indefinitely. Then the homeowners stated their final demand: they demanded that Gilreath Hill not be included on the pilgrimage tour. The garden club faction was furious at the homeowners' demands. Harriet Dixon was speechless; neither Ethel Kelly nor Mary Louise Metcalf wanted to confront Miller and Annie Barnum. Lallie Adams informed George Kelly that the garden club faction was weakly represented at the meeting, and Dixon asked to table the demands by the homeowners for the next meeting. After the meeting, Dixon and Moore countered the homeowners' demand by offering 60 percent of the gross profits to them; they then raised their offer to two-thirds of the profits. They ignored Miller's salary and power demands, and they did not budge on Gilreath Hill. The homeowners forcefully refused the counteroffer. "ALL OR NOTHING!" was Miller's reply. The Natchez Garden Club was in complete disarray, with many bruised feelings among all of the women.

Roane Byrnes was skeptical about whether Katherine Miller actually compiled the list of demands. Instead, she, George Kelly, and Lallie Adams agreed that someone else was behind it: they suspected Balfour Miller, who was well known for making such demands and by living by the motto "rule or ruin." Byrnes was particularly hurt by her best friends like Catherine Feltus siding with Katherine Miller. The division between the women seriously challenged the feasibility of future pilgrimages. The homeowners had twenty-five villas on the tour; the twenty-fifth villa, Dunleith, belonged to Amelia Carpenter. Byrnes suspected that Miller and Barnum had negotiated a special deal with Carpenter to gain her support. Miller knew Barnum held considerable sway over most of the homeowners, since her husband, Hubert, was an executive in the City Bank & Trust. Whether or not Miller contrived the plan for absolute control of the pilgrimage is not clearly known, but she never wavered from her demands. In fact, she became more resolute over time.

George Kelly labeled the two warring factions in his descriptions to Ethel Kelly: he referred to the homeowners as "the drinking & grasping crowd" and the garden club faction as "the temperance people." He also identified the two groups through their financial obligations: the homeowners were the "City Bank & Trust (Carpenter and Barnum families)" crowd while the garden club faction he labeled as the "Britton & Koontz (Learned family)" crowd. This attribution is telling due to the fact that the Depression placed all the villa owners in a precarious financial state. Even the churches were aligned with the factions. Most members of the garden club faction belonged to Trinity Episcopal Church, while the majority of the homeowners worshipped at First Presbyterian Church.[88] Despite the threats by Miller and Barnum to lead the homeowners to form a competing pilgrimage, no one on either side of the feud was willing to completely commit to the idea in 1935 and most of 1936; so the garden club faction agreed to deliberate over the homeowners' demands.

The NGC members agreed to table the discussion until the next meeting, which was to be held at Lansdowne. When it was announced where the next meeting was to be held, George Kelly reported that "a perfect, derisive laugh went up!" Mary Louise Metcalf tried to cancel the meeting but was outvoted by the membership. George conveyed her sentiments to Ethel Kelly, saying she wished his wife was back but was glad that she was escaping "the disagreeable circumstances."[89] After the meeting, the homeowners regrouped to propose a counteroffer to the membership at the meeting. As this was going on, tensions built as the homeowners like Alma Kellogg adamantly remained NGC members, while, at the same time, defiantly planning to form a splinter group.

Before the next NGC meeting was held, Katherine Miller campaigned across the town to try to discredit the club. Her first objective was to convince Natchez women who were not involved in the NGC how it unjustly treated the homeowners. Her objective was to turn Natchez against the garden club faction and then enforce her will on the club. On October 10, 1935, she addressed the Natchez Garden Center, a group of Natchez women who were actually interested in gardening.[90] In her speech, Miller beseeched them to back her and the homeowners and "stand up against the nefarious Garden Club." The Natchez Garden Center did not have a quorum and used this technicality in order to hear from the garden club faction before taking a position in the debate.[91] Mary Jones, a garden center member, remembered that in Miller's address she talked for three hours about herself.[92] But after extolling all of her accomplishments to the garden center women, Miller declared that "there were dignified misrepresentations of facts" in the *Natchez Democrat* about the controversy within the NGC. She never specified what the misrepresentations were. Nevertheless, she made her case for the homeowners and her own interests to anyone who would listen.

On the following day, Roane Byrnes was invited to present the garden club faction's case to the garden center women. Not to be outdone,

Miller conspicuously placed pamphlets that listed the homeowners' demands all around the meeting venue. The *Natchez Democrat* headlined the homeowners' battle cry: "RELEASE THE HOME OWNERS STILL BOUND TO THEM! [Natchez Garden Club]." After hearing from Miller and Byrnes, the garden center voted to remain neutral and not support either side in the pilgrimage feud.[93]

The garden club faction continued to present its case that the homeowners were out of line with their demands. Harriet Dixon and Edith Moore presented talks on why the NGC was committed to restoration projects like Gilreath Hill. On October 13, 1935, a group of loyal NGC homeowners published an open letter reaffirming their commitment to the club. The headline of that day's *Natchez Democrat* read "Home Owners of Garden Club to Remain in Club."[94]

Roane Byrnes reported to George Kelly that the October 23rd NGC meeting at Lansdowne was a "love feast, wreathed in smiles!" It made Byrnes, Metcalf, Dixon, and Moore all the more suspicious. Byrnes also informed George that nothing had been resolved at the meeting because there was a full attendance of garden club faction supporters, and she felt that the "obstreperous recalcitrants would have been outvoted." As president of the club, Dixon most likely wanted to avoid an ugly incident at the meeting; she continued to informally negotiate with Katherine Miller, Annie Barnum, and Ruth Beltzhoover. Miller and others in her faction presented a "paper" specifying a two-year contract for the homeowners. The NGC did not act on the proposal. It agreed to continue with the year-to-year agreement between all of the homeowners.

There was reason for optimism at the next meeting. Dixon reached an agreement of profit division with Miller and the homeowners: one-third for the club and two-thirds for the homeowners. With an agreement in hand, Dixon called for another NGC meeting on October 28.[95] At that meeting, the club agreed in concept with the Dixon-Miller proposal, but members were hesitant to grant complete approval. Details needed to be addressed and agreed to by the club before the issue was to be resolved. Effie Lacy Hale proposed to appoint Ethel Kelly, Roane Byrnes, and Harriet Dixon to review the homeowners' proposal and present their findings and recommendations to the club membership. But at the meeting, the club women voted that there would be no "chairman" of the pilgrimages, the division of profits was settled at one-third for the club and two-thirds for the homeowners, and that the ad hoc committee on the pilgrimage was the final authority on the pilgrimage matter. They also voted that no one in the club would receive a salary. Everyone seemed delighted and relieved that the feud was coming to a workable solution—everyone except Katherine Miller.[96]

Peace and harmony proved to be short-lived in Natchez. According to George Kelly's letters, the homeowners intended to work with the offer "only as long they can agree!" And they refused to acknowledge that there was no one-year or two-year limit or contract between the homeowners and the NGC. Effie Lacy Hale informed George that she was hopeful everyone would return to working in harmony and that the club was again a "unit." George had his doubts: perhaps everything would go back to normal, including "the small cliques that buzz-buzz, each to itself." However, by November, NGC outsiders had intervened to avoid the collapse of the pilgrimage idea. In late November, Mayor Saul Laub interceded to develop a solution, which included long-term contracts with the homeowners. Most of the NGC women were appreciative of his work and acknowledged him with a standing ovation, but not everyone was happy. Mary Louise Metcalf noted that garden club faction member Theodora Marshall refused to yield, and most of the homeowners refused to work with the mayor—most notably, Ruth Beltzhoover and Katherine Miller's sister, Bessie Rose Grafton Pritchartt. Miller was noticeably absent at the meeting, having announced days earlier that she was going to Vicksburg and taking charge of *their* newly planned pilgrimage.[97]

The Christmas holidays provided a much-needed respite for the arguing factions, but the fight soon resumed in early 1936. Miller continued to market the Natchez Spring Pilgrimage, but she was now consulting for the city of Vicksburg on how to start a competing pilgrimage there. Dixon continued to manage the peace between the garden club faction and the disgruntled homeowners.

It may have appeared to some in town that Roane Byrnes was not only influencing the club in restoring the old Gilreath Hill building but influencing the town government as well. Miller, Barnum, and other homeowners were outraged over the Gilreath Hill project during 1935 and could see the profits from the pilgrimage dwindle away. The actual cost for renovating was unknown before the work commenced. How much damage due to decay and vandalism would be found in the old building? The damage would only manifest itself when Stietenroth began his renovation. Although Byrnes secured the approval to purchase the building from Sanders in December 1934, she had persuaded the NGC to work with the city of Natchez for services and projects on the building prior to the purchase. On behalf of the club, the city secured WPA labor to clean up Gilreath Hill and clean out any debris from the building. The city also funded a gravel drive to the building's entrance. This outraged Miller and Barnum, who felt that the club should have been consulted about the project from the beginning.

Roane Byrnes also went on a publicity campaign, explaining in the *Natchez Democrat* her detailed plans after the old building was restored.[98] In her article, she presented the idea that the house would become a museum with a garden spot on top of the hill. She stressed how, in other parts of the country, historic buildings were being converted into museums to attract tourists. She suggested that the old building could be open year-round, and the club could charge a quarter per person to tour it; it could also be included on the pilgrimage tour. Most people were skeptical, but they also remained interested in the project.

Tensions mounted during the summer of 1936, and the crisis between the homeowners and the garden club faction came to a final climax. Annie Barnum, on behalf of herself and Katherine Miller, presented a letter to the NGC threatening that the homeowners would withdraw from the pilgrimage and set up their own tour. Harriet Dixon remained cool but firm and called their bluff, replying officially to Barnum's letter:

> [The Natchez Garden Club] wishes to acknowledge receipt of Mrs. Barnum's letter, dated May 30, 1936; this letter sets forth the plans of the homeowners [to set up their own tour]. Her letter [was] presented to a special call meeting of the Natchez Garden Club meeting on June 9, 1936. After deliberation by the NGC, it voted unanimously to accept the following motion: "That the Natchez Garden Club accept with regret the withdrawal of the Home Owner's Association from participation in the Garden Club Pilgrimage."

Dixon then informed Barnum that the NGC passed the following motions: "That the Natchez Garden Club accept the offer made by the owners of Melrose, Clover Nook, The Briars, Oakland, Magnolia Vale, Elms Court, and Rosalie to participate in the Sixth Annual Pilgrimage conducted by the Natchez Garden Club." But she also informed Barnum that the club left the option for the homeowners to return to the club and the pilgrimage: "[The club approved] an invitation be extended to all home owners who had participated in the last Garden Club Pilgrimage to join with the Natchez Garden Club in its Sixth Annual Pilgrimage, exclusive of any other Pilgrimage." Ever so polite, Dixon conveyed to Barnum that, at the meeting, she expressed her personal regret at the decision of the homeowners' association to withdraw from the Natchez Garden Club Pilgrimage.[99]

The homeowners of Melrose, Elms Court, The Briars, Auburn, and Rosalie, to name but five, aligned with the NGC and were determined to have the 1937 pilgrimage with or without the protesting homeowners, whose homes included Green Leaves, Hope Farm, Monmouth, The Elms, and Arlington. Friends in town soon turned on each other.

George Kelly reported to Ethel Kelly that Russie Butts, who had been very close to Balfour Miller, was deeply hurt by his insults at a cocktail party, all because Butts's wife had sided with the NGC. "All my friends have deserted me!" she cried.

The homeowners wasted no time in announcing that they wanted to conduct a rival pilgrimage to the one held by the NGC. Harriet Dixon swiftly reacted and reserved the city's Memorial Hall auditorium for the 1937 pilgrimage balls and tableau. In correspondence with the city alderman, the city clerk summarized the situation by saying that Dixon requested use of Memorial Hall for the NGC's tableau and Confederate Pageant as they had done in previous years during the pilgrimage, from March 28 through April 4. But another local association, that of the homeowners, also asked to reserve the public venue for its tableau and balls. To complicate manners, the homeowners had not decided on the dates when they wanted to reserve the venue. For most in Natchez, it appeared that a separate pilgrimage experience was in the works, and the homeowners were planning for it; but no one knew for sure.[100]

Despite the ongoing animosity that summer, Katherine Miller, Annie Barnum, Ruth Beltzhoover, and the other homeowners chose to remain members of the NGC. But by September, Miller acted. On behalf of the homeowners, she applied to the Garden Clubs of Mississippi for the right to form a new garden club in Natchez. By now, the homeowners had begun informally calling themselves "the Pilgrimage Garden Club." Dixon, Byrnes, and Moore were horrified at the thought of a competing pilgrimage and garden club in Natchez. In a letter to the honorary president of the Garden Clubs of Mississippi, Dixon asked for personal favor in the matter and requested that their correspondence be confidential; she personally appealed to the state president to reject Miller's application.[101] Dixon's ploy worked. In late October, Barnum received a letter from the Garden Clubs of Mississippi membership committee chairwoman that the executive committee deliberated over the homeowners' application and decided not to vote on making the homeowners' association a garden club. The executive committee based its decision on Article 1 of the association's bylaws, which stipulated that a garden club must demonstrate that it had been in existence for at least one year. And while the committee concurred that the "Pilgrimage Garden Club" had been organized for at least a year, it stated that there had been a time when the group was known by another name, "Home Owners Association." The state organization expressed regret to Barnum that it had learned about "the discord within the membership of the Natchez Garden Club." The executive committee expressed hope that "all differences can be resolved and the club will heal since the Natchez Garden

Club had done great work promoting Mississippi charm, especially in Natchez."[102] Undaunted, Miller, Barnum, and Alma Kellogg proceeded to form a rival club to the Natchez Garden Club called the Pilgrimage Garden Club.[103]

In a letter dated November 5, 1936, to the Natchez Garden Club, Miller formally resigned from the Natchez Garden Club. She reasoned that it is "neat and proper to do so due to conflicting interests." She enclosed a check for $1.00 for all outstanding debts she owed to the club and thanked the membership for their support and cooperation in the past. Barnum and Beltzhoover soon followed and resigned their membership, but Kellogg chose to defiantly remain, much to the disdain of her fellow NGC members.[104] Miller, the self-proclaimed founder of the Spring Pilgrimage and an original member and past president of the Natchez Garden Club, relinquished her position and embarked to start a new pilgrimage organization—completely on her terms. The ramifications were felt throughout the rest of the 1930s and early 1940s.

THE RESTORATION OF CONNELLY'S TAVERN

As all this was going on, Roane Byrnes continued with the restoration of the Gilreath Hill historic structure, the initial cause of the strife between the NGC women. Along with purchasing the building and hiring William Stietenroth as the restoration contractor, she relied on Dick Koch to be the consulting restoration architect and supervise the restoration.[105] Byrnes described how Koch worked on the project: "For over a year he came up several times a month to advise and oversee the progress of the work. For this he charged $150 plus his expenses. As he drove up in his own car and very often visited various members of the club, these expenses were small."[106] He frequently stayed at Ravennaside and was entertained by Roane and Ferriday Byrnes when he was in Natchez. Over the next two years, Koch and the Byrneses became close friends. During his time working on Gilreath Hill, he most likely documented the old building. There are measured drawings of the building in the Historic American Buildings Survey (HABS), for which his protégé, A. Hays Town, and draftsmen Theodore Granberry, Jay T. Liddle Jr., and others are credited as the delineators of the set. But the date of the completed set, January 1934, which was only two weeks after the HABS had been approved as a federally funded project by Interior Secretary Harold Ickes, proves that it was impossible that the Mississippi HABS team measured and documented the building (this will be discussed in greater detail in Chapter 4). It appears that Koch produced the measured

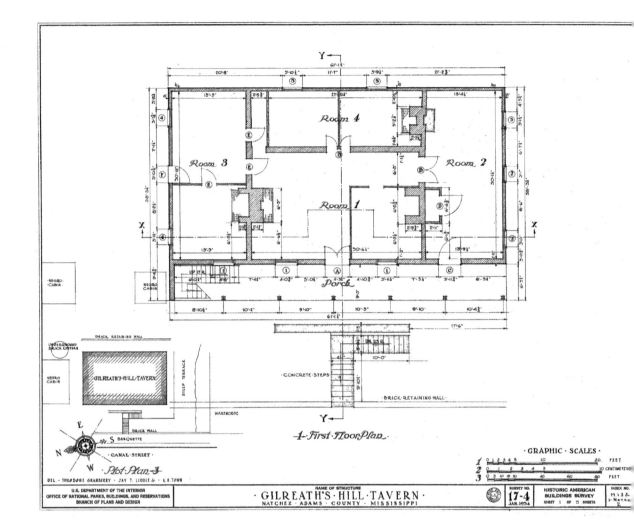

Figure 3.30: First-floor plan, Gilreath's Hill Tavern, HABS No.: 17-4. (Library of Congress, Prints & Photographs Division, Historic American Buildings Survey, HABS MISS,1-NATCH,2-)

sketches of the building and gave the measurements and even the pencil underlay drawings, along with the credit of the drawings, to Town.

The Gilreath Hill tavern HABS architectural drawings are perhaps some of the most elegant drawings of a historic structure in the HABS collection of the 1930s. In these, we learn not only about the condition of the building before its renovation but also the nature of the neighborhood around it. In the first-floor plan, a small site plan notes "negro cabins" adjacent to its north and east sides and a warehouse on its southside, facing Canal Street (figure 3.30). The steep hill and terrace are noted along with the brick retaining wall, which held back the river bluffs from it. Smaller rooms flank the large center section of the building on the north and south sides. The front porch, spanning the entire west side, is where the house's only staircase is located, an architectural characteristic that Koch and, later, historian Paul Goeldner described as

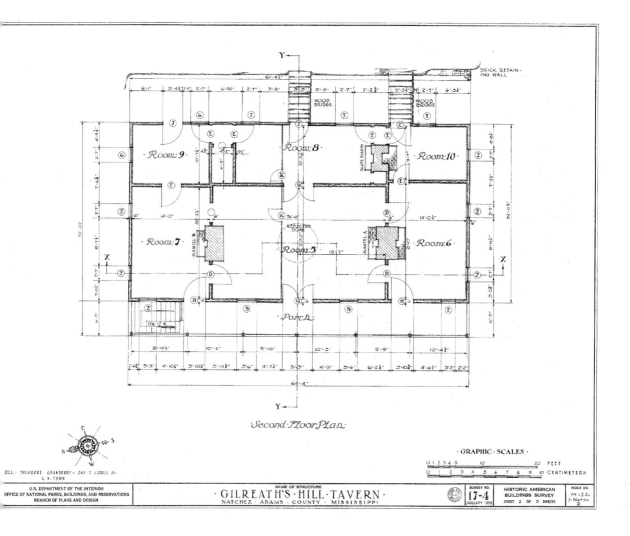

Figure 3.31: Second-floor plan, Gilreath's Hill Tavern, HABS No.: 17-4. (Library of Congress, Prints & Photographs Division, Historic American Buildings Survey, HABS MISS,1-NATCH,2-)

a feature found in Louisiana historic vernacular architecture more than Mississippi or Natchez architecture.

On the second-floor plan drawing, the delineators elegantly illustrated the way the drawbridges engage the steep bank on the east side. We can also see how the structure is now timber, not brick. The building's distinctive interior dome is dashed in the center of room five, and the three fireplaces are shown bricked up in order to better accommodate coal rather than wood fires (figure 3.31).

Town, Granberry, and Liddle elegantly render the main and west façades. Lost and cracked stucco is carefully rendered on the drawing, and certain details, such as the doors and windows, are meticulously drawn. But other features are shown that were not in their proper place in late 1933 and early 1934, when the building was documented. Several porch posts were missing on the porch, at both levels.

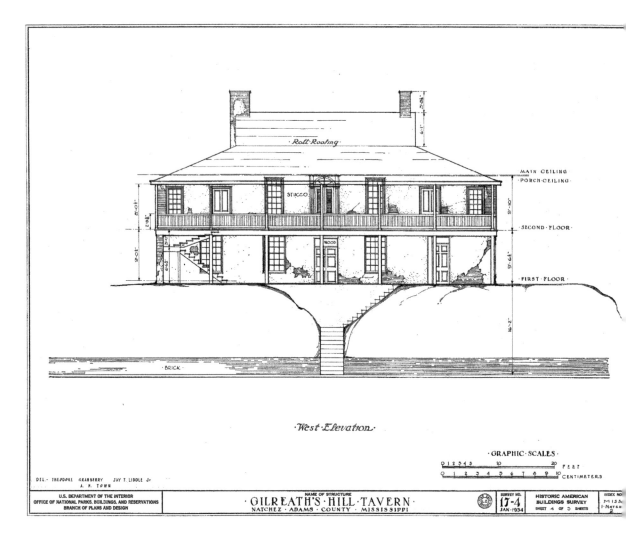

Figure 3.32: West elevation, Gilreath's Hill Tavern, HABS No.: 17-4. (Library of Congress, Prints & Photographs Division, Historic American Buildings Survey, HABS MISS,1-NATCH,2-)

A couple of the posts were found as debris on the site.[107] Also, the second-floor railings were either warped or missing. Finally, modern screen doors were installed on all of the exterior doorways. All of this suggests that the HABS façade drawing was directly traced from Koch's design drawings, or the drawings were intended to be more for publicity purposes of the club than an archival record for the National Park Service (figure 3.32).

Town and Granberry continue their graphic approach, which is more illustrative than informative, in the north elevation of the tavern. Here, we see the brick and stucco whimsically depicted but in juxtaposition with drawing of the temporary supports, placed to hold up the crumbling east brick wall and note stating, "2–2×8 STRUTS TO SUPPORT CAVING WALL." If we thoroughly examine the drawings, it is evident that the delineators' intent was not to accurately depict the existing condi-

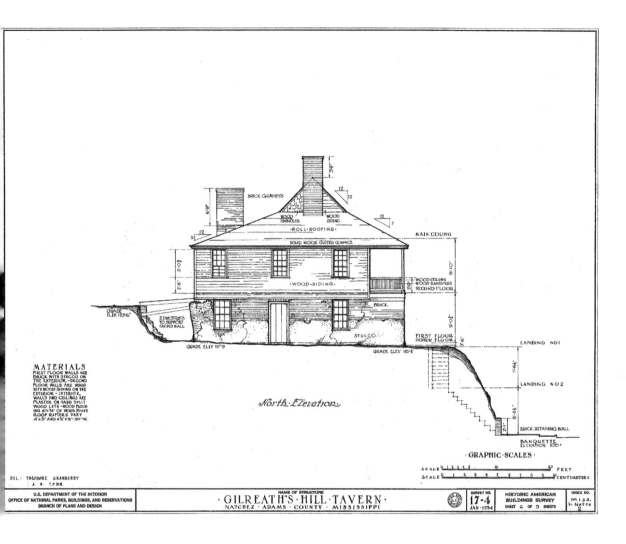

Figure 3.33: North elevation, Gilreath's Hill Tavern, HABS No.: 17-4. (Library of Congress, Prints & Photographs Division, Historic American Buildings Survey, HABS MISS,1-NATCH,2-)

tions, but the drawings do not explicitly describe how the building was to be restored either (figure 3.33).

The east elevation is more confusing for the viewer. Some of the windows are depicted as if they are restored; others are depicted with modern sashes in the original window frames. The collapse and the temporary shoring of the crumbled wall are delineated; however, there are few dimensions shown on the drawing, which an architect or architectural historian would rely on to carefully examine the building in a graphic depiction (figure 3.34).

The south elevation drawing combines the building elevation with exterior details, and the drawing sheet is composed in the finest Beaux Arts tradition of architectural drawing. The sophistication in describing the architectural elements suggests that the delineator, Beverly Martin, was highly trained. The section through the east parlor, "Section A-A," which

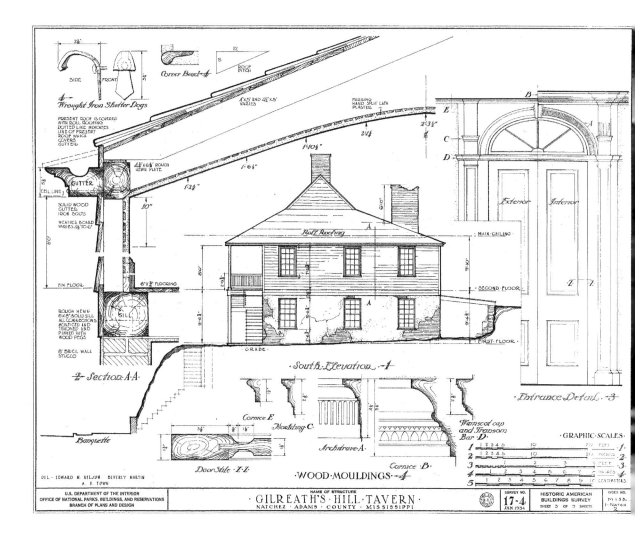

Figure 3.34: South elevation, details and molding profiles, Gilreath's Hill Tavern, HABS No.: 17-4. (Library of Congress, Prints & Photographs Division, Historic American Buildings Survey, HABS MISS,1-NATCH,2-)

describes a finished curved ceiling, suggests a finished design for a renovation and not a recordation of existing conditions. This suggests that the drawing set was perhaps a design and not a HABS record (figure 3.35).[108]

The last sheet of the set, "the Longitudinal Section and Interior Details," is the most informative and elegantly composed drawing sheet of the HABS set for Gilreath Hill. Logan C. Kline and A. Hays Town are credited as the delineators. The juxtaposition of molding profiles, portal elevations, and mantel details with the overall building section embodies what architectural graphics aspired to be prior to World War II. The drawing describes in great detail how the building was constructed, depicting the framing for the center dome and barrel-vaulted ceilings in the north and south parlors on the second floor (figure 3.36).[109]

From 1935 until the 1937 pilgrimage, Roane Byrnes managed as the owner's representative on behalf of the NGC for the restoration, and

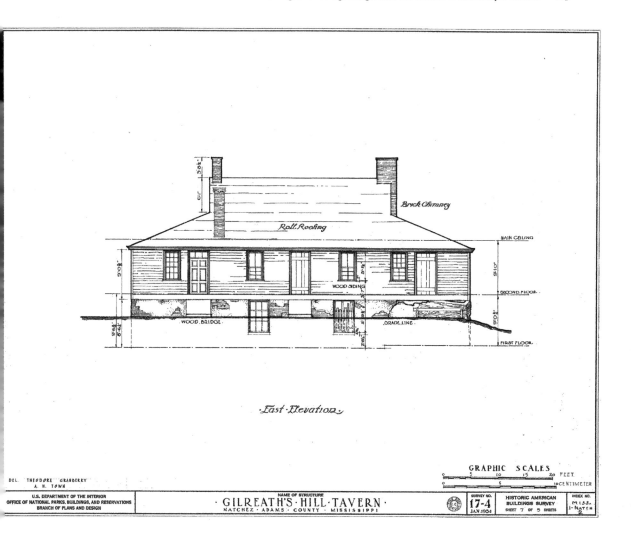

Figure 3.35: East elevation, Gilreath's Hill Tavern, HABS No.: 17-4. (Library of Congress, Prints & Photographs Division, Historic American Buildings Survey, HABS MISS,1-NATCH,2-)

through this experience she became acquainted with the elite architects and historians in American historic preservation and National Park Service officials. She relied heavily on Koch for guidance, and through his tutelage she became an effective construction manager, a skill that she used for the rest of her career. She learned how to manage a construction budget, how to manage design professionals, how to schedule a project's completion and move-in, how to manage the expectations of her fellow garden club members, and more importantly, how to manage unexpected, but inevitable surprises, that occur in a complicated and extensive historic building restoration.

Before the restoration, Byrnes was right in describing Gilreath Hill as a "buzzard's roost." The old building had not been properly maintained for nearly a hundred years. Sanders never kept it up, and the conditions in which his mill employees were forced to live were scandalous. The

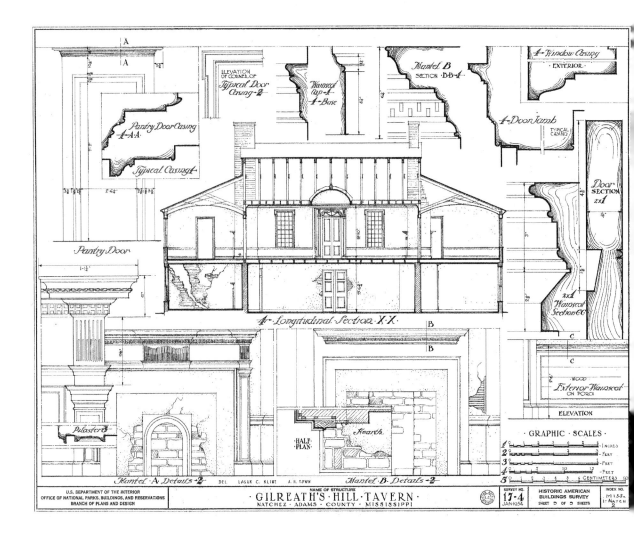

Figure 3.36: Longitudinal section, mantel and door details, Gilreath's Hill Tavern, HABS No.: 17-4. (Library of Congress, Prints & Photographs Division, Historic American Buildings Survey, HABS MISS,1-NATCH,2-)

interior plaster walls crumbled, windows were shattered, and fireplaces were inoperable. Cheap pine and beaver board partitions, built by the tenants, divided up the rooms. It was structurally unsound, with a leaky roof; vermin inhabited the building. In her writings on Connelly's Tavern, Pearl Vivian Guyton best summarized the condition of the building when the garden club took on its restoration: "[The building] underwent all the ravages of destruction which are always imposed on vacant property or on premises rented to such poor tenants as frequently were housed on Ellicott Hill" (figure 3.37).[110]

Koch urged Byrnes to restore the old building utilizing the scientific-based approach for restoring an important historic building. She followed his advice. She had the NGC employ a testing laboratory to analyze the historic plaster in order to replicate it for the restoration.[111] But as the project progressed, Koch's visits to Natchez became less frequent.

Figure 3.37: South parlor before restoration, Gilreath Hill, 1934. (Thomas H. and Joan W. Gandy Photograph Collection, Mss. 3778, Louisiana and Lower Mississippi Valley Collections, LSU Libraries, Baton Rouge, Louisiana)

Throughout 1936, the HABS project in Louisiana was well underway, and he was the district officer for the project. He may also have been ill or exhausted at this time. He apologized to Byrnes for being absent in February 1937 and stated that he had spent several days at a healing spring near Natchez called Brown's Wells.[112]

STARK YOUNG AND THE MARKETING OF CONNELLY'S TAVERN

Throughout late 1936 and early 1937, Byrnes played an ever more active role in managing the restoration, relying less on Koch and becoming more confident in her decision-making abilities. She also marketed the building to the public as work progressed. By winter 1937, Gilreath Hill became Connelly's Tavern, to not only local people in Natchez but to the entire nation. No one helped more to market it than Stark Young (figure 3.38).[113] In 1933, Young visited Natchez to research background material on what became his most popular and noteworthy novel, *So Red the Rose*. He was introduced to Byrnes by several Natchez women because, as Mavis Feltus recalled, "visitors never failed to be charmed by her."[114] Roane and Ferriday Byrnes entertained Young on January 6 at Ravennaside; Young, who considered himself the type of person who easily made friends, was charmed by Roane. In a note to her mother, Stark wrote, "I hope to see you again, and feel that I have three good friends in you and Mrs. Byrnes and Mr. Byrnes."[115] Roane toured Young through the Connelly's Tavern restoration and sold him on the idea that it could

Figure 3.38: Stark Young, novelist and playwright, in 1939. Young wanted Connelly's Tavern to become a museum for his most popular novel, *So Red the Rose*, and worked with Roane Fleming Byrnes to make the historic Natchez building a popular tourist attraction. (Library of Congress, Library of Congress, Prints & Photographs Division, LC-USZ62-117540)

be a historic tavern museum and a tourist attraction for Natchez. Young was enthralled with the idea and agreed to her request to sell a special "Natchez Trace" edition of *So Red the Rose* and to personally autograph five hundred copies of the book, for the 1935, 1936, and 1937 pilgrimages. With *So Red the Rose* set in Natchez, the special editions were a popular souvenir item at the pilgrimages and sold quickly.[116] He was fascinated with the Connelly's Tavern restoration. He was interested in its becoming not only a historic tavern museum but also a marketing center for *So Red the Rose*. He began sending Roane posters advertising the novel and planned to send mementos he collected while conducting research for it—letters, earlier manuscripts, fans, and four chairs that once belonged to Pauline Bonaparte.[117]

During Young's January 1937 visit to Natchez and Connelly's Tavern, Roane Byrnes informed him of the ongoing feud between the garden club and the homeowners. Young was horrified at the thought of a possible split among these women, fearing that the shrine to his novel at Connelly's Tavern would not happen. He urged Byrnes to have the garden club make whatever concessions were necessary to the disgruntled homeowners, but, at the same time, he wanted to keep his name and his reputation out of the feud. He pushed Byrnes hard to complete the Connelly's Tavern restoration in time for the 1937 Spring Pilgrimage. And after he returned to New York, he sent more objects—including a glass swan, two Bohemian glasses, a luster pitcher, a brocade stole, and a Spanish bowl—all intended to be displayed in the restored tavern. When Byrnes informed him that news about Connelly's Tavern was spreading across the nation, he volunteered to help promote the restoration by contacting the leading newspapers in the Northeast. He even nominated the Natchez Garden Club for a service award from a national women's magazine.[118]

In most restoration projects, complications arise, and the Connelly's Tavern renovation was no exception. The new plaster, for which Byrnes had had a testing laboratory develop a recipe to match the historic plaster, did not cure properly and completely fell from the ceilings. The plaster recipe had to be reconsidered, and new plaster had to be reapplied to the old wall lath. Then a new brick retaining wall, intended to support a new terrace on the north side of the, collapsed. One morning, workman entered the building and found that the newly plastered walls were covered with soot. Byrnes remembered this moment in her unpublished work on the restoration: "We thought of vandals and reproached the caretaker who lived on the hill. We were examining the windows and door for signs of a break-in when a bird flew across the ceiling. A Chimney Swift! A flock of swifts had lodged in the chimney and at night had come down into the room. We had the chimneys covered and that was settled."[119]

Dick Koch did return to the project to advise Byrnes as it neared completion. She was very grateful to him and updated him soon after Young had toured the tavern, writing:

> Since then Ellicott's Hill has passed through troubles and excitements too numerous to enumerate here, but we have managed to weather the various storms and expect to open the place with ceremonies during the Pilgrimage, between March 28–Apr. 4. The house and the hill are attracting a great deal of interest wherever they are advertised especially among artists, writers, etc. Stark Young seems crazy about the place and has given us some very interesting relics. By the way he told us he had met you and said some very nice things about you.

She also let him know that Garden Club women still held him in high regard:

> The Garden Club, of course, expects you as one of its honor guests for the Pilgrimage and we certainly hope you will be able to arrange to be present. We owe you a debt which we can never repay and I, personally, hate to

think what I would have done without you. This past eight or nine months without your advice has really been hard, in fact we have not accomplished very much. The grounds are terraced and graded and the brick [steps] are built (I know you are not going to like them, but we did the best we could), but practically nothing has been done in the house since you were here last.

But of course, she continued to prod him, using her charm, to provide his expertise in finishing the restoration:

I hope you remember that you promised us one more visit to advise us about the shelves for the niche and the mantels and a few other things. There are so many different ideas floating about [in our committees], the house will probably be wrecked if you can't come. Of course, we realize that the roads are too bad at present for a motor trip, but do you think that you could stand it on the train? Ferriday and I will be delighted if you will stay with us during your visit here and you can use his car for running about in. Ferriday still regards you as a brother architect and is looking forward to seeing you.[120]

Through his consulting on the Tavern restoration, Dick Koch brought the work of the garden club and Roane Byrnes to the attention of the leading historians, architectural historians, and restoration architects in the nation. He contacted Thomas Tileston Waterman, one of the leading architectural historians and architects for the Colonial Williamsburg Restoration and an architect for Henry Francis du Pont's home, Winterthur in Delaware, to help him "make the looks for the house."[121] He also introduced Byrnes to two other important individuals from the National Park Service: Verne E. Chatelain, chief park historian for the service, and Stuart Cuthbertson, the historical technician for the Vicksburg National Military Park. After touring the tavern, Chatelain proclaimed, "Connelly's Tavern on Ellicott's Hill was the most historically interesting place in Natchez." And while Katherine Miller had succeeded in presenting Natchez to popular culture, Roane Byrnes, through the restoration of Connelly's Tavern, succeeded in presenting Natchez to the American intellectual class and, more importantly, the federal government. Byrnes was well aware of what she was doing and emphasized the national notoriety Connelly's Tavern and the Natchez Garden Club were receiving in her *Natchez Democrat* article on the restoration.[122]

As it neared completion, Byrnes set out to furnish the tavern. She chaired the Furnishing Committee for Connelly's Tavern, which consisted of Lallie Adams, Mavis Feltus, and herself. Together, the three women based the interior design of the tavern not on any factual research

Figure 3.39: Exterior view of Connelly's Tavern in 1937. The Natchez Garden Club made the restored tavern its headquarters and a historic museum, which became the embodiment of the narrative they created for Natchez during the 1930s. (Roane Fleming Byrnes Collection [MUM00057], Department of Archives and Special Collections, J. D. Williams Library, The University of Mississippi)

Figure 3.40: Second-floor gallery before restoration, Gilreath's Hill, 1934. (Thomas H. and Joan W. Gandy Photograph Collection, Mss. 3778, Louisiana and Lower Mississippi Valley Collections, LSU Libraries, Baton Rouge, Louisiana)

Figure 3.41: First-floor gallery after restoration, Connelly's Tavern, 1937, Richard Koch, Architect, William Stietenroth, Contractor. The architect and the contractor paid close attention to the architectural elements and the historic finishes in restoring the historic building. (Thomas H. and Joan W. Gandy Photograph Collection, Mss. 3778, Louisiana and Lower Mississippi Valley Collections, LSU Libraries, Baton Rouge, Louisiana)

but on their own tastes and whims. The repurposed use for Connelly's Tavern was twofold: a historic museum that showed visitors how the early Natchez pioneers lived and traveled, most notably on the Natchez Trace, and the Natchez Garden Club's "headquarters," which had previously consisted of a couple of rooms in the Eola Hotel (figure 3.39).[123]

Despite the fact that the building was nearly a ruin when the restoration began, Byrnes and others always celebrated the wondrous qualities in it to the public (figure 3.40). They extolled the remarkable architectural integrity still found in Connelly's Tavern. As Pearl Vivian Guyton wrote, "Almost miraculously, even the imported glass over the doorway is still in good condition. Only one mantel, one door, shutter hinges, door knobs, gutters, the bridges at the back, a roof and the front steps have had to be replaced. And a sufficient part of the original of each of these was left to serve as a model for the preservation."[124]

In reality, a significant amount of the architectural integrity had been lost through decades of neglect in the building. William Stietenroth took a conservative and practical approach to repairing and rebuilding the existing elements in both the exterior and interior of the tavern (figure 3.41).

Dick Koch also took a straightforward approach and steered away from any conjectural designs in the tavern. Elements that could be found onsite were restored. Float-finished plaster work replaced the

Figure 3.42: Ballroom near completion of the restoration, Connelly's Tavern, Richard Koch, Architect, William Stietenroth, Contractor. Koch took a conservative approach in interpreting the historic finishes for the interiors. (Library of Congress, Prints & Photographs Division, Historic American Buildings Survey, HABS MISS,1-NATCH,2-)

existing plaster that had remained through the years that the tavern was neglected, and door and window hardware based on the existing hardware was installed. Both the interior and exterior trim and the walls were painted a flat white to avoid the suggestion of a color or finish that could not be verified (figure 3.42).

Roane Byrnes and the Furnishing Committee ignored Koch's conservative preservation approach in decor; instead, they decorated the tavern in the "let's pretend" approach they embraced in creating their narrative of Natchez, its culture, and its architecture. They believed that the upper floor was built for the elegant gentlemen and ladies arriving by stagecoach down the Natchez Trace, and the lower floor was outfitted for what they referred to as the "toughs"—the rough and rowdy frontiersmen from Kentucky or Tennessee. Byrnes rationalized that the drawbridges and the upper-level driveway allowed both privacy and separation from the "toughs." Upon entering the tavern, the well-heeled travelers enjoyed furnishings by Duncan Phyfe, Sheraton and Hepplewhite, and Hitchcock in the ballroom. In the dining room, the women imagined the cultured travelers dining on a Sheraton mahogany table, sitting on Trafalgar chairs, using Staffordshire china, beneath a Waterford chandelier, which they claimed came from Concord, the home of Governor Gayoso. (That home burned to the ground in 1901, and it appears highly unlikely that the chandelier came from it.) A portrait of a Natchez gentleman was placed over the south fireplace mantel, and a Spanish lady gazed down upon them from above the north mantel. A Currier and Ives print depicting the Marquis de Lafayette's American tour was prominently placed in the room to remind visitors that Lafayette had spent a day in Natchez.

They outfitted one of the south rooms as a bedroom with a "four-poster bed out of china berry and a trundle bed made by slaves and rolled half way from under the grand four-poster bed, all made by slaves on a nearby plantation. In the bedroom, there is also small oval trunk used during stagecoach travel and a plantation book, both dated 1815–1817."[125] Other rooms on the upper level included one for the headquarters of the Natchez Garden Club and the room promoting Young's *So Red the Rose*.

The lower level was outfitted for the rough boatmen and backwoodsmen. The rules of taverns of that day were stated in this area: "Four pence a night for a bed. Six pence with Supper. No more than five to sleep in the Wash House. No beer allowed in the Kitchen. No Razor Grinders or Tinkers taken in."[126] Simple, rough, handmade chairs and tables were placed around the lower level. There were no beds for these travelers; the women assumed that they slept on mats they owned and placed on the floor. The committee women outfitted the kitchen with what they considered early pioneer utensils and pots, situated around a large cooking fireplace.

The most outrageous and completely conjectural feature in Connelly's Tavern was the Tap Room. According to Pearl Guyton, an old bar—given to the Natchez Garden Club by the owner of a half-deserted building, which he believed had been a tavern located in Natchez Under-the-Hill—was the centerpiece of this room. She went on, saying that ancient jugs, bottles, demi-johns, and "all kind of containers" were scattered about the room. To give it an even more rustic feel, the women placed in the room a table with a soapstone top, a "hint of early days and primitive life, since it furnished a convenient piece on which the hunter might cut up his game." Finally, they placed high-backed chairs and crude benches—all purportedly made by enslaved persons on a plantation—toward the back of the room. More than any other room in the building, the Tap Room embodied Roane Byrnes's joy in pretending history instead of actually depicting it. It became another place where the Natchez narrative could be depicted in promotional photographs and slides, like the ones Katherine Miller had previously used to market the pilgrimage (figure 3.43).[127]

As they had done in nearly every way in promoting Natchez and the pilgrimage, Roane Byrnes, Edith Moore, and Pearl Guyton rationalized Connelly's Tavern's mundane and utilitarian appearance to both the

Figure 3.43: Tap room at Connelly's Tavern, 1937. The Natchez Garden Club women re-created a version of a "Natchez Under-the-Hill" tavern using an old bar found in a deserted Under-the-Hill tavern. The men from the town dressed in period costumes and pretended to be riverboat gamblers fraternizing in the antebellum tap room. (Courtesy of the Archives and Records Services Division, Mississippi Department of Archives and History)

tourists and the locals. They stated that the tavern's sturdy construction was the reason it survived through the nineteenth century, and its rugged beauty epitomized the pioneer Natchez days instead of what Guyton called the "columned mansions of the romantic period just prior to the War Between the States." They continued to distinguish it from the grander antebellum villas; as Guyton wrote, "utility rather than beauty seems to have been the chief motive in the construction of this ancient tavern." But, she continued, "inner touches of delicate beauty were probably added when early Americans converted it into a home." Guyton concluded by saying, "Connelly's Tavern is an architectural gem of its own day, and equally important in our own times."[128]

The restoration of Connelly's Tavern was nearly complete in February 1937, and Harriet Dixon, Edith Moore, and Theodora Marshall decided to use it as a preemptive strike at the newly formed Pilgrimage Garden Club. Their objective was to outshine and outclass the splinter group. Dixon and Moore wanted to offer Connelly's Tavern as a bonus attraction for the 1937 Spring Pilgrimage tourists.

With the split in the Natchez Garden Club and the formation of the Pilgrimage Garden Club, two separate pilgrimages were held in 1937. The Pilgrimage Garden Club planned its event for the week of March 13–20, a week before the planned "official" spring pilgrimage by the Natchez Garden Club. It was Katherine Miller and Annie Barnum's attempt to reduce attendance at the NGC event, which would be both an embarrassment and a financial calamity for that long-standing club. Using their newly restored tavern and headquarters, the women of the NGC counterattacked and planned the celebration of the opening of the tavern on March 30 as a climax to their pilgrimage, scheduled for March 28–April 4. The tavern had only been partially furnished, and the grounds, intended to be what Byrnes called a "virtual paradise of flowers" (irises, roses, azaleas, japonicas, redbuds, etc.), were only partially planted. But it didn't matter; the NGC women were going to overwhelm Miller and the Pilgrimage Garden Club women with an extravaganza at Connelly's Tavern on Ellicott's Hill.[129]

As always, the NGC women reached out to anyone who could provide them assistance in promotion and marketing. Harriet Dixon began soliciting free posters from the newly established Federal Art Project on October 10, 1936. In a letter replying to her request, the program's director in Washington, DC, Helger Cahill, stated that federal artwork can only be produced to promote federally owned or supported projects; since the Natchez Garden Club was a civic organization, it did not qualify for graphic promotion work by the federal government.[130]

Byrnes and Dixon wanted the Connelly's Tavern opening and dedication to be both special and memorable. They came up with the idea of bringing a descendant of Andrew Ellicott to speak at the dedication; their rationale was that this would reaffirm the national significance of Ellicott's Hill and establish Connelly's Tavern as a national shrine to the independence of the US.[131] What better way to do this than having the descendant of George Washington's handpicked emissary wax poetically about the tavern and the proud raising of Old Glory in front of Spanish Fort Rosalie? Their promotional idea nearly backfired.

Dixon first reached out to Professor Andrew Ellicott Douglass, who at the time was interim president of the University of Arizona. He never replied to her invitation and request.[132] Undeterred, Dixon and Byrnes approached another Ellicott descendant, William Miller Ellicott III, who was the great-grandson of Andrew Ellicott's first cousin. He eagerly accepted the women's invitation to represent his famous ancestor and speak about the dedication of Connelly's Tavern and how it was the scene of an important moment in American history.[133] Ellicott said he was excited to represent Andrew Ellicott, but, apparently, he was not

Figure 3.44: William M. Ellicott III and his wife, Anna Campbell Ellicott, dressed in eighteenth-century period costume for the dedication and celebration of Connelly's Tavern, April 4, 1937. A wealthy heir to the Ellicott Mills Flouring Company in Baltimore, Maryland, Ellicott was distantly related to Andrew Ellicott, who defiantly pronounced Natchez was part of the United States in 1797. He was an architect, who was chair of the American Institute of Architects Historic Resources Committee, and an avid environmentalist. (Roane Fleming Byrnes Collection [MUM00057], Department of Archives and Special Collections, J. D. Williams Library, The University of Mississippi)

very attentive to the women's correspondence. After Byrnes and Dixon repeatedly wrote letters requesting his confirmation that he was to attend and partake in the Connelly's Tavern dedication ceremonies, he embarrassingly admitted in his reply that he had misplaced their original letter. Nevertheless, he stated that he and his wife were enthusiastic in joining the women as they commemorated the flag-raising ceremony at Connelly's Tavern.

The women were ecstatic about having Andrew Ellicott's descendant at the event. Wanting to make the commemoration as authentic as possible, they then made this request: "It would please us very much indeed to have your picture taken in costume, so when it is convenient you may forward same to us." He did it. He and his wife, Anna, posed in a portrait wearing an elaborate eighteenth-century costume, much more stylish than his Quaker ancestor would ever wear, for the event's program. Byrnes and Dixon also requested a portrait of his famous ancestor, Andrew Ellicott, but he did not have one in his possession (figure 3.44).[134]

The Natchez Garden Club held the dedication ceremony for Connelly's Tavern, its new headquarters and the first historic building museum in Natchez, on March 30, 1937. Everyone attending the event enjoyed it, and in the end, Andrew Ellicott's descendant's appearance was a success.[135]

Six years and six pilgrimages placed Natchez back in the national spotlight. The NGC women had accomplished an impressive feat, making their town a cultural tourism attraction—a historyland, when historylands were just beginning to be developed for automotive-based middle-class tourism. Who wants to come to Natchez? A lot of people did. These women navigated through a fluid chain of events and overcame formidable obstacles: poor roads into their town, a profound lack of hotel accommodations and dining, and most significantly, a lack of a cohesive sense of place in which tourists could readily comprehend. Roane Byrnes saw the enchantment of a place beyond its current shabby appearance and sought to instill her vision of the past—those "far-off balmy days" of antebellum Natchez—in the imagination of her readers and tourists. Like Katherine Miller, she wanted to present not just the gardens but also the architecture. And also like Miller, Byrnes invited visitors to use their imagination and, in so doing, to put themselves "under the spell of the place,"[136] visualizing Natchez as it used to be: with belles in hoop skirts and "dashing beaux of the sixties whispering goodbyes to their sweethearts in the shade of an old summer house, before they rode off to the war which was to change the world for them."[137] Each of these women utilized their innate skill sets to put Natchez back on the nation's cultural map. Edith Moore contrived a history of Natchez, and Katherine Miller sold it—but Roane Byrnes captured its mythology.

Through her instinctive sense of marketing and flamboyant salesmanship, Miller convinced thousands of women and their families from across the mid-South and the Midwest to travel to Natchez during the early spring each year, escaping the doldrums of industrial America during the Great Depression. Her provocative slides and the sheer force of her commanding personality left her audiences spellbound. Friends, colleagues, and newspapermen all succumbed to her determination. Miller truly believed in Natchez; more importantly, she convinced others in town to believe in Natchez and open the doors of their decaying villas to "receive" the tourists. She and Byrnes understood the power of the Natchez narrative, and they never wavered from it.

People came to enjoy the beautiful architecture; and they also came to reaffirm their heritage and cultural identity. By the end of the second decade of the twentieth century, southerners, both Black and white, had started migrating to northern cities for jobs in burgeoning factories. The dim memory of the antebellum South and the near-ruinous state of

Figure 3.45: Bedroom in Connelly's Tavern, 1937. (Thomas H. and Joan W. Gandy Photograph Collection, Mss. 3778, Louisiana and Lower Mississippi Valley Collections, LSU Libraries, Baton Rouge, Louisiana)

places like southwest Mississippi lulled them to believe that their heritage was a romantic and lost one. A diaspora, created out of mythmaking, predominantly by people like these Natchez women, compelled them to visit Natchez during the pilgrimages. If they came to Natchez and then realized that the NGC women had re-created Confederate officers and their ladies into kings, queens, dukes, and duchesses, then so much the better. It was part of the escapist lure that became Natchez, but it came at a cost: racial superiority of white over Black was reaffirmed.

Roane Byrnes's transformation of the dilapidated tenant building on Gilreath Hill into the chimerical Connelly's Tavern not only introduced Natchez to the professional-based architectural restoration, but it also embedded the intangible and illusory Natchez narrative into a tangible actual artifact. In 1937, the bygone Spanish colonial days in Natchez had returned, and it was an attraction to tour. The ramifications of the fabricated narrative from Natchez had yet to be felt, not just in Mississippi but in the nation as a whole. They soon would be.

By 1936, the Natchez Garden Club had accomplished an incredible record of success in economic development and tourism. Local leaders and business owners took notice of what they had done, and the pilgrimage had become a significant source of income for the city during a time of financial crisis. State leaders took notice as well and in that same year created the Mississippi Tourism Bureau. The new state agency identified two places in Mississippi for the new emerging tourism economy: the beaches of the Mississippi Gulf Coast and the culture and history of Natchez. But just as it seemed that Natchez tourism was on the cusp of ever greater success, calamity happened. The women feuded over the very crux of the pilgrimage idea: idealism through civic improvement versus survival through monetary gain. As news traveled, first through the state and then through the country, the intrigue of what would become the "War of the Hoop Skirts" became a captivating part of the Natchez narrative. Why were the women, who were once friends, fiercely fighting each other? What was the future of the pilgrimage? What would happen in the next five years became legend.

And even as the strife between Miller, Byrnes, Dixon, Beltzhoover, and Barnum increased, greater opportunities for them to have an even greater impact on preserving Natchez emerged. From 1936 until the advent of World War II, these Natchez women worked with national and international leaders to save their town. Their exploits became sensational, and the way they preserved and marketed their historic architecture continued to fabricate a mythology of the American South. Franklin Roosevelt's New Deal became the way they made all this happen. Unknown to anyone in 1936, these Natchez women were about to the change the course of history and historic preservation in the US in the twentieth century (figure 3.45).

Chapter 4

DISTRICT 17

WASHINGTON, DC, 1916-33

Throughout the 1930s, history and preservation became popularized and commercialized in American culture, and new governmental changes at both the federal and state levels significantly expanded history and historic preservation as well. It was a time when the nation was reconsidering its history and its historic places. Academics, in both history and architecture, were involved in developing a history and preservation program at the national level. As these academics began to engage more in the public realm, a conflict between professional historians and architects and amateur and entrepreneurial preservationists, like the women of the Natchez Garden Club, emerged. The struggle stemmed from the most foundational level of preservation and history: the narrative of place. To put it plainly, the group that controlled the narrative controlled how the history and sense of place were perceived and experienced by both local inhabitants and tourists. Furthermore, the narrative determined how a place was preserved. In Natchez, the struggle for narrative control pitted the NGC members, as budding preservationists and entrepreneurs, against Washington policymakers, who arrived accidentally in Natchez because of New Deal programs. This clash lasted nearly a decade. By the late 1930s, Natchez had been transformed into a historic destination, a result of marketing and accepting of local legend as historic fact by historians and architects working for the National Park Service.

The professionals' attempt to establish a scientific or scholarly controlled narrative was challenged by consumerism, which was developing simultaneously through the early enterprises of cultural tourism like the Natchez pilgrimages. These approaches to historic preservation clashed in Natchez, when projects funded by the National Recovery Administration were implemented in 1934. By 1942, the Natchez Garden Club women influenced the outcome of these projects. Indeed, arguably no other private group had as much of an impact on the New Deal cultural programs as they did. They profoundly influenced the Historic American

Buildings Survey and the Works Progress Administration's Writers' Project, and they physically changed the landscape in Mississippi, northwest Alabama, and central Tennessee, spearheading development of the Natchez Trace Parkway from an idea into a lucrative reality.

In 1933, the second year of the Natchez Spring Pilgrimage, a group of men in the US National Park Service, the Library of Congress, the Civil Works Administration, and the Department of the Interior began to develop a narrative of American architecture that involved Natchez, the state of Mississippi, and the United States. Professionalism, the way in which trained individuals dominated historic preservation, was the means by which these men aspired to conceive this narrative.[1] Most of them had only a fleeting idea of Natchez and its architecture at this time; they soon learned about it and the narrative that the NGC women invented. What they attempted—a systemized narrative of American architecture and history—would be the most conspicuous expression of professionalism ever attempted in the fields of history or architecture in America. From 1934 until 1942, when World War II interrupted their work, these men attempted to make historic preservation a professional field, as it was first envisioned twenty years earlier by William Sumner Appleton Jr. but now was becoming embedded into the mission of the National Park Service.

It was Appleton who first brought a scientific process into the practice of American historic preservation, and in founding the Society for the Preservation of New England Antiquities, he instituted a framework to bring preservation to a regional scale. By bringing professionalism into historic preservation, the independently wealthy Appleton distinguished himself from other preservationists. As preservation scholar Michael Holleran best described him, "Appleton was not America's first full-time preservationist—that was surely Ann Pamela Cunningham, of the Mount Vernon Ladies' Association—but he became the first professional preservationist. He brought to the field systematic methods and a standing institution independent of any particular cause."[2]

Men like Appleton believed that professionalism in historic preservation, like architecture, brought stability and the civility of social systems to the field. By removing the amateurs—usually women—from the interpretation and restoration process of historic preservation, Appleton and others argued that an accurate and correct treatment of historic monuments could be achieved. Appleton felt strongly that professionalism promoted an image of competence—guaranteed by education—to historic preservation.

Appleton's professionalism was based on two ideas: first, object-focused scientific inquiry, and second, managerial division of labor, based on an institutional and corporate hierarchy of administration in which educated experts deployed contracted labor to document, manage, and restore historic monuments and buildings. He modernized preservation mainly by evaluating material and aesthetic authenticity and placing an emphasis on documentation and dissemination of architectural knowledge of early American architecture, specifically colonial architecture in New England.[3] It coincided with a never-ending attempt to categorize architecture, based on mutually agreed-upon stylistic labels that were developed by architectural historians, in a similar manner to how biologists classify the taxonomic process of plant and animal life.

During Appleton's time, he was considered a wealthy amateur, but by founding the Society for the Preservation of New England Antiquities in 1910, he is now credited with advancing historic preservation toward a scientific method-based professional standard. His efforts coincided with similar efforts made to professionalize architecture and engineering.[4] In the 1930s, the architecture profession was still in its embryonic stage across the US, particularly in regions away from American urban centers like the Deep South.

If professionalism did create an image of stability within historic preservation and architecture, it also conveyed an elitist image. Historic preservation became an ideology that sought to dominate the study of architecture and control the interpretation of architectural history, along with American history. Appleton had a top-down approach to historic preservation: he and his followers wanted to control the narrative of American architecture history. While their impact was scattered, we nevertheless see its effects today in academic and professional societies, such as the Society of Architectural Historians and the Association for Preservation Technology International—two organizations that not only strive to disseminate knowledge among their members but also shape how that knowledge is conveyed to the public. In the early twentieth century, professionalism contradicted personalism; men exclusively adhered to professionalism, not women. But the men's control of a scientific or scholarly controlled narrative was challenged by consumerism, which was developing through the early enterprises of cultural tourism by women.

PERSONALISM VERSUS PROFESSIONALISM

These men underestimated the commercial appeal of historic places and cultural tourism in America during the Great Depression. On one hand, categorizing history and historic vernacular architecture seemed straightforward, especially when applying the scientific method of observation and recording results. But on the other hand, mobilizing a nonacademic population to apply professionalism to history and architecture, when it had never been done before and never at a continental scale, was quite another challenge. Historic preservation proved to be a much more elusive endeavor to systemize, and the NGC women's personalism philosophy proved to be a formidable obstacle to overcome in obtaining objective and factual information. Moreover, to complicate matters, the men had to overcome their own personal biases, prejudices, and professionally based rivalries to accomplish their ultimate objective: define and categorize American architecture and American history. Ultimately, they failed to accomplish their goal, and the ramifications of their attempts and failure are still being felt today.

Prodigious change in how the US managed its historic sites and monuments occurred in 1933 when the National Park Service (NPS) expanded its stewardship mission to include historic monuments. Established in 1916, the NPS's original sole mission was to manage the natural parks in the American West (among them, Yellowstone, Yosemite, Grand Canyon, and Zion). Less than twenty years after its founding, the NPS's mission expanded from natural resources management to include historic monuments management. During the early twentieth century, these sites were predominantly associated with American military history—forts, battlefields, and significant military-associated gravesites. Before the NPS controlled historic sites, they were managed by the US War Department and, in rare cases, the Department of Agriculture. During World War I, the War Department used battlefields like Gettysburg as training grounds for military officers.[5]

In 1933, national historic monuments were transferred to the NPS, when Franklin Roosevelt reorganized the duties of the executive branch shortly after his inauguration. NPS director Horace M. Albright had already made heritage management a primary objective in the NPS at the beginning of his tenure in 1928. Taking control of battlefields and old forts from the War Department was not heartily embraced by most of the NPS administrators, but under Albright's directive, preparations were made for managing these sites during the Hoover administration, anticipating the NPS's expansion of its role into history. Unlike his western-focused naturalist colleagues, Albright wanted the small governmental agency, which relied on precarious legislative appropriations and was firmly embedded in the Department of the Interior, to have a larger physical presence in the nation's capital and along the more populated East Coast. He reorganized the NPS to include historic monuments, and, more importantly, he sought to attract a different type of visitor to the national parks, one who enjoyed history as much as natural beauty.⁶ Soon after he became director, Albright established the History Division in the service's Branch of Research and Education, along with physical sciences, geology, and biology. He later included architecture and architectural history in the branch.

Earlier that year, Albright had personally accompanied Roosevelt and Department of the Interior secretary and Public Works Administration director Harold L. Ickes on a tour of the construction of Skyline Drive next to Virginia's Shenandoah Valley. During the same trip, they traveled to Virginia's tidewater region to tour the reconstruction of Wakefield, George Washington's birthplace. They also viewed the work being undertaken at Colonial Williamsburg, construction of the Colonial National Monument at Yorktown, and many of the eighteenth-century colonial plantation manor homes along the James River.⁷ An avid history lover, Roosevelt thoroughly enjoyed the trip and approved Albright's idea to assign the administration of historic sites to the NPS. Ickes was initially skeptical of broadening its mission, possibly distracting it from natural areas' management in the West. But Roosevelt was convinced that it was a good idea and overruled Ickes. Albright recalled during his tour for the president, "I had my foot not only in the door for historic preservation, but I had it in the White House."⁸ At the end of the tour, FDR instructed Albright to draft two executive orders: the first was for the transfer of historic monuments in the District of Columbia from the War Department to the NPS, and the second was for the transfer of fifty-seven historic sites from the War Department to the NPS.⁹

Albright realized early on that the National Park Service could flourish as a federal agency if it took administrative control of historic monuments. He stated clearly his objectives when taking the NPS post in 1928 and began a cultural tourism entrepreneurial venture. He was fascinated with history and saw the potential for cultural tourism at historic monuments. As early as 1916, middle-class tourists began driving to national parks in the West, and interest grew in historical tourism in the East as well. ¹⁰

Albright instructed the Branch of Research and Education in the NPS to "coordinate with the other divisions of the National Park Service" and develop science-based philosophical approaches to land and facilities management.¹¹ Harold C. Bryant, an ornithologist from the University of California, Berkeley, was appointed its first director. While nature conservation and biology remained the primary mission of the NPS, with the establishment of national parks in the East, most of which were historic place-based, it became apparent that expertise in history could become as important as natural science expertise in the agency.

Even though tourist interest in historic sites like Gettysburg increased in the early twentieth century, accurate historical interpretation was

Figure 4.1: Verne E. Chatelain, first park historian for the US National Park Service. Chatelain was professor of history and chair of history and social sciences at Nebraska State Teachers College prior to his appointment as the first National Park Service historian by Horace Albright. Chatelain saw the potential for growth in cultural tourism in the historic monuments the Park Service had received from the War Department when President Franklin Roosevelt transferred management of battlefields and fortresses to it. (US National Park Service, Washington, DC)

Figure 4.2: Arno Cammerer, third director of the US National Park Service, 1933–1940. Cammerer succeeded his mentor, Horace Albright, as director of the National Park Service on August 10, 1933, the same day as the transfer to the National Park Service historic sites and Washington, DC, national parks from the War and Agriculture Departments. Interior Secretary Harold Ickes despised Cammerer, and the rift caused strains between the park service and the Interior Department during the 1930s. (US National Park Service, Washington, DC)

lacking. In short, a national historical interpretation program simply did not exist.[12] Albright realized this problem early on and sought to address it in the same systemized management system that had been used in the way the NPS managed natural resources. Soon after the Branch of Research and Education was established, the NPS employed academic historians and began building a History Division to match its Science Division. In 1931, Verne E. Chatelain was appointed the chief historian of the NPS (figure 4.1).

Chatelain worked under Albright for a short period. Albright retired from the NPS in 1933 after negotiating the service's acquisition of historic monuments from the War Department. He considered this accomplishment the high point of his career. When Albright retired, his longtime assistant director, Arno Cammerer, replaced him (figure 4.2). Albright's retirement came at a crucial time for the historic monument management in the NPS; he left the agency just as the conflict between the two competing education missions, nature versus American history, emerged. Among his outside naysayers was Ickes, who, as a moderate midwestern Republican, was steadfast in wanting to keep the NPS within its budget while the country suffered through the Great Depression *and* focused on its original mission, management of natural parks in the West. Ickes was not interested in seeing the NPS's mission or budget increase. To complicate matters more, Ickes despised Cammerer.

Soon after Chatelain became chief park historian, he began developing a power base within the Branch of Research and Education and throughout the NPS. He was among a predominant group of midwestern men in the NPS who were educated at the University of Minnesota. Even though he was an academic, Chatelain understood how popular interpretation at historic sites could bolster tourism in the park system. But he was adamant in making his case that historians should be the primary planners for historic parks development. His goal was simple: develop history-based tourism in the parks and design interpretation projects for each park, with historians supervising both the design and implementation. Led by Chatelain, NPS historians began implementing an interpretative and property acquisition program in such a way in which "pegs could be placed on which American history could be conveniently hung."[13] Chatelain firmly believed that sound and professional surveying and documentation by professional historians were the keys in building a national historic parks program. He was savvy in persuading the NPS administration and Washington politicians that his approach was the right one.

Chatelain understood both politics and loyalty. He was a masterful politician within the agency's bureaucracy. He knew that what he was developing had not been done before in the federal government. Chatelain later remarked, "Nobody had thought in their wildest moments about appointing historians."[14] Understanding that academics may not fit well within the NPS bureaucracy, he urged his recently hired, newly degreed PhD historians to always be diplomatic when working with NPS staff and Washington politicians. Chatelain was a demanding administrator; he expected loyalty and only hired men that he understood and were loyal to him.

Ronald Lee became Chatelain's right-hand man and the public spokesman for the History Division in the Branch of Research and Education. Like Chatelain, he was an alumnus of the University of Minnesota (figure 4.3). Whereas Chatelain approached someone in a brusque and commanding manner, Lee employed a reasonable and agreeable approach in dealing with staff and the public. Chatelain considered Lee a "real Park

Figure 4.3: Ronald F. Lee, assistant chief historian, US National Park Service, 1933–1936. Lee was one of six PhD historians from the University of Minnesota who were hired by Verne Chatelain, alumnus of the history department at the University of Minnesota. Chatelain appreciated Lee's tact and easygoing demeanor and considered him a "park service man." (US National Park Service, Washington, DC)

Service man," and he also hired Carlton Qualey, who worked with him to develop the master plan for interpreting American historic monuments.[15]

During the first one hundred days of the Roosevelt administration, New Deal programs developed in a fluid and reactionary manner to remedy the unemployment most Americans were experiencing. Chatelain understood this period as an incredible opportunity. By 1930, 25 to 30 percent of the American workforce was unemployed, and 30 percent of the workforce was underemployed. Soon after Roosevelt's inauguration, Ickes and Harry Hopkins, the Works Progress Administration (WPA) director, began planning large-scale construction and cultural projects, designed to provide economic relief through short-term employment to as many unemployed Americans as possible. University graduates in the humanities received opportunities working in the federal government like never before.

The national parks became the serendipitous beneficiaries of the work performed by the New Deal work relief program, the Civilian Conservation Corps (CCC). Under the terms of the Emergency Conservation Work Act of 1933, all work by the CCC had to be designed by knowledgeable professionals. By the summer of 1933, trained historians and design professionals were hired to manage the new federal historic preservation program, which was mainly funded by the Emergency Conservation Work program. After his retirement, Chatelain remembered in interviews to scholars that "the New Deal was just made to order for us," and "I was hiring Ph.D.'s a dime a dozen."[16] That year,

Figure 4.4: WPA poster for Fort Marion National Monument, St. Augustine, Florida, 1935. The National Park Service marketed historic forts as tourist attractions during the Great Depression. (Library of Congress, Prints & Photographs Division, WPA Poster Collection, LC-DIG-ppmsca-13396)

Chatelain convened a history conference in Washington, and through it, a set of recommendations ware submitted to Cammerer. Among the recommendations were that historical activities were a significant part of the educational program of the NPS and historians should be key contributors in developing and promoting educational content for historic monuments through research, publication, archival collections, and public outreach and education. This included the management of historic sites and new facilities design to support them.[17] Chatelain felt strongly that "the historical work of the National Park Service is dependent upon a history-focused point of view. He urged the administration to leave interpretation problem-solving to the "historically minded."[18] He was convinced that academically trained historians should form the narrative, explaining American history to the public through historic places. He sought to develop this singular narrative in the NPS through a balance of historical documentation, based completely on archival collection and evaluation, and sound facilities management. He proposed that the NPS should utilize "the uniquely graphic qualities, which inhere in any area where stirring and significant events have taken place to drive home to the visitor the meaning of those events showing not only their importance in themselves but their integral relationship to the whole history of American development." Furthermore, he emphasized that the interpretative mission of the NPS was "to breathe the breath of life into American history and to re-create for the average citizen something of the color, the pageantry, and the dignity of our national past."[19]

Chatelain advocated doing surveys of historic sites, which would document "specifically local, regional state, national, and international importance."[20] Historians would then determine a site's importance within the perspective of the national narrative. For Chatelain, the survey and the historian-produced narrative, which followed a set template, were only the first component of a grander objective. Ultimately, he wanted the NPS to plan a national historical educational program into which each of the park units could be fitted for the maximum of educational efficiency.[21] With this new direction in the service's mission, history became public history, and professionalism now had to coexist with personalism, a concept that the professional men not only did not acknowledge but that caught them completely off guard (figure 4.4).

Roosevelt's reorganization of monuments management, which unified national parks and historic monuments into one system through his executive order as well as his New Deal emergency and relief programs, coincided with the nation's resurging fascination with its past. This enabled the embryonic and hastily assembled NPS historical program to grow significantly throughout the 1930s, albeit in an ad hoc manner. In 1933, the agency received an appropriation of $11 million[22] and, in 1939, $27 million.[23] The influx of funding enabled the NPS to hire professional architects, landscape architects, engineers, and historians to manage historic sites. Not all of the service's staff believed that academically trained historians should plan the interpretation of history-based parks or create a national history narrative. The most prominent critic of Chatelain's approach was a young midwestern architect named Charles E. Peterson.

Known to his friends and colleagues as "Pete," Peterson was literally plucked out of obscurity by Albright, who met him out west in 1928 when Peterson was a young architecture student paying his way through college working as a land surveyor (figure 4.5). Albright immediately liked Peterson and placed him on a career path in the NPS that would impact historic preservation in the US for the remainder of the twentieth century. During his initial years, Pete Peterson was a young man on the rise in the NPS hierarchy. In his doctoral dissertation, Wilton Corkern summarized Peterson's ambitions by quoting a Williamsburg architect who said this in 1933: "Peterson is one of those fellows in the civil service who suddenly finds himself, through this expansion [of the park service

Figure 4.5: Charles E. Peterson, senior landscape architect, US National Park Service (center in the photograph), 1929 in Sequoia National Park. Peterson was chief of the Eastern Division of the Office of Planning in the National Park Service when he proposed the Historic American Buildings Survey for New Deal funding in 1933. (Athenaeum of Philadelphia, Philadelphia, Pennsylvania)

into the east], in a position of power and influence. His qualifications are way ahead of his background."[24]

Like Chatelain, Lee, and Qualey, Peterson had graduated from the University of Minnesota, but as an architect, not a PhD historian.[25] His first assignments for the NPS were out west, where he designed entry structures for the parks. He was soon transferred to Washington, and by 1933 he was chief of the Eastern Division of the NPS Office of Planning. In this role, he worked with Chatelain and his historians. Peterson soon developed a negative assessment of the NPS historians' work and even their purpose in the agency. He dismissed their reports, saying that "most of them were rubbish . . . they just didn't have any grasp of what they were doing."[26] He added, "their reports were a product of the hurrying which was done during that time." He dismissed Chatelain, saying "he wanted a brick station with six historians at every entrance to every military park."

The clash of personalities between Chatelain and Peterson was only part of a larger problem in developing a holistic public history and historic preservation program for the nation within the National Park Service. Inflexibility within the bureaucracy was another one. The two NPS subunits—the History Division and the Office of Planning—were placed, respectively, in two distinctively different and larger units—the Branch of Research and Education and the Branch of Plans and Designs. Chatelain quickly developed a culture in the History Division with its own set of values, an academic-based identity, and its own ambitious agenda. Chatelain regarded himself first as history scholar and second as a history teacher. By necessity as the facilities planning and management NPS office, the Office of Planning was programmatic in its problem-solving approach. Peterson regarded himself first an architect and second as a preservationist in the Appleton tradition. Chatelain embraced the challenge of creating the American history narrative for the general public to not only learn but enjoy. Peterson was more interested in the actual ways historic buildings were constructed and not necessarily how historic buildings could become simply reasons for discussing American history. More importantly, Peterson argued that the correct approach to historic preservation should be scientific, not commercial. Chatelain sought to teach Americans their history using the monuments as props. Intellectual and sensitive to criticism, Chatelain personified the academic stereotype; he often sulked when he was denied his way. Having come from a humbler background, Peterson epitomized the plain-talking, frank midwesterner.[27]

But even as Peterson advocated for Appleton's objective approach to understanding the "builders' art," he was attracted to the built patrimony by personalism, even though he refused to admit it throughout his life. He was not alone. Numerous intellectuals during the Great Depression sought the idealized memory of America's preindustrial past as an answer to the threats to American life—consumerism, industrialism (especially Fordism), and urbanization. Folklorists, including B. A. Botkin and John Collier, had a nostalgic view of farming and agrarian life. Even Henry Ford shared this viewpoint. For Peterson, craft in building was a precious and fast-disappearing characteristic on the American landscape. Historians like Chatelain vehemently disparaged this idea.[28]

The conflict between history and heritage, which emerged in the early 1930s at the NPS, not only obfuscated the agency's public history mission; it influenced how historic preservation evolved in the US.

Under the Emergency Conservation Work (ECW) program, the NPS was assigned the responsibility of providing economic relief to one of the professions most affected by the Great Depression: architecture. Through the NPS, ECW program administrators placed a call for projects in the building professions. More specifically, they wanted employment programs that directly engaged the government with the private sector. The call for projects was not embraced by the Department of the Interior. Ickes protested the service's expanded role, but he was overruled. Peterson reacted quickly to the ECW call for projects. In a dramatic move, he proposed creating the Historic American Buildings Survey (HABS) to the NPS top administration and, later, to the ECW administrators. No single program was more audacious in interacting with the architectural profession, the federal government, and the general public than HABS. What was originally established to aid unemployed or underemployed architects and draftsmen soon became a tool for an elite group of professional men, trained in architecture and history, to gather the architectural documentation that was necessary in constructing their ultimate goal: a holistic narrative of American architecture. But underqualified workers, national and regional politics, a rigid and unyielding bureaucracy, breakdowns in management between Washington and rest of the country, and established competing narratives formed by personalism undermined their efforts. In the end, the American architecture narrative that they envisioned was incomplete and erroneous. Perhaps nowhere else in America did personalism distort the attempted professionalized narrative more so than in Natchez, Mississippi. Not only did women like Edith Wyatt Moore, Roane Fleming Byrnes, and Katherine Grafton Miller know and understand their local heritage, but by 1933, they had already begun reshaping it for commercial gain. *They* controlled the story of Natchez, and they eventually controlled HABS in Mississippi.

Like most twentieth-century preservation initiatives (including the Natchez Spring Pilgrimage), HABS is steeped in as much legend as fact. Like the pilgrimage, its story can be best defined as "heritage," and it continues to be perpetuated by the professional class of preservationists working for the National Park Service and the leading architects specializing in historic preservation in the American Institute of Architects (AIA).[29] But before HABS, there had never been an intentional plan of what to document of the built patrimony of America. In fact, selection of buildings to be documented had been arbitrary. It is only when you learn the politics behind which buildings were selected to be measured and drawn that you begin to understand the significance of HABS. It is not an accurate survey of American architecture; it is the result of political wrangling and the persistence of a locale's conjured narrative. Nowhere is this more the case than in Natchez.

Legend has it that, upon learning about the ECW funding, two young NPS design professionals, Charles E. Peterson and his friend and colleague Alston G. Guttersen, spent the weekend together in Peterson's Washington apartment and created the HABS idea. Their weekend goal: to submit their idea for historic building documentation to NPS director Arno Cammerer by the following Monday morning. Peterson called his idea "the Historic American Buildings Survey," and the title of the project never changed. He intended for HABS to accomplish two objectives: utilize unemployed architects across the nation to document America's historic architecture and provide them some financial relief, and become the "complete resume of the builder's art" of America.[30] His second objective was quite ambitious, and it relied heavily on his first one. Peterson philosophically justified his idea in his memorandum. He pleaded to Cammerer: "Our architectural heritage of buildings diminishes at an alarming rate. The ravages of fire and natural elements, together with demolition and alterations caused by real estate 'improvements,' form an inexorable tide of destruction destined to wipe out the great majority of the buildings which knew the beginning and first flourish of the nation." He emphatically continued, "It is the responsibility of the American people that if the great number of antique buildings must disappear through economic causes, they should not pass into unrecorded oblivion."[31]

Peterson scrawled his objectives and his ideas for implementation for the program on notepads, and Guttersen developed its budget, working late into the night of Sunday, November 12, 1933. In his memorandum, Peterson proposed a national undertaking that utilized the talents of AIA members to document historic buildings of national significance that were facing demolition. This architectural documentation was to be deposited in federal archives, and the program managed by the National Park Service.[32]

On the morning of November 13, Peterson arrived at the director's office with his handwritten memorandum for Cammerer's review and approval, but the director was away from his office on that day. Instead, the proposal was immediately typed and forwarded to NPS associate director Arthur E. Demaray. He approved Peterson's idea without any changes and forwarded it to Ickes on Wednesday the fifteenth. In the meantime, Peterson gave a copy of his memorandum to William Graves

Perry, senior architect of the Colonial Williamsburg Restoration, who was in Washington from Boston for a meeting of the Williamsburg Advisory Committee of Architects, and requested that he present the idea to the committee. The committee endorsed the idea on the afternoon of the fifteenth. The proposal was then presented to Ickes, along with the Williamsburg Advisory Committee endorsement, on November 17. Ickes immediately approved it, and it was then submitted to CWA administrator Harry Hopkins on November 28. On December 1, 1933, Hopkins approved the funds for HABS. The CWA allotted $448,000 for HABS, the exact amount Peterson and Guttersen had calculated, and it was classified as a "cultural program," a work initiative designed for professionals in artistic and literary fields.[33] The original HABS program officially started on December 12, 1933, and it lasted six months.[34]

This story is only partially true.

While Peterson claimed ownership of the HABS idea with his eureka moment of weekend brainstorming session in his apartment, neither surveying and documenting historic American architecture nor employing unemployed architects to produce historic architectural documentation was a new or revolutionary idea. It is also untrue that HABS was the nation's first systematic and comprehensive historic preservation effort. Throughout the first two decades of the twentieth century, there were years of discussion, development, activity, and lobbying among the nation's elite architects, historians, and policymakers in making the concept of measuring and drawing America's historic architecture a reality.[35]

Upon accepting the chair position of the AIA's Committee on Preservation of Natural Beauties and Historic Monuments in 1915, Philadelphia architect Horace W. Sellers urged state chapters to establish historic preservation committees. He intended for AIA chapters to "document buildings of historic or architectural interest through surveys and photographs of buildings that will inevitably be demolished in the progress of the City's development."[36] The primary motive for the AIA and architects to study and learn from historic architecture was to emulate it or re-create elements of it in new design. Patriotism was another motive. And while Sellers and other committee members applauded the idea and made it a high priority for the committee, there was no funding for it from the AIA. Therefore, the survey project idea languished throughout the 1920s.[37]

Documentation of American historic buildings in New England began twenty years earlier than HABS by the construction industry, mainly as a marketing ploy. In 1914, the White Pine Bureau, a joint venture of the Northern Pine Manufacturer's Association of Minnesota, Wisconsin, and Michigan and the White Pine Manufacturers of Idaho, was promoting the use of pine lumber for residential buildings.[38]

Building surveying continued to be a big idea in the architecture profession during the 1920s, but in the interest of better utilizing limited resources, architects opted to focus only on major, nationally important buildings. No one epitomized this change more so than Sellers's 1923 successor as chair of the renamed Committee on Preservation of Historic Buildings: University of Virginia architecture professor Fiske Kimball. Kimball led by example and thoroughly documented Thomas Jefferson's Monticello, the University of Virginia's Academical Village, and Stratford Hall, birthplace of Robert E. Lee. Collecting, dismantling, and reconstructing architectural antiquities, which Kimball profited from as an architect and later championed as director of the Philadelphia Museum of Art, became a popular hobby among wealthy antiquarians. Architects traveled across the country to document historic buildings with the intent of re-creating their details and features in new buildings for wealthy clients. For example, in 1929, as a young apprentice, the pioneer preservation architect and educator James Marston Fitch traveled to Natchez to measure and draw the details of the Natchez villa Auburn; he later replicated these details for a wealthy client who was building a comparable, but modern, Auburn in Nashville, Tennessee.[39]

Measuring and drawing, which were based on the French model for architectural education and the nation's reflective mood on its colonial past compelled the talented and educated architecture designers to continue examining historic vernacular buildings in their region and using the lessons they learned from them as precedents and ideas in their design. Richard Koch, whose assistance Roane Byrnes found critical in the restoration of Connelly's Tavern, readily comes to mind as an example.

Peterson had been educated in this tradition at Minnesota, but he also saw firsthand how beneficial historic architectural documentation was for the profession and for historic preservation. As head of the Eastern Division of the NPS's Branch of Plans and Designs, he supervised restorations at the Colonial National Monument at Yorktown, Virginia, and at Wakefield. Both of these sites were in close proximity to Williamsburg, Virginia, where an extensive restoration, financed by John D. Rockefeller Jr., had been underway since 1926. Peterson knew the architects, who were working for the Boston firm Perry, Shaw & Hepburn and were documenting the historic buildings in measured drawings. These architects considered themselves on the cutting edge of professionalism, developing modern approaches to scholarly restorations. They not only measured and documented the buildings in Williamsburg; they also documented pre-Revolutionary buildings still standing in the

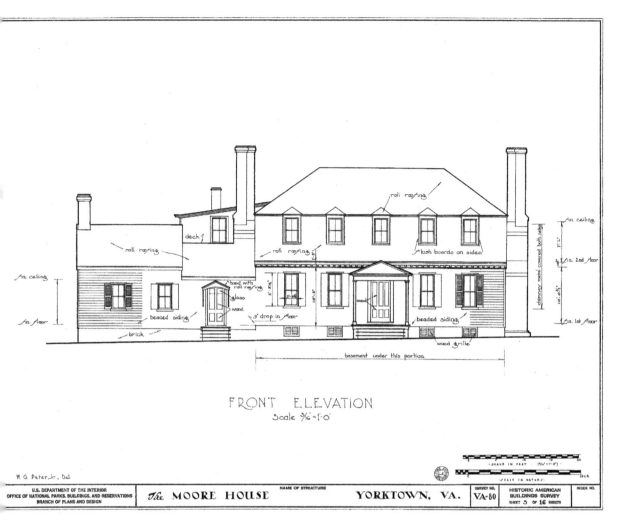

Figure 4.6: The Moore House, Yorktown, Virginia. Charles Peterson learned the value of historic architectural recordation while supervising the restoration of this famous eighteenth-century house, which was the site of the terms of surrender by Lord Cornwallis to George Washington. Peterson was following the work of Perry, Shaw & Hepburn on the Colonial Williamsburg restoration. (Library of Congress, Prints & Photographs Division, Historic American Buildings Survey, HABS VA,100-YORK.V,1-)

nearby Virginia and Maryland countryside. They used this information as sources for ideas for the new buildings proposed for construction in what became Colonial Williamsburg (figure 4.6).

Observing the work of Perry, Shaw & Hepburn, young Pete Peterson realized that the National Park Service lacked the ability to gather the historical architectural information it needed to accurately restore historic monuments in its parks. He carefully observed the way the firm developed documentation, which was a system its architects had adopted from the Royal Institute of British Architects. He considered the measuring and drawing approaches used by Perry, Shaw & Hepburn for architectural documentation as the standard to emulate and began using it himself on weekend jaunts, documenting historic Virginia colonial buildings.

But Peterson also realized that the Williamsburg drawings were the exclusive property of Perry, Shaw & Hepburn. And once its architects had mined them for ideas, as Peterson put it, "[they] placed them in wooden boxes and nailed them up. They didn't know what to with them." Peterson knew how he wanted to manage the archive: "We knew what we had to do with them. First of all, we had to take them away from the guys that drew them, because they're never through. There's always something they want to change in them, no matter how long they have them. Chatelain wanted to get his hands on them, too."[40] Peterson was determined that Chatelain not have any of the drawings.

Therefore, prior to submitting his handwritten memorandum to Cammerer's office, he met with the chair of the AIA National Committee on the Preservation of Historic Buildings and chief of the Division of Fine Arts at the Library of Congress, Leicester B. Holland. In him, Peterson found a steadfast ally in developing a federal program for historic architectural documentation.

No one in 1930s Washington personified professionalism in architecture and historic preservation more than Leicester B. Holland (figure 4.7). Holland literally grew up in modern American professionalism. His family was part of the emerging professional class in late nineteenth-century America. Born in Louisville, Kentucky, he soon moved with his family to Philadelphia. His father, James W. Holland, was a noted physician and later became dean of the Jefferson Medical College in Philadelphia. Young Leicester originally intended to become as a doctor as well but changed his career path and earned a bachelor's degree in architecture in 1904 at the University of Pennsylvania. He remained at Penn and earned his master's degree in architecture in 1917 and a doctoral degree in architecture in 1919. Holland joined the architecture faculty at Penn but also served as chief of the Division of Fine Arts and holder of the Carnegie Chair at the Library of Congress. In 1913, he joined the AIA and became active in the AIA's Committee on the Preservation of Historic Buildings, chairing the committee in 1931. With his Beaux Arts architecture training and his interest in architectural history and archaeology, along with his apprenticeships working for Wilson Eyre in Philadelphia and Cram, Goodhue, and Ferguson in Boston, Holland developed an interest in recording and cataloging early American architecture. In 1918, he proposed that the AIA become involved in documenting historic architecture throughout the US. In his position as chief of the Division of Fine Arts at the Library of Congress, Holland wielded considerable influence

Figure 4.7: Leicester B. Holland, chief of the Division of Fine Arts, holder of the Carnegie Chair at the Library of Congress, and chair of the AIA Committee on the Preservation of Historic Buildings, 1933. Holland was a proponent of professionalism in both architecture and historic preservation during the 1930s. (Frances Benjamin Johnston Photograph Collection, Library of Congress, Prints & Photographs Division, LC-DIG-ppmsca-35579)

both in the architectural profession and in the federal government, especially in the NPS.[41]

Peterson approached Holland with the idea of the Library of Congress becoming the repository for the HABS collection before any drawings had been produced. Holland enthusiastically agreed. Peterson also proposed to Holland that the AIA provide the labor for the survey. He enlisted William Graves Perry to endorse the AIA component of the survey. Peterson then proposed that the NPS manage the survey. He envisioned a "tri-partite" agreement, which was unique to the New Deal programs. He proposed that HABS be administered by the NPS, that the drawings be produced by the AIA, and the resulting drawings be cataloged and archived in the Library of Congress. With this proposal, Peterson had succeeded in taking Chatelain and his historians out of the HABS project. The NPS Office of Planning was to manage the project, and the final products, the drawings, would be placed in the public realm in the Library of Congress.

Peterson nearly destroyed the project idea as it was making its way through the federal bureaucracy for final approval. After Ickes approved the HABS memorandum, it was sent to Harry Hopkins, the executive supervisor of the Civil Works Administration (CWA), who allocated federal emergency work relief funding for projects like HABS. But before

Figure 4.8: Thomas C. Vint, chief landscape architect and architect of the National Park Service Branch of Plans and Designs. Vint served as the chief administrator for HABS from its beginning in late 1933 until his retirement in 1961. He also managed development of the new national parks in the East: Colonial (Yorktown, Virginia), Salem Maritime (Salem, Massachusetts), and Hopewell Furnace (Elverson, Pennsylvania). (US National Park Service, Washington, DC)

Hopkins even had a chance to review the proposal, on November 28, the *Washington Post* carried a story with this front-page headline: "Survey Asked of America's Old Buildings, Ickes Urges $500,000 CWA Funds to Guard Historic Treasures." The article featured a photograph of Peterson and the caption read "Charles E. Peterson, Government Planner and Architect who will direct the proposed survey of Antique Buildings."[42] The article suggested that the HABS project was already approved and that Peterson had been appointed to manage it. This was by no means the case. It was not approved by the CWA, nor had Peterson, or anyone at the time, been appointed to lead it. To make matters worse, the article stated that the project was to employ 1,200 architects for six months. Peterson recalled that Ickes was "mad as hell" that the story had been leaked to the newspaper, and he blamed the ambitious Peterson for providing a false story. Peterson denied any part in leaking the story and accused Ickes's staff of passing the news item to the *Post* prematurely. Despite the embarrassment, Hopkins approved the $448,000 (the exact amount Peterson and Guttersen had proposed), and HABS was now officially underway. But Peterson's political blunder proved costly for him and HABS. Ickes directed Cammerer to assign chief architect and director of the Branch of Plans and Designs (and Peterson's direct reporting executive) Thomas Vint to lead the project (figure 4.8). Vint conferred with Peterson, and they both agreed that staff architect John P. O'Neill should directly manage the project.[43]

John P. O'Neill worked under Peterson in the Eastern Division of the Branch of Plans and Designs in the National Park Service. As the manager of HABS, O'Neill engaged in the day-to-day operations of the program throughout his tenure. He sought to apply a top-down managerial approach to a program that was innately decentralized and undertaken at a national scale. In a proper bureaucratic manner, O'Neill prepared regular reports, based on his correspondence with district officers and later regional managers. But he never understood the challenges facing the HABS program regionally, both logistically and in how to accomplish Washington's objectives in the program. This proved to be particularly problematic in rural states and especially in the South. Little or no historical research had been done before 1933 on architecture. Local lore was typically the only basis for history in rural states.[44]

Peterson worked directly under Vint throughout 1934; in 1935, he was reassigned as senior landscape architect to the Jefferson National Expansion Memorial in St. Louis, where he worked until he joined the US Navy in World War II. Fellow NPS architect James C. Massey remembered that the two men had a close friendship, with Peterson as the maverick and Vint as the calm mentor who kept Peterson out of trouble.[45] Despite this move, Peterson remained engaged in the HABS project, often advising Vint.[46]

Peterson's exit in 1935 provided an opportunity for Holland to seize control of HABS. In his memorandum, Peterson called for a "National Advisory Committee" and a management structure for establishing architecture teams based on the membership of the AIA. While Peterson was shepherding the HABS idea through the NPS and then the CWA, Holland was putting together an advisory committee, and he instructed national AIA executive secretary Edward C. Kemper to submit to Cammerer. Holland, through Kemper, proposed the following members of the advisory committee: Holland, as chair; William Graves Perry, principal architect of the Boston architectural firm Perry, Shaw & Hepburn; Albert Simons, the leading restoration architect in Charleston, South Carolina; and John Gaw Meem, the leading restoration and commercial architect in Santa Fe, New Mexico.[47] Upon reviewing the list, Ickes added four other members who were not architects to the advisory committee: Dr. Waldo G. Leland, executive secretary of the American Council of Learned Societies; Miss Harlean James, executive secretary of the American Civic Association; Dr. Herbert E. Bolton, professor of history, University of California, Berkeley; and I. T. Frary, curator, Cleveland Museum of Art. Ickes also added one other architect to the committee, Chicagoan Thomas E. Tallmedge.[48] Although Ickes tried to balance the membership of the HABS advisory committee, Holland retained firm control.

Peterson envisioned how the AIA membership would be utilized in executing HABS. He proposed that each chapter of the AIA nationwide would be designated a "district" and each AIA chapter would nominate a "district officer." The district officer would then assemble a team of unemployed architects and draftsmen and mobilize the team to go out into the field and document the historic buildings in their state. Although Vint realized that the success of the program relied on the effectiveness of the AIA chapters in the states, he and other NPS staff had misgivings about handing over that much authority to the AIA.[49]

Vint and Peterson envisioned that a district advisory committee would guide the district officer in determining the standards of archival research and graphic clarity and in determining which historical monuments were worthy of being documented. Vint and Peterson assumed that the advisory committee would adhere to the highest ethical standards inspired by HABS and would avoid any "local political encroachment" either in the selection of employees or buildings documented.[50]

But without an overarching thematic plan to record historic buildings across the country, "local political encroachment" became a persistent problem in the HABS program. In Mississippi, this proved problematic because "local political encroachment" was commonplace. Moreover, in 1934, most politicians, all of whom were male and white, were uninterested in documenting the state's architecture; they ceded this responsibility to privileged white women in the state—specifically, the Natchez Garden Club women.

In setting up the parameters for which each building was to be documented, Peterson allowed his own sense of personalism to influence how HABS functioned. By expressing his personal bias about what is and is not a historic building, he undermined the premise of the program before it was even started. In his memorandum, he stated that HABS teams were directed to measure and document buildings erected before and up to 1860. His reasoning revealed his personalism, which was based on his ideas about historic regional architecture.[51]

Ickes recognized early on that there was a need to develop a national historic preservation and public history program in the National Park Service but was unable to cajole Cammerer into developing a coordinated effort between the Office of Planning and the History Division. Early on in the HABS program, the personal rivalry between Peterson and Chatelain made any coordination effort impossible. If there was anything that Peterson and Chatelain agreed on, it was this: HABS was an architecture program. Later in his life, Peterson recalled with pride that "HABS was designed by architects for architects." Chatelain was more cynical in his assessment of the program: "The Historic American Buildings Survey was . . . an architect's dream. . . . It [was] never too closely tied to our program and for that reason I think it failed to do some things that it could easily have done at the time it was carried on." Staff members such as Ronald Lee went on to further dismiss what HABS accomplished: "I don't think HABS had any effect on the park development. HABS was a concept to put unemployed architects to work, recording historic structures, to develop a record of worthwhile buildings that might be useful in the future. It was a good idea, it did have its effect eventually in historic preservation, but I don't think it had any great marked effect immediately."[52]

Men in the National Park Service in Washington all agreed that a national documentation project of America's built patrimony, from the beginning of colonization to 1860, was an important undertaking, and from this project a science-based professional narrative of American architectural history and perhaps American history could be developed to teach Americans about their history. But bureaucratic intransigence and personal infighting compelled historians and architects to conduct their own surveys without any coordination. To complicate matters, Peterson, Vint, and O'Neill abdicated their authority to determine which buildings were to be documented to the AIA state chapters. And while some states were able to prioritize historic monuments that possessed high architectural and historical significance and were threatened by development, other states allowed "local political encroachment" to happen, which distorted the architectural history of the state. When historians began using the collection, mistakes in it became all the more glaring. Although shoddy documentation is partly to blame for these discrepancies, so is a politically driven personalized narrative created in each state. As HABS mobilized to work in Mississippi, the Natchez Garden Club women had developed their narrative, which corrupted HABS's objective-based mission. This resulted in a focus on Natchez, completely controlled by the NGC women, which skewed the architecture archive of Mississippi.

JACKSON AND NATCHEZ, MISSISSIPPI, 1934

HABS history in Mississippi is as steeped in legend as the national HABS history and as much as the history of historic preservation in Natchez. Much of its story was conveyed by the people who were part of the HABS program in 1930s Mississippi, and it is a story that has been perpetuated and romanticized by preservationists and people who knew these individuals firsthand. It is a convoluted story that happened during a brief period of time, and while many of its characters are celebrated, many more talented architects, builders, and draftsmen are forgotten. But the reasons why this story remains important is what these individuals produced in 1934: a captivating drawings collection of historic Mississippi buildings, almost exclusively in Natchez, in the HABS collection in the Library of Congress. The drawings are the manifestation of the Natchez narrative and not only spearheaded historic preservation in the Deep South but also inspired regional southern architecture in the twentieth century.

In January 1934, HABS implemented a financial model to hire nearly eight hundred people with the $448,000 allocated by the CWA. O'Neill devised an employment chart for each district that had a mandated salary structure: a district chief and head architect received a salary of $200 per month (approximately $3,700 in 2019); architects and draftsmen made between ninety cents and a little more than a dollar an hour (depending on the percentage of time committed to the program); clerks and secretaries earned $125 per month (approximately $2,300 in 2019); and stenographers earned $100 per month ($1,829.03 in 2019). Based on statistics by the Department of Labor, O'Neill forecast that Mississippi would employ eighteen architects and draftsmen plus one district chief, one clerk, and one stenographer. District chiefs were expected to furnish office space; most of them incorporated HABS into their own offices. Draftsmen were expected to use their own drawing tools and instruments.[53]

Mississippi suffered severely from the economic upheavals caused by the Great Depression. Mississippi's credit rating plummeted. Construction across the state, both in the private and public sectors, came to an abrupt halt. Several architecture offices failed during this time and closed their practices.[54] During these dire times, securing the district officer position was more than an honor; it was a means to survive.

There were many accomplished architects practicing in Mississippi during the Great Depression who could have led the HABS program.[55] But Noah Webster Overstreet wanted the HABS program for his office. With little competition from his professional peers and being the president of the Mississippi chapter of the AIA, he secured the state HABS program, designated by the NPS as District 17. A native Mississippian who was very interested in the state's architectural heritage and one of the first professional architects in Mississippi, Overstreet commanded influence within the state's architecture profession, and his office was the best qualified to lead the state's HABS initiative (figure 4.9).[56]

Overstreet's partner, Albert Hays Town, was one of the most celebrated HABS architects in the 1930s. Drawings that he either delineated or managed are considered some of the most exquisite in the entire HABS collection. Later in his life, Town drew on his HABS experience to design some of the most noteworthy neotraditional residential architecture in Louisiana and Mississippi during the 1990s and early 2000s.

Figure 4.9: Noah Webster Overstreet, Architect. Overstreet is considered the dean of the architectural profession during the twentieth century in Mississippi. His firm designed many of the most notable modern buildings in the state, and he was a charter member and first president of the Mississippi Chapter of the American Institute of Architects from 1929 until 1936. (University Archives Photographs, Collection A1985-119, University Archives, Special Collections Department, Mississippi State University)

His sensitivity to the vernacular architectural tradition and his use of traditional and even recycled building materials inspired generations of architects that came after him. His involvement with HABS became the stuff of legend, which only obfuscates the HABS story in Mississippi.

Town was born and raised in southern Louisiana and first enrolled to study engineering at Southwestern Louisiana Institute (now the University of Louisiana) in Lafayette in 1918. In 1921, he secured a scholarship to study architecture at Tulane. There, he excelled in its Beaux Arts curriculum. Nathaniel Curtis and William Spratling were his instructors.[57] Tulane's curriculum, which assigned Beaux Arts *analytiques* and *esquisses*, emphasized conceptual design and graphic mastery. Overstreet found in Town a talented conceptual designer who complimented his own technical bent toward architecture.[58]

By 1931, the only ongoing large-scale construction project in the state was the Mississippi State Mental Hospital. It was in its construction phase, meaning that the largest portion of architecture fees had been used. Overstreet began laying off employees, and by 1933, he had laid off all his employees except Town. Overstreet admired Town: in the younger man, he saw how his firm could survive and rebuild. In lieu of a salary, Overstreet offered to share whatever revenues the firm might take in during these lean times. Town accepted the offer, and the name of the firm was changed from N. W. Overstreet and Associates to Overstreet and Town. The new firm moved out of its large office in the Mississippi Fire Insurance Building, which Overstreet designed, to a smaller office in the Standard Life Building.[59]

Overstreet and Town needed a project to carry them through 1934. The HABS program bought them time, and Overstreet saw that Town was more qualified than he was to be the district officer. The $200 monthly salary for Town and the hourly wages for draftsmen kept the firm intact. Town could keep the office in functioning order while Overstreet supported the firm through construction administration of the state hospital. Overstreet then began marketing for new work in earnest, using his political connections in the state. To Overstreet and Town, HABS was exactly what the CWA and Hopkins had intended it to be: a temporary project to employ unemployed or underemployed architects. Town was hired as district officer in January 1934 and immediately began building a HABS team for measuring and drawing historic buildings.

The 1934 HABS program in Mississippi was exactly what Peterson and Chatelain described: "a program created for architects by architects" and "an architect's dream." Town certainly viewed it that way. He documented buildings that he liked in the region of the state was most familiar to him and in a town that promised private architectural commissions for the firm—Natchez. Without any coordination with the NPS's History Division, the first HABS Mississippi program lacked any direction from Washington. Peterson gave the district officers one criterion in documenting historic buildings: document buildings built before and up to 1860. For all the states, O'Neill and the NPS staff relied on state advisory boards to determine a state's building list. The thoroughness of building lists greatly varied from state to state, and state advisory boards greatly varied in engagement. The Mississippi Department of Archives and History and the Mississippi state AIA chapter appointed Emmett Hull as chair of the Mississippi HABS advisory board, along with four board members: Eugene Drummond, Jason R. Stevens, Frank P. Gates, and Ellie Earl Norwood.[60] The advisory board then abjured its role of selecting historic buildings to the WPA Writers' Project and Town.

At the request of Vint, Chatelain visited Natchez in January 1934 at the beginning of the HABS project. Chatelain toured Natchez and met with the NGC women to discuss how to record Natchez's history. He was charmed by these women and the city, which he described as a "gold mine." He also concurred with Katherine Miller, Roane Byrnes, and Ruth Beltzhoover that measures needed to be undertaken to preserve the city's historic architecture. He exclaimed, "There should be some method in preserving and developing in a historical way the plans for the City of Natchez. I am interested in the development of that [of the city] more than any other thing." But he did not follow up on the method for preserving the city, and he did not provide any guidance for documenting its history. Instead, Chatelain assigned Vicksburg National Park historian and technician Stuart Cuthbertson to manage Edith Moore in her research on Natchez's history. No one in the NPS's History Division scrutinized her work.[61]

The WPA Writers' Project for Mississippi was directed by Eri Douglas, who hired local historians to research history and folklore in the state. No one was more productive in compiling the history of a Mississippi locale than Edith Moore. She began researching Natchez's architecture history in 1934, and with the success of the first two pilgrimages, the advisory board gave her the opportunity to select buildings that were worthy of HABS documentation. Moreover, Town was drawn to Natchez for two reasons: first, he identified with the city's architecture and found it similar to his native Louisiana and New Orleans; second, as soon as he became Mississippi's district officer, he began working and collaborating with his old mentor from his time at Tulane, Richard Koch. During his work on Connelly's Tavern, which was being restored at this time, Koch mentioned to Roane Byrnes that he was meeting with Town and showing him historic buildings in Natchez in early 1934. Later in the year, Town was consulting for the Louisiana HABS team.[62] Town's attraction to southwest Mississippi and Natchez, coupled with Moore's taking control of guiding the HABS project, focused the program on Natchez. By now, the state embraced the idea of Natchez and its architecture being *the* historic place of Mississippi—despite the fact that it did not represent the state's regions and national sectionalism, which are diverse, both geographically and culturally. To men like Overstreet, Drummond, Gates, and Norwood, as progressive new architecture replaced historic buildings in Mississippi cities like Jackson and Meridian, Natchez was the obvious place for history—the state's "historyland."

Town wasted little time assembling the District 17 HABS team for what would become a six-month project, although it was originally set by the CWA to last only three months. All of his team members were native Mississippians; some were recently graduated architects, while others were builders or out-of-work architects. Some of them came to work with him in the Standard Life Building in Jackson, while others lived in either Natchez or Vicksburg and worked on buildings there. All of them needed employment and were ready to work. Several of the young architects went on to have impactful architectural careers in Mississippi. After the 1934 HABS program was completed, none of them remained in the Overstreet and Town office.[63] Most of them joined rival Mississippi firms or opened offices in other Mississippi towns and cities, and a couple of them left the state entirely.[64] But during the first half of 1934, these men produced an impressive collection of drawings and photographs.[65]

Town hired Jackson photographers Ralph H. Clynne and James Butters to produce the architectural photography for the HABS program.[66] Together, they produced some of the most iconic photographic images in the Depression-era HABS collection.[67]

Town assembled a capable team to measure and delineate the drawings of historic buildings in Natchez. He and the state advisory committee let Edith Moore produce the historic research on the HABS buildings in Natchez. Moore took great pride compiling the history of historic buildings in Natchez.

Frankly, Moore was not the person who should have been entrusted to document Natchez's history and write for the WPA Writers' Project programs on the history and heritage of Natchez and Mississippi. Even before the beginning of the project, as early as 1931, she was focused on celebrating Natchez's Spanish colonial period. She paid little attention to, and even expressed her disdain of, later architecture periods—most notably, the antebellum one. It was not until tourists demonstrated their fascination with that period that she embraced Natchez's antebellum architecture. Moore wanted to write about what Natchez should have been, not what it actually was. She deliberately twisted facts, emphasized some facts over others, and flat-out fabricated stories about historic buildings in Natchez that she found more useful to the Natchez narrative than others.[68] Although Moore presented herself as earnest and serious-minded, she was prone to romanticism.

With an official role in chronicling the history of Natchez, Moore embedded the Natchez narrative into the HABS official historical record. Her erroneous work was also archived in the WPA Writers' Project. Both in the documentation of historic architecture in Natchez and Adams County and her interviews with formerly enslaved persons, she skewed historical fact to fit the narrative she had created. Through her questioning, she led the interviewee to answer her questions the way she wanted them answered.[69]

In 1934, Moore began compiling records of the historic houses and buildings in Natchez. Fellow Natchez Garden Club members Katherine Perrault and Louise Hernandez assisted her. The records consisted of typed 3×5 cards organized by county and labeled "Number 622," the project code for the Writers' Project guidebook program. Moore was very productive; out of the approximately one thousand card entries for the eighty-two Mississippi counties, 128 cards are in the Adams County folder.[70]

The typed 3×5 cards are cryptic, but they state what Moore and her friends wanted to convey about specific buildings in Natchez for the WPA Writers' Project. They describe Arlington as a century-old

Roman villa. Auburn, a significant Federal-style building built by Levi Weeks, is only mentioned as the ancestral home of the Duncans and that it was opened daily for tours. Moore gave "The Burn" only a brief entry, but she elaborated on Beverly (owned by Roane Byrnes's father, James Fleming Sr.) even though the mansion burned down "years ago but almost in a perfect state of preservation." She did not explain how it is preserved, which only makes the description confusing. She also mentioned romantic tidbits, such as the "lady" of the manor, Jane Ann Beverly, being a "refugee from pitiful scandal in Va."

Laurel Hill, a plantation on the Lower Woodville Road south of Natchez, is another catalog entry by Moore in which she again erroneously emphasized the Spanish architectural influence in Natchez. She stated that the plantation predated the American Revolution and the rooms and wings of the manor house were built during the Spanish era, giving it a "Spanish atmosphere." She mentioned an "exquisite" small chapel, built as a memorial to the original owner's granddaughter, Anna Ellis Mercer, which featured rose windows and marble statuettes.[71]

Subsequent documentation of Laurel Hill proved Moore wrong. Although the manor house was destroyed by fire in the 1960s, the similarly built east and west dependency buildings survived (figure 4.10). With its mid-level brick course and symmetrical fenestration composition, these brick buildings are conclusively Federal in their design, and they reflect the tastes of early Anglo-American settlers in Natchez, not Spanish ones. The chapel, known as St. Mary's Chapel, to which Moore barely gave attention, was built by Natchez builder and architect James Hardie in 1839. It is one of the earliest examples of American Gothic Revival architecture in Mississippi (figure 4.11).[72] Why did it merit only a mention? It was not built in the late eighteenth century, and it was not Spanish. She omitted entirely other notable buildings on the plantation—most notably, the chapel's parsonage, the antebellum carriage house, and the billiard hall.

There are other homes that Moore declared to be "pure Spanish architecture": Texada and Saragossa.[73] While Texada was built during the Spanish period, she neglected to document that it also housed the first legislative session in the newly created state of Mississippi in 1817 (figure 4.12)[74] She alleged that Spanish governor Gayoso built Saragossa as a military fort, and she described it as a "quaint Spanish dwelling" (figure 4.13).[75] Although it was built in the late eighteenth century, Saragossa was not a military fort, and it was not built in the Spanish tradition. Architectural historian and Historic Natchez Foundation executive director Mary Warren "Mimi" Miller later documented Saragossa and stated that it was built in the West Indian vernacular tradition. In respond-

Figure 4.10: Laurel Hill Plantation, Jefferson County, Mississippi. (Library of Congress, Prints & Photographs Division, Historic American Buildings Survey, HABS MISS,32-ROD.V,1-)

Figure 4.11: St. Mary's Chapel, 1839, James Hardie, Architect-Builder, Laurel Hill Plantation, Adams County, Mississippi. (Photograph by the author)

ing to Moore's misinformation and clarifying the history of Saragossa, Miller stated, "Although historians unfamiliar with the unique history of Natchez often characterize such buildings [Saragossa] as Spanish in architectural character (Spain having governed Natchez from 1779 until 1798), the West Indian tradition is substantiated historically."[76]

In her role as a WPA historian, Moore submitted to Town a list of buildings to document in Natchez for HABS, and Town concentrated District 17's efforts on recording Natchez's architecture in 1934. The NPS assigned historian Stuart Cuthbertson to work with Moore and produce

Figure 4.12: Texada, Natchez, Mississippi, photographed by Lester Jones, 1940. (Library of Congress, Prints & Photographs Division, Historic American Buildings Survey, HABS MISS,1-NATCH,24-)

Figure 4.13: Saragossa, Natchez, Mississippi, photographed by James Butters, 1934. (Library of Congress, Prints & Photographs Division, Historic American Buildings Survey, HABS MISS,1-NATCH.V,14-)

the data sheets for the buildings. These included a listed description consisting of the date when the building was built, the architect who designed it, and the building's builder; they also recorded its present condition, the size of the building, and the building's material. A brief history of the building was included in the data sheets for the 1934 Natchez HABS program. The first building numerically assigned by Town was Rosalie (figure 4.14). Moore recorded family and local lore about the building. She wrote that the mansion was built by Peter Little, Mississippi's first lumber king, on the site of the old French fort where the

Figure 4.14: Rosalie, Natchez, Mississippi, photographed by Ralph Clynne, 1934. (Library of Congress, Prints & Photographs Division, Historic American Buildings Survey, HABS MISS,1-NATCH,1-)

infamous bloody American Indian massacre occurred. She asserted that the "real" designer of Rosalie was his brother-in-law, James Griffin, and that the mansion "is nearly all American." Questions arise when reading this summary. If Griffin was the real designer, who then claimed to have designed it earlier? And what does Moore mean in saying that the building "is nearly all American"? Moore placed higher regard on the early Spanish buildings. She then mentioned legendary stories about Little and his (first) ward and (then) young bride, Eliza; she elaborated on Rosalie's most illustrious guest, Ulysses Grant, who briefly resided in the villa during his visit and during the Union army's occupation of Natchez in 1863. But ever the canny and market-minded southern lady, Moore also stated that the "lady" of the house during the Civil War was loyal to the southern cause, even entertaining Jefferson Davis at Rosalie, but also struck up a cordial friendship with her northern occupiers.[77]

Edith Moore's summary of Gloucester exemplifies Silver's later assessment that she had difficulty "writing with a flourish" and failing to distinguish fact from fancy.[78] In actuality, Moore was very deliberate about blurring the facts and writing the stories she wanted to tell about them. In the following summary she dispensed with facts and instead imagined the grandeur of the villa: "The color of 'Gloucester' is exactly

Figure 4.15: Gloucester, Natchez, Mississippi, vicinity, photographed by Ralph Clynne, 1934. (Library of Congress, Prints & Photographs Division, Historic American Buildings Survey, HABS MISS,1-NATCH.V,1-)

right for its semi-tropical setting. The dark red brick, dull green blinds and aged white woodwork and stuccoed columns, blend into an undescribable picture. It is easy to understand that a few years later builders of 'Rosalie' and 'Arlington' had difficulty expressing their own originality, with such an inspiration so close at hand." She goes on to say, "Either the designer of 'Gloucester' was a Spanish builder, or he had made an intensive study of the earlier examples around Natchez, for certainly the house shows great Spanish colonial influence in both plan and detail." Then she made a confusing and conflicting argument:

> The interior is interesting in detail. Most all of the mouldings are similar to the early Spanish details. The mantels are especially fine. The library mantel is of Adam design, is white marble bodied with colored Italian marble inlaid panels, and hand carved marble corner inserts. Still all of this fine detail seems unimportant and is apt to be overlooked even by Architectural students, for the walls are literally covered by enormous oil paintings, some by the old masters, and the library shelves are filled with rare editions of fine books.[79]

As much as Moore wanted to believe that Gloucester had been built by a Spanish builder and embodied the finest qualities of Spanish architecture, and that the builders of Rosalie and Arlington struggled to express their own originality because they were American not cultured Spaniards, Gloucester is, and always has been, a decidedly American building, built in the Federal style (figure 4.15). In her description, she showed that she cannot reconcile her desire to make Gloucester Spanish with the actual details, especially as she mentioned the unambiguously English Adamesque interior features throughout the villa. Also in her description, she glossed over its famous owner, Winthrop Sargent, the first territorial governor, American Revolution patriot, and Massachusetts native, who purchased the suburban villa from the original builder, Abijah Hunt, another New Englander, and renamed it from Bellevue to Gloucester in honor of his Massachusetts birthplace. Hardly a Spanish enclave.[80]

In her typed full-page history reports for HABS, Moore expressed her opinion on Natchez architecture. In her report about Linden, she expressed her preference for the Spanish colonial period over the more recent antebellum one or even the early American period in Natchez: "The old Spanish colonial homes were more livable than the larger and more pretentious houses which were built following the evacuation [of the Spanish]. Of this class, 'Linden' stands to remind us of 'Concord' and others of the finer Spanish homes that have passed." She continued in describing Linden: "the detailed carving and mouldings are very much of the same as other Spanish examples; and recall 'Gilreath,' 'The Evans Home,' '313 Market Street,' 'Springfield,' and others" (figure 4.16).[81]

Moore's assertion that Linden was built by a Spaniard was based on family lore, conveyed to her by Mavis Feltus, and it was completely erroneous.[82] Similarly, by referring to the "Evans Home," Moore misled historians that the home of Lewis Evans, which was Arlington, was built by Spanish builders. Evans purchased the land on which Arlington stands after the US acquired West Florida from Spain in 1806. With the "Evans Home" and "Arlington" names, Moore intentionally confused the history of the villa.[83]

While Moore succeeded in skewing the record of Natchez's architectural history, Town exacerbated the situation by focusing nearly the entire HABS project on Natchez. With little to no oversight from either O'Neill in Washington or the HABS advisory committee in Jackson, Town was free to choose the buildings he wanted the District 17 team to measure and delineate. There were several reasons for the buildings he chose. With only what turned out to be six months to perform the HABS project, he obviously chose buildings that were convenient and easy to access. He was also attracted to the Mississippi historic buildings that more closely resembled the historic architecture of his native Louisiana. The District 17 team never measured any building north or east

Figure 4.16: Interior of the dining room and the "Punkah" at Linden, Natchez, Mississippi, photographed by James Butters, 1934. (Library of Congress, Prints & Photographs Division, Historic American Buildings Survey, HABS MISS,1-NATCH,6-)

of Madison County (central Mississippi). Town overlooked distinctive Mississippi architecture such as Longwood (1860) in Natchez or Waverley (1840) in West Point. He never considered documenting buildings that were located only blocks away from the Standard Life Building in Jackson (where District 17 worked), the Governor's Mansion and the Old Mississippi Capitol, or more eclectic and Victorian buildings such as The Oaks (Boyd House) and the Manship House, and he never considered documenting any historic building built on Mississippi's Gulf Coast. In a report to O'Neill in 1936, Town stated his preference for only documenting buildings in and around Natchez, and he requested that the District 17 team exchange territory, across state lines, in Tennessee and Louisiana.[84]

Town was so much more interested in documenting the historic architecture of southwest Mississippi and Louisiana that he even worked as a consultant for Koch and Louisiana's HABS District 18. As noted earlier, by 1934, Natchez had become the historic town for the state. He also had an easy working relationship with Edith Moore, who eagerly produced the history outline reports for each building District 17 recorded

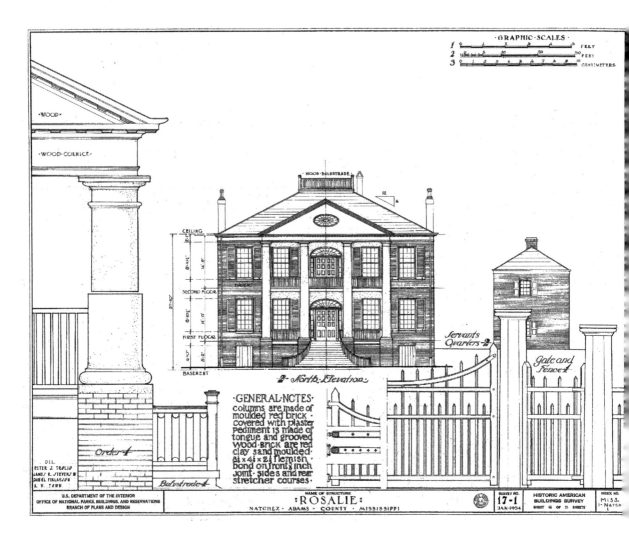

Figure 4.17: North elevation and details of Rosalie, HABS 17-1, Natchez, Mississippi, delineated by Peter J. Trolio, James R. Stevens III, Daniel Finayson, and A. Hays Town, measured in January 1934, delineated in March 1934. (Library of Congress, Prints & Photographs Division, Historic American Buildings Survey, HABS MISS,1-NATCH,1-)

in Natchez. The success of the pilgrimages brought in cultural tourism; leaders in Jackson saw the economic development in what the NGC women were doing there. Finally, Town and Overstreet were interested in cultivating working relationships there and secure work renovating the historic villas.

Town also wanted to measure and draw buildings he found interesting—those he could learn from and with historic details he could reproduce in his new designs. Trained in the same tradition as Peterson, Town understood the value of learning how a historic building was built. But unlike Peterson, who adhered to the Appleton ideas of professionalism in historic preservation, Town was an architect, who preferred designing new buildings over restoring old ones. Town's preference for designing new buildings based on historic buildings was in stark contrast to what preservationists like Peterson were advocating—preserving the

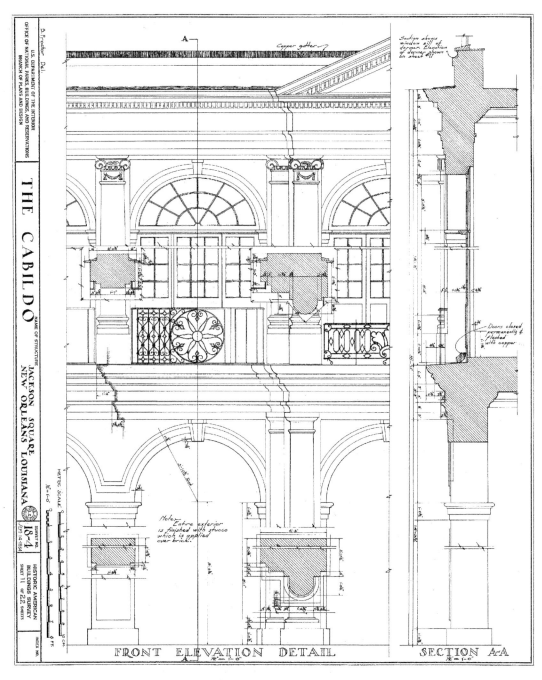

Figure 4.18: Front elevation and section details, The Cabildo, HABS 18-4, New Orleans, Louisiana, delineated by B. Proctor, measured in January 1934, delineated in November 1934. (Library of Congress, Prints & Photographs Division, Historic American Buildings Survey, HABS LA,36-NEWOR,4-)

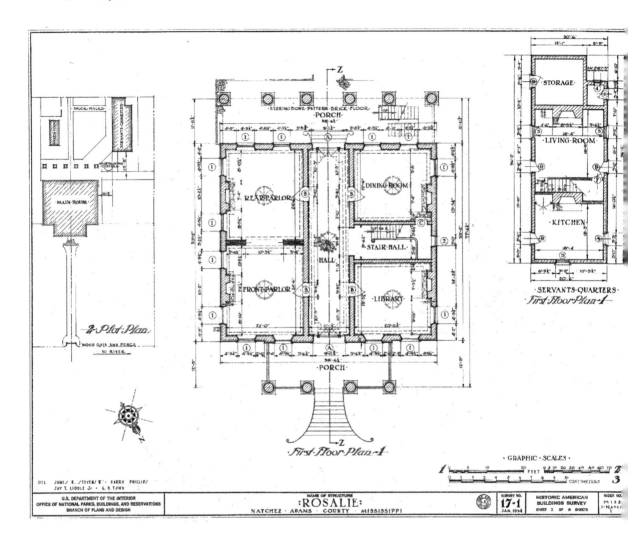

building in a way that reflects how it evolved. And like Koch, Town enjoyed using the Beaux Arts graphic technique known as *analytique* for documenting and delineating buildings. The *analytique* was a façade drawing graphic, which sometimes combined plan and section drawings juxtaposing entablature details and window and door details, and it demonstrated how the five orders of classical architecture were used in a building design or an existing building.[85]

The north elevation of Rosalie (HABS 17-1) shows how Town used the *analytique* technique in building documentation (figure 4.17). Details of the front portico, column, entablature, and railing are juxtaposed with the building elevation. Town placed the landscape elements, specifically the front gate, around the front façade and the north elevation of the dependency building. Town took some license in composing the drawings, which made it more of a compelling work of art and less of a technical recording of a historic building.

Figure 4.19: First-floor plan and plot plan of Rosalie, HABS 17-1, Natchez, Mississippi, delineated by James R. Stevens III, Harry Phillips, Jay T. Liddle Jr., and A. Hays Town, measured in January 1934, delineated in March 1934. (Library of Congress, Prints & Photographs Division, Historic American Buildings Survey, HABS MISS,1-NATCH,1-)

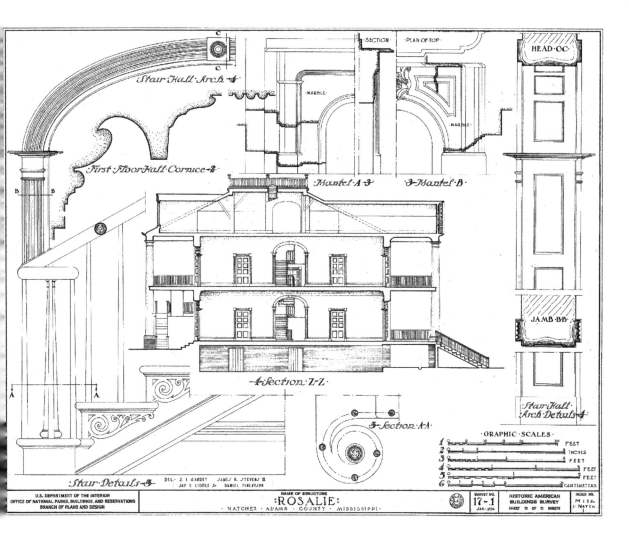

Figure 4.20: Section drawing of Rosalie, HABS 17-1, Natchez, Mississippi, delineated by J. I. Gaudet, James R. Stevens III, Daniel Finlayson, and Jay T. Liddle Jr., measured in January 1934, delineated in March 1934. (Library of Congress, Prints & Photographs Division, Historic American Buildings Survey, HABS MISS,1-NATCH,1-)

Dick Koch also used the *analytique* technique, but in the District 18 (Louisiana) 1934 HABS drawings he used it in a more academic manner. While Town explored elements as a designer, Koch documented the historic buildings in New Orleans in the same way as the French nineteenth-century architect Paul Letarouilly delineated the great buildings of Rome, which was more straightforward and intended for the historian as much as for the architect. Even the fine lineweight of District 18's detail drawings of the typical building bay of the Cabildo (HABS 18-4) mimicked Letarouilly's engraved drawings (figure 4.18).

Town's District 17 drawings are more illustrative than technically informative. The first-floor plan of Rosalie shows exquisite lettering; brick paving patterns are carefully depicted, but the plot plan, located to the left side, omits landscaping elements and the surrounding context (figure 4.19).

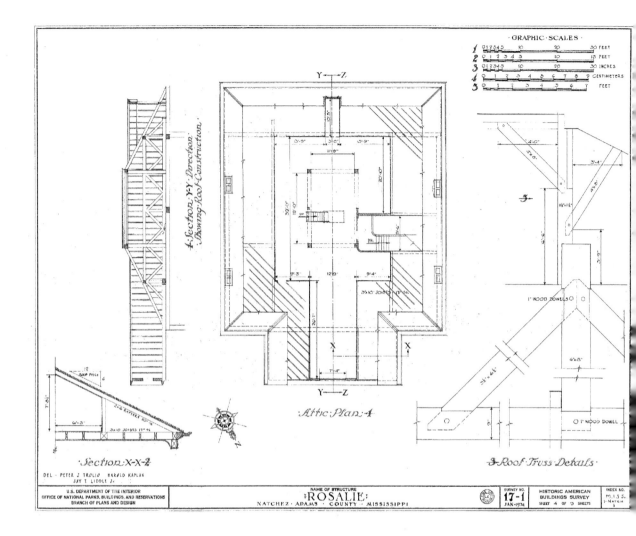

Figure 4.21: Attic plan and roof structural details of Rosalie, HABS 17-1, Natchez, Mississippi, delineated by Peter J. Trolio, Harold Kaplan, and Jay T. Liddle Jr., measured in January 1934, delineated in March 1934. (Library of Congress, Prints & Photographs Division, Historic American Buildings Survey, HABS MISS,1-NATCH,1-)

The sectional drawing of Rosalie demonstrates Town's preference for the *analytique* as an artistic expression and suggests that he may have intended to produce the HABS set not only for the men in Washington but as promotional graphics to be used by the NGC women as well. The NGC women used the HABS drawings in several brochures, most notably in promoting Connelly's Tavern (figure 4.20).

Unlike Koch's District 18 drawings, even technical drawings like the roof structure and attic plan drawing for Rosalie are more graphically illustrative than technically informative (figure 4.21). Key dimensions for the overall height of the roof structure are omitted. The dimensions stated on the drawings provide only marginal information on how the building was constructed. In short, one could not replicate the structure using this drawing.

District 17 documented only two of its eleven buildings outside of Natchez: Shamrock (HABS 17-2) in Vicksburg and the Chapel of the

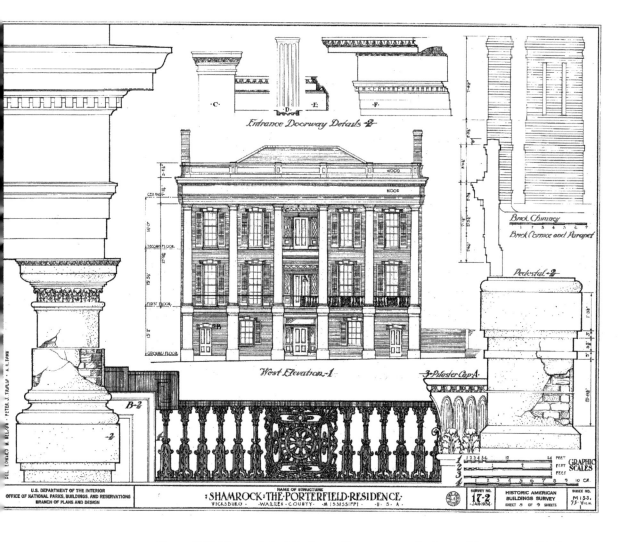

Figure 4.22: West elevation and architectural details of Shamrock, HABS 17-2, Vicksburg, Mississippi, delineated by Edward M. Nelson, Peter J. Trolio, and Jay T. Liddle Jr., measured in February 1934, delineated in April 1934. (Library of Congress, Prints & Photographs Division, Historic American Buildings Survey, HABS MISS,75-VICK,1-)

Cross (HABS 17-3) in Madison County near Jackson. Town most likely included Shamrock on the HABS list for fellow architect William Stanton, who lived and worked in Vicksburg. Stanton measured Shamrock, and he and Town delineated it in a four-sheet set. In his historic building report, Stanton stated that "the house today is almost a complete wreck, and is probably condemned as unsafe by the City of Vicksburg." He also noted that, "in all probability, if no attempt at restoration is made, another decade will find only a mass of ruins on the site of a show place of long ago" (figure 4.22).[86]

The Chapel of the Cross in Madison County was the only building Town and his team documented that was built in the English Gothic style. The small chapel is located only fifteen miles north of Jackson and was thus convenient for the team members to travel to and measure. Town was personally fond of the small plantation church, which was based on Saint Michael's, a twelfth-century church in Long Staunton,

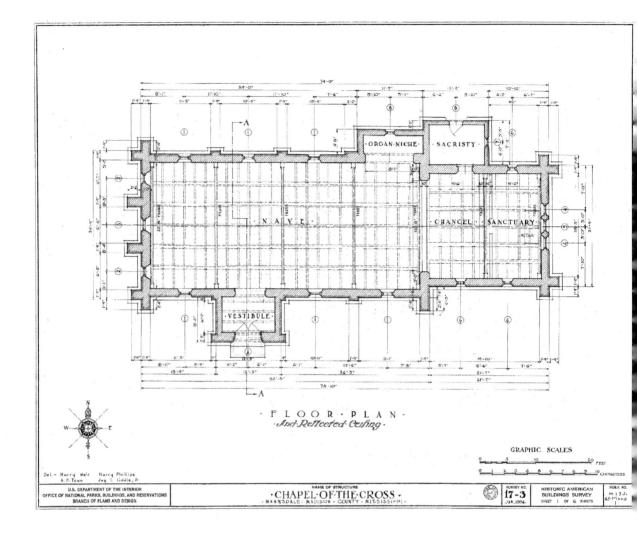

Figure 4.23: Floor plan of the Chapel of the Cross, HABS 17-3, Mannsdale, Mississippi, delineated by Harry Weir, Harry Phillips, Jay T. Liddle Jr., and A. Hays Town, measured and delineated in January 1934. (Library of Congress, Prints & Photographs Division, Historic American Buildings Survey, HABS MISS,45-MAND,1-)

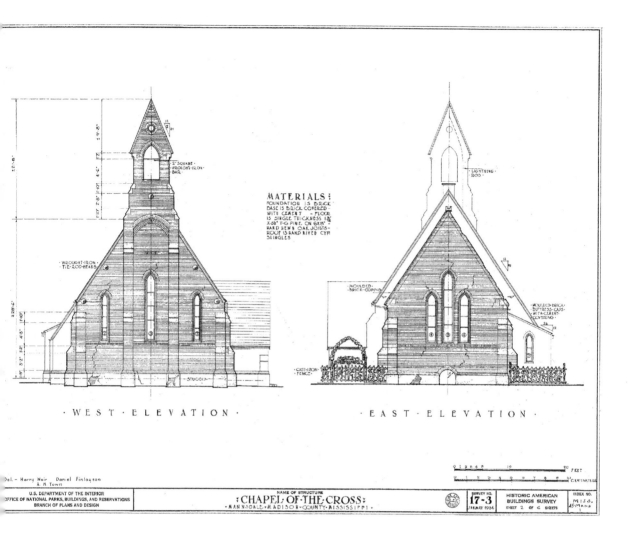

Figure 4.24: West and east elevations of the Chapel of the Cross, HABS 17-3, Mannsdale, Mississippi, delineated by Harry Weir, Daniel Finlayson, and A. Hays Town, measured and delineated in January 1934. (Library of Congress, Prints & Photographs Division, Historic American Buildings Survey, HABS MISS,45-MAND,1-)

Cambridgeshire, England. The Episcopal Diocese of Mississippi believed that the chapel had been designed by an English architect in 1849, but it was later determined that New York architect Frank Wills designed it (figure 4.23).[87]

The elevations for the Chapel of the Cross also contain pertinent technical information. Roof pitches and building heights are noted (figure 4.24). Brick, stucco, and cast iron are rendered, and a brief statement of all of the materials is centered in the west and east elevation drawings. Even the lightning rod is located in the belfry.

Town painstakingly drew the cross section of the chapel and interior details on what can be easily agreed was one of the most elegant and skillful HABS sheets ever produced (figure 4.25). The windowsills and jambs are drawn, as well as the way the interior plaster finish was applied to the building's brick shell.

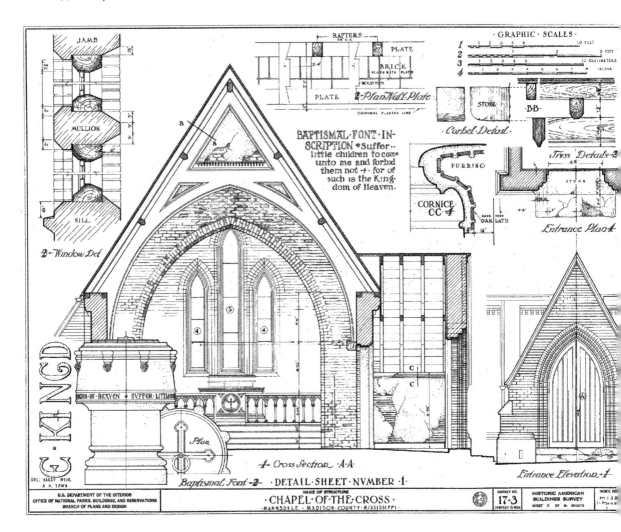

Figure 4.25: Cross section and interior details of the Chapel of the Cross, HABS 17-3, Mannsdale, Mississippi, delineated by Harry Weir and A. Hays Town, measured and delineated in January 1934. (Library of Congress, Prints & Photographs Division, Historic American Buildings Survey, HABS MISS,45-MAND,1-)

Figure 4.26: Railing details of the Chapel of the Cross, HABS 17-3, Mannsdale, Mississippi, delineated by Harry Weir and A. Hays Town, measured and delineated in January 1934. (Library of Congress, Prints & Photographs Division, Historic American Buildings Survey, HABS MISS,45-MAND,1-)

With the large-scale elevations of the cast-iron gates, which were made to resemble oak branches, the Chapel of the Cross HABS set is the most comprehensive in the District 17 collection (figure 4.26). Town and his staff measured and produced the six-sheet set stunningly fast and extremely thoroughly. It is obvious that Town was quite smitten with the small English-inspired church, and he wanted to document its design for use in a future design of a new building. Drawing as record and inspiration was what Peterson saw while working with Perry, Shaw & Hepburn in Williamsburg and Yorktown; Town learned how to measure historic buildings from Koch.

The District 17 collection varies in its depiction of historic buildings, from the technically detailed to the illustrative, but for the exception of Shamrock and the Chapel of the Cross, the collection is exclusively of domestic buildings in Natchez. Drawings of Gloucester follow the

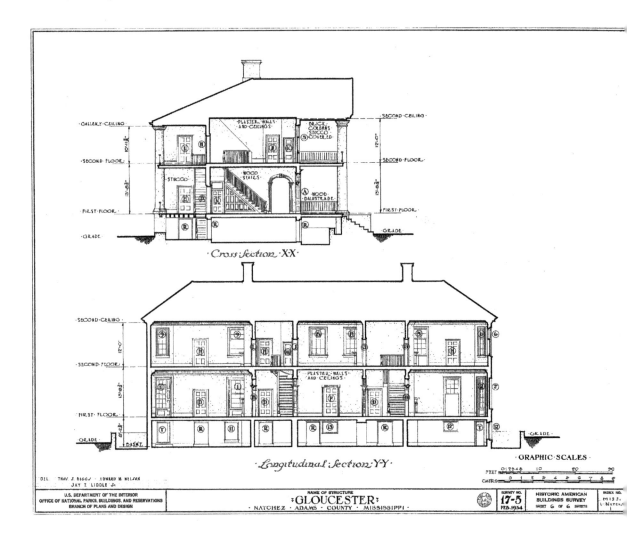

Figure 4.27: Building sections of Gloucester, HABS 17-5, Natchez, Mississippi, delineated by Thomas J. Riggs, Edward M. Nelson, and Jay T. Liddle Jr., measured in February 1934, delineated in April 1934. (Library of Congress, Prints & Photographs Division, Historic American Buildings Survey, HABS MISS,1-NATCH.V,1-)

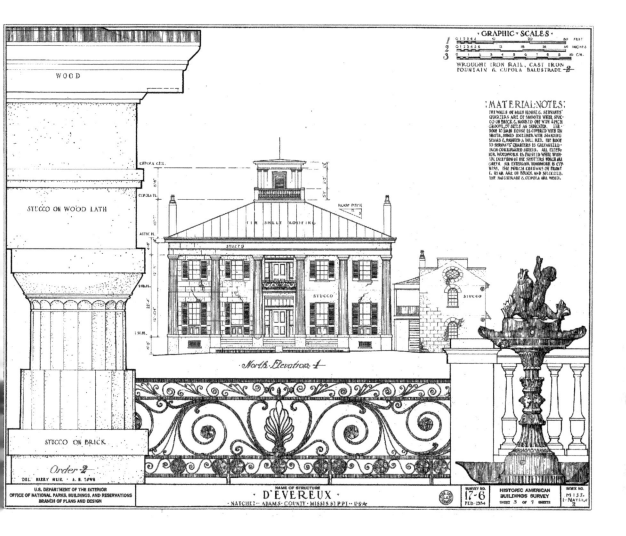

Figure 4.28: North elevation and architectural details of D'Evereux, HABS 17-6, Natchez, Mississippi, delineated by Harry Weir and A. Hays Town, measured in February 1934, delineated in April 1934. (Library of Congress, Prints & Photographs Division, Historic American Buildings Survey, HABS MISS,1-NATCH.V,2-)

National Park Service's intent of detail: its building sections are factual, and the recording is informative. One can understand the spatial and formal arrangement of the Federal period villa (figure 4.27).

The drawing set for D'Evereux reflects Town's fondness of the illustration more than the technical drawing. District 17 followed Town's template for the HABS *analytique*—the portico details paced on the left side of the sheet and the cast-iron railing elevation grounding the composition (figure 4.28).

After completion of the first sets of drawings for Gilreath's Hill Tavern (Connelly's Tavern), Shamrock, and the Chapel of the Cross, District 17 documented Arlington in a straightforward fashion and four Natchez buildings (Van Court House, Arrighi, Linden, and 311-313 Market Street) in a more illustrative manner; this difference suggests that they intended that these four building sets be used to promote the NGC women's bud-

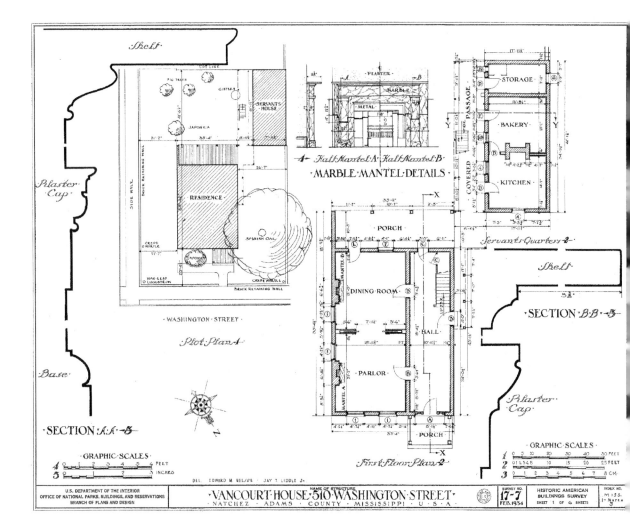

Figure 4.29: First-floor plan of the Van Court House, HABS 17-7, Natchez, Mississippi, delineated by Edward M. Wilson and Jay Liddle Jr., measured in February 1934, delineated in April 1934. (Library of Congress, Prints & Photographs Division, Historic American Buildings Survey, HABS MISS,1-NATCH,3-)

ding tourist enterprise. While these buildings were not featured in the first pilgrimages, the NGC women felt that they were worth preserving and perhaps would be featured in future pilgrimages after being renovated. With the exception of the Arlington set, the drawings are illustrations and not technical drawings of the buildings. With the Van Court House, Town and his young architects were more audacious in using the *analytique* technique, but they also included pertinent technical information.

With its simple double-pile parlor and side hall layout, the Van Court House is a typical Federal-style townhouse, much simpler than the grand villas Gloucester, Rosalie, and D'Evereux. It could easily be mistaken for a townhouse in Alexandria, Virginia, or Annapolis, Maryland. But District 17 used the Van Court House to demonstrate its architects' mastery of the *analytique*. The first-floor plan incorporates a detailed site plan to the left of the simple plan. Interior pilaster and cornice profiles frame

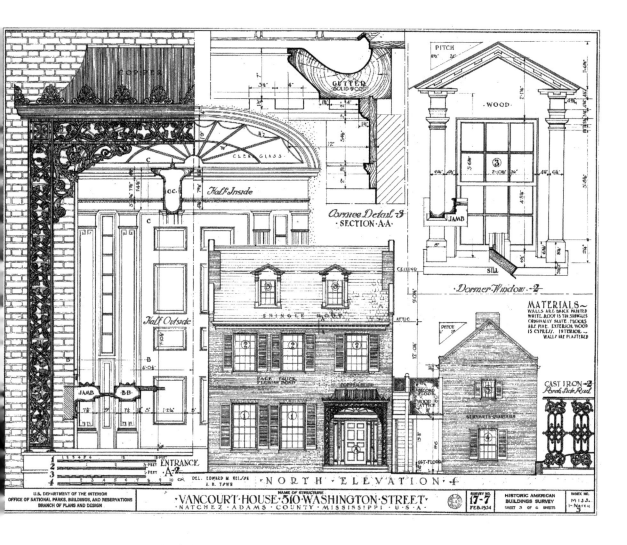

Figure 4.30: North elevation and exterior details of the Van Court House, HABS 17-7, Natchez, Mississippi, delineated by Edward M. Wilson and A. Hays Town, measured in February 1934, delineated in April 1934. (Library of Congress, Prints & Photographs Division, Historic American Buildings Survey, HABS MISS,1-NATCH,3-)

the left and right sides of the sheet. An elevation, displaying half elevations of two mantels, is drawn above the floor plan (figure 4.29).

The north elevation of the Van Court House is perhaps one of the most famous HABS sheets ever produced.[88] HABS director Catherine Lavoie displayed this drawing sheet in her exhibition celebrating the seventy-fifth anniversary of HABS in 2009. Town created an *analytique* drawing of rich complexity but also simple clarity. The elaborate cast-iron and copper front porch, along with the front door elevation, seamlessly slips behind the much smaller scale north elevation. The main gutter and cornice detail and the dormer elevation occupy the top right of the sheet. Profiles of door and window jambs are interspersed, and the large-scale drawing of the brick wall juxtaposed against the smaller-scale elevation drawing is compelling. Quite simply, it is a drawing that you want to spend time studying (figure 4.30).

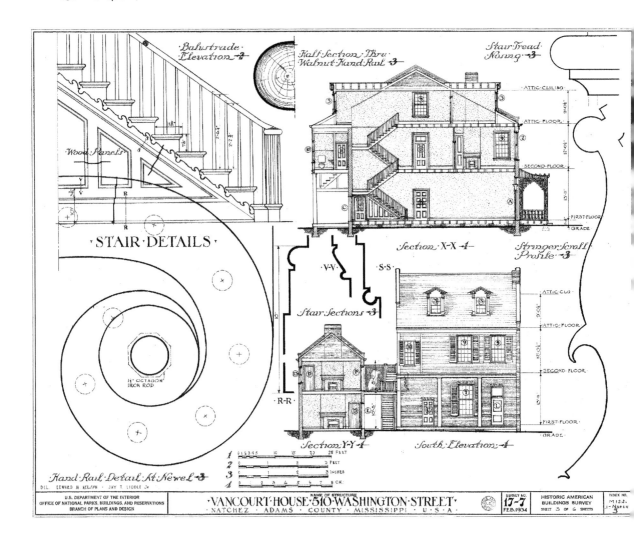

Figure 4.31: South elevation, building section, and stair railing details of the Van Court House, HABS 17-7, Natchez, Mississippi, delineated by Edward M. Wilson and Jay Liddle Jr., measured in February 1934, delineated in April 1934. (Library of Congress, Prints & Photographs Division, Historic American Buildings Survey, HABS MISS,1-NATCH,3-)

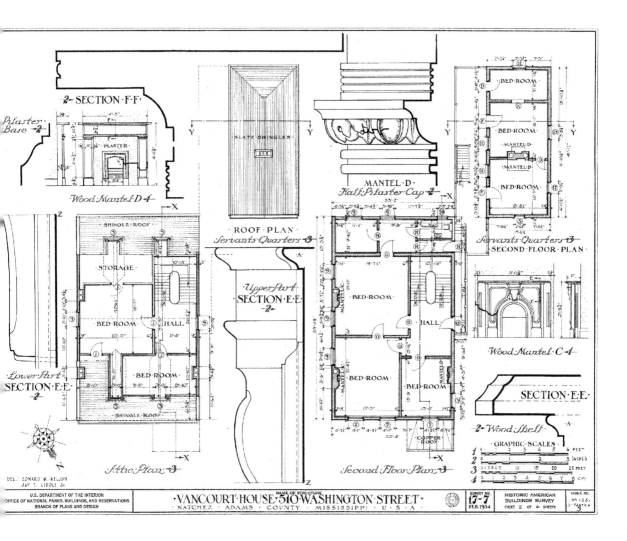

Figure 4.32: Second-floor plan, attic plan, and interior details of the Van Court House, HABS 17-7, Natchez, Mississippi, delineated by Edward M. Wilson and Jay Liddle Jr., measured in February 1934, delineated in April 1934. (Library of Congress, Prints & Photographs Division, Historic American Buildings Survey, HABS MISS,1-NATCH,3-)

The sheet showing the south elevation and the building section presents historical architectural details of the house along with modern conveniences (such as the toilet and sink in the bathroom). This suggests that Town was more interested in cataloging the building for his own design library than he was in providing the National Park Service and the Library of Congress with a record drawing of the house (figure 4.31).

The sheet with the second-floor plan and attic floor plan is another example of how Town used the *analytique* method to convey to the viewer as much information as possible (figure 4.32). But unlike Koch's Cabildo drawings, in which the historian is the intended viewer, Town is presenting the Van Court House for the architect and the designer. This is a set of drawings intended for an architect to study and from which to draw ideas for a new design.

252　Chapter 4

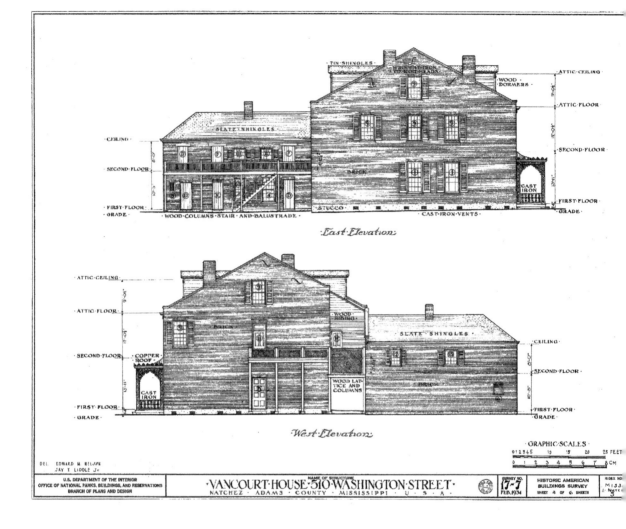

Figure 4.33: East and west elevations of the Van Court House, HABS 17-7, Natchez, Mississippi, delineated by Edward M. Wilson and Jay Liddle Jr., measured in February 1934, delineated in April 1934. (Library of Congress, Prints & Photographs Division, Historic American Buildings Survey, HABS MISS,1-NATCH,3-)

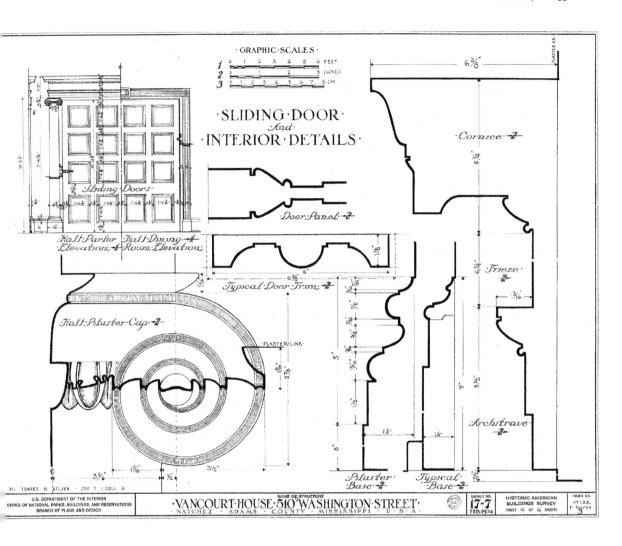

Figure 4.34: Interior details of the Van Court House, HABS 17-7, Natchez, Mississippi, delineated by Edward M. Wilson and Jay Liddle Jr., measured in February 1934, delineated in April 1934. (Library of Congress, Prints & Photographs Division, Historic American Buildings Survey, HABS MISS,1-NATCH,3-)

When we consider the scale and detail found in the Van Court House, it is reasonable to assume that Town was recording this building much in the same way Fitch recorded Auburn five years earlier—to generate ideas for a new design. For Town, Natchez was the font of ideas for residential design for clients in the wealthier capitol city, Jackson. It seemed reasonable to him to not only send the drawings to Washington but also keep a set of them in his office. Town recognized the suitability of a design like the Van Court House for emerging automobile-based suburbs and neighborhoods in Jackson, such as the twentieth-century streetcar suburb Fondren. What better precedent to use than a Natchez nineteenth-century suburban villa for a new modern southern suburb (figures 4.33 and 4.34)?

Arrighi (HABS 17-9) most certainly reminded Town of his days as a student at Tulane, measuring and drawing the historic store buildings

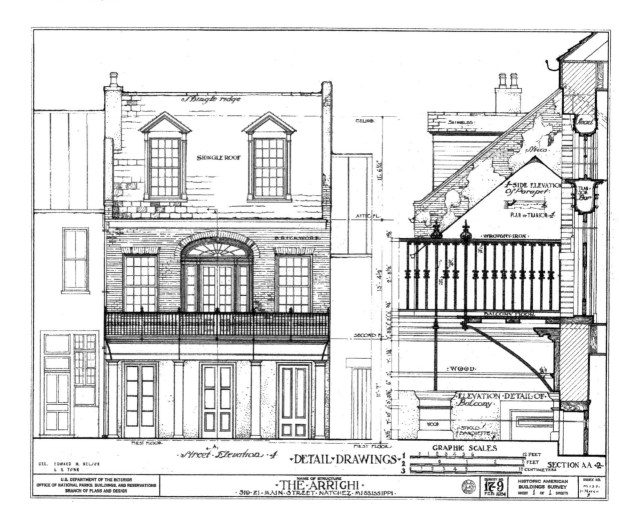

Figure 4.35: North elevation and details of the Arrighi, HABS 17-9, Natchez, Mississippi, delineated by Edward M. Wilson and A. Hays Town, measured in February 1934, delineated in April 1934. (Library of Congress, Prints & Photographs Division, Historic American Buildings Survey, HABS MISS,1-NATCH,5-)

in New Orleans's French Quarter. The use of brick and stucco, the iron balcony, and the intimate two-story façade is reminiscent of the eighteenth-century architecture found in the Crescent City. Only recording it on one architectural sheet, delineated an *analytique* that captured its architectural character (figure 4.35).

Toward the end of the busy six-month period of the first HABS program, District 17 had developed a template in the *analytique* for producing HABS drawings, which was based on National Park Service criteria specified in the HABS Circulars and Town's and his District 17 team's interest. The Linden (HABS 17-10) drawing set combined technical information, which Peterson and O'Neill stipulated for HABS drawings, and the designer-focused *analytiques*, which Town favored (figures 4.36 and 4.37).

The same artistic mastery and technical virtuosity are found in the Arlington record (HABS 17-8), but in this HABS set, like the one for Lin-

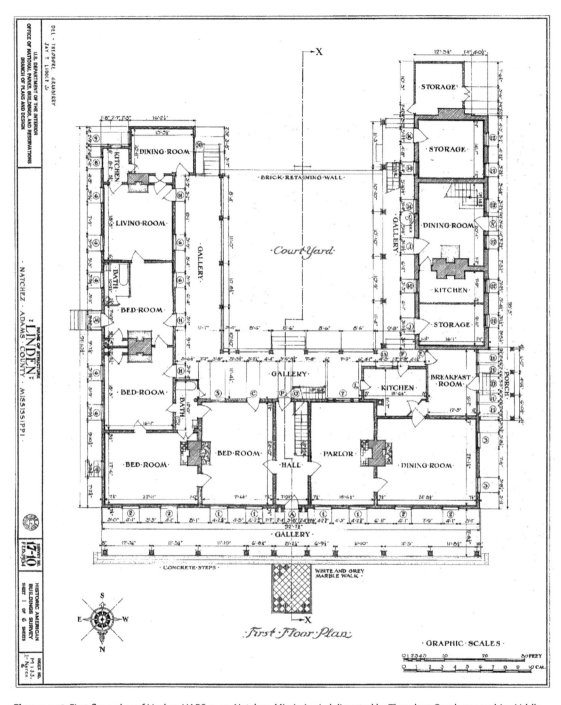

Figure 4.36: First-floor plan of Linden, HABS 17-10, Natchez, Mississippi, delineated by Theodore Granberry and Jay Liddle Jr., measured in February 1934, delineated in April 1934. (Library of Congress, Prints & Photographs Division, Historic American Buildings Survey, HABS MISS,1-NATCH,6-)

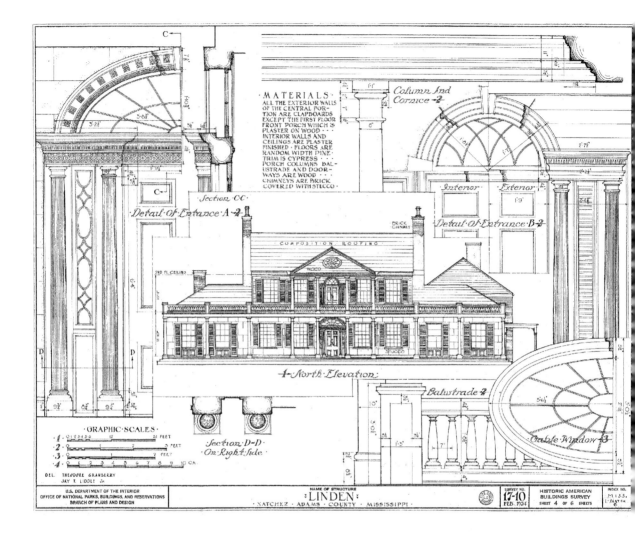

Figure 4.37: North elevation and exterior details of Linden, HABS 17-10, Natchez, Mississippi, delineated by Theodore Granberry and Jay Liddle Jr., measured in February 1934, delineated in April 1934. (Library of Congress, Prints & Photographs Division, Historic American Buildings Survey, HABS MISS,1-NATCH,6-)

den, Edith Moore produced erroneous information, partly based on what Annie Barnum told her and partly based on her imagination (figures 4.38 and 4.39). Moore stated that "according to authentic papers kept by the Natchez chapter of the D.A.R., Arlington was designed by noted Elizabethtown, New Jersey, architect John Hampton White, who was a cousin of the noted late nineteenth century architect, Stanford White."[89] She claimed that John Hampton White came to Natchez during the Spanish regime; in 1808, he married Jane Surget and spent the next eleven years building Arlington, but died before it was completed. Jane, as a widow, spent the next five years completing the home and then planned a lavish housewarming party on June 30, 1825. But the morning after the party, Jane was found murdered, and her diamonds were missing. Moore claimed an enslaved person committed the murder and reported that Jane's sister, Charlotte Surget Bingaman, inherited the villa.[90]

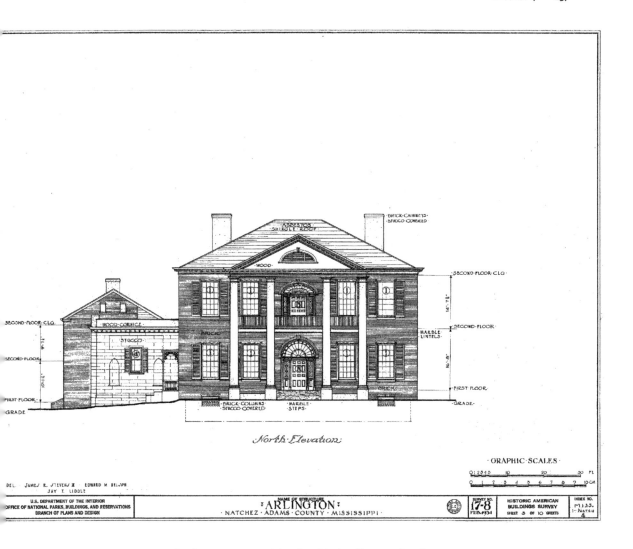

Figure 4.38: North elevation of Arlington, HABS 17-8, Natchez, Mississippi, delineated by James R. Stevens III, Edward M. Nelson, and Jay Liddle Jr., measured in February 1934, delineated in April 1934. (Library of Congress, Prints & Photographs Division, Historic American Buildings Survey, HABS MISS,1-NATCH,4-)

Perhaps unsurprisingly, this is all completely untrue.

Through archival research conducted in 1973, Mississippi Department of Archives and History architectural historian Ronald Miller determined that Arlington was not built by John Hampton White for his wife, Jane. Instead, it was built by Lewis Evans, who later sold it to Jonathan Thompson, who most likely added the Federal-style improvements.[91] According to tradition, the house was designed by John Hampton White, a native of New Jersey, and was constructed in 1816–21 for his wife, Jane Surget White. In his National Historic Landmark Nomination of the house, NPS survey architect Paul Goeldner acknowledged the "much-quoted tradition" that White designed the villa, but he then reinforced Ronald Miller's argument by stating that deed records showed that Thompson built Arlington and that it was built in 1820.[92] The Federal style of the house broadens the range of when it was constructed,

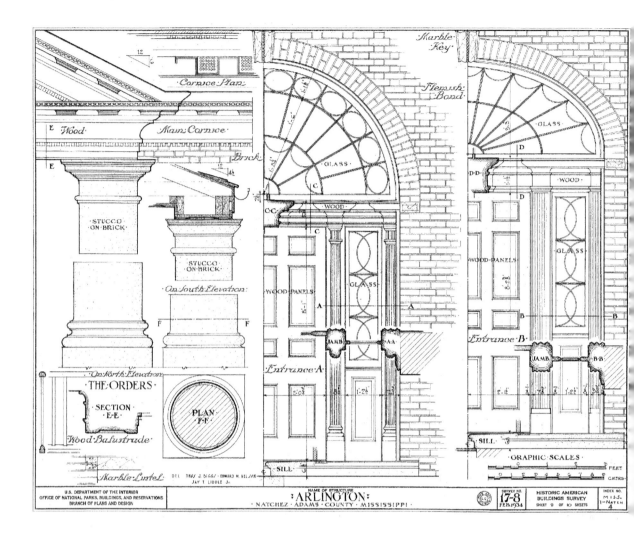

Figure 4.39: Exterior details of Arlington, HABS 17-8, Natchez, Mississippi, delineated by Thomas S. Biggs, Edward M. Nelson, and Jay Liddle Jr., measured in February 1934, delineated in April 1934. (Library of Congress, Prints & Photographs Division, Historic American Buildings Survey, HABS MISS,1-NATCH,4-)

between 1816 and 1821.[93] Due to many inaccuracies such as those regarding Arlington, architectural historians for the rest of the twentieth century were correcting Edith Moore's false reports. By the end of 1934, NPS staff began to grow suspicious of Moore's ability as a historian and Cuthbertson's ability to manage Moore, but no one intervened to verify her histories of Natchez architecture.

Perhaps the most outlandish and flawed set of records produced by Hays Town and Edith Moore was for 311-313 Market Street (HABS 17-11), also known as "the Priest House." Documentation of this rather humble building demonstrates how closely Moore worked with Town (figure 4.40). Today, the HABS set and additional photography of 311-313 Market Street are more confusing to the novice historian than any other HABS set produced by District 17. 311-313 Market Street is no longer located at the address it's known by; instead, it was moved by the Nat-

Figure 4.40:
Photograph of 311-313 Market Street, HABS 17-11, Natchez, Mississippi, by Ralph Clynne, February 1934. (Library of Congress, Prints & Photographs Division, Historic American Buildings Survey, HABS MISS,1-NATCH,7-)

chez Garden Club (at the behest of Roane Byrnes) in 1956 to its current location, near the House on Ellicott's Hill, 205 Canal Street. It is now part of "Lawyer's Row" (figure 4.41).

At the upper right corner of the title sheet for 311-313 Market Street, Town stated that the building was erected in 1787 for Father William Savage. However, in the fact sheet of the historical report, Town called the building "Parish House (Home of San Salvador)," and the building was erected in 1786, three stories in height and built out of wood and brick. He then added under additional details: "This house is of provisional Spanish

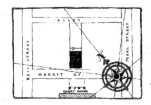

architectural design. Built by order of the Spanish King, for 4 selected priests who came to teach the English-speaking people Catholicism."⁹⁴

Moore provided the most detailed history of Priest House/311-313 Market Street. She noted that Market Street was laid out prior to 1787, and where the street intersected Pearl Street, the Spanish Market once stood (it had been demolished in the previous decade). She stated that it was "without doubt, one of the oldest houses in Natchez, erected in all probability about 1788." She based her argument on information she claimed she found in the "Archives of the Royal Treasury of the Island of Cuba"—in spite of never having traveled to Cuba to research this archive—and stated that the king of Spain appointed Catholic priests William Savage, Michael Lamport, Gregory White, and Constantine MacKenna to establish a Catholic church in Natchez. She quoted Don Jose del Rosario Naltes, honorary provincial intendant and general custodian of the Archives

Figure 4.41: Title sheet for 311-313 Market Street, HABS 17-11, Natchez, Mississippi, delineated by Harry Weir, measured in February 1934, delineated in March 1934. (Library of Congress, Prints & Photographs Division, Historic American Buildings Survey, HABS MISS,1-NATCH,7-)

Figure 4.42: South and north elevations for 311-313 Market Street, HABS 17-11, Natchez, Mississippi, delineated by Harry Weir and A. Hays Town, measured in February 1934, delineated in March 1934. (Library of Congress, Prints & Photographs Division, Historic American Buildings Survey, HABS MISS,1-NATCH,7-)

of Cuba: "It was therein declared, among the other things, to be the will of His Majesty that parochial stations of Irish priests should be established in Natchez and such other places in the said province as might be deemed suitable, for the purpose of attracting the English and American settlers, their children, and families to our religion." She further stated that Father William Savage became the priest in charge of the parish of Holy Savior of Natchez in 1789 and that he built the old house on Market Street.[95]

Moore reiterated her argument that the simple residence on Market Street was most definitely Spanish-built, citing a petition to the royal governor from Father Francisco Lennan in 1794, which mentioned the building in a request for more land for it, to be used for gardens. She wrote that Father Lennan became the head priest after Father Savage left with the Spanish troops and that 313 Market Street then became the property of "Uncle Sam."

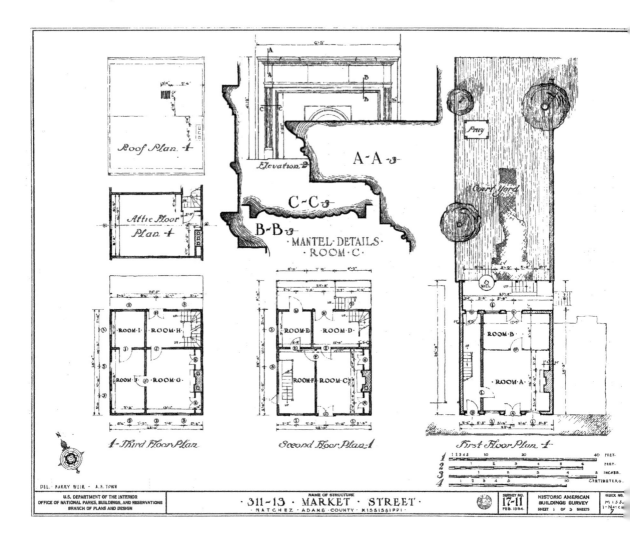

Figure 4.43: Floor plans and site plan for 311-313 Market Street, HABS 17-11, Natchez, Mississippi, delineated by Harry Weir and A. Hays Town, measured in February 1934, delineated in March 1934. (Library of Congress, Prints & Photographs Division, Historic American Buildings Survey, HABS MISS,1-NATCH,7-)

Town provided a detailed description of the house, but he rationalized his assessment in saying at the outset, "The old Catholic Priest's Presbytery is almost different from other Spanish examples in Mississippi, although there is a likeness in woodwork details and in construction methods." He then described the building: it had a lower story built of red brick, and in the center of the second-floor façade, there was a beautiful doorway with an elliptical fan light surrounded with a "dentiled" rake cornice, supported by fluted pilasters. He remarked that in its existing condition it had wood railing, but he had little doubt that the door once entered onto a balcony with a delicate hand-wrought iron railing. He stated that the original roof was covered with slate and that the exterior details matched the ones found on the "Spanish Tavern" also known as Gilreath's Hill, and said the house was likely painted white and the shutters were dark green, "typical of the original Spanish Types" (figure 4.42).[96]

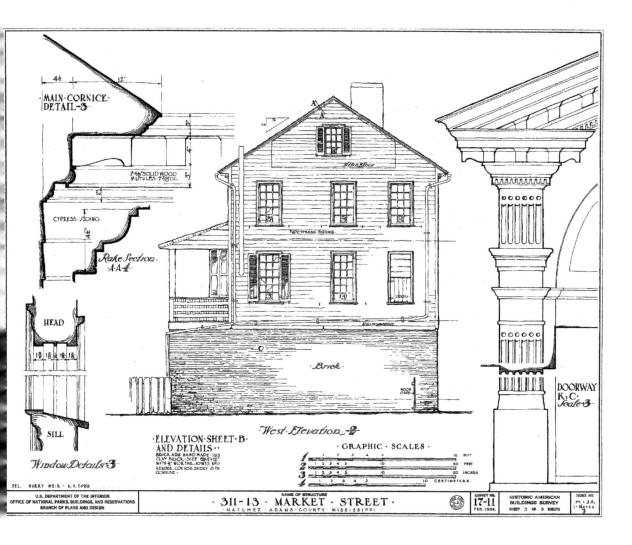

Figure 4.44: West elevation and details for 311-313 Market Street, HABS 17-11, Natchez, Mississippi, delineated by Harry Weir and A. Hays Town, measured in February 1934, delineated in March 1934. (Library of Congress, Prints & Photographs Division, Historic American Buildings Survey, HABS MISS,1-NATCH,7-)

Town went into great detail describing the Spanish courtyard, with its high brick walls and original brick cistern. In describing the interior, he stated that the original woodwork and mantels remained in the dilapidated building (figures 4.43 and 4.44).

The HABS set for 311-313 may be one of the most fallacious entries in the entire HABS archives. Nearly everything recorded about it is incorrect. 311-313 Market Street was never the "Parish House" or the "Home of San Salvador." It was not built by the Spanish in 1787. Neither Father Savage nor Father Lennan ever lived in it, and "Uncle Sam" did not take possession of it after the Spanish army left Natchez. It never had a balcony. Even today, the listing of it in the Library of Congress is misleading in two archives: HABS and the Francis Johnston Photography Collection. The history report for HABS 17-11 proves how far Moore went in trying to prove that Natchez was a Spanish colonial city. It exemplifies the confusing Natchez narrative.

What Moore called the Priest House is actually the James Andrews House, and it was built in 1806, not 1786 or 1787 or 1788 or 1789. Andrews, an American, was a prominent local merchant, and it only makes sense that he located his residence and ground-level business near the old Spanish Market. Father Savage did come to Natchez, and in the eighteenth century the land, which the house was later built on, was owned by a Catholic priest. But the actual priest's house was located across the street from 311-313 Market Street, on the site of the Adams County Courthouse. The wood frame house may have been built by an American builder, Alexander Miller, in the American Federal style. The fanlight doorway, with fluted pilasters, was actually the front door of the building at the ground level. The one-story first floor, with antique brick walls that Town described, was built after 1820, when, like many streets in Natchez, Market Street was graded. The jigsaw railing, placed in front of the door, is Italianate in its detailing and was added after 1870. It may have had either a rear balcony or a double-tiered porch on the rear elevation, since an original doorway with double-leaf doors and a fanlight now opens onto nothing.[97] The interior woodwork and mantel are Federal in style, embodying the tastes of Americans during the first decades of the Republic.[98]

Town's drawings are misleading as well. He depicted the building in artistic illustrative drawings, containing little technical information. The drawings are more sketch-like than a technical architectural record. Town seemed enamored of glorifying the near-ruinous state of the building. Shutters are shown shattered, and some of the detailing, including the mullions in the windows, are dashed lightly, as one might do in a sketch. In the plans, dimensions are shown but are not emphasized, and the merging of mantel profiles with mantel elevations along with the rendered site plan makes the drawing difficult to comprehend. The raised brick basement, shown in the west elevation, does not convey that this part of the house is not original.

PERSONALISM AND HABS

Edith Moore's personalism altered the history of James Andrews House so much so that it continues to convey a story of Natchez that never was. As an artist-architect rather than a preservationist, Town produced captivating drawings, but the technical information (dimensions and the way these buildings were built) is lacking. Later historic building surveys and recordation projects of Natchez continued to incorrectly call it the "Priest House."[99] Recent guidebooks, such as *The Majesty of Natchez* (reprinted in 2007), describe it as the "Priest's House" built in 1783—it keeps getting older!—and claim it was "the home of the beloved Father Lennan for more than fifteen years" and "the first in Natchez to change hands under the American regime."[100]

Did Moore maliciously attempt to distort the history of Natchez? No. In 1934, she wanted to value a heritage in Natchez that she preferred—the Spanish one.[101] She was not a trained or knowledgeable historian; she relied upon chains of title for establishing dates and prior ownerships, and she never considered that a prior building on the site may have been demolished or if the site had been subdivided. She never actually fabricated whole histories of historic Natchez buildings, but she most definitely embellished them. She was following the zest to embrace this romantic heritage in the same way that Roane Byrnes dressed up like a Spanish señora and told tall tales about Spanish Natchez at "Saragossa." Moore's belief in Natchez's heritage compelled her to write the histories that she wrote.[102] As Lowenthal reminds us, "History is the past that actually happened, heritage is a partisan perversion, the past manipulated for some present aim."[103] In 1934, Moore wanted to construct a narrative that told Natchez history the way she wanted to be. Her aim was to make Natchez appealing to herself, the NGC women, and the tourists, who sought to escape to a romanticized past of "let's pretend."

Town approached the HABS project the way Peterson and Chatelain later described it: he embraced the idea that it was a project created by architects for architects and, for him, it was an architect's dream. Town sought to record Natchez architecture as a designer and an architect. District 17's artistically composed drawings captured Town's designer flair, but not always the existing buildings. Furthermore, as seen in the Van Court House, Town was not only creating archival records for the NPS and the Library of Congress but also for his own personal archive, to mine the ideas District 17 recorded for designs he produced later in his career.

Why did Town select these eleven buildings? He was following the accepted perception by Mississippians that Natchez was the state's historic town. But why did he select these nine buildings in Natchez? Other obvious landmarks, such as Stanton Hall, Melrose, the Commercial Bank, Longwood, Choctaw, and Cherokee, among many others, were not architecturally recorded. Even Levi Weeks's Auburn was not measured and delineated by District 17. Town worked with Edith Moore, Katherine Miller, Roane Byrnes, and Mary Louise Metcalf, all of whom shared the idea that eighteenth-century Natchez should be preserved and celebrated. The extent of this partnership was that these women told him which buildings to document in Natchez. When a villa like Linden or Arlington did not have a Spanish history attached to it, Edith Moore invented one. Without explicit instructions from the NPS, specifying what buildings should be documented and how they should be documented, and without any oversight from the state district advisory committee, HABS districts like District 17 had great discretion on how to implement the program in their state. The sheer force of personalities of the NGC women made the 1934 HABS program a record of the narrative they created. At the end of the first CWA-funded HABS program, the Washington men O'Neill, Vint, and Holland questioned what Town and District 17 were doing.

WASHINGTON: 1935–41

No sooner was the 1934 HABS program launched than it was nearly shuttered. Realizing that the economy was beginning to improve, Roosevelt directed Harry Hopkins to begin dismantling the CWA, which funded HABS. Vint was notified that HABS would not be extended beyond the original termination date of February 15. Vint successfully lobbied CWA officials to extend HABS until May 1. The CWA stipulated that the number of personnel in the program be immediately reduced to 596 architects and draftsmen, with a 10 percent reduction in personnel in each succeeding week. O'Neill closed districts that never began working (mostly in northern regions, where the winter prohibited field measuring) and instructed district officers to begin laying off workers as they completed work. On July 14, 1934, the National Park Service's HABS office was dissolved, but this was not the end of the program.[104]

Vint understood the precariousness of federal funding for HABS. At the program's outset, he consulted Holland and the national advisory committee and planned for the survey's continuation after the original funding expiration. With Peterson now working in St. Louis, Holland began to take control of the HABS mission. Representing the advisory committee, Holland lobbied Ickes to continue the program, stating that HABS had exceeded all expectations and that the project had lifted the morale of the American architectural profession. Holland went on to say that, without the HABS program, the talents of unemployed architects across the nation may have been lost in recording America's historic architecture. Holland then supported Vint's proposal for a national exhibition of the work. The exhibit opened in the US National Museum (later named the Smithsonian Institution) in April 1934. Holland informed Ickes that the Library of Congress's Division of Fine Arts planned to catalog the drawings, beginning in the summer. Holland then boldly asked for nearly double the funding originally proposed by Peterson only a few months earlier.[105]

During this period of inactivity, after the first HABS program ended in 1935, Holland and Vint formalized the "tri-partite" arrangement that Peterson originally proposed with Holland. The agreement among the AIA, the National Park Service, and the Library of Congress standardized procedures for processing measured drawings for the NPS and the library's Division of Fine Arts. Vint also kept all of the circulars and HABS directives in place and urged the most enthusiastic district officers to continue measuring and drawing, suggesting to them that they solicit their state governments for financial support.[106] For the rest of 1934, HABS operated through an informal network of district officers, some of whom had state funding while others had not completed spending down their federal allocation. The latter was the case for District 17.[107]

Ickes knew the value of HABS and kept it in a dormant state in anticipation of the passing of the first significant federal legislation for historic preservation in the US, the Historic Sites Act of 1935. The act authorized the secretary of the Interior to establish an advisory board on national parks, historic sites, buildings, and monuments; it also instructed the Department of the Interior to conduct surveys of historic places, acquire historic property, and support restoration projects.[108]

Ickes saw that HABS was an already established program by which the Department of the Interior could implement a historic buildings survey and a historic preservation plan. Chatelain pushed hard for the NPS's History Division to develop the survey program, and he was frustrated that his efforts failed to persuade Ickes or Cammerer. Throughout 1935, the National Park Service reorganized and restarted HABS; Vint reassigned O'Neill to manage the HABS program and allocated only $5,200 to the survey.

O'Neill used this time, and the paltry funding, to assess the drawings received and organize better program management. During the 1934 HABS program, district officers were given much leeway in documenting buildings. O'Neill recognized that some district officers, like Town, focused only on a region of their state, while others did not produce any quality drawings. By June 1935, O'Neill had only $1,200 of Ickes's allocation. He asked Peterson to intercede, and Peterson argued for more funding on behalf of O'Neill.[109]

HABS was allocated $20,000 for O'Neill to revive the program. The NPS then applied to the Works Progress Administration (WPA), which replaced the CWA in 1935, for HABS funding. The WPA provided $600,000 for the survey, justifying the expenditure as a work relief program.[110]

O'Neill reorganized the HABS office in Washington, establishing the positions of an assistant director review architect to review submitted reports and a historian to review historic reports, and divided the country into regions and selected regional officers to manage district officers. Thomas Tileston Waterman became the assistant director of HABS in 1936, reviewing and approving drawings, reports, and photographs. Frederick Doveton Nichols was hired to catalog the HABS collection at the Library of Congress.[111]

O'Neill implemented a divisional management structure to HABS, which assigned division chiefs to monitor district officers. Along with managing their own district work, the divisional chiefs would regularly travel to the other states in their district and examine the progress of the HABS work. They submitted reports in letters to O'Neill. In turn, O'Neill communicated directives from the NPS and the advisory committee to the divisional chiefs.

O'Neill selected Marvin Eickenroht as the Southern Division HABS chief in 1936. The Southern Division was comprised of Texas, Louisiana, Arkansas, Mississippi, Tennessee, Alabama, and Georgia. A University of Texas and MIT graduate, Eickenroht was the Texas district chief (District 33) and had an architectural practice in San Antonio. Eickenroht became a tireless manager of the Southern Division and kept O'Neill apprised of work in the southern states.[112]

O'Neill carefully documented and evaluated the 1934 production statistics from all of the districts. Vint and O'Neill were concerned that CWA employment requirements had not been followed and that the district officers had not been rigorous in their hiring practices of qualified unemployed architects. Town was straightforward about his sole hiring criterion: "Any man who needed work was qualified as far as I was concerned."[113] Although Town did not spend Mississippi's allocation, he was inefficient in the cost of producing the drawings, reports, and photographs. When the CWA-funded program was terminated on April 28, 1934, District 17 had employed seven draftsmen and one woman, who worked as both stenographer and secretary. They had worked 949 "Grand Total Man-days," costing $4,287.00. O'Neill believed that District 17 production was problematic, and there were several projects that were not finished. He was also annoyed that District 17 spent more than a third over the national average to produce an eighteen by twenty-four inches drawing sheet. Town responded to O'Neill's concern, stating in a progress report that "all of the men employed are taking a great deal of interest in the program, and are doing everything they can to expedite it and live within the budget."[114] When HABS resumed, O'Neill expected that teams like District 17 would be more efficient in their production.[115]

Most district officers were not only committed to the HABS idea but were enthusiastic about it.[116] But what was a dire economic situation in 1933 was not the same by 1936. Funding from the WPA had begun to have an impact in the American construction industry. Architects and draftsmen were employed once again as more new private construction became available, and WPA-funded projects, such as new schools and government buildings, were planned. On April 10, 1936, O'Neill sent out "Circular Letter to All District Officers and Deputies" that announced that the NPS had received funding from the WPA to revive HABS. Not everyone was pleased or interested in resuming HABS—especially Hays Town.

In 1935, when HABS went dormant, Overstreet's marketing efforts had finally paid off. With the help of Senators Pat Harrison and Theodore Bilbo, WPA funding for public school buildings was appropriated for Mississippi. Overstreet and Town were back in business designing high schools and high school gymnasiums.[117] When O'Neill and Eickenroht directed Town to reactivate the dormant HABS program in Mississippi, Town recalled, "I told them there was no reason to reinstate it, because if any draftsmen were out of work I would hire them." O'Neill refused to accept Town's response and instructed Eickenroht to travel to Jackson and personally convince Town to resume the HABS program. Later in his life, in an interview with Wilton Corkern, Town recollected what Eickenroht told him: "This thing's not over yet. . . . If you don't get this [HABS project] started, and business gets bad, there will be no place for these boys to go [when you lay them off]. You owe it to them to do this."[118]

Town reluctantly agreed to revive the program, but he demanded that the NPS do most of the paperwork for him. Town then began assembling a new district team in early 1936 and once again received a $200 monthly salary as the district officer, but he became less and less interested in submitting reports on District 17's progress to Eickenroht.[119] In the summer of 1936, Eickenroht and O'Neill informed Town that if he wanted to keep getting paid as the district officer, he would have to put in a full forty-hour work week. Town was furious and immediately resigned the district officer position. He recalled later, "I was just keeping it going because they asked me to, because they were right, something might happen." Town was correct in his opinion about unemployed architects and draftsmen in Mississippi; only two architects and one draftsman received federal employment relief in 1935. Town then resigned as district officer, and O'Neill directed Eickenroht to find someone in Mississippi to replace Town.[120]

Eickenroht went to Jackson and hired J. Preston Waldrop, who did not find measuring and drawing historic buildings particularly interesting and had little in common with Town, who enjoyed the artistic aspects of architectural drawing and was an effective manager. More importantly for the HABS project, Waldrop did not relish the challenges of managing an office of draftsmen and regularly submitting paperwork to the National Park Service.[121]

Eickenroht wanted Waldrop to succeed as district officer. At first, he regularly expressed his confidence in him to O'Neill. But as the revived HABS program progressed, Eickenroht's confidence in Waldrop's abilities waned. Despite his managerial acumen, Town had left HABS and District 17 in disarray. There were several buildings that had been measured but not delineated, and reports were incomplete. Town had approached HABS as a six-month project and nothing more. If HABS was to return, Town was more than happy for someone else to deal with the work his district team had produced. He and Overstreet were back in the business of designing new buildings, not measuring and drawing old ones. Eickenroht concentrated on making sure Waldrop managed District 17 effectively and that drawings and reports were completed. Soon after hiring Waldrop, Eickenroht returned to Jackson and reported back to O'Neill that District 17 was woefully behind in completing its HABS documents.[122]

But just as Waldrop was just beginning to familiarize himself with the HABS project, the entire scope of the project drastically changed. In the fall of 1936, frustrated that Ickes and Congress were not consulting the History Division, Chatelain resigned from the National Park Service. With Chatelain no longer working for the NPS and Peterson away from Washington, Holland took control of the direction of HABS. He had high goals for the new HABS program and conveyed them to O'Neill.[123]

With the support of his fellow advisory members, Holland proposed an audacious experiment utilizing the manpower of the AIA to accomplish an ambitious academic goal: creating an American architecture history narrative and publishing it for the American public. Holland followed the educational practices in architecture that dated back to the French Enlightenment and proposed a different type of professionalism: "progressivism," the use of scientific procedure, relying entirely on observation and rational criticism, to define American architecture history up to the present. He believed that empirical science and Hegelian dialectic categorization, similar to categorizing in biology by genus and species, were the only way architectural history should be taught. At the end of the nineteenth century in the US, architectural categorization motivated historians to develop a canonical and rational narrative for architecture, and this approach became the primary way architecture history was taught in the academy. Banister Fletcher's figurative diagram, "The Tree of Architecture," epitomized this idea of progressivism: allegorical

Figure 4.45: "The Tree of Architecture" by Sir F. Banister Fletcher in *A History of Architecture.*

figures as Grecian maidens—Geography, Climate, Religion, Social, and History—determine the trees' branches, which yield the fruit of distinctive architecture, beginning with ancient societies and later branching out to modernity. Categorization was the objective of professionalism, not only in the way historians like Holland envisioned it, but it also compelled preservationists to embrace conjectural restoration approaches to historic preservation (figure 4.45).[124]

Making a canonical narrative of architecture history was not a new concept in 1936, but implementing a canon systematically across the country was. This initiative directly collided with a new concept of the 1930s: developing a heritage-based narrative for tourism. Three years earlier, Chatelain had proposed an American history narrative that used the national parks as teaching tools; Holland proposed a similar narrative, using HABS as a teaching tool. In Europe, along with Ward's survey of French architecture, Nikolaus Pevsner had published *An Outline of European Architecture* and was conducting a county-by-county architecture survey of Britain, resulting in *The Buildings of England*.[125]

But Holland proposed that HABS do something even more ambitious than Pevsner's survey, which took him twenty years to produce in a country the size of Louisiana; Holland wanted to employ working architects and draftsmen to conduct research for an academic project on a continental scale. HABS districts were, along with recording historic buildings, to produce an "outline"—a sparse set of drawings of building features, verbal building descriptions, and maps of regions of the state, all of which delineated the uniqueness of a state's historic and vernacular architecture. After collecting all of the outlines from the HABS districts, the National Park Service or the AIA would compile a book or series of books describing American architecture. Holland envisioned it to be the penultimate book on historic American architecture.

Instead of waiting to receive and then examine the outlines in order to assess and describe historic architecture, Holland anticipated how the book would be written. To complicate matters more, he, along with Meem, Simons, and Perry, already had in mind what American architecture should be.[126] While some HABS architects understood and produced Holland's survey, there were others who either did not have the skill or simply were not interested in it. Holland directed O'Neill to produce the regional surveys; he then directed his divisional chiefs like Eickenroht to push the district officers in producing their state's survey outlines.

Holland's HABS idea languished in Mississippi. Uncertainty in HABS funding, bureaucratic paperwork, and then trying to complete unfinished HABS sets frustrated Waldrop and encumbered the survey assignment in Mississippi. Eickenroht noted, "Mr. Waldrop has had a fairly large-sized job on his hands getting everything straightened out, but I can say, now more than ever, that his appointment to District Officer in Mississippi will be of lasting benefit. Unfortunately, however, the Mississippi budget will cramp him (unless he loses one of his workers temporarily) because of a little higher than the normal overhead, which I see no way to avoid."¹²⁷ And while Eickenroht sympathized with Waldrop's budget challenges, Waldrop did not help things by failing to submit monthly budget reports to Eickenroht. Changes suggested by Eickenroht in the HABS numbering system, along with new WPA employment forms requiring listed quotas of relief and nonrelief workers, only confused Waldrop; by the end of 1936, he had practically ceased in producing work.¹²⁸ In January 1937, Eickenroht was concerned about Waldrop's abilities to produce the HABS work.¹²⁹

By 1937, enthusiasm in the HABS districts had waned, not only in Mississippi but throughout the Deep South. Eickenroht was very unhappy with the work in Florida, which he regarded as graphically mediocre and careless in accuracy. Koch's District 18 continued to produce good drawings, but Koch had paid little attention to Holland's requirements for the survey outline. In Alabama, Professor Walter Burkhardt was making progress on drawings but not on the outline. And HABS was languishing in Tennessee, Arkansas, and Georgia—either the district officers did not understand the survey outline requirement, or they chose to ignore it completely.¹³⁰

Shortly after updating O'Neill from New Orleans, Eickenroht traveled to Jackson and inspected the HABS progress in the District 17 office.¹³¹ But as much as Eickenroht wanted Waldrop to produce acceptable work, he continued to submit unsatisfactory work, and it was submitted late. Thomas Waterman rejected Waldrop's priority cards for building surveys and outline drafts. Frustration increased, both in the NPS and the districts, when the WPA terminated funding for HABS in June 1937. Throughout the summer, Eickenroht pushed Waldrop to wrap up the district's work without pay.¹³² Waldrop submitted his pencil drawings, photographs, and the outline. Waterman rejected everything Waldrop submitted and marked the materials as being "inadequate and in need of rewriting and amplification." O'Neill commiserated with Eickenroht; the sudden termination of HABS made it difficult to receive survey work from the districts. He expressed hope that Waldrop was committed to the project and that the NPS would at least receive the district's photographs from him. The NPS never received a completed draft of the Mississippi outline. Arkansas and Georgia also failed to submit their outlines, and Holland was not pleased with the finished outlines from Louisiana, Alabama, and Tennessee. Under Waldrop's management, District 17 did not complete a single HABS set. After the second HABS program termination, Waldrop left HABS.¹³³

Eickenroht went back to running his firm in San Antonio when the program ended in 1937. O'Neill appealed to the WPA to continue the "Outline of the Development of Early American Architecture," saying "that it would constitute one of the most important contributions of the Survey." The WPA awarded a $16,000 grant to complete the outline, and O'Neill produced a pamphlet that explained what the survey outline would entail, but it was never completed and never published.[134]

On June 30, 1939, the WPA grant was exhausted, and all national work in HABS ceased. O'Neill was "furloughed" and left the National Park Service.[135] HABS went dormant, but it was to be revived again. Vint and Peterson proposed a new management model for the project to Cammerer. Instead of districts documenting what their states determined to be important, these men proposed a new system comprised of four mobile units, based in Boston, Massachusetts, Richmond, Virginia, Santa Fe, New Mexico, and St. Louis, Missouri, and consisting of forty-nine architectural technicians and supplementary workers. Each unit would have a station wagon, a camera, and drafting tools that would allow the workers to travel throughout their regions and document buildings that had been missed by previous efforts.[136]

Charles Peterson became the regional HABS director for the Mississippi Valley, working out of his St. Louis office. Finally, he had some control over the survey. He assessed the work produced by Town and Waldrop. He listed the projects by Town and made notes—for example, for Arlington, "James Harranton White (?)," and for Arrighi, "American Spanish?" At the bottom of his handwritten note, he scrawled, "Almost all of the buildings are in Natchez." Peterson realized that most of the Mississippi survey was inaccurate and mainly comprised of Natchez villas. With only his four-member team and a station wagon, Peterson knew that he had to rely on NPS managers at historical monuments and battlefields, as well as the old AIA district officer infrastructure, if he was going to produce more HABS documentation in Mississippi and other states in his region. In December 1939, he explained the situation to Malcolm Gardner, who had been managing the Vicksburg National Battlefield Park and now was managing the building of the Natchez Trace Parkway, and requested that he evaluate the state of the HABS archive in the state. He wrote, "the state of Mississippi is not well enough represented in the collection and it is hoped that one of our field parties can secure material there this winter. Please look over the enclosed copy of the 'Priority List' and list of the subjects already measured and photographed. You will note that all the buildings so far measured are, with one exception, at Natchez." Peterson then expressed to Gardner how weighted the survey was toward the Natchez villas and his Appleton-influenced principles regarding the built patrimony, noting, "The humble cabin type is just as important for our purposes as the planters' mansions and it is hoped that all types can be represented."[137]

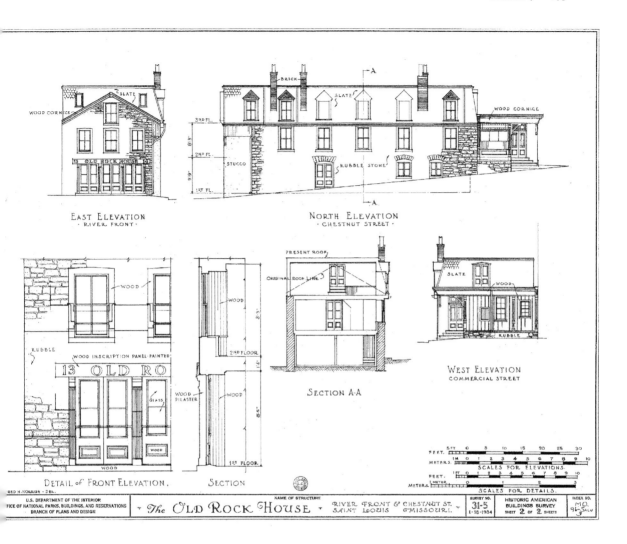

Figure 4.46: Elevations and sections of The Old Rock House, HABS 31-5, St. Louis, Missouri, delineated by Alfred H. Norrish, measured and delineated in January 1934. (Library of Congress, Prints & Photographs Division, Historic American Buildings Survey, HABS MO,96-SALU,5-)

Gardner passed Peterson's request to Assistant Research Technician Dawson Phelps. Phelps examined the entire collection and replied to Peterson: "A list of forty-one houses which do not appear on the Mississippi 'Priority List' has been compiled and is submitted herewith. This list has been selected from the Federal Writers' Project, *Mississippi, The Magnolia State*. The historical information seems for the most part, to be local tradition, and should be accepted only after it has been verified by further research."[138]

First Waterman had flagged the inaccurate and Natchez-focused HABS survey, and now Phelps. But no one returned the erroneous reports to Town or Waldrop or to Edith Moore. By 1939, it was too late. The Natchez narrative conjured up by Moore, Katherine Miller, and Roane Byrnes had then been archived in the Library of Congress and was accessible to anyone.

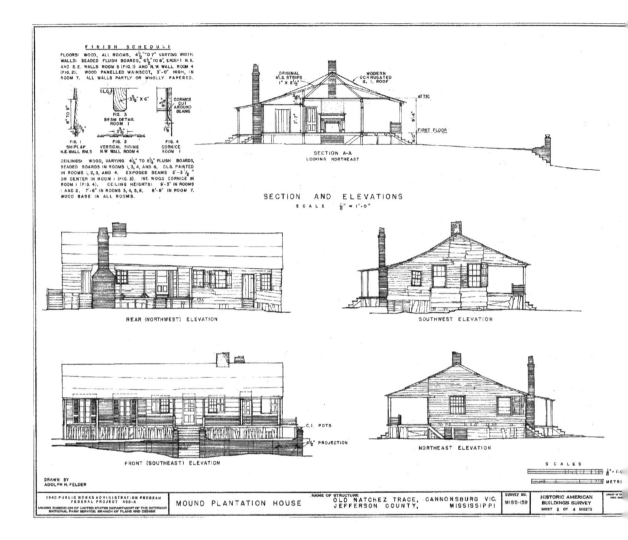

Figure 4.47: Elevations and building section of Mound Plantation House, HABS MISS-159, delineated by Adolph H. Felder, measured in February 1940, delineated in October 1940. (Library of Congress, Prints & Photographs Division, Historic American Buildings Survey, HABS MISS,32-CANB.V,1-)

Peterson attempted to make the Mississippi collection more balanced and wanted to document buildings that represented Mississippi, not just Natchez. Working with Gardner to measure and draw a farmstead, known as "Mound Plantation," on the planned Natchez Trace Parkway in Jefferson County, he shared with Gardner his technical and less artistic approach to HABS documentation by saying that it could only be thoroughly documented if the "architect has had an opportunity to open up the walls and get every bit of evidence which might be found" (figure 4.46).[139] Peterson's statement summarized his approach to historic preservation. Throughout his career, he was a restoration architect, who sought the best approaches to restore a building, often to a conjectural appearance (figure 4.47).

Peterson's involvement in managing the St. Louis HABS regional office was short-lived. He relinquished its management to F. Ray Leimkuehler. Emmett Hull took charge of District 17 in 1940 and had a marginal role in HABS. And although Peterson was no longer in charge of the St. Louis office, as the senior landscape architect for the National Park Service's midwest office, he was still involved with HABS, most notably with the Mound Plantation in Jefferson County and the Old French Fort in Pascagoula. Peterson originally requested Hull's District 17 office to delineate the Mound Plantation, working off the field notes produced by Peterson's team, but progress on the set languished in Hull's office. Peterson asked Gardner, who wanted the drawings in order to plan the building's restoration for the Natchez Trace Parkway, to pressure Hull. Finally, in December 1940, Hull sent a copy of the HABS set to Gardner and the original drawings to Waterman in Washington. But to Waterman's annoyance, Hull failed to send the photographic negatives. Hull mismanaged District 17, and mishaps, such as the missing negatives, were a common occurrence.[140]

Interestingly, Peterson was also fascinated with Mississippi's Spanish colonial past. At this time, he had not begun to directly work with the NGC women, but like them, he appreciated the patina of the old architecture and was less interested in mid-nineteenth-century buildings during his career in the NPS in the 1930s. He most likely sought to document and preserve them because these buildings were the oldest and most deteriorated buildings, and he and others may have regarded the mid-nineteenth-century buildings as largely in good condition and there were more of them than eighteenth-century buildings.

He inquired about the Old French Fort in Pascagoula to William D. McCain, director of the Mississippi Department of Archives and History. McCain could not find any information about the building but told Peterson he would welcome any article Peterson wished to publish about it in the *Journal of Mississippi History*. Peterson sent his team from St. Louis to document the simple three-room structure. The team's drawings reflect Peterson's interest in construction: included with the building sections are sectional framing diagrams and three-dimensional vignettes, which explain timber joinery found in the building (figure 4.48). The set illustrates what Peterson envisioned for HABS—technical drawings that explain the construction of historic buildings.

But while the drawings demonstrated Peterson's rigor in accurate documentation, the historical data report, written by team member Adolph Felder, relied on local heritage and contained numerous inaccuracies conjured up in 1907 by John Hanno Deiler.[141] Based on Deiler's cryptic notes, Felder could not determine if the building should be called the "Old French Fort" or the "Old Spanish Fort" or if it was a fort at all. He also guessed about the year when it was built, which he determined

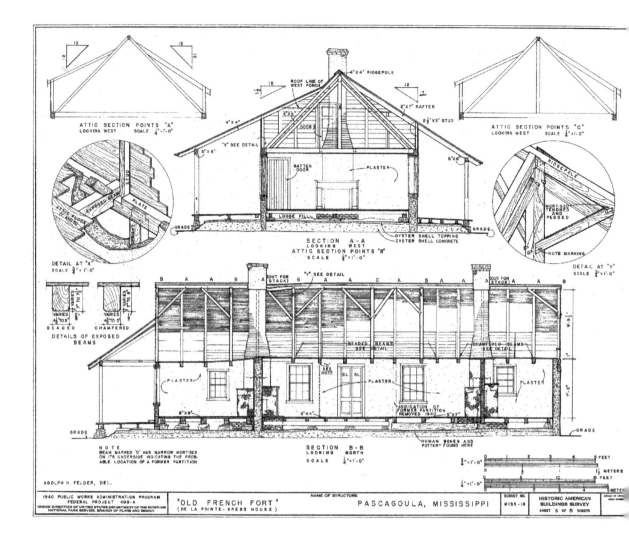

Figure 4.48: Building sections and details of Old French Fort (De La Point-Krebs House), HABS MISS-18, delineated by Adolph H. Felder, measured in March 1940, delineated in May 1940. (Library of Congress, Prints & Photographs Division, Historic American Buildings Survey, HABS MISS,30-PASCA,3-)

was 1721. Later, through dendrochronology, experts concluded that it was built in 1757.[142]

As district officer, Hull never initiated a HABS project. He signed off on work produced by Peterson's team and hurriedly completed an unfinished set, started by Town's team, for an important Natchez villa, Katherine Miller's Hope Farm. During Town's tenure, Miller saw how having her villa documented by HABS was yet another way to enhance her status as the leading "lady" in town. Interestingly, she had helped Town, Edith Moore, and Roane Byrnes in writing the erroneous history of Connelly's Tavern; she seemed to have been impressed with the work produced by the District 17 team. Town had not scheduled Hope Farm, but he did have his team measure it and produce field notes. After Town left HABS, Waldrop was too unorganized to mobilize a team to travel from Jackson

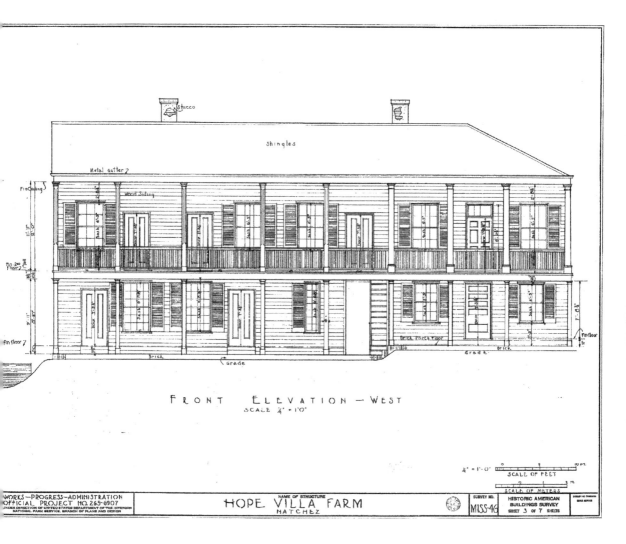

Figure 4.49: West elevation of Hope Villa (Farm), HABS MISS-46, Natchez, Mississippi, field party and delineators unknown, measured and delineated in 1936. (Library of Congress, Prints & Photographs Division, Historic American Buildings Survey, HABS MISS,1-NATCH.V,7-)

to measure it. But Hull did direct the District 17 team to complete the set. Unfortunately for Miller, it is the poorest quality set in the entire Mississippi collection (figure 4.49). Miller sought to call her residence "Hope Villa," de-emphasizing the "Farm" label, since the site had evolved from being an approximately 240-acre farm to a villa with fifteen acres and was built by Don Carlos de Grande Pré in 1789.[143] Later in her life, when Hope Farm/Villa was nominated for listing on the National Register of Historic Places, Miller convinced Mississippi Department of Archives and History historian Elizabeth Reynolds to state that it may have been built even earlier, possibly in 1782. Reynolds did just that, but with a caveat—noting the date of construction was based on local tradition.[144]

By 1941, having read about the NGC women's accomplishments and adventures in Natchez, Peterson wanted to learn more about their preservation activities. But, interestingly, he did not contact them; instead, he wrote to Natchez mayor William J. Byrne, asking him: "How many historic buildings in Natchez and vicinity are publicly owned?" "How many are owned by special private or semi-public organizations?" And his last question: "If entrance fees are collected who receives the revenue and is it applied to the maintenance of the buildings?"[145] Peterson was aware that the women had established their tourism enterprise and their preservation initiative. Perhaps he did not want to bother himself discussing historic buildings with a group of middle-aged society women, most notably Edith Moore, who had fabricated so much inaccurate history of the place? Or perhaps he did not want to get involved in their feud over the pilgrimages? Regardless, it would not be until after World War II that Peterson worked with Katherine Miller and Roane Byrnes.

Mayor Byrne replied to Peterson by simply sending him copies of the previous year's pilgrimage programs. It must have seemed self-explanatory for him. Undaunted, Peterson contacted the Natchez Association of Commerce's Thomas J. Reed, requesting the same information. Reed also sent him copies of the pilgrimage programs.[146]

Peterson and the National Park Service men in Washington were too preoccupied with managing HABS to correct all of the discrepancies found in the District 17 sets. Holland's outline project distracted the NPS and the districts. In Mississippi, Waldrop and then Hull were not effective or dependable managers. Then, federal funding waned as the nation began readying itself for possible entry into World War II. As early as 1939, Vint realized that HABS was not going to receive any additional appropriations and planned to produce a comprehensive catalog of the HABS collection. He assigned Waterman to assess drawings, reports, and photographs received by the NPS, and he assigned Frederick Nichols to work with Holland on the HABS catalog at the Library of Congress. The catalog was published in March 1941, and the New Deal era of HABS effectively ended.[147]

The New Deal HABS collection in the Library of Congress is more of an archive of the attitudes of people about their built patrimony than the archival record of America's historic buildings. Essentially, through their personal motives, people like Edith Moore, Roane Byrnes, Katherine Miller, and Hays Town corrupted it as a true historical archive. But the Mississippi 1934–36 collection is not the only section that contains false information. There are countless errors in it from every state that participated in the first HABS program.

As Charles Peterson stated in his proposal memorandum, nothing like it had ever been proposed, and certainly not on a national scale. Peterson and, later, Leicester Holland misjudged the AIA members and their employees' abilities to produce record drawings of historic buildings across the country. Skill levels varied wildly from region to region, and the more rural a state was, the fewer skilled architects were available. The "tri-partite" arrangement among the National Park Service, the Library of Congress, and the AIA was a flawed one. The NPS and the Library of Congress had difficulty coordinating catalog and record standards, and men like O'Neill and Peterson attempted to micromanage the loosely associated chapters of the AIA. During the WPA-funded HABS program, Holland's idea to solicit architects, photographers, and draftsmen to research and produce factual information to produce a scholarly narrative of historic American architecture proved disastrous. The comprehensive book on American architecture Holland envisioned was never published.[148]

The NPS men misjudged three important conditions in 1934 America. First, they overestimated the number of talented available architects, which dwindled dramatically as the WPA programs had an impact on the national economy. Second, they misjudged the influence of state politics in determining what were the historic buildings in the state. Lastly, they completely underestimated the influence of local participants in skewing the record of HABS, most especially in District 17.

In 1934, Mississippi's construction industry had ground to a halt, but Democratic political allies of Franklin Roosevelt brought appropriations to the state that built numerous federally funded buildings, from school buildings to housing to government buildings. Architects like Town and Overstreet did need work in early 1934, but Overstreet's gamble to use HABS to buy some time paid off. When real design work came into their office, Town and Overstreet were more than happy to shed their District 17 responsibilities. By leaving the selection of historic buildings to the state's advisory committees, who later designated this responsibility to the WPA Writers' Project and who later relied on district officers and local historians for selecting buildings, the NPS lost control of the survey. Chatelain and the History Division were not involved in HABS. It is evident that Town cared little about northern Mississippi, and he even tried to broker a deal with Frazer Smith of Memphis to cede it to Tennessee. He also wanted to work with his mentor Dick Koch. Furthermore, he and Overstreet understood what the NGC women were doing and wanted to solicit work from them. Once in Natchez, Town and his team measured and delineated buildings that Town wanted, buildings like Arrighi, which allowed him to create a compelling *analytique*, and Chapel of the Cross, which was a valuable record he used to design a new church building. Town was not an academic; he was a businessman, architect, and designer.

But the most critical mistake the National Park Service men made was underestimating the influence of the NGC women. The men's professional approach to historic preservation, influenced by the French academy and later by Appleton, was no match for the personalism adhered to by Edith Moore, Roane Byrnes, and Katherine Miller. Dawson Phelps's assessment of Moore's history reports is telling: they were "local tradition." Thomas Waterman described them as local tradition but also pitiful. Historians who followed Moore in writing about historic buildings in Natchez had to stipulate that some of their information was local tradition.[149]

Shils notes that local historiography is local tradition: the recordation of it originated in ancient Greece, and the practice carried over to ancient Rome. He contends that national history originated in modern times and its proponents sought to put "antiquities in order—scientifically identify, classify and critically scrutinize for accuracy local history."[150] By the nineteenth century, American historians were convinced that they were meeting the needs of their society and were providing affirmation of the value of the nation's past. Chatelain and his staff followed this ideal, but even in the best of circumstances, it was a formidable challenge. And due to Chatelain's personal feuds with Peterson, then Vint, Cammerer, Ickes, and finally, Congress, the National Park Service's History Division did not participate in HABS, and no one scrutinized any of the information pertaining to the history of the buildings documented. Edith Moore's writings were not verified for accuracy, and the NGC women's fascination with Spanish Natchez became accepted as fact, ingrained into the story behind the nine buildings HABS recorded in the city. Natchez men first ceded cultural political power to the NGC women, then Mississippi men in Jackson ceded it; finally, the NPS ceded it to them. Moore, Roane Byrnes, and Katherine Miller established the Natchez tradition, which first became local history and then heritage. Lowenthal was right: heritage is the perversion of history. This is clearly evident in the 1934–40 HABS Mississippi program.

Although the Washington men professed the virtues of professionalism in historic preservation, they were not immune to personalism. Peterson's fascination with Spanish and French colonial history in Mississippi drove him to direct his regional team to measure and delineate the "Old French Fort," also known as the "Old Spanish Fort," in Pascagoula, which may not have been a fortified residence. He was inspired by Appleton's beliefs that the nitty-gritty details of early American construction were as valuable as the artistry of elite designers and refined culture. He said as much in his correspondence with Malcolm Gardner. But beneath the impartial image Peterson conveyed, he shared Edith

Figure 4.50:
Photograph of the front of Hope Villa (Farm), HABS MISS-46, Natchez, Mississippi, by James Butters, April 8, 1936. (Library of Congress, Prints & Photographs Division, Historic American Buildings Survey, HABS MISS,1-NATCH.V,7-)

Moore's romance with the Spanish colonial period and Town's artistic bent in drawing. This may explain why the northern and eastern sections of the state were not documented. There were plenty of notable examples of buildings built before 1860 (Peterson's only criterion for documentation), and he chose two colonial buildings to document.[151]

Leicester Holland's idea was also a flawed one. Local historians like Moore and professional architects like Town were not suitably educated to produce the researched material for an academic history publication. More importantly, architects like Town were also businessmen, and scholarly research was not their primary objective. Making a living designing buildings was their goal. Vint and O'Neill were naïve in thinking that managers like Waldrop were capable of both managing the production of drawings and editing an outline, all of which was ambiguously conveyed to them. Finally, the instability of financial support for the project and the bureaucracy, partly embedded within the National Park Service and partly created by O'Neill, inhibited the project's progress. But Holland's expectations, shared by Meem, Simons, and Perry, became an obstacle to the book project's success. Everyone on the advisory committee shared a view about the built past, which weighed heavily on revising it to conform to what they thought it should be, both in the way it was depicted in history books and how it was to be preserved and restored. At the same time Holland's survey outline program was being implemented, Meem oversaw multiple demolitions of historic buildings in Santa Fe and replaced them with his idea of Spanish southwestern Colonial Revival architecture. Simons's revisionist designs changed Charleston, South Carolina; and Perry's Colonial Williamsburg altered several Victorian buildings and made them "Colonial" while at the same time he created buildings based completely on conjecture, including the Colonial Virginia Capitol, the Governor's Palace, and the Old Gaol, to name but a few. Holland managed to salvage the project in publishing a portfolio of great Georgian American houses, which was edited by the talented historicist architect, William Lawrence Bottomley.

For the most part, the HABS archives of the 1930s are a collection of beautifully delineated drawings of historic buildings, a record of how architects used to draw but rarely do today. The collection is respected as the finest archive of drawings of historic architecture in the world because, by and large, no other country has produced a similar archive of this scale. In it there are discrepancies. Some are simple errors, but others, like the majority of the Mississippi collection, were politically driven and were the result of the NGC women and the narrative they created. From 1934 until 1939, as Town and later Waldrop and Hull were working on the project, Roane Byrnes was busy working on the NGC's most audacious project, creating a scenic parkway from Nashville, Tennessee, to Mexico City, centered around Natchez. In 1935, she began creating the Natchez Trace Parkway (figure 4.50).

Chapter 5

CREATING THE NATCHEZ TRACE PARKWAY

Harnett Kane remarked that Katherine Miller met her lifelong career through the Natchez Spring Pilgrimage. In helping to create the Natchez Trace Parkway, Roane Byrnes met her lifelong adventure. She did not seek to spearhead the construction of what would eventually be a billion-dollar and over four-hundred-mile-long parkway, but was caught up in the momentum surrounding the project. And while at first no one ever thought she was up to the task, herself included, Byrnes rose to the challenge with guile, grace, and grit. In leading the effort to develop the Natchez Trace Parkway, she played a critical role in changing the geography and heritage of Mississippi. She parlayed the Natchez Garden Club women's Natchez narrative into part of the national narrative of heritage. Its success was the catalyst for developing a thriving automobile-based tourist economy for both Natchez and the state of Mississippi (figure 5.1).

Like the Natchez narrative, the Natchez Spring Pilgrimage, and the first HABS projects in Mississippi, the original story of the Natchez Trace and the modern Natchez Trace Parkway is steeped more in legend and lore than in fact. The Natchez Trace exemplifies the creation of heritage on a continental scale. Initially, Roane Byrnes's motive to build the parkway was the same as most of her fellow Mississippians—she wanted a modern automobile highway in the state, and she especially wanted one that connected Natchez to the wider world. She had always been acutely aware of Natchez's physical isolation from the rest of the country. Frustration with the condition of roads throughout Mississippi was a shared sentiment. Indeed, roads barely existed. At the end of her life, she justified her initial motives, saying, "At the beginning we needed a road and the way to get it seemed to be through what . . . became the Natchez Trace Association."[1] Throughout the first half of her life as she witnessed the decline of river transportation, Byrnes understood that if Natchez was to survive in the twentieth century, it would have to have good roads connecting it to Jackson, Vicksburg, Baton Rouge, and New Orleans. But

Figure 5.1: Cover rendering of the Natchez Trace Parkway promotional brochure, May 1945, US National Park Service. (Roane Fleming Byrnes Collection [MUM00057], Department of Archives and Special Collections, J. D. Williams Library, The University of Mississippi)

as she became more and more involved in the parkway project, she came to realize that the Natchez Trace Parkway could be much more than a utilitarian highway: it could be an elongated parkway, spanning diagonally across the state, which celebrated both the natural beauty and the history of the place she loved.

As the president of the citizen-based Natchez Trace Association, Byrnes worked with some of the most prominent and colorful men of the state, region, and country. She associated with two types of powerful men: the most influential power brokers in Tennessee and Alabama, and the most blatantly racist and corrupt politicians in Mississippi (and perhaps in American history). And Byrnes had to deal with two personalities: an outrageous yet imaginative charlatan, and a dismissive elitist. She strategically deployed her gracious southern charm to lobby the leaders of the National Park Service (NPS) and the Department of the Interior and several Mississippi governors, along with artists, writers, design professionals, and everyday folk to champion the building of the parkway. She became a student of highway engineering and converted her library and pantry at Ravennaside into map rooms, which she (not

Figure 5.2: Harold L. Ickes, US Secretary of the Interior, 1933–1946. (Library of Congress, Prints & Photographs Division, photograph by Harris & Ewing, LC-DIG-hec-38720)

entirely) jokingly called "war rooms." She understood how her talents could be best utilized and developed a productive partnership with a young lawyer, Ralph Landrum, who worked behind the scenes and handled the endless details necessary to keep the project going. She encountered numerous setbacks but never visibly conveyed her disappointment or frustrations; instead, she was determined in her enthusiasm, and she inspired dozens of women to become leaders of their own causes. From the ground-breaking ceremony in 1938, when Governor Hugh White placed a spade of Mississippi earth into a silver urn that she held, to her last ribbon-cutting ceremony in 1969, when she prominently stood in front of the important Mississippi and NPS men, dressed in high heels, pearls, and a feminine hat, Byrnes was the purposeful southern lady.

It did not to matter to Byrnes (or to many of the others involved in the project) if the Natchez Trace as a single road may have never actually existed. She loved the romance of it as an idea and how it could be monetized: an NPS-managed parkway could be an economic asset for Mississippi. In promoting the construction, she often claimed that it would become "our Yosemite" and that it would not only employ hundreds of

Mississippians but also would become a tourist destination. Her ambitions for the parkway did not start in Nashville and end in Natchez. She wanted it to be a vital stretch of a grander parkway, sited on the nearly forgotten historic trails of El Camino Real[2] and the Wilderness Road—a road that would connect Washington, DC, with Mexico City. Through her sheer audacity, Byrnes traveled to Mexico City, met with officials of the Mexican government, and negotiated an initial agreement to build a Pan-American parkway. Only World War II stopped her plans and her momentum.

From 1933 until 1942, Mississippians, Alabamians, and Tennesseans envisioned an impressive parkway across their states. Their motives varied, but all of them shared the same goal—pave the 444 miles between Natchez and Nashville, known in the region's folklore as the Natchez Trace. They worked together to cajole a very skeptical NPS team of historians, architects, landscape architects, and engineers. Scheming with some of the savviest politicians of the day, they outmaneuvered their most outspoken national critics in Washington, most notably Secretary of the Interior Harold Ickes (figure 5.2). And working with prominent writers of the day, they reintroduced the legend of a long-forgotten pioneer road to mainstream America. Byrnes never saw the completion of the parkway—she died in 1970—but her political and promotional groundwork sustained the project through the war and through the rest of the twentieth century, until its completion south of Nashville in 2005.

THE OLD NATCHEZ TRACE

The Natchez Trace Roane Byrnes knew consisted of ruined fragments of a pre-Columbian footpath that had been widened by the early American pioneers and later made into rough farm roads.[3] It was a series of ancient ruts in the forests of the Deep South, connecting the Lower Mississippi River Valley to the Cumberland River Basin in Tennessee. This trace predated human occupation, originally created by bison and other large animals that followed a small ridge that led to salt licks along the Cumberland River.[4] American Indians, predominantly the Creek tribe, who lived in what is now middle Tennessee, followed the animals, beat out this trail, and traveled this route to trade with tribes like the Natchez, in lower Mississippi. Numerous prehistoric settlements were established along the trace, most notably the Pharr Mounds located near present-day Tupelo, Mississippi. An unnamed French explorer in 1742 was the first European known to travel the trace, and he made note of its "miserable conditions." The British documented the route in the 1770s and referred to it as the Path to the Choctaw Nation.

Although the Natchez Trace ended at the Mississippi River, another road, El Camino Real ("the Royal Road"), resumed the main transportation route in Spanish colonial Mississippi, Louisiana, and Texas. The road linked Natchez to Natchitoches, Louisiana, then San Antonio de Béxar in Texas, and eventually culminated at Mexico City. Like the Natchez Trace, El Camino Real was an animal trail that was later established as a trading route for the Hasinai Confederacy, who traded with the Caddo Indians in what became Louisiana. Early Spanish explorers found the trail, but it was not until 1770 that it was mapped by Athanase de Mézières, a Frenchman employed by the Spaniards. Texas founders Moses Austin and his son Stephen, Jim Bowie, Davy Crockett, and Sam Houston all traveled El Camino Real, as well as the Natchez Trace. Known as the Old San Antonio Road in Texas, El Camino Real was romanticized by Americans in the late nineteenth century.[5]

After the end of the American Revolution in 1783, the Natchez Trace was the answer for American frontiersmen to the challenges posed by the region's geography, economy, and eighteenth-century Spanish colonial governmental policy in settling Mississippi. Pioneers from Virginia arriving in the newly created town of Nashville from the Wilderness Road began using it as they settled into the Old Southwest. Along it, they built villages, farms, and taverns, and it became one of the most significant wilderness roads in the newly established United States. At the end of the eighteenth century, it was a point of contention between the US and the Choctaw, Cherokee, and Creek tribes, and it was also a focal point in the international rivalry among the US, Spain, Great Britain, and France.

The trace was in its heyday from 1800 to 1830. During the decade after the US took control of the Mississippi Territory in 1798, the early US Postal Service used the road, and it became the vital means of communication between the territorial capital in Natchez and Washington, DC. It was also the scene of brutal robberies and violence and the famous backdrop of several of America's earliest legendary pioneer stories and romantic stories of military glory. Returning from his transcontinental exploration, Meriwether Lewis committed suicide along it, south of Nashville at Grinder's Inn.[6] Andrew Jackson used it to march his army of Tennesseans and Kentuckians to New Orleans to defeat the British in 1815. Kentucky and Illinois boatmen floated down to Natchez on log rafts with goods and sold their crude rafts when they arrived. With the money they earned, they walked or rode the trace back home. Some of them were robbed and even murdered along the wilderness road.

From 1828 until 1861, Isaac Franklin and John Armfield, the two most prominent and successful slave traders in the US, drove an estimated one million enslaved African Americans down the Natchez Trace, where they were sold to plantation owners at the Forks of the Road Slave Market in Natchez. During this time, the Natchez Trace became also known as the "Slave Trail" and the scene of one of the largest mass deportation events in American history. The number of African Americans, shackled and chained to each other and forced to march at gunpoint, was double the number of Native Americans forced to march to Oklahoma in the Trail of Tears. Organized in "coffles," the African Americans left Alexandria, Virginia, marched to the Wilderness Road at Nashville, and then embarked on the Natchez Trace. Franklin and Armfield became multimillionaires, so much so that in 1832, 5 percent of all commercial credit available through the Second Bank of the United States had been extended to their firm. The Civil War brought not only an end to the slave trade in Natchez but also to the trace as a usable road.[7] By the end of the nineteenth century, the Natchez Trace was absorbed into the farms and towns along its path.[8]

Eventually, the Natchez Trace was all but forgotten. Tennesseans, Mississippians, and Alabamians who had traveled or lived along it passed on its gory and adventurous stories to their children and grandchildren. These stories became part of the region's folklore, but never captured the nation's interest. Other frontier roads—the Wilderness Road, the Old National Road, the Santa Fe Trail, and the Oregon Trail—were celebrated by fiction writers and historians.[9]

A group of motivated women revived the idea of the Natchez Trace. In 1905, Elizabeth Jones of Holly Springs, the first native Mississippian member of the Daughters of the American Revolution (DAR), proposed at the first Mississippi DAR statewide conference to commemorate the trace. She proposed erecting granite markers in every county in Mississippi that the trace ran through, and the state chapter of the DAR approved the proposal. Natchez Trace historian Dawson Phelps speculated that Jones may have been inspired by John Swain's "The Natchez Trace," which was published in the September 1905 issue of *Everybody's Magazine*, but he acknowledged that the article contained few historical facts. It is entirely likely that Jones was inspired by the stories she heard from her elders while growing up along the old road. There were other DAR women who had heard about the trace and wanted it memorialized, most notably, Edith Moore. After approving Jones's proposal, the Mississippi DAR women urged their counterparts in Alabama and Tennessee to also commemorate the trace with stone markers.[10]

The DAR raised $230 ($6,563 in 2019 dollars) and in 1909 erected the first granite marker in Bluff Park, overlooking the Mississippi River in Natchez (figure 5.3).[11] The next year, they erected a similar granite

Figure 5.3: Mississippi Chapter of the Daughters of the American Revolution granite marker commemorating the Natchez Trace near Tupelo in Lee County, Mississippi, erected in 1914. (Library of Congress, Prints & Photographs Division, Historic American Engineering Record, HAER MS-15)

marker in Port Gibson. The third was erected in 1912 in Kosciusko, and the fourth was erected on the Alabama-Mississippi state line in Tishomingo County in 1913. The Alabama DAR chapter contributed half the cost of this monument. In 1914, near Tupelo, they erected their fifth granite marker.[12]

By 1915, the cost of erecting large granite monuments along the trace began to take its toll on the DAR treasury, and the DAR women turned to the Mississippi state legislature for financial assistance in funding their project. Although the legislature had in the past funded Confederate memorials at the Vicksburg National Battlefield and the Shiloh National Battlefield, its members showed little interest in funding monuments along the forgotten road, and the DAR's request was denied. Undaunted, the DAR women turned to another group, the Daughters of the War of 1812, who agreed to share in the monument costs. Their counterparts in Tennessee decided to erect bronze markers, which cost less, along their portion of the trace. The Alabama chapter of the DAR followed suit. By 1933, the three state chapters of the DAR had fulfilled Elizabeth Jones's dream of marking the trace.

The advent of the automobile coincided with the DAR women's efforts to reintroduce the forgotten highway to the public. Highway automobile travel began as a fad among wealthier Americans from the Northeast. They first began traveling down the Atlantic seaboard during the winter months to places like Jekyll Island, Georgia, and St. Augustine, Florida, to enjoy the balmy spring weather. The miserable road conditions, which Roane Byrnes and so many others complained about in southwestern Mississippi, were not uncommon. Indeed, during the early twentieth century in the South, the roads were deplorable. In *Dixie Before Disney*, Tim Hollis describes how it took American Automobile Association (AAA) mapmaker R. H. Johnston, in preparing the first AAA guidebook to the South in 1908, twenty-five days to travel from Philadelphia to Savannah, Georgia, by automobile.[13] The roads were so bad and so confusing that Johnston had to ask some two hundred people how to get to Chattanooga, Tennessee, from Atlanta. Automobile-based tourism did not motivate southern legislatures to improve or actually build roads—but farming did. Legislatures funded the construction of roads in rural parts of their states, which allowed farmers to bring their produce to nearby town markets. Throughout the first half of the twentieth century, rail remained the preferred way to travel; however, passenger travel always yielded to freight travel, thereby making passenger rail travel unreliable.

In some states, interstate travel was practically nonexistent. The mid-Atlantic states first worked together and built the National Highway (1909) and the Capitol Highway (1910). The National Highway attempted to link New York to Atlanta, and the Capitol Highway tried to link Washington, DC, to Atlanta. Neither road was completely paved or continuous. Millionaire Carl Fisher, who first developed Miami Beach, tried to develop the first transcontinental highway, the Lincoln Highway, from New York to San Francisco. Then he attempted to build the Dixie Highway, from Sault Ste. Marie, Michigan, to Miami. Both roads were only partially completed and moderately successful.[14]

The memory of trails from the colonial days became a starting point for people championing good roads in the states. Nostalgia for the colonial past was a motive for reusing the historical roads; also, there was the perception that the states still owned these roads' rights-of-way. The "Better Roads" movement was spurred by two types of men: wealthy men who wanted roads to travel leisurely in the countryside in their expensive automobiles, and progressive-minded men who equated good roads with improvement. In October 1915, a group of automobile enthusiasts met in Mobile, Alabama, and formed the "Old Spanish Trail Highway Association." Their objective: pave the mythical old Spanish trail from St. Augustine, Florida, to San Diego, California. During the 1920s, chambers of commerce throughout the country joined the highway associations and began championing good roads in their states.

In 1916, the Natchez Chamber of Commerce initiated a highway lobbying group called the Natchez Trace Association, located at Kosciusko, Mississippi; its objective was to pave a highway connecting Nashville to New

Orleans. At the same time, a competing highway association emerged, the Jackson Military Highway Association, which proposed paving the same route. This group's intent was to memorialize the route traveled by Andrew Jackson on his way to the Battle of New Orleans and military glory. Both organizations existed for only a few months. That same year, the US Congress passed the Federal State Aid Road Act. After that, interstate roads were managed and partially supported by the federal government. The legislation brought about the establishment of state highway departments. Ten years later, the Federal Bureau of Highways introduced a new system for organizing roads. Historical road names were changed into numbered highways. El Camino Real became US Route 82. The Old Spanish Trial became US Route 90.[15] The Natchez Trace did not become a numbered interstate highway because, at the time, it essentially did not exist.

World War I suspended any road activity in the US. But in 1920, the DAR women resumed placement of their markers, siting another marker at Old Greenville in Jefferson County near Natchez. During the last half of the 1920s, they completed their mission and had placed eight stone commemorative boulders along the trace. By then, the patriotic stories of the trace had taken hold throughout the state. The DAR members' dedication ceremonies were ready-made campaign events for Mississippi politicians seeking election. What better way for a politician to express and reaffirm his patriotic values than dedicating a granite marker in the memory of Andrew Jackson and the heroes of the Battle of New Orleans in front of the women of the Daughters of the American Revolution and the Daughters of the War of 1812? The DAR became adept at making its ceremonies events worthy of front-page news coverage in the state's newspapers. And in 1932, at a marker dedication event in Webster County, Mississippi, the future of the Natchez Trace forever changed.

THE "INTERNATIONAL HOBO"

In January 1932, the DAR women invited Mississippi state representative and Webster County, Mississippi, native Thomas A. Bailey to give the dedication address for their newest Natchez Trace monument near Matheson, Mississippi. Ned Lee, editor of the local newspaper, the *Webster Progress*, attended the ceremony and became interested in the history of the trace and the DAR's efforts to celebrate its history. Lee may have also spotted an opportunity to rid himself of a very annoying pest. He suggested to one of his "reporters," Jim Walton, that he devote his efforts to writing about the trace—specifically, to determine its actual route through Mississippi.

"Colonel" Jim Walton was certainly the most colorful, if not most peculiar, individual associated with the Natchez Trace Parkway. Yet, he perhaps did more than anyone to make it a national parkway. Walton had a shady past that he greatly embellished. He claimed to be a colonel, but how he had earned this honor was never known. He also professed to be an itinerant piano tuner and a well-known journalist. He averred that he fought valiantly for the Confederacy and fled the US during Reconstruction. He then traveled the world, supposedly having been entertained by the Russian czar in St. Petersburg and surviving a shipwreck off the coast of Mozambique. In 1886, he maintained that he became a journalist, writing travel articles for newspapers in Charleston, Atlanta, and New York, known throughout the world as the "International Hobo."[16] Now in his eighties, he settled in nearby Europa in Webster County.[17]

Walton loved the newspaper assignment and wrote a series of articles about the trace in his column, "Bits and Tidbits." He relished hyperbolizing what was already convoluted local lore about the trace. In one article, he claimed "that the old Natchez Trace is probably the oldest highway in the world" and boasted that Mayans and Incas traveled it long before Columbus had arrived in America. He asserted that the claims he made in his articles were substantiated by scientists from the Smithsonian Institution, who had found four thousand-year-old Indian pictures on a stone along the trace. He began following the activities of the Good Roads association in Mississippi, Alabama, and Texas, and he realized that new highway road construction was becoming an important idea across the US. This convinced him to make it his last goal: take up the cause of paving the Natchez Trace and making it a modern highway.[18]

In 1933, Walton called on US congressman Thomas Jefferson Busby at his Houston, Mississippi, office and later US senator Hubert Stephens in New Albany, Mississippi. Busby met with him, but Walton was unable to meet with Stephens, who perhaps wanted to avoid him. In his meeting with Busby, Walton described what the DAR had accomplished with its marker program and the illustrious history of the forgotten road.[19] Walton suggested to Busby that he propose a bill in Congress for a survey of the old trace, which would be the basis for a newly paved trace, a continuous paved highway from Nashville to Natchez. Busby remembered that Walton expressed little hope in the bill getting passed, but he thought it would be a pleasing gesture of support for the "ladies of the DAR," something that would give them recognition for their hard work over the past twenty years. Walton most likely used false humility in convincing Busby to propose the highway bill.[20]

Busby was an ambitious lawyer and politician, and he was facing reelection for his fifth, and final, term in Congress when Walton met

Figure 5.4: Thomas Jefferson Busby, US Congressman from the Fourth District, Mississippi, 1923–1935. Busby proposed the Natchez Trace Parkway in an appropriations bill that was part of the National Park Service federal appropriation in February 1934. (Library of Congress, Prints & Photographs Division, LC-DIG-npcc-09868)

with him (figure 5.4).[21] Busby knew that winning a federally funded highway would benefit his district and Mississippi, as well as greatly aid his reelection campaign. He researched the Natchez Trace in the Library of Congress and soon realized that Walton had greatly embellished its history, but he nevertheless concluded that it was indeed a historic old road. Cognizant that a new highway could bring employment to hundreds of Mississippians out of work during the Great Depression, he wasted little time drafting the Natchez Trace road bill. He knew that through the National Recovery Act of 1933 (which, among many projects, funded the Historic American Buildings Survey), there was money available for highway and infrastructure work. When he returned to Webster County, Busby told his constituents about his bill in Congress and that they needed, as he later put it, "to whoop and holler" so that Congress would realize that the state desperately wanted a new road.[22]

No one "whooped and hollered" about the proposed paved Natchez Trace more than Jim Walton. In what was probably the most outrageous publicity stunt in modern southern history, Walton set out to bring together the DAR and other patriotic women's groups, county boards of supervisors, chambers of commerce, and good roads advocates from across the state to meet in Jackson for the first statewide conference of the "Natchez Trace Military Highway Association," which only existed in Walton's imagination. Somehow, he managed to arrange for Jackson's most modern hotel, the Edwards Hotel, to be the meeting venue for the "association" conference in early January 1934. He proclaimed to all these stakeholders that the objective was to rebuild the trace as a modern military highway.[23]

Using his talents as a publicist, Walton promoted the conference through a series of press releases and marketing stunts. In press releases, he announced that Mississippi governor Mike Conner, US senator Pat Harrison, the entire Mississippi congressional delegation, the heads of the departments of archives and history in Mississippi and Alabama, the staff from the National Park Service, Alabama's US senator John S. Bankhead, and more importantly, Bankhead's glamorous movie star niece, Tallulah Bankhead, all planned to attend the meeting. Walton then hired two dozen men to begin "cutting a right-of-way" for the new trace from Mathison, Mississippi, to French Camp, Mississippi. He claimed in his newspaper article that "a hundred men" were busy cutting the right-of-way, and the massive road project had begun. All of this was completed fabricated, but people from across the state descended on Jackson and met at the Edwards Hotel, including Governor Conner, Senator Harrison, and two lesser-known individuals, Alma Kellogg and Roane Byrnes.[24]

Walton's caper accomplished two things: first, it brought good roads proponents and preservationists together to lobby for a heritage-inspired modern road, built through the state; and second, it completely discredited him. Roane Byrnes recalled how she was told to stay away from Walton during the January meeting and that he was "crazy."[25] People may have been duped into coming to the meeting, but they remained there and began to work together to make the highway project a reality. Progressive men recognized how focused the DAR members were on paving the trace and that they shared the same goal. Earlier in August 1933, at the last marker dedication in Thomastown, DAR regent Lucille Mayfield proposed not only to pave the trace but to make it into a parkway. She attended the Edwards Hotel meeting and met an ambitious young lawyer from Kosciusko, Ralph L. Landrum, who came to play an important role in the making of the Natchez Trace Parkway and influenced Roane Byrnes's life. During the third day of the conference, the group resolved to become an actual organization and aspired for even greater things than paving the trace from Nashville to Natchez—they sought to pave not only the trace but also the historic Wilderness Road and El Camino Royal, thereby making a grand highway from Washington, DC, to Mexico City, one that would run through Natchez. Most attendees were excited and motivated to urge the federal government to rebuild the trace, but there were others who questioned whether it could actually be done. One of the most prominent skeptics was Dunbar Rowland, director of the Mississippi Department of Archives and History, who was conspicuously absent from the meeting (although his office was only a few blocks away). He expressed "very serious doubts . . . as to the feasibility or wisdom . . . of attempting to induce the federal government to reopen and pave the old Trace"; after all, according to him, most of the road was still in use.²⁶ But the Mississippi legislature did not share Rowland's concerns. While meeting during the same evening as the Natchez Trace Association meetings, legislators unanimously passed a joint resolution requesting that the US Congress appropriate funding "to pave the Old Trace."²⁷ Meanwhile at the Edwards Hotel Natchez Trace Association conference, the attendees organized themselves into a lobbying group and discussed how to build a new trace.

Representing the National Park Service, Stuart Cuthbertson and Olaf Hagen explained how the agency would work with the newly formed Natchez Trace Association and the state government. Then the association elected Lucille Mayfield as its first president and Pontotoc newspaperman E. T. Winston as vice president; Ralph Landrum was named secretary-treasurer.²⁸ In perhaps an act of sympathy, the members also elected the unpredictable Colonel Walton as field director.²⁹ The association's first two objectives were to rally statewide support for building the trace and then enlist the support of the two other states the old trace passed through—Alabama and Tennessee.

Congressman Jeff Busby may have originally sought to make the trace a commercial highway, but it appears that Lucille Mayfield convinced him to propose a parkway, similar to the Blue Ridge Parkway. Mayfield had been moving up the chain of command in the national DAR. On one of her visits to Washington, she learned about the parkway concept, which was designed to be more scenic and prohibited commercial vehicles on it. But few people in Mississippi, most notably the state legislature, understood what a parkway was and what requirements it entailed.³⁰

Soon after the meeting at the Edwards Hotel, Mayfield reached out to good roads advocates and DAR members in Alabama and Tennessee, urging them to start similar trace associations and to contact their congressional delegations. This began a loosely organized but effective network for lobbying for the trace. Meanwhile, Walton, along with Mayfield and Ralph Landrum, began a promotional tour in 1934 promoting the trace, which could be the first phase of building an international parkway to Mexico.³¹

On February 14, 1934, Busby introduced two appropriation bills in the House of Representatives for the Natchez Trace. His first bill was to appropriate $50,000 for a survey for a road "to be known as the Natchez Trace Parkway." The second proposed a separate act that would appropriate $25 million for constructing the parkway. Busby spoke of the unique history of the old road, emphasizing its crucial role in Andrew Jackson's victorious Battle of New Orleans during the War of 1812. He assured his congressional colleagues that rebuilding the trace would be "an advantageous and useful investment by the National Government for all the people." He made note in his presentation that there was strong support in Mississippi, Alabama, and Tennessee for the project.[32]

Five days later, Senator Hubert D. Stephens proposed identical bills in the US Senate. Both the House and Senate bills were referred to the House Committee on Roads. Committee chairman Wilburn Cartright scheduled two days of hearings, beginning on March 5, 1934. During the hearing, Busby rationalized the building of the road, balancing the recreation with practical use:

> It is a scenic highway, but it also is a utility proposition, a project of great usefulness. People of the country must find the best way they can from New Orleans, Baton Rouge, and points in Texas across to Nashville, Paducah, and other sections of the North and East; but there is no system of roads that is adequate to this particular territory and there is not likely to be any for many years to come.[33]

The entire Mississippi congressional delegation testified during the hearing and voiced their support of the trace proposal. Congressional representatives from the neighboring states in which the trace passed also testified. Then Busby arranged for members of the Natchez Trace Association to explain to the committee the importance of the Natchez Trace. They included Lucille Mayfield, E. T. Winston, Ralph Landrum, and George Maynard of Tupelo. Walton was not invited to Washington to testify in favor of the trace project. After the Edwards Hotel Natchez Trace Association meeting, he had harbored ill feelings towards Busby, Mayfield, and especially Landrum, who he felt cheated him out of the position of association treasurer. Landrum always believed that Walton "looked with longing eyes at the treasury of a few hundred dollars, and he immediately lost interest."[34] Apparently, Walton believed that he had riches waiting for him with his scam. It also appears that Busby felt that Walton's flamboyant exploits might hurt the project more than help it in the congressional hearings. It was at this juncture of the Natchez Trace Parkway project that Walton's involvement in the project ended. At the suggestion of Mayfield, Busby arranged for the authority on the history of the Natchez Trace, Edith Moore, to testify in front of the roads committee.[35]

Among all of the congressmen and senators from Mississippi, none had more sway in Congress than Senator Pat Harrison, the powerful Senate finance committee chairman. In his testimony, he stated: "The people of My State are deeply interested in this proposed legislation. They are interested not only because of commercial benefits but also because it will mean the marking of a very historic trail."[36]

Figure 5.5: View looking south of the George Washington Memorial Parkway at Wellington, Virginia. Built in 1930, the George Washington Memorial Parkway epitomized the convergence of landscape architecture, patriotic virtues, and historic preservation. (Library of Congress, Prints & Photographs Division, Historic American Engineering Record, HAER VA,30-,8-)

The roads committee approved the proposal and forwarded it to the House floor. The House and the Senate then authorized the two appropriation bills to the Bureau of Budget for an opinion. At this juncture of the legislative process, Secretary of the Interior Harold Ickes stated that the proposal was flatly "not in accord" with President Roosevelt's New Deal program and he advised the president to veto the bill. Harrison arranged a meeting with Roosevelt, bringing along with him Busby and the rest of the Mississippi delegation. Harrison convinced Roosevelt not to veto the survey bill, and Roosevelt authorized that the survey be financed from the 1935 National Park Service's Roads and Trails appropriation. Ickes was furious.[37] The bill for the survey was signed on May 21, 1934, but the $25 million road construction bill was defeated. Encouraged that the idea had made it that far, Busby, Harrison, and the Natchez Trace Association came away optimistic, but the appropriation for the Natchez Trace survey came with one very significant stipulation—it was to become a parkway, not a highway.[38]

How the Natchez Trace became a parkway and not a highway is yet another story of how several Mississippi and Natchez women changed the state's landscape and preserved its built heritage. Through her involvement in the DAR, which later would take her from Mississippi to Washington, Lucille Mayfield embraced the predominantly East Coast idea of linking the pragmatic concerns—safe, efficient automotive-based travel—with the symbolic concerns and symbolic landscapes that epitomized America's historic virtues and ideals. In her travels through Virginia, Mayfield experienced the Mount Vernon Memorial Highway (now the George Washington Memorial Parkway), which links McLean, Virginia, and George Washington's Mount Vernon. Mayfield envisioned the Natchez Trace Parkway being a similar patriotic excursion (figure 5.5).

Parkway design and development employed sophisticated design strategies in landscape architecture and aggressive government intervention. The intent was to produce a road within a landscape, embedded with both elite and popular imagery of a romanticized vernacular countryside, which embodied the values of hard work, honesty, and steadfastness. Long-distance roads like this had never existed before. Limited in scope and located in or near urban centers, parkways were viewed as primarily respites, placed in park settings and away from disorderly, loud, and dirty city streets. As the automobile became more and more part of everyday American life and pleasure travel, integral to modern tourism, the parkway as an interstate roadway was first conceived and built beginning with the Mount Vernon Memorial Highway (1928), then the Colonial Parkway (1930) and Skyline Drive (1930), all in Virginia. The first long-distance parkway built was the CCC-funded Blue Ridge Parkway (1935), from Rockfish Gap, Virginia, to Oconaluftee, North Carolina; it was 469 miles in length. By the time the Natchez Trace Parkway was proposed in 1934, the design ideas for making a parkway were established.[39]

Parkways built and managed by the National Park Service during the Great Depression became very popular with the American public, who were using the automobile more and more for tourism activities. Soon after they were built, they were considered "showcases of landscape engineering." They were also a definitive response to the calamitous effects of the Great Depression, as their construction immediately provided work for hundreds of unemployed men. And because they were separate appropriations from those for a specific state, congressmen coveted these projects and sought them. And while Ickes was critical of the NPS for wanting to build functional roads in the national parks, he was enthusiastic about the building of parkways.[40] As a trained landscape architect and a preservationist, chief NPS planner Thomas Vint had strong ideas regarding the design and construction of parkways. For him, a national parkway design "should preserve and protect the scene at one of the great moments in our national history." He believed that the best way to accomplish this objective was to hold the scene of the moment frozen in time, making both the scene and the moment important.[41]

Figure 5.6: View of the log fire lookout and a "buck" or "yankee" fence in the foreground at Groundhog Mountain, Blue Ridge Parkway, Patrick County, Virginia, built in 1942. (Library of Congress, Prints & Photographs Division, Historic American Engineering Record, HAER NC,11-ASHV.V,2-88)

There were practical reasons to combine historic buildings and moments with the cultural landscape in creating the ideal American parkway. NPS landscape architect Stanley Abbott recollected that the designers soon realized that most motorists would find hundred-mile stretches of unrelenting natural scenery extremely boring.[42] Historic structures and farmsteads intermittently placed along the parkway broke the monotony of automotive travel at a leisurely speed. Also, by utilizing the existing, and historic, vernacular landscape, construction costs could be mitigated. Vint, Abbott, and others were convinced that by merging historic monuments and cultural landscapes, the NPS could provide the relaxation, inspiration, and cultural reassurance that Americans sought during the Great Depression. The NPS's approach brought about two significant challenges to parkway design. First, by attempting to isolate the motorist from modernity, provocative tensions were produced between what historian Timothy Davis refers to as an "institutional vernacular" (figure 5.6)[43] and modern commercial roadside landscapes, which were growing in numbers and scale with each passing year of the automobile. Second, combining cultural landscapes, landscape architecture, and historic monuments with civil engineering required a tremendous amount of land, a minimum of eight hundred feet of absolute wide right-of-way, along with another four hundred feet of easement from development, spanning hundreds of miles. Mississippians, Alabamians, and Tennesseans had never experienced such a large-scale seizure of private property for a public works project in their history, and most of them reacted negatively to the idea of losing possibly large portions of their land. State or federal governments had never used eminent domain at this scale before in the Deep South. And to make matters worse, most of them had little or no idea why the parkway had to be a designed landscape.

Originally, most Mississippians, including Roane Byrnes, only wanted a functional road to cross through Mississippi. Now, the legislation, for a meager funding of $50,000 for a preliminary survey, stipulated that the states of Mississippi, Alabama, and Tennessee promise the federal government the required rights-of-way to receive any future funding for the project. In short, no right-of-way, no Natchez Trace Parkway. This was Byrnes's first and most formidable challenge when she assumed the presidency of the Natchez Trace Association.[44]

MADAME PRESIDENT

On March 26, 1935, in a happenstance meeting in downtown Natchez, Melrose owner George Kelly congratulated Roane Byrnes for being elected "Madame President" of the Natchez Trace Association. Byrnes laughed and shared with Kelly the story of how DAR state regent Mrs. Robert Henry wanted the DAR to take total control of the trace initiative. Byrnes shared with Kelly how, in her meeting at the Edwards Hotel in Jackson, Henry was "just as sweet as honey and shared with me the rumor that the Natchez Trace Association had fallen through." Byrnes replied, "Oh! No! We have 300 members, more than all the rest of the states put together." But Kelly feared that Henry's ploy was just another way for people in Jackson to take over a Mississippi project. Byrnes assured him that would not happen. Natchez women like Edith Moore and Harriet Dixon were well positioned in the organization, and Byrnes had the support of the Kosciusko delegation, who disliked Jacksonians as much as Kelly did. For Kelly, the idea of the city of Jackson getting involved in planning the trace was "despicable politics!" As he remarked to Ethel Kelly, "after all, Andy Jackson didn't march through Jackson on his way to fight the British in New Orleans."[45] But Byrnes had greater challenges than regional rivalries in leading the Natchez Trace Parkway project. Where exactly was the trace located? How was she going to convince the state of Mississippi to purchase the large right-of-way and easement required by the NPS to build it? And how was she going to convince the state and federal government to fund its construction?

Byrnes had become involved in the Natchez Trace Association completely by accident. During the association's meeting in July 1934, she agreed to attend the meeting in Jackson and give a report from the Natchez chapter as a favor to Harriet Dixon, who was ill at the time. The last agenda item at the association meeting was to hold an election to replace E. T. Winston, who was stepping down as vice president. Byrnes recalled how a group in the association asked her to be vice president. At first, she flatly refused, saying, "Oh No! I've never even presided at a church meeting. I can't do it."[46] But Lucille Mayfield assured Byrnes that there was not anything to the job, and she would not have to actively participate in the meetings. Reluctantly, Byrnes accepted the position.

Mayfield had a strategic motive in enlisting Byrnes into the leadership of the Natchez Trace Association. As a fellow member of the DAR, Byrnes understood Mayfield's ideas for making the trace more than a commercial road—to make it a monument to Mississippi heritage. Byrnes also displayed enthusiasm for paving the trace, and Mayfield took note. She suggested submitting articles to newspapers and magazines throughout the country, extolling the history of the trace. Mayfield saw Byrnes's leadership potential, but she also understood that having another woman leader counterbalanced the male-dominated good roads contingent in the association. Lastly, Mayfield knew that a *Natchez* woman could carry a considerable amount of power and influence within the organization and in the state.[47]

Byrnes's motivation may have come from her deep sense of civic obligation or her frustration with the state of poor roads in the state. But her sense of adventure and wanting to embrace a challenge may also have attracted her to the cause. Further, the brewing strife between the homeowners, led by Katherine Miller, against the Natchez Garden Club over the ongoing restoration of Connelly's Tavern was an unpleasant experience for her. Throughout her life, Byrnes either deflected conflict away from her or avoided it all together, and the feud between her and Miller had been a fierce one. After four years of working with together, Byrnes and Miller parted ways. Byrnes concentrated on the Natchez Trace, and Miller took control of the Natchez pilgrimage.

In November 1934, Mayfield was offered a position at the DAR national headquarters in Washington and accepted it. Byrnes was made interim president of the Natchez Trace Association in Mississippi from December 1934 until March 1935, when she was elected to the first of her many terms as president of the association. Prior to leaving for Washington, Mayfield tutored Byrnes on the politics and political figures involved in the trace project (figure 5.7).

There were several men that Byrnes soon learned she had to work with in making the parkway a reality. How she managed and persuaded them was an important part of her success in the project. Mayfield con-

Figure 5.7: Roane Fleming Byrnes, Natchez Trace Association President, seated in front of the DAR Natchez Trace Monument in Natchez, Mississippi. Pictured are, from left to right seated: Mrs. Murrell, Mrs. Ed Ratcliff, Mrs. Ben Cameron, Elizabeth Jones, Roane Fleming Byrnes, Gerard Brandon, Mrs. Hugh Jenkin (standing), Miss Charlie Compton; second row, standing: Natchez mayor William Byrne, Charles Engle, two unidentified women, Walter Abbott, and Florence Sillers Ogden. (Thomas H. and Joan W. Gandy Photograph Collection, Mss. 3778, Louisiana and Lower Mississippi Valley Collections, LSU Libraries, Baton Rouge, Louisiana)

Figure 5.8: Senator Pat Harrison of Mississippi, 1919–1941. (Library of Congress, Prints & Photographs Division, photograph by Harris & Ewing, LC-DIG-hec-29242)

Figure 5.9: Senator Theodore Bilbo of Mississippi, 1935–1947. (Library of Congress, Prints & Photographs Division, photograph by Harris & Ewing, LC-DIG-hec-29179)

fided to Byrnes that Congressman Jeff Busby, who wrote the first bill in Congress for the trace and had proved to be an able and competent politician, was not politically powerful enough to make the parkway a reality.[48] It was Senator Pat Harrison who was making things happen, both in Congress and in the Roosevelt White House (figure 5.8).[49]

Another Mississippi senator Byrnes had to work with was Theodore Gilmore Bilbo.[50] In the Senate, he was not as persuasive as Harrison in convincing his fellow senators to support legislation. He often accused them of being "farmer murderers," "poor-folks haters," and "spitters on our heroic veterans." Although Bilbo was a supporter of Roosevelt and the New Deal, FDR and his fellow Democrats had little use for him. However, he was supported by segregationists throughout the South.[51] Bilbo intensely hated Harrison, viewing him as a friend of the wealthy and an enemy of the "common folk." When asked by Harrison's aide to support Harrison's bid to become Senate majority leader, Bilbo angrily replied, "Tell the son of a bitch I wouldn't speak to him even if it meant the presidency of the United States" (figure 5.9).[52]

Byrnes had to persuade and then manage the self-absorbed US senators, and she also had to manage an unruly Mississippi congressional delegation consisting of career politicians who, like Bilbo, were blatant racists. The two congressmen who did not fan racial hatred were A. L. Ford and Wall Doxey.[53] Doxey was Harrison's most reliable colleague in championing the Natchez Trace Parkway in Congress. He also was a steadfast supporter of Harrison and succeeded him in the Senate after Harrison's death in 1941.[54]

The other six Mississippi congressmen were avid supporters of Bilbo and shared his racist views. John Rankin of Tupelo was a New Deal Democrat but also a white supremacist and a member of the Ku Klux Klan.[55] William M. Whittington of Greenwood, William M. Colmer of Moss Point, Dan R. McGehee of Meadville, and Ross A. Collins of Meridian were all white supremacists. Overall, because of their racism and racially based legislation in Congress, the Mississippi delegation was largely dismissed by their congressional colleagues. Only Harrison, Doxey, and Ford had the credibility with Congress and the Roosevelt White House to obtain the appropriations for the Natchez Trace Parkway.

Byrnes's primary contact in the state government was Governor Hugh White. He wanted to bring New Deal jobs in Mississippi. An avid recreational motorist, White saw the benefits of having a parkway in his state, especially if the federal government financed it.

Byrnes also had counterparts, fellow presidents of Natchez Trace Associations in Alabama and Tennessee. The three "divisions" of the association coordinated their efforts in soliciting federal support for building the project. Paul Coburn, the editor and publisher of the *Tuscumbia Reporter* in Tuscumbia, Alabama, was president of the Alabama division of the Natchez Trace Association. He became interested in the parkway project because the majority of the thirty-three miles of it that runs through Alabama crossed his home county of Colbert County. As a newspaperman, Coburn was renowned for "horse trading" in the Alabama legislature. It was because of his "calling in favors" that the state of Alabama purchased the rights-of-way and easements for the project.[56] Coburn was always very cordial and supportive of Byrnes and how she was leading the Mississippi division of the association. Often the two would jokingly tease each other in their correspondence.

Byrnes's counterpart in Tennessee, however, was very skeptical of her abilities. The president of the Tennessee division of the Natchez Trace Association was Patrick Mann (P. M.) Estes (1872–1947), an upper-class corporate attorney from Nashville. Somber and stern, he was the antithesis of the effervescent Roane Byrnes. Estes may not have preferred Byrnes to be his counterpart in Mississippi, but he had no choice but to rely on her to be the leader of the three states' efforts since most of the old trace crossed Mississippi. He looked down on Mississippians and once remarked to Byrnes that Tennessee had a more developed public road system than Mississippi. He was general legal counsel of the Life and Casualty Insurance Company of Tennessee and a prominent member of the Belle Meade Country Club in Nashville. Estes was a lifelong Republican who despised Roosevelt and the New Deal, and he often claimed bitterly that Roosevelt and his people were wasting tax dollars. But he was also a motor enthusiast who enjoyed pleasure driving. During the 1920s and 1930s, he was president of the upper-crust Nashville Automobile Club. Thus, despite his disdain for the Democratic Party, Estes knew that there was an opportunity for Tennessee to receive federal funding for a new road. Because of his experience lobbying for the insurance industry, he knew how to get legislation through the state legislature and Congress, often thoroughly researching any issue he lobbied for in Congress and the politicians he solicited for support. His motorist hobby was what attracted him to the project, but, like the Natchez Garden Club women, he also understood the potential of developing the local heritage for economic development.[57]

Despite their differences in personality, Estes and Byrnes learned to work well together. His pragmatism kept her focused and grounded, and her optimism and enthusiasm motivated him to carry on when situations appeared dour for the parkway project. Initially considering the trace as just another road funded by what he saw as the ill-conceived New Deal, Estes felt that if the federal government was going to spend money on infrastructure, then it might as well happen in Tennessee. Unlike Byrnes, who reached out to as many people as possible to help her on the parkway project, Estes was essentially a one-person Natchez Trace Association for Tennessee, much to the dismay of many Tennesseans who supported the project. But with his political connections, it appeared that the lone Estes was enough of a factor to effectively bring Tennessee into the cooperative agreement with Mississippi and Alabama to make the parkway a reality.

Byrnes's partner in the Mississippi division of the Natchez Trace Association was Ralph Landrum. Landrum was a young and aggressive attorney from Kosciusko, Mississippi. Like Byrnes, he was a natural promoter, with an infectious enthusiasm for the project and an unshakeable good humor. But what Byrnes lacked was his eye for detail. As both secretary and treasurer of the Natchez Trace Association, Landrum made sure that dues were paid by the local chapters, records were kept, and lines of communication remained open between all of the interested trace parties. But his most important skill was to always make sure that the right people attended crucial meetings, and he consistently wrote letters inviting and reminding key politicians to attend important meetings. As a practicing lawyer, at times his professional tact was instrumental in keeping the association together.

Byrnes was savvy enough to delegate contact with politicians among her friends and Landrum. Following Mayfield's advice, she kept in constant contact with Pat Harrison, but realizing the animosity between Harrison and Bilbo, she asked her husband, Ferriday, to correspond with Bilbo. Ferriday enjoyed Bilbo's populist rants in Washington, and perhaps because of his financial calamities caused by his heavy drinking, he identified with Bilbo's ideas regarding the championing of the forgotten poor white man. Ferriday enthusiastically accepted his wife's request to handle Bilbo. This marked the start of a productive relationship between Ferriday and Roane during their middle-age years and at the end of his legal career.[58] Ferriday, along with Anne Alexander and Lallie Lawrence, traveled throughout the state and across the country to tout the benefits of the Natchez Trace Parkway.

Roane Byrnes relied on A. L. Ford to lead the state's House of Representatives delegation in passing appropriation bills for the parkway. Although a junior congressman, Ford quickly demonstrated that he was an effective politician. Landrum developed productive relationships with members of Congress and the Mississippi legislature. He also actively worked on getting support from local governments and civic groups.

Both Roane Byrnes and Ralph Landrum had a productive working relationship with Malcom Gardner, who had been head historian at the Vicksburg National Battlefield Park but now was assigned by Thomas Vint to manage the development of the parkway idea. They also worked closely with other members of the NPS staff: Stuart Cuthbertson, who at the time was working with Edith Moore on the HABS project in Natchez, and NPS historian Olaf Hagen. Later in the project, they worked with his successor, Dawson Phelps. The speed with which Byrnes and Landrum organized the Natchez Trace Association and developed effective communication with their counterparts Estes and Coburn was impressive. It had to be. Once Roosevelt signed the bill appropriating the survey, the Natchez Trace Parkway project was put in motion, and events happened quickly.

A ROAD "EASY TO TRAVEL AND HARD TO FOLLER"

Jeff Busby's bill for a survey of the Natchez Trace Parkway in 1934 was more than merely a survey; it was a comprehensive historical study, a civil engineering study, and a preliminary design for the parkway. After signing the legislation, Roosevelt instructed the NPS to allocate $50,000 from its 1934 Roads and Trails appropriation and set up an ad hoc group to answer the following questions: Where was the original Natchez Trace located? What would be the design of the modern parkway? How much would the project cost? And finally, what would be the required rights-of-way that Mississippi, Alabama, and Tennessee had to provide in order to make the parkway a reality? But there was also a strategic issue that should have been considered. Beginning with the Mount Vernon Memorial Highway, then the Colonial Parkway, and then the Blue Ridge Parkway, the National Park Service managed parkways centered around two ideas—history and natural scenery. The Natchez Trace had neither of these qualities, and this proved to be problematic.

Determining the location of colonial roads proved to be perplexing and elusive. For Depression-era historians and archaeologists, colonial roads like the Natchez Trace, the Spanish Trail, and El Camino Real were frustrating to precisely locate because they did not exist as roadways as we define them today. Essentially, there were many "Spanish Trails" and many "Natchez Traces," and no one could declare with any certainty which trail or path was the real road. Early travelers never adhered to one distinct path because one singular road was never built. Rather, they traveled the path of least resistance. Early Americans walked around mudholes, avoided swamps and steep hills, and bypassed fallen trees or overgrown thickets. There were few colonial-era maps for the NPS historians to examine, and those that existed were inaccurate. To complicate matters more, when the metes and bounds information were indicated on the maps, the referenced landmarks (e.g., an old pine tree, rock outcropping) had long ago been removed. But the legislation clearly stipulated the survey's intent was to locate the Natchez Trace "as near as practicable to its original route."[59]

From the beginning of the project, NPS administrators were dubious about whether the Natchez Trace should be part of its parkway system. But the decision was not theirs to make. Mississippians, Alabamans, and Tennesseans wanted a road that the federal government would pay for and build. With influential politicians connected to Roosevelt, like Senators Harrison of Mississippi and John H. Bankhead II of Alabama, Speakers of the House Joseph W. Byrns of Tennessee and then William B. Bankhead of Alabama, the political muscle behind making the trace a parkway was formidable.

Much to Ickes's ire, $40,000 of the $50,000 from the NPS's survey budget was allocated to the Bureau of Public Roads in the Department of Commerce. Prior to any design work, historical research had to be conducted. NPS head historian Verne Chatelain's historians were mobilized to determine the historical significance and actual location of the old trace, but only after Harrison and Bilbo applied pressure (on behalf of Roane Byrnes) on Ickes to make the project a priority.[60] Chatelain had not planned for the project in early 1935; in fact, he and Ronald Lee were still organizing the History Division, which had only been implemented in the NPS in 1934. Lee hastily assembled a group of recently graduated, academically trained historians and assigned them the project. In addition to their other work, Chatelain authorized them to produce new historical interpretation plans for the parks. After departmental infighting and bureaucracy, the trace's historical survey finally began in February 1935. The final research document that was submitted to Vint and Cammerer was a neglected and poorly construed one. Unfortunately, it became the basis of the planning process for the parkway.

Lee assigned NPS historian Ruth E. Butler to research the trace in the Washington, DC, federal archives; Olaf Hagen was assigned to research it in Mississippi; and Randle Truett was assigned to research it in Alabama and Tennessee. Butler examined documentation about the trace in the Library of Congress, the US Geological Survey, the War Department archives, and the General Land Office. Hagen and Truett reviewed the original state surveys in Alabama and Mississippi, but in Tennessee, the only map that mentioned the trace was a military map prepared by James Wilkinson prior to the War of 1812. Despite the extensive research effort in federal archives, identifying the road was elusive.

Frustrated by the dead ends he encountered, especially in the Old Natchez District, Hagen consulted Edith Moore. He was dubious about her claims about the trace, however. Finally, he toured all of the counties where the trace was believed to have crossed. Hagen most likely experienced the same frustrations that others had before him. In "The Natchez Trace," published in the September 1905 issue of *Everybody's Magazine*, John Swain described how difficult it was to locate the fabled road:

> In humility, my mind went back to the advice I had received from an old woman at [a place called] She Boss (expressively named hamlet!) some four hours earlier.
>
> "You're going a mighty crooked road," she had said, "and maybe you'll keep to it all right. But I reckon you'll find the Natchez Trace easy to travel and hard to foller. You better ask everybody you see if you're on it."[61]

By April 1935, the three historians had run out of time and were forced to compile their findings and submit them to Gardner, who then forwarded the revised report to Vint and Cammerer. They reviewed it and suggested revisions, and the final version was then forwarded to the House Committee on Roads.[62] Chatelain did not supervise the historians (and most likely was contemplating retiring and leaving the NPS during this time). It appears that Lee had only minimal involvement. The lack of senior-level management proved to be very problematic for conceiving a history-based Natchez Trace Parkway. Parkway historian Dawson Phelps summarized their work and its impact on the parkway development:

Figure 5.10: John Nolen, landscape architect and city planner. Nolen created the conceptual design of the Natchez Trace Parkway. (Library of Congress, Prints & Photographs Division, LC-DIG-ggbain-06138)

The three inexperienced historians who were assigned the job of locating the Natchez Trace on a map and then flagging this location on the ground worked under a misconception that proved to be a serious, but not fatal, handicap. They were seeking a road that never was, which had acquired a name, retrospectively, many years after it and its component parts had lost those characteristics assigned to it in the preamble of Busby's resolution of 1934.[63]

Despite the report's findings, which stated a meager, even tenuous, basis for historic site development anywhere along the old trace route, and the acknowledgment that it was impossible to identify and locate the Old Natchez Trace, Cammerer and Vint arrived at a solution that would justify the project within the mission of the NPS and accommodate the political pressure they felt to make the project happen: by building this parkway, the NPS would not conserve or restore what likely never was a singular path; rather, they would memorialize the Old Natchez Trace.[64] The decision forever changed the mission of the NPS. By compromising on the lack of historical integrity in the old trace and lacking a picturesque landscape, but accepting that the trace would be memorialized, the NPS compromised its mission.

The Bureau of Public Roads assigned civil engineer Frank L. Brownell to lead the engineering design. Vint assigned NPS landscape architect Edward S. Zimmer to coordinate the landscape design and the historical research for the project and then forward it to Brownell. As the historians completed their work, they sent mapping information to Brownell, who compiled a map and instructed engineers to use red paint to mark trees and fence posts on the ground to show the approximate location of

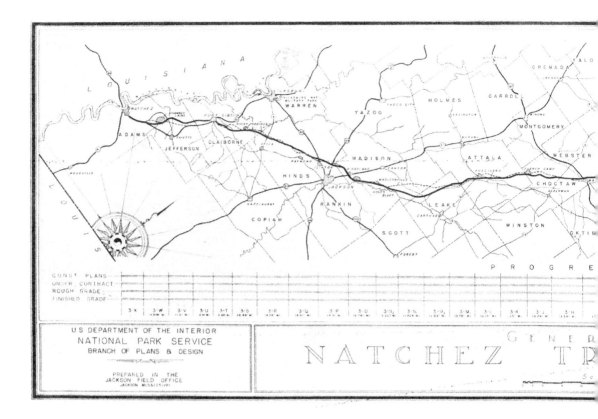

Figure 5.11: Conceptual map of the Natchez Trace Parkway design, 1940, Branch of Plans & Designs—Eastern Division, Branch of Education & Research—Historical Division, National Park Service and the Bureau of Public Roads, Department of Commerce. (Mississippi Department of Archives and History)

the trace. On March 14–21, 1935, NPS administrators Hillary A. Tolson, Vint, and Chatelain, accompanied by Zimmer, Hagen, and Truett, but not Ruth Butler, conducted an inspection party for the parkway project. Joining the team was landscape architect John Nolen (figure 5.10).[65] Together, the men agreed to the approximate location of the parkway. The NPS commissioned Nolen to produce the conceptual design.[66]

With Nolen's consultation, the National Park Service developed a conceptual route design of the memorialized parkway (figure 5.11). The design was divided into four units. "Unit One" began west of Natchez and ended near Raymond, Mississippi. There, the parkway ended and resumed east of Ridgeland, Mississippi, which began "Unit Two"; it passed northeast of Kosciusko, Mississippi, and ended at Tupelo. "Unit Three" was the parkway's portion in Alabama; it passed northwest of Florence and ended in Iuka, Alabama. There, "Unit Four" began and concluded near Franklin, Tennessee. The unit division of the parkway design was a sensible approach in designing for the diverse topogra-

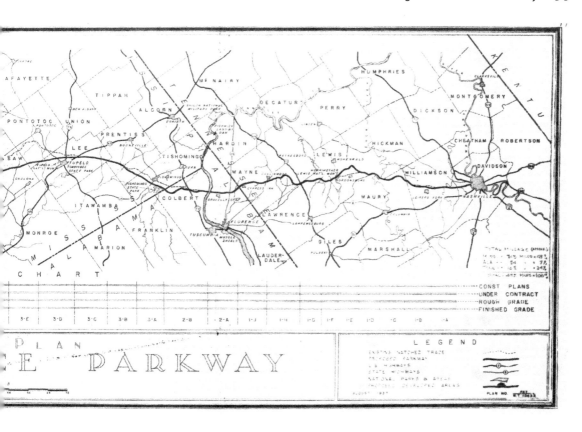

phy—low Mississippi River swampland, central Mississippi pine forest land, and the limestone outcropping landscape of the northern corner of Alabama and central Tennessee—that was encountered along the proposed 444-mile parkway. The route was now set, and the NPS requested from the states dedicated eight hundred-foot rights-of-way and four hundred-foot easements adjacent to the proposed parkway. This proved to be a daunting challenge for the three southern states.

The March 1935 Natchez Trace Association meeting in Jackson was an important one in the history of the parkway. First, Roane Byrnes was elected president of the association, a position she would hold for the remaining thirty-five years of her life. Second, Olaf Hagen explained how the relationship between the federal government and the states worked in building a parkway. The first and most daunting challenge was for the states to provide the required rights-of-way to the federal government. Regulations established by the Bureau of Public Roads required a clear title to the land for the road, the right-of-way, and the easements before construction could not only begin but also at the time construction appropriations were considered by Congress. The total cost for purchasing rights-of-way in Mississippi was estimated at $500,000.[67] The staggering cost for land acquisition caused great alarm among Mississippi politicians, especially Governor Hugh White. To complicate matters, both Estes and Coburn informed Byrnes that since Mississippi possessed the majority of the trace within its boundaries, Tennessee and Alabama would wait for Mississippi's lead in making the parkway a reality.[68]

Two obstacles had to be surmounted. Although Wilkinson, Jefferson, and Hinds Counties in Mississippi readily secured rights-of-way, administrators in the remaining nine counties in the parkway project had no idea how to go about securing them. A statewide program had to be established for parkway land acquisition. Byrnes also had to persuade a sticker-shocked Mississippi legislature and a skeptical public that the parkway was a good state investment. Ralph Landrum worked with the counties in developing local land acquisition offices, which were coordinated by the Mississippi highway office. And Byrnes began her over three-decade promotional program for the project, beginning with rights-of-way acquisition.

She immediately utilized the Natchez Spring Pilgrimage to rally support for the project. Occurring simultaneously with the land acquisition debates in Jackson was the Connelly's Tavern dedication, held in March 1936, so she planned to feature the parkway project during the event. She arranged for Stark Young and Charles Scribner's Sons to publish five hundred special Natchez Trace commemorative copies of *So Red the Rose*, although the novel only mentioned the trace. The special editions were personally signed by Young. Combined with the tavern dedication, the presence of this initiative galled Katherine Miller, Ruth Beltzhoover, and the rest of the homeowners, who protested that the tavern project had happened at all. To them, Byrnes was now using it, and the Natchez pilgrimage, to promote another of her projects.[69]

Byrnes was able to build her confidence in leading the parkway funding campaign through the Connelly's Tavern promotion. Afterward, she devoted her energy to campaigning across the state for the Mississippi legislature to pass an appropriations bill to fund parkway land acquisition. She gave talks to civic groups, was interviewed on radio broadcasts, and wrote newspaper articles. She created a statewide high school essay contest, and she planned rallies in Natchez, Kosciusko, Mathiston, and Tupelo. She, Landrum, and others fabricated a state holiday, "Natchez Trace Day," on June 21, 1935, and urged supporters to organize rallies for the trace. Finally, she routinely sent letters and telegrams to state politicians, always reminding them about how important and exciting the parkway project was.[70]

Figure 5.12: Cover image, "Why the Natchez Trace Should Be Constructed," prepared by the Natchez Trace Association, Mississippi Division, Natchez, Mississippi, November 6, 1935. (National Park Service, Natchez Trace Parkway Archives, Tupelo, Mississippi)

Byrnes and Landrum also produced a brochure, "Why the Natchez Trace Parkway Should Be Constructed," and handed out copies to civic group members and politicians (figure 5.12). In it, she developed another narrative, loosely based on factual history, and listed the reasons why the parkway needed to be funded and built. She claimed that the trace was an ancient trail used by the Choctaw and Chickasaw Indians, who were "staunch friends of the United States," and that the modern roadway would be a commemoration to their memory of their friendship with the United States.[71] Further, not only was the old trace important to the settling of America, but it was traveled by some individuals prominent in US history: Meriwether Lewis, Aaron Burr, Andrew Jackson, Lafayette, and Jefferson Davis. In her telling, not only was it the route that Jackson took to defeat the British at New Orleans; it was also a vital road in supplying American troops during the Mexican War. She concluded her history by emphasizing its close proximity to the Vicksburg and Shiloh National Battlefields and "several famous battlefields in Tennessee." And then she promoted her hometown: "Natchez, Miss., name town of the Trace, is one of the most famous historic shrines of America, and its well-preserved Antebellum mansions attract thousands of visitors annually."

In the brochure, Byrnes rationalized paving the trace by asserting its regional and national significance and "outstanding and undisputed historic value," which alone she thought should be sufficient reason for preserving this ancient American Indian trail as a national parkway.[72] But she also made an argument to pave it for practical and economic reasons: "the historic road would greatly benefit not only Mississippi but all sections of the United States." She reiterated her dream that the new parkway would be part of an important highway system, linking Washington, DC, to Mexico City, thereby further developing the friendship between the US and Mexico. Only the Mississippi River could encumber the motorist, but she reassured readers that "There is excellent free ferry service at Natchez and there has been promised by the State a new bridge." She also mentioned the promise of well-paying construction jobs and that, to date, the federal government had paid very little attention to the Mississippi counties the trace would cross. Finally, she maintained that the parkway would repair relations between the North and the South: "Roads are the ties which bind a nation together."

In her summary of the status of the development of the project in the brochure, Byrnes exaggerated the facts. She claimed that the parkway was adopted by the National Park Service and approved by the WPA and President Roosevelt, and that the survey that located the ancient trail had been completed. Then she claimed that the Mississippi Allotment Board had allocated $500,000 for engineering design between Natchez and Tupelo, and that road work was underway between Tupelo and Clinton, costing over $1 million. But she reminded readers, "The government contemplates the completion of the project, but we cannot relax in our efforts to keep the matter before the attention of our senators and representatives." Finally, she concluded her brochure, stating in bold: "NOTE: Funds for the Natchez Trace Parkway are not derived from the funds allotted to our State, but will be an extra gift from the Federal Government to Mississippi."[73]

In promoting the parkway idea, Byrnes pressed the Natchez narrative on the rest of Mississippi. She also launched Natchez heritage into the public discourse before NPS historians could verify and disseminate a researched history on the trace. She understood that the NPS's mission was to showcase American history and nature, and if they had accepted that the new parkway was only going to memorialize the trail, then so be it. Using the Natchez narrative, she was determined to make the old trace more historic than it ever was.

And then there are her problematic claims about the future of the parkway. Byrnes needed grassroots support in Mississippi to pressure

Harrison, Bilbo, Ford, and Governor White. She was willing to stretch the truth to generate enthusiasm in Mississippi for the project.

Byrnes also wanted to prove that the old trace was already being experienced by motorist tourists. She asked Edith Moore to write a driving guide for the trace in 1936, which focused entirely on Natchez. Moore, now appointed by the WPA Writers' Project as "Government Historical Technician of the Natchez Territory," provided a point-of-interest tour around Natchez on the old trace in her brochure, "Path of the Natchez Trace in the Country of the Natchez Tribes." Using the HABS reports she was compiling, Moore started the tour at the DAR monument at Bluff Park, which she stated was long known as the "Esplanade" and where soldiers from Spain, France, and Britain, as well as the United States, paraded. She then mentioned Rosalie and the ancient Spanish house on Gilreath Hill, which was being restored at the time (it had not become Connelly's Tavern just yet), where Ellicott raised the flag (the site later became known as Ellicott's Hill[74]) and Burr committed treason. Next, she mentioned King's Tavern and claimed that a young Abraham Lincoln most likely had patronized the establishment. She declared that Summerset plantation was where the first cotton was produced for export. But unlike her writings about Natchez history, grandeur, and architecture, Moore introduced a new facet of the narrative—treachery. On St. Catherine's Street, she told of "Huge Oaks" and described how the severed head of the notorious bandit and murderer, Samuel Mason, was brought to these trees and identified by the terrorized local gentry in 1804. And at the corner of the Kingston Road and Lower Woodville Road, where a filling station was standing, she determined, through her examinations of several old maps, that was where the White Horse Tavern had stood, the rendezvous point for the murderous Murrell gang. Byrnes and Moore were claiming that these and other unsavory intrigues happened along the old trace—all of which may have occurred.[75]

Throughout 1935 and 1936, Byrnes was under a considerable amount of stress. Both her parents died; her brother Jim and husband, Ferriday, were difficult alcoholics; and she was engaged in a feud with Katherine Miller and Annie Barnum over Connelly's Tavern. Along with all of these challenges, she was managing an elaborate lobbying campaign to secure millions of dollars for the trace and was the *de facto* leader of the drive for the project in two other states. Coburn waited on her before he solicited political support, saying that if Mississippi was committed, then Alabama would be as well. Estes, on the other hand, doubted Byrnes's political abilities to convince the Mississippi legislature to purchase the rights-of-way or Congress to fund the project. He wrote to her, "I cannot see from newspaper reports at Washington that we are making any progress with respect to [the] Natchez Trace."⁷⁶ Never one to admit defeat, she responded buoyantly to his pessimistic letters.

But Byrnes's tireless needling of Governor Hugh White eventually paid off, as he began to fully support the project. Ferriday Byrnes and Ralph Landrum also wrote letters to key Mississippi politicians. Harrison assured Roane Byrnes and Governor White that he was making headway in passing the road construction appropriation in Congress. And on October 1, 1935, in an extra session, the Mississippi legislature passed a bill appropriating $200,000 for the purchase of rights-of-way, with matching funds to be furnished by the counties through which the trace passed. In a state that received little direct federal appropriation and, in fact, was wary of federal involvement, the commitment to the parkway project was extraordinary. More importantly, Byrnes and Landrum had convinced the politicians that the eight hundred feet of rights-of-way, along with the four hundred feet of scenic easement, were necessary for the project. In its next term, the legislature passed a bill creating a three-member board called the Natchez Trace Commission, appointed by the governor, to oversee the purchase of rights-of-way.⁷⁷ White and key members of the state legislation only had Harrison's word that the federal money was coming for the project. Legislators and association members cast aspersions upon Harrison's power in Congress. P. M. Estes bluntly expressed his skepticism that the efforts would ever pay off.⁷⁸

But Harrison proved that he was more than capable of securing the funding for the project. On November 21, 1935, he sent a telegram to Byrnes informing her that Roosevelt had approved a $1.5 million allotment for the Natchez Trace Parkway. This was only a small initial amount for the estimated $25 million parkway, but it was a start. In securing it, Harrison bypassed Congress altogether and went directly to Roosevelt and WPA director Harry Hopkins for the emergency stop-gap funding. In the bill, Mississippi received $1.2 million, and the remaining funds were allocated to Tennessee.⁷⁹

Landrum realized that the entire Mississippi delegation had to be united in pursing the federal construction funding; he also understood the animosity between Harrison and Bilbo. He worked behind the scenes to get the two senators to work together on the parkway. He proposed a meeting between the two in Mississippi, where they would meet with Roane Byrnes and Edith Moore and other prominent members of the Natchez Trace Association. He ended his letter to Byrnes by saying, "In the meantime, if you think it might be well, some of you who are fairly close to Senator Bilbo, both in distance and politically, might see him and talk about the Natchez Trace." Byrnes asked her husband to begin a dialogue with Bilbo, and he did contact the senator. The meeting was held, and Harrison described to the association how he was going to propose the funding bill. The delegation pledged its support to Harrison.[80]

In Natchez, Byrnes reassured everyone that the project would be funded. Estes remained skeptical.[81] He wrote to Byrnes, "I have received your optimistic reports, but I cannot feel that they are justified. They are certainly different from anything that I have been able to learn here."[82] Nevertheless, Byrnes's victory in the Mississippi began to motivate Estes and Coburn to get busy in securing the rights-of-ways in their states.

Throughout 1935, Byrnes and the Mississippi delegation pushed for the full parkway appropriation. Ford and Harrison introduced the parkway bill in Congress, requesting $25 million for construction, and it was met with strong opposition, especially from Ickes, who was vehemently against the parkway. Ickes's approval was vital because he influenced how the National Emergency Council voted, and Roosevelt listened to him as well. Worried that the bill might be defeated, Landrum and Natchez Trace Association vice president Ashton Toomer went to Washington and met with the delegation. After meeting with them, Landrum concluded that if Harrison could not secure the funding, then no one could.

Harrison understood that the project would probably not receive the full appropriation, so he decided to try another approach. He had the parkway included in a $20 million parkway appropriations bill for fiscal years 1938 and 1939. Cammerer and Vint were not pleased with the idea that part of the federal parkway appropriation would go to a project they considered unworthy of becoming a parkway. Nevertheless, they developed a formula, on a mileage and cost basis, to allocate funding between the Blue Ridge Parkway, the Rocky Mountain Road, and the Natchez Trace Parkway. In the bill, Mississippi would receive $3 million in fiscal year 1937 and $3.4 million in fiscal year 1938.

Meanwhile, in Jackson, the rights-of-way acquisition had stalled. The Natchez Trace Commission reported to the legislature that it was having difficulties securing land in Madison County, and its members were even experiencing difficulties securing rights-of-way in Roane Byrnes's Adams County. To complicate matters more, the counties were either unable or refused to match the state's allocation for funding rights-of-way.

Byrnes had misjudged the degree to which Mississippians had accepted the Natchez narrative that she presented in selling the parkway. Most farmers in distant places, like Lee and Tishomingo Counties and where the old trace may have crossed, were outraged that their farms could be severed in two by the very wide NPS-mandated eight-hundred-foot right-of-way on each side of the road, plus four-hundred-foot wide additional scenic easement. Moreover, many farmers became enraged when the Zimmer landscape architecture team proposed the memorial design scheme, which veered away from the original trace as much as six miles in some areas. Byrnes received protest letters complaining that many stretches of the proposed parkway would run across the best farming fields in the state, and that the wider right-of-way was going to force some farmers to abandon their homes and country stores. Even an old established post office was slated for demolition, one farmer claimed.[83]

Farmers also complained that the National Park Service prohibited farm trucks and tractors on the proposed parkway. At the designated sixty-mile-per-hour speed limit, one protester doubted that any tourist would stop and spend money in his county. He mockingly suggested to Byrnes, "Perhaps it would be better to call it the Natchez Trace Speedway?"[84] She responded to nearly all of the protest letters, reassuring irate farmers that the new parkway would greatly benefit them.

Byrnes and Landrum decided that the only way to overcome the land acquisition obstacle was to persuade the Mississippi legislature to pass a new appropriations bill to purchase all of the rights-of-way. Time was of the essence: if Harrison could not present to Congress that the state had purchased the rights-of-ways and the easement, then the project was most certainly would not be funded. Byrnes persuaded Governor White to support the bill, which was up for debate in a special session. She then wrote letters to politicians and civic group leaders urging them to back the appropriation bill. Finally, she wrote an op-ed article in the Natchez *Democrat* putting White on notice to fully support the bill.[85]

In promoting the appropriations bill, Byrnes was once again not averse to exaggerating the importance of the parkway project. In her article, entitled "Mississippi Must Have the Natchez Trace Parkway," published in the September 1935 issue of *Mississippi Highways*, she earnestly pleaded:

> It is hard to realize just how much the construction of this project will mean to Mississippi. The Natchez Trace is not to be just a highway, but an elongated park reaching from the famous little town of Natchez in Southern Mississippi, through Alabama near Muscle Shoals, to Nashville, Tennessee. In addition to playing its part as a splendid modern road, a vital link in a highway system connecting Canada and Mexico City, it is to be one of the highly-prized showplaces of the nation, a Mecca for tourists where there will be preserved for the patriot a romantic page from the history of our country.[86]

In September 1936, Byrnes used her abilities as a hostess to lobby state politicians and highway administrators. Her parties at Ravennaside became the stuff of legend. One of her friends, novelist Alice

Walworth Graham, quipped that the Natchez Trace Parkway was paved with moonshine and meatloaf.[87] Byrnes recalled that meatloaf was an easy recipe for her long-serving cook, Charlotte Green, to prepare at a moment's notice (Byrnes had never learned how to cook), and moonshine was inexpensive and readily accessible in Depression-era Natchez. Young legislators, as well as NPS officials like Malcolm Gardner and Frank Brownell, loved coming to her parties. Often, the NPS planners would spread their drawings out on the floors of Byrnes's dining room and living room and discuss the project over moonshine.[88]

As the October date of the special session of the Mississippi legislature approached, Byrnes and Landrum planned for a large meeting and rally of the Natchez Trace Association at the Edwards Hotel in Jackson. In her letter to the general membership, she stressed how important this session was for the future of the Natchez Trace Parkway.[89]

Byrnes knew of the uncertainties in funding the construction and obtaining the needed right-of-way, but she was not afraid to exaggerate the truth. In her pleasant way, she responded to critics of the project, writing, "A reasonable and patriotic attitude on the part of these landowners in regard to land values along the right-of-way will practically assure us of the Trace and we feel sure that no right-thinking individual would be willing to obstruct a project which means so much to Mississippi."[90]

With dramatic flair, Byrnes opened the Natchez Trace Association meeting in Jackson by reading a telegram from Senator Harrison: "The immediate acquiring of rights of way for the Parkway is of vital importance, for otherwise the appropriation will be lost."[91] But promising news soon arrived at the meeting. The House Committee on Highways and Highway Financing approved $500,000 for right-of-way purchase, and on October 18, 1936, the Mississippi legislature approved using $500,000 from the gasoline tax fund on right-of-way.[92] With the right-of-way issue resolved, now the association could focus on the legislation in Washington. No one was more shocked at Byrnes's accomplishment than P. M. Estes, who congratulated her, but now realized that he had to lead Tennessee in acquiring right-of-way. Paul Coburn had to get to work in Alabama as well.[93]

In 1937, Byrnes's accomplishment was noticed by people not only in Mississippi but throughout the South. Women, among them Ethel Childress of Nashville, were inspired by her astuteness and moxie. Childress was frustrated by Estes's inactivity and conveyed it to Byrnes in several letters. In one letter, she said, "I was pleased to have all that information about the Trace in Mississippi, and took it down to Mr. Springfield in the Automobile Club to read. He and I talked it over and decided we were going to get behind Mr. Estes, President of our Trace Asso., so strong he would have to do something or resign. . . . Isn't it dreadful that our hands are tied by having as our President a man who doesn't do a thing and yet holds on to the office? I am surely going to get busy."[94]

Estes ignored complaints from his fellow Tennessee association members and pressed on with the parkway in Tennessee. Working first with Governor Hill McAliser and then Governor Gordon Browning, he was able to secure Tennessee's right-of-way acquisition for the parkway by May 1937.[95] With rights-of-way in Mississippi and Tennessee secured, Coburn had little trouble persuading the Alabama legislature to purchase the rights-of-way for the thirty-three miles of parkway in the northwest portion of the state.[96]

Male leaders in Natchez soon praised Byrnes for her accomplishment. The City Bank and Trust gave her its silver trophy for outstanding service to Natchez and Adams County. In the December 30, 1936, *Natchez Democrat*, the editorial praised and also inflated the scale of the project, stating that it was a fifty-million-dollar parkway.[97]

Although the Mississippi legislature enacted appropriations to remedy the rights-of-way issue, Washington did not regard it as sufficient to fund the construction of the parkway. The Bureau of Budget did not recommend that it receive funding due to the lack of acquired rights-of-way. Byrnes pressed Mississippi's Natchez Trace Commission to purchase it as soon as possible and promised Harrison that all of the rights-of-way along the trace would be ready in time of the funding authorization. Finally, by July 1937, all of the parkway rights-of-way and easements had been secured by the three states. The deeds for them were submitted to the National Park Service, and the Bureau of Budget authorized the initial construction of the parkway.[98] With her work completed in Mississippi, Byrnes's next objective was to convince the US and Mexico to extend the Natchez Trace Parkway all the way to Mexico City.

MEXICO CITY

In July 1937, Natchez society was buzzing with excitement regarding the news that one of their own, Roane Byrnes, was traveling across the country promoting Mississippi. In a letter to Ethel, George Kelly shared the news that Mary Louise Metcalf had busied herself coloring promotion brochures of the pilgrimage for Byrnes to take with her on the first westward transcontinental train trip of her life on the "Know Mississippi Now" train. According to George, she was traveling for two weeks and making twenty-nine stops from Jackson to Los Angeles and back. Roane's husband, Ferriday, was going with her. But before she would leave on the train, heading north and then west, she was going to Jackson to visit and contact several state officials about the parkway project.[99] Three years earlier, Byrnes had been a civic-minded housewife; now she was planning to represent the United States in developing an over two-thousand-mile-long parkway that would link the US and Mexico with a landscaped scenic design and heritage-themed road from Washington to Mexico City.[100]

Byrnes had convinced the state tourism office to fund the trip west to Mexico City for her to meet with the Mexican government and discuss the possibility of developing the old El Camino Real, linking it to the Natchez Trace Parkway, and then developing the Wilderness Road, building a parkway connecting Washington, DC, and Mexico City. Paul Coburn wished Byrnes a pleasant trip and expressed hope that the Mexican government "may investigate a plan to carry the Trace to Mexico City." He then quipped, "Better watch Mr. Byrnes or some Senorita may get him."[101]

With Harrison already occupied with pushing the appropriations bill, Roane Byrnes asked Ferriday to contact Bilbo to have the State Department arrange a meeting between her and Mexican president Lázaro Cárdenas del Río. Neither Ferriday nor Roane had heard from Bilbo about the status of the meeting when they departed on the train in Jackson, but when they arrived in Monterey, Mexico, on July 21, 1937, a telegram from Bilbo was waiting for them at the station. The State Department had arranged for her to meet Cardenas on July 23.[102]

Prior to traveling to Mexico, Byrnes and two of her fellow Natchez Garden Club members, Mary Lambdin and Anna Alexander, made presentations about the Natchez Spring Pilgrimage to garden clubs throughout Texas, New Mexico, Arizona, and southern California. Before she returned to Natchez, Byrnes shared her experience in Mexico City in a letter to *Natchez Democrat* news editor Ned Smith. She recalled that the train was eight hours behind schedule when it arrived in the Mexican capitol, and she and Ferriday then hurried to the presidential palace. When they arrived, they were disappointed to learn that President Cárdenas had been called out unexpectedly late the night before to help settle a railway strike in the Yucatan. She added, "It seems he attends personally to such things, and is a busier man even than President Roosevelt—so we were told at the American Embassy."[103]

Through his secretary, President Cárdenas conveyed to them that he would be happy to meet with them on the following Monday, but it was impossible for Roane and Ferriday to remain in Mexico City over the weekend as the train was scheduled to leave on Saturday evening. The president's secretary arranged for Roane to meet Cárdenas's right-hand man, General Francisco José Múgica, who was Cárdenas's secretary of the national economy and his ideological advisor. Roane told Smith that it was said that the leftist Múgica was "more of a Red than Trotsky."[104]

Staff members from the American embassy escorted Byrnes and her husband to Múgica's office in the lavish marble-floored federal building. Múgica had contacted Ickes in Washington to inquire who this middle-aged woman was and the reason she wanted to meet with him. Byrnes commented that neither Múgica nor Cárdenas understood any English, but Múgica's secretary, Concepcion de Pogos, spoke fluent English. Byrnes liked her and remarked to Smith that she was very pretty.[105]

The meeting went well. Byrnes remarked that Múgica "was very agreeable and gallant in his manners, and seemed much interested and pleased with the idea of the Natchez Trace Parkway as a link in an International Highway connecting Washington, D.C., and Mexico City." He also informed her that the president was especially interested. Byrnes then invited President Cárdenas to Natchez to see the town and the old trace and to meet Natchez Trace Association and NPS members. Múgica explained to her that the Mexican constitution prohibited the president from leaving the country except under extraordinary situations, but he would send a representative to attend the fall association meeting. Múgica also expressed to Byrnes that he would like to visit Natchez in the near future. He then introduced her to Juan Vasquez, who was the executive of the Mexican Railway. Vasquez also expressed interest in Natchez and agreed to visit the town the following May and be entertained by Roane and Ferriday at Ravennaside. As the couple left Mexico City and headed back to Jackson and then home to Natchez, a group of Mexican dignitaries gave Roane a gold medal and dozens of letters of goodwill. She also received a telegram from Harrison stating that he had secured the emergency $1.5 million for funding the parkway project.[106]

Roane Byrnes charmed everyone she met in Mexico City, and several expressed to her their gratitude for her affection for Mexico and Mexicans. Concepcion de Pogos was impressed by how Byrnes tried to speak Spanish with her and General Múgica and expressed to her how much she enjoyed touring Byrnes around the city. Múgica was also impressed with Byrnes, referring to her as the "pleasant American Lady." She succeeded in generating interest by the Mexican government in the Natchez Trace Parkway and its potential of being part of a larger international parkway.[107] Neither American ambassador Josephus Daniels nor Ickes was concerned that she met with top Mexican governmental officials. It did not occur to Ickes that Cárdenas was at all interested in seriously pursuing the international parkway idea.

By late summer of 1937, the Natchez Trace Parkway had received over $4 million in federal appropriations, and work began on September 16, 1937, near Madisonville, Mississippi. There was no certainty that the entire project would be funded; nevertheless, Mississippi and the National Park Service had construction funding for a parkway design and small sections of the road. Byrnes and Ralph Landrum planned an elaborate groundbreaking ceremony, intending to generate publicity for the parkway. The ceremony included speeches by Congressman A. L. Ford and Highway Commissioner Brown Williams; a group of Choctaw Indians performed a ceremony, recognizing how their ancestors first created the ancient trail.[108] Hundreds of association members and supporters attended. Governor White gave the main speech and then shoveled the first spade of earth into a silver urn that Byrnes was holding. She then spoke to the crowd, exclaiming, "It's the most valuable earth ever dug in Mississippi or perhaps the whole South for it means that the object for which we have all worked for so many years has been attained—the ancient Natchez Trace is to be preserved as one of the greatest national parkways in the United States." When she returned to Natchez, she placed the urn on the mantel in the ballroom in Connelly's Tavern.[109]

Byrnes did not consider the groundbreaking ceremony in Madisonville to be the major celebration for the building of the Natchez Trace Parkway. She had grander ideas. Working with Anna Alexander and Lallie Lawrence, she planned an elaborate event that would feature a Mexican diplomatic delegation, led by General Múgica, and include the Mexican ambassador to the US, Francisco Castillo Nájera. Byrnes and General Múgica's communication office corresponded about scheduling his visit to Natchez in the spring of 1938.[110] Byrnes's objective for the visit was to celebrate the international parkway initiative with Governor White, Senator Bilbo, Congressman Dan McGehee, and NPS officials Malcolm Gardner, Olaf Hagen, and Stuart Cuthbertson. Byrnes also asked her husband to ask Bilbo to invite President Roosevelt. He did but added his own request to Bilbo to bring up a Navy gunboat from New Orleans to Natchez to "show the Mexicans who's boss." Bilbo replied to Ferriday Byrnes, saying that it might be best if Roane invited the president to the event, but he added, "I think it is altogether possible to arrange for the boat trip from New Orleans to Natchez if the Mexican Government will send the representative as suggested."[111] Ickes, Secretary of State Cordell Hull, and Roosevelt designated Department of the Interior undersecretary Charles West to represent the Roosevelt administration. Roane made sure that the event was sufficiently covered by newspapers and the media.[112]

Figure 5.13: Cover of *Ingeniería e Industria* magazine, November-December 1937 issue. The cover photograph shows the dedication of the Mexican and American collaboration on the Natchez Trace Parkway as part of an international parkway connecting Mexico City to Washington, DC. From left: Mexican general Francisco Múgica, General Múgica's translator Carolina Esudero, engineer Carlos Santacruz, Governor Hugh L. White, and Roane Fleming Byrnes. (National Park Service, Natchez Trace Parkway Archives, Tupelo, Mississippi)

Roane Byrnes asked Anna Scheffy Alexander to host the ceremony at her home, Brandon Hall, one of the grandest Greek Revival buildings east of Natchez, near Washington, Mississippi. It was close enough to Natchez and the old trace to be a suitable site for the ceremony. Byrnes conceived of the idea that an American contingent would greet the Mexicans at the Mexican border and escort them in a motorcade for the nearly seven-hundred-mile journey to Natchez. Everything went as planned until a Louisiana state trooper, who was assisting the motorcade, struck a cow on US 84, which delayed the guests from arriving in Natchez. Once they entered the city, they were greeted to a "royal welcome."[113] The Mexican dignitaries were brought to Stanton Hall, and Mayor William J. Byrne presented General Múgica the key to the city.

The next day's event was touted as the first of its kind to happen in Natchez since Marquis de Lafayette visited it more than a century ago. The event featured musical entertainment, speeches by dignitaries, a barbecue, a dance to honor the Mexican delegation, and a memorial tree-planting event with a tree from Mexico and every state the proposed parkway would cross. White, Charles West, and Bilbo spoke at the event; Bilbo, represented the US, planted a tree during the ceremony. Múgica made his remarks in Spanish; they were translated into English by his brother, who was a newspaper reporter in San Antonio. The event was a success, and it was covered by newspapers throughout the country and in Mexico (figure 5.13).

A RECREATIONAL PARKWAY, NOT A HISTORICAL ONE

After meeting with the Mexicans, Roane Byrnes returned to spearheading the parkway project. She had led the charge to secure the rights-of-way for the parkway, and Harrison had successfully negotiated a piecemeal approach to funding construction of it in Congress. Mississippi had been the leading state in making the parkway a reality; now, Tennessee was lagging behind in survey work and purchasing rights-of-way. During the first half of 1937, the National Park Service had only tentatively developed the parkway design. Without a definite route established, it was impossible to begin acquiring rights-of-ways and easements or determine the actual cost of them.[114] Several women who were active in the Tennessee division of the Natchez Trace Association became frustrated with the secretive and inattentive P. M. Estes. Ethel Childress, who also was a prominent member of the state Democratic National Committee, pleaded for Byrnes to come to Nashville and help them obtain their land for the parkway.[115]

Eventually, Estes was able to push the NPS to finalize the parkway design in Tennessee and procure the rights-of-way and thus receive federal construction funding to build the parkway there. But he had to admit that a woman from Mississippi outmanaged him and delivered results to the Natchez Trace Parkway. He wrote to Byrnes, "you can rely upon the fact that I am going to push the matter as much at this end, as I am able."[116]

Although funding had been established in 1937, the Natchez Trace Parkway was still not considered a permanent, federally funded project.[117] But Harrison had been working behind the scenes to secure permanent funding for the parkway, and on May 13, 1938, Congress finally established the Natchez Trace Parkway as a permanent part of the National Park Service (figure 5.14).[118]

Unlike the building of national parkways in Virginia, roadway construction was sporadic and minimal from 1937 until America's entry into

Figure 5.14: Natchez Trace Parkway, located between Natchez, Mississippi, and Nashville, Tennessee, at Tupelo, Mississippi. (Library of Congress, Prints & Photographs Division, Historic American Engineering Record, HAER MS-15)

World War II. Thomas Vint authorized relocating the parkway headquarters from Jackson to Tupelo soon after Congress added the Natchez Trace Parkway to the NPS parkway network. Also, at Tupelo, WPA director Harry Hopkins combined the roadwork with a WPA housing project that only produced modest success. There were also problems obtaining rights-of-way at reasonable prices, so much so that the state highways commission relocated its men to Mathiston. Despite all of the delays in obtaining rights-of-way and construction funding, Ralph Landrum remained optimistic that the construction progress was well underway.[119] By 1943, the NPS had built small stretches of roadway near Natchez, a discontinuous road originating near Canton to past Kosciusko, a small stretch of road near the Tupelo headquarters, and a short segment of the road at the Alabama-Tennessee state line. And while construction was proceeding, NPS historians continued to research the

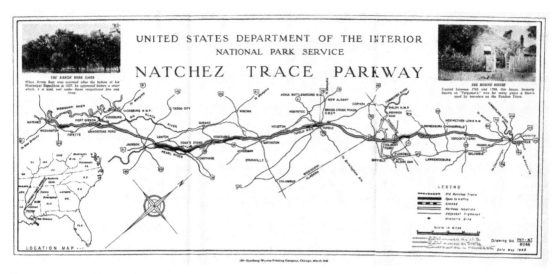

Figure 5.15: Map of the Natchez Trace Parkway, annotated May 1943. The map shows possession of rights-of-way and construction progress at the outbreak of World War II. (National Park Service, Natchez Trace Parkway Archives, Tupelo, Mississippi)

history and historic buildings of the old Natchez Trace, albeit with minimal accuracy (figure 5.15).

At the end of 1937, Roane Byrnes was confident that the Natchez Trace Parkway was going to be built and it was going to be a historic road, preserving American history. In an op-ed for the Clarksdale, Mississippi, *Register*, she enthusiastically declared, "Construction has now commenced on the Natchez Trace Parkway. The ancient trace, path of the bison and Indian through the primeval forest and road of the pioneers who developed the old Southwest, is now to be preserved as a national parkway; a modern paved road winding through landscaped parked areas and past historic inns, churches, mansions, forts and battlefields, all of which are to be restored for future generations."[120]

But in reality, National Park Service historians and planners had much different opinions of the historic trace. Dawson Phelps summarized their frustration by recounting a conversation he had at an NPS meeting at the Great Smoky Mountains National Park information desk: "To the inquiry: 'Where are you from?,' he confessed with some pride to being a Service man stationed at the Natchez Trace. To his astonishment the Ranger replied, 'I certainly feel sorry for you!' Dr. Phelps [asked,] 'Why?, [and] the Ranger replied, 'Because you have nothing for visitors to see.'"[121]

NPS historians and planners knew that much of what had been said about the old trace was embellished folklore. But in convincing the influential Washington politicians from Mississippi, Alabama, and Tennessee to push the project through Congress and then have it signed off by Franklin Roosevelt, Roane Byrnes and Edith Moore had succeeded in embedding the Natchez narrative into the Natchez Trace Parkway and influencing the heritage of Mississippi.

Vint and Lee had never encountered a problem like the Natchez Trace Parkway before. In developing historic monuments, especially for battlefields like Antietam, Chancellorsville, Gettysburg, Vicksburg, and Saratoga, historians and planners had a wide array of sites that told the history of the place from which to select and use in their plans. More often than not, it was practically impossible to contain all of the land over which armies had fought. The old trace was different. Research made it clear early on in the planning process that there was meager, perhaps tenuous, physical evidence of historic site development along the old road. Some NPS historians contended that there may have not been any Natchez Trace at all. Lastly, the historians concluded that no single event had an overpowering historical significance to the nation. No battle was fought on it. No national figure was directly linked to it, and it was not a work of craft, architecture, or engineering. Nevertheless, Byrnes and the Natchez Trace Association had succeeded in turning a civic-minded activity by the Mississippi DAR into a multimillion-dollar historic preservation and civil engineering project, which the National Park Service was authorized to build and then manage.

Planner Edward Zimmer and historian and administrator Malcolm Gardner faced a daunting challenge: how to make the Natchez Trace Parkway a history-based parkway worthy of being a unit in the National Park Service. Essentially, less than 10 percent of the estimated forty-five thousand acres of parkway was considered historic.[122] Beginning in the 1920s, when Albright secured battlefields from the War Department, the National Park Service believed it had two types of units to manage, natural beauty parks in the West and historic monuments and sites in the East. NPS administrators concluded that the Natchez Trace was neither. Moreover, beginning with the Mount Vernon Memorial Highway and the Colonial Parkway, administrators like Arthur Demaray believed that parkways had historic events embedded in them. In the case of the Blue Ridge Parkway, natural beauty and vernacular culture (e.g., historic farmsteads found on the mountains of the Blue Ridge) was the justification of its existence. With the trace's flat terrain in Mississippi, Vint, Demaray, and especially Ickes did not consider its natural beauty worthy of being part of the National Park Service system. But it was not their choice. Congress and Roosevelt authorized that it become a parkway.

The challenge for the National Park Service's Eastern Division of its Office of Planning was also to develop the historic sites that visitors would

Figure 5.16: Mound Plantation, Jefferson County, Mississippi. (Library of Congress, Prints & Photographs Division, Historic American Buildings Survey, HABS MISS,32-CANB.V,1-)

experience driving along the parkway. And it is in this planning that the narratives created by NPS architects, landscape architects, and historians clashed with the Natchez narrative. NPS architects and landscape architects did not see the old trace as a road where mansions and pastoral farms were the attraction. Instead, they wanted to highlight the vernacular architecture of most of the state with rustic buildings that reflected the subsistence reality of nineteenth-century Mississippi, Alabama, and Tennessee. Charles Peterson especially wanted to preserve this architecture and felt that there were enough of the grand Natchez mansions to depict the world of the landed gentry, which the NGC women not only loved but were using in a profitable tourist industry (figure 5.16).

From the beginning of the parkway project, there were women like Elizabeth Brandon Stanton who saw the federally funded parkway as a way to make a profit on their inherited land. She especially wanted to rid herself of her dilapidated home, called Windy Hill Manor, near Washington, Mississippi, which was not directly on the trace (figure 5.17). Stanton and her sisters, Beatrice and Maude, all unmarried women, inherited the eighteenth-century home from their father, General Robert Stanton. Elizabeth Stanton had been the Edith Moore of her generation. Serving as historian of the Colonial Dames of Mississippi, she had spun stories of Natchez romance and even wrote a historical novel on the Aaron Burr conspiracy titled *Fata Morgana*. Described as "tall, willowy and dictatorial," she was used to getting her way, bullying her sisters Beatrice, whom she saw as silly and vacuous, and Maude, whom she saw as berated and beleaguered.[123]

Figure 5.17: Windy Hill Manor, Adams County, Mississippi. (Frances Benjamin Johnston Photograph Collection, Library of Congress, Prints & Photographs Division, LC-DIG-ppmsca-23950)

Elizabeth Stanton contacted Roane Byrnes and asked her to propose to the National Park Service that it acquire Windy Hill Manor. But the NPS, already wary of veering off the old trace to accommodate political whims, would not consider the offer.[124] Even if it was one of the oldest residences in Adams County, and even if it may have housed Aaron Burr during his treason hearing and was where he fell in love with the attractive daughter of a widow neighbor, the NPS planners would not consider including it. Both Stanton and Byrnes were disappointed with the decision, and the Stanton sisters continued to live in it, even after woodpeckers had nearly destroyed the second floor and the beams holding up the dining room ceiling began to sag alarmingly.[125]

When Charles Peterson stated that "the humble cabin is just as important for our purposes as the planters' mansions," he was also expressing an opinion shared by others in the National Park Service, like Gardner, Phelps, Zimmer, and landscape architect Stanley Abbott. They were convinced that, as professional architects and landscape architects, they knew what was historic and worthy of preserving and what should be discarded. But these men were in some ways no different from the Natchez Garden Club women in that they both created a narrative to design around. This became a challenge for the NPS professionals who wanted to apply academic-based design strategies, which utilized their assumptions of what authentic vernacular landscapes were like, within their nearly quarter-mile required easements. All of this produced what landscape architecture historian Timothy Davis refers to as "institutional vernacular"—a sanctioned substitute—that mixes vernacular and elite precedents for traditional roadside land-

Figure 5.18: Interior of the Mount Locust Inn and Plantation, Natchez Trace Parkway, Adams County, Mississippi. (Library of Congress, Prints & Photographs Division, photograph by Carol M. Highsmith, LC-DIG-highsm-42684)

Figure 5.19: Northwest corner of the Billie Eaton House, Old Natchez Trace, Tishomingo, Tishomingo County, Mississippi. (Library of Congress, Prints & Photographs Division. Historic American Buildings Survey, HABS MISS,71-TISH.V,5-)

scapes.[126] Beginning with John Nolen and carried through by Edward Zimmer, physical deficiencies and visual incongruities were corrected on the Natchez Trace Parkway. The compromise of making the parkway "memorialize" the old trace, and thereby not having to restore or reconstruct it, enabled the designers to have more freedom in developing it as a new design on the southern landscape.

The institutionalized approach extended into the preserving and restoring of historic buildings that the National Park Service preserved

Figure 5.20: Evolution of the Natchez Trace Parkway as described by the Historic American Engineering Record. (Library of Congress, Prints & Photographs Division, Historic American Engineering Record, HAER MS-15)

along the Natchez Trace Parkway. Gardner, working with Peterson, directed the restoration of the Mount Locust Inn near Natchez. Both the interior and exterior were meticulously restored; every visual discrepancy was corrected. Would the wearied pioneer William Ferguson and his family have kept the Mount Locust in such a pristine condition during the nineteenth century? Probably not. Mount Locust's restoration was the application of the NPS's developed institutional vernacular, which related to actual vernacular structures like the Billie Easton House in Tishomingo County, Mississippi, only cleaner and more pristine. How different were Peterson's and other professional architects' and landscape architects' ideas for "let's pretend" than the one promoted by Roane Byrnes and Katherine Miller (figures 5.18 and 5.19)?

Through the Natchez narrative and the NPS narrative, the Natchez Trace Parkway was created in the 1930s. Folklore, telling tales of bison and Indigenous people carving out the trail from the wilderness and explorers and then pioneers using it to build the Old Southwest, was made into heritage. The Natchez Trace Parkway became synonymous with the heroes and villains that traveled on it. The parkway became a pathway through history.

But it was not the Natchez Trace. It was a memorial parkway for the trace idea (figure 5.20).

In his essay "Paving the Trace," Jack D. Elliott Jr. bluntly summarized the motives and methods for creating the Natchez Trace Parkway:

> Individuals and organizations developed and then manipulated the image of the Natchez Trace, all within the context of heritage organizations, road promotion schemes, and the pursuit of federal dollars. Within this context the dimensions of the Trace's meaning was [sic] changed from a historical geographical phenomenon to a heritage symbol within the national mythos. This idealistic image was in turn transformed into a propaganda symbol to promote road-building efforts, and from such "smoke and mirrors" a confused mandate for a parkway emerged that the NPS was obligated to make sense of. In the course of this process, something was lost.[127]

To the parkway creators, heritage was a means to an end, and that end was a pleasurable road.

Conceptually, the Natchez Trace Parkway became the institutionalized manifestation of the Natchez pilgrimage. Its historic resources, Meriwether Lewis's gravesite, and structures like the Gordon House and Mount Locust, along with the ancient Emerald Mound, were, in Chatelain's words quoted earlier, "pegs placed on which American history could be conveniently hung."[128] And like the way the Natchez Garden

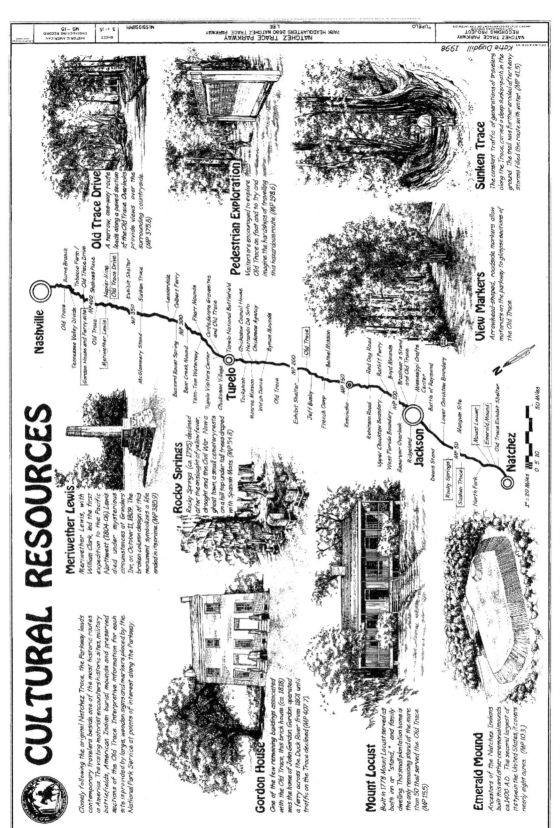

Figure 5.21: Cultural resources along the Natchez Trace Parkway as described by the Historic American Engineering Record. (Library of Congress, Prints & Photographs Division, Historic American Engineering Record, HAER MS-15)

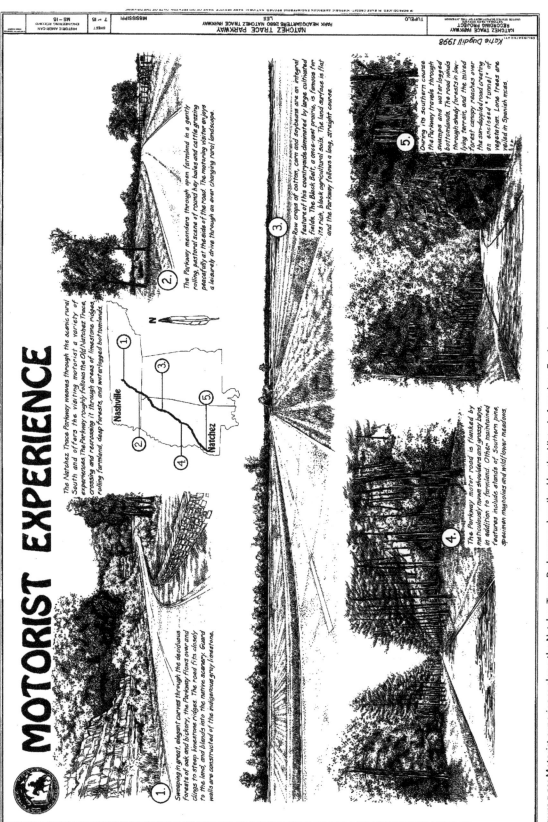

Figure 5.22: Motorist experience along the Natchez Trace Parkway as described by the Historic American Engineering Record. (Library of Congress, Prints & Photographs Division, Historic American Engineering Record, HAER MS-15)

Club women created their pilgrimage, all of these historic sites were only accessible by automobile (figure 5.21).

The Natchez Trace Parkway is a designed landscape from the days when landscape architects and civil engineers aspired to build grand visions of idealized and controlled landscapes. To this day, its shoulders are meticulously mown, and views carefully designed. In the north, near Franklin, Tennessee, it gracefully hugs the topography with guardrails built out of the native limestone, which was quarried nearby. As it approaches Natchez, elegant views of moss-draped live oaks frame the horizon (figure 5.22).

Manipulation of history as Elliott describes aside, the Natchez Trace Parkway is what Busby originally intended: a scenic highway, a utilitarian proposition, and a project of great usefulness. As planning and then construction progressed on the parkway, Vint understood that it broadened the mission of the National Park Service to include more than what Albright had envisioned twenty years earlier: natural beauty and historic sites. The Natchez Trace Parkway did not neatly fit into either of these categories. But Vint acknowledged this by saying, "It was a road that is entirely built for recreation, one that is built to display certain natural landscapes or historical country." He added that the parkways supplemented but never competed with national parks.[129] With that said, the National Park Service expanded its original mission of preserving natural and historic sites to include recreation. During the 1950s, as automobile-based tourism came into its own, this new updated outlook boded well for the National Park Service in seeking appropriations to upgrade existing and declining infrastructure.[130]

In four years, from 1934 until 1938, Roane Byrnes had succeeded in broadening the appeal of Natchez on a national stage. By incorporating the Natchez narrative into the Natchez Trace Parkway, she influenced southern heritage and made Natchez a predominant feature in it. As she traveled and worked with politicians, supporters, and NPS administrators, the Natchez Trace and Natchez were becoming part of the country's popular culture. In addition to Stark Young's *So Red the Rose*, *New York Times* art critic Robert M. Coates published *The Outlaw Years: The History of the Land Pirates of the Natchez Trace*, a salacious and violent book about the bandits that roamed the old trace in the nineteenth century. Both books were published in 1936. Byrnes worked with these authors to promote the Natchez Trace Parkway and Natchez in popular fiction. Other books and films followed, most notably Eudora Welty's *The Robber Bridegroom* (1942). For the rest of her life, Byrnes devoted herself to completing the parkway. But during these crucial years, while she struggled to promote the parkway idea, Katherine Miller, Ruth Beltzhoover, and Annie Barnum back in Natchez clashed with Harriet Dixon and Edith Moore over the future of heritage tourism in their city. The media and Hollywood would also discover Natchez, and the "Old South" would become a commodity. Only World War II stopped the garden club women from accomplishing their objectives.

Figure 6.1: Katherine Grafton Miller, 1938. (From *Natchez of Long Ago and the Pilgrimage* by Katherine Grafton Miller [Natchez: Relimak Publishing Co., 1938])

Chapter 6

FEUDING AND BRANDING

In 1938, Katherine Miller published her version of the Natchez narrative, *Natchez of Long Ago and the Pilgrimage*. She sent copies to friends she had made throughout the country, often with her handwritten inscription on the inside cover, "How do you like my little book."[1]

A photograph of Miller in antebellum period dress features prominently. Her pose and look are deliberately both feminine and authoritative. With Roane Byrnes preoccupied with the Natchez Trace Parkway, Miller was now the preeminent "southern lady" of Natchez (figure 6.1).

In 1937, Katherine Miller and Annie Barnum transformed the insurgent Homeowners' Association into the Pilgrimage Garden Club. They then established a second pilgrimage to that of the Natchez Garden Club—a direct competitor to the original pilgrimage. This incited a legendary feud known as the "Battle of the Hoop Skirts." Miller and Barnum, aided by Alma Kellogg and Ruth Beltzhoover, led the fight to not only control the pilgrimage but also the entire heritage tourism enterprise in Natchez. They pitted themselves against Edith Moore, Harriet Dixon, Ethel Kelly, and Kate Brandon of the now-diminished Natchez Garden Club. Roane Byrnes was still an active participant in the NGC, but her involvement was secondary to her primary cause, the Natchez Trace Parkway. The fighting between the women was personal. And given the economic success of the pilgrimage, the stakes were high. Each group accused the other of undermining their pilgrimages; family and friends glared at each other on the street and in social gatherings; and the clubs tried to outdo each other in winning over tourists. Eventually, the feud landed in court in 1941, a denouement no one could have imagined ten years earlier when the women invented the pilgrimage tourism event.

Ironically, Miller and Barnum, who were so critical of Byrnes's Connelly's Tavern project, did exactly what she was advocating but on an even grander scale. After founding the Pilgrimage Garden Club (PGC), they immediately purchased and renovated Stanton Hall for their rival clubhouse. It was an obvious ploy to outdo the NGC and another one of Miller's demonstrations of her power in Natchez. Mayor Joseph Byrne was among those who dreaded the escalation in hostilities between the women; state economic promoters were also alarmed that the now-lucrative business venture in Natchez could collapse. But the national press loved it. They wrote about the "private war" between the women and humorously chronicled how the NGC pilgrimage was conducted from early to the third week in March and the PGC pilgrimage was held from the third week of March until early April. Then, in February 1941, Miller took the gloves off and persuaded the PGC to conduct its pilgrimage at the same time as the NGC one.[2] By the 1941 trial, the feud between the club women had become part of the Natchez narrative—now synonymous with the "Old South" and historic preservation in the South throughout the nation. Whether they intended it or not, the "Battle of the Hoop Skirts" was an ingenious publicity stunt.

As the feud escalated, America's fascination with the mythic "Old South" also increased, and Natchez became part of the country's popular culture. But it was Margaret Mitchell's *Gone with the Wind* (1936)—although set in Clayton County, Georgia, not Natchez—that stirred national interest in the romanticized version of the antebellum South. It was the architecture and landscapes in and surrounding Natchez that, in turn, influenced the movie version of the book.

During this time, Natchez was also being chronicled through photographs by some of the leading photographers in the country. Prominent photographer Frances Benjamin Johnston photographed Natchez on a grant from the Carnegie Corporation—and with Leicester Holland's support—in 1938. Although Johnston photographed the villas that the NGC women wanted to use to market Natchez to the world, she also photographed the lesser-known and vernacular buildings in Natchez. Working for the US Farm Security Administration, noted Depression-era photographers Walker Evans and Ben Shahn documented the poverty that was pervasive in Natchez and the rest of the rural Deep South. The images these three photographers took of Natchez became part of the national narrative of the hardship experienced during the Great Depression, which are now intriguingly perceived as scenes from a long-ago time by succeeding generations of Americans. New Deal technocrats funded the photographers to tell a different narrative of places like Natchez—places that were trapped within their rural past and damned to poverty. It was a counternarrative from the one Moore, Miller, and Byrnes were creating and was by no means a place of "let's pretend" (figure 6.2).

Despite their animosity toward each other, these Natchez women innately understood the need to brand and market Natchez. Tourists were amused by the stories they read about their escapades, and the publicity it generated only made them want to make the long drive south and experience it for themselves. As modern and very enterpris-

Figure 6.2: "Advertisements for Popular Malaria Cure, Natchez, Mississippi," Ben Shahn, Photographer, 1938. Shahn recorded Natchez during the Great Depression for the US Farm Security Administration, Resettlement Administration. His images became an important visual portrayal of the Great Depression in the South. (Library of Congress, Prints & Photographs Division, Farm Security Administration/Office of War Information Collection, LC-DIG-fsa-8a16479)

ing women, these women capitalized on their own notoriety and that of their narrative. Lillie Boatner and Ethel Kelly sold the idea of developing a Melrose silverware pattern, and Boatner marketed to Old South Toiletries an idea for a perfume called "Natchez Rose Jar." Important national figures, among them Eleanor Roosevelt and Henry Ford, came to see the storied architecture and what the NGC women had created in the pilgrimage. And then the women captured Hollywood's attention. In 1939, they persuaded short film producer James A. FitzPatrick to produce the brief travel movie piece "Old Natchez on the Mississippi," which depicted their tableaux and their villas. But they really captured the nation's imagination through the production of a far greater movie. In that same year, set designers and researchers created the Georgia scenery for *Gone with the Wind* from what they gleaned from the architecture and landscapes of Natchez.

But as the Natchez narrative became more popularly known, it also became more scrutinized. Although National Park Service architectural historians did not question Edith Moore's findings, administrators from the WPA Writers' Project did. NGC women like Harriet Dixon stood up for Moore, writing a protest letter to the NPS about how its administrators were treating her. In protecting Moore, one of the most prominent creators of the narrative, Dixon and Miller protected their brand.

Figure 6.3: Anne Conner standing at the front door of Linden in Katherine Grafton Miller's *Natchez of Long Ago and the Pilgrimage*. Miller carefully choreographed the ideal of southern charm next to the most refined architectural elements in Natchez, such as the front door of Linden. (From *Natchez of Long Ago and the Pilgrimage* by Katherine Grafton Miller [Natchez: Relimak Publishing Co., 1938])

But with all of their success came challenges. Outsiders began to purchase villas from the old families. Kitschy tourist attractions like Old Fort Rosalie and Mammy's (renamed Mammy's Cupboard in the 1990s) were built. And more ominously, the attitudes of white Natchez toward race became an issue the women could no longer easily dismiss or ignore, especially after World War II. In 1942, their efforts to create the Natchez narrative and then commercialize it ended abruptly. World War II caused a break in their activities. In some ways, the interlude caused by the war provided the women time to heal old wounds and learn to work together again. But during the postwar period, they soon realized that Natchez was a different place. They had made it into a historyland, which brought them prosperity but also change.

The Natchez narrative became part of Madison Avenue and part of Hollywood. As a marketing ploy during the Great Depression, it was uniquely accessible for middle-class Americans living in places from which one could travel to Natchez by automobile. For these Americans, it was both glamorous and comforting. One could easily indulge in the warm early spring and "lost" days of the antebellum South; or one could return from the industrialized North and reaffirm a life they left behind, which never really existed (figure 6.3). Natchezians learned all of this from their visiting tourists, and they capitalized on it. But soon after World War II ended, the modernity these women had long sought—better roads, more industries, and progress—came to their town and, with it, progressive national ideas, particularly regarding racial relations. The new ideas clashed with the older established ones that they held so dear regarding social order. The civil rights movement would determine the future of the town, and it eventually changed the "Old South" Natchez that was branded in popular culture during the two years leading up to America's entry into World War II.

THE "BATTLE OF THE HOOP SKIRTS"

Connelly's Tavern brought the issue of who controlled the pilgrimage to a head in 1935. On the surface, it was, as George Kelly wryly summarized, a struggle between the "drinking and grasping crowd" and the "temperance people."[3] The Connelly's Tavern renovation brought to the forefront what the mission of the Natchez Garden Club should embody. Initially, there was an understanding that part of the profits from the pilgrimage went to the owners of the historic villas and part was allocated for the betterment of the city. Roane Byrnes had forced the issue with Connelly's Tavern. She had persuaded the NGC to reinvest the profits allocated for civic improvement back into Natchez, in projects like the Connelly's Tavern renovation. Katherine Miller, Annie Barnum, and Ruth Beltzhoover objected to her and her idea. The next year, the NGC women quarreled and were at a crossroads: Should the NGC obtain historic buildings and renovate them in order to improve Natchez? Or should the NGC give the profits back to homeowners, who had to maintain their expensive villas and annually endure thousands of tourists trampling through them and their gardens? But both camps, the NGC and the soon-to-be PGC, agreed on one important idea, even though it was lost in the heat of their row: all of them wanted to preserve Natchez and profit from their efforts.

The tussle, even if it seems humorous now, came down to a tradition-based idea—the political power of ownership. Edward Shils and others have pointed out that, throughout history, ownership of historic monuments has testified to the importance and power of the owner.[4] This has always been the case in Natchez. And this was the crux of the conflict: should the NGC women who owned the villas control the pilgrimage? For the antagonists in the struggle, the lines had always been clearly drawn. Miller, Barnum, and Beltzhoover, the leaders of the homeowners, owned historic houses that were showcased during the Spring Pilgrimage. Byrnes, Harriet Dixon, and Edith Moore did not own any of the historic villas. Barnum summarized the homeowners' frustration: "They own the homes, pay the taxes and they are willing to do the work and finance the Pilgrimage, give a certain percentage away, they ought to run it in their own way."[5] Agnes Gardner was more critical, remembering how unjust she felt Byrnes, Dixon, and Moore were during the early days of their feud: "they took all the money. They didn't want the homeowners to have anything. We felt we had to keep up the homes, and buy things for them, and keep them looking pretty. We thought it was taxation without representation."[6] Why should the women who did not own villas control the pilgrimage now that it was established and profitable?

A wary compromise was reached in 1936 that allowed the pilgrimage that year to go on as before. But after the 1936 Spring Pilgrimage, tensions rose. The city remained transfixed on what would happen the next year. As president of the NGC, Dixon reserved the city's Memorial Hall for the tableau of the 1937 pilgrimage and confronted the city council. Suspicious of Miller and Barnum, she implied to the council the prospect of what the homeowners may intend to do: start a rival pilgrimage to the NGC one. Dixon speculated that Miller and her friends had attempted to reserve the performance space for their tableau. She and Moore were upset and assumed that Miller intended to undermine the NGC and its pilgrimage. They were right in their assumptions.[7]

Dixon's apprehensions grew through 1936, especially when she learned that Miller had contacted the Garden Clubs of Mississippi, inquiring about applying for new membership for a garden club in Natchez. Dixon wrote Mrs. Robert Henry, president of the Garden Clubs of Mississippi, stating that she was seeking her advice—but most likely she was attempting to stop Miller from leading the splinter group of homeowners away from the NGC. In her letter, she reiterated that the NGC tried to do everything to be an outstanding civic organization and that Miller's group was only interested in financial gain. As did most people who knew about the ongoing row, the state president remained neutral in her response and her opinion.

Dixon had reason to worry about the future of the pilgrimage and support for historic preservation in Natchez. Gossip about the feud between the NGC and the homeowners was beginning to make state politicians and administrators nervous. In September 1936, she received news from Lieutenant Governor James B. (Billy) Snider that the newly established Mississippi Advertising Commission was not going to publish a magazine issue on the Spring Pilgrimage. Although he acknowledged that the pilgrimage had become one of the leading tourist attractions in the state, he felt investing in promoting it at this time was not a prudent way to spend the limited funding the commission had.[8] Soon after receiving this letter from Snider, she received a letter from the state advertising director, Ed Lipscomb, conveying apprehension about funding a promotional film on Natchez and the pilgrimage.[9] Suddenly, all the hard work the women had given to the pilgrimage appeared to be in jeopardy.

Katherine Miller was also on the move. She and Annie Barnum met with the other nine disgruntled homeowners and planned to split off from the NGC and develop their own pilgrimage. But before she could begin her new campaign, she had to disassociate herself from the Natchez Garden Club. On November 5, 1936, she formally resigned her membership from the Natchez Garden Club. In her letter, she stated that it was the "neat and proper" thing to do given that she may now have conflicting interests with the club. She also enclosed a check for $1.00 for outstanding dues she owed to the club and then ended her letter thanking the NGC "for their support and cooperation in the past." But in true Miller character, she let it be known that she was up to something—she used a letterhead from a group called "Participants and Descendants of the Campaign, Siege, and Defense of Vicksburg, Mississippi." She had tried to establish a competing pilgrimage in Vicksburg but with little results.[10]

Like Dixon, Miller realized that the feud was discouraging support from the state government and private companies. A month after her resignation, she also received a letter from Lipscomb stating that he had canceled orders for plates and placemats designed to celebrate the pilgrimage and tourism in Mississippi. Moreover, he noted that he had canceled the feature story in the Mississippi Advertising Commission magazine about the 1937 pilgrimage. He relayed his decision to Dixon as well. In concluding his letter to Miller, he urged her to "heal the breech that has occurred there."[11]

Miller and Barnum ignored all pleas from Natchez businessmen and political leaders and state politicians and established the Pilgrimage Garden Club. Barnum was elected the first president of the PGC, Charlotte Surget (who owned Gloucester) was vice president, Mary Henderson Lambdin (who owned Edgewood) was secretary, and Kellogg was treasurer (figures 6.4 and 6.5). Miller was permanently made "director of the Pilgrimage," which provided her a cash honorarium and a travel allowance.

Dixon made every effort to discredit the newly founded Pilgrimage Garden Club and defend the accomplishments of the Natchez Garden Club. Motivated to present her case after reading an editorial about the infighting between the women written by *Greenville Democratic Times* editor Ernest Smith, she stated in her rebuttal that some of the homeowners were dissatisfied with the two-thirds to one-third homeowners

Figure 6.4: Annie Barnum and her daughter, Anne Gwin, at Arlington during the 1937 pilgrimage. Barnum was critical of Natchez Garden Club members who did not own historic villas shown during the pilgrimages. She and Katherine Grafton Miller led the movement by the Natchez homeowners to split from the Natchez Garden Club and establish the Pilgrimage Garden Club in 1936. (From *Natchez of Long Ago and the Pilgrimage* by Katherine Grafton Miller [Natchez: Relimak Publishing Co., 1938])

Figure 6.5: Alma Kellogg standing in front of The Elms in 1937. Kellogg was the first treasurer of the Natchez Garden Club, and she became the first treasurer of the Pilgrimage Garden Club. (From *Natchez of Long Ago and the Pilgrimage* by Katherine Grafton Miller [Natchez: Relimak Publishing Co., 1938])

to NGC profit-sharing agreement and wanted all of the profits for themselves. She bitterly noted that while the homeowners had pulled out of the NGC pilgrimage to form the rival PGC, they continued to be members of the NGC and refused to relinquish their offices on the NGC executive board. Continuing, Dixon reminded Smith and the newspapers' readers that the NGC was a civic organization working on the beautification and preservation of historic Natchez. She said that the club had recently purchased the historic Spanish inn on Ellicott's Hill and had spent over $15,000[12] "on the restoration of this unusual place." She boasted that the club had bought period furniture for the Natchez city-owned Auburn. She then chided the PGC by saying that they were merely a private organization out for personal gain and that their application for membership in the Federation of Garden Clubs had been denied.[13]

At this point, Natchez businessmen and -women not involved in the pilgrimages were truly alarmed that the fight was going to ruin the profitable pilgrimage and marketing support from the state. Prominent Natchez attorney Charles F. Engle interceded on behalf of Natchez and complained about Lipscomb's reluctance to invest in marketing the 1937 pilgrimage. In a letter to Lt. Gov. Snider, he blamed Snider for Lipscomb's "hands off" attitude towards Natchez and stated that it did not benefit either Natchez tourism or its rich history. He urged Snider to make Lipscomb advertise the two pilgrimages impartially.[14]

In 1937, the two clubs planned for two separate pilgrimages; the NGC planned its first pilgrimage for March 28–April 4, 1937, and the PGC held its pilgrimage the week after. Miller convinced the owners of Airlie (Merrill), D'Evereux (Smith), Dunleith (Carpenter), Elgin (Beane), Homewood (Kaiser), King's Tavern (Register), Lansdowne (Marshall), Linden (Feltus), Monteigne (Kendall), and Richmond (Shelby Marshall family)[15] to leave the NGC and open their homes with the PGC pilgrimage. Miller was confident that the homeowning members of the NGC like Ethel Kelly and Mary Britton Conner (owner of Clover Nook) would realize that the NGC pilgrimage would be greatly diminished and therefore join the PGC. But Dixon, Byrnes, Moore, and Effie Hale countered the PGC threat and augmented their pilgrimage by adding Mt. Repose (Shields), Melmont (Ayres), Propinquity (Rebecca Miller), Cottage Gardens (Katie Foster and Mrs. Earl Norman), Myrtle Bank (Chamberlain), Pleasant Hill (Postelthwaite), and The Parsonage (Metcalfe). Dixon was confident that the Connelly's Tavern's dedication would upstage anything the PGC had planned for the 1937 pilgrimage, remarking that if the PGC had planned any civic-based preservation project, its members had not announced it.[16]

She was mistaken. Miller had ambitious plans to upstage Connelly's Tavern and the NGC's preservation mission. At one of the first meetings held by the newly established Pilgrimage Garden Club in early 1937, she convinced the membership to purchase the opulent Stanton Hall from the Clark family and make it the PGC's clubhouse, rivaling the nearby Connelly's Tavern, the NGC's nearly restored clubhouse. With only eight-seven cents in the PGC treasury, Miller convinced the club to take out a loan for $28,000,[17] a substantial amount of money during the Great Depression.[18] She envisioned a restored Stanton Hall as a place to entertain PGC friends and out-of-town visitors, not necessarily a period house museum but a historic clubhouse with exquisite furnishings placed in it.[19] Miller's establishment of the PGC's home at Stanton Hall is telling. With it, the garden club women established two tangible places that embodied their particular versions of the Natchez narrative. The

Figure 6.6: View of the portico of Stanton Hall, Natchez, Mississippi. Katherine Grafton Miller led the effort to purchase the Greek Revival mansion and convert it into the headquarters of the newly formed Pilgrimage Garden Club in 1937. (Frances Benjamin Johnston Photograph Collection, Library of Congress, Prints & Photographs Division, LC-DIG-ppmsca-23957)

Natchez Garden Club's headquarters at Connelly's Tavern represented the colonial Spanish heritage narrative of the town, while the Pilgrimage Garden Club's Stanton Hall headquarters epitomized the mythic "Old South" narrative (figure 6.6).

Kate Brandon became president of the NGC after Harriet Dixon's term ended in 1937 and continued the skirmish with Annie Barnum on the scheduling of future pilgrimages between the two clubs. Mayor Byrne intervened and attempted to facilitate a compromise. Brandon was known for being feisty, and she dismissed the mayor's plan as hearsay, even though he had presented it to both clubs. In concluding her rejection of a possible compromise in a letter to Barnum, she stated her defiance in a thinly veiled southern lady manner.[20]

For the next three years, the two clubs conducted separate pilgrimages. And by then there was true animosity between the women of the two clubs. While some in the press referred to the quarrel as the "Battle of the Hoop Skirts" or the "Hoop Skirt War;" locals called it the "Big Split."[21] The national press covered the row, and the coverage brought an immense amount of publicity to Natchez. Writing for the *Atlanta*

Constitution, Ralph McGill described how the women "are fighting it out who can show their homes as grimly as Grant did at Vicksburg."²²

By 1940, the two clubs were sparring through the newspapers. The greatest point of contention was over which club actually created the pilgrimage idea. Writing for the *Atlanta Constitution*, Sally Forth stated that both clubs claimed credit "as founders of the annual invasion of the deep south." She then explained how the NGC claimed the credit by reacting to the now-infamous cold spell before the Garden Club Federation visit in 1931. She reported that Miller claimed to have come up with the idea; and when she, along with Barnum, Kellogg, and others, split from the NGC, they took the pilgrimage idea credit with them to the PGC. Sally Forth then stated that the two clubs used their historic homes as weapons for battle: "Antiquity as the common battle flag, splendor the emblem, and the password to all visitors, 'Glad to meet you, honey, call again.'"²³

After the "Big Split," the NGC and PGC agreed to hold their pilgrimages on separate weeks with the NGC alternating between two-week blocks of time during the early spring. They also agreed that while one club was holding its event, the other club would close its operations. The increased timeframe and the increase of homes opened during the springtime event gave a tremendous boost to the event. In the *New York Times*, August Loeb summarized what was a brilliant, and accidental, marketing breakthrough for the women: "Natchez is so rich in historic resources that there will be virtually no duplication in the tours of the two clubs." Other garden clubs, throughout the Deep South, he noted, had copied the Natchez pilgrimage and were conducting their events in direct competition with the two clubs. For most of the spring, there was at least one pilgrimage going on somewhere in the state of Mississippi, but by then, he concluded, Natchez had established itself in the national press as "that great storehouse of Southern tradition."²⁴ The increased numbers of tours and homes allowed both groups of garden club women to stay ahead of their competition.

Prior to the 1941 pilgrimage, the fighting took a nasty turn. The PGC announced that its members would conduct their tours during the same week as the NGC and brazenly relocated its pilgrimage headquarters a half a block from the Masonic Building, which served as the NGC's pilgrimage headquarters. The PGC members were now sparring with the NGC on Main Street. The two clubs raised up similar banners, used similar tour signage, held similar tableaux, and even had rival African American bands play Dixieland music in their galleries.²⁵ The PGC members claimed they had the consent of the NGC, but the NGC vehemently disagreed. The NGC sued the PGC to prohibit its members from showing their homes during the same week of the NGC pilgrimage. Hearing the complaint, Judge A. B. Anderson ordered the PGC to close its operations. The PGC promptly threatened to countersue.

But then Anderson reversed his order and explained through a supplemental fiat "that the original fiat to close the Pilgrimage Garden Club tours through a law suit from the Natchez Garden Club was hastily done and that the Pilgrimage Garden Club tours can resume."[26] The PGC reopened its operations; confusion and frustration then ensued.

The complaint was rewritten and presented to Judge J. B. Barbour. In it, the NGC did not hold anything back. Its members individually sued members of the PGC and stated how they had wronged the NGC for over five years. Among the defendants they singled out were Frances Beane, the PGC president at that time; Katherine Miller; Annie Barnum; Barnum's daughter, Anne Gwin; Elizabeth Stanton; Mary Louise Kendall; Rebecca Fauntleroy; and Harriet Laub. Therein, they stated their version of the chain of events. First, they noted that the PGC members separated their houses from the tour and competed with the NGC. The PGC tours were injurious and tortious to the NCG, they claimed, and the NGC had lost business and profits from the competition. Second, they declared that the PGC had reneged on the agreement that it would remain closed while the NGC members conducted their pilgrimage. Third, they claimed that the PGC charged the same price for admission, $2.50, and used similar banners and advertisements as the NGC. They particularly wanted the PGC banners removed from the balustrade of the Elks Club, as the NGC traditionally placed its banner just a half a block away on the Masonic Building.[27]

On March 28, 1941, Judge Barbour ordered the PGC to stop its tours and remove their banners. But the PGC refused and continued to sell tickets to its pilgrimage. Barbour then instructed the Adams County Sheriff's office to post a "cease and desist" order on the doors of The Elms, Arlington, Lexington, King's Tavern, and Elgin. The PGC women were outraged. Several of them were quoted in the *Jackson Daily News* decrying these tactics: "Think of it, they used nails and large ones, too. That is an example of what 'they' are trying to do to us." Another PGC member was quoted saying, "We are going through Sunday just as though nothing happened."[28] Harnett Kane of the *Times-Picayune* summarized the climatic confrontation with great literary flair:

> Thick faced deputies started out, nailing notices to Georgian doors. One chatelaine, not knowing what was happening, saw the Law coming up the walk and mistook it for a tourist. She dropped him a deep bow, "and then he handed me an injunction!" That, sire, was hardly the act of a gentleman.

Certain ladies scurried around town, fleeing justice; and rode to the Devil's Punchbowl, where bandits of the Natchez Trace used to hide out when the Law was tailing them. Town officials, pressed to "do something," stared at the ground. The mayor found he had business in New York and left for a week; many husbands wished they could follow him.[29]

For the next two days, tourists were confused, tempers flared, and nerves were frayed. Mayor Byrne, who also ran an insurance agency in town, told *Time* magazine that he was leaving town for the weekend.[30] Sheriff H. R. Jenkins refused to give a quote to any newspapers. The *Atlanta Constitution* relished covering the feud:

> The good women are fighting—no blows struck yet—for the patronage visitors to the antebellum homes and azalea-lined streets. They're divided up into camps of the "Pilgrimage Garden Club" and "The Natchez Garden Club." "Don't see her old home," a pretty thing tells a prospective sight-seer. "My old home is better than her old home." It's gotten so bad that Mayor William J. Byrne says he won't run for re-election when he finishes out his term in a couple of years. The Pilgrimage Garden Club was supposed to run its tours from March 2 through March 23, with the Natchez Garden Club running from March 22 to April 6. But the Pilgrimage Garden Club is still running its tours right into the dates of the rival organization, with the explanation that the extension was "due to prolonged bad weather."[31]

By March 30, events took a turn for the surreal. The day before, Judge Barbour had clarified his ruling, stating that although the PGC could not conduct a pilgrimage at the same time as the NGC pilgrimage, individual homeowners may open their homes for tours. Katherine Miller struck fast and came up with the idea that the PGC members advertise their homes individually, thereby indirectly conducting a pilgrimage. The March 31 *Natchez Democrat* published individual announcements for private home tours during the pilgrimage but stipulating no relationship to the PGC.[32]

The NGC members were furious. Throughout that turbulent week, tourists and townspeople became very annoyed by the women's behavior. Many tourists packed their bags and left the town. There was even a tourist who apparently suffered a heart attack from all of the excitement. The Freemasons met during the week and voted to refuse to let the NGC use their building for future pilgrimages.

The NGC was still angry at the PGC, and once again filed suit. The case was tried in August 1941 with Chancellor Richard W. Cutrer presiding. At this trial, the NGC members charged that the PGC benefited from their advertising and that the PGC had lured away their paying tourists. The PGC members countered that claim in saying that their homes were "more attractive" and had more "originality." The NGC members asked the court to reward them for the loss of their ticket sales after March 23, when the PGC had begun conducting its pilgrimage. The PGC countered in its suit and sought $4,000 in damages for wrongfully closing its headquarters. The trial took two and half days, and at the end, Cutrer ruled that the injunction filed by the NGC was wrongfully issued and that the club was not entitled to damages from the PGC.[33] He then ruled that the PGC was also not entitled to any damages from the NGC.[34]

Neither club was pleased with Cutrer's rulings. The NGC filed an appeal with the Mississippi Supreme Court. But by December 1941, circumstances had drastically changed with America's entry into World War II. The appeal was dropped, and the feud stopped. One more pilgrimage was held by both clubs in 1942, after Pearl Harbor, with the proceeds being donated by both clubs to the American Red Cross and the war effort. The "War of the Hoop Skirts" ended as the war effort became a more urgent calling for all Americans. But the "Big Split" remained.[35]

THE NATCHEZ NARRATIVE IN POPULAR CULTURE

Throughout the 1930s, Roane Byrnes and Katherine Miller entertained national literary, cultural, and political dignitaries in Natchez. And through these liaisons, they promoted the town. By 1940, Byrnes had become well known for her free-for-all parties. Miller built the Carriage House Restaurant and the PGC clubhouse behind Stanton Hall and entertained guests there and in the restored east wing of Hope Farm. Mavis Feltus remembered that when celebrities arrived in town, they were introduced to Byrnes. She always enjoyed hosting and charming well-known guests, who left Natchez with a very favorable impression of the place.[36]

On one of her tours across the country, Eleanor Roosevelt toured Natchez in March 1939. Roosevelt was very impressed with Natchez and the garden club women. These women, who were all very politically conservative, were less impressed with Roosevelt. She was making early presidential campaign stops for her husband along the lower Mississippi River. She arrived in Baton Rouge, began her tour of Mississippi in Vicksburg on March 7, and arrived in Natchez the following day. The garden club women had a special pageant performed for her in the auditorium that evening. Alma Kellogg remembered that Roosevelt left in the middle of the program "to go down some place in lower Mississippi to see some college"; since this happened "while the tableaux were going on," Kellogg speculated that the king and queen were not very happy to see her walk out.³⁷ Rebecca Benoist humorously recalled the rumor that Roosevelt found herself stuck in her bathtub while staying in the Eola Hotel.³⁸

In her syndicated newspaper column, "My Day by Eleanor Roosevelt," the first lady stated that her entourage traveled a newly paved road, funded by the WPA, from Vicksburg to Natchez. In Natchez, she met a woman who voiced her objection to the new road, saying that she wanted people to linger in Natchez. But recognizing how physically isolated Natchez was, Roosevelt felt it was fortunate for Natchez to have a paved road going to it. She then met with a woman from the WPA, most likely Edith Moore, who urged Roosevelt to convince the federal government to fund restoration projects on the historic villas in town. After lunch, Roosevelt marveled at the beautiful Natchez gardens; she particularly enjoyed the gardens at Monteigne. She concluded her column with a strong endorsement of the work by the garden club women: "Never tell me that women are not able in business. Natchez is being built up financially by a woman's idea carried out by women. They have obtained good publicity and they have one great advantage, the houses they display are really homes. They are lived in today and frequently the mistress receives you herself."³⁹

Henry Ford also visited Natchez and admired its architecture and the garden club women's entrepreneurial spirit. People drove in their automobiles from across the state to see the famous tycoon. Rebecca Benoist recalled that there were so many automobiles that it was impossible for Ford's entourage to pass through.⁴⁰ Ironically, Ford had to return to Detroit by train. But while in Natchez, he and his wife, Clara, were entertained by George and Ethel Kelly at Melrose.

Popular authors came to Natchez during the 1930s, and by associating with the women, especially Roane Byrnes and Edith Moore, they helped incorporate the Natchez narrative into the national mainstream. By 1940, Natchez had gone from being an unknown town to a place marketed for its historic architecture and history. No one incorporated the Natchez narrative into their published work more than Stark Young. Young first met Byrnes while researching in Natchez and Woodville, Mississippi, for his novel *So Red the Rose*, and he directly incorporated into the novel two stories Byrnes told him about her family during the nineteenth century. The first story was how her ornery grandmother, Zuleika Lyons Metcalfe, hid food and ammunition beneath her hoop skirts and walked down the ravine near her home, Ravenna. Once she arrived at the Confederate lines, she delivered her smuggled loot to the Confederate troops defending the town from the Union army during the Civil War. The federal soldiers eventually arrested her and ordered her and her family to vacate Ravenna. Undeterred, she hurled insults at any of the federal soldiers long after the Union army first occupied Natchez.[41]

Young also based one of his characters in the novel, a feisty old cousin of the Bedford family named Mary Cherry, on Byrnes's grandmother. The novel recounts how Cherry stole a horse and buggy in Hernando, Mississippi, and hid boots, shoes, and quinine beneath her hoop skirts. The family patriarch, Malcolm Bedford, ends the story by saying that the federal sentries let her pass their battle lines because they lacked the courage to confront the Bedfords' combative cousin.[42]

Borrowing from Byrnes's story of her great-great grandfather, John Cox, Young incorporated the Ibrahima story into his novel:

> "There's a story for you," the host said, as the colonel leaned over to see into the centre of a lotus flower. The lotus seed had been sent from Africa to his father by an ex-slave named Prince. He told the colonel the story of a man who, after years as a slave, wrote a letter in Arabic to the consul at Tangier, speaking of his rank among the Timboo tribe, his capture in battle and his sale. The consul sent the letter to President Adams who in turn had Henry Clay inquire for what he could be bought. The owner presented the slave with his freedom; diverse Natchez citizens raised a sum to purchase his wife and a Moorish costume, and the two set off by way of Washington for Morocco.[43]

Roane Byrnes's zeal for telling stories convincingly impressed Young. Like all good historical novelists, he used these stories to give his novel depth and history-based content. By incorporating them into his novel, he helped bring the Natchez narrative into popular entertainment. Moreover, Young used the Natchez architecture as other characters in his novel. And while he invented the Bedfords' villa, Portobello, McGehee's plantation named Montrose was an actual Natchez villa. Young prominently featured the descriptions of real Natchez villas—Monmouth, Arlington, Rosalie, Richmond, D'Evereux, and Windy Hill Manor.

His sentimental and nostalgic novel was a national sensation when it was published in 1934. The next year, Hollywood director King Vidor directed a film version of it starring Margaret Sullavan and Randolph Scott. Edith Moore consulted for Paramount Films, providing historical background.[44] Although the film was not popular at the box office, it was the first "talkie" movie that introduced the public to Natchez and the first one to present the Natchez narrative (figure 6.7).

While Young's *So Red the Rose* celebrated the gallant and romantic aspects of Natchez, Robert M. Coates's pulp true crime book *The Outlaw Years: The History of the Land Pirates of the Natchez Trace* presented

Figure 6.7: Movie poster for *So Red the Rose*, starring Margaret Sullavan and Randolph Scott, distributed by Paramount Pictures in 1935. (University of Illinois Library, Urbana, Illinois)

Figure 6.8: Robert M. Coates, author of *The Outlaw Years: The History of the Land Pirates of the Natchez Trace*. (Library of Congress, Prints and Photographs Division, New York World-Telegram & Sun Newspaper Photograph Collection, LC-USZ62-118207)

to the public the darker and more lurid history and lore of Natchez, Natchez Under-the-Hill, and the Natchez Trace (figure 6.8).[45] While most critics agreed that Coates selectively chose the most gruesome stories about the horrible Harpes Brothers, the twisted and bloodthirsty Mason, and the genteel murderer Murrel, they agreed that he captured the dark mood and dangerous times along the Natchez Trace and Natchez Under-the-Hill.[46] Readers loved the sensational violence and dark descriptions that Coates presented in the book. It also inspired other writers to make the Natchez Trace a part of the national myth, most notably Eudora Welty.

Mississippi native and one of the state's most lauded writers, Eudora Welty learned about *The Outlaw Years* from a member of her book club, known as the Night-Blooming Cereus Club. Welty found the book riveting, and it inspired her to write two novellas, *The Wide Net* and *The Robber Bridegroom* (1942).⁴⁷ Welty had also become familiar with Natchez and the Natchez Trace in the mid-1930s; she worked briefly for Overstreet and Town while the HABS project was underway, and she had been a photographer for the WPA. The combination of Coates's gory stories and her familiarity with Natchez's architecture inspired her to write a Mississippi version of Grimm's fairytale.⁴⁸

The branding of Natchez went beyond popular literature. Motivated by Katherine Miller, many women—most successfully Lillie Boatner, the secretary of the NGC—marketed their town's architecture and its furnishings and decor to the public. As early as 1936, Boatner was contacting furniture, perfume, and cutlery company executives to push the wealthy white women's Natchez villas lifestyle, which she defined as *the* Natchez lifestyle. She first sent a portfolio of Norman photographs that featured the exteriors and interiors of the Natchez villas to William Tomilson of the High Point Furniture Company, who expressed interest in developing a Natchez-themed furniture line.⁴⁹ She persuaded New York-based cosmetic company Old South Toiletries to develop a new perfume fragrance called "Natchez Rose Jar."⁵⁰ She and Ethel Kelly also convinced the Gorham Manufacturing Company to produce a silverware pattern based on the family pattern at Melrose.⁵¹ The hard work in marketing paid off. By the end of the 1930s, *House and Garden* was selling a Natchez-inspired bedspread, and the Mobil Oil Company featured the villas on its calendars.⁵²

The Natchez marketing and branding campaign fueled a fascination across the country for wealthy white southern decor. Writing for the *Atlanta Constitution*, Elizabeth McRae Boykin stated, "It looks as though even Yankees were going to have Southern accents before it's over, not in speech, perhaps, but at least in-home decorations."⁵³ She then noted that, due to the restorations of Colonial Williamsburg and the rediscovery of Natchez, interior design had become "southern." At an exhibit on furnishing that she attended, she saw a living room with marble mantels, ceiling to floor windows, and Hepplewhite and Sheraton furniture—called "Natchez."

Boatner was not the only one who sought to make Natchez villas well known. As early as 1934, Effie Hale tried to convince movie producers to come to Natchez and film the tableaux during the pilgrimage. Silent movies were filmed in Natchez before 1930. The first one, *A Gentleman from Mississippi* (1914), included scenes shot at D'Evereux. Interior

Figure 6.9: South elevation of Homewood, Natchez, Mississippi, photographed by James Butters, 1936. Hollywood director-producer D. W. Griffith filmed scenes for *Birth of a Nation* on the porches and lawns of Homewood. In 1940, the villa was gutted by fire. (Library of Congress, Prints & Photographs Division, Historic American Buildings Survey, HABS MISS,1-NATCH.V,13-)

scenes for *Slippy McGee* (1921) were filmed at Melrose. D. W. Griffith filmed scenes on the porches and lawns at Homewood (figure 6.9) for his now-infamous film, *Birth of a Nation* (1915).[54]

In 1938, Boatner, Hale, and Dixon set out to make the Natchez narrative a movie event. When they needed Byrnes to charm the movie producers, she was glad to assist them.[55] They began a letter-writing campaign to convince popular travel documentary producer James A. FitzPatrick to film one of his documentaries on Natchez and the pilgrimage.[56] After countless letters from the three women, FitzPatrick agreed to film the pilgrimage and scenes of life and characters in Natchez. He called his Natchez documentary "Old Natchez on the Mississippi."

The scene-by-scene breakdown is an important piece of documentation of not only the tangible heritage of 1930s Natchez, but also the racism found in the city and in the pilgrimages. FitzPatrick, who narrated all of his documentaries, opened the film by promoting the Natchez Garden Club: "In Natchez, Mississippi, we experience the flavor of antebellum days. The Natchez Garden Club restores old homes, and it hosts a spring pilgrimage featuring costumes, song, and dance to celebrate the Old South." The documentary exhibits both the patriotic and escapist ideas prevalent during the Great Depression.[57]

The opening scene from a rooftop vantage point shows the downtown, with its Texaco filling station and the Mississippi River before the US 84 bridge was built. The red roof of the courthouse clearly delineated the center of town. The next scene in the film is of the opulent villas: Dunleith, Rosalie, and Ravenna. Then, a cut to the Natchez Garden Club women scurrying along the porches of Connelly's Tavern. The movie then proudly shows the raising of the American flag on Ellicott Hill, behind Connelly's Tavern, honoring Andrew Ellicott, and NGC member Blanche Robinson saluting it while "Dixie" plays in the background. The next scene is of the picnic scene tableau at Edgewood. Boatner persuaded FitzPatrick to feature her daughter, Kathie; other Natchez children perform "Ring Around the Rosie" dressed in antebellum attire. There are scenes recreating when the Swedish Nightingale, Jenny Lind, sang in the parlor of The Briars. FitzPatrick juxtaposes the elegance of the parlor scene with a scene of "happy" African Americans dancing in front of their cabin. It focuses on two older African American women. The first one is described as "Mammy," and she is kissing a child; she is Jane Johnson, the formerly enslaved woman who had helped save Melrose forty years earlier. This scene is clearly meant to contrast with the elegance of the wealthy white women. "The Hunt" tableau and the ballet tableau by Trebby Poole, "Audubon, the Dancing Master," both performed in front of Melrose, are featured in the next scene. The final scene is a romantic sunset over the Mississippi River.[58]

The FitzPatrick documentary was shown in at least seventeen thousand theaters across the nation and abroad. It made the historic architecture and the Mississippi River the main attractions. It also reinforced racial stereotypes that were pervasive in 1930s America. Racism across the country coincided with many white people's nostalgia for the lost cause of the Confederacy. Nevertheless, the documentary became a vehicle for promoting Natchez through the burgeoning American film industry. FitzPatrick was so taken with the place that he suggested using it as background scenes for the grandest movie ever made about the mythic "Old South" and one of grandest films ever produced—*Gone with the Wind*.

NATCHEZ AND *GONE WITH THE WIND*

In a letter to famed Hollywood producer David O. Selznick, Marjorie Taylor of Columbia, Tennessee, suggested that he visit Natchez during the pilgrimage to develop ideas for the movie he was about produce from Margaret Mitchell's *Gone with the Wind*.[59] When Vivien Leigh accepted the part of Scarlett O'Hara, Lillie Boatner invited her to Natchez. The NGC named a japonica bush at Melrose after Vivien Leigh and then mailed her red blossoms from the bush. Leigh was photographed holding the flowers. Thus, began a mutually beneficial publicity campaign for the film and Natchez in 1939.[60]

Gone with the Wind commercialized the architecture of Natchez. In making the movie, the set designers did more than just research the HABS architectural archives; they used it to manufacture a consumable product that has ever since warped our understanding of historic architecture and architectural documentation. HABS in Natchez and the manipulation of it by Hollywood were something that Charles Peterson did not foresee when he conceived the idea of the archive. He envisioned it as an archive to be used for architectural historians. But like most historical records, they are open to the making of fictional ideas. Drawings of historic architecture can be used to understand history. They can also be used as precedents for new construction. But they could also be used to create fantastical places. In the case of Natchez and *Gone with the Wind*, HABS helped produce Tara.

The Tara that Margaret Mitchell envisioned when she was writing *Gone with the Wind* (*GWTW*) did not have colossal Greek Revival-style columns. It was a rather humble Federal-style, wood-framed residence. The inspiration for Mitchell's Tara was her maternal great-grandfather Fitzgerald's home, called Rural Home (figure 6.10). Built in 1831, it was a simple, wood-framed Federal-style single-pile, center hall structure consisting of four rooms, where Phillip Fitzgerald and his wife, Eleanor, raised seven girls. It was located in Clayton County between Jonesboro and Lovejoy, Georgia, approximately twenty miles southwest of Atlanta. Like most of the real antebellum South, the plantations were humble and crude. "Tara Country" was not the opulent suburban world of Natchez. In fact, nowhere in the antebellum South was Natchez. Antebellum Natchez was a haven for wealthy planters who typically owned multiple plantations. After Mitchell sold the movie rights to her novel to David O. Selznick in 1936, she initially took an interest in the film's production. The next summer, she persuaded Wilbur G. Kurtz Sr., a friend of her father and a prominent amateur historian and accomplished painter, to accompany her on a tour of Clayton County to photograph antebellum homes for the movie. The humble utilitarian homes, like the Fitzgerald Home, did not impress Selznick, who made it clear to her that he wanted a grander Tara than what she had written about in her novel (figure 6.11).

Mitchell was horrified that Tara was not going to be based on the authentic historic architecture of western Georgia. "I grieve," she wrote as the movie production began, "to hear that Tara has columns. Of course,

Figure 6.10: Tara in the movie *Gone with the Wind*. The grand plantation home with its tetrastyle portico and two-story columns was not what novelist Margaret Mitchell envisioned for the home of her heroine, Scarlett O'Hara. (John Springer Collection/Getty Images)

Figure 6.11: Rural home, the Phillip Fitzgerald House, Clayton County, Georgia, 1831. The utilitarian Federal-style wood-frame residence was the home of Margaret Mitchell's maternal great-grandfather, Phillip Fitzgerald. It was a single-pile, center hall, and it had four rooms. (Photograph courtesy of Tommy H. Jones)

it didn't and looked ugly like Alex Stephens' Liberty Hall."[61] For Mitchell, survival was the theme of the book. Realizing that Selznick wanted to make the southern scenery more glamorous than that in western Georgia, she politely bowed out of the production of the movie, but she convinced Selznick to hire Kurtz as the film's technical advisor and historian.[62]

Wilbur Kurtz jokingly referred to himself as a "transplanted Yankee," and he viewed himself as an impartial observer of the South. He was a midwesterner, born in the downstate Illinois small town of Oakland

Figure 6.12: Historian Wilbur G. Kurtz Sr. and actress Ona Munson at the *Gone with the Wind* pre-premiere press reception at the Georgia Terrace Hotel in Atlanta, Georgia. Margaret Mitchell urged David O. Selznick to hire Kurtz as a history and technical advisor for the *Gone with the Wind* movie production. (Kenan Research Center at the Atlanta History Center)

and raised in rural Greencastle, Indiana. He studied art at DePauw University and later at the Art Institute of Chicago. After finishing at the Art Institute, Kurtz worked in Chicago as a draftsman, engraver, professional illustrator, and architectural renderer. At the turn of the century, he became fascinated with the famous Andrews Raid, which happened near Atlanta, in 1862, and involved "the General," a large locomotive used by the Confederacy. He first visited Atlanta in 1903 while researching the Andrews Raid and was charmed by the "quiet, pleasant town, full of churches, where they rolled up the sidewalks at dark every night." He moved permanently to Atlanta in 1912 (figure 6.12).[63]

Along with consulting about historical authenticity in movies, Kurtz advised Selznick on the general feeling and truth of "southern-ness." He dismissed the "Lost Cause" myth of the Confederacy, and he stated that Mitchell never intended for *GWTW* to resurrect the Lost Cause myth or even glorify it. He also reiterated that Mitchell never intended to stir up old animosities. Instead, she wrote a book that "would give the very age and body of the time his form and pressure," but more importantly, tell a story that the book-buying public would enjoy. In other words, it would use the region's heritage as a tool for entertainment. And like any movie, he contended, "If no one in the South—happens to enjoy the Atlanta scene as presented—then what of it?"[64]

Kurtz then argued that, in creating Scarlett O'Hara, Mitchell set out to discredit the "southern lady" ideal that had been so well crafted through two generations of women in Natchez and throughout the South. He stated:

> To say the society that the war brought to an end, consisted largely of vain, empty-headed young girls, whose only object in life seemed to be to flirt and finally capture a husband; while the young men—were mostly occupied in hunting and getting drunk, not even having minds enough to stay in college when they were sent there. The sooner such a society was broken up, the better, it would seem.[65]

Kurtz's comments are telling. He made the claim that the white antebellum woman was never a glamorous southern lady. In his research, he submitted to Selznick evidence to the contrary, like the "Southern Girls Song," which extolls the homespun dress and palmetto hat of the hardworking Christian girl who labored on the farm while her brave lad fought for southern freedom. It was hardly the southern belle created by Katherine Miller and many others during the 1930s.[66] From his time living in Atlanta from 1912 until 1938, when he temporarily moved to Culver City, California, for the production of *GWTW*, Kurtz did not acknowledge the southern lady that Anne Firor Scott and Drew Gilpin Faust documented; instead, he knew the modern woman like Mitchell, who was educated at Smith College, sexually liberated, twice married, and a reporter for the *Atlanta Journal*. For Kurtz, the history of the Civil War was important, and he dismissed the myth of the gallantry of southern gentlewomen. For him, that character type was all nonsense, though he saw no harm in making it entertaining for the movie-watching public. It was Hollywood, and people went to the movie to escape reality. And Selznick did just that.

Unlike Stark Young, who wrote extensive descriptions of the fictional Portobello and Montrose and of real villas like Monmouth and Rosalie, Mitchell wrote only brief descriptions of the landscapes of Clayton County and a single paragraph describing Tara:

> The house had been built according to no architectural plan whatever with extra rooms added where and when it seemed convenient, but with Ellen's care and attention, it gained a charm that made up for its lack of design. The avenue of cedars leading from the main road to the house—that avenue of cedars without which no Georgia planter's home could be complete—had a cool dark shadiness that gave a brighter tinge, by contrast, to the green of the other trees. The wisteria tumbling over the verandas showed bright against the whitewashed brick, and it joined with the pink crêpe myrtle

bushes by the door and the white-blossomed magnolias in the yard to disguise some of the awkward lines of the house.[67]

Her description provided several clues that Tara and western Georgia were not as opulent as the movie presented them to be. Mitchell was forthright that the fictional Tara was a vernacular building and, like most vernacular structures, had not been planned. Her description coincided with the rough and new development of Clayton County and western Georgia. And while slavery and the plantation-based economy were prevalent across the antebellum South, few planters were wealthy enough to build a grand manor home. The typical plantation resembled a rural home; it often consisted of simple structures, much smaller than the Natchez villas. Natchez was created as a suburban oasis and, ironically, the place "Where the Old South Still Lives" was never the real antebellum South. That was Mitchell's Clayton County.

Mitchell did provide some descriptions that enabled Selznick and his staff to develop a Hollywood Tara. The avenue of cedars from the main road to the house, "without which no Georgia planter's home could be complete," provided the art designers something to work with in designing the house. The greenery she described also was a device with which the house could be developed without being perceived as awkward. But despite this description, Selznick knew that the movie plot required something grander, and he set out to build a set design team that would provide him the scenery for the movie.

In early 1938, Selznick hired Joseph B. Platt to be the head of art and setting design for the movie.[68] Along with Kurtz, Selznick's most trusted staff member, Lillian Deighton, researched and collected the historical information for the movie. During the production, Platt and others consulted multiple archives, from women's fashion libraries in the northeast to the Historic American Buildings Survey.[69]

Uninspired by the scenery of the real Tara country captured by Mitchell and Kurtz, Platt and Deighton followed FitzPatrick's advice and toured Natchez and the surrounding countryside. They quickly realized that the area possessed the scenic inspiration for the movie, more so than the descriptions from the book. Their research in Natchez dramatically departed from the landscapes and circumstances of Mitchell's book. *Gone with the Wind* was no longer a story of survival of a middle-class heroine in hardscrabble Clayton County, Georgia, during the Civil War but of Scarlett O'Hara, a heroine within the grand world of the southern lady of Natchez.

Ironically, the red earth of Tara, which Scarlett O'Hara clutched in her hand at the movie intermission, was not from Georgia. It was from

Figure 6.13: Belmont, Liberty Road, Natchez, Mississippi, Joseph B. Platt, Photographer. On the back of this photograph, Platt wrote: "Tara." Belmont was not a prominent villa in Natchez, but the Asher Benjamin-inspired architecture and its setting evidently inspired Platt to suggest that it become the inspiration of Scarlett O'Hara's west Georgia home. (David O. Selznick Collection, Harry Ransom Center, The University of Texas at Austin)

near Natchez, Mississippi.[70] Platt took several color photographs of the Mississippi cotton fields and attached to the photographs small plastic bags containing the samples of red clay found near Natchez. It was all a deliberate effort to pattern the landscape and architecture for the movie setting after Natchez. Live oaks, which are not prevalent in northwest Georgia, replaced cedars, and flat Mississippi cotton fields replaced the rolling hills of Georgia topography.[71]

Of all the grand Natchez villas on which Platt and Deighton could have based Tara, they were most captivated by a villa that was not featured in the Natchez pilgrimage and was not owned by any of the Natchez women of either the Natchez Garden Club or the Pilgrimage Garden Club. Platt wanted Tara in the movie to be based on Belmont, located on Liberty Road not far from Melrose (figure 6.13).[72]

Belmont, more than most of the other Natchez villas, resembles the Greek Revival architecture found not only in the South but throughout the country. The Mississippi Department of Archives and History determined that it was built in approximately 1845 and was based on the

Figure 6.14: The driveway approach to Belmont, Joseph B. Platt, Photographer. With its alley of moss-draped cedars, the approach to Belmont most resembles Margaret Mitchell's Tara description among all of the villas in Natchez. (David O. Selznick Collection, Harry Ransom Center, The University of Texas at Austin)

pattern designs published by Vermont architect Asher Benjamin.[73] New Englander Platt may have found the villa more to his northeastern liking than other villas such as Hope Villa or The Burn.

Belmont was featured in Nola Nance Oliver's *Natchez: Symbol of the Old South*, which was published in 1940, the year after the film's release. Interestingly, that is the only instance when this villa is featured in any book about Natchez, and it was not recorded at all by the HABS team in the 1930s. Oliver stated that Louisiana planter Loxley Thistle built it in the early 1840s and that it was built in a sturdy way to withstand tornados, which Oliver suggested was what compelled Thistle to move to Natchez and build it in the first place. Edith Moore noted that Belmont probably had more owners than any other antebellum mansion in Natchez. It may have been built as early as 1838 for Israel Leonard.[74]

What perhaps captivated Platt more than anything about Belmont was the thirty-three-acre grounds surrounding it. Oliver described its entry drive: "The approach to Belmont is a majestic line of moss-draped cedars and giant oak trees standing sentinel-like over the gardens of days long passed."[75] The approach matched Mitchell's Tara description (figure 6.14).

Selznick hired set designers Lyle R. Wheeler[76] and William C. Menzies[77] to work with Platt in building the sets for the movie. The set designers did not concur with Platt that Belmont was the appropriate precedent for the movie version of the plantation manor. Wheeler and Menzies also understood that Margaret Mitchell had intended for Tara not to be more impressive than Ashley Wilkes's Twelve Oaks. In order to provide the movie with a more realistic feel, Tara was built as a freestanding building. Working with Lillian Deighton, who directly reported to Selznick, they began designing the manor house as authentically as possible and built it on a film lot in Culver City, California.

Facing a tight production schedule, Wheeler and Menzies needed to work fast in designing Tara. How they accomplished it was perhaps the first time the Historic American Buildings Survey was blatantly used to fabricate a fictional place based on heritage. Wheeler, an architect, learned through the AIA that the HABS project was underway, and as for so many aspects of the movie production, from period signage to women's fashion, Deighton contacted various libraries, archives, and historians to obtain ideas for images, costumes, and props that would make *Gone with the Wind* appear authentic.[78]

On December 27, 1938, Menzies asked Deighton to order the Historic American Buildings Survey Catalog from the US Government Printing Office. The next day, Wheeler ordered the catalog from Washington. Together, the two set designers perused the listings for Natchez, Mississippi, following Platt's advice to use Natchez as the precedent for the movie sets. For Wheeler and Menzies, HABS—specifically Hays Town's District 17 work that had been produced four years earlier—was what Chatelain had sneeringly referred to as "an architect's dream." They picked from various detailed drawings among the Natchez HABS drawings and photographs to create Tara.[79]

Wheeler and Menzies used a simpler and more vernacular precedent than Belmont. They studied Annie Barnum's Monmouth (figure 6.15). Its stark white stucco finish and bold square piers supporting the tetrastyle portico coincided with their imagined version of Mitchell's description. Wheeler quickly created a schematic design for the plantation house, which was approved by Platt and Selznick. He stylized its entablature, and instead of designing the portico's Greek Revival tympanum, he proposed making a shed roof for the portico. He then added one-story wings on either side, and to make the composition more picturesque than classical in appearance, he added on the right wing, porch, and colonnade that terminated with a small dependency building. These first conceptual gestures enabled the house to strike a balance between the high style and glamorous look that Selznick wanted and the vernacular structure Mitchell envisioned (figure 6.16).

The design proposal was approved, and Wheeler and Menzies quickly developed it into a buildable design for the Tara movie set. The layout of the plan resembled more of the contemporary residential designs of the 1930s than the strict symmetrical design of floor plans found in Greek Revival residences of the 1840s and 1850s. The meandering placement

Figure 6.15: Monmouth, Natchez, Mississippi, Ralph Clynne, Photographer. (Library of Congress, Prints & Photographs Division, Historic American Buildings Survey, HABS MISS,1-NATCH,29-)

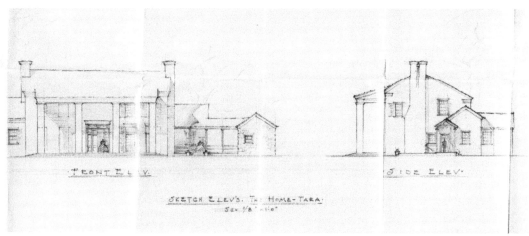

Figure 6.16: Lyle Wheeler, "Sketch Elev's. The Home—Tara," January 1939. (David O. Selznick Collection, Harry Ransom Center, The University of Texas at Austin)

of the building's components, an asymmetrical arrangement designed for picturesque effect, shifted the portico to the right side of the building and added a curved colonnade, which culminated with an octagonal dependency building (figure 6.17). On the left side, the designers proposed a two-story porch, similar in scale to the one built for Homewood (see Figure 6.9). The plan layout was designed with the filming scenes in mind. After all, Tara was a film set, not an actual plantation manor.

Wheeler and Menzies used details that they examined from the District 17 HABS documentation to make their Tara appear authentic. They designed a much more affordable (for the film production and in the spirit of Mitchell's novel) portico than the Asher Benjamin-inspired Belmont portico; it was an edited and simpler version of the Monmouth portico (figure 6.18).

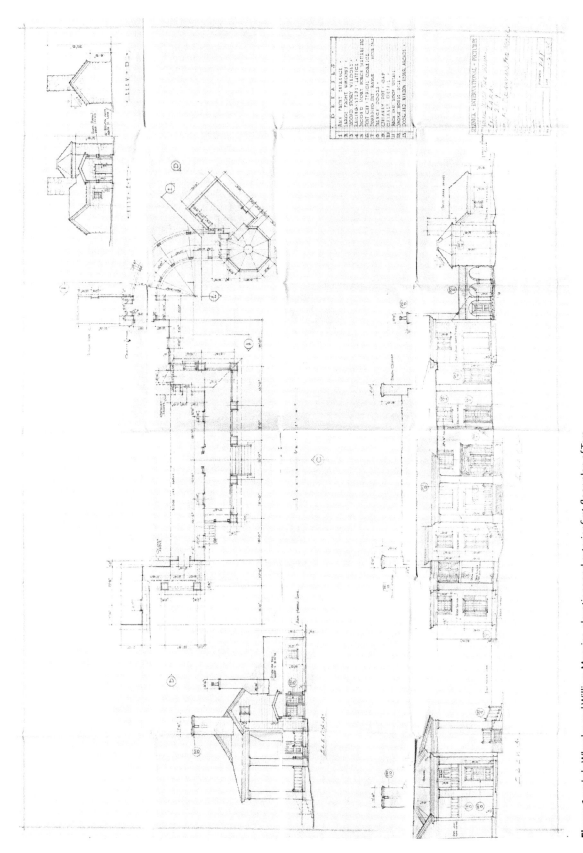

Figure 6.17: Lyle Wheeler and William Menzies, elevations and exterior first-floor plan of Tara. (David O. Selznick Collection, Harry Ransom Center, The University of Texas at Austin)

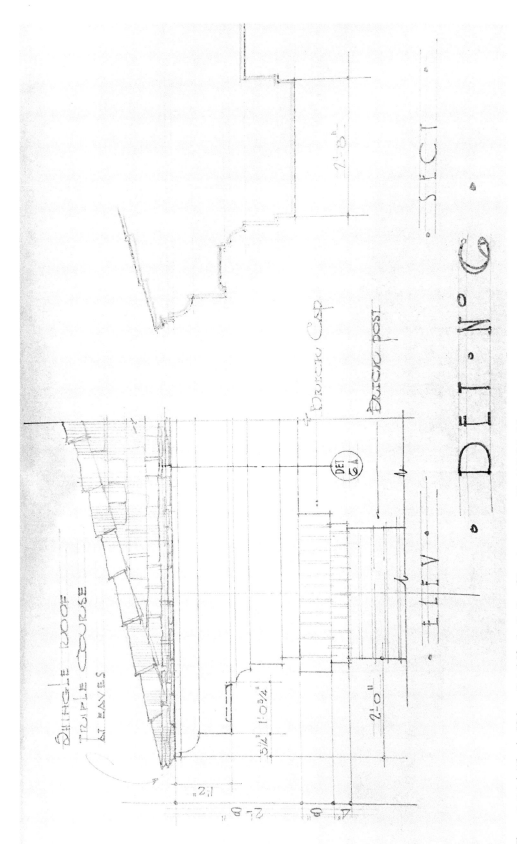

Figure 6.18: Lyle Wheeler, "Column Details" for the Portico of Tara, January 1939. (David O. Selznick Collection, Harry Ransom Center, The University of Texas at Austin)

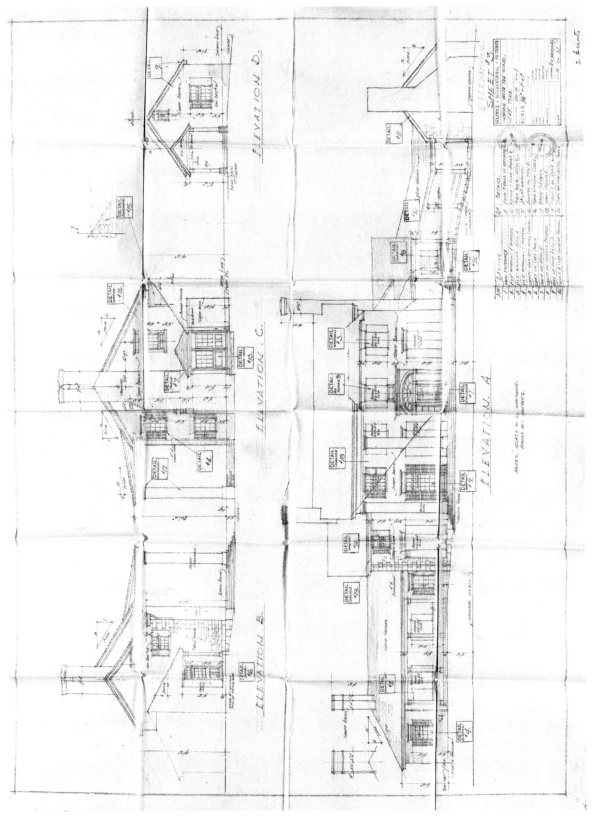

Figure 6.19: Lyle Wheeler and William Menzies, exterior elevations of Tara, February 1939. (David O. Selznick Collection, Harry Ransom Center, The University of Texas at Austin)

Figure 6.20: Lyle Wheeler and William Menzies, detail sketch of the front elevation of Tara, February 1939. (David O. Selznick Collection, Harry Ransom Center, The University of Texas at Austin)

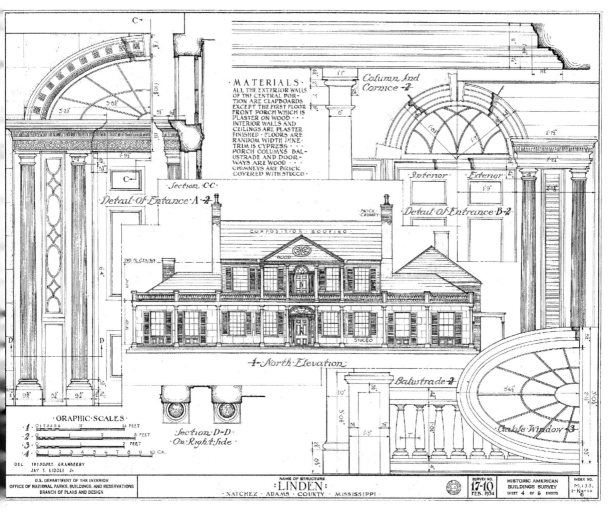

Figure 6.21: Theodore Granberry and Jay T. Liddle Jr., elevation and details of Linden, HABS 17-10, February 1934. (Library of Congress, Prints & Photographs Division, Historic American Buildings Survey, HABS MISS, 1-NATCH,6-)

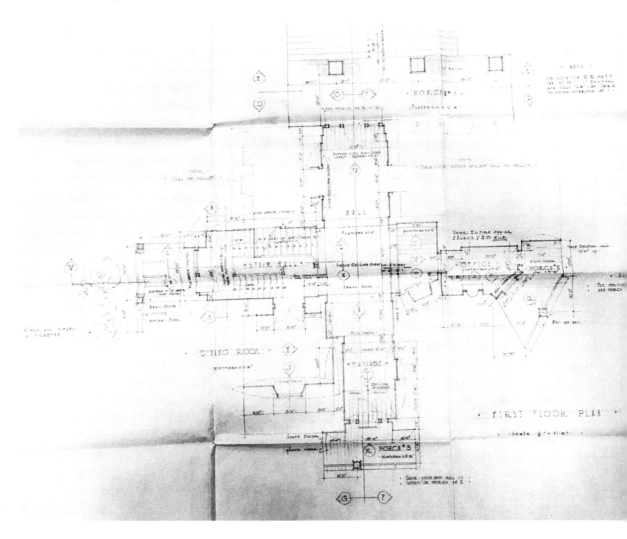

Figure 6.22: Lyle Wheeler and William Menzies, interior floor plan of Tara, February 1939. (David O. Selznick Collection, Harry Ransom Center, The University of Texas at Austin)

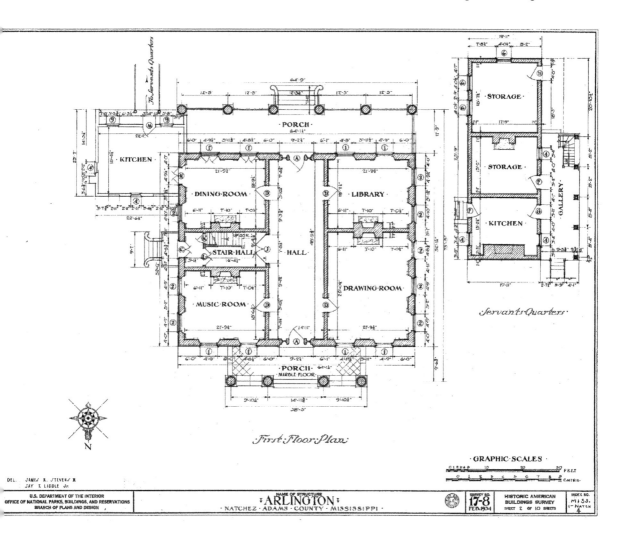

Figure 6.23: Theodore Granberry and Jay T. Liddle Jr., floor plan of Arlington, HABS 17-8, February 1934. (Library of Congress, Prints & Photographs Division, Historic American Buildings Survey, HABS MISS,1-NATCH,4-)

The final design simplified the one-story colonnade and outbuilding located on the right side of the building. But as their design became more detailed, the two designers relied on the Natchez HABS set of drawings (figure 6.19). They copied the front entry from the Linden HABS set, which Edith Moore had declared was an excellent example of Spanish Colonial architecture found in Natchez, and transformed it into the most iconic "Old South" door ever created (figures 6.20 and 6.21).

Wheeler laid out the interior plan based on the important Natchez villas. He examined both Arlington and Rosalie and arranged the rooms for the movie set around a center hall, which went through the entire building and had a front and a rear door and porch (figure 6.22). The grand iconic staircase was placed on the side of the building, similar to what is found in Natchez villas (figure 6.23). The District 17 drawings provided him immediate precedents to follow, which he needed since production of the movie was scheduled for less than a year.

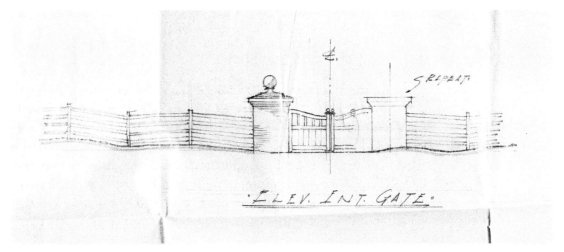

Figure 6.24: Lyle Wheeler, elevation of the entrance gates at Tara. (David O. Selznick Collection, Harry Ransom Center, The University of Texas at Austin)

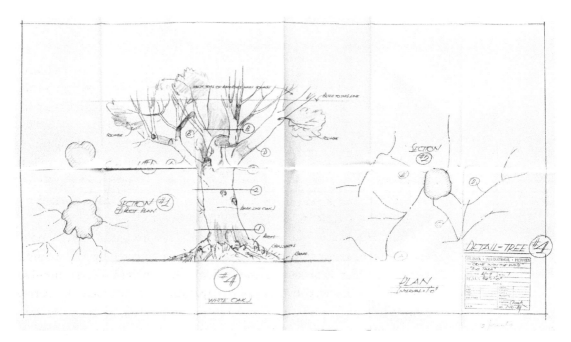

Figure 6.25: Lyle Wheeler, elevations and plans of the tree at Tara. (David O. Selznick Collection, Harry Ransom Center, The University of Texas at Austin)

The movie scenery was also inspired by Natchez (figure 6.24). Wheeler studied the entrance gates and the dependency buildings found in Natchez and created similar ones for the movie scenery. With its large brick piers and timber gates, it resembled what Annie Barnum built for the entrance of Monmouth after the first pilgrimages.[80]

He even designed the famous oak tree that Scarlett stands beneath at crucial times during the movie after trees such as the Aaron Burr Oaks found in Natchez (figure 6.25).[81] The large gnarly oak tree resembled more of the Natchez live oak trees than any of the red or white oak trees that grow in western Georgia.

Wheeler won an Academy Award for Art Direction for his designs and set construction for *Gone with the Wind*. Menzies won an Academy Honor Award for his work on lighting and stage design as well. They received these accolades in spite of Platt's attempt to claim all the credit for the design of the movie.[82] After the movie was released in 1940, Natchez's branding in popular culture as the place "Where the Old South Still Lives" was complete. People all over the world equated the architecture and landscapes of Natchez with the movie and the stereotypical idea of the antebellum South. Natchez was now set apart from other southern cities—Savannah, Charleston, Mobile, and New Orleans—for its "southern-ness." Although women like Edith Moore and Roane Byrnes, and even Katherine Miller, had set out to create a Natchez narrative that celebrated its Spanish colonial history, Natchez became the embodiment of the "Old South" after the movie adaptation of *Gone with the Wind*.

But antebellum Natchez was never the quintessential southern place. Natchez was a suburban enclave of very elaborate villas built by a small set of wealthy planters. Margaret Mitchell and Wilbur Kurtz were correct in their objections about creating a grander Tara. Clayton County was similar to a lot of the rural South prior to the Civil War; it was a poorer and cruder place than Natchez. But the creators of the movies, and even Kurtz, understood what their audience wanted—the glamour and romance of a lost age. And so, by using Natchez, they created an image of the mythic "Old South" that resonates today.

Using HABS as a resource to create the "let's pretend" world of movies instead of an archive for architectural research is telling. One should remember that Charles Peterson developed the idea for the archive after he was inspired by the documentation work produced by Perry, Shaw & Hepburn for the re-created Colonial Williamsburg. No one should be surprised to realize that archival collection could be used in numerous ways.

Despite the brilliant and serendipitous way in which the garden club women marketed Natchez and how it was portrayed by Hollywood, on Madison Avenue, and in literature during the late 1930s, the real Natchez of that time was still an impoverished and isolated place. Other photographers and writers came to the place and recorded a grimmer Natchez, where racial conflict prevailed. These individuals created a counternarrative to the one that the garden club women created, and their work became part of the American visual and literary narrative of the Great Depression.

A DISTRESSED NATCHEZ

At the same time the Natchez Garden Club women created their narrative and branded their place as a cultural tourism destination, outside scholars, photographers, and writers came to Natchez and documented a different place from what was published in brochures, shown on postcards, and featured in movies. A team of University of Chicago sociologists—Allison Davis, Burleigh Gardner, and Mary Gardner, two of whom were African American—selected Natchez for interviews based on their initial assessments that it was the best place to study the southern mindset on society and race. The team came to Natchez and used "free associative" techniques to interview people, both African American and white, to examine the place within the social context of 1930s Natchez in order to understand how Natchez society "worked." They asked few questions, relied on their observation work, and collected statistical data on social gatherings from what they read in the *Natchez Democrat.*

Based on their findings, they described a caste-class system in the town, comprised of white and African American citizens. Within each caste, six social classes and subclasses were identified, but all of them identified as part of the "Old City" or the "Old County." What the group believed skewed its field material was implementation of the New Deal's Agricultural Adjustment Act. It provided new opportunities from outside the elite white social order, namely through tenant farming changes, which compelled many of the poorer African Americans to leave Natchez and seek better opportunities elsewhere.[83] Even as Natchez was creating its "Old South" brand, the demographics were apparently changing.

The Chicago sociologists were substantiating what Yale sociologist John Dollard had discovered four years earlier, in 1934, in the Mississippi delta town of Indianola: the white elite caste subordinated African Americans and denied them their legal rights to vote as American citizens. The result was that two separate caste systems existed in Natchez, and while African Americans could move upward in their caste, they could never move economically upward as much as their white counterparts. But what made the Davis, Gardner, and Gardner study a groundbreaking research project is that they recognized the importance of private property ownership in all of Natchez. They concluded that the distinction between the villas and the impoverished quarters of Natchez was a visual sign of power in the city. They also noted contradictions caused by economic conditions; for example, white shopkeepers in Natchez who depended on African American business showed deference to their African American customers. The researchers noted that wealthier whites in town were either hostile or oblivious to the plight of their Afri-

Figure 6.26: Frances Benjamin Johnston, 1938. (Frances Benjamin Johnston Photograph Collection, Library of Congress, Prints & Photographs Division, LC-USZ62-120443)

can American counterparts. As the tourism economy grew in Natchez, the deference decreased.[84]

The caste system in Natchez was captured visually during the 1930s through three photographers, each of them wanting to document the poverty and decay they saw in Natchez. What they eventually produced was another narrative that specifically addressed Depression-era Natchez. Some of the landscapes and historic buildings they photographed were preserved, but most was lost as the buildings fell into disrepair or were replaced with modern buildings.

WPA-funded agencies and private foundations financed noted photographers and gave them the directive to produce a photographic record of the city, not only its brilliant architecture but also the city's mundane and vernacular features. The photographs they produced show a starker Natchez narrative, one of poverty and racial injustice; and, as was the case with District 17, the garden club women could not control them or manage this narrative.

In 1938, funded by a Carnegie grant, noted photographer Frances Benjamin Johnston[85] arrived in Natchez to photograph many of the grand villas. However, she was not interested in recording the opulence; rather,

Figure 6.27: Choctaw, 1938, Frances Benjamin Johnston, Photographer. (Frances Benjamin Johnston Photograph Collection, Library of Congress, Prints & Photographs Division, LC-DIG-ppmsca-23941)

she was capturing the villas in their state of decline. In her photograph of Choctaw, with is peeling paint and cracked stucco, she recorded the Natchez that tourists found fascinating. The declining place possessed a romance that was brought about by decay. This was the Natchez of the Great Depression. She was compelled to photograph grand villas like Choctaw as a record of their existence, realizing that it may be demolished; but she, like so many tourists who experienced the pilgrimages, was captivated by their decay.

But what made Johnston's work in Natchez so important today is that she did not focus exclusively on the Natchez villas; she also recorded the middle-class and vernacular buildings found in the city (figure 6.28). More importantly, she photographed buildings that no one in Natchez considered worthy of recording and preserving. In one picture, she recorded the brick foundation, hewed log construction, and clapboard-clad shed addition of a cabin located south of Natchez in Adams County (figure 6.29). She photographed several middle-class houses, like 821 Main Street, which although it had an overgrown front lawn, had numerous architectural features that defined the Natchez's architectural character—the deep porch and slender columns, tall windows, and Federal period dormers (figure 6.30).

As a noted architectural photographer of her time, Johnston was introduced to Katherine Miller, Roane Byrnes, Edith Moore, Ethel Kelly, and other garden club women, who provided her the introductions she

Figure 6.28: Unidentified house, Natchez vicinity, Adams County, Mississippi, 1938, Frances Benjamin Johnston, Photographer. (Frances Benjamin Johnston Photograph Collection, Library of Congress, Prints & Photographs Division, LC-DIG-ppmsca-23942)

Figure 6.29: Unidentified cabin, Natchez vicinity, Adams County, Mississippi, 1938, Frances Benjamin Johnston, Photographer. (Frances Benjamin Johnston Photograph Collection, Library of Congress, Prints & Photographs Division, LC-DIG-ppmsca-23944)

Figure 6.30: House, 821 Main Street, Natchez, Mississippi, 1938, Frances Benjamin Johnston, Photographer. (Frances Benjamin Johnston Photograph Collection, Library of Congress, Prints & Photographs Division, LC-DIG-ppmsca-32369)

Figure 6.31: Windy Hill Manor, Natchez vicinity, Adams County, Mississippi, 1938, Frances Benjamin Johnston, Photographer. (Frances Benjamin Johnston Photograph Collection, Library of Congress, Prints & Photographs Division, LC-DIG-ppmsca-32379)

Figure 6.32: Spanish Priest's House, 311-313 Market Street (now known as the James Andrews House), Natchez, Mississippi, 1938, Frances Benjamin Johnston, Photographer. (Frances Benjamin Johnston Photograph Collection, Library of Congress, Prints & Photographs Division, LC-DIG-ppmsca-32377)

needed to access villas like Richmond, Elms Court, and Longwood. She photographed Hope Farm for Miller, and she granted Byrnes's request to photograph Windy Hill Manor. In another photograph, she artfully captured the wrecked state in which Elizabeth Brandon Stanton and her sisters lived (figure 6.31).

Johnston listened to Edith Moore and photographed the "Spanish Priest's House" at 311-313 Market Street, which Moore and Hays Town had incorrectly labeled. Why she photographed and documented it the same way District 17 had done two years earlier is not known. Having worked closely with Waterman, she could have coordinated this work with HABS, but she took a picture from a similar vantage point as the picture taken by HABS photographer James Butters. Clearly, Moore, Miller, and Byrnes felt strongly that the James Andrews House was worthy of recordation. To this day, both the HABS recordation and Johnston's photograph of this historic Natchez building are erroneously labeled the "The Parrish House" and the "Spanish Priest's House" (figure 6.32).

Two other photographers, Walker Evans (figure 6.33)[86] and Ben Shahn,[87] recorded Natchez during the Great Depression as part of a national record on the state of the country for the federal government's Farm Security Administration (FSA). Evans and Shahn photographed the poor who lived on the city's streets. Their work, along with Johnston's photographs, captured the conditions of a different Natchez, one that none of the garden club women wished to share with the outside world. It is a powerful irony to consider that, at the same time Katherine Miller was instructing Natchez photographer Earl Norman to photograph the

Figure 6.33: Walker Evans, 1938. (Library of Congress, Prints & Photographs Division, Farm Security Administration/Office of War Information Collection, LC-DIG-fsa-8a14702)

grandeur of Natchez's antebellum villas, Evans and Shahn were photographing the abject poverty of the place only a couple of blocks away.

Evans wanted to capture the authoritative truth of the moment in his photographs. In a 1974 interview with William Ferris, he emphasized that he regarded himself as more of a photojournalist than an artist, saying, "I'm serving a great tradition of reporting, anything from reporting all the way up to literature."[88]

In Natchez, Evans's photographs for the FSA archive are the Lum Brothers Livestock Building and the Commercial Bank on Main Street (figure 6.34). Standing in front of the stark Greek Revival temple bank building are two young African American men; behind them, painted on the limestone wall, is one word: "Signs." Evans photographed the mundane way the grand Greek Revival landmark was used and maintained. The image explains how historic antebellum buildings like the Commercial Bank were used in 1930s Natchez.

In Natchez, Shahn photographed the racial discrimination prevalent throughout the city. In his photograph "Negro Child in Front of Badly Rundown House," Shahn captured the severe poverty found in the African

Figure 6.34:
Commercial Bank, Main Street, Natchez, Mississippi, 1935, Walker Evans, Photographer. (Library of Congress, Prints & Photographs Division, LC-USZC4-1795)

Figure 6.35: "Negro Child in Front of Badly Rundown House," Natchez, Mississippi, 1935, Ben Shahn, Photographer. (Library of Congress, Prints & Photographs Division, Farm Security Administration/Office of War Information Collection, LC-DIG-fsa-8a16477)

Figure 6.36: "Scene in Lower Natchez, Mississippi," 1935, Ben Shahn, Photographer. (Library of Congress, Prints & Photographs Division, Farm Security Administration/Office of War Information Collection, LC-DIG-fsa-8a16481)

American areas of Natchez. An African American toddler stands alone, perhaps even abandoned, in front of a dilapidated house (figure 6.35). In "Natchez Under-the-Hill," Shahn photographed an elderly African American man sitting in front of an unkempt commercial building; a dog walks in front of the man in the photograph's foreground (figure 6.36).

Shahn also photographed buildings in Natchez but not the exquisite landmarks that the garden club women showcased or the District 17 scenes that Johnston and Evans recorded. He photographed the banal vernacular buildings of everyday life in the city. Like Evans, he photographed the Lum Brothers building (figure 6.37). Evans focused in on

Figure 6.37: "Lum Brothers Livestock Barn," Natchez, Mississippi, 1935, Ben Shahn, Photographer. (Library of Congress, Prints & Photographs Division, Farm Security Administration/Office of War Information Collection, LC-DIG-fsa-8a16554)

Figure 6:38: "Church at Natchez, Mississippi," 1935, Ben Shahn, Photographer. (Library of Congress, Prints & Photographs Division, Farm Security Administration/Office of War Information Collection, LC-DIG-fsa-8a16557)

one bay of the tripartite building; but, using an oblique viewpoint, Shahn photographed the entire front façade, which include haphazard signage and a large horseshoe in its gable.[89] The building was demolished, and the Natchez Convention Center was built at its location on Main Street. Shahn composed his photograph of the Bethel A.M.E. Church similarly to photographs of the historic buildings that Earl Norman had made (figure 6.38).

Shahn's photography captured not the "let's pretend" Natchez but the real one of 1937—a place where business was conducted between Black

Figure 6.39: "Scene in Natchez, Mississippi," 1935, Ben Shahn, Photographer. (Library of Congress, Prints & Photographs Division, Farm Security Administration/Office of War Information Collection, LC-DIG-fsa-8a16398)

Figure 6.40: Ethel "Russie" Blanks, Katherine Grafton Miller, Emily Marks Calvert, Helen Ballou Bruce, Josephine Davis Walker, and Carlotta Searles McIlhenry at Hope Farm, 1937. Photograph featured in Miller's book, *Natchez of Long Ago and the Pilgrimage*. (From *Natchez of Long Ago and the Pilgrimage* by Katherine Grafton Miller [Natchez: Relimak Publishing Co., 1938])

and white residents, and a place that was definitely not antebellum (figure 6.39). Contemporary critics accuse the photographic record of Evans, Shahn, and Lange as showing evidence of situational manipulation, a conscious act to influence the viewer's feelings towards a specific subject through composition. But throughout the 1930s, as photography became more persuasive in modern society, advertising and marketing began to use this tool in a more pervasive manner and create not only a message but a brand. One can argue that photography was widely used to manipulate public opinion, and this was one of the FSA's objectives. As the brands became accepted—in this case produced by Johnston, Evans, or Shahn—brand personalities emerged. Marketing professor Jennifer Aaker contends that these brand personalities become associated with the personality expressions of consumers. In the case of 1930s Natchez, she argues, two brand personalities emerged: the first one, produced by the garden club women, was the grandeur of the "Old South" (figure 6.40). The second one was produced by the FSA: the poverty and racial injustice found in the rural South. Both realities existed in 1930s Natchez. According to Aaker, the garden club women did create an intangible heritage of their place that commodified what a certain consumer wanted to embrace about the South and perhaps expressed in their mannerisms, architecture, and home decor; but the brand that the FSA created helped educate the American public about the social problems facing many of its rural citizens during the Great Depression.[90] Self-expression of the photographers and the garden club women created both brands, which were two separate but coexisting narratives of a place.

As the 1930s concluded and the fame of Natchez increased as an "Old South" tourist place, tourist traps were built that capitalized on the pilgrimage. Modernity, mainly through the New Deal programs, began to encroach on the once-isolated small town. Two tourist destinations in particular manipulated the colonial narrative and the mythic "Old South" one: Old Fort Rosalie and Mammy's Cupboard.

KITSCH AND THE NATCHEZ NARRATIVE

By 1940, the development of state highways, which began in 1916, started to influence cultural tourism in the South, and it was changing Natchez. The first pilgrimages were experienced by wealthy tourists from the North and the South, who could afford to travel leisurely to Natchez, even on the unreliable passenger trains. But travel to Natchez soon changed. Even though the Natchez Trace Parkway was slowly being built, state highways like US 61 were improved. New Deal funding was paving roads, and all this allowed middle-class tourists to easily travel throughout the South for recreation. This development fostered the emergence of family-owned, folksy, and completely unregulated roadside tourists' attractions. As Tim Hollis noted in *Dixie Before Disney*, this was the era of the manufactured tourism destination.[91]

Natchez was not immune to roadside kitsch built during the World War II, automobile-based tourism era. But what made these attractions compelling that still exist today is that they were reactions to the colonial and antebellum narratives that the Natchez garden club women created.

Figure 6.41: Old Fort Rosalie Gift Shop, Natchez, Mississippi, 2006. (Library of Congress, Prints & Photographs Division, Historic American Buildings Survey, HABS ms-274)

Old Fort Rosalie and Mammy's Cupboard demonstrate that these women's narrative of their place was firmly established and commercially profitable in Natchez by 1940.

Entrepreneurs who did not associate with the Natchez elite recognized what the women had accomplished and built attractions that capitalized on their success. No one was more aggressive or flamboyant in building an amusement venture than Jefferson Davis Dickson Jr., a Natchez native who returned to the city and purchased a large tract of the Natchez bluff west of Rosalie from William A. Cauthen and soon built his idea of a reconstruction of the French Fort Rosalie, the same historic fort that Roane Byrnes, Edith Moore, and Katherine Miller made famous with the restoration of Connelly's Tavern. Dickson had nothing to study or on which base his version of the lost fort, and it did not matter to him. Old Fort Rosalie was a log cabin stockade constructed of small logs. The complex included a log blockhouse and at least six log cabins with wood shingle gable roofs. It resembled Hollywood's version of Daniel Boone's Boonesboro more than an eighteenth-century fort in any country. In December 1940, Dickson bought a lot that fronted Canal Street and built the Old Fort Rosalie Gift Shop, which served as the formal entrance to the reconstructed fort (figure 6.41).

Dickson owned Old Fort Rosalie only for a brief period. After the US entry into World War II, he rejoined the army as an intelligence officer and was killed in Germany in 1943. The attraction ceased operations during the war, after which the Natchez Historical Association reopened and operated Old Fort Rosalie until 1950 when it was demolished.[92]

Figure 6.42: Mammy's Cupboard, 555 Highway 61 South, Natchez, Mississippi, 2006, James W. Rosenthal, Photographer. (Library of Congress, Prints & Photographs Division, Historic American Buildings Survey, HABS MS-277)

While Dickson was building Old Fort Rosalie, local gas station owner Henry Gaude built something less ambitious in size but kitschier in appearance. Capitalizing on the "Old South" craze in Natchez, he built a gas station that was called Mammy's Cupboard in the 1990s (figure 6.42). Annie Davis Bost, wife and draftsman of Natchez's most prolific prewar architect, Robert E. Bost, designed the hoop skirt building with a woman's head and torso on top. She originally designed it to be an African American servant with a tray in her arms and was most likely inspired by actress Hattie McDaniel, who portrayed Mammy in the *Gone with the Wind* movie. Inside the station, Gaude served southern food, fried chicken, and pies.[93]

The racial stereotyping in Mammy's Cupboard reflected attitudes about race not only of many white Natchezians but also of its tourists. White exploitation of African Americans for entertainment purposes was a long-established tradition, dating back to the last decades of the nineteenth century. The Natchez Garden Club women used them for this purpose in the pilgrimage, and by the outbreak of World War II, this stereotype was assimilated into the tourism narrative.

Roadside kitsch articulated the two city narratives in the most blatant way. Old Fort Rosalie embodied the Spanish colonial narrative, and Mammy's Cupboard represented the antebellum narrative. Did it matter to anyone that the fictional fort was located adjacent to the historic Rosalie villa? Did it matter that nothing like the caricature of Mammy had ever existed anywhere prior to 1940? No. At the end of 1941, Natchez was profiting on the pilgrimage and its "Old South" brand. The "Battle of the Hoop Skirts" created national publicity for the city. All of this, created between 1934 and 1941, made Natchez a tourism destination, and as long as the money kept coming, no one seemed to mind.

◆ ◆ ◆

In ten years, the Natchez Garden Club women transformed the city and changed its meaning for its inhabitants and the outside world. The period from 1936 to 1942 was an incredibly dynamic time in the history of Natchez; even the Civil War had not impacted the city as much as the later years of the Great Depression. During this time, garden club women led by Katherine Miller continued to expand the pilgrimage. Lillie Boatner successfully marketed the place to Hollywood and Madison Avenue. Roane Byrnes continued to help create the Natchez Trace Parkway, and Edith Moore continued to provide her "expert" knowledge about its history, which she had in actuality fabricated. Buildings like Stanton Hall were purchased and saved, and celebrities came and marveled at the historic architecture of the Greek Revival architecture and the ingenuity of these women in marketing it.

But it all came to a halt soon after the bombing of Pearl Harbor. America's entry into World War II brought the Great Depression to an end and, with it, programs like the Historic American Buildings Survey, the Federal Writers' Project, and the Farm Security Administration photographic work. America was finished self-reflecting about itself and preserving its historic architecture, and it became too busy fighting a war to enjoy a vacation in a place like Natchez. Both women's clubs held a pilgrimage in 1942 and donated their profits to the American Red Cross and the war effort, but they ceased having any pilgrimages until 1946, after the war had ended. During the war years, Ruth Beltzhoover remembered that there was a seriousness in the country and "everyone was worried and unhappy because their sons were overseas."[94] The war provided a break in the activity and the animosity that occurred in Natchez. In 1946, the garden club women, like all of America, experienced a new era, one that forever moved nineteenth-century Natchez into history.

Figure 7.1: Pilgrimage headquarters at the Elks Lodge, corner of Pearl and Franklin Streets, Natchez, Mississippi, 1940. (Thomas H. and Joan W. Gandy Photograph Collection, Mss. 3778, Louisiana and Lower Mississippi Valley Collections, LSU Libraries, Baton Rouge, Louisiana)

Chapter 7

AFTERMATH

World War II ended the Great Depression, and it ended the garden club women's embracive preservation and marketing efforts in Natchez. The war years provided a respite from their quarreling, and the clubs ceased having pilgrimages after 1942. In 1946, they revived the Spring Pilgrimage and extended it throughout the month of March. Alma Carpenter was the Confederate Pageant queen that year, and Annie Gwin took over Monmouth for the pilgrimage from her mother, Annie Barnum. A new generation of elite white Natchez women were poised to carry on the enterprise. By 1946, the Natchez narrative was complete, and the city was nationally known as the place where the "Old South Still Lives" (figure 7.1). The postwar boom came to the nation and Natchez, and for the next fifteen years, it changed the city. Racial tensions in the wake of the passage of federal antilynching laws increased. At first, both Natchez and the nation tried to ignore the tensions; but by the 1960s, the conflict came to a head.[1]

The garden club women were now older and faced their own decline and the loss of their loved ones. But they controlled the city's class structure and a significant portion of the local economy. By the 1960s, they were equated with historic Natchez—so much so that, in 1977, Natchez historian Ronald Miller remarked that "unfortunately the remarkable and commendable efforts of the women have resulted locally in a feeling that preservation is a sexually and socially exclusive activity."[2] Katherine Miller led the Pilgrimage Garden Club to even greater heights, and the Natchez Garden Club waned. By the 1950s, the philosophical differences between their narratives had been ignored and replaced with a caricature of what the national press portrayed of the women: the PGC members indulged in drinking and partying, and the NGC members were teetotalers.

Roane Byrnes spent the remaining twenty-four years of her life relentlessly advocating for completion of the Natchez Trace Parkway. At one of her final Natchez Trace Association meetings in 1967, she enthusiastically declared, "I want to ride on the Natchez Trace all the way before I have to ride on the golden streets."[3] But also, during the 1950s, she found time to lead the effort to move and restore the "Parish House," consulting with Charles Peterson, who never questioned whether the American-built James Andrews House was the home of eighteenth-century Catholic priests in Natchez.

Throughout the late 1940s and 1950s, *Gone with the Wind* became the embodiment of the national idea of the "Old South," and Natchez became the tangible place of this southern myth. Natchez continued to be the subject of literature and movies. Harnett Kane published *Natchez on the Mississippi* in 1947; Edith Moore published *Natchez Under-the-Hill* in 1958; and, in 1985, Jonathan Daniels published his version of the Natchez Trace story, *The Devil's Backbone*. Hollywood produced a B movie called *The Natchez Trace*.

During this time, Natchez experienced both Black and white diasporas. Native Natchez African Americans who had moved to places like Chicago returned to the city and reconnected with family and friends. White southerners who had left the region to search for jobs in Midwest factories came back to Natchez to reaffirm their southern identity. As the generation that first enjoyed *Gone with the Wind* grew older, they were interested in visiting the city's antebellum villas.

The new architecture that guided Natchez building during the postwar years reflected the "Old South" narrative. For the construction of elementary schools to motels, architects selectively copied ideas from the villas, and they awkwardly attached facsimiles of the villas to modern buildings. Modernity brought prosperity to Natchez and Mississippi. The Eisenhower administration led the effort to build the interstate highway system. By the mid-1970s, Mississippi had modern highways that finally connected the state; even though an interstate highway system did not pass near Natchez, it was accessible at nearby Vicksburg, and Highway 61 was substantially improved. "Mission 66," the Eisenhower-funded program to refurbish the national parks, funded a significant portion of the paving of the Natchez Trace Parkway. River commerce improved in Natchez, and in the 1960s and 1970s, the petroleum industry prospered, but the garden club women firmly communicated that they and their families were the city's wealthy elite, which was not true.[4]

During the mid-1970s and the presidency of Jimmy Carter, America once again was fascinated with the South. But by this time, Natchez was more of a "historyland" and less of an actual place. National newspaper reporters flocked to Natchez to cover the pilgrimage and comment on the splendid decadence of the Natchez elite. The garden club women and the men who had created the narrative of the place and helped preserve the city now developed a narrative about the work they did forty years earlier. Katherine Miller, Ruth Beltzhoover, and Edith Moore solidified their reputations as the women who saved Natchez. Charles Peterson and Hays Town defined their careers partly by their HABS involvement. Peterson wrote about his work in Natchez and in establishing HABS. Town reinvented his career as a "neotraditionalist" and "neo-Creole" architect and used the details he recorded during the District 17 days for designing new expensive houses in the 1970s, '80s, and '90s.

With the passage of the National Historic Preservation Act in 1966, the Mississippi Department of Archives and History established a comprehensive statewide historic preservation program. But its initial efforts were weighted toward Natchez, which by this time had become one of the state's preeminent historic places, along with the Vicksburg National Battlefield and the battlefields near Tupelo. President Ronald Reagan signed legislation to create the Natchez National Historical Park, which originally consisted of Melrose and the Fort Rosalie site. Later the William Johnson Home was added to it to honor the African American heritage in the city. District 17 had been a leader in HABS documentation in its initial period, but during the postwar era, when the National Park Service revived the project, Mississippi lagged behind the nation in recording historic buildings for HABS.

Personalism and then professionalism were applied to preserving the historic architecture of Natchez and then Mississippi through the creation of the Natchez Trace Parkway. As heritage became a viable tourism-based economy, personalism persevered over professionalism. People believe the southern myth more than actual fact during the middle part of the twentieth century. But at the beginning of the twenty-first century, the perception of Natchez and Mississippi's antebellum architecture and Civil War monuments changed. Americans began to acknowledge the role slavery played in creating the exquisite villas and how Jim Crow laws perpetuated and displayed white power and privilege in places like Natchez. Eventually all of this became part of the significance of the place. Today, we now face two challenges in Natchez: How will we continue to preserve this historic city? And what period of significance should we preserve it to—the nineteenth-century antebellum era or the 1930s Depression era?

THE RETURN OF THE PILGRIMAGE

After the hiatus during the war effort, the garden club women renewed the pilgrimage in 1947. By then the two clubs had agreed to work together and hold a single month-long event. The national press continued to make light of the women's feuding. *Los Angeles Times* reporter Horace

Figure 7.2: African American band playing music at Hope Farm during the 1952 Spring Pilgrimage. (From *The Lufkin Line* XXVII: 1, 1952. Courtesy The History Center, Diboll, Texas)

Sutton called the two clubs "two rival dandelion societies" that emerged from the "holocaust." In his article, he also jokingly described how the town mediators called in the "U-all N" and negotiated a peace. It was all amusing, but the women understood what the stakes were: $500,000[5] of tourism revenue for the city's economy. And even though the "Big Split" remained, the two clubs worked together. As Sutton reported, they managed to alternate in selecting kings and queens for the pageant and staging events; but during the immediate postwar years, the PGC presence grew, showcasing twenty-five houses, while the NGC presence waned, opening just five houses.[6]

In the late 1940s, racial tensions were not often acknowledged in the national press, and the garden club women denied that any conflict between African Americans and whites existed at all. After the 1947 pilgrimage, the *Chicago Daily Tribune* praised what it defined as all the citizens of Natchez, homemakers, businessmen, Junior Leaguers, and "top shelf society matrons, for their impressive display of southern hospitality." The writer also noted how easy it was to wander into the kitchens of these grand mansions and chat with "the help," and she praised the supposed racial harmony that she contended existed in Natchez, declaring that Black and white residents were "united in one vast heaveho to the stay of every pilgrim completely happy."[7]

White tourists may have wanted to believe that Natchez was this kind of utopian place, but the reality was that African Americans remained

Figure 7.3: Katherine Grafton Miller at Hope Farm, 1947. (Courtesy of the Archives and Records Services Division, Mississippi Department of Archives and History)

Figure 7.4: Katherine Grafton Miller at Hope Farm, 1952. (From *The Lufkin Line* XXVII: 1, 1952. Courtesy The History Center, Diboll, Texas)

subjected to Jim Crow laws. Moreover, the garden club women manipulated African Americans, making them part of a narrative that relegated them to playing servants during the tourists' show. But after twenty-five years of conducting the pilgrimage, everyone in Natchez understood that a little "southern hospitality" could go a long way in earning tourists' dollars (figure 7.2).

Figure 7.5: Katherine Grafton Miller, Balfour Miller, and Ruth Audley Beltzhoover enjoying a night at the Copacabana Club in New York, circa 1956. (Photograph from the Pritchartt Collection, Natchez, Mississippi)

Though women like Annie Barnum served as presidents of the PGC, Katherine Miller was firmly in charge of the club and influenced the tourism industry (figure 7.3). She spearheaded expansion of the PGC's facilities at Stanton Hall to include the Carriage House Restaurant, with a formal clubhouse wing and a swimming pool for the exclusive enjoyment of the club members. More importantly, she made the mythic "Old South" the theme of Natchez, and she became the matronly southern lady (figure 7.4).

During the 1950s, Miller solidified her fame and power in Natchez. President Eisenhower appointed her a delegate to the US National Commission of UNESCO in 1953, and she received the 1954 Amy Angell Collier Montague Medal from the Garden Clubs of America.[8] The state of Mississippi awarded her a "Missy" distinguished service award in 1959; she was the first female recipient for her work in the state's tourism industry.[9] In Natchez, she continued to rule the PGC with a velvet-gloved iron fist, often leading efforts to decorate Stanton Hall and arrange parties there. Away from Natchez, she basked in her glory with Balfour (figure 7.5). These were the heady days of Natchez. Highways connected it to the rest of the world; its river port was redeveloped, and the petroleum industry was bringing jobs and financial prosperity to the city. As Miller said to the *Ladies' Home Journal* in 1947, "We've got three industries in Natchez—cotton, oil, and the Pilgrimage"; the article's author added, "And never believe that the last of these isn't a practical crop."[10]

Figure 7.6: Katherine Grafton Miller with General Douglas MacArthur at Stanton Hall, 1952. MacArthur came to the pilgrimage shortly after he stepped down as commander of United Nations-led forces during the Korean War. (Photograph from the Pritchartt Collection, Natchez, Mississippi)

But perhaps Miller felt her greatest triumphs were hosting dignitaries and Hollywood movie stars in Natchez and at Stanton Hall. In 1952, soon after General Douglas MacArthur returned from his command during the Korean War, Miller and the rest of Natchez welcomed him for a visit.[11] Alma Kellogg, who was president of the PGC at the time, rode with the general in a horse-drawn carriage and remembered how he complained about the cold weather. PGC vice president Margaret Ware rode in a separate carriage with MacArthur's aide and the mayor. MacArthur's son, Arthur, rode with pilgrimage queen Kathie Blankenstein. Miller greeted MacArthur and his wife at Stanton Hall. The great southern lady was hosting the great wartime general—something she considered a major accomplishment in her life (figure 7.6).[12]

After the World War II, when Miller solidified her reputation as the quintessential Natchez southern lady, Ruth Beltzhoover became the modern southern woman. Married to wealthy Melchoir Beltzhoover, whose family owned the Britton and Koontz Bank, she initially was protected from the financial hardships of the Great Depression and spent her winters at Green Leaves (figure 7.7) and her summers at her husband's family home in Irvington-on-the-Hudson, New York, called Rochroane (the family sold it in 1927). But when Melchoir was stricken by a rare and life-ending disease in the late 1930s, Ruth found herself with no financial assets other than the majority shares of a local department store called the Famous & Price Store.[13]

Figure 7.7: Green Leaves, Natchez, Mississippi. (Library of Congress, Prints & Photographs Division, Historic American Buildings Survey, HABS MISS, 1-NATCH,9-)

Ruth Beltzhoover used the tenacity she had shown in creating a restaurant in her villa, Green Leaves, and reinvented the declining department store into one of the most popular women's clothing stores in the Deep South. She put her three children through college, nursed her husband in his declining days, saved Green Leaves, and stayed active in the PGC, using her payments from the pilgrimages to preserve her villa.

In an article about Beltzhoover's life in the *Ladies' Home Journal*, writer Struthers Burt presented her as the gentle southern lady who worked effortlessly in the male-dominated world of business:

> Her soft voice, her gentle manners, her constant feminine appeal to the supposed superior practical wisdom of men are typically Southern. So is her appearance. She says deprecatingly she has "no head for figures." Perhaps; but she has a very clear and imaginative head for buying and selling, and feminine styles; and for ten years she has run the biggest store of its kind in Natchez, and one of the leading stores in that part of the South: the Beltzhoover store, now known as the Natchez Department Store.[14]

In reality, Beltzhoover was not known in Natchez for her soft voice and gentle manners. Quite the contrary, she was irascible and outspoken. But as America began to adapt to the changing postwar reality, which had

Figure 7.8: "Yesterday's enchantment lives today Natchez hospitality," from "Meet the Beltzhoovers, of Natchez, Mississippi," *Ladies' Home Journal*, January 1947. (University of Illinois Library, Urbana, Illinois)

both opportunities and challenges, Natchez, a place known for female entrepreneurship, where domesticity and history went hand-to-hand, became a place where modern feminine virtue could be celebrated. Eleanor Roosevelt had first proposed this modern southern woman ideal in her nationally syndicated article eight years earlier after she visited Natchez. But Struthers Burt's article about Beltzhoover attempted to contextualize the Natchez narrative into the postwar national paradigm that eventually became Second Wave Feminism. In the *Ladies' Home Journal* article, Beltzhoover is portrayed as the modern American woman, a southern lady who can run a successful business in a man's world, raise children, and preserve an iconic historic home. Furthermore, she was proof that southern feminine virtue still existed, especially in Natchez (figure 7.8).[15]

Burt suggested that the gracious "Old South" Natchez lifestyle and the benevolent treatment of African American house servants allowed Beltzhoover to accomplish all that she did. The ever-dependent elderly Crissie, who kept up Green Leaves, prepared all of the Beltzhoovers' meals and was not only taking care of Ruth Beltzhoover but also her son, Melchoir, and his family. Burt noted that Crissie remained devoted to Beltzhoover. He also presented the Confederate Ball not as a celebration of the Lost Cause but as a reaffirmation of American values and reminded readers that even though the young men dressed in Confederate officer attire, waved the Confederate flag, and sang "Dixie," they had earlier been wearing the American Army uniform and fighting in Germany and Japan for the stars and stripes. The national press had now updated the Natchez narrative for the post–World War II era.[16]

Natchez emerged from World War II poised to reap the benefits of all the hard work that women like Miller, Beltzhoover, and Barnum had accomplished in making the city the epitome of the "Old South" myth. They employed historic preservation and an uncanny knack for promotion to market outdated furnishings and antique collectibles to the nation, making Natchez a place worthy of being included with other American cities known for their architecture and refined taste, such as New Orleans, Savannah, Baltimore, Philadelphia, and even New York. Harnett Kane declared, "Natchez has become a plantation museum without parallel in the South."[17] And one that could be easily traveled to by automobile.

ROANE FLEMING BYRNES AND THE NATCHEZ TRACE PARKWAY

During World War II, the Natchez Trace Parkway and the Natchez Trace Association (NTA) were dormant. In May 1942, Ralph Landrum reported that the NTA had only $30 in its treasury and that he was paying any outstanding expenses before temporarily shutting down the organization.[18] The war squashed any lobbying momentum to build the parkway to Mexico City. During the war, Mexico experienced several presidential turnovers, and the Mexican government lost interest in the project. In that same time frame, Landrum moved to Jackson and became prominent in civic affairs in the capitol city but remained active in the NTA leadership for the rest of his life.[19] For the next twenty-five years, he took a more prominent role in negotiating with Mississippi and Washington politicians to make the parkway a reality. Meanwhile,

Figure 7.9: Roane Fleming Byrnes cuts the ribbon at the dedication ceremony for the new section of the Natchez Trace Parkway near Kosciusko, Mississippi, in 1951. From left to right: Kosciusko mayor Alton Massey, Natchez Trace parkway superintendent Malcolm Gardner, Roane Fleming Byrnes, and Jackson, Mississippi, mayor Allen Thompson. (Roane Fleming Byrnes Collection [MUM00057], Department of Archives and Special Collections, J. D. Williams Library, The University of Mississippi)

he was more than happy for Roane Byrnes to continue to be the spokesperson for the project.

The NTA reorganized in 1947, and Byrnes presided over its first postwar meeting in Kosciusko, Mississippi, that October.[20] The Alabama and Tennessee NTA divisions also met that year. But P. M. Estes had died in February 1947 in an automotive accident while returning from the Belle Meade Country Club, and the Tennessee division did not have a president for several years. Roadwork on the parkway resumed in September 1947 with repair work in Madison County. Byrnes was present at the dedication ceremony (figure 7.9).[21]

Although the war stopped activity in building the parkway, the problems with building the parkway had not been resolved. As late as February 1950, no new land had been conferred to the National Park Service by the state of Mississippi.[22] In Mississippi, rights-of-way remained unpurchased, and in Washington, appropriations were uncertain. Senator Pat Harrison died in 1941, and Senator Theodore Bilbo died in 1947. A new Mississippi congressional delegation emerged after the war. James Eastland replaced Harrison and John Stennis replaced Bilbo as the state's senators. The challenge had also changed. In 1930s, the push was to pave the trace; in 1947, it was imperative to complete the Natchez Trace Parkway. By now all three states realized the parkway benefits, and each of them pledged to obtain all of the rights-of-way needed by the NPS, even though Mississippi was slow in using the $100,000 it appropriated for the project. Obtaining federal appropriations also remained problematic.[23]

Congressman Thomas G. Abernathy and Senator John Stennis took the lead in securing federal appropriations for the parkway. Often, they were frustrated with the political obstacles they encountered and referred to the Natchez Trace Parkway as a "stepchild" of the national parkway system.[24] Federal appropriations were sporadic for the parkway in the late 1940s and early 1950s. Acting NPS director Hillary Tolson stated that the service received $811,900 for the Mississippi portion of the parkway, a meager appropriation for the unfinished parkway. Maintenance on ten years of existing roads had to be done; comfort stations and an orientation center needed to be built; and of course, significant sections of it had to be built, even though rights-of-way had not been secured. Tolson decided that, with this paltry allocation, construction had to be curtailed. No one in Mississippi was happy with this news. But at Roane Byrnes's urging, the Mississippi State Highway Department continued to pursue rights-of-way acquisition.[25]

Byrnes understood that rights-of-way acquisition was the necessary component in receiving funding from the federal government to complete the parkway project, and she began working in earnest to convince the state highway department to expedite the process, using any means necessary. In a June 1949 publicity stunt, she arranged for a team of six oxen to pull a wagon loaded with eight women dressed as pioneers across the parkway near Adams County in front of a motorcade. Unfortunately, the demonstration did not go well. The oxen broke the tongue of the wagon, and the women shrieked in terror.[26]

After the failed demonstration, Byrnes met with Malcolm Gardner from the National Park Service and John Smith and Tom Robbins from the state highway department. The decades-old rights-of-way problem became a sore point of contention at the meeting. Smith and Robbins argued that the acquisition program disrupted other state highway projects. Gardner was offended and accused them of not being more diligent in purchasing the needed land for the parkway. Byrnes ended the two-hour meeting without a resolution.[27] But even though acrimony continued in Mississippi, Abernathy bought the project some extra time by amending the Postwar Highway Act to increase parkway construction from $5 million to $10 million.[28] Stennis met with Byrnes and Natchez Commerce Association president Stan Murphy and informed them that Congress would probably not authorize construction funds until all needed rights-of-way in the state were secured. Byrnes intensified her lobbying campaign through her connections in the Mississippi legislature, urging legislators to pressure the state highway department to acquire the rights-of-way. As she contended with bureaucratic red tape from the state highway department, construction on the Natchez Trace Parkway remained sporadic for the rest of 1951 and all of 1952.

After twenty years of Democratic control of the presidency, a Republican was elected president in 1952, bringing tremendous change for the Natchez Trace Parkway and alarming Byrnes and Landrum. President Dwight Eisenhower's first national budget called for complete elimination of the Natchez Trace Parkway; he even suggested it be completely abandoned. The 1952 election also gave full control of Congress to the Republicans. Abernathy, Stennis, and Eastland struggled to keep a token appropriation for the parkway. Testifying at the House Subcommittee on Appropriations, Abernathy reaffirmed that Mississippi had secured the rights-of-way for the Natchez Trace Parkway and chastised the federal government for failing to honor its commitment to complete the parkway. Byrnes sent to him a signed NTA resolution urging Congress to complete the project.[29] The ploy worked. It bought the parkway project time. The 1954 budget included a trifling $651,000 road appropriation. But later that year, Abernathy managed to secure nearly $3 million for the parkway in a separate NPS bill, and this funding allowed road construction to resume.[30]

In 1955, Byrnes and Landrum received promising news about the parkway. Reacting to Eisenhower's ambitious ten-year Interstate Highway Program, National Park Service director Conrad Wirth proposed a similar ten-year program to rebuild the park system called "Mission 66." After the New Deal funding, which ended in 1938, the NPS had received very little funding to operate during the war years and soon after. The amount of deferred maintenance reached a critical point by the mid-1950s, and the public was outraged at the poor state of roads in the national parks, the lack of natural conservation, and the lack of park amenities. Historian Ethan Carr noted that Wirth, who had been working for the NPS his entire career and was a skilled Washington bureaucrat, understood what Congress wanted to hear, and he proposed a ten-year program to rebuild the park system, culminating at the half-century anniversary mark of the National Park Service in 1966. Wirth's proposal worked, albeit in annual federal appropriations. According to Carr, Congress appropriated funding for projects like the Natchez Trace Parkway until the late 1960s, when domestic funding was frozen to offset costs for waging the Vietnam War.[31] For the first "Mission 66" appropriation, over $4 million was allocated to the parkway.[32] Road construction, but more importantly much-needed support building and amenities construction, soon followed. Byrnes remained active in not only lobbying for funding but also communicating building projects to the local construction industry.[33]

In 1956, Ferriday Byrnes died. Roane Byrnes had devoted almost all of her time to the Natchez Trace Parkway, but at sixty-six, she was not as effective in spearheading the final stages of the project. Like Roane, Ferriday had found purpose and adventure on the parkway project; the NTA appreciated his dedication to it. Working with his wife had allowed him to leave his law practice, which he had never liked, and to travel across the country. As the garden club women grew older and more accomplished, their husbands, like Ferriday Byrnes and Balfour Miller, became content to support them and share in their accomplishments. Once Ferriday Byrnes passed away, Roane relied on her oldest friend and cousin, Lallie Adams, as her confidant.[34]

When Bern Keating visited Roane Byrnes in 1968 at Ravennaside, two years before her death, for an article on the parkway for *National Geographic*, she projected the elderly but confident southern lady to him. He noted, "Mrs. Byrnes received me in her Natchez home, Ravennaside, at midmorning in a floor-length velvet gown adorned with a superb red-and-white candy-striped camellia blossom. Her soft accent and manner belied the iron under the velvet glove—the iron that has persuaded two generations of state and Federal officials that paving a few more miles of the Trace Parkway offers the easiest way out."[35]

Keating then noted the hand-tinted photomurals of trace scenes and the pen she proudly displayed: the one Franklin Roosevelt had used to establish the Natchez Trace Parkway in 1938. Byrnes offered Keating a mint julep and showed him her annotated parkway map, and she told him that National Park Service officials often dropped by Ravennaside, enjoyed a mint julep, and updated the road construction on the map for her. He described the small pantry, now converted into a map room and a bar, as a "war room."[36]

Byrnes remained the face of the lobbying efforts for the Natchez Trace Parkway for the remainder of her life. Even as arthritis took its toll, she never wavered in traveling across the state and the country, championing the parkway. During the 1960s, in dozens of ribbon-cutting ceremonies, wearing her elegant dresses and hats, she stood out among the older gray men wearing dark suits.

ROANE BYRNES, EDITH MOORE, AND THE NATCHEZ GARDEN CLUB

While Katherine Miller became the face of the Pilgrimage Garden Club and imprinted her flamboyant personality on the organization after World War II, Edith Moore became the face of the Natchez Garden Club. Somber and serious in bearing, Moore's personality projected her as the public perception of the NGC. The press enjoyed labeling the PGC as the "Partying Club" and the NGC as the "Teetotaling Club."[37] This was not the case. While Miller did like to plan festive events, other PGC women like Ruth Beltzhoover and Annie Barnum were not known for planning boisterous parties. On the other hand, Roane Byrnes enjoyed putting on parties and keeping up a stocked bar. Bern Keating recollected how she offered him a highball glass of bourbon at eight in the morning. "Ordinarily, I don't offer a drink before 9 a.m.," she said, "but for a writer of your stature, I am forced to make an exception."[38]

Edith Moore was the only Natchez woman who had served her country during World War II. At sixty-nine years of age, she joined the Women's Army Corps and assisted in editing the Napier Airfield's newsletter, "The Flash News," and another newsletter, "The Skyfighter," for the Fourth US Army Air Force.[39] After the war, Moore returned to Natchez and resumed her work as the historian for the NGC and for the Adams County division of the Natchez Trace Association. She remained committed to the Spanish Colonial narrative, and during the 1950s, she persuaded the NGC and Byrnes to expand the narrative through preserving and relocating the erroneously labeled "Priest's House."

In January 1950, Moore wrote an article in the *Natchez Times* about the "Priest's House" and the eighteenth-century Catholic priest Father Lennan. Essentially, she rehashed what she had submitted to HABS in 1934.[40] The next month, a local hotel owner and owner of the old dilapidated "Priest's House" on Market Street, Tom Radigan, informed Moore and Byrnes of his intentions to demolish it for a new parking lot for his hotel. Despite her preoccupation with lobbying for the Natchez Trace Parkway, Byrnes felt compelled to preserve what she believed was the "Old Parish House." She asked Radigan how much it would cost to buy the building and then investigated the feasibility of moving it. Moore and Byrnes convinced the NGC to finance relocation of the building to NGC-owned land adjacent to Connelly's Tavern. In April 1950, Byrnes and Moore presented their plan to relocate the old Parish House to Canal Street adjacent to Connelly's Tavern.[41] Although the NGC did not have enough money to move and restore it, they agreed to the project and signed a loan for it. Byrnes contracted a house mover to relocate the building from Market Street to Canal Street. Byrnes's old friend Richard Koch designed a new foundation for the house at its new location on Canal Street.[42]

On June 14, 1950, a house-moving company relocated the old structure. Byrnes, Moore, Mayor Audley Conner, and Bishop Richard O. Gerow of the Natchez Catholic Diocese gave brief remarks before its front stoop in its new location. Conner declared that the moving of the building was "the finest thing the Garden Club had undertaken." Nevertheless, an extensive restoration was required for a building that had been neglected for over fifty years.[43]

Byrnes's preservation strategy was to restore the old building enough for it to be suitable for occupation. Throughout the 1950s, the NGC financed small projects such as a new roof, restoring windows and doors, replastering walls, and painting. When workmen tore into a plaster wall in the main parlor, they discovered a large arch, originally built to connect it to the rear parlor. Excited about the found arch, Byrnes and Moore asked the priests from St. Mary Basilica to examine it. Based on the detailing of the arch, they all concluded that the first floor had been used by the priests as a chapel. In actuality, the first floor was built to be a small shop.[44]

Work slowly progressed until NGC member Laura Belle Hooks rented the building for her antique business, and the rent helped pay for the restoration. As her business grew, Hooks asked the NGC about making an addition to the building. Roane Byrnes asked Malcolm Gardner for advice regarding an addition to the relocated 311-313 Market Street structure, and Gardner referred the request to Charles Peterson, who was working on Mount Locust in Jefferson County on the Natchez Trace Parkway.[45]

Because of the fame the city had gained through its association with *Gone with the Wind*, Peterson begrudgingly acknowledged the historic Natchez created for the pilgrimages, saying in an article for the *Journal of the Society of Architectural Historians*, "We suppose that our greatest aggregation of ante-bellum mansions is to be found here, providing an opportunity well known to Hollywood producers of moonlight and magnolia epics." But he also recognized what these women had accomplished: "To the women of Natchez belongs the credit of the recognition and appreciation which has saved them."[46]

Peterson had always been interested in preserving and restoring Mount Locust, and he shared Edith Moore's interest in the Spanish colonial period. He argued that Mount Locust shared Louisiana French architectural characteristics with Connelly's Tavern and Selma Plantation, located in Washington, Mississippi.[47] Neither French nor Spanish builders had built either building. Rather, Peterson like Moore saw what he wanted to see in Natchez's historic architecture; however, he did express his concern that Moore's research was suspect. He stated, "The Natchez region has never been seriously studied and written up by architectural historians and we found that most of the houses purporting to have been in the 18th century are either dated too early or have been more or less denatured by 'improvements.' We have been tempted to start here a corpus on the subject."[48]

In 1955, Peterson brought with him National Park Service architect Henry Judd to meet with Byrnes and Moore and examine the Parish House, and they called the building "a rare specimen of early provincial architecture." Together, they concluded that an addition could be built on the building's south side elevation. Judd provided sketches for the addition, and Byrnes had local contractor Dix Fowler build it in 1957 for around $5,000.[49]

Although Peterson was dubious about the historical accuracy of Moore's research in Natchez, he was interested in the city's early American architecture more than its mid-nineteenth-century antebellum architecture. The *Gone with the Wind* sensation made him dismiss the importance of the mid-nineteenth-century architecture, although he was fascinated by the oddity that was Longwood; he only expressed interest in the city's earlier buildings like the Priest's House, Mount Locust, and Selma Plantation. And while Peterson always projected himself as a professional preservationist, he was still lulled into believing that buildings in Natchez had an older history than they actually had, perhaps agreeing with Moore's findings. And because of his acquiescence, by 1960, Moore's account of Natchez architectural history became accepted as fact by architectural historians in the National Park Service.[50]

In 1961, the relocated house had a new neighbor when Moore and Byrnes convinced the NGC to relocate the old Judge Josiah Winchester law office, known as Lawyer's Lodge. The one-story, gable-ended, four-room law office had also been located on Market Street, and because Winchester was famous for tutoring a young Varina Howell Davis, they were excited to relocate the building to the corner of Canal and Franklin Streets. Once again, Byrnes led the efforts to relocate it and restore its finishes. Moore had persuaded the Natchez Garden Club to build a complex comprised of Connelly's Tavern, the Priest's House, and Lawyer's Lodge to counter the domain of the Pilgrimage Garden Club's Stanton Hall. It was the tangible heritage of the intangible Spanish heritage of the historic city. But neither the House on Ellicott's Hill nor the James Andrews House nor Lawyer's Lodge was built by Spaniards. Architects and historians have determined that the House on Ellicott's Hill was built in the late eighteenth century, but they agree that an Anglo-Saxon American most likely built it. And because two of the houses were relocated to this corner and away from the courthouse and Market Street, people are often confused about their presence and purpose. It was not until after Moore died in 1970 that the Natchez Garden Club expanded its mission's period of significance to include antebellum architecture. In 1974, the NGC created "The Preservation Society of Ellicott Hill" as its nonprofit arm and made it the legal owner of the buildings on Ellicott

Figure 7.10: Magnolia Hall, the Henderson-Britton House, Natchez, Mississippi, 2018. The large villa was used as a nursery and elementary school by Trinity Episcopal Church until 1974. In 1976, the Preservation Society of Ellicott Hill, a nonprofit organization created by the Natchez Garden Club, took ownership and began restoring it. (Photograph by the author)

Hill. During this time, Mrs. George Armstrong donated to the society Magnolia Hall, the Henderson-Britton House, a grand Greek Revival villa, built in 1859 (figure 7.10). Throughout the twentieth century, maintaining the grand villa was problematic. During the early 1930s, George Kelly owned it for a brief time. He sold it to the Britton and Koontz Bank to save what equity he had in the building. The bank then sold it to the Wheeler family, who let it decay. The house was then owned by the Learned and Armstrong families, along with Trinity Episcopal Church, which used it as a nursery and elementary school until 1974; the NGC took it over in 1976 and continues to restore it to this day.[51]

"WE CALL OURSELVES THE *REAL* SOUTH"

Katherine Miller, Ruth Beltzhoover, Lillie Boatner, and the Natchez Garden Club and Pilgrimage Garden Club women never wavered from the mythic "Old South" narrative throughout the 1960s, despite the fact that the conflict arising from the civil rights movement uncovered an uncomfortable truth about race in Natchez. After nearly forty years of the pilgrimage and preservation of antebellum architecture, Miller willed Natchez to be the place where America would find more than just the "Old South" but what she viewed as the "Real South," both in the city's architecture and the manners of its elite white social class. "We call ourselves the *real* South. . . . Some people think Florida is the South, but you just find tourist types there. And New Orleans is so cute and French and sweet and Spanish and you love the people but that is not the real South, either. Natchez is because we are the American South," she explained in an interview with Judy Klemesrud for the *New York Times*.[52]

As Miller had seen over the decades, the national fascination for the place waxed and waned, but America once again became fascinated with the South in the 1970s. *Gone with the Wind* enjoyed a comeback. It was now a classic movie. And with the election of Jimmy Carter in 1976, the "New South" of oil wealth and Sun Belt cities like Atlanta, Nashville, and Charlotte and Raleigh, North Carolina, "southern" became both chic and kitsch. The "southern lady" became an iconic stereotype, but it was also referred to as the "Steel Magnolia" persona. There was even an Off-Broadway play that lampooned the garden club women and the "War of the Hoop Skirts." Did all of this annoy Miller? Certainly not. She welcomed the attention to both her and her native city.

Americans and the national press were also enamored with the house tour aspect of the pilgrimage. Instead of being impressed by the rare antiques and antebellum architecture, tourists were fascinated by the spectacle of it all: the wealthy elite families—who, in reality, were not that wealthy or elite—opening up their homes and lives to thousands of intermeddlers. Americans appreciated the richness of the city's villa architecture, and they admired the tenacity of the garden club women in preserving it. Natchez was a unique town that made its uniqueness an event for four decades.

But unlike the celebratory way the national press covered the pilgrimages and Natchez shortly after World War II, 1970s reporters described Natchez with irony to a skeptical American public, and the New Journalism was used to probe the practices of Natchez.[53] At the end of the 1977 Spring Pilgrimage, Blair Sabol of the *New York Times* wrote an expansive article explaining what the pilgrimage had become.[54] She attended the wild after-tableaux parties held by Natchez teenagers, met with the drunken younger generation of the Natchez elite, and participated in the pilgrimage. Kate Don Adams persuaded her to don a hoop skirt and work as a guide at Oakland. And, most especially, she enjoyed lunch with Katherine Miller at the Carriage House restaurant, located behind Stanton Hall.

At eighty-three years of age and having lived through two world wars and the Great Depression, instigated the "Big Split," and created a multi-million-dollar tourism industry, Miller was more than comfortable with herself and her legacy. On that day in the restaurant she created, she enjoyed her plate of fried chicken, adjusted her hearing aid, reapplied her lipstick, lit an unfiltered Camel cigarette, and candidly expressed her opinion of Natchez and feminism:

> You know, the Pilgrimage is a religion for me. Why don't you find looking at all the Southern history enriching? Doesn't our town inspire you and fill you with hope? There is no place like Natchez. Where else in the South can you see and learn what life was all about? There is the real South. There is no other Jimmy Carter and his gang here, [they are] not the South I know and love.

She continued:

> You know why there's all this sudden interest in us? 'Cause we have always known how to live in the great style. We love luxury and we never bother ourselves with politics. We also love fine furniture—but only early American, Empire, and Sheraton are allowed in our tour homes. Of course, some Texans moved into one of our finer mansions and I swear they redid it terribly—all pink and green and outrageous décor. Well, what can you expect! They are not from Natchez!

Miller also shared her opinion on being an old southern lady in Natchez, saying, "Why most of the people in these homes were born here and will no doubt die here. In the Old South we don't send our aged off to homes and condominiums. They become royalty." And finally, she expressed her opinion about the modern feminist movement and being a southern lady in Natchez:

> Well Northerners [women] are more practical. We had more servants than they did and I still can't make a bed. And yes, it's true we are all flirts, but in the South, we women love being women. That's why we don't wear pants the way you Northern girls do. As for Women's Lib, well, we've been in power in Natchez for years but we don't want the men and the Chamber of Commerce to think we think that.[55]

Miller was not the only one who played up the southern lady act. Alma Carpenter, who later in life became the grand southern lady of

Natchez in the twenty-first century, slyly acknowledged that she was only a member of the DAR and not the Colonial Dames of America, saying, "I have been divorced and they don't take in us wanton women." Mary Louise Kendall Goodrich demurely stated that she was not eager to marry a northern man because they were "a little cold," even though she had been involved in Democratic national politics and with northern men since the Roosevelt administration. She also married a man from New York.[56]

By the end of the 1970s, the Natchez pilgrimage, which was now being conducted both in the spring and the fall, was bringing $35 million annually into Natchez. Only the oil boom generated more money for the city.[57] At Miller's urging, the PGC took control of King's Tavern in 1969. The McAdams Foundation of Austin, Texas, sold Longwood to the PGC in 1970.[58]

For the rest of the twentieth century, historic preservation, which started out as a movement in Natchez and the entire country, became a professional enterprise. In 1974, the Historic Natchez Foundation was founded, and in 1979, Ronald Miller became its first executive director. Mimi Miller began documenting the historic buildings and often correcting Edith Moore's erroneous histories of its buildings.[59] At eighty-eight, Katherine Miller died in her hometown of Natchez in 1983.

Historic preservation continued in Natchez throughout the twentieth century. Petroleum businessman John Callon purchased and restored Melrose and made it a home for his family. It later became a bed and breakfast. President Ronald Reagan established Natchez National Historical Park in 1988. It initially included the Fort Rosalie site and Melrose; the William Johnson House, a free African American residence, was added to the park in 1991. The Pilgrimage Garden Club created Natchez Pilgrimage Tours as its business management arm for the spring and fall pilgrimages.

In 1991, the Natchez Association for the Preservation of African American Culture (NAPAC) opened the Natchez Museum of African American History and Culture in the former Waterworks Building on Market Street; it was later moved to the old Natchez Post Office. Through the work of the Historic Natchez Foundation and NAPAC, the heritage narrative became more balanced and more three-dimensional than the mythic "Old South" narrative; now, tourists can learn about the African American experience and both its tangible and intangible heritage. Still, people arrive to Natchez Under-the-Hill on riverboat cruises, drive along US 61 and the Natchez Trace Parkway, and experience the pilgrimages and villas like Stanton Hall and Melrose, which are open year-round. But plantation tourism is not as popular as it once was, and industries from petroleum to river shipping have waned as well. Other tourism industries have entered the city. Casino gambling has been established, and festivals like the balloon festival and the crepe myrtle festival are promoted to tourists who may not be interested in antebellum southern architecture. Like other historic southern towns such as Charleston and Savannah, Natchez has become a popular place to have an elaborate wedding. As a tourist destination, twenty-first-century Natchez must become a multivenue and multi-event-based city. Today's tourists expect nothing less.

CONCLUSION

In season 6, episode 6 of the hit PBS historical drama *Downton Abbey*, Violet, the dowager countess of Grantham, is shocked when her family agrees to open its grand manor house for tours by the lower-class village folk as a fundraising event for the village hospital. More importantly, she is completely dumbfounded that "common" people would want to pay for a ticket to see the family's house and fine furnishings. For Violet, the house is just so . . . ordinary. And yet, when the open house day arrives, people line up outside the front door to pay six pence and gawk inside the grand edifice—a place they were once forbidden to enter. The fundraising event is such a hit that Branson, the former chauffeur turned estate manager, wants to open Downton Abbey regularly to the public and charge admission. The irony of the episode is that the owners of the real Downton Abbey, Highclere Castle, opened its doors long ago to tourists so it could stay afloat.[60]

What was it that compelled ordinary Americans in the 1930s to make the effort to tour the grand Natchez villas, so much so that they dressed up as if they were personal guests of the owner? As most people in Natchez told Katherine Miller in 1932: Who wanted to come to Natchez? Who wanted to see these near-dilapidated houses? Voyeurism was the primary motive for middle-class Americans to come to Natchez in 1932. Because of financial distress, the elite owners had to do something to try to keep the grand places they had inherited from falling in all around them. And like the working class from the village in *Downton Abbey*, tourists now had an opportunity to see firsthand what had once been forbidden: to enter the gates of Melrose or Dunleith and experience the life of a perceived higher class of people. But in 1932, after decades of neglect, the grandeur had not been maintained. Ernie Pyle was right: the rugs were frayed, there was chipped paint on the wood trim, and many rooms were mere storehouses. But the garden club women came up with a brilliant idea—a narrative to share with tourists about a bygone era of a romantic south in Natchez; and they, the descendants of these gentlepeople, were perpetuating their refined and exotic ways. All the tourist had to do was to play "let's pretend." It was what Americans wanted—an accessible escape from a dreary industrial existence to a graceful place and a kinder time, never mind that it never really existed. The garden club women capitalized on all this and used personalism to embellish and embed their story into the heritage of Natchez. They made a living being "the living that occupy the past."

As Judy Klemesrud wryly noted nearly forty years ago, "In this historic Mississippi River city, whose motto is 'Where the Old South Still Lives,' there are two things that really matter socially: One's home and one's family name, and probably in that order."[61] As Shils pointed out, ownership is an expression of power in the western idea of tradition.[62] The Natchez Garden Club women used their tradition-based idea of homeownership and combined it with another tradition-based idea, that of southern womanhood, and seized the initiative from their husbands and other Natchez men, saving their town through historic preservation. From 1932 to 1939, a startlingly active seven-year period, they controlled or influenced not only a significant portion of the town's economy but also the state's tourism economy. They shaped Mississippi's image to the nation and the world. And with this impressive feat, through their building of the Natchez Trace Parkway, they literally changed the geography of three states: Mississippi, Alabama, and Tennessee. Unless men were outside consultants, like Richard Koch and later his partner Samuel Wilson, or National Park Service staff, like Malcolm Gardner or Stuart Cuthbertson, a man had difficulty breaking into the preservation business in Natchez. In Natchez, the NGC women controlled historic preservation.

But there were other reasons that enthralled so many people to come to Natchez during the early and middle decades of the twentieth century. Forty years ago, architectural historian Michael Fazio observed that the richness of visual and symbolic imagery found in the South attracted people from outside of the region to visit it. Citing David M. Potter, he wrote that there was peculiarly strong and sentimental loyalty by Americans to "Dixie" and the "Lost Cause of the Confederacy" and that because of a "persistent, haunting nostalgia," the South was an enigma.[63] Historian Paul H. Buck stated it best—the South became the place where "nostalgic Northerners could escape the wear and tear of expanding industry and growing cities and dwell in a Dixie of story books which had become the Arcady of American tradition."[64]

On April 1, 1935, at the end of a long day of pilgrimage tours at Melrose, George Malin Davis Kelly encountered an elderly woman and a thirty-year-old man whom he presumed was her son at his front door. Apologizing for calling on him at the end of the day, the son asked Kelly if they could tour the house, saying his mother had always wanted to see Melrose. Kelly reluctantly agreed to personally give a tour of his home. He noted that the elderly woman was visibly moved by the architecture, and she informed him that she was a native Mississippian who, since her husband had died, had been living with her daughter in Ohio. After thanking him profusely, Kelly noted that the elderly woman gave "an aristocratic toss to her head," then said she was going back to what was now her home and "TELL THOSE DURNED YANKEES THAT WE STILL HAVE IN MISSISSIPPI THINGS WHICH THEY CAN'T EQUAL IN OHIO!!!!!"[65]

Many African Americans and whites left the South during the middle decades of the twentieth century, in what James Gregory calls a southern diaspora.[66] Although through their migration into African American-concentrated neighborhoods in Chicago and Detroit, southern African Americans profoundly changed the political and social conditions of these cities, even more whites migrated into northern industrial cities. The difference, according to Gregory, is that southern whites did not settle in concentrated neighborhoods and, for obvious racial reasons, assimilated into northern white society.[67] But like their African American counterparts, the transplanted southern white middle class clung to their traditions, especially identity and religious beliefs, and returned periodically to places like Mississippi.[68] In 1930s Natchez, the NGC women capitalized on both the white and Black diasporic people. Through their narrative, they tapped into the nostalgia of the "lost South" felt by many transplanted white southerners, and, as in the case of Ruth Beltzhoover's restaurant venture at Green Leaves, they provided short-term business opportunities to diasporic African Americans, who briefly returned from Chicago to visit their families. Both whites and African Americans reaffirmed their roots when they came back to Natchez during the pilgrimage, but there were considerable differences between the races. Whites returned to the northern cities comforted in knowing that what they saw as southern "grace and grandeur" still existed in Natchez, while Blacks were often haunted with the feeling of loss.

Throughout the 1940s and '50s, many members of the national press enjoyed writing about the rows and infighting among the garden club women. It became comedic entertainment featured in the nation's leading newspapers. Former war correspondent Ernie Pyle remarked that he did not know who was winning war between these women, but he thought it was a fine war.[69] The "War of the Hoop Skirts," also known as "The Big Split," was less about money and more about the power of the

Figure 7.11: Eola Hotel stationary, 1940. By the beginning of World War II, Natchez had embraced its antebellum tourism brand that Katherine Grafton Miller created. (Roane Fleming Byrnes Collection [MUM00057], Department of Archives and Special Collections, J. D. Williams Library, The University of Mississippi)

homeownership tradition in Natchez and the struggle between Miller, Barnum, Byrnes, Moore, and Shields over the two narratives. Why would Miller and the Pilgrimage Garden Club go into profound debt purchasing Stanton Hall and making it their clubhouse if the rift was only about money? Women like Barnum believed that their ownership of Arlington and Monmouth should hold considerably more sway over decisions in the Natchez Garden Club. Essentially, why should those women like Moore and Byrnes who did not own historic villas determine how the pilgrimage was managed? For Barnum, Beltzhoover, and Alma Kellogg, the answer was simple: they should not have any control at all over it. But it was Miller's definitive vision of what the pilgrimage and Natchez were to become that changed the course of the history of the NGC, the PGC, and Natchez (figure 7.11). Through her marketing trips, wearing bangles and hoop skirts, she learned what the country wanted, and it was definitely not old Spain in Natchez. It was antebellum Natchez. More than anyone, she understood that the country's fascination with the pre-Civil War South was growing during the mid-1930s. *So Red the Rose* and *Gone with the Wind* only validated her conviction. Even at the end of her life, Miller never wavered from her deep belief that Natchez was the essential southern place in America, and as the national press came back to her, during the country's on-again, off-again infatuation with the South, she claimed that Natchez and its architecture were the "real South."

Americans were preoccupied with their history and their architecture during the 1930s, and the New Deal programs gave architects and intellectuals the means to categorize and try to define what historic American architecture was. These male-dominated circles found the National Park Service, with its expanding mission to include historic sites management, to be the venue to carry out this agenda. But Verne Chatelain failed in accomplishing Horace Albright's objective of creating a public history program in the National Park Service that would vet local lore and history and create a national history-based narrative of the country. And Charles Peterson's Historic American Buildings Survey fell prey to the philosophy it attempted to discredit: personalism. Leicester Holland and his board of advisors, who applied their idea of what historic places should be into actual historic places, wanted to create a systematic catalog for American architecture that would rival what Banister Fletcher accomplished in cataloging world architecture. They attempted to use the AIA to help them classify American architectural elements, found not only in the South but also in New England, the Midwest, and the West. But the continental country that is the United States was too large to allow the project to be successful with its limited funding, and the research and documentation skills of the AIA-HABS districts were inadequate. More importantly, local political agendas, derived by personalism, as was the case in Edith Moore's documentation and Hays Town's interest in documenting buildings that inspired him as a designer, completely skewed HABS. In the end, HABS was what Chatelain had surmised: it was "an architect's dream" and not an accurate archive of American architecture. Peterson was naïve in believing it was anything else than that when he created it.[70] But the use of HABS for commercial gain—from creating Tara for *Gone with the Wind* to Town's replicating the Chapel of the Cross in his design of the Church of the Accession in Lafayette, Louisiana, in 1957—perhaps made HABS a tool to convolute our understanding of architectural heritage more than anything else.[71]

As early as 1941, concern was raised that HABS was not effectively managed as a comprehensive archive of American architecture. At the Society of Architectural Historians Roundtable meeting that year, noted architectural historian Henry-Russell Hitchcock publicly chastised Thomas Vint regarding the lack of oversight of HABS by architectural historians. He urged Vint to accept an idea to appoint a roundtable of historians to recommend selection of monuments and buildings that should be recorded. He noted that HABS suffered from an "all-too-prevalent regional myopia and that selections sponsored by local groups often showed a great lack of historical perspective." He gave examples: there was a tendency to only record Greek Revival buildings, and the NPS made excessive efforts to preserve seventeenth- and eighteenth-century buildings without any regard to "essential architectural merit." He concluded his admonition by saying, "A nation-wide group of watchful architectural historians could perform valuable civic service in warning of danger weight [demolition] with those responsible of an endangered building."[72]

Vint did not respond to Hitchcock because everything he said was true. The National Park Service did not develop priorities regarding HABS documentation, and local groups selected buildings that they wanted documented. Then, district managers like Town selected the ones that they found visually appealing. Peterson was correct in concluding that District 17's HABS work was concentrated too much in Natchez. This was Town's intent. Town had no interest in documenting historic buildings north or east of Madison County, and District 17 never visited the Mississippi coast. Town even proposed a deal to John O'Neill to give up north Mississippi to Frazier Smith and lead District 17 across the Mississippi River to document buildings similar to the Natchez villas in the east parishes of Louisiana. But more damaging than Town's motives for HABS was Edith Moore's motives to make sure that only what she regarded as primarily Spanish colonial buildings were documented by HABS. To complicate matters more, other architecture documentation projects were misrepresented. To this day, both in the HABS archive and in the Frances Benjamin Johnston photography archive in the Library of Congress, the James Andrews House remains incorrectly named 311-313 Market Street (Parish House), even though it was never a Catholic priest's house and it no longer is located on Market Street in Natchez.[73]

Personalism, espoused by people like Moore and Town, made HABS a corrupted archive. Examination of District 17's work is only a case study. There are numerous errors and discrepancies in the archive, so many that it may be impossible to rectify the collection of drawings.[74]

Mississippi remains undersurveyed by HABS. After World War II, HABS activity was sporadic nationally and did not occur at all in Mississippi. National Historic Preservation Act Section 106 mediation work, National Park Service HABS documentation at Natchez National Historical Park, engineering works (USS Cairo and Waterways Experimentation Station), and five projects documented for the Mississippi Department of Archives and History are the historical resources that have been added to HABS from Mississippi from the postwar period to today. In 2011, historian Virginia Price noted that Mississippi ranked forty-first in the nation in HABS documentation. And as visually appealing as District 17's drawings truly are, technical information about any of the buildings cannot be accurately understood.[75]

HABS was not the only project affected by the Natchez narrative. Without a proactive history program to vet and counteract it, the National Park Service was not prepared for the political maneuvering by some of the most powerful congressional members of the Great Depression to build the Natchez Trace Parkway. Much to the annoyance of Secretary of the Interior Harold Ickes, an initially flippant idea pitched by the old con-man Jim Walton and proposed by the young ambitious congressman Jeff Busby became an interstate parkway project. By the time NPS historians Ruth Butler, Olaf Hagen, and Randle Truett concluded that the legendary Natchez Trace did not actually exist, it was too late. Senators Pat Harrison and Theodore Bilbo, along with Congressman A. L. Ford and Speaker of the House William Bankhead of Alabama, garnered the necessary support in Congress and, most importantly, the backing of Franklin Roosevelt to build the parkway. By the 1940s, Thomas Vint was forced to redefine the NPS mission, which he had always envisioned as focusing solely on nature conservation and history education, to include "recreation" since there was little nature or history to feature on the Natchez Trace Parkway.

The men in Washington completely misjudged the tenacious and audacious Roane Fleming Byrnes. Initially driven by a simple aspiration to have a modern roadway to connect Natchez to the outside world and armed only with the Natchez narrative, Byrnes browbeat two generations of politicians and charmed or stunned male chauvinists like P. M. Estes. She even shocked Secretary of State Cordell Hull and Ickes when she met with the Mexican government to try to make the Natchez Trace Parkway part of an international parkway connecting Washington with Mexico City. Today, it seems hard to imagine that Theodore Bilbo, perhaps the most racist senator in history, enthusiastically supported building a pastoral parkway across Mississippi and into the heart of Mexico. And yet, if not for the onset of World War II, it might have happened.

Thanks to Lillie Boatner and Harriet Dixon, the Natchez narrative became a commercialized brand. They convinced furniture manufacturers, cutlery manufacturers, soap and perfume makers, and house builders to embed the concept of antebellum Natchez into their products. Roane Byrnes influenced Stark Young as he wrote *So Red the Rose*, and Natchez and its lore are prominently featured in the novel. But it was Boatner and housewives across the country who loved the "Old South" Natchez who influenced the producers of *Gone with the Wind* to study and copy Natchez's architecture for its movie sets, most notably, for building Tara. Tourists instantly connected the set of the movie with the city's antebellum architecture. When *Chicago Daily Tribune* travel writer Marguerite Lyon noted, "The homes are enchanting, giving one the feeling walking thru the movie sets of Gone With the Wind," she was actually closer to experiencing the movie sets than she may have realized.[76]

The narrative, popular culture, and architecture cross-fertilized, and new buildings emerged that reflected the narrative. Mammy's Cupboard represents the kitsch that came about from the narrative and the new automobile-based highway tourism culture, but the narrative also influ-

Figure 7.12: William H. Braden Elementary School, Homochitto Street, Natchez, Mississippi, Beverly W. Martin and Robert W. Naef, architects, 1949. (Library of Congress, Prints & Photographs Division, Historic American Buildings Survey, HABS MS-283)

enced more serious architecture in Natchez. In 1949, Natchez architect Beverly Martin collaborated with Jackson architect Robert W. Naef to design the William H. Braden Elementary School in Natchez (figure 7.12). Martin had relocated to Natchez in the 1930s and was part of the HABS District 17 team led by Town. It is evident in the school's design that Martin was influenced by the HABS work of the 1930s. The center of the school is a temple form, with a tetrastyle Greek Doric portico, a pyramidal roof capped with a square, and a pyramidal roof form cupola bearing an uncanny resemblance to D'Evereux. The building's regal center is probably the only aspect of the school that Martin designed because the institutional brick two-story wings read "elementary school." Although the components of the building composition are incongruent, it is pleasing to view, so much so that the building was recognized on the "List of Outstanding School Buildings" in the 1950–51 edition of *American School and University*.[77]

As more commercialized buildings were constructed in Natchez, some of them were based on the narrative, but modernist buildings were built as well. Conceptually similar to the William H. Braden Elementary School but poorly designed, the Bellemont Motor Hotel also combined the Greek Revival villa with modern wings—in this case featuring single motel rooms. Behind the austere front was a swimming lagoon, and inside the rooms were "Greek Revival"-style television cabinets—everything the postwar family needed on the motorized vacation to Natchez.[78]

But the Malt Shop, built in 1955 on Homochitto Street, demonstrated how modernism was changing the landscape in Natchez (figure 7.13). Katherine Miller, Mary Louise Shields, and Ruth Beltzhoover did not

Figure 7.13: The Malt Shop, 1955, Homochitto Street, Natchez, Mississippi. (Library of Congress, Prints & Photographs Division, Historic American Buildings Survey, HABS MS-286)

welcome the twentieth century's march into what they viewed as an antebellum city, but automobile-based urbanism and architecture had arrived in the 1960s, and there was little they could do about it.

After over thirty years of commercial architecture in Jackson and then in Baton Rouge, Hays Town reinvented his practice, focusing on residential architecture that eventually was described as "neo-Creole" and "neo-Traditional." While his designs were innovative in using recycled building materials such as timbers and brick from demolished Louisiana rice and sugar factories and were evocative in their traditional design, Town also reintroduced into southern residential architecture architectural details found in Natchez villas, notably mantels and entries, and often directly applying HABS detail drawings in his designs. As a young architect working in Jackson, Kansas State University professor David Sachs became enamored with the work of Overstreet and Town. In his PhD dissertation on Overstreet and Town and later his book on Town's work, Sachs created a legend around Town's work in HABS, one that Town cajoled Sachs to establish. Sachs gives the impression that Town was heroically committed to HABS in Mississippi during the Great Depression. Town actually was not all that committed to HABS. He and Web Overstreet found more profitable work as soon as they could, and Town quit HABS in 1936. Jefferson Waldrop, whom Marvin Eickenroht hired to replace Town, is a forgotten figure in the HABS story. When Town died at the age of 102 in 2005, his work on HABS had become the stuff of legend. His stories of his valiant leadership were shared among architects, and they were, by and large, untrue. The history of HABS during the Great Depression is steeped in more legend than history; each AIA-HABS district has lore tied to it.

Charles Peterson also lived long enough to determine how his legacy was conveyed. Like Town's, his HABS story is a complex one. He became a revered figure in historic preservation, most notably in historic building technology. The legend of the weekend when he and Alston Guttersen created HABS continues to be told by HABS National Park Service staff, and the Peterson Prize for Student Architectural Documentation bears his name. But Peterson never actually ran HABS. His relocation from Washington to St. Louis very soon after he proposed the program was under dubious circumstances at best. Vint was fond of him and most likely shielded him from the brunt of Ickes's temper after Peterson was featured as the leader of the HABS project on the front page of the *Washington Post*. Peterson's work in St. Louis and later in Philadelphia has never been considered in detail by preservation scholars. One can argue that his job at both the Jefferson National Expansion Memorial and Independence National Park was to demolish the historic buildings that were in the way of the expansive commemorative malls. In the mid-1950s, Peterson resurrected the HABS idea, this time utilizing inexpensive student labor from nearby Philadelphia architecture schools to document the dozens of Victorian buildings that were demolished to make way for the mall in front of Independence Hall.

Peterson later taught with James Marston Fitch at Columbia University, helped establish the Association for Preservation Technology, and served as a delegate representing the US when the Venice Charter was drafted. And like Town, he relied on his reputation with HABS to convey his expertise in historic building design during the 1970s, '80s, '90s, and early 2000s. More often than not, projects he consulted on were restored in the best way possible, but there were others, such as the Mississippi Governor's Mansion, for which he proposed ill-conceived ideas that obliterated historic features.

The generation that lived through the Great Depression was the bridge that connected the Victorian generation with the modern one. All of the women and men involved in making Natchez a historic place were first motivated to preserve it, and through their efforts, they transformed their built patrimony and history into a heritage, which they and others commodified. Had they not done this, Natchez would have been lost. But their legacy is a complicated one that continues to challenge us, specifically in regard to America's history of slavery. The rituals and events the NGC women created are now intangible heritage, and the restored or conjecturally built landmarks are now historic in their own right. Now that southern heritage is being contested, how should we preserve and convey places like Natchez?

After the protest over the Robert E. Lee statue in Charlottesville, Virginia, in 2017 and then the removal of the Confederate monument at the University of North Carolina at Chapel Hill known as "Silent Sam" in 2019, preservationists have been oddly silent over the issue of heritage and monuments. In an essay appreciating the scholarship of David Lowenthal, Richard Longstreth explains that preservationists have been notoriously non-introspective, and the reason for this lack of self-reflection is that professionals and activists have been preoccupied and focused on "getting concrete things done." But after over a century of preservation, and with it, heritage making, perhaps we should weigh in on not only how our predecessors preserved our landmarks but why. Furthermore, he argues, we should consider the ramifications of preserving these landmarks after we learned more about the original motives for their preservation.[79] As Natchez continues to face growing scrutiny over what it has become known for and perhaps becoming a declining tourism place, I believe that we must understand how its heritage tourism industry was first created to rectify the grievances against it and how it will continue to be a heritage place.[80]

As Shils and Lowenthal noted, we are compelled to preserve monuments for many reasons. We perpetuate patrimony to reaffirm our identity—either national, tribal, or religious. We commemorate great moments in our history, or great people, by connecting them to a place. But we also preserve for economic and commercial gain; this is what happened in Natchez during the 1930s. The Natchez Garden Club women were a demonstration of the way Lowenthal said heritage making happens—the women clarified their shared pasts and infused them with their present purposes and financial needs.

What is ironic is that Natchez, Mississippi, was never "Where the Old South Still Lives" because it was never really the "Old South." In the early nineteenth century, it was considered the "Southwest," later known as the "Old Southwest." And there was nowhere in the antebellum South that resembled it; it was a suburban enclave of freestanding villas built in the Ruskin tradition.[81] And Margaret Mitchell was right to grieve that Tara was going to have Natchez columns on it. The Georgia she knew as a girl only had small and humble farmhouses; there certainly were no grand villas there. Natchez was the exception, a river town and community of planters who chose to live in the town instead of on their plantations. The rest of the South was mostly poor and primitive. Moreover, the region that we refer to as the "South," the old Confederacy, is a geographically diverse one, from the Low Country of South Carolina to the

Hill Country of Texas. But what the garden club women did in the 1930s was to showcase their villas and inspire some of the wealthier Americans to emulate them. Along with Colonial Williamsburg, Natchez became a model for suburban living across the country. The Belle Meade neighborhood near Nashville, Fondren in Jackson, Mississippi, and Buckhead in Atlanta were inspired by the suburban setting of villas found in Natchez. There are even Natchez-inspired villas found in Urbana, Illinois, and Beverly Hills, California. Natchez inspired "Where the Old South Still Lives" in the minds of mid-century Americans more than the real antebellum South.

In contextualizing the commodification of Natchez, Michael Fazio quotes the southern secessionist William L. Yancey: "Our poetry is our lives: our fiction will come when truth has ceased to satisfy." As Fazio explains, Katherine Miller subscribed to this idea and used the architecture of her native town to develop a unique American visitor experience during the Great Depression. Fazio argues that fascination with the South is not fictional; it is real and very potent, and the garden club women were innately aware of this fascination. Miller discovered it touring the country—to showcase the pilgrimage and the awareness of place, the consciousness of mystery, and the understanding of nostalgia were the forces that formed the Natchez narrative.[82]

Did it matter to the garden club women that it was all heritage and only loosely based on history? No. The end, a successful tourism industry, justified the means. It was also the justification for politicians to build a parkway. But today, as we consider the legacy of the Natchez pilgrimage, historiography of southern architecture and southern historic preservation should be a critical field of cultural inquiry. Through our historical analysis, we can then consider how and what of the cultural history of the twentieth-century South should be preserved and featured in the public realm. But if we continue to seek out places that are historic, distinctive, memorable, and real, we must accept that there may be a darker, more sinister heritage attached to them. If we purge this heritage and replace it with one of our making, like the "Crossroads Sign" (Chapter 1) in Clarksdale, Mississippi, we may create something that may confuse us or insult our intellect. Preservationists cannot be the sole arbiter of heritage; we must provide the expertise and the facts to the public forum, where heritage decisions can be adjudicated in an established manner.

Today, Natchez remains a southern tourism town, but it is also much more. It is a Mississippi River town, one of the best-preserved towns on the river. People come to see balloon races and antique car shows there, and they enjoy its rich and diverse cuisine. And while female house museum guides still dress in hoop skirts and describe the city's antebellum architecture, Blacks and whites learn about their history by touring places like the William Johnson House and the Natchez Museum of African American History and Culture. But like most small towns in America, it faces the challenges of an aging and declining population and diminishing economic opportunities. But no one can argue that what the Natchez Garden Club and the Pilgrimage Garden Club did during the twentieth century saved the town from being forgotten. As found in places throughout America, women primarily created what we call today historic preservation. This is definitely the case in Natchez.

The Natchez that these women aspired to create was never completed. They hoped that John D. Rockefeller Jr. or some other millionaire would finance its restoration, as was done at Colonial Williamsburg. It never happened. And the dream of paving the Natchez Trace to the bluffs of the Mississippi River—an idea held so dear by first Elizabeth Jones and then Lucille Mayfield and Roane Byrnes—never happened, and perhaps never should happen. Instead, the Natchez Trace Parkway awkwardly ends at Liberty Road, southeast of the downtown. But by urging us to "let's pretend," these women accomplished an extraordinary feat: creating an industry from the past. And through it all, they entertained famous celebrities and important figures of their day. They engaged in international diplomacy, and they saw the world. They are also remembered in Mississippi. Katherine Miller's portrait is displayed in the Mississippi Hall of Fame in the Old Capitol Museum in Jackson. The Mississippi Department of Archives and History placed a roadside plaque that commemorates Roane Byrnes in front of her home, Ravennaside, recognizing her work in creating the Natchez Trace Parkway. Miller and Byrnes were rivals during the 1930s, and their rivalry brought out the best of them. It improved and expanded Natchez's heritage tourism industry.

As I researched and wrote this book, I often asked myself which of the women I would have liked to have met. Would I have wanted to dine on fried chicken with Katherine Miller, who may have flirted with me or curtly disregarded me? I am confident that the encounter would have been very memorable. Would I have wanted to be served a bourbon by Roane Byrnes in her "war room" and talk about the Natchez Trace? I am sure I would have come away with some interesting stories—some of them might even be true. Would I have wanted to discuss Natchez architectural history with Edith Moore? I am sure she would have readily dismissed me for having the audacity to inquire about her research.

Figure 7.14: The Mississippi River at Natchez, Mississippi, 2008. (Library of Congress, Prints & Photographs Division, photograph by Carol M. Highsmith, LC-DIG-highsm-12528)

Raised during the later decades of the Victorian era and shaped by the Great Depression and two world wars, these women were part of a generation best described as formidable (figure 7.14). The Pilgrimage Garden Club website implies that this idea that we call Natchez—false as we now know it was—was formed by a "group of very determined women."

So very true.

AUTHOR'S NOTE AND ACKNOWLEDGMENTS

Every spring, I introduce my theory of historic preservation course to my students by reciting this quote from D. H. Lawrence: "Different places on the face of the earth have different vital effluence, different vibration, different chemical exhalation, different polarity with different stars: call it what you like. But the spirit of place is a great reality." Beyond the shrines to great people, the battlefields across the country, and the works of great architecture, I love to experience the unique places I encounter in the world that are embedded with history and tradition and are interpreted through heritage. Natchez is this kind of a unique place. I do not support the idea of ridding ourselves of these places and things, no matter what painful meanings they suggest to us; instead, I urge us to reinterpret and contextualize their heritage in order to educate future generations that human values evolve with time. Sinister motives did not always create degrading heritage; our ancestors' long-forgotten traditions and human memory also developed it. Preceding generations created heritages for the world they understood and existed in. A sanitized built heritage is similar to a pedestal without a statue—empty and confusing.

I have always been inspired by preservationists who were passionate about the place that they lived in. For them, the past is alive, and it is relevant to their existence. They see value in it, and they refuse to accept that their town, church, school, or home is left behind, bypassed by progress. Through dogged hard work and despite great hardship, they succeeded in transforming their built patrimony, which is then enjoyed by succeeding generations and visitors. We should study their stories and learn why they preserved and how they preserved. The story of the women of the Natchez Garden Club and, later, the Pilgrimage Garden Club is part of the rich, but mostly unrecognized, history of historic preservation. With the passing of the last of the original garden club women, Mary Louise Kendall Goodrich Shields in 2015 at the age of 109, their impact in changing Natchez and Mississippi is now being considered.

Eleanor Roosevelt was right in saying, "Never tell me that women are not able in business. Natchez is being built up financially by a woman's idea carried out by women." These women were part of my grandmothers' generation, and I understood them as I researched them. And while they may be perceived today as being subservient to the men in their lives, they were anything but that. They were independent, entrepreneurial, and determined. They also understood the severity of the times they were living in, from World War I to the Great Depression to World War II and the Cold War and the civil rights movement. And as they marketed Natchez's past, they adapted the city for its future. This book, I hope, neither glorifies nor vilifies these Natchez women but instead presents their story considerately, using their words and their images.

I did not originally set out to write the history of historic preservation in Natchez. I first became fascinated with Depression-era Natchez through my examination of the beautifully delineated drawings produced by the District 17 Team of the Historic American Buildings Survey from 1934 until 1936. I thought a book about the architectural drawings would be an interesting project to undertake. However, architectural historian Todd Sanders from the Mississippi Department of Archives and History suggested that I look beyond the drawings and learn about the remarkable women who transformed Natchez from a forgotten Mississippi town into a cultural tourism destination. I am indebted to him for his thoughtful advice.

As I was researching for this book, I had the pleasure of experiencing the celebrated Natchez hospitality and the city's joie de vivre. I had the great privilege of giving a talk about my book on William Nichols at the 2017 Natchez Antique Forum. During my two-day stay, Eugenie and Michael Cates entertained me at their lovely home, the Governor Holmes House on Wall Street. I enjoyed my tours of Melrose and Stanton Hall. The reception and dinner party at the Burn were exceptional, and the evening party at Longwood was memorable. The women of the Pilgrimage Garden Club were very gracious, and I will always remember fondly my talk at the Carriage House Restaurant.

In researching for this book, I found many archives and libraries were very helpful. I am grateful to Leigh McWhite, Archivist, Department of Archives and Special Collections at the University of Mississippi, Mark Martin, Public Services Librarian, Louisiana State University Libraries, and Cristina Meisner at the Harry Ransom Center at the University of Texas at Austin. At the Mississippi Department of Archives and History, I am indebted to Clinton Bagley for his insights on Natchez. Independent scholar and Mississippi College adjunct professor Charles Weeks provided me important documentation about the many colonial trails and routes that crossed Mississippi, Louisiana, and Texas. I am especially indebted to Mimi Miller and Carter Burns at the Historic Natchez Foundation for sharing with me the archival records, collections of letters, and the photographs of Natchez, the Natchez Garden Club, and the Spring Pilgrimage. Natchezian Elodie Pritchartt was very gracious in sharing with me photographs of her great-aunt, Katherine Grafton Miller. In Franklin, Tennessee, I am indebted to Tony Turnbow, who provided me important information from the Natchez Trace Association Archives, and Christina Smith, who helped me find important information in the Natchez Trace Parkway Archives in Tupelo, Mississippi.

I wish to acknowledge the James Marston Fitch Charitable Foundation, the National Endowment for the Humanities, and the University of Illinois Research Board for providing me the financial support to write this book. I particularly wish to thank Martica Sawin and Mary Dierickx from the Fitch Foundation for their opinions on the multiple drafts of this book.

This is my second book that I published with the University Press of Mississippi. I've always appreciated the guidance that Craig Gill gave me while I wrote the book, and Emily Bandy was very professional and conscientious, an exemplary editor. I wish to thank Kiezha Ferrell for editing the manuscript and Lynn Whittaker for her excellent copyediting service.

There are many wonderful friends who helped me write this book. First, I want to acknowledge and give a heartfelt "thank you" to Maria Gillombardo in the Office of Research Advising and Project Development at the University of Illinois at Urbana-Champaign. Without Maria's help, I would not have earned the National Endowment for the Humanities Fellowship or the James Marston Fitch Fellowship; these fellowships gave me the time and the resources to write this book. But Maria did much more for me. She reviewed multiple chapter drafts and provided me very good consultation on how to approach this project at times when I needed it the most. I also wish to thank Craig Koslofsky and Carol Symes at the Office of Research Advising and Project Development at Illinois for their editorial suggestions. Finally, I want to thank Cynthia Oliver, Associate Vice Chancellor for Research & Innovation—Humanities at the University of Illinois at Urbana-Champaign for supporting my book project.

I am especially grateful to have so many friends at Illinois, across the country, and abroad who were with me as I wrote this book. Each of them gave me moral support and suggestions on how to improve my ideas. Helaine Silverman and Cele Otnes were so generous with their time, and I enjoyed their wit and enthusiasm. Virginia Price shared with me her insights on HABS and Natchez, and Roger White shared with me his opinions on how this book could be received in the UK. David Chasco, Steve Hartley, Lauren Bricker, Robert Young, and Michael Tomlan were all there when I needed them. I want to personally thank Jennifer Arthur, Kristien Anderson, and Bill Leftwich for providing me a quiet and comfortable place to write at the Pittsylvania County Public Library in Chatham, Virginia. I also want to thank them for providing me all the affordable coffee—"knowledge nectar"—that I could drink.

As always, I am thankful to my family, Wendy and John Paul. They are everything to me.

I dedicate this book to the memory of my mother, Emily Lureese Evans Kapp. She was one of the last of the southern ladies.

APPENDIX: BIOGRAPHICAL NOTES

(Listed in Alphabetical Order)

Annie Shotwell Green Barnum (1881–1960) owned Arlington and Monmouth and was an original member and a vocal critic of the Natchez Garden Club. Together with Katherine Grafton Miller, she founded the Pilgrimage Garden Club in 1937.

Ruth Audley Beltzhoover (1897–1991) owned Green Leaves. As one of the founders of the Natchez Garden Club and the Natchez Spring Pilgrimage of Antebellum Homes, she originated the "Confederate Pageant." After World War II, she owned and managed the Famous & Price Store and made it into one of the most successful women's retail businesses in the Deep South.

Lillie Vidal Boatner (1899–1987) was a founding member of the Natchez Garden Club and an early promoter of Natchez. She persuaded Hollywood documentary producer James A. FitzPatrick to film *Old Natchez on the Mississippi* in 1939 and developed the idea for a perfume, "Natchez Rose Jar." She and Ethel Moore Kelly marketed the Melrose silverware pattern to the Gorham Manufacturing Company in 1948.

Kate Doniphan Brandon (1899–1983) was a steadfast member of the Natchez Garden Club and a vocal critic of Katherine Grafton Miller and Annie Green Barnum.

Roane Fleming Byrnes (1890–1970) was declared the "Queen of the Natchez Trace Parkway" by the Natchez Trace Parkway Association in 2012 for her work in spearheading the efforts for building the scenic parkway from Nashville, Tennessee, to Natchez, Mississippi. Gregarious and enthusiastic, she became an exceptionally effective lobbyist for the Natchez Trace Parkway in Washington, DC, Jackson, Mississippi, and Mexico City. She led the effort of renovating Gilreath Hill into Connelly's Tavern in 1936 and relocating and renovating the Parish House during the 1950s.

Verne E. Chatelain (1895–1991) became the National Park Service Chief Historian and Director of the History Division in the National Park Service's Research and Education Branch in 1931. Prior to coming to the National Park Service, he was Chairman of the History and Social Sciences Department at Nebraska State Teachers College. Chatelain's primary goal was to develop a thematic program for historic interpretation at the national parks.

Harriet Shields Dixon (1890–1986) was President of the Natchez Garden Club when the Pilgrimage Garden Club split from the club in 1937. She helped manage her husband Joseph F. Dixon's paint, wallpaper, and housewares store and did not own a historic Natchez home. She was known as a facilitator within the Natchez Garden Club and along with Lillie Vidal Boatner marketed Natchez to numerous corporations and Hollywood studios.

Marvin Eickenroht (1898–1969) was the Chief of the Southern Division of HABS from 1936 to 1939. In 1934, he was appointed District Officer for District 33 in Texas for HABS.

Leicester B. Holland (1882–1952) was the Chief and Carnegie Chair of the Division of Fine Arts at the Library of Congress and Chair of the AIA National Committee on the Preservation of Historic Buildings. He was also Professor of Architecture at the University of Pennsylvania. Holland was an enthusiastic supporter of the Historic American Buildings Survey and agreed to have the Library of Congress become the repository of the HABS drawings, photographs, and reports. He was the Chair of the HABS Advisory Committee from 1935 until 1942.

Alma Cassell Kellogg (1889–1986) was the longtime treasurer of the Natchez Garden Club and later the Pilgrimage Garden Club. She was born at The Elms, and her father, Albert Gallatin Cassell, was a druggist. She inherited The Elms and was married to City Bank and Trust Company Vice President Joseph Bentley Kellogg. A natural-born accountant, she took great pride in keeping accurate books.

Ethel Moore Kelly (1878–1975) helped restore Melrose with her husband, George Malin Davis Kelly. She was born in New York, moved to Natchez with Kelly, and made it her full-time home in 1909 after he had taken her there on their honeymoon in 1901. She was a founding and loyal member of the Natchez Garden Club and spent several months during the year visiting her family in New York and later her daughter,

Marion Kelly Ferry, and her family in Grosse Pointe, Michigan, during the 1930s.

George Malin Davis Kelly (1877–1946) came from the wealthy Davis family of Natchez and inherited Melrose, Concord, Choctaw, and Cherokee when he was a child. He grew up in New York, graduated from Columbia University, and had a lifelong interest in singing. In 1901, he brought his bride, Ethel Moore Kelly, to Natchez, and they eventually made Melrose their home. He wrote his wife daily informing her of all the activities of the Natchez Garden Club and, most notably, the feud between the Natchez Garden Club and what eventually became the Pilgrimage Garden Club.

Richard Koch (1889–1971) was the leading restoration architect in New Orleans from the 1930s until the late 1960s. He consulted on numerous restoration projects in Natchez—most notably, Connelly's Tavern. He was an Adjunct Architecture Professor at his alma mater, Tulane University, and helped train A. Hays Town. He was the District Officer of the Louisiana Historic American Buildings Survey district office from 1934 until 1936.

Ralph L. Landrum (unknown–1976) was named the first secretary-treasurer of the Natchez Trace Association in January 1934. Landrum was an attorney who first practiced in his native town of Kosciusko, Mississippi, and later in Jackson, Mississippi. Focused and detail-oriented, Landrum was a trusted colleague of Roane Fleming Byrnes.

Katherine Grafton Miller (1894–1983) was one of the founders of the Natchez Garden Club in 1931 and was a leader in creating the Natchez Spring Pilgrimage of Antebellum Homes. Born into an established but financially challenged Natchez family, she was very ambitious and audacious. She had a lifelong passion for preserving historic Natchez and toured the country promoting it. In 1937, she led a group of homeowners to split off from the Natchez Garden Club and establish the Pilgrimage Garden Club. In 1953, President Dwight Eisenhower appointed her a delegate to the US National Commission of UNESCO, and in 1959 she was the first woman recipient of the "Missy" distinguished service award from the state of Mississippi.

Edith Wyatt Moore (1885–1973) considered herself the historian of Natchez, Mississippi. She was one of the original founders of the Natchez Garden Club and the Natchez Spring Pilgrimage of Antebellum

Homes. During the first pilgrimages, she wrote historical sketches about historic Natchez homes, which appeared in special "Pink Editions" of the *Natchez Democrat*. She also wrote a newspaper series for the *Natchez Democrat* entitled "Fondly I Roam." She was a historian for the Works Progress Administration Writers' Project in 1934.

John P. O'Neill (1898–1969) was the Director of the Historic American Buildings Survey (HABS) in the National Park Service (NPS) office in Washington, DC, from 1933 until 1939. He was trained at the University of Notre Dame and worked for Chicago architect David Adler. He coordinated funding for HABS with the Works Progress Administration and was the interface between the NPS and the states. He produced regular progress reports of the program for the WPA and the NPS based on his correspondence with NPS field officers and district officers.

Noah Webster Overstreet (1888–1973) was the managing partner in the architecture firm Overstreet and Town and the first president of the Mississippi chapter of the American Institute of Architects (AIA). Overstreet used his political connections in the AIA to secure the district officer position for his partner A. Hays Town and thus provided operating revenue for his firm during the bleakest times of the Great Depression.

Charles E. Peterson (1906–2004) was Deputy Chief Architect of the Eastern Division of the National Park Service (NPS) Branch of Plans and Designs when he conceived and proposed the Historic American Buildings Survey (HABS) to the Civil Works Administration in 1933. Although he is credited as the author of the initial proposal, he had a more tangential relationship with HABS during its initial years. He began his NPS career in 1929 working in the western regional office in San Francisco under Thomas Vint. From 1930 until 1933, he served as the resident landscape architect in Yorktown, Virginia, which was then established as the Colonial National Monument (designated as Colonial National Historical Park in 1936). In 1934, he was assigned to the Jefferson National Expansion Memorial in St. Louis.

Mary Louise Kendall Goodrich Shields (1906–2015) was the youngest and longest-living member of the Natchez Garden Club and later the Pilgrimage Garden Club. She was active in politics and in 1936 was a Democratic National Committeewoman representing Mississippi.

Albert Hays Town (1903–2005) was hired as the first district officer for District 17, covering the state of Mississippi, for the Historic American

Buildings Survey (HABS) in January 1934. Town was a partner in the Overstreet and Town architectural firm in Jackson, Mississippi. A gifted artist and delineator, Town was one of the most celebrated HABS architects in the 1930s. He was a Louisiana native and a Tulane graduate and was a student and close colleague of New Orleans architect Richard Koch.

Thomas C. Vint (1894–1967) was Chief Architect of the National Park Service Branch of Plans and Designs. He served as the chief administrator for HABS from its beginning 1933 until his retirement in 1961. Vint joined the NPS in 1922 as an assistant landscape engineer for Yosemite National Park. In 1927, he was appointed Chief Landscape Architect of the NPS in San Francisco. In 1933, he was reassigned to Washington, DC, to oversee the development of new national parks in the East such as Colonial (Virginia), Salem Maritime (Massachusetts), and Hope Village (Pennsylvania), along with battlefield parks transferred from the War Department to the NPS.

J. Preston Waldrop (1909–1946) was hired as the second HABS District 17 officer for Mississippi in 1936. He trained at Georgia Institute of Technology as an industrial designer and an architect. Prior to managing the Mississippi HABS program, he worked in Los Angeles and established an industrial design business in Atlanta that failed during the Great Depression.

"Colonel" Jim Walton (birth and death dates unknown) suggested creating the Natchez Trace Parkway to US congressman Thomas Jefferson Busby in 1933. An elderly man, Walton was a news reporter working for the *Webster Progress,* but he claimed to be a well-known journalist and an itinerant piano tuner. He boasted that he had traveled the world and called himself "the International Hobo." Walton staged several publicity stunts during the first meeting of the Natchez Trace Association in January 1934.

NOTES

INTRODUCTION

1. Mary Swain Hoover, "Cane and Cotton Kingdoms," in *Visiting Our Past: America's Historylands*, ed. Daniel J. Boorstin et al. (Washington, DC: National Geographic Society, 1977), 283.

2. Hoover, "Cane and Cotton Kingdoms," 283.

3. Quoted in Hoover, "Cane and Cotton Kingdoms," 284.

4. Hoover, "Cane and Cotton Kingdoms," 286.

5. Paul K. Goeldner, "House on Ellicott's Hill/Connelly's Tavern," National Register Form, 1974. Through court records, the Historic Natchez Foundation determined that Patrick Connelly acquired five lots in downtown Natchez (Lot 1, square 31, Deed Book A, p.5; Lot 4, square 34. Deed Book A, p. 272; Lot 3, square 32. Deed Book C, p. 352; Lot 4, square 33. Deed Book C, p. 426; Lot 1, square 18. Deed Book C, p. 434). Deed Book A, p. 223 documents Connelly's lease of a tavern and inn, which is likely the main source of Edith Moore's erroneous history. Historic Natchez Foundation to author, June 11, 2021.

6. Quoted in Goeldner, "House on Ellicott's Hill/Connelly's Tavern."

7. Quoted in Joann Culver, "NGC Home Not Connelly's Tavern," *Natchez Democrat*, June 20, 1974.

8. Quoted in Culver, "NGC Home."

9. David Lowenthal, *The Heritage Crusade and the Spoils of History* (Cambridge, UK: Cambridge University Press, 1998), xvii.

10. Bette Barber Hammer, *Natchez' First Ladies: Katherine Grafton Miller and the Pilgrimage* (New York: L. Kinter, 1955), 2.

11. James Marston Fitch, *Historic Preservation: Curatorial Management of the Built World* (Charlottesville: University of Virginia Press, 1992), 41–42, 221–24.

12. John A. Jakle, *The Tourist: Travel in Twentieth-Century North America* (Lincoln: University of Nebraska Press, 1985), 298.

13. Kenneth Hudson, *Museums of Influence* (Cambridge, UK: Cambridge University Press, 1987), 77–80.

14. Jakle, *The Tourist*, 4.

15. Daniel J. Boorstin, Introduction, in *Visiting Our Past: America's Historylands*, ed. Daniel J. Boorstin et al. (Washington, DC: National Geographic Society, 1977), 11.

16. Built patrimony is our inheritance from previous generations of historic buildings and monuments, which society considers cultural assets.

17. David W. Blight, *Race and Reunion: The Civil War in American Memory* (Cambridge, MA: Belknap Press of Harvard University Press, 2001), 1.

18. Quoted in Jakle, *The Tourist*, 298.

19. Ernie Pyle, "Touring with Ernie Pyle," newspaper clipping, n.d., Natchez Garden Club Scrapbooks, NGC Headquarters, Natchez, MS.

20. Chris Wilson, *The Myth of Santa Fe: Creating a Modern Regional Tradition* (Albuquerque: University of New Mexico Press, 1997), 3.

21. Wilson, *Myth of Santa Fe*, 4.

22. Pyle, "Touring with Ernie Pyle." In his newspaper article, Pyle said this about downtown Natchez: "There are lots of stores, and nice shops. It impresses me as one of the most modern towns in the South. And there's a tall, modern hotel that was as good as New York City."

23. Verbie Lovorn Prevost, "Roane Fleming Byrnes: A Critical Biography" (PhD diss., University of Mississippi, 1974), 100.

24. Georgie Wilson Newell and Charles Cromartie Compton, *Natchez and the Pilgrimage* (Kingsport, TN: Southern Publishers, 1935), 21.

25. David L. Cohn, "Natchez Was a Lady," *Atlantic Monthly*, January 1940.

26. Katherine Grafton Miller, *Natchez of Long Ago and the Pilgrimage* (Natchez, MS: Rellimak Publishing Co., 1938), 48.

27. "Charles IV and the French Revolution," *Encyclopedia Britannica*, Vol. 28 (London: Encyclopedia Britannica, 2005), 53. Charles IV never visited Spanish Louisiana or West Florida during his reign as the king of Spain. In 1799, he authorized Prussian aristocrat and scientist Alexander von Humboldt to travel across Spanish America and record his findings. In 1807, he tried to flee to America, but he was caught by supporters of his son, Ferdinand, and forced to abdicate the Spanish throne. By this time, the US controlled Natchez, West Florida, and Louisiana.

28. Mary Louise Geddes, interview by Graham Hicks, August 4, 1981, Mississippi Department of Archives and History, Jackson, MS.

29. Lloyd Lewis, "Perils of Progress," *Chicago Daily News*, April 10, 1936, Roane Fleming Byrnes Papers, Folder 5, University of Mississippi Archives, Oxford, MS.

30. Edith Weigle, "Departed Glory of Natchez Now Being Restored: Garden Club Starts . . . ," *Chicago Tribune*, December 27, 1936, F6.

31. Roane Fleming Byrnes, "People Entertained (When lobbying for the Trace—Mississippi Legislators from all over the state, principally Chairman of Committee)," Roane Fleming Byrnes Papers, Folder 4, University of Mississippi Archives, Oxford, MS.

32. "More Fights Mean Better Pilgrimages for Natchez," *Jackson Clarion-Ledger*, March 22, 1941; and "Natchez Club War Has Casualties," *Atlanta Journal-Constitution*, March 29, 1941.

33. "'Hoopskirts' War Ends," *Natchez Democrat*, November 15, 1946.

34. "Centuries of Charm: Rich in History, the Tucked-Away Town of Natchez, Mississippi, Has Many Stories to Tell—with Plenty Still Being Written," *American Airlines American Way Magazine*, September 2016, 44–45.

35. Blight, *Race and Reunion*, 4.

36. David Lowenthal, "The American Way of History," *Columbia University Forum* 9 (Summer 1966): 27.

37. Edward Shils, *Tradition* (Chicago: University of Chicago Press, 1981), 210.

38. Jack E. Davis, "A Struggle for Public History: Black and White Claims to Natchez's Past," *The Public Historian* 22, no. 1 (Winter 2000): 45.

CHAPTER 1: A PLACE CALLED NATCHEZ

1. An esplanade is a long, open, level area, usually next to a river or large body of water, where people walk, usually for leisure purposes.

2. In *The South-West by a Yankee*, published in 1835, travel writer Joseph H. Ingraham mentions the "noble green esplanade along the front of the city," which he says, "not only adds to its [Natchez's] beauty, but is highly useful as a promenade and parade ground." Ingraham, *The South-West by a Yankee* (New York: Harper & Brothers, 1835), 22–23.

3. Frederick Law Olmsted, *The Cotton Kingdom: A Traveler's Observations on Cotton and Slavery in the American Slave States* (New York: Knopf, 1953), 436. Olmsted is considered the father of American landscape architecture.

4. The first pilgrimage cost $1.50.

5. Through the efforts of the Historic Natchez Foundation and the National Park Service, heritage tourism in Natchez has begun to change from the southern-focused narrative to a more progressive one that includes African American tourism. See Susan T. Falck, *Remembering Dixie: The Battle to Control Historical Memory in Natchez, Mississippi, 1865–1941* (Jackson: University Press of Mississippi, 2019), 225–50.

6. Historic Natchez Foundation to author, June 11, 2021.

7. *The New Encyclopedia of Southern Culture* defines cultural tourism as the deliberate act of using the South's history and cultural activities to attract visitors and thereby generate wealth. Charles Reagan Wilson, "Tourism, Cultural," in *The New Encyclopedia of Southern Culture: Volume 16: Sports and Recreation*, ed. Harvey H. Jackson (Chapel Hill: University of North Carolina Press, 2011), 227–30.

8. John Ruskin, "The Poetry of Architecture; Or the Architecture of the Nations of Europe, Considered in Its Association with Natural Scenery and National Character. No. 3 The Villa (Continued.) IV. The British Villa-The Cultivated or Blue Country-Principles of Composition," *The Crayon* 1, no. 21 (May 23, 1855): 325–27.

9. Building "townhouses" was not uncommon for the southern planter elite. Virginia planters, such as the Tayloe family, built homes in Williamsburg and Washington, DC, in order to enjoy the social season in the town during the winter months.

10. David Lowenthal, "The American Way of History," *Columbia University Forum* 9 (Summer 1966): 27.

11. "Geographic Identifiers: 2010 Demographic Profile Data (G001): All Places within Mississippi," US Census Bureau, American Factfinder, accessed February 27, 2018, https://factfinder.census.gov/faces/tableservices/jsf/pages/productview.xhtml?src=bkmk.

12. George Malin Davis Kelly to Ethel Moore Kelly, October 13, 1936, George Malin Davis Kelly Papers, Natchez Historical Foundation, Natchez, MS. George Kelly complained about the passenger rail service in Natchez. It could take as much as four hours to travel ninety miles to Jackson on rail during the 1930s.

13. The Treaty of Doak's Stand was an accord between the United States and the Choctaw Indian Tribe in which the Choctaw agreed to cede one-half of their remaining homeland in what is now Mississippi to the US. Andrew Jackson and Thomas Hinds represented the US; chiefs Pushmataha, Mushulatubbee, and Apuckshunubee represented the Choctaw. The treaty was signed on October 18, 1820, at a place known as Doak's Stand on the Natchez Trace. Robert V. Remini, *The Life of Andrew Jackson* (New York: Harper Perennial, 1999), 105–15.

14. Denver Service Center, National Park Service, US Department of the Interior, *Environmental Statement for the Natchez Trace Parkway: Tennessee-Alabama-Mississippi*, Vols. I and II, June 20, 1978, 21–42.

15. James A. Crutchfield, *The Natchez Trace: A Pictorial History* (Franklin, TN: Territorial Press, 2011), 7.

16. Robert Leroy Johnson (1911–38) was an American blues singer, songwriter, and musician in the Mississippi Delta. Bessie Smith (1894–1937) was nicknamed the "Empress of the Blues" and was the most popular female blues singer of the 1920s and 1930s.

17. Philippe Margolin and Jean-Mitchell Guesdon, *Bob Dylan, All the Songs: The Story Behind Every Track* (Philadelphia: Running Press, 2015), 45.

18. Matthew Potteiger and Jamie Purinton, *Landscape Narratives: Design Practices for Telling Stories* (New York: Wiley and Sons, 1998), 307–12.

19. Jason S. Alexander, Richard C. Wilson, and W. Reed Green, "A Brief History and Summary of the Effects of River Engineering and Dams on the Mississippi River System and Delta," US Department of the Interior, US Geological Survey, last modified 2021, https://pubs.usgs.gov/circ/1375/.

20. George Malin Davis Kelly to Ethel Moore Kelly, July 17, 1936, George Malin Davis Kelly Papers, Natchez Historical Foundation, Natchez, MS.

21. Todd Sanders in discussion with author, February 3, 2016.

22. Robert Lubin, a Virginia attorney, proposed renovating the Eola Hotel in 2019. Once completed, it will include seventy to eighty new hotel rooms and several top floor apartments. Scott Hawkins, "Owner: Eola Work to Resume Soon," *Natchez Democrat*, March 24, 2019, https://www.natchezdemocrat.com/2019/03/24/owner-eola-work-to-resume-soon/; and Historic Natchez Foundation to author, June 11, 2021.

23. On February 1, 2019, United Mississippi Bank foreclosed on the historic Dunleith and Castle Restaurant. Kevin Cooper, "Natchez Bank Purchases Historic Dunleith Inn and the Castle," *Natchez Democrat*, February 1, 2019, https://www.natchezdemocrat.com/2019/02/01/natchez-bank-purchases-historic-dunleith-inn-and-the-castle/.

24. Ronald W. Miller and Mary W. Miller, *Great Houses of Natchez* (Jackson: University Press of Mississippi, 1986).

25. Mary Warren Miller, "Natchez On-Top-of-the Hill Historic District," National Register of Historic Places Nomination Form, May 31, 1979.

26. Sabrina Robertson, "City Considers Next Steps for Arlington," *Natchez Democrat*, January 24, 2019, https://www.natchezdemocrat.com/2019/01/24/city-considers-next-steps-for-arlington-property/.

27. Historic Natchez Foundation to author, June 11, 2021.

28. Local architect John Munce designed the renovation, and master builder George Williams built these features for it. Miller, "Natchez On-Top-of-the Hill Historic District."

29. "Welcome to St. Mary Basilica," St. Mary Basilica, last modified 2018, http://www.stmarybasilica.org; "Our History," Trinity Church, last modified 2018, http://www.trinitynatchez.org/our-history.html; and R. O. Gerow, *Cradle Days of St. Mary's at Natchez* (Natchez, MS: St. Mary's Cathedral, 1941).

30. The First Presbyterian Church was originally built in 1829 and substantially renovated and expanded in 1851 by James Hardie; then it was altered again in 1859. Historic Natchez Foundation to author, June 11, 2021.

31. Historic Natchez Foundation to author, June 11, 2021.

32. MDAH Historic Resources Inventory Database, accessed May 17, 2018, http://www.apps.mdah.ms.gov/Public/search.aspx.

33. Historic Natchez Foundation to author, June 11, 2021.

34. "Ashlar" refers to the technique of laying stone blocks, which are carefully cut into rectangular blocks and set into a wall in an organized bond pattern.

35. Mills Lane et al., *Architecture of the Old South: Mississippi and Alabama* (New York: Abbeville Press/Beehive Press, 1989), 62–65; and Marion K. Schlefer, ed., "Commercial Bank (First Church of Christ, Scientist): HABS No. MS-190 Photographs Written Historical and Descriptive Data," Historic American Buildings Survey, Library of Congress, Washington, DC.

36. In classical architecture, "in antis" denotes a temple type of building with side walls extending to the front face of the portico.

37. MDAH Historic Resources Inventory Database, accessed May 18, 2018, http://www.apps.mdah.ms.gov/Public/search.aspx.

38. Minard Lafever, *The Beauties of Modern Architecture* (New York: Appleton, 1835).

39. Paul Goeldner, "Stanton Hall," National Register of Historic Places Nomination Form, January 8, 1974; and Historic Natchez Foundation to author, June 11, 2021.

40. Albert D. Kirwan, "Politics and Human Slavery," in *The Civilization of the Old South: Writings of Clement Eaton* (Lexington: University Press of Kentucky, 1968), 107–34.

41. William Nemoyten, "John Wood Mansion," National Register of Historic Places Nomination Form, January 15, 1970. In 2007, the Illinois Chapter of the American Institute of Architects recognized the John Wood Mansion as one of the "150 Most Important Buildings in Illinois" during the Sesquicentennial Anniversary of the AIA. The Society of Architectural Historians recognizes it on the society's website, "SAHARCHIPEDIA," accessed May 3, 2018, http://sah-archipedia.org/detail%2Fcontent%2Fentries%2FIL-01-001-0046.xml?q=%28type%3Amansions%29%20AND%20style%3A%22Greek%20Revival%22%20sort%3Arelevance.

42. Mills Lane, *Architecture of the Old South: Kentucky and Tennessee* (Savannah, GA: Beehive Press, 1993), 116–22.

43. Lane et al., *Architecture of the Old South: Mississippi and Alabama*, 53–56.

44. Stanley B. Kimball, "The Mormons in Illinois, 1836–1846: A Special Introduction," *Journal of the Illinois State Historical Society* 64, no. 1 (1971): 4–21. Joseph Smith, Brigham Young, and architect-builder William Weeks adapted the Greek Revival style in building all of the buildings in the first preeminent city and home of the Church of Latter Day Saints, Nauvoo, Illinois, from 1836 until it was abandoned by the Mormons in 1846.

45. Steven Hoelscher, "'Where the Old South Still Lives': Displaying Heritage in Natchez, Mississippi," in *Southern Heritage on Display*, ed. Celeste Ray et al. (Tuscaloosa: University of Alabama Press, 2003), 218–19.

46. Michael Hennen, "The Elms: Time Capsule of Natchez and Vicksburg Urban Life," *The Primary Source* 25, no. 1, art. 3 (2003): 9–10; and Alma Cassell Kellogg Carpenter (1926–2005) Obituary, *Jackson Clarion Ledger*, September 5, 2005.

47. Jennifer Baughn, "The Elms Historic Survey Fact Sheet 2007," Mississippi Department of Archives and History Historic Preservation Database, accessed June 14, 2018, https://www.apps.mdah.ms.gov/Public/prop.aspx?id=470&view=facts&y=823. Photographs recorded during the 2007 Natchez Study Tour by MDAH depict The Elms in an advanced state of disrepair. Repair projects included the reconstruction of the fireplace in the main parlor, evaluations for repair, replacement, and repainting of the porch roof balustrade, replacement of the terne metal standing seam roof, and photographs of mantelpieces in abandoned rooms in the building.

48. Miss Alma's daughter, Esther Carpenter, has restored The Elms. It is now a bed and breakfast that caters to tourists during the pilgrimages and throughout the year.

49. Hoelscher, "'Where the Old South Still Lives,'" 219.

50. Volume 11, 2016, of the *Journal of Heritage Tourism* was a special issue dedicated to Plantation Heritage Tourism. Articles include Perry L. Carter, "Where Are the Enslaved?: Trip Advisor and the Narrative Landscapes of Southern Plantation Museums," Amy E. Potter, "She Goes into Character as the Lady of the House: Tour Guides, Performance, and the Southern Plantation," Condace Forbes Bright and Perry Carter, "Who Are They? Visitors to Louisiana's River Road Plantations," Derek H. Alderman and E. Arnold Modlin Jr., "On the Political Utterances of Plantation Tourists: Vocalizing the Memory of Slavery on River Road," and Matthew R. Cook, "Counter-Narratives of Slavery in the Deep South: The Politics of Empathy Along and Beyond River Road." In these articles, the authors note that interpreters and docents at historic plantations continue to change the content of their tour presentations to accommodate tourists.

51. Judith Adler, "Travel as Performed Art," *American Journal of Sociology* 94, no. 6 (May 1989): 1366–91.

52. Michael Bowman, "Performing Southern History for the Tourist's Gaze: Antebellum Home Tour Guide Performances," in *Exceptional Spaces: Essays in Performance and History*, ed. Della Pollock (Chapel Hill: University of North Carolina Press, 1998), 142–58.

53. Marion Kelly (Mrs. Dexter) Ferry interview with Graham Hicks, November 17, 1981, Mississippi Department of Archives and History.

54. Natchez Garden Club, "Seventh Annual Pilgrimage Sponsored by the Original Natchez Garden Club, March 26–April 3, 1938, Natchez, Mississippi, Where the Old South Still Lives," Mississippi Department of Archives and History.

55. Ben Hillyer, "Is Pilgrimage Addressing Changing Face of Tourism?," *Natchez Democrat*, March 15, 2018, https://www.natchezdemocrat.com/2018/03/15/is-pilgrimage-addressing-changing-face-of-tourism/.

56. Jennifer L. Eichstedt and Stephen Small, *Representations of Slavery: Race and Ideology in Southern Plantation Museums* (Washington, DC: Smithsonian Books, 2002).

57. Edward A. Modlin, "Tales Told on the Tour: Mythic Representations of Slavery by Docents at North Carolina Plantation Museums," *Southeastern Geographer* 48, no. 3 (2008): 265–87.

58. Bette Barber Hammer, *Natchez' First Ladies: Katherine Grafton Miller and the Pilgrimage* (New York: L. Kinter Publishers, 1955), 3.

59. Allison Davis, Burleigh B. Gardner, and Mary B. Gardner, *Deep South: A Social Anthropological Study of Caste and Class* (Chicago: University of Chicago Press, 1941), 252–55.

60. Amy E. Potter, "She Goes into Character as the Lady of the House: Tour Guides, Performance, and the Southern Plantation," *Journal of Heritage Tourism* 11, no. 3 (2016): 251–52.

61. Potter, "She Goes into Character," 250.

62. Potter, "She Goes into Character," 251.

63. Potter, "She Goes into Character," 253.

64. Potter, "She Goes into Character," 255.

65. Andreas Huyssen, *Twilight Memories: Marking Time in a Culture of Amnesia* (New York: Routledge), 2–3; and Shelly Hornstein, *Losing Site: Architecture, Memory, and Place* (London: Routledge, 2012), 36–48.

66. Historic Natchez Foundation to author, June 11, 2021.

67. Hoelscher, "'Where the Old South Still Lives,'" 229.

68. Paul Connerton, *How Societies Remember* (Cambridge, UK: Cambridge University Press, 1989), 73.

69. Lowenthal, "American Way of History," 30; and Mike Robinson, "Intangible Industrial Heritage: Ironbridge International Institute for Cultural Heritage Lecture Series," University of Birmingham, February 12, 2014. See also the UNESCO definition of intangible heritage, accessed June 28, 2018, https://ich.unesco.org/en/home.

70. Hoelscher, "'Where the Old South Still Lives,'" 229.

71. Roane Fleming Byrnes Archives, "Historic Natchez: Where the Old South Still Lingers," unpublished manuscript, Roane Fleming Byrnes Archives, n.d., Box 15, Folder 26, University of Mississippi Archives, Oxford, MS.

72. Potter, "She Goes into Character," 254.

73. Potter, "She Goes into Character," 256–57.

74. Natchez Pilgrimage Tours, accessed July 2, 2019, https://natchezpilgrimage.com.

75. In nineteenth-century America, the tableau was also strongly associated with nudity as a sort of means to get around obscenity by recreating famous nude works of art.

76. Robert M. Lewis, "Tableaux Vivants: Parlor Theatricals in Victorian America," *Revue Française D'etudes Américaines* 36 (1988): 280–84.

77. David Glassberg, *American Historical Pageantry: The Uses of Tradition in the Early Twentieth Century* (Chapel Hill: University of North Carolina Press, 1990), 16–18.

78. *Biographical and Historical Memoirs of Mississippi: Authentic and Comprehensive Account of the Chief Events in the History of the State, and a Record of the Lives of Many of the Most Worth and Illustrious Families and Individuals*, 2 vols. (Chicago: The Goodspeed Publishing Co., 1891), 657; and *Vicksburg Evening Post*, August 24, 1887. The kirmess was an outdoor fair or festival developed in Belgium and Holland in the sixteenth century. In the US, it consisted of a fair and indoor entertainment. Ms. C. C. Campbell, Miss Annie Hackler, and Mr. Luther Manship organized the 1887 kirmess in Natchez to raise funding for the Natchez Hospital.

79. Prevost, "Roane Fleming Byrnes," 62.

80. Ben Hillyer, "Changes Planned for Tableaux to Tell Entire Natchez Story," *Natchez Democrat*, February 15, 2015, http://www.natchezdemocrat.com/2015/02/15changes-planned-for-tableaux-to-tell-entire-natchez-story/. In 2000, the "Confederate Pageant" was renamed the "Natchez Historical Pageant." Today, the pageant attempts to exhibit the entire history of Natchez, and it has become more racially diverse, featuring African American performers and African American themes.

81. Cecelia Moore, "Outdoor Dramas," accessed July 2, 2018, https://www.ncpedia.org/outdoor-dramas.

82. Marion Kelly (Mrs. Dexter) Ferry interview with Graham Hicks, November 17, 1981, Mississippi Department of Archives and History.

83. Marion Kelly (Mrs. Dexter) Ferry interview.

84. Roane Fleming Byrnes interview with Graham Hicks, September 5, 1973, Mississippi Department of Archives and History.

85. It is anticipated the Forks of the Road will be acquired by the Natchez National Historical Park. Historic Natchez Foundation to the author, June 11, 2021.

86. Rugel Michael, "Natchez Burning: Anniversary of the Rhythm Club Fire," in *Nobody Knows Where the Blues Come From: Lyrics and History*, ed. Robert Springer (Jackson: University Press of Mississippi, 2007), 76–107.

87. Mary Warren Miller, "Brumfield High School," National Register of Historic Places Nomination Form, June 20, 1993.

88. Mississippi Museum of Art, "Mapping a Modern Mississippi," Natchez Museum of African American History and Culture, accessed September 12, 2018, http://msmuseumart.org/index.php/map/place/natchez-museum-of-african-american-history-and-culture.

89. Karen L. Cox, *Goat Castle: A True Story of Murder, Race, and the Gothic South* (Chapel Hill: University of North Carolina Press, 2017). Cox presents the most comprehensive story of the "Goat Castle Murder" and how the nation viewed the Gothic South in all of its decay during the 1930s.

90. David Glassberg, "Public History and the Study of Memory," *The Public Historian* 17, no. 2 (Spring 1996): 17–19.

91. Henry Glassie, *Passing the Time in Ballymenone: Culture and History of an Ulster Community* (Philadelphia: University of Pennsylvania Press, 1982), 664.

92. Randy Hester, "Subconscious Landscapes of the Heart," *Places* 2 (1985): 10–22.

CHAPTER 2: THE EVOLVING NARRATIVE

1. Roane Fleming Byrnes Papers, Folder 8, University of Mississippi Archives, Oxford, MS.

2. Newell and Compton, *Natchez and the Pilgrimage*, 13.

3. Diane L. Barthel, "Nostalgia for America's Village Past: Staged Symbolic Communities," *International Journal of Politics, Culture, and Society* 4 (1): 79–93.

4. Kevin Lynch, *What Time Is This Place?* (Cambridge, MA: MIT Press, 1972), 64.

5. Diane L. Barthel, "Historic Preservation: A Comparative Analysis," *Sociological Forum* 4 (1): 102.

6. Scott W. Poole, "Memory," in *The New Encyclopedia of Southern Culture: Volume 4: Myth, Manners, and Memory*, ed. Charles Reagan Wilson (Chapel Hill: University of North Carolina Press, 2006), 105.

7. Maurice Halbwachs, *The Collective Memory*, trans. Francis J. Ditter Jr. and Vida Yazdi Ditter (New York: Harper and Row, 1980).

8. Falck, *Remembering Dixie*.

9. Dennis Dulling, "Memory, Collective Memory, Orality, and Gospels," *HTS Theological Studies* 67 (1): 4.

10. Cornelius Holtorf, "On Pastness: A Reconsideration of Materiality in Archaeological Object Authenticity," *Anthropological Quarterly* 86, no. 2 (Spring 2013): 430–32.

11. Anne Firor Scott, *The Southern Lady* (Chicago: University of Chicago Press, 1970), 4.

12. Roane Fleming Byrnes graduated from Stanton College for Girls, which occupied Stanton Hall. Theodora Britton Marshall and Catherine Dunbar Marshall graduated from the Natchez Institute. Emmett J. Hull, *The Mississippi Educational Advance* (Jackson, MS: Tucker Printing House, 1914).

13. Hull, *Mississippi Educational Advance*, 7. Scott, in *Southern Lady*, cites "Anonymous Diary of a Young Woman Living near Natchez," Manuscript Department, William R. Perkins Library, Duke University.

14. During the mid-nineteenth century, most white upper-class women in Mississippi were educated in finishing schools, which embraced the Southron movement. Inspired by Sir Walter Scott, southerners believed that as "Southrons" they followed a higher moral code than other Americans and, therefore, they believed they were

superior. Women educated within the Southron idea learned high Christian morals, some aspects of classical education, and homemaking skills.

15. Scott, *Southern Lady*, 23–44.

16. Drew Gilpin Faust, "Altars of Sacrifice: Confederate Women and the Narratives of War," *Journal of American History* 76, no. 4 (March 1990): 1220–27.

17. Drew Gilpin Faust, *Mothers of Invention: Women of the Slaveholding South in the American Civil War* (Chapel Hill: University of North Carolina Press, 1996), 7.

18. Scott, *Southern Lady*, 220.

19. Scott, *Southern Lady*, 221–22.

20. *Natchez, Mississippi on Top: Not "Under the Hill"* (Natchez, MS: Daily Democrate Steam Press, 1892), 6.

21. James C. Giesen, "The Truth about the Boll Weevil: The Nature of Planter Power in the Mississippi Delta," *Environmental History* 14, no. 4 (October 2009): 693–94.

22. Suzanne T. Dolensky, "Natchez in 1920: On the Threshold of Modernity," *Journal of Mississippi History* 73, no. 2 (Summer 2011).

23. George Malin Davis Kelly to Ethel Moore Kelly, January 22, 1932, George Malin Davis Kelly Papers, Natchez Historical Foundation, Natchez, MS.

24. George Malin Davis Kelly to Ethel Moore Kelly, September 11, 1934, George Malin Davis Kelly Papers, Natchez Historical Foundation, Natchez, MS.

25. George Malin Davis Kelly to Ethel Moore Kelly, January 24, 1933, George Malin Davis Kelly Papers, Natchez Historical Foundation, Natchez, MS.

26. George Malin Davis Kelly to Ethel Moore Kelly, January 5, 1932, George Malin Davis Kelly Papers, Natchez Historical Foundation, Natchez, MS.

27. George Malin Davis Kelly to Ethel Moore Kelly, March 16, 1933, George Malin Davis Kelly Papers, Natchez Historical Foundation, Natchez, MS.

28. Susan T. Falck, "Black and White Memory Making in Postwar Natchez, Mississippi, 1865–1935" (PhD diss., University of California, Santa Barbara, 2012), 176–83. See also Karen L. Cox, *Dixie's Daughters: The United Daughters of the Confederacy and the Preservation of Confederate Culture* (Gainesville: University Press of Florida, 2003).

29. James M. Lindgren, "A New Departure in Historic Patriotic Work: Personalism, Professionalism, and Conflicting Concepts of Material Culture in the Late Nineteenth and Early Twentieth Centuries," *The Public Historian* 18, no. 2 (Spring 1996): 43–49.

30. Lindgren, "New Departure," 51–53.

31. The Garden Club of America traces its beginning to when Elizabeth Price Martin founded the Garden Club of Philadelphia in 1904.

32. Jean Gould Bryant, "From the Margins to the Center: Southern Women's Activism, 1820–1970," *The Florida Historical Quarterly* 77, no. 4: 413.

33. The first organized women's garden club was the Ladies Garden Club of Athens, Georgia, in 1910, but the movement first became popular in the Northeast. Recording, drawing, and enjoyment of American gardens by women, along with their conservation and interest in horticulture, became the clubs' primary objectives. By 1913, twelve garden clubs from the Northeast and Midwest formed the Garden Guild, which later changed its name to the Garden Club of America. Virginia A. Smith, "The Vigorous Garden Club of America," *Philadelphia Inquirer*, accessed August 24, 2018, http://www.philly.com/philly/archives/.

34. Alice G. B. Lockwood, *Gardens of Colony and State: Gardens and Gardeners of the American Colonies and of the Republic Before 1840*, vols. 1 and 2 (New York: Charles Scribner and Sons, 1931).

35. Dorothy Hunt Williams, *Historic Virginia Gardens* (Charlottesville: University of Virginia Press, 1975), 3–6.

36. Katherine Grafton Miller Scrapbook, Historic Natchez Foundation.

37. The "Old Spanish Market" in Natchez was built in 1837 and was designed by Andrew Brown. The Grecian building also served as the city hall, jail, and market with the open market area distinguished by a roof supported by large Greek Doric columns. Historic Natchez Foundation to author, June 11, 2021.

38. Historical Architecture, Cultural Resources Division, *Natchez National Historical Park, Old Fort Rosalie Gift Shop, Historic Structure Report* (Atlanta: US National Park Service, Cultural Resources Division, 2006), 7.

39. Clinton Bagley in discussion with author, July 20, 2016.

40. "An Interview with Mrs. Mary Louise Geddes and Mr. William A. Adams" by Graham Hicks, August 4, 1981, Mississippi Department of Archives and History, Jackson, MS, 7.

41. George Malin Davis Kelly to Ethel Moore Kelly, August 14, 1933, George Malin Davis Kelly Papers, Natchez Historical Foundation, Natchez, MS.

42. Prevost, "Roane Fleming Byrnes," 204.

43. Susan T. Falck, "The Garden Club Women of Natchez: 'To Preserve the South We Love'" (Master's thesis, California State University, Northridge, 2003), 100–149.

44. In settling in Spanish West Florida, this suggests that the Graftons may have had Tory leanings during the American Revolution.

45. Thomas Grafton was a former Confederate officer and a founding member of the Confederate Memorial Association. It seems ironic, then, that as the editor of the Natchez *Democrat*—and the paternal grandfather of the woman who helped brand Natchez as the place "Where the Old South Still Lives"—he penned an article praising Abraham Lincoln in 1890. However, this article reflected the ambivalence that wartime Natchezians felt regarding the Civil War, the Union, and the Confederacy. Most of the Natchez planters were either transplanted northerners or invested in northern industry before the advent of the Civil War. Grafton also published numerous essays on Natchez history. In one piece, he described Natchez as "the garden of the South, the favorite land of the emigrant hunting a home." Falck, "Garden Club Women of Natchez," 130–40.

46. Sarah Dunbar Smith, "Thomas Rose: A Nineteenth Century Master Builder in Natchez, Mississippi" (Master's thesis, Tulane University, 1993).

47. Karen L. Cox, "Revisiting the Natchez Pilgrimage: Women and the Creation of Mississippi's Heritage Tourism Industry," *Journal of Mississippi History* 74, no. 4 (Winter 2012): 353.

48. George Malin Davis Kelly to Ethel Moore Kelly, October 2, 1935, George Malin Davis Kelly Papers, Natchez Historical Foundation, Natchez, MS.

49. Hammer, *Natchez' First Ladies*, 3.

50. Miller Family File, Judge George W. Armstrong Library, Natchez, MS.

51. Miller, *Natchez of Long Ago*, 24.

52. Miller, *Natchez of Long Ago*, 24.

53. Katherine Grafton Miller (Mrs. Balfour) interview, February 18, 1971, transcript, Mississippi Department of Archives and History.

54. Quoted in Cox, "Revisiting the Natchez Pilgrimage," 353.

55. Quoted in Jack Davis, *Race Against Time: Culture and Segregation in Natchez Since 1930* (Baton Rouge: Louisiana State University Press, 2001), 68–69.

56. Pyle, "Touring with Ernie Pyle."

57. Cox, "Revisiting the Natchez Pilgrimage," 349–72.

58. Quoted in Falck, "The Garden Club Women of Natchez," 130–40.

59. Prevost, "Roane Fleming Byrnes," 22–23.

60. William Harris was a commission merchant, real estate developer, planter, and Natchez alderman. Harris purchased the Ravenna property in 1835 (Adams County Deed Book W:401); it was described as a fifteen-acre lot in which, as noted in county records, "the said Harris is now building for a residence" (Adams County Deed Book X:102). Historic Natchez Foundation to author, June 11, 2021.

61. Historic Natchez Foundation to author, June 11, 2021, 10.

62. Roane Fleming Byrnes, "Autobiographical Sketch," rough draft submitted as Lesson I, Juvenile Story Writing, Columbia University Extension, Box 1, Roane Fleming Byrnes Archives, University of Mississippi.

63. Prevost, "Roane Fleming Byrnes," 35.

64. James Register, *Jallon: Arabic Prince of Old Natchez, 1788–1828* (Shreveport, LA: Mid-South Press, 1968). Register chronicles Rahahman's story as a prominent African Muslim prince in Natchez and substantiates that Cox did free him.

65. Roane Fleming Byrnes, "Autobiographical Sketch," Box 2, Roane Fleming Byrnes Archives.

66. Terry Alford, *Prince Among Slaves*, 2nd ed. (Oxford: Oxford University Press, 1986), 4.

67. Prevost, "Roane Fleming Byrnes," 57.

68. Box 2, Roane Fleming Byrnes Archives, University of Mississippi Archives.

69. Mable L. Robinson to Roane Fleming Byrnes, letter, April 20, 1926, Box 2, Roane Fleming Byrnes Archives, University of Mississippi Archives.

70. James Fleming had been a prominent member of Natchez society. He was the vice president of the Britton and Koontz National Bank, secretary of the Natchez Building and Loan Association, and member of the Adams County Board of Supervisors. He was a deacon in the First Presbyterian Church, a Freemason, and a member of the Knights Templar. In 1906, his business success allowed him to build a Queen Anne-style Victorian home near his wife's family home, Ravenna, which he named Ravennaside. There, he moved his wife, Anna, and their two teenage children, Roane and Jim (James Jr.); they continued to reside there as adults and after Roane's marriage to Charles Ferriday Byrnes in 1913. Roane Fleming Byrnes, "Autobiographical Sketch," Box 2, Roane Fleming Byrnes Archives.

71. George Malin Davis Kelly to Ethel Moore Kelly, March 22, 1935, George Malin Davis Kelly Papers, Natchez Historical Foundation, Natchez, MS. George refers to Ferriday as a "leech." He warns his daughter, Marion, to not get involved with him in any professional matters.

72. George Malin Davis Kelly to Ethel Moore Kelly, October 21, 1936, George Malin Davis Kelly Papers, Natchez Historical Foundation, Natchez, MS.

73. Lawrence Adams, Interview, Natchez, Mississippi, April 4, 1974; and Mavis Feltus, Interview, Natchez, Mississippi, April 24, 1974, Roane Fleming Byrnes Archives, University of Mississippi.

74. Roane Fleming Byrnes Archives, University of Mississippi Archives.

75. Prevost, "Roane Fleming Byrnes," 52.

76. "Interview with Mrs. Mary Louise Geddes and Mr. William A. Adams," 7.

77. Historic Natchez Foundation to author, June 11, 2021.

78. Ellen Hampton, "'Lawdy! I Was Sho Happy When I Was a Slave': Manipulative Editing in the WPA Former Slave Narratives from Mississippi," *TOC: Journal L'Ordinaire des Ameriques* 215 (2013): 23–32.

79. Norman Yetamn, "Ex-Slave Interviews and the Historiography of Slavery," *American Quarterly* 36, no. 2 (1984): 187.

80. Cox, "Revisiting the Natchez Pilgrimage," 367.

81. Natchez National Historical Park, "Julia Davis Portrait Returns to Melrose," US National Park Service, March 17, 2012, https://www.nps.gov/natc/learn/news/julia-davis-portrait-returns-to-melrose.htm. Julia Davis's father, George Malin Davis, acquired Melrose in 1865 from John McMurran, who owed Davis a large debt. McMurran and Davis amicably settled the debt after the Civil War. McMurran repaid Davis with Melrose and additional money. Historic Natchez Foundation to author, June 11, 2021.

82. Historic Natchez Foundation to author, June 11, 2021.

83. David Hasty, *Cultural Landscape Inventory for the Melrose Estate at Natchez National Historical Park, Adams County, Mississippi* (Atlanta: US National Park Service, 2013), 4–138; Mary Warren Miller in discussion with the author, April 4, 2017; Ann Beha & Associates, Inc., *Melrose Estate Historic Structures Resource Study* (Atlanta: US National Park Service, 1996), 5–7; and Historic Natchez Foundation to author, June 11, 2021.

84. The Historic Natchez Foundation has printed and digital copies for scholars to research.

85. George Malin Davis Kelly to Ethel Moore Kelly, September 16, 1934, George Malin Davis Kelly Papers, Natchez Historical Foundation, Natchez, MS.

86. George Malin Davis Kelly to Ethel Moore Kelly, March 17, 1933, George Malin Davis Kelly Papers, Natchez Historical Foundation, Natchez, MS.

87. George Malin Davis Kelly to Ethel Moore Kelly, March 31, 1935, George Malin Davis Kelly Papers, Natchez Historical Foundation, Natchez, MS.

88. Joseph Kellogg became vice president of the City Bank and Trust Company of Natchez.

89. Hennen, "The Elms," 8–10.

90. James B. Lloyd, "Marshall, Theodora Britton," in *Lives of Mississippi Authors, 1817–1967* (Jackson: University Press of Mississippi, 1981), 326.

91. University of North Carolina at Chapel Hill Libraries, Southern Historical Collection; *Southern Women and Their Families in the 19th Century: Papers and Diaries, Part I: Mary Susan Ker Papers, 1785–1923* (Chapel Hill: University of North Carolina Libraries, 2013), 1–3; and Catherine Dunbar Papers, University of North Carolina Libraries, Southern Historical Collection, Chapel Hill, NC.

92. "Mary Louise Netterville Kendall Goodrich Shields Obituary," *Natchez Democrat*, November 3, 2015; and Interview with Mary Louise Kendall Goodrich by Graham Hicks, January 27, 1982, Mississippi Department of Archives and History, Jackson, MS.

93. Falck, "Garden Club Women of Natchez," 139.

94. Newell and Compton, *Natchez and the Pilgrimage*, II.

95. Hammer, *Natchez' First Ladies*, 3.

96. "Will Distribute Flowers Friday" and "Clean-Up Drive with Good Response," *Natchez Democrat*, March 13, 1931.

97. Roane Fleming Byrnes, "The Purchase of Ellicott's Hill," Rough Draft, 16, Box 4, Roane Fleming Byrnes Archives.

98. Natchez Garden Club, "Natchez' First Pilgrimage," *Over the Garden Wall* 8 (March 1955): 4.

99. Historic Natchez Foundation to author, June 11, 2021.

100. Dolensky, "Natchez in 1920," 136. In Dolensky's telephone interview with Mimi Miller, executive director, Historic Natchez Foundation, Miller emphasized, "No freezing!

No freezing!" in regard to the story that a late frost killed off the gardens, so the Natchez Garden Club women decided to open their homes to the state garden club women.

101. Miller, *Natchez of Long Ago*, 30.

102. Miller, *Natchez of Long Ago*, 29.

103. Leigh McWhite, archivist, University of Mississippi, in discussion with author, May 17, 2016.

104. Historic Natchez Foundation to author, June 11, 2021.

105. Miller, *Natchez of Long Ago*, 26.

106. Miller, *Natchez of Long Ago*, 26.

107. Roane Fleming Byrnes, "Description Given of Many Homes to be Visited Here," *Natchez Democrat*, March 20, 1931.

108. Miller, *Natchez of Long Ago*, 28.

109. Byrnes, "Description Given of Many Homes."

110. Jakle, *The Tourist*, 5. Jakle summarizes the spirit of travel throughout the US by quoting John Steinbeck: "A trip is an entity. It has personality, temperament, individuality, uniqueness. Trips are things in themselves." See also Alfred Haworth Jones, "The Search for a Usable Past in the New Deal Era," *American Quarterly* 23, no. 5 (December 1971): 710–24.

111. Cox, "Revisiting the Natchez Pilgrimage," 359.

112. Hammer, *Natchez' First Ladies*, 5.

113. During the antebellum period, there were several pleasure gardens in villas like Melrose, but by the 1930s none of them survived. Falck, *Remembering Dixie*, 155–58.

114. Miller, *Natchez of Long Ago*, 32.

115. Cox, "Revisiting the Natchez Pilgrimage," 349.

116. Roane Fleming Byrnes, "The Natchez Pilgrimage," rough draft as for an article, 3, Roane Fleming Byrnes Archives, University of Mississippi Archives, Oxford, MS.

117. Historic Natchez Foundation to author, June 11, 2021. The state historic marker in front of King's Tavern mistakenly reads "by 1789." The Historic Natchez Foundation determined that the building was actually built between 1797, when Richard King acquired the property to build the building, and 1799, when he received his tavern license.

118. "People and Events," *Natchez Democrat*, April 7, 1933.

119. Edith Wyatt Moore Notes for the WPA Writers' Project, 1932–1936, Mississippi Department of Archives and History, Jackson, MS.

120. Newell and Compton, *Natchez and the Pilgrimage*, 5.

121. Newell and Compton, *Natchez and the Pilgrimage*, 9–11.

122. Newell and Compton, *Natchez and the Pilgrimage*, 11.

123. George Malin Davis Kelly to Ethel Moore Kelly, March 9, 1935, George Malin Davis Kelly Papers, Natchez Historical Foundation, Natchez, MS. George shares his frustration with Ethel about how persistent and annoying Katherine Miller is in coming unannounced to Melrose with photographers.

124. Newell and Compton, *Natchez and the Pilgrimage*, 13–14.

125. Newell and Compton, *Natchez and the Pilgrimage*, 19.

126. Newell and Compton, *Natchez and the Pilgrimage*, 15, 17. Rosalie Beekman was the name of the girl killed in Natchez during the Civil War, and she was seven years old. Historic Natchez Foundation to author, June 11, 2021. During the Civil War, Natchez was known as a Unionist town with many Union sympathizers among the planter elite.

127. Newell and Compton, *Natchez and the Pilgrimage*, 15.

128. Newell and Compton, *Natchez and the Pilgrimage*, 19, 21.

129. Newell and Compton, *Natchez and the Pilgrimage*, 23.

130. Marion Kelly (Mrs. Dexter) Ferry interview with Graham Hicks, November 17, 1981.

131. George Malin Davis Kelly to Ethel Moore Kelly, March 25, 1935, George Malin Davis Kelly Papers, Natchez Historical Foundation, Natchez, MS. George complains to Ethel about how slow and difficult it is to travel by passenger rail out of Natchez.

132. Newell and Compton, *Natchez and the Pilgrimage*, 13.

133. Newell and Compton, *Natchez and the Pilgrimage*, 17.

134. Newell and Compton, *Natchez and the Pilgrimage*, 13, 17, 19, 34.

135. June Newman Graham, "Social Graces: The Natchez Garden Club as a Literacy Sponsor" (PhD diss., Louisiana State University, 2011), 83–93.

136. A "punkah" is a large, swinging, screen-like fan hung from the ceiling and is moved by a servant pulling on a pulley and rope. Punkahs were widely used in dining rooms of plantation manor houses and operated by servants. The "Great Punkah" is a showpiece in the dining room at Melrose.

137. George Malin Davis Kelly to Ethel Moore Kelly, March 26, 1935, George Malin Davis Kelly Papers, Natchez Historical Foundation, Natchez, MS.

138. Newell and Compton, *Natchez and the Pilgrimage*, 13.

139. Nola Nance Oliver, *Natchez: Symbol of the Old South* (New York: Hastings House, 1940), 3.

140. Oliver, *Natchez*, 4.

141. University of Houston Public History Program, "Children and the Great Depression," accessed May 6, 2019, http://www.digitalhistory.uh.edu/active_learning/explorations/children_depression/human_meaning.cfm. The economic crisis caused by the Great Depression overwhelmed private charities and local governments. In south Texas, the Salvation Army provided a penny per person each day in 1932.

142. Historic Natchez Foundation to author, June 11, 2021.

143. Oliver, *Natchez*, 25.

144. Oliver, *Natchez*, 31.

145. Attaching ghosts and legends to places to increase their tourism value was not unique to Natchez. Mrs. Hansell Hilyer, wife of the president of the Savannah Gas Company, converted an eighteenth-century Savannah residential structure into the Pirate's House restaurant and claimed that Captain Flint, a pirate mentioned in Robert Louis Stevenson's *Treasure Island*, died in its second-floor bedroom and his ghost haunts the restaurant to this very day. A scintillating story, but it neglects to acknowledge that *Treasure Island* is fiction and Captain Flint and his ghost never existed. Nevertheless, tourists found stories tied to places like King's Tavern and the Pirate's House captivating during the 1930s and 1940s. Alan Brown, *Haunted Places in the American South* (Jackson: University Press of Mississippi, 2002), 77.

146. Cox, *Goat Castle*.

147. Oliver, *Natchez*, 48.

148. Oliver, *Natchez*, 96–97.

149. Nola Nance Oliver, *This Too Is Natchez* (New York: Hastings House Publishers, 1953), 5.

150. Mary Warren Miller, "Texada," "Texada Tavern," "Old Spanish House," Mississippi Department of Archives and History Resources Inventory, accessed October 14, 2018, http://www.apps.mdah.ms.gov.

151. Oliver, *This Too Is Natchez*, 18, 53–54, 71–72.

152. Hoelscher, "Where the Old South Still Lives," 224.

153. T. H. Gallaudet (Thomas Hopkins), 1787–1851, *A Statement with Regard to the Moorish Prince, Abduhl Rahhahman* (New York: D. Fanshaw, 1828), University of North Carolina Libraries, https://docsouth.unc.edu/neh/gallaudet/menu.html.

154. J. D. B. DeBow, *DeBow's Review*, vol. 29 (New Orleans: Southern States, 1860), 503.

155. Anne Chamberlain, "Son of Roots?," *Washington Post*, October 20, 1977; and Hollie I. West, "Out of Time's Shadow: Seven Years' Research for a Prince Among Slaves," *Washington Post*, August 6, 1978.

156. Charles S. Sydnor, "The Biography of a Slave," *South Atlantic Quarterly* 36 (January 1937): 59–73.

157. Mississippi Department of Archives and History, *Ninth and Tenth Annual Reports, Archives and History, Mississippi, 1910–11* (Jackson, MS: MDAH), 45.

158. Alford, *Prince Among Slaves*.

159. Alford, *Prince Among Slaves*. Alford states that after the plantation was sold to the Henderson family, it was renamed Greenwood Plantation. There is in Natchez a Greenwood Plantation Road near the southeast corner of the city.

160. Steven Brooke, *The Majesty of Natchez*, 2nd ed. (Gretna, LA: Pelican Publishing Co., 2007), 2. Brooke's guidebook was first published in 1969; it was subsequently reprinted in 1982, 1999, 2001, and 2007.

CHAPTER 3: THE MAKING OF THE PILGRIMAGE AND THE INVENTION OF CONNELLY'S TAVERN

1. $55,000 in today's money.

2. $13,000 in today's money.

3. "An Interview with Mrs. Ruth Audley Britton Wheeler Beltzhoover" by Graham Hicks, August 4, 1981, Mississippi Department of Archives and History, Jackson, MS, 2–4.

4. "Interview with Mrs. Ruth Audley Britton Wheeler Beltzhoover," 2.

5. "Historic Garden Week," accessed December 13, 2018, https://www.vagardenweek.org.

6. "Historic Garden Week," 4.

7. Roane Fleming Byrnes Papers.

8. "An Interview with Mrs. Hunter Goodrich" by Graham Hicks, Mississippi Department of Archives and History, Jackson, MS, 2.

9. "Interview with Mrs. Hunter Goodrich," 3.

10. $3,400 in today's dollars.

11. Melchoir Beltzhoover was president of the Britton & Koontz Bank. "Interview with Mrs. Ruth Audley Britton Wheeler Beltzhoover," 5; and "Dollar Times Calculator," accessed December 3, 2018, https://www.dollartimes.com/inflation/inflation.php?amount=200&year=1932.

12. "Interview with Mrs. Ruth Audley Britton Wheeler Beltzhoover," 6.

13. Miller, *Natchez of Long Ago*, 35.

14. Miller, *Natchez of Long Ago*, 43.

15. "Interview with Mrs. Mary Louise Geddes and Mr. William A. Adams," 4.

16. "An Interview with Mrs. Margaret Persell Marshall Macilroy" by Elliot Trimble, September 26, 1981, Mississippi Department of Archives and History, Jackson, MS, 2.

17. "An Interview with Mrs. Rebecca Fauntleroy Benoist" by Graham Hicks, August 26, 1981, Mississippi Department of Archives and History, Jackson, MS, 8.

18. "Interview with Mrs. Ruth Audley Britton Wheeler Beltzhoover," 12.

19. Ruth Audley Britton Wheeler Beltzhoover, "The Historic Natchez Pageant, 1932," p. 1, Natchez Garden Club, Natchez, MS.

20. The Natchez Garden Club and the Pilgrimage Garden Club changed the name of the "Confederate Pageant" to the "Natchez Historic Pageant" in 1995. Graham, "Social Graces," 137–39.

21. Miller, *Natchez of Long Ago*, 46.

22. "An Interview with Mrs. Alma (Mrs. Joseph) Kellogg" by Elliot Timble, August 15, 1981, Mississippi Department of Archives and History, Jackson, MS, 3–6.

23. "Interview with Mrs. Hunter Goodrich," 4.

24. Edith Wyatt Moore, "Natchez Plans a 'Pilgrimage to Paradise': Century Old Homes and Gardens to Be Opened to Public This Spring," *Chicago Tribune*, February 28, 1932.

25. "Interview with Mrs. Margaret Persell Marshall Macilroy," 3.

26. Miller, *Natchez of Long Ago*, 35.

27. "Interview with Mrs. Hunter Goodrich," 4.

28. "Interview with Mrs. Hunter Goodrich," 4; and "Interview with Mrs. Rebecca Fauntleroy Benoist," 2.

29. Miller, *Natchez of Long Ago*, 46.

30. "Interview with Mrs. Rebecca Fauntleroy Benoist," 3; and Miller, *Natchez of Long Ago*, 60.

31. Jakle, *The Tourist*, 288.

32. Ivan S. Cobb, *Roughing It Deluxe* (New York: Doran, 1914), 8.

33. "Interview with Mrs. Margaret Persell Marshall Macilroy," 3.

34. The Natchez Garden Club women used *Godey's Lady Book*, a fashion book and magazine that was published by Louis A. Godey in Philadelphia from 1830 to 1878 and featured dress patterns of antebellum hoopskirts. "Interview with Mrs. Hunter Goodrich," 10; and Anne C. Rose, *Voices of the Marketplace: American Thought and Culture, 1830–1860* (New York: Rowman & Littlefield Publishers, 2004), 75.

35. "Interview with Mrs. Ruth Audley Britton Wheeler Beltzhoover," 8.

36. "Interview with Mrs. Hunter Goodrich," 12.

37. William R. Cullson, "Tulane's Richard Koch Collection—A Visual Survey of Historic Architecture in the Mississippi Delta," *Louisiana History* 18 (Fall 1977): 453–71; and Jessie Poesch and Barbara SoRelle Bacot, *Louisiana Buildings 1720–1940* (Baton Rouge: Louisiana State University Press, 1997), 51–90, 226–54. Richard Koch (1889–1971) was a native of New Orleans and spent his career preserving and restoring the city's historic architecture, most notably, the buildings in the Vieux Carré. In 1910, he graduated from Tulane University, where he was taught architecture in the Beaux Arts tradition. He continued his studies in Paris for two years at the Atelier Bernier. From 1912 until 1916, he worked in several architectural firms in New York and then returned to New Orleans, where he immediately formed an architectural firm with Charles Armstrong, a classmate from Paris. He focused on restoring and reusing the city's historic architecture and is considered a pioneer in adaptive use architecture, not only in New Orleans but throughout the US. Koch utilized his education from Tulane and in Paris to document New Orleans's historic architecture. As an adjunct professor at Tulane, he led students in field measuring and drawing the city's most significant historic buildings, like the Cabildo. He was also an accomplished architectural photographer, and he understood the importance of architectural photography in recording historic buildings. In the 1920s, he designed the restoration of two of Louisiana's most iconic landmarks, Shadow-on-the-Teche and Oak Alley.

38. Roane Fleming Byrnes Papers.

39. "Interview with Mrs. Hunter Goodrich," 10.

40. "Interview with Mrs. Hunter Goodrich," 10.

41. Historic Natchez Foundation to author, June 11, 2021.

42. "Dyed" margarine, colored to look like butter, was made illegal to serve in Mississippi and thirty-two other states in 1902. The ban was not lifted until World War II.

43. Saul Laub was mayor of Natchez from 1929 until 1936. C. F. Engle was city solicitor during the 1920s and 1930s.

44. "Interview with Mrs. Ruth Audley Britton Wheeler Beltzhoover," 10.

45. George W. Healy Jr., *A Lifetime on Deadline: Self-Portrait of a Southern Journalist* (Gretna, LA: Pelican Publishing, 1976), 89–90.

46. Miller, *Natchez of Long Ago*, 38–40.

47. Miller, *Natchez of Long Ago*, 38–40.

48. George Malin Davis Kelly to Ethel Moore Kelly, April 6, 1933, George Malin Davis Kelly Papers, Natchez Historical Foundation, Natchez, MS.

49. George Malin Davis Kelly to Ethel Moore Kelly, April 6, 1933.

50. Roane Fleming Byrnes, "History of the Natchez Pilgrimage," Rough Draft for an Article, 2–5, Roane Fleming Byrnes Archives, University of Mississippi Archives, Oxford, MS.

51. $116,750 in today's money.

52. $1,682.71 in today's money.

53. Alma Kellogg Treasurer Reports, Natchez Garden Club, 1935, Mississippi Department of Archives and History, Jackson, MS.

54. It is also known as Magnolia Hall.

55. Byrnes, "History of the Natchez Pilgrimage."

56. Historic American Buildings Survey, "Photographs and Descriptive Data, Gilreath's Hill Tavern, Ellicots [sic] Inn, Natchez, Miss.," HABS No. 17–4.

57. It was known to the Spanish as Fort Panmure.

58. John C. Van Horne, "Andrew Ellicott's Mission to Natchez (1796–1798)," *Journal of Mississippi History*, August 1983, 160–85; and WPA Writers' Project Notecard Collection, Mississippi Department of Archives and History.

59. Goeldner, "House on Ellicott's Hill/Connelly's Tavern." In Goeldner's nomination, which was written shortly after it was determined that the house on Ellicott's Hill was not Connelly's Tavern, he states that while Ellicott's raising of the American flag at Natchez must have occurred very near the building, it happened before the building was built in 1800.

60. National Park Service historian Dawson Phelps determined in a 1952 report that the American flag was raised by Ellicott on the site of the house on Ellicott's Hill. Historic Natchez Foundation to author, June 11, 2021.

61. Stuart Cuthbertson, Edith Wyatt Moore, and Katherine Grafton Miller, "Photographs, Written Historical and Descriptive Data of Gilreaths [sic] Hill Tavern, Ellicotts [sic] Inn, Natchez, Miss., HABS 17-4," Historic American Buildings Survey, Library of Congress, Washington, DC.

62. A brief description of Connelly's Tavern on a postcard printed in 1940 states: "Legend: Treasure is supposed to be buried beneath the house, and the floors of the lower rooms have often been found dug up." Mississippi Postcard Collection, University of Mississippi Archives.

63. Sanders built on his father's accomplishments and developed a cotton mill empire in the state (including a mill near the Gilreath Hill building in Natchez); he also coined the state's industrial development motto: "What Mississippi Makes—Makes Mississippi."

64. William D. McCain, *The Story of Jackson* (Jackson, MS: Hyer Pub. Co., 1953), 63–67.

65. Roane Fleming Byrnes, "The Purchase of Ellicott's Hill," Rough Draft, 18, Roane Fleming Byrnes Archives.

66. A self-educated architect and builder, William Stietenroth was respected for his work in Natchez; he built the parish hall building for Trinity Episcopal Church and was the architect and builder for the Natchez Elks Club Building.

67. Mississippi Department of Archives and History Database, accessed January 19, 2017.

68. Roane Fleming Byrnes, "Gilreath Hill," rough draft of a speech presented to the Natchez Garden Club, 1934, Roane Fleming Byrnes Archives.

69. Byrnes, "Gilreath Hill."

70. Prevost, "Roane Fleming Byrnes," 52–54.

71. Hammer, *Natchez' First Ladies*, 12.

72. George Malin Davis Kelly to Ethel Moore Kelly, April 6, 1935.

73. George Malin Davis Kelly to Ethel Moore Kelly, March 26, 1935.

74. George Malin Davis Kelly to Ethel Moore Kelly, March 31, 1935.

75. George Malin Davis Kelly to Ethel Moore Kelly, April 6, 1935.

76. $342,000 in 2019.

77. George Malin Davis Kelly to Ethel Moore Kelly, April 12, 1935.

78. The gate was composed of brick posts, which were built out of bricks from her dilapidated dairy building and outhouse. White concrete caps were placed on top of the piers, and there were iron gates on each side between the posts. George Malin Davis Kelly to Ethel Moore Kelly, April 6, 1935.

79. Roane Fleming Byrnes, "The Natchez Pilgrimage," rough draft as for an article, 3, Roane Fleming Byrnes Archives, University of Mississippi Archives, Oxford, MS.

80. "The Old South Lives Again in Famous Natchez Pilgrimage," *Atlanta Constitution*, April 28, 1935.

81. George Malin Davis Kelly to Ethel Moore Kelly, April 2, 1935.

82. George Kelly complained to Ethel Kelly that the men working the gates expected to be provided endless bottles of Coca-Cola and an endless supply of cigarettes, along with an hourly wage. George Malin Davis Kelly to Ethel Moore Kelly, April 4, 1935.

83. George Malin Davis Kelly to Ethel Moore Kelly, April 4, 1935.

84. George Malin Davis Kelly to Ethel Moore Kelly, March 26, 1935.

85. George Malin Davis Kelly to Ethel Moore Kelly, April 4, 1935.

86. George Malin Davis Kelly to Ethel Moore Kelly, October 3, 1935.

87. This amount was based on the 1934 pilgrimage and would be $15,000 in today's money.

88. George Malin Davis Kelly to Ethel Moore Kelly, October 8, 1935.

89. George Malin Davis Kelly to Ethel Moore Kelly, October 8, 1935.

90. The Natchez Garden Center was a local women's club whose mission was only enjoying gardening. Susan T. Falck wrote that there were also numerous women in the Natchez Garden Club who were interested in gardening. Falck, *Remembering Dixie*.

91. George Malin Davis Kelly to Ethel Moore Kelly, October 10, 1935.

92. Natchez Garden Club Archives, Mississippi Department of Archives and History, Jackson, MS.

93. George Malin Davis Kelly to Ethel Moore Kelly, October 13, 1935.

94. The following homeowners (using the specified names) signed the open letter supporting the Natchez Garden Club: Mrs. G. M. Kelly of Melrose, Mrs. J. D. McDowell

of Oakland, Mrs. R. E. Ratcliffe of Ravenna, Miss Annie Wilson of Rosalie, Mr. David L. McKittrick of Elms Court, Mrs. William W. Wall of The Briars, and Mrs. Lem Conner. "Home Owners of Garden Club to Remain in Club," *Natchez Democrat*, October 13, 1935; and Natchez Garden Club Files, Mississippi Department of Archives and History, Jackson, MS.

95. George Malin Davis Kelly to Ethel Moore Kelly, October 23, 1935.

96. George Malin Davis Kelly to Ethel Moore Kelly, October 28, 1935.

97. George Malin Davis Kelly to Ethel Moore Kelly, November 1, 1935.

98. Roane Fleming Byrnes, "The Gilreath Hill Project," Roane Fleming Byrnes Archives, University of Mississippi Archives, Oxford, MS.

99. Harriet Dixon to Annie Barnum, June 16, 1936, Natchez Garden Club Files, Mississippi Department of Archives and History, Jackson, MS.

100. Official Correspondence from the City of Natchez, July 14, 1936, Natchez Garden Club Files, Mississippi Department of Archives and History, Jackson, MS.

101. Harriet Dixon to Mrs. Robert Harvey, Honorary President, The Garden Clubs of Mississippi, September 18, 1936, Natchez Garden Club Files, Mississippi Department of Archives and History, Jackson, MS.

102. Mrs. J. D. Duncan to Mrs. Hubert Barnum, October 28, 1936, Natchez Garden Club Files, Mississippi Department of Archives and History, Jackson, MS.

103. Kate Don Brandon Adams, "Natchez Pilgrimage Collection, 1932–1988 (Manuscript)," Mississippi Department of Archives and History, Jackson, MS.

104. Katherine Grafton Miller to Harriet Dixon and the Natchez Garden Club, November 5, 1936, Natchez Garden Club Files, Mississippi Department of Archives and History, Jackson, MS.

105. Pearl Vivian Guyton, *The Story of Connelly's Tavern on Ellicott Hill: A National Shrine Owned by the Natchez Garden Club, Natchez, Mississippi* (Jackson, MS: Hederman Bros., 1942), 41–43.

106. Prevost, "Roane Fleming Byrnes," 113.

107. Guyton, *Story of Connelly's Tavern*, 42.

108. Beverly Warner Martin (1910–81) was a recent graduate of the architecture program at Georgia Tech in 1932. A native of Neshoba County in northeast Mississippi, Martin worked for architecture firms in Jackson, most notably, the office of E. L. Malveny, who likely introduced him to Koch. By 1933, he had relocated to Natchez and was working on Gilreath Hill. MDAH Database, "Martin, Beverly W.," accessed February 15, 2019, https://www.apps.mdah.ms.gov/Public/rpt.aspx?rpt=artisanSearch&Name=Martin&City=Natchez&Role=Any; and George S. Koyl, ed., *AIA Architect's Directory* (New York: R. R. Bowker Co., 1962), 465.

109. HABS staff member Logan Kline provided this information for the drawing. Before the Depression, Kline was a builder for railroad companies, building commercial buildings in railroad towns; he built buildings for the Mobile and Ohio Railroad. During the 1920s, he and business partner Henry Morton built commercial brick buildings in Shuqualak (pronounced *sugar lock*) in northeast Mississippi. Kline most likely was out of work, due to the scarcity of construction projects during the Great Depression, and worked for Stietenroth on the restoration. Dennis M. Murphy, "Central Shuqualak Historic District National Register of Historic Places Nomination Form," September 7, 1979, https://www.apps.mdah.ms.gov/nom/dist/100.

110. Guyton, *Story of Connelly's Tavern*, 45.

111. Mrs. S. A. Beatner to the Shillsbone Testing Laboratory, Jackson, MS, August 24, 1936, Mississippi Department of Archives and History, Jackson, MS.

112. Richard Koch to Roane Fleming Byrnes, January 28, 1937, Mississippi Department of Archives and History, Jackson, MS. Brown's Wells was a healing mineral resort, established in 1852 and located near Hazlehurst, Mississippi, in Copiah County. It is located east of Natchez. David Clement, "A Program for Brown's Wells Health Resort in Hazlehurst, Mississippi in Copiah County" (B. Arch. thesis, Texas Tech University, 1987).

113. Stark Young (1881–1963) was a notable playwright, literary critic, and former professor of English at several universities, but most notably at Amherst College. In 1921, he left academia and became a celebrated novelist. Born in Como, Mississippi, he was the most popular southern novelist and essayist during the late 1920s.

114. Prevost, "Roane Fleming Byrnes," 114.

115. Stark Young to Anna Metcalfe Fleming, letter, n.d., BC.

116. Prevost, "Roane Fleming Byrnes," 115.

117. Prevost, "Roane Fleming Byrnes," 117.

118. Prevost, "Roane Fleming Byrnes," 120.

119. Roane Fleming Byrnes, "The Purchase of Ellicott's Hill," rough draft as for a manuscript, 20, Roane Fleming Byrnes Archives, University of Mississippi Archives, Oxford, MS.

120. Roane Fleming Byrnes to Richard Koch, January 22, 1937, Natchez Garden Club Files, Mississippi Department of Archives and History, Jackson, MS.

121. Richard Koch to Roane Fleming Byrnes, March 11, 1937, Natchez Garden Club Files, Mississippi Department of Archives and History, Jackson, MS.

122. Roane Fleming Byrnes, "Restoration on Ellicott's Hill Started by Club," *Natchez Democrat*, July 19, 1936, Natchez Garden Club Files, Mississippi Department of Archives and History, Jackson, MS.

123. Natchez Garden Club Files, Mississippi Department of Archives and History, Jackson, MS.

124. Guyton, *Story of Connelly's Tavern*, 42–43.

125. Guyton, *Story of Connelly's Tavern*, 43.

126. Tinkers were known as questionable travelers. Razor grinders were known as shady men who carried knives.

127. Guyton, *Story of Connelly's Tavern*, 44–45.

128. Guyton, *Story of Connelly's Tavern*, 44–45.

129. Roane Fleming Byrnes, "History of the Natchez Pilgrimage," rough draft for an article, not dated, Roane Fleming Byrnes Archives, University of Mississippi Archives, Oxford, MS.

130. Harriet Dixon to Helger Cahill, October 10, 1936; and Harriet Dixon to Thomas C. Parker, January 13, 1937, Mississippi Department of Archives and History, Jackson, MS.

131. Natchez Garden Club Files, Mississippi Department of Archives and History, Jackson, MS.

132. Harriet Dixon to Roane Fleming Byrnes, December 13, 1935, Mississippi Department of Archives and History, Jackson, MS.

133. William M. Ellicott (1863–1944) was the heir to the wealthy Ellicott Flour Milling Company empire, which also established Ellicott City, Maryland. Ellicott was born in Philadelphia, attended Haverford College, but then transferred to the University of Pennsylvania, where he earned a bachelor's degree in architecture in 1887; the next year, he studied at the École des Beaux Arts in Paris. Upon his return to the US, he moved to Portland, Oregon, and joined Edgar M. Lazarus, a prominent Jewish architect in

Portland, in an architectural firm, which lasted from 1890 until 1895. Richard E. Ritz, "Ellicott, William M.," *Architects of Oregon: A Biographical Dictionary of Architects Deceased—19th and 20th Centuries* (Portland: Lair Hill Publishing, 2003), 123.

134. Harriet Dixon to William M. Ellicott, January 12, 1937, Mississippi Department of Archives and History, Jackson, MS.

135. Roane Fleming Byrnes to William M. Ellicott, January 25, 1937, Mississippi Department of Archives and History, Jackson, MS.

136. Byrnes, "Gilreath Hill."

137. Byrnes, "Natchez Pilgrimage."

CHAPTER 4: DISTRICT 17

1. Julia Everts, "The Concept of Professionalism: Professional Work, Professional Practice and Learning," in *International Handbook of Research in Professional and Practice-Based Learning*, ed. Stephen Billet et al. (Dordecht, The Netherlands: Springer, 2014), 29–56.

2. Michael Holleran, *Boston's Changeful Times* (Baltimore: Johns Hopkins University Press, 1998), 218.

3. Charles B. Hosmer, *Preservation Comes of Age: From Williamsburg to the National Trust, 1926–1949* (Charlottesville: University of Virginia Press, 1981).

4. Professional architecture education was first introduced by the Massachusetts Institute of Technology in 1865. The University of Illinois soon followed, establishing an architecture studies program in 1867. In 1897, the state of Illinois was the first to implement an architecture licensure law. Other states followed, albeit slowly, over the next fifty years, according to the National Architectural Accreditation Board.

5. Carlo D'Este, *Eisenhower: A Soldier's Life* (London: Macmillan, 2003), 127–38. In World War I, Eisenhower trained army officers in tank maneuvers at Camp Colt at Gettysburg, Pennsylvania. The training exercises were conducted on the Civil War battlefield, which was managed by the US War Department.

6. John Ise, *Our National Park Policy: A Critical History* (Baltimore: Johns Hopkins University Press, 1961), 187–89.

7. Horace M. Albright, "Origins of National Park Service Administration of Historic Sites: A Reminiscence," Eastern National Park and Monument Association, 1971, 5–7.

8. Donald M. Swain, "Albright, Ickes, and the Hundred Days," *The Pacific Historical Review* 34 (November 1965): 460.

9. Executive Order 6288, Section 2—National Parks, Buildings, and Reservations, Executive Order 6288, Section 2—National Parks, Buildings, and Reservations, 48 Stat. 369 Fed, accessed November 12, 2018, https://www.archives.gov/federal-register/codification/executive-order/06166.html.

10. Horace Albright stated his history-based park objectives in a letter to Robert Sterling Yard: "consolidate our gains [acquiring parks in the West], finish rounding out of the Park system, go rather heavily into the historical park field, and get such legislation as is necessary to guarantee the future of the system on a sound permanent basis where the power and the personality of the Director may no longer have to be controlling factors in operating the Service." Albright to Robert Sterling Yard, December 20, 1928. Quoted in Wilton C. Corkern Jr., "Architects, Preservationists, and the New Deal: The Historic American Buildings Survey, 1933–1942" (PhD diss., The George Washington University, 1984), 52.

11. US National Park Service, "Annual Report, 1929," 169, Old History Division Files, Washington, DC, Office, US National Park Service, Washington, DC.

12. Denise D. Meringlo, *Museums, Monuments, and National Parks: Toward a New Genealogy of Public History* (Amherst: University of Massachusetts Press, 2012), 113.

13. Meringlo, *Museums, Monuments, and National Parks*, 113.

14. Meringlo, *Museums, Monuments, and National Parks*, 114.

15. Meringlo, *Museums, Monuments, and National Parks*, 112–15.

16. Corkern, "Architects, Preservationists, and the New Deal," 52.

17. "Historical Conference," November 27, 1931, Old History Division Files, Washington, DC Office, US National Park Service, Washington, DC.

18. Harlan D. Unrau and G. Frank Williss, "To Preserve the Nation's Past: The Growth of Historic Preservation in the National Park Service during the 1930's," *The Public Historian* 9, no. 2 (Spring 1987): 20–23.

19. Verne E. Chatelain, "History and Our National Parks," June 1935, Old History Division Files, Washington, DC Office, US National Park Service, Washington, DC.

20. Chatelain, "History and Our National Parks."

21. Chatelain, "History and Our National Parks."

22. $12 billion in 2019.

23. Meringlo, *Museums, Monuments, and National Parks*, 112.

24. Corkern, "Architects, Preservationists, and the New Deal," 63.

25. Charles Peterson was an influential figure in historic preservation; he is credited for conceiving the idea of a historical architect. During his renowned career, he represented the US at the Second International Congress of Architects and Technicians of Historic Monuments in 1964. He contributed and helped shaped the first graduate degree program in historic preservation at Columbia University in 1964, he helped establish the Association for Preservation Technology International in 1970, and he wrote several books on historic construction technology. He had an impactful thirty-year career at the National Park Service including working on the Colonial National Historic Park at Jamestown and Yorktown, Virginia, and as a senior landscape architect working on the Jefferson National Expansion Memorial (now known as the Gateway Arch National Monument) in St. Louis, Missouri. He was also instrumental in the planning of the Independence Hall National Park in Philadelphia. John G. Waite, "In Memory of Charles E. Peterson, 1906–2004," *APT Bulletin* 37, no. 1 (2006): 5. See also Nicholas Gianopolis, "In Memory of Charles E. Peterson, 1906–2004," *APT Bulletin* 37, no. 1 (2006): 3.

26. Meringlo, *Museums, Monuments, and National Parks*, 117.

27. Michael A. Tomlan conversation with author, December 5, 2018. Tomlan was a student of Peterson at Columbia University's Historic Preservation Program during the early 1970s. He recalled that Peterson did not put on "airs" about himself.

28. Michael A. Tomlan conversation with author, 118.

29. For the past eighty-five years, HABS has produced an impressive body of work, documenting thousands of buildings, and later, landscapes and engineering works. It continues to be one of the most popular archival collections visited by the public at the Library of Congress. It has been used to document the vanishing American landscape, employ unemployed or underemployed design professionals, and, since passage of the National Historic Preservation Act, a way to mitigate the "adverse effect" on a historic monument. Mark Schara, "Preserving Our Early Architecture: The Historic American Buildings Survey in the District of Columbia, 1933–1942," *Washington History* 30, no. 1 (Spring 2018): 30.

30. Catherine C. Lavoie, "Architectural Plans and Visions: The Early HABS Program and Its Documentation of Vernacular Architecture," *Perspectives in Vernacular Architecture* 13, no. 2 (2006): 15–18.

31. Official Records of Charles E. Peterson, RG 515 Stack Area: 150, Row: 63, Compartment: 26, National Archives, College Park, MD.

32. Charles E. Peterson to Arno B. Cammerer, November 13, 1933, Record Group 79, Central Classified Files, Series 614, Surveys, HABS, National Archives, College Park, MD.

33. Memorandum of Agreement, July 23, 1934, US Department of the Interior, Washington, DC, US National Park Service, Office Files. The term "cultural programs" was applied to other projects funded by the WPA for professional and artistic fields. The Federal Theatre Project, the Federal Art Project, the Federal Writers' Project, and the Historic Records Survey were WPA projects that historians group together in what became known as "Federal Project Number One." HABS became part of what became known as "Federal Project Number Two."

34. Lavoie, "Architectural Plans and Visions," 17.

35. Measuring and recording historic architecture are practices as old as the modern architectural profession itself. Soon after its founding in 1857, the American Institute of Architects called for surveys of architecturally significant buildings across the nation. Charles B. Hosmer, *Presence of the Past* (New York: Putnam Publishing, 1965), 207. Architecture schools, from the late nineteenth century until after World War II, made measuring and drawing historic buildings a required course in their curricula. In 1917, Columbia University Architecture School dean Richard F. Bach proposed that the AIA produce a comprehensive survey of colonial architecture in the US, specifically in New England, New Orleans, California, Arizona, and New Mexico. Frank H. Bosworth and Roy C. Jones, *A Study of Architectural Schools* (New York: Charles Scribner and Sons, 1932), 5.

36. Horace W. Sellers to the Committee on Natural Beauties and Historic Monuments, September 17, 1915, AIA Archives, Washington, DC.

37. Richard F. Bach, "Books on Colonial Architecture: Part VII—The Final Record," *Architectural Record* 40 (January-June 1917): 486–91.

38. The White Pine Bureau hired architect Russell F. Whitehead and photographer Julian Buckly to draw and photograph colonial houses. Their documentation work was featured in bimonthly publications aimed at architects and draftsmen. In a ploy to appeal to American nostalgia and perhaps to not be burdened with accurately documenting the buildings they studied, Whitehead and Buckly created the fictional and historically idyllic town of Stotham, Massachusetts, as the home to all of this historic architecture. It was not until twenty years after the "White Pines" series was published that it was disclosed that Stotham never existed. John F. Harbeson, "Stotham, the Massachusetts Hoax, 1920," *Journal of the Society of Architectural Historians* 23, no. 2 (May 1964): 111–12. See also Lavoie, "Architectural Plans and Visions."

39. Martica Sawin email to author, September 20, 2018. James Marston Fitch worked for the Rogers interior design firm in Nashville, Tennessee, around 1929. One of his projects was the replica of Auburn built for a private client in Nashville. Fitch went to Natchez to make drawings of the details in Auburn, and he brought several carpenters with him to figure out how to re-create key architectural elements for the new residence.

40. Meringlo, *Museums, Monuments, and National Parks*, 120.

41. Charles E. Peterson, "Leicester Bodine Holland, 1882–1952," *Journal of the Society of Architectural Historians* 11, no. 2 (May 1952): 24.

42. Corkern "Architects, Preservationists, and the New Deal," 78–80.

43. Lavoie, "Architectural Plans and Visions," 15–18.

44. Lavoie, "Architectural Plans and Visions," 18–19.

45. Elise Vider, "The Historic American Buildings Survey in Philadelphia, 1950–1966" (Master's thesis, University of Pennsylvania, 1991), 26–27.

46. Corkern, "Architects, Preservationists, and the New Deal," 82–84; *Washington Post*, November 29, 1933; Charles E. Peterson, "American Notes," *Journal of the Society of Architectural Historians* 16, no. 3 (October 1957): 31; and Lavoie, "Architectural Plans and Visions," 18.

47. Edward C. Kemper to Arno B. Cammerer, November 28, 1933, Record Group 515, Central Classified Files, Series 63, Surveys, HABS, National Archives, College Park, MD.

48. Harold Ickes to Arno B. Cammerer, December 4, 1933, Record Group 515, Central Classified Files, Series 63, Surveys, HABS, National Archives, College Park, MD.

49. Thomas G. Vint, "Progress Report to Civil Works Administration, January 31, 1934," Record Group 69, Central Classified Files, Series 54, Records of the Works Projects Administration, National Archives, College Park, MD.

50. Thomas G. Vint, "Memorandum to Dr. Herbert E. Bolton, Albert Simons, Thomas Tallmedge, and I. T. Frary, January 5, 1934," Record Group 515, Central Classified Files, Series 63, Surveys, HABS, National Archives, College Park, MD.

51. Peterson stated in his memorandum: "[The date was chosen because] after that time, the sectional characteristics of the country became less and less distinct. Steadily increasing movements of population and accelerated distribution of information broadened architectural taste, and local differences in design and construction methods disappeared. There is little sectional difference in our architecture of today." Charles E. Peterson to Arno B. Cammerer, November 13, 1933, Record Group 515, Central Classified Files, Series 63, Surveys, HABS, National Archives, College Park, MD.

52. Meringlo, *Museums, Monuments, and National Parks*, 118–21.

53. John P. O'Neill, "Employment Chart 1934," Record Group 515, Central Classified Files, Series 63, Surveys, HABS, National Archives, College Park, MD.

54. Between 1929 and 1933, the value of cotton fell from $190 million to $46 million. Bank savings fell from $101 million to $48 million, and retail sales dropped from $413,000 in 1929 to $140,000 in net profits in 1933. David Helborn Sachs, *The Life and Work of the Twentieth Century Louisiana Architect A. Hays Town* (Lampeter, Ceredigon, Wales: Edwin Mellen Press, 2003), 40–44.

55. Emmett J. Hull was a prominent architect in Jackson and the son of Francis D. Hull, the owner of the state's largest contracting companies. Hull studied architecture at Cornell University and was a charter member of the state AIA chapter, but at the time HABS was introduced, he was considering a job for the Federal Housing Authority. MDAH Database, "Hull, Emmett J.," accessed February 12, 2019, https://www.apps.mdah.ms.gov/Public/rpt.aspx?rpt=artisanSearch&Name=Hull&City=Jackson&Role=Any. Edgar L. Malvaney, trained at Washington University in St. Louis and an accomplished architect in the Beaux Arts tradition, was qualified to be the district officer, but in 1934, he was busy planning the move of Coldwater, Mississippi, to a new site to make way for the new Arkabutla Lake. MDAH Database, "Malvaney, Edgar Lucian," accessed February 12, 2019, https://www.apps.mdah.ms.gov/Public/rpt.aspx?rpt=artisanSearch&Name=Malvaney&City=Jackson&Role=Any.

56. Noah Webster Overstreet was born in Eastibouchie, Mississippi, twelve miles north of Hattiesburg. His father owned the town's general store and named his children after its bestselling items. Apparently, *Webster's Dictionary* sold well in Harvey Overstreet's store. Known as "Web," he was a large man, well over six feet tall, outgoing,

and gregarious. He first studied mechanical engineering at Mississippi A&M College (now Mississippi State University); after working for the Reuben H. Hunt, an architect in Chattanooga, Tennessee, he earned an architectural engineering degree at the University of Illinois in 1910. At the time, Illinois was one of the leading architecture schools in the nation. Its founding professor, Nathan Ricker, based its curriculum on the German polytechnic tradition instead of the French Beaux Arts one. Structural analysis and building systems integration were emphasized in the curriculum, along with the other practical aspects of architecture, rooted in emerging technology in building construction. Overstreet was fascinated with these ideas in architecture and sought to design progressive modern buildings throughout his long career. After briefly working for Urbana, Illinois, architect Joseph W. Royer, he moved to Jackson and established his practice, first with Raymond Spencer of Overstreet and Spencer. After Spencer left the firm in 1912, it became N. W. Overstreet, Architect, in 1915. Web Overstreet enjoyed solving building problems more than doing conceptual architectural design. He managed the office and construction administration of his projects. He was also very interested in engineering buildings using new materials, most notably reinforced concrete. This interest reflects the influence his education at Illinois had on his career. He enjoyed marketing. Overstreet used his societal connections—the Mississippi A&M Alumni Society, the Jackson Rotary Club, and the Belmont Hunting Club—to market for architectural commissions. Overstreet was a proud Mississippian who admired the state's history and its architectural tradition, but at the same time, he aspired to be a modern, progressive architect, interested in building in the emerging modernist style of the early twentieth century. David Helburn Sachs, "The Work of Overstreet and Town: The Coming of Modern Architecture to Mississippi" (PhD diss., University of Michigan, 1986), 21–27; and Paul S. Kruty, "Walter Burley Griffin and the University of Illinois," *Reflections: The Journal of the School of Architecture at Urbana-Champaign* 9 (Spring 1993): 33.

57. William Spratling was a renowned artist and drawing instructor at Tulane University. He illustrated the books *Old Plantation Houses in Louisiana* and *Sherwood Anderson and Other Famous Creoles*. During the 1920s, he was close friends with William Faulkner and Sherwood Anderson. In 1927, Spratling designed Anderson's home in Grayson County, Virginia, called Ripshin. Sachs, "Work of Overstreet and Town," 18–20; and Calder Loth, *The Virginia Landmarks Register* (Charlottesville: University of Virginia Press, 1999), 198.

58. As a student, Town was captivated by the old buildings he encountered in New Orleans's French Quarter and spent his free time sketching and learning from them. During his summers from 1922 until 1925, he worked for Richard Koch, who became a mentor to him. While working for Koch, Town worked on the restoration of Oak Alley Plantation and on the Horace Grima House in New Orleans. Koch helped Town early in his career and introduced him to Natchez in 1934. Sachs, *Life and Work of the Twentieth-Century Louisiana Architect A. Hays Town*, 20–24.

59. The most famous building designed by Overstreet and Town, Bailey Junior High School in Jackson, was lauded by Lewis Mumford as a master work in reinforced concrete. But even though they were attracted to designing in the "modern style," both men admired the nineteenth century architecture of their native states of Mississippi and Louisiana. Sachs, *Life and Work of the Twentieth-Century Louisiana Architect A. Hays Town*, 40–43.

60. Marvin Eickenroht to John P. O'Neill, May 1, 1936. Eickenroht states that the members of the Mississippi HABS advisory committee were reappointed. Virginia Price,

"Drawing Details: Taking Measure of the HABS Collection," *Preservation Education & Research* 4 (2011): 53–68; MDAH Database; and Ted Ownby and Charles Reagan Wilson, *The Mississippi Encyclopedia* (Jackson: University Press of Mississippi, 2017). Price states that the advisory committee consisted of Emmett Hull, Claude Lindsley, Frank P. Gates, Dunbar Rowland, and Judge Andrew H. Longino. Lindsley listed his residence in the Mississippi AIA directory as "Washington, D.C." Rowland was the first director of the Mississippi Department of Archives and History, but in 1934 he was actively campaigning to establish the National Archives and spent most that year in Washington. Longino was the thirty-fifth governor of Mississippi, 1900–1904. He helped establish the Mississippi Department of Archives and History during his term. By 1934, he had retired from public life.

61. Sara Amy Leach, "The Daughters of the American Revolution, Roane F. Byrnes, and the Birth of the Natchez Trace Parkway," in *Looking Beyond the Highway*, ed. Claudette Stager and Martha Carver (Knoxville: University of Tennessee Press, 2006), 110.

62. WPA Writers' Project, *Mississippi: A Guide to the Magnolia State* (New York: The Viking Press, 1938), 10; Richard Koch to Roane Fleming Byrnes, February 10, 1934, Roane Fleming Byrnes Archives, University of Mississippi Archives, Oxford, MS; and Sachs, *Life and Work of the Twentieth-Century Louisiana Architect A. Hays Town*, 47.

63. A. Hays Town's two most productive draftsmen were Harry Edmiston Weir (1907–79) and Jay Tunis Liddle Jr. (1906–67). Weir was a delineator, a draftsman, and later an architect who never attended architecture school; he attended Cumberland University from 1926 to 1928 and then worked for architect Frank Fort. He knew Overstreet and Town well and applied to work for them. When the only thing they had to offer him was HABS, he readily accepted their offer. MDAH Database, Harry Edmiston Weir, accessed February 11, 2019, https://www.apps.mdah.ms.gov/Public/rpt.aspx?rpt=artisanSearch&Name=Weir&City=Any&Role=Any; and MDAH Database, Jay Tunis Liddle, accessed February 11, 2019, https://www.apps.mdah.ms.gov/Public/rpt.aspx?rpt=artisanSearch&Name=Liddle&City=Any&Role=Any.

64. Jay Liddle graduated a year after Town at Tulane. He first worked for P. J. Krouse in Meridian, Mississippi, and then worked as the chief draftsmen for Carey and Dowling Architects in Mobile, Alabama. Like Town, Liddle was trained in Tulane's Beaux Arts curriculum; he understood and was very capable of producing the kind of drawings Town wanted in his HABS program. MDAH Database, Jay Tunis Liddle.

65. Thomas J. Biggs (1912–99) and Harold Kaplan (1910–93), along with Beverley Martin (1910–81), graduated from Georgia Tech in 1931. MDAH Database, Beverley W. Martin, accessed February 13, 2019, https://www.apps.mdah.ms.gov/Public/rpt.aspx?rpt=artisanSearch&Name=Martin%2C%20Beverley&City=Any&Role=Any. Peter J. Trolio (1910–51) was a recently graduated architect, having earned his architecture degree from the University of Notre Dame. A native of Canton, Mississippi, Trolio returned to Jackson and worked for District 17. MDAH Database, Peter J. Trolio, accessed February 13, 2019, https://www.apps.mdah.ms.gov/Public/rpt.aspx?rpt=artisanSearch&Name=Trolio&City=Any&Role=Any. Trolio and Jay Liddle were partners in a Jackson, Mississippi, architecture firm from 1947 until 1952.

66. Birth and death dates for Ralph Clynne and James Butters are unknown.

67. "Minnie B. Clynne Obituary, October 16, 1980," *Jackson Clarion-Ledger*, Journalism Library, University of Illinois Library, Urbana, IL.

68. In reviewing her book *Natchez Under-the-Hill* in 1956, Professor Jack Silver of the University of Mississippi summarized Moore's scholarship: "The author's occasional attempts at writing with a flourish never quite come off, and her obvious use of poetic

license makes it difficult at times to draw the line between fact and fancy." Jack W. Silver, "Natchez Under-the-Hill by Edith Wyatt Moore: Book Review," *Journal of Southern History* 26, no. 2 (May 1960): 246–47.

69. Edith Moore transcribed one set of comments in the following way: "Dey all had different ways ob thinkin' bout hit but most ob'em wuz like me, dey didn't know what freedom meant. Hit wuz jest a word dats all. Folks dat ain't ebber bin free don't rightly know de feel ob bein' free, or de meanin ob hit." Edith Wyatt Moore, "Transcript of Interview with James Lucas," Microfilm Records, 37102 and 37013, Mississippi Department of Archives and History, Jackson, MS. See also Norman R. Yetman, "Ex-Slave Interviews and the Historiography of Slavery," *American Quarterly* 36, no. 2 (1984): 187.

70. Edith Wyatt Moore, Katherine Perrault, and Louise Hernandez, "Adams County Sites Index Cards, WPA Writer's [sic] Project, Historic Homes and Sites Cards, n.d.," Series 1509/Box 12656, Vol, Info: 12656: Historic Buildings and Sites, WPA Records (RG. 60), Mississippi Department of Archives and History, Jackson, MS.

71. Edith Wyatt Moore, "Laurel Hill," "Adams County Sites Index Cards, WPA Writer's [sic] Project, Historic Homes and Sites Cards, n.d.," Series 1509/Box 12656, Vol, Info: 12656: Historic Buildings and Sites, WPA Records (RG. 60), Mississippi Department of Archives and History, Jackson, MS.

72. Mary Warren Miller, "Laurel Hill Plantation National Register of Historic Places Nomination," December 21, 1981.

73. Edith Wyatt Moore, "Spanish House," "Adams County Sites Index Cards, WPA Writer's [sic] Project, Historic Homes and Sites Cards, n.d.," Series 1509/Box 12656, Vol, Info: 12656: Historic Buildings and Sites, WPA Records (RG. 60), Mississippi Department of Archives and History, Jackson, MS.

74. Mary Warren Miller, "Natchez On-Top-of-the Hill Historic District," National Register of Historic Places Nomination Form, May 31, 1979.

75. Edith Wyatt Moore, "Sara Gossa," "Adams County Sites Index Cards, WPA Writer's [sic] Project, Historic Homes and Sites Cards, n.d.," Series 1509/Box 12656, Vol, Info: 12656: Historic Buildings and Sites, WPA Records (RG. 60), Mississippi Department of Archives and History, Jackson, MS.

76. Mary Warren Miller, "Saragossa National Register of Historic Places Nomination," September 14, 1980.

77. Stuart Cuthbertson, Edith Wyatt Moore, and Mrs. Rumble, "Photographs Written Historical and Descriptive Data, Rosalie, Natchez, Adams County, Mississippi, HABS No. 17–1," Historic American Buildings Survey, Library of Congress, Washington, DC; and Norman Chronister and William C. Allen, "Rosalie National Register of Historic Places Nomination," June 24, 1976.

78. Silver, "Natchez Under-the-Hill," 246.

79. Stuart Cuthbertson and Edith Wyatt Moore, "Photographs Written Historical and Descriptive Data, Gloucester, Natchez, Adams County, Mississippi, HABS No. 17–5," Historic American Buildings Survey, Library of Congress, Washington, DC.

80. William C. Allen, "Gloucester National Register of Historic Places Nomination," August 23, 1976.

81. Stuart Cuthbertson and Edith Wyatt Moore, "Photographs Written Historical and Descriptive Data, Linden, Natchez, Adams County, Mississippi, HABS No. 17–5," Historic American Buildings Survey, Library of Congress, Washington, DC.

82. In his 1976 National Register nomination, Mississippi Department of Archives and History historian William Allen disproved the Spanish connection to its construction. Basing his argument on examination of deeds to the property, he argued that the

tract on which Linden was eventually constructed did not have any building on it in 1803 and that the center part of the villa was constructed in 1818, ten years after the Spanish ceded Natchez to the US and a year after Mississippi became a state. He reinforced his determination through an analysis of its Federal-style woodwork. William C. Allen, "Linden National Register of Historic Places Nomination," August 23, 1976.

83. Ronald W. Miller, "Arlington National Register of Historic Places Nomination," November 13, 1973.

84. A. Hays Town to John P. O'Neill, May 1, 1936, Record Group 515, Correspondence Files, Series 63, Box 8, HABS, National Archives, College Park, MD.

85. Sachs, *Life and Work of the Twentieth Century Louisiana Architect A. Hays Town*, 12–13.

86. William A. Stanton, "Photographs Written Historical and Descriptive Data, Shamrock, Vicksburg, Warren County, Mississippi, HABS No. 17–2," Historic American Buildings Survey, Library of Congress, Washington, DC.

87. Sachs, *Life and Work of the Twentieth Century Louisiana Architect A. Hays Town*, 47; Lane et al., *Architecture of the Old South: Mississippi and Alabama*, 150; and Episcopal Diocese of Mississippi, "Chapel of the Cross Near Madison, Madison County, Mississippi, HABS 17-3," Historic American Buildings Survey, Library of Congress, Washington, DC.

88. Lavoie, "Architectural Plans and Visions," 18.

89. Stanford White was born in 1853 in New York City and is considered one of the greatest architects of the late nineteenth century. He was a partner in the architectural firm McKim, Mead & White. No relation has ever been determined between him and James Hampton White, who lived in Natchez during the early nineteenth century.

90. Stuart Cuthbertson and Edith Wyatt Moore, "Photographs Written Historical and Descriptive Data, Arlington, Natchez, Adams County, Mississippi, HABS No. 17–8," Historic American Buildings Survey, Library of Congress, Washington, DC.

91. Miller, "Arlington National Register of Historic Places Nomination."

92. Paul Goeldner, "Arlington National Historic Landmark Nomination," December 26, 1973.

93. Historic Natchez Foundation to author, June 11, 2021.

94. A. Hays Town, Stuart Cuthbertson, and Edith Wyatt Moore, "Photographs Written Historical and Descriptive Data, 313 Market Street, Natchez, Mississippi, HABS 17-11," Historic American Buildings Survey, Library of Congress, Washington, DC. The historical report for this HABS file states "the Parrish House." This is most likely a typographical error.

95. Town et al., "Photographs Written Historical and Descriptive Data."

96. Town et al., "Photographs Written Historical and Descriptive Data."

97. Historic Natchez Foundation to author, June 11, 2021.

98. Todd Sanders and Paul Hardin Kapp, "311-313 Market Street (Parish House), Natchez, Adams County, Mississippi, HABS MISS, 1-NATCH, 7, Correctly Renamed the James Adams House Relocated to 205 Canal Street, North Natchez, Adams County, Mississippi," unpublished book chapter, September 19, 2015, 1–4; Mississippi Department of Archives and History Database, accessed on September 17, 2015; and 1925 Sanborn Map of Natchez, Mississippi, Mississippi Department of Archives and History. Architect Samuel Wilson made the attribution that Miller designed the house for Andrews based only on the fact that Miller had done work for James Andrews after Andrews had sold this house on Market Street. Historic Natchez Foundation to author, June 11, 2021.

99. Mary Warren Miller, "Natchez On-Top-of-the-Hill Historic District," National Register of Historic Places Nomination. In the National Register nomination, the Andrews House is still incorrectly called the "Parish House." Ronald Miller to Mrs. Grace MacNeil, July 2, 1974, James Andrews House File, Historic Natchez Foundation, Natchez, MS. See also Arch R. Winter and Samuel Wilson Jr., "Architectural-Historical Historic Natchez Building Survey-1973," James Andrews House File, Historic Natchez Foundation, Natchez, MS; and Arch R. Winter and Samuel Wilson Jr., "Priest's House, Natchez Metropolitan Planning Commission—Adams County Landmarks Inventory-1974," James Andrews House File, Historic Natchez Foundation, Natchez, MS. It is unclear when the James Andrews House was raised and a brick basement built underneath it. Miller determined that this alteration was done between 1805 and 1822. The wind-blown silt (loess soil) was prone to erosion, so to alleviate the problem, the streets were gradually cut through the hills, which left some early buildings sitting on top of banks along the streets. See also Fortesque Cuming, *Cuming's Tour to the Western Country, 1807–1809* (Cleveland: Arthur H. Clark Co., 1904).

100. Brooke, *Majesty of Natchez*, 20.

101. Amateur historians throughout the Southwest and in California were fascinated with Spanish colonial heritage.

102. Edith Wyatt Moore, "Spanish House," "Adams County Sites Index Cards, WPA Writer's [*sic*] Project, Historic Homes and Sites Cards, n.d."

103. Lowenthal, *Heritage Crusade and the Spoils of History*, 94, 102.

104. Thomas G. Vint to District Officers, "Special Communication to All District Officers, February 19, 1934," Record Group 515, Central Classified Files, Series 63, Surveys, HABS, National Archives, College Park, MD; and Arthur E. Demaray to Harold Ickes, September 14, 1934, Record Group 515, Central Classified Files, Series 63, Surveys, HABS, National Archives, College Park, MD.

105. Leicester B. Holland, Harlean James, and Waldo B. Leland to Harold Ickes, March 9, 1934, Record Group 79, Historic American Building Engineering Record, 1934–1988, Box 2, National Archives, College Park, MD.

106. "HABS Bulletin No. 32—Historic American Buildings Survey as a Permanent Plan, April 6, 1934," Record Group 79, Historic American Building Engineering Record, 1934–1988, Box 2, National Archives, College Park, MD.

107. Arthur E. Demaray to Harold Ickes, September 14, 1934, Record Group 79, Historic American Building Engineering Record, 1934–1988, Box 2, National Archives, College Park, MD.

108. David L. S. Brook, *A Lasting Gift of Heritage: A History of the North Carolina Society of the Preservation of Antiquities, 1939–1974* (Raleigh: Division of Archives and History, North Carolina Department of Cultural Resources, 1995), 16–17.

109. Charles E. Peterson to Hillary A. Tolson, June 27, 1935, Record Group 79, Historic American Building Engineering Record, 1934–1988, Box 2, National Archives, College Park, MD.

110. Leicester B. Holland to Harry L. Hopkins, September 7, 1935, Record Group 69, Records of the Work Projects Administration, 1935–1942, Box 11, National Archives, College Park, MD.

111. Fredrick Doveton Nichols proved so valuable at this task that Vint arranged for his military service to be deferred at the beginning of World War II so he could complete his work. Lavoie, "Architectural Plans and Visions," 18; and Price, "Drawing Details."

112. Daughters of the Republic of Texas Library, San Antonio, Texas, "Marvin Eickenroht Papers, 1904–1969," *Austin Seminary Archives, Stitt Library* (San Antonio: Southwest Publications, 1952), 257.

113. Corkern, "Architects, Preservationists, and the New Deal," 102.

114. A. Hays Town to John P. O'Neill, "Progress Report to Civil Works Administration," May 15, 1934, Record Group 79, Historic American Building Engineering Record, 1934–1988, Box 2, National Archives, College Park, MD.

115. John P. O'Neill, "Employment Survey of the HABS Program on May 15, 1934," Record Group 79, Historic American Building Engineering Record, 1934–1988, Box 2, National Archives, College Park, MD.

116. The district officer for Central Illinois, Edgar E. Lundean, summed up the sentiment of his cohort: "The Historic American Buildings Survey shouldn't just be extended, it should be enlarged. We are just getting warmed up, DON'T STOP NOW." John P. O'Neill, "Progress Report from the National Park Service to the Civil Works Administration, January 15, 1935," Record Group 79, Historic American Building Engineering Record, 1934–1988, Box 2, National Archives, College Park, MD.

117. Sachs, *Life and Work of the Twentieth-Century Louisiana Architect A. Hays Town*, 49–50.

118. Corkern, "Architects, Preservationists, and the New Deal," 133, 149.

119. Marvin Eickenroht to John P. O'Neill, September 1, 1936, Record Group 79, Historic American Building Engineering Record, 1934–1988, Box 2, National Archives, College Park, MD.

120. Corkern, "Architects, Preservationists, and the New Deal," 134.

121. McCain, *Story of Jackson*, 218.

122. Eickenroht conveyed several of his concerns in a letter: "My visit to Mississippi was timely; Mr. Waldrop, while becoming familiar with his professional duties, had permitted the personnel supervisor to continue handling all contracts and business with the WPA, a very unsatisfactory and uneconomical arrangement. We requested that the personnel supervisor be relieved of his duties at the end of the month, and an architectural worker put on in his stead. These changes will be more conducive to a more economical and efficient setup there. I emphasized to Mr. Waldrop the importance of completing unfinished records, bringing the priority card file up to date, etc. before undertaking much of anything else. As I told you before, the photographs there are good, and the histories are pitiful, and it seems like very few priority and index cards have ever been completely prepared. The whole project should operate smoothly now, with two draftsmen, a photographer, a secretary and the District Officer. I expect to visit Jackson again on my Division trip, after which I shall be able to tell better how things are working out." Marvin Eickenroht to John P. O'Neill, September 26, 1936, Record Group 79, Historic American Building Engineering Record, 1934–1988, Box 2, National Archives, College Park, MD.

123. John P. O'Neill to Marvin Eickenroht, October 30, 1936, Record Group 79, Historic American Building Engineering Record, 1934–1988, Box 2, National Archives, College Park, MD.

124. Carroll William Westfall, *Architecture, Liberty, and Civic Order: Architectural Theories from Vitruvius to Jefferson and Beyond* (Farnham, UK: Ashgate, 2015), 40–45. See also Giedon Sigfired, *Space and Architecture* (Cambridge, MA: Harvard University Press, 1944), Part I.

125. Nikolaus Pevsner, *The Buildings of England* (New York: Penguin, 1951–1974). In the 1940s Pevsner found that architectural history was not embraced as serious scholarship in academic circles and that architectural information was limited for tourists, so he proposed a survey series of English architecture to Penguin books founder Allen Lane.

126. Wilson, *Myth of Santa Fe*. Wilson described how Meem created Santa Fe in a way that did not represent actual Pueblo building tradition. Simons and Perry re-created English colonial architecture that was more conjectural than factual.

127. Marvin Eickenroht to John P. O'Neill, October 29, 1936, Record Group 79, Historic American Building Engineering Record, 1934–1988, Box 2, National Archives, College Park, MD.

128. Marvin Eickenroht to John P. O'Neill, October 29, 1936.

129. Marvin Eickenroht to John P. O'Neill, January 29, 1937, Record Group 79, Historic American Building Engineering Record, 1934–1988, Box 2, National Archives, College Park, MD.

130. Marvin Eickenroht to John P. O'Neill, March 19, 1937, Record Group 79, Historic American Building Engineering Record, 1934–1988, Box 2, National Archives, College Park, MD.

131. Marvin Eickenroht to John P. O'Neill, March 29, 1937, Record Group 79, Historic American Building Engineering Record, 1934–1988, Box 2, National Archives, College Park, MD.

132. John P. O'Neill to Marvin Eickenroht, May 26,1937, Record Group 79, Historic American Building Engineering Record, 1934–1988, Box 2, National Archives, College Park, MD; and Marvin Eickenroht to John P. O'Neill, June 7, 1937, Record Group 79, Historic American Building Engineering Record, 1934–1988, Box 2, National Archives, College Park, MD.

133. Marvin Eickenroht to John P. O'Neill, June 22, 1937, Record Group 79, Historic American Building Engineering Record, 1934–1988, Box 2, National Archives, College Park, MD.

134. John P. O'Neill to "Mrs. Cole," March 15, 1937, Record Group 69, WPA Central Files Box 214, HABS, National Archives, College Park, MD.

135. Arthur E. Demaray to Charles C. Adams, October 27, 1939, Record Group 515, Central Classified Files, Series 63, Surveys, HABS, National Archives, College Park, MD.

136. The cost of the new regional model was $122,000. Ickes approved the proposal in August 1939.

137. Charles E. Peterson to Malcolm Gardner, December 12, 1939, Record Group 79, Historic American Building Engineering Record, 1934–1988, Box 4, National Archives, College Park, MD.

138. Dawson A. Phelps, "Memorandum for the Acting Superintendent" [Natchez Trace Parkway Project], December 26, 1939, Record Group 79, Historic American Building Engineering Record, 1934–1988, Box 4, National Archives, College Park, MD.

139. Charles E. Peterson to Malcolm Gardner, December 12, 1939.

140. Malcolm Gardner to F. Ray Leimkuehler, December 2, 1940, Record Group 79, Historic American Building Engineering Record, 1934–1988, Box 4, National Archives, College Park, MD.

141. John Hanno Deiler was a German immigrant and educator who was obsessed with promoting ideas of German culture in the Deep South. The Historic New Orleans Collection, "J. Hanno Deiler," accessed May 8, 2019, https://www.hnoc.org/research/j-hanno-deiler.

142. The "Old French/Spanish Fort" may have been built under the supervision of Sieur Joseph Simon de la Pointe, hence the "Old French Fort" name, and it may have been used as a fortified residence by Spanish officer Don Enrique Grimarest, hence the "Old Spanish Fort" name; but no one could find any factual evidence to make either conclusion. It later was known as the LaPointe-Krebs House (Krebs explains

Deiler's fascination with its German ownership). Once again, unverified stories from local tradition provided misleading information, which was accepted as fact and archived in the Library of Congress. Although the set was produced by Felder from the St. Louis Central Unit office, it was submitted to Washington by Hull of District 17 from Jackson, who was directed by Leimkuehler to "mail the documented to the NPS Chief of Planning as soon as possible." Adolph H. Felder, "Photographs, Written Historical and Descriptive Data of the "Old French Fort," HABS No. MISS-18, HABS MISS 30-PASCA-3, Historic American Buildings Survey, Library of Congress, Washington, DC. See also Dawn Maddox, "Old Spanish Fort (Old French Fort) National Register of Historic Places Nomination," May 13, 1971; Grant Harley, "Dendrochronology Report at La Point-Krebs House, 2016," University of Southern Mississippi; and F. Ray Leimkuehler to Emmett J. Hull, November 12, 1940, Record Group 79, Historic American Building Engineering Record, 1934–1988, Box 5, National Archives, College Park, MD.

143. Historic Natchez Foundation to author, June 11, 2021. Several early Natchez villas such as Concord and Gloucester were once plantation houses.

144. A. Hays Town, "Photographs, Written Historical and Descriptive Data of Hope Villa Farm, Balfour Miller Home," HABS No. MISS-46, HABS MISS 1-Natch V7, Historic American Buildings Survey, Library of Congress, Washington, DC; and Elizabeth P. Reynolds, "Hope Farm National Register of Historic Places Nomination," June 5, 1975.

145. Charles E. Peterson to Mayor, Natchez [William J. Byrne], February 8, 1941, Record Group 79, Historic American Building Engineering Record, 1934–1988, Box 5, National Archives, College Park, MD.

146. Charles E. Peterson to Thomas J. Reed, February 17, 1941, Record Group 79, Historic American Building Engineering Record, 1934–1988, Box 5, National Archives, College Park, MD.

147. Charles Peterson enlisted in the US Navy, and Nichols was drafted into the US Army. In 1942, Noah Webster Overstreet was listed as HABS district officer for Mississippi; he most likely agreed to serve to sustain it if the program was ever brought back, but it was never revived in Mississippi. HABS District Officers Roster, February 24, 1942, Record Group 79, Historic American Building Engineering Record, 1934–1988, Box 5, National Archives, College Park, MD.

148. Holland's committee, now called the Architect's Emergency Committee, published a two-volume portfolio publication titled *Great Georgian Houses of America*. In it, the committee included the Natchez villa Arlington.

149. Thomas J. Waterman to Thomas G. Vint, March 5, 1942, Record Group 79, Historic American Building Engineering Record, 1934–1988, Box 5, National Archives, College Park, MD.

150. Shils, *Tradition*, 58-60.

151. Lindgren, "New Departure in Historic Patriotic Work," 52.

CHAPTER 5: CREATING THE NATCHEZ TRACE PARKWAY

1. Jack D. Elliott Jr., "Paving the Trace," *Journal of Mississippi History*, Fall 2007, 227.

2. There were two versions of "El Camino Real," one running from Mexico to California and the other from Mexico City to Texas, Louisiana, and Mississippi. The latter one is the focus of this part of the chapter.

3. The term "trace" is derived from the Old French word for trail: *tracier*. Bern Keating, "Today Along the Natchez Trace," *National Geographic* 134 (November 1968): 641.

4. Ernie Price, National Park Service, "Natchez Trace," *Mississippi Encyclopedia*, accessed March 28, 2019, https://mississippiencyclopedia.

5. Charles A. Weeks, "Plano de una parte de la Provincia de la Luisiana y de otra de la Florida Occidental y de la Provincia de Texas," unpublished essay, 2016; and Mrs. Lipscomb Norvell, "The Gate-Way Across Texas to Mexico City Combining: A Royal Empire Trail, Natchez Trail, San Antonio Trail, El Camino Real Today—Old San Antonio Road," essay for the US Good Roads Association in Texas, 1933.

6. In 1807, President Thomas Jefferson appointed Meriwether Lewis as governor of the Louisiana Territory, and he settled in St. Louis. He had a mixed record of success and failures during his three-year term, and this may have led to his depression and suicide.

7. Edward Ball, "Retracing Slavery's Trail of Tears: America's Forgotten Migration—The Journey of a Million African-Americans from the Tobacco South to the Cotton South," *Smithsonian Magazine*, November 2015, http://www.smithsonianmag.com/history/slavery-trail-of-tears-180956968.

8. Dawson Phelps, "The Natchez Trace Indian Trail to Parkway," *Tennessee Historical Quarterly* 21, no. 3 (September 1962): 203–5; and Isabel Howell, "John Armfield, Slave Trader," *Tennessee Historical Quarterly* 2, no. 1 (1943): 3–29.

9. In *Commerce of the Prairies*, published in 1844, Josiah Gregg wrote about the Santa Fe Trail. Francis Parkman's *Oregon Trail* was published in 1849. These stories became the basis of the pioneer story in history books for generations of American children, yet no one published anything substantive about the Natchez Trace. Dawson Phelps, "The Administrative History of the Natchez Trace Parkway," unpublished manuscript, 1965, US National Park Service, Tupelo, MS, II-2.

10. Phelps, "Administrative History," II-2.

11. "Marking the Natchez Trace," *Atlanta Constitution*, October 20, 1907.

12. Eron Rowland. "Marking the Natchez Trace," *Publications of the Mississippi Historical Society* 11 (1910): 345–61.

13. Tim Hollis, *Dixie Before Disney: 100 Years of Roadside Fun* (Jackson: University Press of Mississippi, 1999).

14. Hollis, *Dixie Before Disney*, 5–8.

15. Hollis, *Dixie Before Disney*, 5–8; and Elliott, "Paving the Trace," 215–17.

16. None of the articles Jim Walton claimed to have written have ever been located in any archive.

17. Phelps, "Administrative History," III-1; and Elliott, "Paving the Trace," 218. Elliott cited several articles published in the *Webster Progress* by Ned Lee, most notably "Col. Jim Walton Had Hectic Youth." Elliott documents that Walton eventually was admitted to the state home for Confederate veterans at Beauvoir on November 2, 1943, and died on August 30, 1947.

18. Phelps, "Administrative History," III-1.

19. Phelps, "Administrative History," III-1.

20. Thomas J. Busby to Charlotte Capers, October 6, 1950, Mississippi Department of Archives and History, Jackson, MS.

21. Thomas Jefferson Busby lost his congressional seat in 1938 but remained in Washington and practiced law with his son, Jeff Busby, until 1958 when he returned to Houston, Mississippi, and practiced law there until his death in 1964.

22. Phelps, "Administrative History," III-2–3.

23. A military highway or road was a type of road proposed in the early twentieth century in the US as one built by the army for transportation of troops and supplies. The road was intended to be used by soldiers and the general public.

24. *Jackson Clarion Ledger*, January 10, 11, and 12, 1934.

25. Byrnes, "Autobiographical Sketch."

26. Elliott, "Paving the Trace," 226.

27. Phelps, "Administrative History," III-2.

28. Byrnes, "Autobiographical Sketch"; Phelps, "Administrative History," III-4; and Florence Sillers Ogden, "Natchez Trace Was First Only a Dream of the DAR," *Jackson Clarion Ledger*, May 26, 1963.

29. Elliott, "Paving the Trace," 226.

30. Tony Turnbow, the Natchez Trace Association, interview with author, July 2017; Lucille Mayfield to Roane Fleming Byrnes, February 5, 1935, Natchez Trace Parkway Archives, Tupelo, MS; and Elliott, "Paving the Trace," 228.

31. Elliott, "Paving the Trace," 226.

32. Phelps, "Administrative History," III-3.

33. Phelps, "Administrative History," III-3.

34. Ralph L. Landrum to Malcom Gardner, October 10, 1963, Natchez Trace Association Archives, Franklin, TN.

35. Ralph L. Landrum to Malcom Gardner, October 10, 1963; and Ogden, "Natchez Trace."

36. U.S. Congress, S. Rept. 106-332.

37. Phelps, "Administrative History," III-4.

38. The term "highway" refers to a main roadway that connects one municipality to another. The term "parkway" refers to a scenic roadway and landscaped thoroughfare. H.R. 7312, 73rd Congress, 2nd Session, "A Bill to provide for an appropriation of $50,000 with which to make a survey of the Old Indian Trail known as the 'Natchez Trace.'"

39. Timothy M. Davis, "A Pleasant Illusion of Unspoiled Countryside: The American Parkway and the Problematics of an Institutionalized Vernacular," *Perspectives in Vernacular Architecture* 9 (2003): 228.

40. Ethan Carr, *Mission 66: Modernism and the National Park Dilemma* (Amherst: University of Massachusetts Press, 2007), 25, 176.

41. Carr, *Mission 66*, 176.

42. H. S. Evison, "Oral History Interview of Stanley W. Abbott, 1958," 23. U.S. National Park Service, Southern Historical Collection, University of North Carolina University Libraries, Chapel Hill, NC.

43. Davis, "Pleasant Illusion."

44. Davis, "Pleasant Illusion," 237.

45. George Malin Davis Kelly to Ethel Moore Kelly, March 26, 1935.

46. William Thomas, "The Queen of the Natchez Trace," *Mid-South: Memphis Commercial Appeal Magazine*, September 7, 1969, 10.

47. Ralph L. Landrum to Roane Fleming Byrnes, August 4, 1934, Natchez Trace Association Archives, Franklin, TN.

48. Lucille Mayfield to Roane Fleming Byrnes, January 5, 1935, Natchez Trace Parkway Archives, Tupelo, MS.

49. Byron Patton "Pat" Harrison (1881–1941) was one of the most prominent and influential southerners in the US Senate. In 1936, *Time* magazine declared that "better than any living man, Senator Byron Patton Harrison of Mississippi represents in his

spindle-legged, round-shouldered, freckle-faced person the modern history of the Democratic Party." Erudite and witty, he was a skilled orator and was dubbed the "Gadfly of the Senate." A native of Crystal Springs on the Mississippi coast, Harrison had been an accomplished lawyer when he was elected to the US Congress, representing Mississippi's Sixth District in 1911. A loyal Democrat and supporter of President Woodrow Wilson, he succeeded in defeating the infamous white supremacist incumbent senator and former governor James K. Vardaman in 1919. Harrison held the senate seat until his death in 1941. "Vardaman Loses Mississippi Race: Senator Opposed by Wilson Apparently Defeated by Harrison," *Atlanta Constitution*, August 21, 1918.

50. Theodore G. Bilbo to Roane Fleming Byrnes, multiple letters, 1935–1938, Roane Fleming Byrnes Archives, Box 4, University of Mississippi Archives.

51. Theodore Gilmore Bilbo (1877–1947) was one of the most egregious white supremacists and segregationists in American political history. Prior to being a senator, he was Mississippi governor twice, in 1916–1920 and 1927–1932. He defeated Hubert D. Stephens in 1934 for his Senate seat. A flamboyant populist, historians have referred to him as the "prince of rednecks" due to his approach to rally support from poor, rural white Mississippians. Because he tended to refer to himself in the third person, friends and foes alike called him "The Man." Short in statue, he wore bright, flashy suits to draw attention to himself. Always attentive to the letters from his constituents, he often closed his response letters with "COMMAND ME!" instead of "Sincerely." Chester M. Morgan, *Redneck Liberal: Theodore G. Bilbo and the New Deal* (Baton Rouge: Louisiana State University Press, 1985), 28–31.

52. "Mississippi Spurning," *U.S. News & World Report*, September 21, 1996, 120.

53. United States Congress, "Aaron L. Ford," *Biographical Directory of the United States Congress* (Washington, DC: United States Congress, 2013).

54. United States Congress, "Wall Doxey," *Biographical Directory of the United States Congress* (Washington, DC: United States Congress, 2013).

55. Kenneth W. Vickers, "John E. Rankin: Democrat and Demagogue" (Master's thesis, Mississippi State University, 1993).

56. Paul Coburn was renowned for "horse trading" in the Alabama legislature. It was because of his "calling in favors" that the state of Alabama purchased the rights-of-way and easements for the project. Phelps, "Administrative History," IV-4.

57. "P. M. Estes Files," Tennessee State Library, Nashville, TN.

58. Theodore G. Bilbo to C. Ferriday Byrnes, May 9, 1935, Natchez Trace Parkway Archives, Tupelo, MS.

59. Phillip A. Grant, "Congress and the Development of the Natchez Trace Parkway, 1834–1946," in *Parkways: Past, Present, and Future*, ed. International Linear Parks Conference (Boone, NC: Appalachian State University, 1987), 157.

60. Pat Harrison to Roane Fleming Byrnes, December 31, 1934; and Theodore G. Bilbo to Roane Fleming Byrnes, January 15, 1935, Natchez Trace Association Archives, Franklin, TN.

61. John Swain, "The Natchez Trace," *Everybody's Magazine*, September 1905.

62. US House of Representatives, "Survey of Old Indian Trail, Natchez Trace": Report 1442 to Accompany H.R. 731, 73rd Congress, 2nd Session, May 2, 1935.

63. Phelps, "Administrative History," VII-2.

64. Memorandum for the Director, National Park Service (Arno Cammerer), June 11, 1935.

65. Phelps, "Administrative History," V-3.

66. John Nolen (1869–1937) is considered the father of modern landscape architecture and city planning. A native Philadelphian, Nolen was one of the first graduates of the Harvard School of Landscape Architecture and was trained by Frederick Law Olmsted Jr. and Arthur Shurtleff. After graduation, Nolen established a prolific landscape architecture and city planning practice, and he was also a member of the Harvard landscape architecture faculty. Among the city plans that he and his office developed are those for Madison, Wisconsin; San Diego, California; Savannah, Georgia; and Schenectady, New York. He also designed campus master plans for the University of Virginia, University of North Carolina, and College of Worcester in Ohio. Following Olmsted's tradition, he was an avowed naturalist. Parkway design was thus an obvious outlet for his design talent, and he was the conceptual designer for the Blue Ridge Parkway project. The Natchez Trace Parkway was one of his final projects. R. Bruce Stephenson, *John Nolen, Landscape Architect and Planner* (Amherst: University of Massachusetts Press, 2015).

67. $9 million in 2019.

68. Natchez Trace Association Meeting Minutes, Jackson, MS, March 21, 1935; US Department of the Interior, "Regulations and Procedures to Govern the Acquisition of Right-of-Way for National Parkways," February 8, 1935, Natchez Trace Association Archives, Franklin, TN; and Paul Coburn to Roane Fleming Byrnes, March 30, 1935, Natchez Trace Association Archives, Franklin, TN.

69. Prevost, "Roane Fleming Byrnes," 166.

70. Prevost, "Roane Fleming Byrnes," 166.

71. Roane Fleming Byrnes and the Natchez Trace Association, Mississippi Division, "Why the Natchez Trace Parkway Should Be Constructed," November 6, 1935, Natchez Trace Parkway Archives, Tupelo, MS.

72. Byrnes, "Why the Natchez Trace Parkway Should Be Constructed."

73. Byrnes, "Why the Natchez Trace Parkway Should Be Constructed."

74. National Park Service historian Dawson Phelps confirmed that it was Ellicott's Hill in his study of the site in 1952. Historic Natchez Foundation to author, June 11, 2021.

75. Edith Wyatt Moore, "Path of the Natchez Trace in the Country of the Natchez Tribes," 1936, Natchez Trace Parkway Archives, Tupelo, MS. Moore may have located the White Horse Tavern on an 1820 map made upon the death of George Overaker, who owned Hope Farm and the White Horse Tavern at the time of his death. Historic Natchez Foundation to author, June 11, 2021.

76. P. M. Estes to Roane Fleming Byrnes, May 20, 1935, Natchez Trace Association Archives, Franklin, TN.

77. Mississippi Legislature, "Extraordinary Session of the Mississippi Legislature Commencing October 1, 1935, Ending December 7, 1935," Mississippi Department of Archives and History, Jackson, MS.

78. P. M. Estes to Roane Fleming Byrnes, August 17, 1935, Natchez Trace Association Archives, Franklin, TN.

79. Roane Fleming Byrnes, Personal Notes, Roane Fleming Byrnes Papers, Folder 4, University of Mississippi Archives, Oxford, MS.

80. Ralph L. Landrum to Roane Fleming Byrnes, August 3, 1935, Natchez Trace Association Archives, Franklin, TN.

81. P. M. Estes to Roane Fleming Byrnes, March 7, 1936, Roane Fleming Byrnes Papers, Folder 5, University of Mississippi Archives, Oxford, MS.

82. P. M. Estes to Roane Fleming Byrnes, October 22, 1935, Roane Fleming Byrnes Papers, Folder 5, University of Mississippi Archives, Oxford, MS.

83. Dan Cohn to Roane Fleming Byrnes, August 20, 1938, Natchez Trace Association Archives, Franklin, TN. Cohn urged Byrnes to tell the National Park Service to locate the parkway as far as possible from US Highway 80 in Lorman, Mississippi. He worried that it would impact his cotton factory, which was located on the highway.

84. George Parke to Roane Fleming Byrnes, date unknown, Natchez Trace Parkway Archives, Tupelo, MS.

85. Roane Fleming Byrnes to Hugh White, August 30, 1936, Roane Fleming Byrnes Papers, Folder 5, University of Mississippi Archives, Oxford, MS.

86. Roane Fleming Byrnes, "Mississippi Must Have the Natchez Trace Parkway," *Mississippi Highways* 5 (September 1936): 16.

87. Prevost, "Roane Fleming Byrnes," 178–80.

88. Prevost, "Roane Fleming Byrnes," 178–80.

89. In her letter, Byrnes stated the following to the Natchez Trace Association in 1936: "The Natchez Trace Parkway has now reached the most critical point in its development. As of course you know Federal Appropriations for the Parkway, mounting into millions, are waiting to be spent; engineers from the National Park Service and the Bureau of Public Roads are in Mississippi ready to begin construction; Mississippi Highway Engineers have prepared acreage maps for two units of construction, but all business is at a standstill awaiting sufficient funds to buy the Trace rights-of-way which must be furnished by the state of Mississippi." Roane Fleming Byrnes to Hyde R. Jenkins, September 9, 1936, Roane Fleming Byrnes Papers, Folder 4, University of Mississippi Archives, Oxford, MS.

90. Roane Fleming Byrnes to Hyde R. Jenkins, September 9, 1936.

91. "Trace Meeting Great Success," *Jackson Clarion Ledger*, October 18, 1936.

92. "Harrison Introduces Natchez Trace Bill, Delegation Enthused," [Corinth, MS] *Corinthian*, February 7, 1936, Box 20, University of Mississippi Archives, Oxford, MS.

93. P. M. Estes to Roane Fleming Byrnes, January 6, 1937, Roane Fleming Byrnes Papers, Folder 6, University of Mississippi Archives, Oxford, MS.

94. Ethel B. Childress to Roane Fleming Byrnes, February 13, 1937, Roane Fleming Byrnes Papers, Folder 5, University of Mississippi Archives, Oxford, MS.

95. C. L. Watkins to O. F. Goetz, April 9, 1937; C. W. Turner to Gordon Browning, May 24, 1937, Natchez Trace Association Archives, Franklin, TN; and Phelps, "Administrative History," IV-3.

96. Paul Coburn to Roane Fleming Byrnes, July 19, 1937, Natchez Trace Association Archives, Franklin, TN.

97. The *Natchez Democrat* stated: "As leader of the movement which made the fifty-million-dollar Natchez Trace Parkway a reality Mrs. Byrnes inspired the entire state with her enthusiasm. Her tact, charming personality and spirit of unselfishness created harmony in every Trace county and obtained the fullest measure of co-operation from officials, patriotic and civic groups and all united to make the influence of the State Natchez Trace Association far reaching and effective not only in the state legislative halls at Jackson but in the national capital itself." Editorial, "Honor Where Honor Is Due," *Natchez Democrat*, December 30, 1936, Roane Fleming Byrnes Papers, Folder 5, University of Mississippi Archives, Oxford, MS.

98. Roane Fleming Byrnes to Ned Smith, July 29, 1937, Natchez Trace Association Archives, Franklin, TN.

99. George Malin Davis Kelly to Ethel Moore Kelly, July 19, 1937, Historic Natchez Foundation, Natchez, MS.

100. Under Governor White in 1936, Mississippi established a state tourism office that was similar in scope to that of neighboring states and promoted two places as tourist destinations: the Mississippi Gulf Coast and Natchez. The office devised a promotional train caravan called the "Know Mississippi Now Train," in which promotional ambassadors from the state in industry and tourism traveled across the country advocating for Mississippi.

101. Paul Coburn to Roane Fleming Byrnes, July 19, 1937; and Ralph L. Landrum to Roane Fleming Byrnes, July 8, 1937, Natchez Trace Association Archives, Franklin, TN.

102. Theodore G. Bilbo to Ferriday Byrnes, telegram, July 21, 1937, Natchez Trace Association Archives, Franklin, TN.

103. Roane Fleming Byrnes to Ned Smith, July 29, 1937, Natchez Trace Association Archives, Franklin, TN.

104. Roane Fleming Byrnes to Ned Smith, July 29, 1937. Francisco José Múgica (1884–1954) was a leftist leader of the Mexican Revolution of 1917. When Roane Byrnes met him in 1937, she understood that he was the likely successor to Lázaro Cárdenas del Río as president of Mexico. But by 1939, he and Cárdenas had lost favor with the Mexican electorate. After Ávila Camacho became president in 1940, Múgica was banished from national politics and appointed governor of Baja Sur, the most remote and undeveloped place in Mexico. In 1946, he retired from politics and government and died in 1954 in Mexico City. Leon Trotsky (1879–1940) was one of the leaders of the Bolshevik Revolution. In 1929, he was exiled from the Soviet Union and was assassinated in Mexico City in 1940.

105. Roane Fleming Byrnes to Ned Smith, July 29, 1937, Natchez Trace Association Archives, Franklin, TN.

106. Roane Fleming Byrnes to Ned Smith, July 29, 1937.

107. Concepcion de Pogos to Roane Fleming Byrnes, July 24, 1937, Natchez Trace Association Archives, Franklin, TN.

108. Associated Press, "Indians Today Travel Old Trace to Mark Its Rebuilding," September 15, 1937, Natchez Trace Association Archives, Franklin, TN.

109. "Natchez Trace Parkway Construction Formally Launched," *Mississippi Highways* 6 (September 1937): 9.

110. Secretario De Comunicaciones Y Orbas Publicas to Roane Fleming Byrnes, October 21, 1937, Natchez Trace Association Archives, Franklin, TN.

111. Ferriday Byrnes to Theodore G. Bilbo, October 5, 1937, Natchez Trace Parkway Archives, Tupelo, MS; and Theodore G. Bilbo to Ferriday Byrnes, October 12, 1937, Natchez Trace Association Archives, Franklin, TN.

112. Prevost, "Roane Fleming Byrnes," 185.

113. Associated Press, "Indians Today Travel Old Trace."

114. M. O. Allen to O. F. Goetz, Department of Highways and Public Works, April 9, 1937, Tennessee State Library and Archives, Nashville, TN.

115. Ethel B. Childress to Roane Fleming Byrnes, April 20, 1937, Natchez Trace Parkway Archives, Tupelo, MS.

116. P. M. Estes to Roane Fleming Byrnes, October 21, 1937, Natchez Trace Association Archives, Franklin, TN.

117. "Road Work Starts on Natchez Trace," *Atlanta Constitution*, October 29, 1937.

118. US Congress, Senate Report 112–106, US Senate, 112th Congress, Washington, DC.

119. Ralph L. Landrum to Roane Fleming Byrnes, October 7, 1938, Natchez Trace Association Archives, Franklin, TN.

120. Roane Fleming Byrnes, "Trace Will Be Part of Road to Old Mexico," *Clarksdale Register,* December 12, 1937, Roane Fleming Byrnes Papers, Folder 5, University of Mississippi Archives, Oxford, MS.

121. Phelps, "Administrative History," VI-3.

122. Phelps, "Administrative History," VI-2.

123. Francois Mignon, "Windy Hill Manor Is a Forgotten Plantation," *Shreveport Times,* February 16, 1975, 106.

124. In 1928, Calvin Coolidge transferred the Meriwether Lewis Gravesite from the War Department to the National Park Service. The Natchez Trace Parkway planners veered the parkway approximately ten miles from its original configuration to include the site in the parkway. The Civilian Conservation Corps reconstructed the Grinder's Stand cabin, where Lewis apparently committed suicide.

125. Elizabeth Brandon Stanton to Roane Fleming Byrnes, November 21, 1936, Roane Fleming Byrnes Papers, Folder 5, University of Mississippi Archives, Oxford, MS; Catherine Van Court, *In Old Natchez* (Garden City, NJ: Doubleday, 1937), 33–35; James B. Lloyd, "Stanton, Elizabeth Brandon," *Lives of Mississippi Authors, 1817–1967* (Jackson: University Press of Mississippi, 1981), 420; and François Mignon, "Windy Hill Is Forgotten Plantation," [Shreveport, Louisiana] *The Times,* February 16, 1975. Mignon said that shortly after Elizabeth and Maude died, oil was discovered on the eroding fields of Windy Hill Manor.

126. Davis, "Pleasant Illusion of Unspoiled Countryside," 228–29.

127. Elliott, "Paving the Trace," 200.

128. Quoted in Meringlo, *Museums, Monuments, and National Parks*, 113.

129. Phelps, "Administrative History," VI-4.

130. Carr, *Mission 66*, 12–27.

CHAPTER 6: FEUDING AND BRANDING

1. Katherine Miller inscribed this note in a copy of *Natchez of Long Ago and the Pilgrimage* to Julia Johnson Eggleston, wife of Joseph Dupuy Eggleston II, president of Hampden-Sydney College from 1919 to 1939.

2. India Moffett, "Natchez—City That Still Is Living in Past," *Chicago Daily Tribune*, March 10, 1940.

3. George Malin Davis Kelly to Ethel Moore Kelly, October 8, 1935.

4. Shils, *Tradition*, 75; and Davis et al., *Deep South*, 71.

5. Natchez Garden Club Files, Mississippi Department of Archives and History, Jackson, MS. Minutes from the joint session held by the Natchez Garden Club and the Pilgrimage Garden Club, November 16, 1936, Natchez Garden Club Papers, Mississippi Department of Archives and History, Jackson, MS.

6. "An Interview with Mrs. Agnes Marshall Gardner," by Elliot Timble, August 10, 1981, Mississippi Department of Archives and History, Jackson, MS: 3.

7. Harriet Dixon to the City of Natchez, July 14, 1936, Natchez Garden Club Papers, Mississippi Department of Archives and History, Jackson, MS.

8. James B. Snider to Harriet Dixon, September 28, 1936, Natchez Garden Club Papers, Mississippi Department of Archives and History, Jackson, MS.

9. Ed Lipscomb to Harriet Dixon, October 8, 1936, Natchez Garden Club Papers, Mississippi Department of Archives and History, Jackson, MS.

10. Katherine Grafton Miller to the Natchez Garden Club, November 5, 1936, Natchez Garden Club Papers, Mississippi Department of Archives and History, Jackson, MS.

11. Ed Lipscomb to Katherine Grafton Miller, December 7, 1936, Natchez Garden Club Papers, Mississippi Department of Archives and History, Jackson, MS.

12. $273,000 in 2019.

13. Harriet Dixon to Ernest Smith, December 7, 1936, Natchez Garden Club Papers, Mississippi Department of Archives and History, Jackson, MS.

14. Charles F. Engle to James B. (Billy) Snider, December 21, 1936, Natchez Garden Club Papers, Mississippi Department of Archives and History, Jackson, MS.

15. The names in parenthesis refer to the families that owned the villas listed. Natchez Garden Club Papers, Mississippi Department of Archives and History, Jackson, MS.

16. Harriet Dixon to Ernest Smith, December 7, 1936.

17. $488,000 in 2019.

18. Falck, "Garden Club Women of Natchez," 130–40.

19. Miller, *Natchez of Long Ago*, 55. Paul Schweizer noted how Miller purchased a reproduction of Thomas Cole's "The Voyage of Life" and featured the four paintings in Stanton Hall. She had purchased them from an estate sale of a historic house in nearby Port Gibson, Mississippi. Schweizer, "Thomas Cole's 'The Voyage of Life' and Stanton Hall," paper given at the Natchez Antique Forum, Pilgrimage Garden Club, Natchez, MS, November 2, 2017.

20. Kate Brandon stated the following in a letter to Annie Barnum: "We most sincerely wish in assuring you that it is our earnest wish to reach a harmonious working basis for the Pilgrimage in Natchez. We are sure many of you have the same wish and hope a plan may evolve which will be acceptable to all concerned." Kate Brandon to Annie Barnum, July 2, 1937, Natchez Garden Club Papers, Mississippi Department of Archives and History, Jackson, MS.

21. Norma Lee Browning, "Quaint Old Natchez: Pre-Civil War Glories Live Again Thru Woman's Dreams," *Chicago Daily Tribune*, March 4, 1951.

22. Ralph McGill, "One Word More: 'There was a Land—,'" *Atlanta Constitution*, December 29, 1939.

23. Sally Forth, "SALLY FORTH Says: Rival Clubs in Natchez Claim Origin of Pilgrimage," *Atlanta Constitution*, March 7, 1940.

24. August Loeb, "Natchez Trips Begin: Cities Along the Mississippi and the Gulf Open Homes and Gardens to 'Pilgrims,'" *New York Times*, February 25, 1940.

25. "To Continue Tours," *Natchez Democrat*, March 21, 1941, Natchez Garden Club Papers, Mississippi Department of Archives and History, Jackson, MS; and "More Fights Mean Better Pilgrimages for Natchez," *Jackson Clarion Ledger*, Harriet Dixon's Scrapbook, Natchez Garden Club Papers, Mississippi Department of Archives and History, Jackson, MS.

26. "Judge Anderson Rescinds Order to Close Pilgrimage Garden Club," *Natchez Democrat*, March 27, 1941, Harriet Dixon's Scrapbook, Natchez Garden Club Papers, Mississippi Department of Archives and History, Jackson, MS.

27. "Text of Application for Injunction: Natchez Garden Club vs. Pilgrimage Garden Club, State of Mississippi, County of Adams," *Natchez Democrat*, March 27, 1941, Harriet Dixon's Scrapbook, Natchez Garden Club Papers, Mississippi Department of Archives and History, Jackson, MS.

28. "Natchez Club Defies Court, Extends Tour," *Jackson Daily News*, March 28, 1941, Harriet Dixon's Scrapbook, Natchez Garden Club Papers, Mississippi Department of Archives and History, Jackson, MS.

29. Harnett T. Kane, *Natchez on the Mississippi* (New York: Bonanza Books, 1947), 346–47.

30. "Mississippi: Civil War in Natchez," *Time*, April 7, 1941.

31. "Fiddle-dee-dee—Natchez Ladies Fighting Over Tourist Trade," *Atlanta Constitution*, March 26, 1941, Harriet Dixon's Scrapbook, Natchez Garden Club Papers, Mississippi Department of Archives and History, Jackson, MS.

32. Individual Announcements, *Natchez Democrat*, March 30, 1941, Lacey Hale's Scrapbook, Natchez Garden Club Papers, Mississippi Department of Archives and History, Jackson, MS. This statement was placed at the bottom of all the advertisements to tour the Homeowner's Association homes.

33. "'Hoop-Skirt War' Claims in Natchez Court," *Times-Picayune*, August 13, 1941, Lacey Hale's Scrapbook, Natchez Garden Club Papers, Mississippi Department of Archives and History, Jackson, MS.

34. In his closing remarks, Cutrer addressed both clubs: "forget your difference and settle this matter in a friendly manner, because I fear that if you do not work out some plan by which both can carry on peacefully and satisfactory you are going to eventually kill both, as the public will not care to take part in your family quarrel." "Chancellor Gives Ruling in Case of Garden Clubs," *Natchez Democrat*, Lacey Hale's Scrapbook, Natchez Garden Club Papers, Mississippi Department of Archives and History, Jackson, MS.

35. "Natchez's Rival Groups Put Tour Dates Together," *Chicago Daily Tribune*, March 4, 1942.

36. In her notes, Roane Fleming Byrnes listed the celebrities that she entertained at Ravennaside: Henry Ford (who she noted in her list that she compiled later was already dead), World War II Admiral Aaron Merrill, Ford Foundation chairman Rowan Galther, Guggenheim Foundation chairman Henry Moc, Putnam publisher Herbert Bolch, and the Australian ambassador to the US though neither she nor Katherine Miller could remember her name. Roane Fleming Byrnes, "People That Visited Ravennaside," Roane Fleming Byrnes Papers, Folder 5, University of Mississippi Archives, Oxford, MS.

37. "Interview with Mrs. Alma (Mrs. Joseph) Kellogg," by Elliot Timble, August 15, 1981, 6.

38. "Interview with Mrs. Rebecca Fauntleroy Benoist," by Graham Hicks, 8.

39. Eleanor Roosevelt, "My Day by Eleanor Roosevelt," March 8, 1939, United Press Syndicate.

40. "Interview with Mrs. Rebecca Fauntleroy Benoist," by Graham Hicks, 8.

41. Prevost, "Roane Fleming Byrnes," 13.

42. Stark Young, *So Red the Rose* (New York: Scribner's, 1934), 235.

43. Young, *So Red the Rose*, 232.

44. Cox, "Revisiting the Natchez Pilgrimage," 367.

45. Robert M. Coates was the art critic for the *New York Times* and the writer who later coined the term "abstract expressionism."

46. Robert M. Coates, *The Outlaw Years: The History of the Land Pirates of the Natchez Trace* (New York: The Macaulay Co, 1930); and Greta Wagle, "Robert M. Coates," in *The Continuum Encyclopedia of American Literature*, ed. Alfred Bendizen (London: Continuum Publishing, 2003), 203.

47. Lisa Newman, "'The Outlaw Years' by Robert M. Coates a Riveting Read," *Jackson Clarion Ledger*, August 30, 2014.

48. Eudora Welty, *The Robber Bridegroom* (New York: Doubleday, 1942).

49. Lillie Vidal Boatner to William A. Tomilson, December 28, 1936, Natchez Garden Club Papers, Mississippi Department of Archives and History, Jackson, MS.

50. "Natchez Rose Jar" was inspired by a poetry book, *The Rose Jar* by Thomas S. Jones Jr. (Portland, ME: Thomas Bird Mosher, 1909).

51. Cox, "Revisiting the Natchez Pilgrimage," 367.

52. Karen L. Cox, *Dreaming of Dixie* (Chapel Hill: University of North Carolina Press, 2011), 155–57.

53. Elizabeth McRae Boykin, "Pleasant Homes: Southern Accent in Home Decorations," *Atlanta Constitution*, April 16, 1937.

54. "Slippy Magee Is Story That Could Have Happened Here," *Natchez Democrat*, June 19, 1921; and George M. Moreland, "Ramblings in Mississippi," *Memphis Commercial Appeal*, January 18, 1925.

55. Thomas Mires to Roane Fleming Byrnes, April 12, 1938, Natchez Trace Association Archives, Franklin, TN.

56. "FitzPatrick Traveltalks" and "Voice of the Globe" were eight-minute films shown before feature movies in theaters across the country and abroad.

57. "Old Natchez on the Mississippi (1939)," IMDB, last modified 2019, http://www.imdb.com/title/tt0164796/.

58. "Natchez Pilgrimage, 1939," Shantybellum Blogspot, last modified 2019, http://shantybellum.blogspot.com/2010/03/natchez-pilgrimage-1939.html.

59. Marjorie Taylor to David O. Selznick, February 28, 1938, David O. Selznick Archives, Harry Ransom Center, University of Texas, Austin, TX.

60. Lillie Vidal Boatner, "27th Birthday of the Natchez Garden Club," Natchez Garden Club Papers, Mississippi Department of Archives and History, Jackson, MS.

61. Darden Pyron, *Southern Daughter* (New York: Harper Perennial, 1992), 479. Liberty Hall was the home of Alexander Stephens, who was vice president of the Confederate States of America. It is located in Crawfordville, Georgia. Built in 1834, it is a large wood frame house with a one-story porch that runs across the front. Greek Revival in its overall design, it is more utilitarian in appearance than ornate.

62. Wilbur J. Kurtz to Mrs. A. B. Smith, May 14, 1937, Wilbur Kurtz Collection, Atlanta History Center, Atlanta, GA.

63. Atlanta History Center, "Wilbur G. Kurtz." Kurtz spent the next fifty-five years of his life as an illustrator and an amateur historian of the South and Atlanta. He painted numerous murals for courthouses; southern history inspired his paintings. He met Margaret Mitchell through her father, who was involved with him in the founding of the Atlanta Historical Society. Along with *Gone with the Wind*, he was also the technical advisor for historical accuracy for Walt Disney's *Song of the South* (1946) and *The Great Locomotive Chase* (1956), which was based on the Andrews Raid. Wilbur G. Kurtz, Sr. Obituary.

64. Wilbur G. Kurtz to Barbara Keon, Inter-Office Communication, Subject: "Remarks on critical articles published by the Society of Correct Civil War Information," December 19, 1938, David O. Selznick Archives, Harry Ransom Center, University of Texas, Austin, TX.

65. Wilbur G. Kurtz to Barbara Keon, 2.

66. Wilbur G. Kurtz, "The Southern Girls Song," 1938, David O. Selznick Archives, Harry Ransom Center, University of Texas, Austin, TX.

67. Margaret Mitchell, *Gone with the Wind* (New York: Macmillan Publishing Co., 1936), 46.

68. In 1934, Joseph B. Platt was considered one of the leading industrial designers in the US. He had been the style director for Marshall Field's department store in Chicago and designed the iconic Parker arrowhead clip fountain pen. Platt had a reputation

for arrogance, and he proposed doing most of his consulting from New York. Selznick refused that proposal and instructed him that his contract would be for four weeks at $200 per week ($3,500 in 2019).

69. David O. Selznick to Mrs. James Barrett, December 31, 1938, David O. Selznick Archives, Harry Ransom Center, University of Texas, Austin, TX; and Carroll M. Gentz, *Design Chronicles: Significant Mass-Produced Designs of the 20th Century* (Atglen, PA: Schiffer Publishing, 2005).

70. "Mississippi File," 1938, David O. Selznick Archives, Harry Ransom Center, University of Texas, Austin, TX.

71. "Mississippi File," 1938.

72. "Tara" File, 1938, David O. Selznick Archives, Harry Ransom Center, University of Texas, Austin, TX.

73. MDAH Database, "Bellmont," accessed June 2, 2019.

74. Historic Natchez Foundation to author, June 11, 2021. Louis Fry acquired Bellmont in 1923. After his death, it was left to his wife and daughter. The house fell into disrepair, and by the early 1970s, the eastern side wall had collapsed. Louis Fry's grandson acquired the house and restored it.

75. Oliver, *Natchez*, 20.

76. Lyle R. Wheeler (1905–90) studied architecture at the University of Southern California; he worked for several architectural offices in Los Angeles and eventually joined Hollywood studios and designed movie sets. He had just started his set design career when Selznick hired him for *Gone with the Wind*. Burt A. Folkart, "Lyle Wheeler, Who Won 5 Oscars for Art Direction, Dies at 84," *Los Angeles Times*, January 12, 1990.

77. William C. Menzies (1896–1957) became famous for directing the "burning of Atlanta" scene in the movie and had experience designing film sets for period movies. Selznick hired him after seeing his work in *The Adventures of Tom Sawyer*. James Curtis, *William Cameron Menzies: The Shape of Films to Come* (New York: Pantheon Books, 2015), 182–87.

78. Lillian K. Deighton to American Library Services, December 30, 1938, David O. Selznick Archives, Harry Ransom Center, University of Texas, Austin, TX; and Annie L. Fuller Kurtz to Mr. John Davidson, January 6, 1939, David O. Selznick Archives, Harry Ransom Center, University of Texas, Austin, TX.

79. Mr. Lambert to Bill Menzies, "Inter-Office Communication," December 27, 1938; and Lyle H. Wheeler to Superintendent of Documents, Government Printing Office, December 28, 1938, David O. Selznick Archives, Harry Ransom Center, University of Texas, Austin, TX.

80. See Figure 3.32.

81. The Aaron Burr Oak at Jefferson College was where Aaron Burr was first tried for treason in 1807.

82. Mr. J. H. Whitney to Miss Katherine Brown, October 23, 1939, David O. Selznick Archives, Harry Ransom Center, University of Texas, Austin, TX.

83. Davis et al., *Deep South*, 155–200.

84. Maurice Robert Stein, *The Eclipse of Community: An Interpretation of American Studies* (Princeton, NJ: Princeton University Press, 1960), 153–74 and William R. Ferris and John Dollard, "John Dollard: Caste and Class Revisited," *Southern Cultures* 10, no. 2 (Summer 2004): 7–18.

85. Frances "Fannie" Benjamin Johnston (1864–1952) is considered one of the first professional female photographers in the US. Over her fifty-year career, she photographed political and social leaders and news events, but she became renowned for her

architectural photography. Born into a wealthy family, she grew up in Washington, DC, and was interested in fine arts. She studied art at the Académie Julian in Paris and the Washington Art Students' League (now the Corcoran Art School). She became interested in becoming a photographer and opened her photography studio in Washington in 1896. Initially, she worked as a photojournalist; by 1913, she dedicated her career to architectural photography. Elizabeth M. Gushee, "Travels Through the Old South: Frances Benjamin Johnston and the Vernacular Architecture of Virginia," *Art Documentation: The Journal of the Art Libraries Society of North America* 27, no. 1 (Spring 2008): 18–23.

86. Walker Evans (1903–75) was a photographer and photojournalist. Born in St. Louis and educated in the East, he dropped out of Williams College and became part of New York's art scene and then spent a year in Paris. He became interested in architectural photography after producing a photo series of Victorian houses in Boston. While working for the FSA precursor agency, the Resettlement Administration, in 1936, Evans produced the photographs for James Agee's groundbreaking book, *Let Us Now Praise Famous Men*. Belinda Rathbone, *Walker Evans: A Biography* (New York: Houghton Mifflin Co., 1995), 11–23.

87. Ben Shahn (1898–1970) was a painter and artist who experimented with photography. Shahn was a Jewish Lithuanian, who immigrated to New York in 1906 with his family. In 1935, he was recommended by friend and former roommate Walker Evans to join with him and Dorothea Lange and photograph the American South. David R. Conrad, "Ben Shahn as Aesthetic Educator," *Journal of Aesthetic Education* 15, no. 2 (1981): 74–80.

88. William R. Ferris, "Walker Evans, 1974," *Southern Cultures* 13, no. 2 (Summer 2007): 49. In his interview with Evans, Ferris remarked that his father bought cows from the Lum Brothers Livestock Barn in Natchez, which Evans and Shahn photographed for the FSA. (See Figure 6.40.)

89. Lum Brothers was demolished, and the Natchez Convention Center was built at its location on Main Street.

90. Jennifer L. Aaker, "The Malleable Self: The Role of Self Expression in Persuasion," *Journal of Marketing Research* 36, no. 1 (1999): 46.

91. Hollis, *Dixie Before Disney*, 23–66.

92. Jefferson Davis Dickson Jr. (1896–1943) was a native Natchezian and an internationally renowned sports promoter. During World War I, he served in the US Army Signal Corps; after the war, he remained in France and developed a successful sports promotion company in boxing, wrestling, and ice hockey. During the 1920s, he built and operated Paris's Palais des Sports, which was highly successful. His Fort Rosalie tourist attraction never was as popular as he had hoped it would be and fell into disrepair. It was demolished in the 1950s. Historical Architecture, Cultural Resources Division, Southeast Regional Office, "Natchez National Historical Park, Old Fort Rosalie Gift Shop, Historic Structure Report," US National Park Service, June 2006. Dickson also built a lavish interpretive center at the White Apple Village mound south of Mammy's Cupboard on Highway 61 South and attempted to create a lesser tourism site on Cemetery Road. Historic Natchez Foundation to author, June 11, 2021.

93. Roadside America, "Mammy's Cupboard," accessed June 7, 2019, https://www.roadsideamerica.com/story/3344; Preservation in Mississippi, "Mammy's Cupboard," accessed June 7, 2019, https://misspreservation.com/101-mississippi-places-to-see-before-you-die/mammys-cupboard-adams-county/; and MDAH Database, "Robert Edgar Bost," accessed June 7, 2019, https://www.apps.mdah.ms.gov/Public/rpt.aspx?rpt=artisanSearch&Name=Bost&City=Natchez&Role=Any.

94. "Interview with Mrs. Ruth Audley Britton Wheeler Beltzhoover," 7.

CHAPTER 7: AFTERMATH

1. "Anti-Lynching Bill Is Passed by House," *New York Times*, January 11, 1940.

2. Ronald Miller, "Historic Preservation in Natchez, Mississippi," *Antiques* 111 (March 1977): 539.

3. Roane Fleming Byrnes, Personal Notes, Roane Fleming Byrnes Papers, Folder 4, University of Mississippi Archives, Oxford, MS.

4. Kermit Holt, "Antebellum Natchez: Colorful City Is a Museum Not Only of the Old South But of Early U.S. History," *Chicago Tribune*, August 31, 1980.

5. $4.4 million in 2019.

6. Horace Sutton, "A Traveler's Diary: Garden Clubs Fight the Battle of Natchez, Call on U. (All) N. to Negotiate a Peace," *Los Angeles Times*, January 26, 1958.

7. Marguerite Lyon, "Fresh from the Hills. . . . Natchez," *Chicago Daily Tribune*, May 18, 1947.

8. Hammer, *Natchez' First Ladies*, 5–7.

9. "Pilgrimages to Start Soon in Mississippi," *Chicago Sunday Tribune*, February 1, 1959.

10. Struthers Burt, *Ladies' Home Journal*, January 1947, 134.

11. "Interview with Mrs. Ruth Audley Britton Wheeler Beltzhoover," 10.

12. "Interview with Mrs. Alma (Mrs. Joseph) Kellogg," 6; and Lindsey Shelton, "Spring Reigns: Queens Remember Past Spring Pilgrimages," *Natchez Democrat*, April 8, 2014.

13. Burt, *Ladies' Home Journal*, 134–36.

14. Burt, *Ladies' Home Journal*, 131.

15. Daphne Spain, *Constructive Feminism: Women's Spaces and Women's Rights in the American City* (Ithaca, NY: Cornell University Press, 2016), 33.

16. Burt, *Ladies' Home Journal*, 160.

17. C. Faye Bennett, "Natchez—Pilgrimage to Yesterday," *The Lufkin Line* 27, no. 1 (January-February 1952): 6.

18. Ralph L. Landrum to Roane Fleming Byrnes, May 13, 1942, Natchez Trace Association Archives, Franklin, TN.

19. Ralph L. Landrum to Roane Fleming Byrnes, October 5, 1944, Natchez Trace Association Archives, Franklin, TN.

20. Ralph L. Landrum to Roane Fleming Byrnes, November 17, 1947, Natchez Trace Association Archives, Franklin, TN.

21. "Resume Work on Natchez Trace Parkway," *Natchez Democrat*, September 7, 1947.

22. Prevost, "Roane Fleming Byrnes," 190.

23. Ralph L. Landrum to Roane Fleming Byrnes, June 13, 1949; and Hillary A. Tolson to Walter Spiva, October 25, 1949, Natchez Trace Association Archives, Franklin, TN.

24. Thomas G. Abernathy to Roane Fleming Byrnes, May 11, 1965, Roane Fleming Byrnes Papers, Folder 8, University of Mississippi Archives, Oxford, MS.

25. Hillary A. Tolson to Thomas G. Abernathy, June 17, 1949, Natchez Trace Association Archives, Franklin, TN.

26. Roane Fleming Byrnes Papers, Folder 8, University of Mississippi Archives, Oxford, MS.

27. Prevost, "Roane Fleming Byrnes," 192.

28. Thomas G. Abernathy to Ralph L. Landrum, June 22, 1949, Natchez Trace Association Archives, Franklin, TN.

29. Thomas G. Abernathy to Roane Fleming Byrnes, May 11, 1965, Roane Fleming Byrnes Papers, Folder 8, University of Mississippi Archives, Oxford, MS.

30. Prevost, "Roane Fleming Byrnes," 194.

31. Carr, *Mission 66*, 47–55.

32. John Stennis to Roane Fleming Byrnes, January 15, 1966, Telegram, Natchez Trace Association Archives, Franklin, TN.

33. Clifford J. Harriman (Acting Natchez Trace Parkway Superintendent) to Roane Fleming Byrnes, May 15, 1956, Natchez Trace Association Archives, Franklin, TN.

34. Natchez Trace Association, "Resolution in Memory of C. Ferriday Byrnes," November 15, 1956, Natchez Trace Association Archives, Franklin, TN.

35. Keating, "Today Along the Natchez Trace," 646.

36. Keating, "Today Along the Natchez Trace," 646.

37. Sutton, "Traveler's Diary."

38. Bern Keating, "Nostalgia in Natchez," *Washington Post*, November 10, 1985.

39. Edith Wyatt Moore, *Natchez Under-the-Hill* (Natchez, MS: Southern Historical Publications, 1958).

40. Edith Wyatt Moore, "Fondly I Roam: Stories of Natchez Homes," *Natchez Times*, January 8, 1950, Roane Fleming Byrnes Papers, Folder 8, University of Mississippi Archives, Oxford, MS.

41. Thomas H. Radigan to Roane Fleming Byrnes, March 25, 1950; and Edith Wyatt Moore, "Historic House to be Restored by Garden Club," *Natchez Times*, April 30, 1950, Roane Fleming Byrnes Papers, Folder 8, University of Mississippi Archives, Oxford, MS.

42. Roane Fleming Byrnes, "Garden Club Purchases Father Lennan's House," *Over the Garden Wall*, September 1950, 5.

43. Byrnes, "Garden Club Purchases."

44. "Bishop Gerow Here for Service Sunday Father Lennan's Home," *Natchez Times*, September 22, 1950, Roane Fleming Byrnes Papers, Folder 8, University of Mississippi Archives, Oxford, MS.

45. After serving in the US Navy during World War II, Charles Peterson returned to the National Park Service and the Jefferson National Expansion Memorial in St. Louis. He became one of the leading historic architects for the NPS, and he began compiling articles in numerous journals about the early architecture of St. Louis, most of the buildings he had documented prior to demolition. Frances Krauskopf, "Reviewed Work: *Colonial St. Louis: Building a Creole Capital* by Charles E. Peterson," *Indiana Magazine of History* 46, no. 2 (June 1950): 216; and Floyd A. McNeil, "Reviewed Work: *Colonial St. Louis: Building a Creole Capital* by Charles E. Peterson," *Mississippi Valley Historical Review* 36, no. 4 (March 1950): 700.

46. Charles E. Peterson, "Notes on Natchez," *Journal of the Society of Architectural Historians* 14, no. 1 (March 1955): 30.

47. In a 1974 HABS project, HABS historian Marion Schiefer deduced that "Selma Plantation" was built in 1805 by Gerard Brandon I. In 1989, Jack D. Elliott confirmed that it was built in 1811 by Brandon. Marion Schiefer, "Photographs, Written Historical and Descriptive Data, Selma, U.S. Highway North 61, Washington vicinity, Adams County, Mississippi," HABS No. MS-198; and Jack D. Elliott Jr., "Selma Plantation House," January 5, 1989, National Register of Historic Places Nomination.

48. Peterson, "Notes on Natchez," 31.

49. Charles E. Peterson to Roane Fleming Byrnes, February 27, 1957; and Henry A. Judd to Roane Fleming Byrnes, May 20, 1957, Roane Fleming Byrnes Papers, Folder 8, University of Mississippi Archives, Oxford, MS.

50. Peterson, "Notes on Natchez," 31.

51. George Malin Davis Kelly to Ethel Moore Kelly, October 23, 1935; and Mary McCahon Shoemaker, Samuel Wilson Jr., and Mary W. Miller, "Henderson-Britton Home, Magnolia Hall," National Register of Historic Places Nomination, February 21, 1978.

52. Judy Klemesrud, "Natchez, Where, They Say, the Old South Still Lives," *New York Times*, March 29, 1970.

53. Encyclopedia Britannica, "New Journalism: American Literary Movement," accessed June 18, 2019, https://www.britannica.com/topic/New-Journalism.

54. Blair Sabol, "A Yankee Pilgrim in the Old South," *New York Times*, April 24, 1977.

55. Sabol, "Yankee Pilgrim."

56. Klemesrud, "Natchez."

57. Julia Cass, "The Old South Comes Alive During the Natchez Pilgrimage," *Boston Globe*, March 27, 1983.

58. Carl A. Ray, "King's Tavern National Register of Historic Places Nomination," April 1, 1971; and Patricia Heintzelman, "Longwood National Register of Historic Places Nomination," May 30, 1975.

59. Ben Hillyer, "Burns Named New Historic Natchez Foundation Director," April 18, 2018, https://www.natchezdemocrat.com/2018/04/18/burns-named-hnf-director/.

60. Jordan Bartel, "Downton Abbey Recap: Open House, Open Wounds," *Baltimore Sun*, February 7, 2016, https://www.baltimoresun.com/entertainment/tv/bal-downton-abbey-recap-open-house-open-wounds-20160207-story.html.

61. Klemesrud, "Natchez."

62. Shils, *Tradition*.

63. Michael Fazio, "Architectural Preservation in Natchez, Mississippi: 'A Conception of Time and Place,'" *Southern Quarterly* 19, no. 1 (Fall 1980): 138–39.

64. Fazio, "Architectural Preservation," 141.

65. George Malin Davis Kelly to Ethel Moore Kelly, April 1, 1935.

66. James N. Gregory, *The Southern Diaspora: How the Great Migrations of Black and White Southerners Transformed America* (Chapel Hill: University of North Carolina Press, 2005).

67. In the 1960s, sociologist John McKnight invented the term "redlining" to describe banks' discriminatory practices against African Americans' investment in real estate. Yves Zenou and Nicolas Boccard, "Racial Discrimination and Redlining in Cities," *Journal of Urban Economics* 48, no. 2 (September 2000): 260–85.

68. Gregory, *Southern Diaspora*.

69. Al Burt, "In Natchez the Old South Lives," *Boston Globe*, January 18, 1976.

70. The Chicago-based architectural firm Rapp and Rapp designed the Orpheum Theater in Champaign, Illinois, in 1914, based on their measured drawings of the Opera House at Versailles.

71. Sachs, *Life and Work of the Twentieth-Century Louisiana Architect A. Hays Town*, 47.

72. Henry-Russell Hitchcock and Turpin C. Bannister, "Summary of the Round Table on the Preservation of Historical Architectural Monuments, Held Tuesday, March 18, 1941, in the Library of Congress, Washington, D.C.," *Journal of the American Society of Architectural Historians* 1, no. 2 (April 1941): 21–24.

73. Charles Peterson also photographed the James Anderson House and labeled it as 311–13 Market Street (Parish House), Natchez, Adams County, MS in 1938. HABS MISS, 1-NATCH, 7-3, Library of Congress Prints and Photographs Division, Washington, DC.

74. The architect of the President's Home at the University of Alabama was incorrectly identified as Thomas Nicholls of Philadelphia, who did not exist. Then it was incorrectly revised to state that William Nichols was credited for its design. Michael Berry was the architect of this building. The history of the building was provided to the HABS team by the National League of American Pen Women. This erroneous record is another example of the discrepancies that remain in HABS. HABS ALA-207, Historic American Buildings Survey, Washington, DC.

75. Price, "Drawing Details," 55.

76. Marguerite Lyon, "Fresh from the Hills . . . Natchez," *Chicago Daily Tribune*, May 18, 1947.

77. MDAH Database, "William H. Braden Elementary School," accessed June 20, 2019, https://www.apps.mdah.ms.gov/Public/prop.aspx?id=2134&view=facts&y=812.

78. Horace Sutton, "Of All Places: The War Between Women and Women," *New York Herald Tribune*, January 26, 1958.

79. Richard Longstreth, "David Lowenthal—An Appreciation," *Preservation Education and Research* 11, no. 1 (November 2019).

80. Suzi Parker, "In Mississippi, Glorifying the Old South No Longer Pays the Bills," *Al Jazeera America*, April 5, 2014, http://america.aljazeera.com/articles/2014/4/5/natchez-antebellumplantation.html.

81. John Ruskin had a contradictory view of suburbia. Initially, he promoted the idea of free-standing villas built in the English countryside; but later, he disavowed suburban living. Sarah Bliston, *The Promise of the Suburbs: A Victorian History in Literature and Culture* (New Haven, CT: Yale University Press, 2019), 79–80.

82. Fazio, "Architectural Preservation," 144–46; and Michael Fazio, "Interpreting Southern Antebellum Architecture in the 1990s," *Journal of Architectural Education* 44, no. 4: 225–34.

SELECTED BIBLIOGRAPHY

ARCHIVAL MATERIAL

Adams County Courthouse, Judge George W. Armstrong Library, Natchez, Mississippi.
    Miller Family Files.
Athenaeum of Philadelphia, Philadelphia, Pennsylvania.
    Philadelphia Architects and Buildings Archive.
Duke University, Perkins Library, Durham, North Carolina.
    Kate D. Foster Diary, Foster Family Papers, 1930–2013.
    Scott, Anne Firor. Papers, 1963–2002.
    Sydnor, Charles S. Papers, 1923–1954.
Hampden-Sydney College, Special Collections Library, Walter M. Bortz III Library, Hampden-Sydney, Virginia.
    Rare Books Library.
Historic Natchez Foundation, Natchez, Mississippi.
    Carpenter, Alma. Papers.
    Kelly, George Malin Davis. Papers.
    Katherine Grafton Miller Scrapbook.
Historic New Orleans Collection.
Library of Congress, Washington, DC.
    Farm Security Administration/Office of War Information Photography Archives.
        Walker Evans Archival Collection.
        Ben Shahn Archival Collection.
    Harris and Ewing Photograph Collection.
    Historic American Buildings Survey: Mississippi.
    Historic American Buildings Survey: Alabama.
    Historic American Buildings Survey: Tennessee.
    Historic American Buildings Survey: Louisiana.
    Historic American Buildings Survey: Virginia.
    Johnston, Frances Benjamin. Photograph Collection.
    National Park Service Office Records.
    United States Congress Committee on Roads Papers.
    United States Congress, *Journal of the House of Representatives of the United States.*
Louisiana State University, Hill Memorial Library, Baton Rouge, Louisiana.
    Norman Photography Archive.
    Thomas and Joan Gandy Photography Collection.
Mississippi Department of Archives and History, Jackson, Mississippi.
    Bell, Robert W., Jr. Papers, 1936–1986.
    Brandon, Gerard. Papers.
    MDAH Historic Resources Database.

Mississippi American Institute of Architects Papers.
Mississippi Legislature Papers.
Natchez Garden Club Papers, 1931–1945.
Natchez Pilgrimage Collection.
Natchez Trace Parkway Papers.
Pilgrimage Historical Association Collection.
WPA Records, Mississippi.
    Historic Homes and Site Index Cards.
    WPA Interviews.

Mississippi State University, Mitchell Memorial Library, Starkville, Mississippi.
    Overstreet Architectural Drawings Collection.

Natchez Garden Club Headquarters, Natchez, Mississippi.
    Natchez Garden Club Scrapbooks, 1930–1950.

Natchez Trace Association, Franklin, Tennessee.
    The Natchez Trace Association Archives.

Natchez Trace Parkway Headquarters, National Park Service, Tupelo, Mississippi.
    Natchez Trace Parkway Administrative Offices Archives.

National Archives, College Park, Maryland.
    National Park Service:
        Bulletins and Circulars. Records of the Historic American Building Survey, Record Group 515, National Archives at College Park, 1933–1938.
        Bulletin No. 15: Historic American Building Survey Index. Records of the Historic American Building Survey, Record Group 515, National Archives at College Park, 1934.
        Holland, Leicester B. *Historic American Building Survey, Catalog of the Measured Drawings and Photographs of the Survey of the Library of Congress.* Washington, DC: United States Government Printing Office, 1941.
        Procedures Manuals for HABS/HAER Data Collection, Records of the Historic American Building Survey, Record Group 515, National Archives at College Park, 1935–1988.
        Records of the District Officer, District and State Correspondence. Records of the Historic American Building Survey, Record Group 515, National Archives at College Park, 1934–1941.
        Records Relating to Field Office Activities of the Historic American Buildings Survey, Mississippi, Records of the Historic American Building Survey, Record Group 515, National Archives at College Park, 1934–1941.
        State Organizational Files. Records of the Historic American Building Survey, Record Group 515, National Archives at College Park, 1933–1950.
        Subject Files Relating to the Historic American Building Survey, Mississippi, 1933–1938. Records of the Historic American Building Survey, Record Group 515, National Archives at College Park, 1933–1938.
        Subject Files Relating to Planning and Administration of the HABS/HAER Program. Records of the Historic American Building Survey, Record Group 515, National Archives at College Park, 1935–1984.

Tennessee State Library and Archives, Nashville, Tennessee.
    Natchez Trace Parkway Archive.
    Tennessean Archive.

University of Illinois at Urbana-Champaign, University Library, Urbana, Illinois.
    Alumni Files.

History, Philosophy, and Newspaper Library.
    School of Architecture Archives.
University of Maryland, Special Collections Library, College Park, Maryland.
    Peterson, Charles E. Papers: HABS History General.
University of Mississippi, Archives and Special Collections, Oxford, Mississippi.
    Mississippi Post Card Collection.
    Roane Fleming Byrnes Papers.
University of North Carolina at Chapel Hill, Southern Historical Collection, Chapel Hill, North Carolina.
    Ker, Mary Susan. Papers, 1785–1958.
    Dunbar, Catherine. Papers.
University of Texas, Harry Ransom Center, Austin, Texas.
    David O. Selznick Archives.
University of Virginia, Albert and Shirley Small Collections Library, Charlottesville, Virginia.
    Garden Club of Virginia Papers.
Tulane University, Southeastern Architectural Archive, New Orleans, Louisiana.
    A. Hays Town Office Records.
    Koch and Wilson Office Records.
    Richard Koch Drawings and Photographs.

NEWSPAPERS AND PERIODICALS

Al Jazeera America
American Way
Associated Press
Atlanta Journal
Atlanta Journal Constitution
Atlantic Monthly
Baltimore Sun
Bluff City Bulletin
Boston Globe
Chicago Daily News
Chicago Daily Tribune
Chicago Tribune
Christian Science Monitor
Clarksdale (Mississippi) *Register*
Corinth (Mississippi) *Corinthian*
Jackson Clarion Ledger
Jackson Daily Clarion Ledger
Jackson Daily News
Ladies' Home Journal
Los Angeles Times
Memphis Commercial Appeal
Mississippi Highways
National Geographic
Natchez Democrat
Natchez Times

New Orleans Times-Picayune
Newsday
New York Herald-Tribune
New York Times
Philadelphia Inquirer
Raleigh News and Observer
St. Louis Post-Dispatch
The Times (Shreveport, Louisiana)
Time Magazine
United Press Syndicate
Washington Post
Watson's Jeffersonian Magazine.

UNPUBLISHED AND PUBLISHED SOURCES, FEDERAL GOVERNMENT

Albright, Horace M. "Origins of National Park Administration of Historic Sites: A Reminiscence." Eastern National Park and Monument Association, 1971.
Allen, William C. "Gloucester." August 23, 1976. National Register of Historic Places Nomination.
Allen, William C. "Linden." August 23, 1976. National Register of Historic Places Nomination.
Beha, Ann, and Associates. "Natchez National Historical Park, Natchez, Mississippi, Historic Resource Study." United States Department of the Interior, National Park Service, 1996.
Butler, Ruth E., Olaf Hagen, and Randle Truett. "The Natchez Trace: Its Location, History, and Development." Unpublished Manuscript, N.P.S., 1936.
Chronister, Norman, and William C. Allen. "Rosalie." June 24, 1976. National Register of Historic Places Nomination.
Denver Service Center, National Park Service. "Environmental Statement for the Natchez Trace parkway, Tennessee-Alabama-Mississippi." Vol. I and II. June 20, 1978.
Elliott, Jack D., Jr. "Selma Plantation House." January 5, 1989. National Register of Historic Places Nomination.
Executive Order 6288, Section 2—National Parks, Buildings, and Reservations.
Goeldner, Paul. "Arlington." December 26, 1973. National Historic Landmark Nomination.
Goeldner, Paul. "House on Ellicott's Hill/Connelly's Tavern." January 10, 1974. National Register of Historic Places Nomination.
Goeldner, Paul. "Stanton Hall." January 8, 1974. National Register of Historic Places Nomination.
Heintzelman, Patricia. "Longwood." May 30, 1975. National Register of Historic Places Nomination.
Historic American Engineering Record (HAER). "The Natchez Trace Parkway: Natchez, MS to Nashville, TN." Draft typescript, Washington, D.C.: NPS, n.d.
Historical Architecture, Cultural Resources Division, Southeast Regional Office, National Park Service. "Natchez National Historical Park, Old Fort Rosalie Gift Shop, Historic Structure Report." June 2006,
Lavoie, Catherine C., ed. *American Place: The Historic American Building Survey at Seventy-five Years.* Washington, DC: United States Government Printing Office, 2009.

Louisiana Department of Transportation and Development. "Louisiana Historic Bridge Inventory."

Maddox, Dawn. "Natchez Bluffs and Under-the-Hill." August 31, 1971. National Register of Historic Places Nomination.

Miller, Mary Warren. "Brumfield High School." June 20, 1993. National Register of Historic Places Nomination.

Miller, Mary Warren. "Edgewood." National Register of Historic Places Nomination, September 24, 1978.

Miller, Mary Warren. "Laurel Hill." December 21, 1981. National Register of Historic Places Nomination.

Miller, Mary Warren. "Natchez On-Top-of-the Hill Historic District." May 31, 1979. National Register of Historic Places Nomination.

Miller, Mary Warren. "Saragoosa." September 14, 1980. National Register of Historic Places Nomination.

Miller, Mary Warren. "Texada Tavern." December 1, 1978. National Register of Historic Places Nomination.

Miller, Ronald W. "Arlington." November 13, 1973. National Register of Historic Places Nomination.

Murphy, Dennis M. "Central Shuqualak Historic District." September 7, 1979. National Register of Historic Places Nomination.

National Park Service. "Historic American Building Survey, Documenting a Legacy," *Journal of the Library of Congress* (1973).

Nemoyten, William. "John Wood Mansion." January 15, 1970. National Register of Historic Places. Nomination.

Phelps, Dawson A. "The Administrative History of the Natchez Trace Parkway." Unpublished manuscript.

Ray, Carl A. "King's Tavern." April 1, 1971. National Register of Historic Places Nomination.

Reynolds, Elizabeth P. "Hope Farm." June 5, 1975. National Register of Historic Places Nomination.

US Department of the Interior. "National Park Service, Parkways: A Manual of Requirements, Instructions for Use in the National Park Service." 1936.

Wallace, Mary Crocker. "Ravennaside." February 7, 1979. National Register of Historic Places Nomination."

Wilson, Samuel, Jr., and Marry Warren Miller. "Henderson-Britton Home, 'Magnolia Hall.'" February 21, 1978. National Register of Historic Places Nomination.

INTERVIEWS

Adams, Lawrence. Interview by Verbie Lovorn Prevost, April 4, 1974, Natchez, Mississippi.

Adams, William A., and Mary Louise Geddes. Interview by Graham Hicks, August 4, 1981, Natchez, Mississippi.

Bagley, Clinton. Multiple Interviews by the Author, July 2016.

Beltzhoover, Ruth Audley Wheeler. Interview by Graham Hicks, August 4, 1981, Natchez, Mississippi.

Benoist, Rebecca Fauntleroy. Interview by Graham Hicks, August 26, 1981, Natchez, Mississippi.

Byrnes, Roane Fleming (Mrs. Ferriday). Interview by Guy Braden and Richard Vance, May 20, 1969, Natchez, Mississippi.

Dixon, Harriet, and Joseph F. Dixon. Interview by Graham Hicks, n.d., Natchez, Mississippi.

Feltus, Jeanette. Interview by the Author, November 1, 2017.

Feltus, Mavis. Interview by Verbie Lovorn Prevost, April 24, 1974, Natchez, Mississippi.

Ferry, Marion Kelly. Interview by Graham Hicks, November 17, 1981, Natchez, Mississippi.

Geddes, Mary Louise. Interview by Graham Hicks, August 4, 1981, Natchez, Mississippi.

Goodrich, Mary Louise Netterville Kendall. Interview by Graham Hicks, January 27, 1982, Natchez, Mississippi.

Kellogg, Alma. Interview by Elliott Trimble, August 15, 1981, Natchez, Mississippi.

MacIlroy, Margaret Percell Marshall. Interview by Elliott Trimble, n.d., Natchez, Mississippi.

MacNeil, Grace. Interview by Graham Hicks, n.d., Natchez, Mississippi.

McWhite, Leigh. Interview by the Author, May 17, 2016, Oxford, Mississippi.

Miller, Katherine Grafton (Mrs. Balfour). Interview by Graham Hicks, February 18, 1971, Natchez, Mississippi.

Miller, Mary Warren (Mimi). Multiple Interviews by the Author, July 2016, Natchez, Mississippi.

Sanders, Todd. Multiple Interviews by the Author, May 2015-August 2017, Jackson, Mississippi.

Swain, Martica. Email correspondence with the Author, February 15, 2019.

Tomlan, Michael A. Interview by the Author, March 26, 2019, via telephone.

Turnbow, Tony. Interview by the Author, July 20, 2017, Franklin, Tennessee.

BOOKS AND NOVELS CONTEMPORARY WITH MAIN PERIODS STUDIED

Bosworth, Frank H., and Roy C. Jones. *A Study of Architecture Schools*. New York: Charles Scribner and Sons, 1932.

Britton, Theodora, and Gladys Crail Marshall Evans. *A Day in Natchez: An Informal Introduction to the Most Romantic Locality in the South*. Natchez, MS: The Reliquary, 1946.

Butler, Pierce, and Carol Howard Pforzheimer. *The Unhurried Years: Memories of the Old Natchez Region*. Baton Rouge: Louisiana State University Press, 1948.

Coates, Robert M. *The Outlaw Years: The History of the Land Pirates of the Natchez Trace*. New York: The Macaulay Co., 1936.

Cobb, Ivan S. *Roughing It Deluxe*. New York: Doran, 1914.

Davis, Allison, Burleigh B. Gardner, and Mary B. Gardner. *Deep South: A Social Anthropological Study of Caste and Class*. Chicago: University of Chicago Press, 1941.

DeBow, J. D. B. *DeBow's Review*, Vol. 29. New Orleans: Southern States, 1860.

Faulkner, William. *As I Lay Dying*. New York: Random House, 1930.

Gerow, R. O. *Cradle Days of St. Mary's and Natchez*. Natchez, MS: St. Mary's Cathedral, 1941.

Goodspeed. *Biographical and Historic Memoirs of Mississippi: Authentic and Comprehensive Account of the Chief Events in the History of the State, and a Record of the Lives of Many of the Most Worth and Illustrious Families and Individuals*. Vols. 1 and 2. Chicago: The Goodspeed Publishing Co., 1891.

Guyton, Pearl Vivian. *The Story of Connelly's Tavern on Ellicott Hill: A National Shrine Owned by the Natchez Garden Club, Natchez, Mississippi*. Jackson, MS: Hederman Bros., 1942.

Guyton, Pearl Vivian. *The Story of Rosalie, Natchez, Mississippi: Historic Shrine, Mississippi Society of the National Society of the American Revolution*. Jackson, MS: Hederman Bros., 1941.

Hamlin, Talbot. *Greek Revival Architecture in America; Being an Account of Important Trends in American Architecture and American Life Prior to the War between the States*. New York: Oxford University Press, 1944.

Hammer, Bette Barber. *Natchez' First Ladies: Katherine Grafton Miller and the Pilgrimage*. New York: Kintner Publishing, 1955.

Ingraham, Joseph H. *South-West by a Yankee*. New York: Harper Brothers, 1835.

Kane, Harnett T. *Natchez on the Mississippi*. New York: William Morrow and Co., 1947.

Lafever, Minard. *The Beauties of Modern Architecture*. New York: Appleton, 1835.

Lockwood, Alice G. B. *Gardens of Colony and State: Gardens and Gardeners of the American Republic Before 1840*. Vols. 1 and 2. New York: Charles Scribner and Sons, 1931.

Marshall, Theodora Britton, and Gladys Crail Evans. *They Found It in Natchez*. New Orleans: Pelican Publishing Co., 1939.

McCain, William D. *The Story of Jackson*. Vol. 2. Jackson, MS: J. F. Heyer Publishing Co., 1953.

Miller, Katherine Grafton. *Natchez of Long Ago and the Pilgrimage*. Natchez, MS: Relimak Publishing, 1938.

Mitchell, Margaret. *Gone with the Wind*. New York: Macmillan Publishing Co., 1936.

Moore, Edith Wyatt. *Natchez Under-the-Hill*. Natchez, MS: Southern Historical Publications, 1958.

Murray, Elizabeth Dunbar. *My Mother Used to Say: A Natchez Belle of the Sixties*. Boston: Christopher Publisher House, 1959.

Natchez Democrat. *Natchez, Mississippi on Top, not "Under the Hill."* Natchez, MS: Daily Democrat Steam Press, 1892.

Newell, Georgie Wilson, and Charles Cromartie Compton. *Natchez and the Pilgrimage*. Natchez, MS: Southern Publishers, Inc., 1935.

Oliver, Nola Nance. *Natchez: Symbol of the Old South*. New York: Hastings House, 1940.

Oliver, Nola Nance. *This Too Is Natchez*. New York: Hastings House Publishers, 1953.

Olmsted, Frederick Law. *The Cotton Kingdom: A Traveler's Observation on Cotton and Slavery in the American Slave States*. New York: Alfred A. Knopf, 1953.

Shields, Joseph D., and Elizabeth Dunbar Murray. *Natchez: Its Early History*. Louisville, KY: J. P. Morton & Co., 1930.

Smith, J. Frazier. *White Pillars: The Architecture of the Old South*. New York: W. Helburn, Inc., 1941.

Stanton, Elizabeth Brandon. *Sidelights on the Picturesque and Romantic History of Ye Old Natchez Trace of the Mysterious Natchez*. Natchez, MS: Self-published, 1934.

Van Court, Catherine. *In Old Natchez*. Garden City, NJ: Doubleday, 1937.

Welty, Eudora. *The Robber Bridegroom*. New York: Doubleday, 1942.

Young, Stark. *So Red the Rose*. New York: Charles Scribner and Sons, 1934.

BOOKS

Aaron, Cindy S. *Working at Play: A History of Vacations in the United States.* New York: Oxford University Press, 1999.

Alford, Terry. *Prince Among Slaves.* New York: Oxford University Press, 1977.

Ausherman, Maria Elizabeth. *The Photographic Legacy of Frances Benjamin Johnston.* Gainesville: University Press of Florida, 2009.

Belasco, Warren James. *Americans on the Road: From Autocamp to Motel, 1910–1945.* Baltimore: Johns Hopkins University Press, 1997.

Bendizen, Alfred. *The Continuum Encyclopedia of American Literature.* London: Continuum Publishing, 2003.

Blight, David. *Race and Reunion: The Civil War in American Memory.* Cambridge, MA: Belknap Press of Harvard University Press, 2001.

Boorstin, Daniel J., Richard R. Beeman, Ray Allen Billington, Joe B. Frantz, Brooke Hindle, Charles Pierce Roland, James Morton Smith, and Wilcomb E. Washburn. *Visiting Our Past: America's Historylands.* Washington, DC: National Geographic Society, 1977.

Brook, David L. S. *A Lasting Gift of Heritage: A History of the North Carolina Society of the Preservation of Antiquities, 1939–1974.* Raleigh: North Carolina Division of Archives and History, North Carolina Department of Cultural Resources, 1995.

Brooke, Steven. *The Majesty of Natchez.* Gretna, LA: Pelican Publishing Co., 2014.

Brown, Alan. *Haunted Places in the American South.* Jackson: University Press of Mississippi, 2002.

Campbell, Edward D. C., Jr. *The Celluloid South: Hollywood and the Southern Myth.* Knoxville: University of Tennessee Press, 1981.

Carr, Ethan. *Mission 66: Modernism and the National Park Dilemma.* Amherst: University of Massachusetts Press, 2007.

Cash, Wilbur J. *The Mind of the South.* New York: Alfred A. Knopf, 1941.

Cobb, James C. *Away Down South: A History of Southern Identity.* New York: Oxford University Press, 2005.

Connerton, Paul. *How Societies Remember.* Cambridge, UK: Cambridge University Press, 1989.

Cox, Karen L. *Dixie's Daughters: The United Daughters of the Confederacy and the Preservation of Confederate Culture.* Gainesville: University Press of Florida, 2003.

Cox, Karen L. *Dreaming of Dixie: How the South Was Created in American Popular Culture.* Chapel Hill: University of North Carolina Press, 2011.

Cox, Karen L. *Goat Castle: A True Story of Murder, Race, and the Gothic South.* Chapel Hill: University of North Carolina Press, 2017.

Crutchfield, James A. *The Natchez Trace: A Pictorial History.* Franklin, TN: Territorial Press, 2011.

Daniels, Jonathan. *The Devil's Backbone: The Story of the Natchez Trace.* New York: McGraw-Hill, 1962.

Davis, Jack. *Race Against Time: Culture and Segregation in Natchez since 1930.* Baton Rouge: Louisiana State University Press, 2001.

Delehanty, Randolph, Van Jones Martin, Ronald W. Miller, Mary Warren Miller, and Elizabeth MacNeil Boggess. *Classic Natchez.* Savannah, GA: Martin-St. Martin Publishing Co., 1996.

Des Jardins, Julie. *Women and the Historical Enterprise in America: Gender, Race, and the Politics of Memory, 1880–1945.* Chapel Hill: University of North Carolina Press, 2003.

D'Este, Carlo. *Eisenhower: A Soldier's Life*. London: Macmillan, 2003.

Eichstedt, Jennifer L., and Stephen Small. *Representations of Slavery: Race and Ideology in Southern Plantation Museums*. Washington, DC: Smithsonian Institution Press, 2002.

Falck, Susan T. *Remembering Dixie: The Battle to Control Historical Memory in Natchez, Mississippi, 1865–1941*. Jackson: University Press of Mississippi, 2019.

Farbe, Michael. *The World of Richard Wright*. Jackson: University Press of Mississippi, 1985.

Faust, Drew Gilpin. *Mothers of Invention: Women of the Slaveholding South in the American Civil War*. Chapel Hill: University of North Carolina Press, 1996.

Faust, Drew Gilpin. *This Republic of Suffering*. New York: Knopf Doubleday, 2008.

Fitch, James Marston. *Historic Preservation: Curatorial Management of the Built World*. Charlottesville: University Press of Virginia, 1992.

Frankebburg, Ruth. *White Women, Race Matters: The Social Construction of Whiteness*. London: Routledge, 1993.

Glassberg, David. *American Historical Pageantry: The Uses of Tradition in the Early 20th Century*. Chapel Hill: University of North Carolina Press, 1990.

Glassberg, David. *Sense of History: The Place of the Past in American Life*. Amherst: University of Massachusetts Press, 2001.

Glassie, Henry. *Passing the Time in Ballymenone: Culture and History of an Ulster Community*. Philadelphia: University of Pennsylvania Press, 1982.

Gleason, David K., Mary Warren Miller, and Ronald W. Miller. *The Great Houses of Natchez*. Jackson: University Press of Mississippi, 1986.

Gregory, James N. *The Southern Diaspora: How the Great Migrations of Black and White Southerners Transformed America*. Chapel Hill: University of North Carolina Press, 2005.

Halbwachs, Maurice. *The Collective Memory*. Trans. Francis J. Ditter Jr. and Vida Yazdi Ditter. New York: Harper and Row, 1980.

Hale, Grace Elizabeth. *Making Whiteness: The Culture of Segregation in the South*. New York: Pantheon Books, 1998.

Healy, George W., Jr. *A Lifetime on Deadline: Self-Portrait of a Southern Journalist*. Gretna, LA: Pelican Publishing, 1976.

Holleran, Michael. *Boston's Changeful Times*. Baltimore: Johns Hopkins University Press, 1998.

Hollis, Tim. *Dixie Before Disney: 100 Years of Roadside Fun*. Jackson: University Press of Mississippi, 1999.

Hornstein, Shelly. *Losing Site: Architecture, Memory, and Place*. London: Routledge, 2012.

Horton, James Oliver, and Lois E. Horton, eds. *Slavery and Public History: The Tough Stuff of American Memory*. Chapel Hill: University of North Carolina Press, 2006.

Hosmer, Charles B. *Preservation Comes of Age: From Williamsburg to the National Trust, 1926–1949*. Charlottesville: University Press of Virginia, 1981.

Howard, Hugh. *Natchez: The Houses and History of the Jewell of the Mississippi*. New York: Rizzoli, 2003.

Hudson, Kenneth. *Museums of Influence*. Cambridge, UK: Cambridge University Press, 1987.

Huyssen, Andreas. *Twilight Memories: Marking Time in a Culture of Amnesia*. New York: Routledge, 2003.

Ise, John. *Our National Park Policy: A Critical History*. Baltimore: Johns Hopkins University Press, 1961.

Jakle, John A. *The Tourist: Travel in Twentieth-Century North America.* Lincoln: University of Nebraska Press, 1985.

Johnson, Joan Marie. *Southern Ladies, New Women: Race, Region, and Clubwomen in South Carolina, 1890–1930.* Gainesville: University Press of Florida, 2004.

Joos, Vincent. *The Natchez Fire.* Chapel Hill: University of North Carolina Press, 2011.

Kammen, Michael. *Mystic Chords of Memory: The Transformation of Tradition in American Culture.* New York: Vintage Books, 1993.

Kapp, Paul Hardin, with Todd Sanders. *The Architecture of William Nichols: Building the Antebellum South in North Carolina, Alabama, and Mississippi.* Jackson: University Press of Mississippi, 2015.

Kirby, Jack T. *Media-Made Dixie: The South in the American Imagination.* Rev. ed. Athens: University of Georgia Press, 2004.

Kirwan, Albert D., ed. *The Civilization of the Old South: Writings of Clement Eaton.* Lexington: University Press of Kentucky, 1968.

Koyl, George S., ed. *AIA Architect's Directory.* New York: R. R. Bowker Co., 1962.

Lane, Mills. *Architecture of the Old South: Kentucky and Tennessee.* Savannah, GA: Beehive Press, 1993.

Lane, Mills, Robert Gamble, Mary Warren Miller, and Ronald W. Miller. *Architecture of the Old South: Mississippi and Alabama.* New York: Abbeville Press/Beehive Press, 1989.

Lindgren, James M. *Preserving Historic New England: Preservation, Progressivism, and the Remaking of Memory.* New York: Oxford University Press, 1996.

Lindgren, James M. *Preserving the Old Dominion: Historic Preservation and Virginia Traditionalism.* Charlottesville: University Press of Virginia, 1993.

Loth, Calder. *The Virginia Landmarks Register.* Charlottesville: University Press of Virginia, 1999.

Lowenthal, David. *The Heritage Crusade and the Spoils of History.* New York: Cambridge University Press, 1998.

Lowenthal, David. *The Past Is a Foreign Country.* Cambridge, UK: Cambridge University Press, 1985.

Lynch, Kevin. *What Time Is This Place?* Cambridge, MA: MIT Press, 1972.

Margolin, Phillipe, and Jean-Mitchell Guesdon. *Bob Dylan, All the Songs: The Story Behind Every Track.* Philadelphia: Running Press, 2015.

Meringlo, Denise D. *Museums, Monuments, and National Parks: Toward a New Genealogy of Public History.* Amherst: University of Massachusetts Press, 2012.

Morgan, Chester M. *Redneck Liberal: Theodore G. Bilbo and the New Deal.* Baton Rouge: Louisiana State University Press, 1985.

Nolan, Charles E. *St. Mary's of Natchez: The History of a Southern Catholic Congregation, 1716–1988.* Vol. 1. Natchez, MS: St. Mary's Parish, 1992.

Ownby, Ted, and Charles Reagan Wilson. *The Mississippi Encyclopedia.* Jackson: University Press of Mississippi, 2017.

Pevsner, Nikolaus. *The Buildings of England.* New York: Penguin, 1951–1974.

Pilkington, John, ed. *Stark Young: A Life in the Arts: Letters 1900–1962.* Vols. 1 and 2. Baton Rouge: Louisiana State University Press, 1975.

Poesch, Jessie, and Barbara SoRelle Bacot. *Louisiana Buildings: 1720–1940.* Baton Rouge: Louisiana State University Press, 1997.

Potteiger, Matthew, and Jamie Purinton. *Landscapes Narratives: Design Practices for Telling Stories.* New York: Wiley and Sons, 1998.

Pyron, Darden. *Southern Daughter.* New York: Harper Perennial, 1992.

Rathbone, Belinda. *Walker Evans: A Biography.* New York: Houghton Mifflin Co., 1995.
Register, James. *Jallon: Arabic Prince of Old Natchez, 1788–1828.* Shreveport, LA: Mid-South Press, 1968.
Remini, Robert V. *The Life of Andrew Jackson.* New York: Harper Perennial, 1999.
Ritz, Richard E. *Architects of Oregon: A Biographical Dictionary of Architects Deceased–19th and 20th Centuries.* Portland, OR: Lair Hill Publishing Co., 2003.
Sachs, David Helburn. *The Life and Work of the Twentieth Century Louisiana Architect A. Hays Town.* Lampeter, Ceredigon, Wales: Edwin Mellen Press, Ltd., 2003.
Scott, Anne Firor. *Making the Invisible Woman Visible.* Urbana: University of Illinois Press, 1984.
Scott, Anne Firor. *Natural Allies: Women's Associations in American History.* Urbana: University of Illinois Press, 1993.
Scott, Anne Firor. *The Southern Lady: From Pedestal to Politics, 1830–1930.* Chicago: University of Chicago Press, 1970.
Shaffer, Marguerite S. *See America First: Tourism and National Identity, 1880–1940.* Washington, DC: Smithsonian Institution Press, 2013.
Shils, Edward. *Tradition.* Chicago: University of Chicago Press, 1981.
Sigfired, Giedon. *Space and Architecture.* Cambridge, MA: Harvard University Press, 1944.
Skates, John Ray. *Mississippi: A History.* New York: W. W. Norton Company, 1979.
Spain, Daphne. *Constructive Feminism: Women's Spaces and Women's Right in the American City.* Ithaca, NY: Cornell University Press, 2016.
Stein, Maurice Robert. *The Eclipse of Community: An Interpretation of American Studies.* Princeton, NJ: Princeton University Press, 1960.
Stephenson, R. Bruce. *John Nolen, Landscape Architect and Planner.* Amherst: University of Massachusetts Press, 2015.
Sussman, Warren. *Culture as History.* New York: Pantheon Books, 2012.
Swain, Martha. *Pat Harrison: The New Deal Years.* Jackson: University Press of Mississippi, 1978.
Vetter, Cyril, and Philip Gould. *The Louisiana Homes of A. Hays Town.* Baton Rouge: Louisiana State University Press, 1999.
Washington, D.C., Historical Society. *Directory of Washington, D.C. Architects.* Washington, DC: Washington, DC, Historical Society, 2015.
Watters, Sam, and Frances Benjamin Johnston. *Gardens for a Beautiful America, 1895–1935.* New York: Acanthus Press, 2012.
West, Patricia. *Domesticating History: The Political Origins of America's House Museums.* Washington, DC: Smithsonian Books, 1999.
Westfall, Carroll William. *Architecture, Liberty, and Civic Order: Architectural Theories from Vitruvius to Jefferson and Beyond.* Farnham, UK: Ashgate, 2015.
Williams, Dorothy Hunt. *Historic Virginia Gardens.* Charlottesville: University Press of Virginia, 1975.
Wilson, Charles Reagan, Martin V. Melosi, Samuel S. Hill, Michael Montgomery, Milton Thomas Inge, Richard Pillsbury, Rebecca Celeste Ray, John T. Edge, Bill C. Malone, and Nancy Bercaw. *The New Encyclopedia of Southern Culture.* Chapel Hill: University of North Carolina Press, 2009.
Wilson, Chris. *The Myth of Santa Fe: Creating a Modern Regional Tradition.* Albuquerque: University of New Mexico Press, 1997.
Works Progress Administration. *The WPA Guide to the Magnolia State.* Jackson: University Press of Mississippi, 2009.

ARTICLES, BOOK CHAPTERS, AND ESSAYS

Aaker, Jennifer L. "The Malleable Self: The Role of Self Expression in Persuasion." *Journal of Marketing Research* 36, no. 1 (1999): 43–54.

Adler, Judith. "Travel as Performed Art." *American Journal of Sociology* 94, no. 6 (May 1989): 1366–91.

Alderman, Derek E., and E. Arnold Modlin Jr. "One the Political Utterance of Plantation Tourists: Vocalizing the Memory of Slavery on River Road." *Journal of Heritage Tourism* 11, no. 2 (2016): 275–89.

Alderman, Derek H., David L. Butler, and Stephen P. Hanna. "Memory, Slavery, and Plantation Museums: The River Road Project." *Journal of Heritage Tourism* 11, no. 2 (2016): 209–18.

Bach, Richard F. "Books on Colonial Architecture: Part VII—The Final Record." *Architectural Record* 40 (January-June 1917): 486–91.

Barnett, Jim, and H. Clark Burkett. "The Forks of the Road Slave Market at Natchez." *Journal of Mississippi History* 63 (Fall 2001): 169–87.

Barthel, Diane L. "Nostalgia for America's Village Past: Staged Symbolic Communities." *International Journal of Politics, Culture and Society* 4, no. 1 (1993): 79–83.

Bowman, Michael. "Performing Southern History for the Tourist's Gaze: Antebellum Home Tour Guide Performances." In *Exceptional Spaces: Essays in Performance and History*, ed. Della Pollock. Chapel Hill: University of North Carolina Press, 1998.

Bryant, Jean Gould. "From the Margins to the Center: Southern Women's Activism, 1820–1970." *The Florida Historical Quarterly* 74, no. 4: 400–19.

Carter, Perry L. "Where Are the Enslaved?: Trip Advisor and the Narrative Landscapes of Southern Plantation Museums." *Journal of Heritage Tourism* 11, no. 2 (2016): 235–49.

Conrad, David R. "Ben Shahn as Aesthetic Educator." *Journal of Aesthetic Education* 15, no. 2 (1981): 74–80.

Cook, Matthew R. "Counter-Narratives of Slavery in the Deep South: The Politics of Empathy Along and Beyond River Road." *Journal of Heritage Tourism* 11, no. 2 (2016): 290–308.

Corkern, Wilton. "Heritage Tourism: Where Public and History Don't Always Meet." *American Studies International* 42, no. 2/3 (2004): 7–16.

Cox, Karen L. "Revisiting the Natchez Pilgrimage: Women and the Creation of Mississippi's Heritage Tourism Industry." *Journal of Mississippi History* 74, no. 4 (Winter 2012): 349–71.

Danson, Mike, and Jim Mather. "Doing Business with the Scottish Diaspora." In *The Modern Scottish Diaspora: Contemporary Debates and Perspectives*, ed. Leith Murray Stewart and Slim Duncan. Edinburgh, UK: Edinburgh University Press, 2014.

Davidson, Lisa Pfueller, and Martin J. Perschler. "The Historic American Building Survey During the New Deal Era." *CRM: The Journal of Heritage Stewardship* 1 (2003): 49–73.

Davis, Jack. "A Struggle for Public History: Black and White Claims to Natchez's Past." *The Public Historian* 22, no. 1 (Winter 2000): 45–63.

Davis, Timothy M. "A Pleasant Illusion of Unspoiled Countryside: The American Parkway and the Problematics of an Institutionalized Vernacular." *Perspectives in Vernacular Architecture* 9 (2003): 218–30.

Dolensky, Suzanne T. "Natchez in 1920: On the Threshold of Modernity." *Journal of Mississippi History* 73, no. 2 (Summer 2011): 110–41.

Driever, Steven L. "From Travel to Tourism: Harry Franck's Writing on Mexico (1916–1940)." *Journal of Latin American Geography* 12, no. 2 (2013): 11–33.

Dulling, Dennis. "Memory, Collective Memory, Orality, and Gospels." *HTS Theological Studies* 67, no. 1: 4.

Elliott, Jack D., Jr. "City and Empire: The Origins of Natchez." *Journal of Mississippi History* 59 (Winter 1997): 271–322.

Elliott, Jack D., Jr. "Paving the Trace." *Journal of Mississippi History* 69, no. 3 (Fall 2007): 199–234.

Fazio, Michael. "Architectural Preservation in Natchez, Mississippi: 'A Conception of Time and Place.'" *Southern Quarterly* 19, no. 1 (Fall 1980): 134–40.

Fazio, Michael. "Interpreting Southern Antebellum Architecture in the 1990s." *Journal of Architectural Education* 44, no. 4: 225–34.

Ferris, William R., and John Dollard. "John Dollard: Caste and Class Revisited." *Southern Cultures* 10, no. 2 (Summer 2004): 7–18.

Ferris, William R. "Walker Evans, 1974." *Southern Cultures* 13, no. 2 (Summer 2007): 40–49.

Forbes Bright, Candace, and Perry Carter. "Who Are They? Visitors to Louisiana's River Road Plantations." *Journal of Heritage Tourism* 11, no. 2 (2016): 262–74.

Fox-Genovese, Elizabeth. "Scarlett O'Hara: The Southern Lady as New Woman." *American Quarterly* 33, no. 4 (Autumn 1981): 391–411.

Gates, Paul. "Portrait of a Classic: A. Hays Town." *Baton Rouge* 6, no. 10 (October 1985): 85–87.

Gianopolis, Nicholas. "In Memory of Charles E. Peterson, 1906–2004." *APT Bulletin* 37, no. 1 (2006): 3.

Gilpin Faust, Drew. "Altars of Sacrifice: Confederate Women and the Narratives of War." *Journal of American History* 76, no. 4 (March 1990): 1220–27.

Glassberg, David. "Public History and the Study of Memory." *The Public Historian* 18, no. 2 (Spring 1996): 7–23.

Grant, Phillip A. "Congress and the Development of the Natchez Trace Parkway, 1834–1946." In *Parkways: Past, Present, and Future*, ed. International Linear Parks Conference. Boone, NC: Appalachian State University, 1987.

Gushee, Elizabeth M. "Travels through the Old South: Frances Benjamin Johnston and the Vernacular Architecture of Virginia." *Art Documentation: The Journal of the Art Libraries of North America* 27, no. 1 (Spring 2008): 18–23.

Hamilton, William B. "Notes." *Journal of Southern History* 10, no. 4 (November 1944): 398.

Hanna, Stephen P. "Placing the Enslaved at Oak Alley Plantation: Narratives, Spatial Contexts, and the Limits of Surrogation." *Journal of Heritage Tourism* 11, no. 2 (2016): 219–34.

Harbeson, John F. "Stotham, the Massachusetts Hoax, 1920." *Journal of the Society of Architectural Historians* 23, no. 2 (May 1964): 111–12.

Hennen, Michael. "The Elms: Time Capsule of Natchez and Vicksburg Urban Life." *The Primary Source* 25, no. 1, art. 3 (2003): 9–10.

Hester, Randy. "Subconscious Landscapes of the Heart." *Places* 2 (1985): 10–22.

Hitchcock, Henry-Russell, and Turpin C. Bannister. "Summary of the Round Table on the Preservation of Historical Architectural Monuments, Held March 18, 1941, in the Library of Congress, Washington, D.C." *Journal of the Society of Architectural Historians* 1, no. 2 (April 1941): 21–24.

Hoelscher, Steven. "'Where the Old South Still Lives': Displaying Heritage in Natchez, Mississippi." In *Southern Heritage on Display: Public Ritual and Ethnic Diversity with Southern Regionalism*, ed. Celeste R. Ray, Melissa Schrift, Helen Reis, Kathryn Van Spanckeren, and Gwen Kennedy Neville. Tuscaloosa: University of Alabama Press, 2003.

Holland, Leicester B. "American Institute of Architects Proceedings, Testimony," *Journal of American Institute of Architects* (May 1930): 130–31.

Holtorf, Cornelius. "On Pastness: A Reconsideration of Materiality in Archaeological Object Authenticity." *Anthropological Quarterly* 86, no. 2 (Spring 2013): 430–32.

Houghton, Melissa, and Barbara Daniels, eds. *Pioneers in Preservation: Biographical Sketches of Architects Prominent in the Field Before WWII*. Washington, DC: AIA Press, 1990.

Howe, Barbara J. "Women in Historic Preservation: The Legacy of Ann Pamela Cunningham." *Public Historian* 12 (Winter 1990): 33–61.

Ivy, Robert, Jr. "Looking Forward to History." *Mississippi Architect* 9, no. 3 (1978): 229–39.

Jones, Alfred Haworth. "The Search for a Usable American Past in the New Deal Era." *American Quarterly* 23, no. 5 (December 1971): 710–24.

Joos, Vincent. "Upbeat Down South: Jimmy Anderson—Natchez Swamp Blues." *Southern Cultures* 16, no. 3 (Fall 2010): 129–36.

Keating, Bern. "Today Along the Natchez Trace." *National Geographic* 134 (November 1968): 630–48.

Keenan, Hugh T. "Heaven Bound at the Crossroads: A Sketch of a Religious Pageant." *Journal of American Culture* 11, no. 3 (Fall 1988): 39–45.

Kimball, Stanley B. "The Mormons in Illinois, 1836–1846: A Special Introduction." *Journal of the Illinois State Historical Society* 64, no. 1 (1971): 4–21.

Krauskopf, Frances. "Reviewed Work: Colonial St. Louis—Building a Creole Capital by Charles E. Peterson." *Indiana Magazine of History* 46, no. 2 (June 1950): 216.

Kruty, Paul S. "Walter Burley Griffin and the University of Illinois." *Reflections: The Journal of the School of Architecture at Urbana-Champaign* 9 (Spring 1993): 30–37.

Lavoie, Catherine C. "Architectural Plans and Visions: The Early HABS Program and Its Documentation of Vernacular Architecture." *Perspectives in Vernacular Architecture* 13, no. 2 (2006–2007): 15–35.

Leach, Sara Amy. "The Daughters of the American Revolution, Roane F. Byrnes, and the Birth of the Natchez Trace Parkway." In *Looking Beyond the Highway*, ed. Claudette Stager and Martha Carver. Knoxville: University of Tennessee Press, 2006.

Lewis, Robert M. "Tableaux Vivants: Parlor Theatricals in Victorian America." *Revue Française D'etudes Americaines* 36 (1988): 280–84.

Lindgren, James M. "A New Departure in Historic Patriotic Work: Personalism, Professionalism, and Conflicting Concepts of Material Culture in the Late Nineteenth and Early Twentieth Centuries." *The Public Historian* 18, no. 2 (Spring 1996): 43–49.

Longstreth, Richard. "David Lowenthal—An Appreciation." *Preservation Education and Research* 11, no. 1 (November 2019).

Lowenthal, David. "The American Way of History." *Columbia University Forum* 9 (Summer 1966): 15–32.

Lowenthal, David. "Historic America—and the Unremarked Past." In *Bending the Future: Fifty Years of Historic Preservation in the United States*, ed. Max Page and Maria R. Miller. Amherst: University of Massachusetts Press, 2016.

Marx, Leo. *The Machine in the Garden: Technology and the Pastoral Ideal in America.* New York: Oxford University Press, 1964.

McNeil, Floyd A. "Reviewed Work: Colonial St. Louis—Building a Creole Capital by Charles E. Peterson." *The Mississippi Valley Historical Review* 36, no. 4 (March 1950): 700.

Michael, Rugel. "Natchez Burning: Anniversary of the Rhythm Club Fire." In *Nobody Knows Where the Blues Comes From: Lyrics and History*, ed. Robert Springer. Jackson: University Press of Mississippi, 2007.

Miller, Ronald W. "Historic Preservation in Natchez, Mississippi." *Antiques* 111 (March 1977): 537–40.

Modlin, Edward A. "Tales Told on the Tour: Mythic Representations of Slavery by Docents at North Carolina Plantation Museums." *Southeastern Geographer* 48, no. 3 (2008): 265–87.

Morgan, Jo-Ann. "Mammy the Huckster: Selling the Old South for the New Century." *American Art* 9, no. 1 (Spring 1995): 86–109.

Peterson, Charles E. "American Notes." *Journal of the Society of Architectural Historians* 16, no. 3 (October 1957): 31.

Peterson, Charles E. "The Historic American Buildings Survey: Its Beginnings." In *Historic America: Buildings, Structures, and Sites*, ed. C. Ford Peatross. Washington, DC: Library of Congress, 2003.

Peterson, Charles E. "Leicester Bodine Holland, 1882–1952." *Journal of the Society of Architectural Historians* 11, no. 2 (May 1957): 24.

Peterson, Charles E. "Notes on Natchez." *Journal of the Society of Architectural Historians* 14, no. 1 (March 1955): 30.

Peterson, Charles E. "Thirty Years of HABS." *AIA Journal*, November 1963, 84.

Potter, Amy E. "She Goes into Character as the Lady of the House: Tour Guides, Performance, and the Southern Plantation." *Journal of Heritage Tourism* 11, no. 2 (2016): 250–61.

Price, Virginia B. "Drawing Details: Taking Measure of the HABS Collection." *Preservation Education and Research* 4 (2011): 53–68.

Price, Virginia B. "Preserving on Paper." *Heritage Conservation in North America Context* 92 (2005): 21–23.

Rowland, Eron. "Marking the Natchez Trace." *Publications of the Mississippi Historical Society* 11 (1910): 345–61.

Ruskin, John. "The Poetry of Architecture; Or the Architecture of the Nations of Europe, Considered in Its Association with Natural Scenery and National Character." *The Crayon* 1, no. 21 (May 23, 1855): 325–27.

Sanders, Todd, and Paul Hardin Kapp. "311-313 Market Street (Parish House), Natchez, Mississippi." Unpublished book chapter.

Schara, Mark. "Preserving Our Early Architecture: The Historic American Buildings Survey in the District of Columbia." *Washington History* 30, no. 1 (Spring 2018): 15–18.

Silber, William L. "Why Did FDR's Bank Holiday Succeed?" *Economic Policy Review* 15, no. 1 (July 2009): 19–30.

Silver, Jack W. "Natchez Under-the-Hill by Edith Wyatt Moore." *Journal of Southern History* 26, no. 2 (May 1960): 1131.

Sydnor, Charles S. "The Biography of a Slave." *South Atlantic Quarterly* 36 (January 1937): 59–73.

Urnrau, Harlan D., and G. Frank Williss. "To Preserve the Nation's Past: The Growth of Historic Preservation in the National Park Service during the 1930's." *The Public Historian* 9, no. 2 (Spring 1987): 15–31.

Van Horne, John C. "Andrew Ellicott's Mission to Natchez (1796–1798)." *Journal of Mississippi History*, August 1983.

Waite, John G. "In Memory of Charles E. Peterson, 1906–2004." *APT Bulletin* 37, no. 1 (2006): 3.

Weeks, Charles A. "Plano de una parte de la Provincia de la Luisana y de otra de la Florida Occidental y de la Provincia de Texas." Unpublished essay, 2016.

UNPUBLISHED DISSERTATIONS AND THESES

Clement, David. "A Program for Brown's Wells Health Resort in Hazlehurst, Mississippi in Copiah County." B. Arch. thesis, Texas Tech University, 1987.

Corken, Wilton C., Jr. "Architects, Preservationists, and the New Deal: The Historic American Buildings Survey, 1933–1942." PhD diss., The George Washington University, 1984.

Davis, Timothy M. "Mount Vernon Highway and the Evolution of the American Parkway." PhD diss., University of Texas, 2000.

Falck, Susan T. "Black and White Memory Making in Postwar Natchez, Mississippi, 1865–1935." PhD diss., University of California, Santa Barbara, 2012.

Falck, Susan T. "The Garden Club Women of Natchez: 'To Preserve the South We Love.'" Master's thesis, California State University, 2003.

Graham, June Newman. "Social Graces: The Natchez Garden Club as a Literacy Sponsor." PhD diss., Louisiana State University, 2011.

Parker, Cynthia J. "Monmouth: The Survival of a Grand Mansion Estate in Natchez, Mississippi, from the Era of Slavery to the Present." Master's thesis, California State University, Northridge, 2010.

Prevost, Verbie Lovorn. "Roane Fleming Byrnes: A Critical Biography." PhD diss., University of Mississippi, 1974.

Sachs, David Helburn. "The Work of Overstreet and Town: The Coming of Modern Architecture to Mississippi." PhD diss., University of Michigan, 1986.

Smith, Susan Dunbar. "Thomas Rose: A Nineteenth Century Master Builder in Natchez, Mississippi." Master's thesis, Tulane University, 1993.

Vickers, Kenneth W. "John E. Rankin: Democrat and Demagogue." Master's thesis, Mississippi State University, 1993.

Vider, Elise. "The Historic American Buildings Survey in Philadelphia, 1950–1966." Master's thesis, University of Pennsylvania, 1991.

INDEX

A

AAA (American Automobile Association), 292
Aaker, Jennifer, 388
Abbott, Stanley, 301
Abbott, Walter, 304
Abdulrahman Ibrahim Ibn Sori (Ibrahima), 86–87, 127–32, 356
Abernathy, Thomas G., 404, 405
Academical Village, University of Virginia, 216
Adam Thoroughgood House, 78
Adams, Bill, 139
Adams, John Quincy, 129, 130, 131
Adams, Kate Don, 411
Adams, Lallie: Connelly's Tavern furnishing committee, 190; Natchez Pilgrimage Parade, 139; NGC, 68; Roane Byrnes, 406; splitting pilgrimage profits with homeowners, 172, 173
Adams, Roane, 132
Adams County Sheriff's office, 97
Adams Light Infantry, 73
African Americans: caste-class system in Natchez, 378–79; collective memories, 66; Great Depression photos of Natchez, 384–85; "Heaven Bound" folk drama, 17, 59, 135; history of, influenced by historic preservation, 21; housing for servants of pilgrimage attendees, 142; Jim Crow laws, 395, 396–97; Miller's slide presentations showing subservience, 150, 151, 155; Natchez Association for the Preservation of African American Culture, 413; Natchez Museum of African American History and Culture, 44, 60, 413; performances reaffirming own cultural identity, 59; poverty during the 1930s, 116–18; subservient role in contrived heritage, 12–13; voting rights denied, 378. *See also* racial relations; racism
Agricultural Adjustment Act, 378
Agricultural Bank, 30
AIA. *See* American Institute of Architects (AIA)
Airlie: PGC 1937 pilgrimage, 349; photo, 1935, 118; pre–Civil War architecture, 30; state garden clubs convention in 1931, 103
Alabama, Natchez Trace associations, 298
Albright, Horace M.: NPS heritage management, 204–7, 210; NPS history-based program, 418
Alexander, Anna (Anne) Scheffy: Mexican diplomatic visit, 325, 326; Natchez Spring Pilgrimage presentations, 323; Natchez Trace Parkway, 308
Alford, Terry: Ibrahima, 130–31; *Prince Among Slaves*, 131
American Automobile Association (AAA), 292
American Colonization Society, 128–29
American Institute of Architects (AIA): Committee on Preservation of Natural Beauties and Historic Monuments, 215, 216; Committee on the Preservation of Historic Buildings, 218, 219; executing HABS project, 221–22; HABS advisory committee, 221; John Wood House (Quincy, IL), 45; Overstreet as MS chapter president, 224, 225; producing HABS drawings, 219, 281
American Red Cross: pilgrimage profits, 39; proceeds from NGC and PGC pilgrimages, 354

504   Index

Amy Angell Collier Montague Medal, 398
analytique technique: A. Hays Town, 238–40; D'Evereux, 247; Van Court House, 248–51, 253
Anderson, A. B., 352
Andrews Raid, 363
antebellum era/style: familiar and sentimental, 11; nostalgia for, 146; pilgrimage costumes, 158; as tangible expression of "Old South" myth/ideal, 124; tourists' fascination with, 228, 417
Anzalone, Sam, 71
Appleton, William Sumner, Jr., 202–3, 212
architectural history: architectural categorization, 270–72; HABS affecting, 23; *Journal of the Society of Architectural Historians*, 408; Society of Architectural Historians, 44, 203, 418; "The Tree of Architecture," 270–71. *See also* Historic American Buildings Survey (HABS)
Arlington: "cease-and-desist" order posted, 352; exterior details, 258; fire destroying, 37, 38; HABS documentation, 254, 256–58; HABS historical research, 228–29; Lewis Evans, 234; narrative of antebellum Natchez, 61; north elevation, 257; pilgrimage in 1937, 177, 348; pilgrimage tours, 110; place as feature of Natchez experience, 52; Stark Young, 356; state garden clubs convention in 1931, 103
Armfield, John, 44, 289–90
Armstrong, Mrs. George, 410
Armstrong family, 410
Arrighi, 253–54
Asher, Benjamin, 367, 368
Association for Preservation Technology International, 203, 423
Atlanta Constitution: "Battle of the Hoop Skirts," 353; Natchez pilgrimages, 350–51
Atlanta Journal, 364
Atlantic Monthly, 103
Auburn: adjacent to Duncan Park Public Golf Course, 38; architectural features, 118–19, 122; early tours of homes, 100; HABS historical research, 229; NGC purchase of furniture for, 348; photo of, 112, 115; pictured on map, 14; pre-Civil War architecture, 30; spiral staircase, 14, 16; Thomas Rose, 82; year-round tours, 27
Audubon, John James, 39
"Audubon, the Dancing Master" ballet tableau, 140, 360
Aunt Hill, 126
Aunt Jemima advertising, 102
Austin, Moses, 289
Austin, Stephen, 289
automobiles: marketing of built heritage in Natchez, 25; Natchez only accessible by, 31; Natchez Trace as a highway, 291–93; parkways, 300; pilgrimage to be experienced by, 52; Roane Byrnes, 88; tourism, 9–10, 102, 388
Ayres family, 349

B

Bacon's Castle, 78
Bailey, Thomas A., 293
Baker, Livie J., 73
"Bal Poudre" ball, 140
Balfour, Catherine Hunt, 83
Balfour, William, 83
Ball of a Thousand Candles, 17
ballet tableaux, 59, 140, 360
balloon festival, 414
Bank of Louisville, Louisville, KY, 44, 46, 47
Banker's House, 30, 41
Bankhead, John S., 296
Bankhead, Tallulah, 296
Bankhead, William, 420
Barbour, J. B., 352, 353
Barnum, Annie Green: Arlington architect, 256; clashes over heritage tourism, 339; daughter taking over Monmouth, 393; formation of PGC, 179, 341; home ownership providing control over pilgrimage, 417; Monmouth and Tara design, 368, 369; Monmouth entrance gates, 376; NGC lawsuit, 352; NGC membership, 98; PGC pilgrimage, 347, 350, 352; resigning from NGC, 179; splitting

pilgrimage profits with homeowners, 170, 171–79, 345–46, 347, 352
Barnum, Hubert, 173
Barrow, Henry, 161
Barthel, Diane, 64
Baton Rouge, LA, 39
Battle of New Orleans, 289, 293, 297
"Battle of the Hoop Skirts," 19–20, 341, 345–54, 416
Beane, Frances, 352
Beane family, 349
Beauties of Modern Architecture, The (Lafever), 43
Belle Meade, Nashville, TN, 425
Bellemont Motor Hotel, 421
Belmont, 366–67, 368, 369
Beltzhoover, Melchoir: death of, 399; idea for house tour, 137; tea room for pilgrimage tourists, 159
Beltzhoover, Ruth Audley: becoming modern southern woman, 399–402; Confederate-style ball, 140–41; control of heritage tourism, 339, 341; Copacabana Club, NYC, 398; first pilgrimage, 136, 137, 138; Green Leaves restaurant, 416; historic preservation, 79–80, 98, 157; home ownership providing control over pilgrimage, 417; meeting with Chatelain, 226; Natchez during war years, 391; NGC membership, 68; resigning from NGC, 179; saving Natchez, 394–95; *So Red the Rose* commemorative copies, 314; splitting pilgrimage profits with homeowners, 171, 345–46; tea room for pilgrimage tourists, 159–60
Beltzhoover, Virginia Roane, 78, 136
Benjamin, Asher, 45
Benoist, Rebecca: Eleanor Roosevelt's visit to Natchez, 355; "The Hunt" tableau, 140
Bethel A.M.E. Church, 386
Beulah Missionary Baptist Church, 59
Beverly, 229
Beverly, Jane Ann, 229
"Big Split, The," 19–20
Bilbo, Theodore Gilmore: corresponding with Ferriday Byrnes, 308; death of,

403; diplomacy with Mexico, 323, 325, 327; funding for public school buildings, 269; Natchez Trace Parkway, 305, 318–19, 420
Billie Eaton House, 333, 335
Bingaman, Charlotte Surget, 256
Biographies of Representative Women of the South (Knight), 69–70
Birth of a Nation (movie), 359
Blankenstein, Kathie, 399
Blankenstein, Mrs. Rawdon, 5
Blanks, Ethel "Russie," 387
Blennerhassett, Harman, 165
Blight, David, 11
Blue Ridge Parkway, 300, 319
"Blues Highway," 33
Bluff Park: Gilreath Hill house near, 164; location of, 25, 38; Natchez Trace Parkway driving guide, 317; stone marker for Natchez Trace, 290
Boatner, Lillie Vidal: branding and marketing Natchez, 343, 358, 359, 360, 391; commercialization of "Old South" narrative, 98, 420; Harriet Shields Dixon, 91; Vivien Leigh, 361
boll weevil infestation, 70
Bolton, Herbert E., 221
Bonaparte, Pauline, 188
Boorstin, Daniel J., 3–4, 9–10
Bost, Annie Davis, 390
Bost, Robert E., 390
Botkin, B. A., 212
Bottomley, William Lawrence, 284
boutique hotels, 36
Bowie, Jim, 289
Boyd House (The Oaks), 235
brand personalities, 387–88
Brandon, Gerard, 304
Brandon, Kate Doniphan: control of pilgrimage, 341; NGC, 68, 98; NGC presidency, 350
Brandon Hall: Greek revival style, 119, 120, 122; Mexican diplomatic visit, 325; pre-Civil War architecture, 30
Briars, The: Federal style mantel, 120, 122; film and TV exposure, 17; "Old Natchez on the Mississippi," 360; pilgrimage in 1937, 177; state garden clubs convention in 1931, 103; Varina

Davis marriage to Jefferson Davis, 108, 120, 122
Britton and Koontz Bank: James Fleming resigning from, 172; Magnolia Hall (Henderson-Britton House), 410; Melchoir Beltzhoover, 399; photo of, 88; splitting pilgrimage profits with homeowners, 174
Brooke, Steven, 132–33
Brooks, Samuel, 166
Brown, Andrew: Commercial Bank and Banker's House, 41; pre-Civil War architect, 30
Brown, Catherine Dunbar, 97–98
Brown, Elise, 139
Brown, George, 98
Brown, Mimi, 155
Brownell, Frank L.: Byrnes hosting, 321; Natchez Trace Parkway engineering design, 311
Browning, Gordon, 322
Browning, Norma Lee, 84
Bruce, Helen Ballou, 387
Brumfield School, 60
Bruton Parish Church, 9
Bryant, Harold C., 205
Bryant, Jean Gould, 76
Buchanan, James, 36
Buck, Paul H., 415
Buckhead, Atlanta, GA, 425
Buildings of England, The (Pevsner), 272
built patrimony of Natchez: antebellum era, 64; commodification for preservation, 62; HABS documentation, 20; heritage influencing, 23; motives for heritage narrative, 10; New Deal programs, 6; personalism in, 75
Burkhardt, Walter, 273
Burns, Emily, 123–24
Burn, The, 229, 367
Burr, Aaron: treason plot at Connelly's Tavern, 4, 165, 166; treason trial, 108, 109, 111; William Burr Howell, 122; Windy Hill Manor, 332
Burt, Struthers, 400, 401–2
Busby, Thomas Jefferson (Jeff): Natchez Trace, 294–95, 297–98, 299; Natchez Trace Parkway, 305, 308, 338, 420
Butler, Ruth E.: Natchez Trace location, 310; Natchez Trace Parkway, 420

Butters, James: Frances Johnston, 383; HABS photography, 228
Butts, Russie, 178
Byers, Jacob, 30
Byrne, Joseph: "Battle of the Hoop Skirts," 353; compromising on two pilgrimages, 350; garden club hostilities, 341; preferring modern look over historic preservation, 157
Byrne, William J.: Mexican diplomatic visit, 326; Natchez Trace Association, 304; questioned about historic buildings, 280
Byrnes, Charles Ferriday (Ferriday): death of, 406; education and marriage, 88; Fleming-Byrnes family budget, 172; George Kelly writing about, 95; Mexican diplomatic visit, 325; Natchez Trace Parkway, 318–19; Richard Koch, 159, 179; Senator Bilbo, 308; Stark Young, 187
Byrnes, Roane Fleming: achieving Natchez Trace Parkway, 420; Alma Cassell Kellogg, 97; capturing Natchez mythology, 198; Charles Peterson, 280; Clarksdale, MS, *Register* op-ed, 329; Connelly's Tavern furnishing committee, 190, 193, 194; controlling HABS in Mississippi, 213; entertaining celebrities, 354, 355–56; erroneous history of Connelly's Tavern, 278; Ethel Kelly, 93; Frances Johnston, 380, 383; fundraising for first pilgrimage, 137; Great Depression, 60; HABS collection in Library of Congress, 280; historic preservation and personalism, 282; historic preservation as purpose, 79–81, 85–89, 157; Ibrahima, 127, 130; Lawyer's Lodge, 409; marketing built patrimony of Natchez, 134; marketing of Connelly's Tavern, 187–94, 196–200; meeting with Chatelain, 226, 227; Natchez narrative and the Natchez Trace Parkway, 330, 338–39; Natchez narrative archived in Library of Congress, 275; Natchez Pilgrimage Parade, 139; Natchez Trace Association, 296, 302–8, 313, 403–6; Natchez Trace Parkway as purpose, 285–88; NGC 1937 pilgrimage, 349;

"Old Parish House," 407; personal issues, 317; plaque commemorating, 426; proposal for Gilreath Hill house, 162–64, 166–70; restoration of Connelly's Tavern, 179, 184–87; Richard Koch, 159; rights-of-way acquisition, 314, 320–21; Spanish colonial period, 377; Spanish-themed house tours, 103, 265; splitting pilgrimage profits with homeowners, 171–78; state garden clubs convention in 1931, 99, 100–102; tourism, 111; Windy Hill Manor, 332; working on Natchez Trace Parkway, 284, 391, 393; working with Mexico, 322–27; working with Town to select buildings to document for HABS, 265; writing articles about historic architecture of Natchez, 144; writing projects, 87

Byzantine influences, 31

C

Cabildo, The (New Orleans, LA), 237, 239
Caddo Indians, 289
Cahill, Helger, 196
Callon, John, 413
Calvert, Emily Marks, 387
Cameron, Mrs. Ben, 304
Cammerer, Arno: HABS advisory committee, 221; HABS proposal, 214, 220; Natchez Trace location, 310, 311, 312; Natchez Trace Parkway funding, 319; NPS divisions, 222; NPS heritage management, 206, 207, 209
Cape Girardeau, MO, 39
Capitol Building, Colonial Williamsburg, VA, 9
Capitol Highway, 292
Cárdenas del Rio, Lázaro, 323
Carpenter, Alma Cassell Kellogg: Confederate Pageant Queen, 393; docent for Natchez Spring Pilgrimage, 48–50, 54; guidebook photo, 12, 112; southern lady ideal, 412–13
Carpenter, Amelia, 173
Carpenter, Amie: house tour during state garden club convention, 136; restaurant for pilgrimage tourists, 160
Carpenter, Nathaniel Leslie, 48–49
Carpenter family, 349
Carr, Ethan, 405
Carriage House Restaurant, 354, 398, 412
Cartright, Wilburn, 298
casino gambling in Natchez, 414
Cassell, Albert Gallatin, 97
Cauthen, William A., 389
CCC (Civilian Conservation Corps), 208
Chamberlain family, 349
Chapel of the Cross, Madison County, MS: cross section and interior details, 243, 244; English Gothic style, 240–45; floor plan, 242; railing details, 245; west and east elevations, 243
Charles IV (King of Spain), 17
Chatelain, Verne E.: Charles Peterson, 212, 218, 222–23, 282; discussing Natchez history with NGC, 226; Natchez Trace location, 309, 310; NPS chief historian, 190, 206, 207–10, 211–12, 219; NPS History Division to develop building survey program, 267; NPS history-based program, 272, 417–18; resignation from NPS, 270
Cherokee: George Malin Davis, 93; pre–Civil War architecture, 30; style of, 42, 43
Chicago Daily News, 19
Chicago Daily Tribune, 396, 420
Chicago Tribune: commending NGC work, 19; Natchez and its preservation, 17; Natchez Pilgrimage, 162; Norma Lee Browning on Katherine Miller, 84
Child Life magazine, 87
Childress, Ethel, 321–22, 327
Choctaw: decline of, 380; George Malin Davis, 93; pre–Civil War architecture, 30; style of, 42, 43
Choctaw Indians: Natchez Trace Parkway groundbreaking ceremony, 325; Treaty of Doak's Stand, 32
Chowning's Tavern, 9
Christian Science Monitor, 17
Christiana Campbell's Tavern, 9
City Bank & Trust: splitting pilgrimage profits with homeowners, 173; trophy given to Byrnes, 322
Civil War: Airlie, 118; antebellum era as familiar and sentimental, 11; Natchez said to be noncommittal, 106–7;

surrender of Natchez, 4; Zuleika Lyons Metcalfe, 86, 355–56
Civil Works Administration (CWA): dismantling, 266; funding of HABS project, 219–20; historic preservation as professional field, 202
Civilian Conservation Corps (CCC), 208
Clarion-Ledger, Jackson, MS: Natchez Pilgrimage, 162; state garden clubs convention in 1931, 99
Clark family, 349
Clay, Henry, 129, 130, 131
Cleaveland, John, 45
Clover Nook: pilgrimage in 1937, 177, 349; state garden clubs convention in 1931, 103
Clynne, Ralph H., 228
CMA (Confederate Memorial Association), 73
Coates, Robert M., 17–18, 23, 338, 356–57
Coburn, Paul: Natchez Trace Association Alabama division, 306, 308; rights-of-way acquisition, 314, 317, 319, 321, 322
Cohn, David, 103
collective memory: different and competing memories, 66; as distinct from history, 66; personalism, 75; uses of, 64–66
Collier, John, 212
Collins, Ross A., 306
Colmer, William M., 306
Colonial Dames of Mississippi, 331
colonial era: first pilgrimage highlighting, 140; glamorization of, 106; Natchez women in 1930s, 79
Colonial National Monument, Yorktown, VA, 216
Colonial Parkway, 300
Colonial Virginia Capitol, 284
Colonial Williamsburg Restoration: Albright and Ickes touring, 205; construction of, 9; Perry, Shaw & Hepburn, 216, 217; Prentis Store, 8; restoration, 190; William Perry, 215
Columbia University: Charles Peterson, 423; George Malin Davis Kelly, 93; Roane Byrnes, 87
Commercial Appeal, Memphis, TN, 162

Commercial Bank: Greek Revival style, 41; photos, 384; pre-Civil War architecture, 30
"Common Glory, The," 58
Compton, Charles (Charlie) Cromartie: "Ballet Tableau," 59; early tours of homes, 100; *Natchez and the Pilgrimage*, 103, 104, 105–16; Natchez Trace Association, 304
Concord: building and destruction of, 92; compared to Linden, 234
Confederacy: later pilgrimage entertainments, 140–41; Miller's slide presentations, 152, 153, 154
Confederate Ball/Pageant: Miller's slide presentations, 154, 155; Natchez Spring Pilgrimage of Antebellum Homes, 17; photos of, 132; post-WWII presentation of, 402
Confederate Memorial Association (CMA), 73
Connelly, Patrick: Connelly's Tavern, 4; Gilreath Hill house, 164, 166
Connelly's Tavern (Ellicott's Hill House/Inn): bedroom scene, 199; Byrnes and Miller feud, 303; colonial Spanish heritage, 350; dedication of, 196–98, 314, 349; Edith Wyatt Moore, 90; erroneous history, 278; exterior view, 191; feud within NGC, 345; furnishing committee, 190, 192, 193–94; marketing of, 187–200; museum and NGC headquarters, 191, 192; myths about, 4–5; Natchez Trace Parkway groundbreaking ceremony, 325; "Old Natchez on the Mississippi," 360; preservation efforts, 80, 162–70; purchase of, 348; Tap Room, 194, 195. *See also* Ellicott's Hill House/Inn; Gilreath Hill House
Conner, Anne, 344
Conner, Audley, 407
Conner, Mary Britton, 349
Conner, Mike, 296
Connerton, Paul, 55
Conti House (Governor Holmes House), 65
Corkern, Wilton: Charles Peterson, 210; Town as HABS district chief, 269

costumes for pilgrimage participants, 157, 158
Cottage Gardens: NGC 1937 pilgrimage, 349; Spanish Colonial period, 121, 122
Couner, Eliza, 53
"Countess of the Steerage, The" (Byrnes), 87
Cox, John Coates: Ibrahima, 127, 128, 356; Roane Byrnes, 86–87
Cox, Karen L.: *Goat Castle*, 60; Katherine Miller dressed for the pilgrimage, 84; "Old South" idea/myth, 102
Cox, Rousseau, 128
Cram, Goodhue, and Ferguson, 218
Creek tribe, 288
crepe myrtle festival in Natchez, 414
Crissie (servant), 402
Crockett, Davy, 289
"Cross and Sword," 58
"Crossroads" sign on US Highway 61, 33, 34
cultural tourism: emergence of, 6–11; factors affecting, 19–20; making historic preservation possible, 144; Natchez women first to commercialize, 137; NPS historic monuments, 205, 206; personalism forming collective memory, 80. *See also* heritage tourism
Cunningham, Ann Pamela: historic preservation, 75; Mount Vernon Ladies' Association, 202
Curtis, Nathaniel, 225
Cuthbertson, Stuart: Mexican diplomatic visit, 325; Moore's Natchez history research, 227, 230–31; Natchez Trace Association, 297; Natchez Trace Parkway, 308; Vicksburg National Military Park, 190
Cutrer, Richard W., 353–54
CWA. *See* Civil Works Administration (CWA)

D

Dakin, Charles, 46, 47
Dakin, James: Bank of Louisville, Louisville, KY, 46, 47; buildings designed by, 47
Dana, Richard, 60, 122–24
Daniels, Jonathan: *The Devil's Backbone*, 394; poverty as a preservative of the past, 12
Daniels, Josephus, 324
DAR. *See* Daughters of the American Revolution (DAR)
Daughters of the American Revolution (DAR): allegorical tableaux, 58; Catherine Brown, 98; founding of Mississippi State Society, 73; Natchez Trace Associations, 296, 298, 302; Natchez Trace monument, 74, 75; Natchez Trace Parkway, 19; stone markers for Natchez Trace, 290–91, 293
Daughters of the War of 1812, 291, 293
Davis, Allison, 378–79
Davis, Elizabeth, 92
Davis, George Malin, 92, 93
Davis, Jack, 21
Davis, Jefferson, 108, 120, 122
Davis, Timothy, 332
Davis, Varina Howell: Josiah Winchester, 409; marriage to Jefferson Davis, 108, 120, 122
de Pogos, Concepcion, 324
Deighton, Lillian, 365, 368
Deiler, John Hanno, 277
Demaray, Arthur E.: approving HABS, 214; nonhistoric nature of Natchez Trace Parkway, 330
Department of the Interior: Harold Ickes, 205; historic preservation as professional field, 202; Historic Sites Act of 1935, 267; NPS, 204
"Derelict, The" (Byrnes), 87
D'Evereux: Braden Elementary School, 421; early tours of homes, 100; *A Gentleman from Mississippi* (movie), 358; Natchez Spring Pilgrimage of Antebellum Homes, 1952, 2; north elevation and architectural details, 247; PGC 1937 pilgrimage, 349; photos of, 51, 112, 113; slides showing, 145, 146; splitting pilgrimage profits with homeowners, 169; Stark Young, 356; state garden clubs convention in 1931, 103
Devil's Backbone, The (Daniels), 394
Devil's Punchbowl, 353

Dickson, Jefferson Davis, Jr., 389
Dinsmoor, Silas, 32
Disneyland/Disney World, as historylands, 7, 9
Dixie Before Disney (Hollis), 292, 388
Dixie Highway, 292
Dixon, Harriet Shields: clashes over heritage tourism, 339; commercialization of Natchez narrative, 420; Connelly's Tavern as bonus for pilgrimage, 195, 196; control of pilgrimage, 341; Edith Moore, 343; historic preservation as purpose, 79–80, 91; Natchez Trace Association, 302, 303; NGC, 68; opposing PGC pilgrimage, 346–48; splitting pilgrimage profits with homeowners, 171–78
Dixon, Joseph F., 91
Dixon Hardware Store, 91
docents for Natchez experience, 54–55
Dockery, Octavia, 60, 122–24
Dollard, John, 378
Douglas, Eri, 227
Douglass, Andrew Ellicott, 196
Downton Abbey, 414
Doxey, Wall, 305–6
Drummond, Eugene, 226, 227
Dumas, Cornelia, 17
Duncan Park Public Golf Course, 38
Dunleith: Alma Carpenter, 48; early tours of homes, 100; film and TV exposure, 17; gates of, 133; house tour during state garden club convention, 136; Miller's slide presentations, 156; Natchez Spring Pilgrimage of Antebellum Homes, 3; "Old Natchez on the Mississippi," 360; PGC 1937 pilgrimage, 349; place as feature of Natchez experience, 52; silent movie, 100; splitting pilgrimage profits with homeowners, 173
Dylan, Bob, 33

E

Eastland, James, 403, 405
economic depression. *See* Great Depression
ECW. *See* Emergency Conservation Work (ECW) Act of 1933
Edgewood: Mary Henderson Lambdin, 347; "Old Natchez on the Mississippi," 360; pre-Civil War architecture, 30; Thomas Rose, 82
Edwards Hotel, Jackson, MS, 295, 321
Eickenroht, Marvin: HABS work, 422; Southern Division HABS chief, 269–70, 272–73
Eidt, Carolyn Davis, 140
Eisenhower, Dwight, 405
El Camino Real: Byrnes working with Mexico, 322–27, 420; Natchez Trace Association, 296; Pan-American parkway, 288, 289; US Route 82, 293; WWII ending plans for, 402
Elgin: "cease-and-desist" order posted, 352; PGC 1937 pilgrimage, 349; state garden clubs convention in 1931, 103
Elks Lodge, 392
Ellicott, Andrew: Connelly's Tavern, 4; "Old Natchez on the Mississippi," 360; Treaty of San Lorenzo (Treaty of Madrid), 165, 166
Ellicott, Anna Campbell, 197
Ellicott, William Miller, III, 196–98
Ellicott's Hill House/Inn: Connelly's Tavern, 4, 5; Gilreath Hill house, 164; NGC purchase of, 348; place as feature of Natchez experience, 52; pre-Civil War architecture, 30; preservation efforts, 80; Richard Koch, 159; site of, 44. *See also* Connelly's Tavern (Ellicott's Hill House/Inn); Gilreath Hill House
Elliott, Jack D., Jr., 335
Elms, The: Alma Cassell Kellogg, 97, 348; "cease-and-desist" order posted, 352; film and TV exposure, 17; guidebook photo, 12, 112; Natchez Spring Pilgrimage tour, 48, 49–50; nonparticipation in 1937 pilgrimage, 177; renovation, 49; state garden clubs convention in 1931, 103; Thomas Rose, 82
Elms Court: Ball of a Thousand Candles, 17; cast iron portico being destroyed by overgrown vines, 11, 12; Frances Johnston, 383; *Natchez and the Pilgrimage* photo, 104; participation

in 1937 pilgrimage, 177; state garden clubs convention in 1931, 103; Thomas Rose, 82
Emerald Mound, 335, 336
Emergency Conservation Work (ECW) Act of 1933: CCC work, 208; NPS to provide relief for architecture, 213
Engle, Charles F., 304, 349
Eola Hotel: abandonment of, 36; Pilgrimage attendees filling, 142; state garden club convention, 135; stationery from, 417; view from, 40
"Esplanade": Natchez bluffs, 24, 25; Natchez "On-Top-of-the-Hill," 38; Natchez Trace Parkway driving guide, 317
Essex (Federal gunboat), 107
Estes, Patrick Mann (P. M.): death of, 403; Natchez Trace Association Tennessee division, 306–7, 308; Natchez Trace Parkway, 420; rights-of-way, 314, 317–18, 319, 321–22, 327
Esudero, Carolina, 326
Evans, Lewis, 234, 257
Evans, Walker, 342, 383, 384, 385–86, 387–88
Everybody's Magazine, 290, 310
Ewald family house, 159
Eyre, Wilson, 218
Eyrich, Clarence, 170–71

F
Fall Pilgrimage, described, 26
Famous & Price Store (Natchez Department Store), 399, 400
Farm Security Administration, 383, 388
farmers: boll weevil infestation, 70; necessity of roads, 292
Fata Morgana (Stanton), 331
Fauntleroy, Rebecca, 352
Faust, Drew Gilpin: southern belle/lady ideal, 364; southern women, 68–69; women's history influenced by historic preservation, 21
Fazio, Michael, 415, 425
Federal Bureau of Highways, 293
Federal State Aid Road Act of 1916, 293
Federal style of architecture: The Briars, 120, 122; Natchez, 28

Felder, Adolph, 277–78
Feltus, Catherine, 173
Feltus, Charlotte, 170
Feltus, Mavis: Connelly's Tavern furnishing committee, 190; entertaining celebrities, 354; Linden, 234; Roane Byrnes, 187
Feltus family, 349
Ferguson, William, 335
Ferris, William, 384
Ferry, Dexter, 95
Ferry, Marian Kelly, 93, 95
First National Bank, Greenville, MS, 70
First Presbyterian Church: Ethel Kelly, 96; Federal/Greek Revival style, 40, 41; pre-Civil War architecture, 30; splitting pilgrimage profits with homeowners, 174
Fisher, Carl, 292
Fitch, James Marston: Auburn, 216; Columbia University, 423
Fitzgerald, Philip, 361, 362
FitzPatrick, James A.: "Old Natchez on the Mississippi" (travel movie), 343, 359–60; *Traveltalks* showing Natchez homes, 17
"Flash News, The," 407
Fleming, Anna Metcalfe, 58
Fleming, James Stockman, Sr.: Beverly, 229; resigning from Britton and Koontz Bank, 172; Roane Byrnes, 87
Fleming, Lalie, 86
Fletcher, F. Banister: systematic catalog for world architecture, 418; "The Tree of Architecture," 270–71
Fondren, Jackson, MS, 425
"For She's a Jolly Good Fellow" (Byrnes), 87
Ford, A. L.: Natchez Trace Parkway, 420; Natchez Trace Parkway groundbreaking ceremony, 325; Natchez Trace Parkway politics, 305, 308, 319
Ford, Clara, 355
Ford, Henry: Greenfield Village as a historyland, 9; idealized memory of America's preindustrial past, 212; visiting Natchez, 20, 343, 355
Forks of the Road slave market, 60, 290
Forsyth Spanish House, 126

Fort, Julian, 70
Fort Marion National Monument, 209
Fort Rosalie: Andrew Ellicott, 4; destruction of, 106; killing of French settlers, 47; Manuel Gayoso de Lemos, 165; Natchez founded in 1716 as a French settlement, 25; Natchez National Historical Park, 395, 413; Old Fort Rosalie reconstruction, 344, 389–90; Visitor Center, 23
Forth, Sally, 351
Foster, Ada, 130
Foster, Katie, 349
Foster, Stephen, 102
Foster, Thomas, 127, 128, 130
Fosters Fields, 131
Foster's Mound, 131
Fowler, Dix, 409
Frank, Melanie, 73
Franklin, Isaac, 44, 289–90
Frary, I. T., 221
French heritage of Natchez, 25, 106
Futa Jalon, 87, 128

G

Gallaudet, Thomas Hopkins, 128–29
Gallier, Charles, 47
Gallier, James: buildings designed by, 46, 47; Government Street Presbyterian Church, Mobile, AL, 46, 47
Gandy, Thomas, 84
Garcia de Texada, Manuel, 125–26
Garden Club of Virginia: "Historic Garden Week," 137; historic gardens, 77, 78
Garden Clubs of America: Amy Angell Collier Montague Medal, 398; modern women, 76
Garden Clubs of Mississippi: catalyst for pilgrimages, 135–36; founding in 1929, 78; PGC membership denied, 346, 348; state convention held in Natchez, 99, 100, 103
"Garden of Dreams" tableau, 58
gardens, landmark value of, 77
Gardens of Colony and State (Lockwood), 76–77
Gardner, Agnes, 346
Gardner, Burleigh, 378–79

Gardner, Malcolm: Byrnes hosting, 321; evaluating HABS archive, 274–76, 277; Mexican diplomatic visit, 325; Natchez Trace location, 310; Natchez Trace Parkway, 308, 330, 404; "Old Parish House" addition, 408
Gardner, Mary, 378–79
Gates, Frank P., 226, 227
Gaude, Henry, 390
Gayoso de Lemos, Manuel: Concord, 92, 93, 193; responsible for Bluff Park, 25, 106; Saragossa, 229; Spanish colonial Governor, 165; Spanish heritage house tours, 103
Gentleman from Mississippi, A (movie), 100, 358
George Washington Memorial Parkway (Mount Vernon Memorial Highway), 299, 300
Gerow, Richard O., 407
Gilreath, J. R., 164
Gilreath Hill House: Connelly's Tavern, 19; disagreement over restoration, 171–72, 176–77; east elevation, 183, 185; first-floor plan, 181–82; longitudinal section and interior details, 184, 186; Natchez Trace Parkway driving guide, 317; north elevation, 182–83; proposal for purchase and restoration, 162–70; restoration of, 179–87; second-floor plan, 181; south elevation, 183–84; unknown cost of renovation, 176; west elevation, 181–82. *See also* Connelly's Tavern (Ellicott's Hill House/Inn); Ellicott's Hill House/Inn
Girault, John, 25
Glasberg, David, 61
Glassie, Henry, 61–62
Glenwood (Goat Castle), 60, 123–24
Gloucester: building sections, 246; Charlotte Surget, 347; HABS documentation, 245–47; HABS historical research, 232–34; state garden clubs convention in 1931, 103
Goat Castle (Glenwood), 60, 123–24
Goat Castle: A True Story of Murder, Race, and the Gothic South (Cox), 60
Godey's Lady Book and Magazine, 158

Goeldner, Paul, 180–81
Gone with the Wind (Mitchell): antebellum era, 342, 417; anti-heroes, 18; romantic Natchez narrative, 23; southern belle/lady ideal, 147
Gone with the Wind (movie): Monmouth as inspiration for Tara, 36, 37; "Old South" myth/ideal, 63, 377; set design for influenced by Natchez, 343, 360–77, 420
Goodrich, Hunter, 98
Goodrich, Mary Louise Kendall, 413
Goodwin, William A. R., 9
Gordon House, 335, 336
Gothic revival style, 105, 112
Government Street Presbyterian Church, Mobile, AL, 46, 47
Governor Holmes House (Conti House), 65
Governor's Mansion, MS, 235
Governor's Palace, Colonial Williamsburg, VA, 9, 284
Grafton, Jennie, 82
Grafton, Kirby W., 82
Grafton, Molly, 82
Grafton, Thomas, 82
Graham, Alice Walworth, 320–21
Granberry, Theodore: Arlington, 375; Gilreath Hill House, 179, 181–83; Linden, 373
de Grand Pré, Carlos: Concord, 92; Hope Villa (Farm), 279
Grant, Ulysses, 232
Great Depression: cultural tourism helping, 60; George and Ethel Kelly, 97; idealized memory of America's preindustrial past, 212; mood of Americans and US tourism, 9–10; Natchez, 70–72; "Old South" myth/ideal, 102; photographing poverty in Natchez, 342, 343; towns "frozen in time," 10, 12
Greek Revival architecture: Belmont, 366; Brandon Hall, 119, 120, 122; Cottage Gardens stairway, 121, 122; Natchez, 28; *Natchez and the Pilgrimage*, 105, 112
Green, Charlotte, 321
Green, Paul, 58

Green Leaves: film and TV exposure, 17; Miller's slide presentations, 152, 153, 154; nonparticipation in 1937 pilgrimage, 177; open for early tours, 137; photos, 78, 136; pre-Civil War architecture, 30; restaurant, 416; Ruth Beltzhoover, 399–400, 402; state garden clubs convention in 1931, 103; tea room for pilgrimage tourists, 159–60
Greenfield Village, Dearborn, MI, 8, 9
Greenlea, 30
Greenville Democratic Times, 347
Gregory, James, 416
Griffin, Cyrus, 130
Griffin, James, 232
Griffith, D. W., 359
guides for Natchez experience, 54–55
Guion, Isaac, 165
Guttersen, Alston G., 214, 220, 423
Guyton, Pearl Vivian: Connelly's Tavern, 186, 192, 194–95; guidebook, 104
Gwin, Anne: Arlington, 348; Monmouth, 393; NGC lawsuit, 352

H

HABS. *See* Historic American Buildings Survey (HABS)
Hagen, Olaf: Mexican diplomatic visit, 325; Natchez Trace Association, 297; Natchez Trace location, 310; Natchez Trace Parkway, 308, 312, 420
Halbwachs, Maurice, 65
Hale, Effie Lacy: marketing for movies in Natchez, 358–59; NGC 1937 pilgrimage, 349; splitting pilgrimage profits with homeowners, 175, 176
Hamilin, Talbot, 100
Hammer, Bette Barber: *Natchez' First Ladies: Katherine Grafton Miller and the Pilgrimage*, 98; "Old South" myth/ideal, 102; presenters as feature of Natchez experience, 53
Hampton, Ellen, 90
Hardie, James: First Presbyterian Church, 40; Laurel Hill, 229, 230; pre-Civil War architect, 30
Harpes Brothers, 357
Harris, Joel Chandler, 102
Harris, William, 86

Harrison, Julie, 17
Harrison, Pat: death of, 403; funding for public school buildings, 269; Natchez Trace Association, 296, 304, 305, 308; Natchez Trace Parkway, 298–99, 420; Natchez Trace Parkway funding, 324; Natchez-Vidalia Bridge, 35; soliciting support for Natchez Trace Parkway, 318, 319
Harrison, William Henry, 166
Hasinai Confederacy, 289
Hazelius, Artur, 7
Healy, George, Jr., 161
Heart of Maryland (movie), 100
"Heaven Bound" folk drama: African American performances, 59; Natchez Spring Pilgrimage of Antebellum Homes, 17; profit from early pilgrimages, 135
Henderson, Ellen, 73
Henderson, John, 50
Henderson family, 131
Henderson-Britton House. *See* Magnolia Hall (Henderson-Britton House)
Henry, Mrs. Robert, 302, 346
heritage: built patrimony and history transformed into, 423–24; commodification of history into, 62; *vs.* history, 212–14, 265, 282; narrative for tourism, 272; Natchez Trace Association, 296; tangible *vs.* intangible, 28–29; tourism-based economy, 395
heritage tourism: clashes over, 339; heritage *vs.* history, 5–6, 20; understanding creation of, 424. *See also* cultural tourism
Hernandez, Louise: historical research, 228; Natchez Trace Parkway map, 15
High Point Furniture Company, 358
Hispanic culture, Santa Fe, NM, 13
Historic American Buildings Survey (HABS): archive of drawings, 218, 219; Charles Peterson proposing, 211, 213; creation of, 214, 423; design of Tara for movie, 361, 368, 369, 377; development of architectural history, 23; enthusiasm waning, 273; falling prey to personalism, 418–19; funding and World War II, 280; funding instability, 283; funding terminated by WPA, 273–74; Gilreath Hill House, 179; lack of oversight by architectural historians, 418–19; Marschalk Printing Office, 131; Natchez drawings, 223–24; Natchez in 1936, 19; NGC influencing, 201–2; previous proposals for documentation of American historic buildings, 215–18; problems with, 213–14; reorganization and restart of, 267; Rosalie, 18; salaries of employees, 224; state advisory boards to select buildings, 226
Historic Natchez Foundation: Arlington, 37; Brumfield School on National Register of Historic Places, 60; founding of, 7, 413
historic preservation: Alice Sims and Jane Johnson, 93; influence on African American and women's history, 21; motives for, 424; narrative's dramatic performance important to, 47–48; national level program, 201; NGC beginning in 1933, 157; NGC controlling, 415; personalism *vs.* professional approach, 282
Historic Sites Act of 1935, 267
historical consciousness: evolution of, 61–62; mission of garden clubs, 76
Historical Society of Quincy and Adams County, 45
history: commodification into heritage, 62; as distinct from collective memory, 66; *vs.* heritage, 212–14, 265, 282; *vs.* heritage tourism, 5–6, 20; narrative to use as teaching tool, 272
"historylands": cultural tourism, 6–11, 13–19; Disneyland/Disney World, 7, 9; Greenfield Village, 8, 9; Natchez as, 13–19, 36, 51, 227; *Visiting Our Past: America's Historylands*, 3–4
Hitchcock, Henry Russell, 418–19
Hoelscher, Steven: performances as cultural expression, 55; *Southern Heritage on Display*, 48–50; "Where the South Still Lives: Displaying Heritage in Natchez, Mississippi," 126–27
Holland, James W., 218
Holland, Leicester B.: American architecture, 272; continuing HABS after

funding expiration, 266; controlling direction of HABS, 270, 272–73, 280–81, 283–84; expectations becoming an obstacle, 283–84; federal program for historic architectural documentation, 218–19, 221; Frances Johnston photographing Natchez, 342; local historians a problem, 283; national exhibition of HABS work, 266–67; overestimated abilities for historic building drawings, 280–81; systematic catalog for American architecture, 418

Holland's Magazine, 53
Holleran, Michael, 202
Hollins College, 48
Hollis, Tim, 292, 388
Holly Hedges, 125
Holy Savior of Natchez Church, 261
Homewood: *Birth of a Nation* (movie), 359; PGC 1937 pilgrimage, 349; William Balfour, 83
Hooks, Laura Belle, 408
Hope Farm (Hope Villa): celebrities entertained at, 354; documentation of, 278–79; Frances Johnston, 383; Katherine Miller photos, 397; nonparticipation in 1937 pilgrimage, 177; photos, 73, 387; place as feature of Natchez experience, 52; purchase of (1927), 83; showing gardens during presentations, 147; southern belle/lady ideal, 22, 148, 156; state garden clubs convention in 1931, 103
Hopkins, Harry: dismantling CWA, 266; funding for HABS, 215, 219–20; Natchez Trace Parkway funding, 318, 328; Works Progress Administration, 208
hotels and housing, Natchez: Bellemont Motor Hotel, 421; boutique hotels, 36; Eola Hotel, 36, 40, 135, 142, 417; Natchez Grand Hotel, 36; Natchez Hotel, 142, 170–71; for Pilgrimage attendees, 142, 157, 170–71
Houmas (plantation home), 47
House and Garden magazine, 358
Houston, Sam, 289
Howell, William Burr, 122

Howells, William Dean, 11
Hull, Cordell: Mexican diplomatic visit, 325; Natchez Trace Parkway, 420
Hull, Emmett, 226, 277, 278–79
Hunt, Abijah, 234
Hunt, David, 83
"Hunt, The" (tableau), 140, 141, 360
Huyssen, Andreas, 55

I

Ibrahima (Abdulrahman Ibrahim Ibn Sori), 87, 127–32, 356
Ickes, Harold L.: approving HABS, 179, 214, 215, 219–20; Arno Cammerer, 206, 207; continuing HABS, 266, 267; critical of Natchez Trace Parkway, 287, 288; Department of the Interior, 205; enthusiasm about parkways, 300; HABS advisory committee, 221; HABS program, 222; Mexican diplomatic visit, 325; Mújica asking about Byrnes, 324; Natchez Trace Parkway, 299, 419, 420; NPS survey budget, 309; opposing Natchez Trace Parkway, 319
Independence National Park, 423
Ingenieria e Industria magazine, 326
Institute Hall, 97
"institutional vernacular" architecture: described, 301, 332–33, 335; Johnston's photographs, 380, 381
intangible heritage: combining with tangible heritage, 28–29; performing narrative, 55; personalism in built patrimony, 75
Interstate Highway Program, 394, 405

J

Jackson, Andrew: Battle of New Orleans, 289, 293, 297; marriage at Springfield, 108, 109
Jackson Daily News, 352
Jackson Military Highway Association, 293
Jagger, Mick, 20
Jakle, John: history as contrived attractions, 9; romanticizing old and historic places, 145
James, Harlean, 221

James Andrews House. *See* 311-313 Market Street ("Priest House," "Spanish Priest's House," Parish House, James Andrews House)
James Moore House, 164. *See also* Gilreath Hill House
Jefferson, Thomas, 216
Jefferson College, Washington, MS: Aaron Burr treason trial, 108, 109, 111; photo of, 112, 114
Jefferson National Expansion Memorial, St. Louis, MO, 221, 423
Jefferson Street Methodist Church, 40
Jenkin, Mrs. Hugh, 304
Jenkins, H. R., 353
Jim Crow laws, 395, 396–97
John Wood House, Quincy, IL, 44, 45
Johnson, Jane: George and Ethel Kelly, 93, 94; "Old Natchez on the Mississippi," 360
Johnson, Robert, 33, 34
Johnston, Frances Benjamin: decline of Natchez, 379–83; Hope Farm (Villa) photo, 73; photographing Natchez, 342; photos misrepresented, 419
Johnston, R. H., 292
Jones, Elizabeth: Natchez Trace, 290; Natchez Trace Association, 304; Natchez Trace monument, 75
Jones, Mary, 174
Journal of Heritage Tourism, 54
Journal of Mississippi History, 277
Journal of the Society of Architectural Historians, 408
Judd, Henry, 409
Junkin, Sally, 12, 112
Junkin, Sophie: NGC, 68; signage for tourists, 169

K

Kaiser family, 349
Kane, Harnett: "cease-and-desist" order for PGC pilgrimage, 352–53; Katherine Miller, 84, 285; *Natchez on the Mississippi*, 23, 394
Keating, Bern, 406, 407
Kellogg, Alma Cassell: control of pilgrimage, 341, 417; Douglas MacArthur, 399; Eleanor Roosevelt's visit to Natchez, 354–55; Ethel Kelly, 93, 97; formation of PGC, 179; garden clubs, 97; historic preservation as purpose, 79–80, 97; Natchez Trace Association, 296; NGC, 48, 68; PGC treasurer, 347, 348; planner during early pilgrimages, 137, 138; purchase of Connelly's Tavern, 167–68; splitting pilgrimage profits with homeowners, 171–79
Kellogg, Joseph Bentley, 97, 167
Kelly, Ethel Moore: 1937 pilgrimage, 349; Alma Cassell Kellogg, 93, 97; branding and marketing Natchez, 343; control of pilgrimage, 341; entertaining Henry and Clara Ford, 355; Frances Johnston, 380; Great Depression, 70; historic preservation as purpose, 79–80, 92–97; Melrose silverware pattern, 343, 358; opening home for tour, 137; splitting pilgrimage profits with homeowners, 173, 175
Kelly, George Malin Davis: Byrnes, and Natchez Trace Association, 302; Byrnes's promotional travel, 322; complaints about *Natchez and the Pilgrimage*, 112; entertaining Henry and Clara Ford, 355; Great Depression, 70–71, 93–97; Magnolia Hall (Henderson-Britton House), 410; splitting pilgrimage profits with homeowners, 169, 170–76; tours of Melrose, 161–62, 415–16
Kelly, Julia Davis, 92, 93
Kelly, Marion, 70
Kelly, Richard, 93
Kelly, Stephen, 93
Kemper, Edward C., 221
Kendall, Mary Louise, 352
Kendall, William, 98
Kendall family, 349
Kerry, William Graves, 221
Kimball, Fiske: AIA Committee on Preservation of Natural Beauties and Historic Monuments, 216; early tours of homes, 100
King's Tavern: bandits, 111; bullet holes, 122, 123; "cease-and-desist" order posted, 352; Natchez Trace Parkway driving guide, 317; Natchez

Under-the-Hill, 4; PGC, 413; PGC 1937 pilgrimage, 349; preservation efforts, 80; site of, 44; state garden clubs convention in 1931, 103
kitsch: Mammy's Cupboard, 22, 23, 344, 389, 390, 420; in Natchez, 388–91; Old Fort Rosalie, 344, 389–90
Klemesrud, Judy, 411
Kline, Logan C., 184
Knight, Lucian Lamar, 69–70
Koch, Richard: A. Hays Town, 227, 235; *analytique* technique, 239; Connelly's Tavern, 179–80, 185, 186–87, 189–90, 192–93; measuring and drawing historic buildings, 216; "Old Parish House" foundation, 407; preservation architect, 159
Ku Klux Klan, 306
Kurtz, Wilbur G., Sr., 361–65, 377

L

Ladies' Home Journal: Katherine Miller, 398; Ruth Beltzhoover, 400, 401–2
Lafever, Minard, 43, 124
Lake St. John, LA, 112, 116
Lambdin, Mary Henderson: Natchez Spring Pilgrimage presentations, 323; *Natchez: Symbol of the Old South*, 116; PGC secretary, 347
Lamport, Michael, 260
land pirates, 17–18, 23, 338, 356–57
Landrum, Ralph L.: Natchez Trace Association, 287, 296, 297, 298, 307, 308, 402; Natchez Trace Parkway groundbreaking ceremony, 325; Natchez Trace Parkway progress, 328; rights-of-way acquisition, 314, 320; soliciting support for Natchez Trace Parkway, 318
landscape architecture: Natchez Trace Parkway landscape design, 311; Natchez Trace Parkway motorist experience, 337, 338; parkways, 300
Lange, Dorothea, 387
Lansdowne: George Marshall, 83; NGC meeting, 174, 175; open for early tours, 137; PGC 1937 pilgrimage, 349; pre-Civil War architecture, 30; state garden clubs convention in 1931, 103

Laub, Harriet, 352
Laub, Saul, 176
Laurel Hill Plantation, 229, 230
Lavoie, Catherine, 249
Lawrence, Lallie: Mexican diplomatic visit, 325; Natchez Trace Parkway, 308; Roane Byrnes, 87
Lawyer's Lodge, 44, 409
Learned family, 410
Lee, Ned, 293
Lee, Robert E., 216
Lee, Ronald F.: dismissing accomplishments of HABS, 223; Natchez Trace location, 309–11; Natchez Trace Parkway problems, 330; NPS, 207–8, 211
Legionnaire's Disease, 36
Leigh, Vivien, 360–61
Leimkuehler, F. Ray, 276–77
Leland, Waldo G., 221
Lennan, Francisco, 261, 407
Leonard, Israel, 367
Letarouilly, Paul, 239
"Let's pretend" tourism, 13, 31–32, 102, 193, 265, 377, 415, 426
Lewis, Kate, 159, 160
Lewis, Lloyd, 19
Lewis, Meriwether, 289, 335, 336
Lexington, 352
Library of Congress: archive of HABS drawings, 219, 281; cataloging of HABS work, 266–67, 280; historic preservation as professional field, 202; Leicester B. Holland, 218–19; Natchez narrative archived in, 275
Liddle, Jay T., Jr.: Arlington, 375; Gilreath Hill House, 179, 181–82; Linden, 373; Natchez map, 14
Life magazine, 162
Lifetime on Deadline: Self-Portrait of a Southern Journalist, A (Healy), 161
Lincoln, Abraham: Illinois home, 10; John Wood, 44; Logan County, IL courthouse, 9
Lincoln Highway, 292
Lind, Jenny, 360
Linden: elevation and details, 373, 375; first-floor plan, 255; HABS documentation, 254, 255, 256; HABS historical research, 234, 235; Miller's slide

presentations, 151, 152, 155; Natchez Spring Pilgrimage of Antebellum Homes, 13; north elevation and exterior details, 256; PGC 1937 pilgrimage, 349; photo of, 112, 114; splitting pilgrimage profits with homeowners, 170; state garden clubs convention in 1931, 103
Lindgren, James, 75
Lipscomb, Ed, 347, 348, 349
Little, Eliza, 232
Little, Peter, 231, 232
Lockwood, Alice G. B., 76–77
Loeb, August, 351
Logan County, IL courthouse, 9
Longstreth, Richard, 424
Longwood: Charles Peterson, 409; Civil War, 124; Frances Johnston, 383; HABS not documenting, 235; juxtaposition of old and new, 31; Moorish Revival, 105; place as feature of Natchez experience, 52; pre-Civil War architecture, 31; preservation efforts, 80; sold to PGC, 413; year-round tours, 27
Los Angeles Times: garden clubs' feuds, 395–96; Natchez and its preservation, 17
"Lost Colony, The," 58
Louisiana State Capitol, Baton Rouge, LA, 47
Lowell, Eva, 100
Lowenthal, David, 424
Lum Brothers Livestock Building, 384, 385–86
Lynch, Kevin, 64
Lyon, Marguerite, 420

M

MacArthur, Douglas, 20, 399
MacKenna, Constantine, 260
Macrae, Ruth Faxon, 104–5
Magnolia Hall (Henderson-Britton House): donation of, 410; pre-Civil War architecture, 30; site of, 44; *This Too Is Natchez*, 125
Magnolia Vale: house tour during state garden club convention, 136; participation in 1937 pilgrimage, 177; pre-Civil War architecture, 30; Richard Koch, 159; state garden clubs convention in 1931, 103
Majesty of Natchez, The (Brooke), 132–33, 264–65
Malt Shop, 421–22
Mammy's Cupboard, 22, 23, 344, 389, 390, 420
Manship House, 235
maps: creation of Natchez as cultural tourist attraction, 14–16; geography of imagination, 14–16; Natchez Trace Parkway, 15, 329
Mardi Gras, 140
Marks, Emma, 68
Marschalk, Andrew, 129–30, 131
Marschalk Printing Office, 131–32
Marshall, Agnes, 137
Marshall, George, 83
Marshall, Levin R., 41
Marshall, Margaret: Edith Bolling Wilson, 143; Natchez Pilgrimage Parade, 140; NGC, 68
Marshall, Shelby, 349
Marshall, Theodora Britton: Connelly's Tavern as bonus for pilgrimage, 195; southern lady and modern woman, 97; splitting pilgrimage profits with homeowners, 172, 176
Marshall family, 349
Martin, Beverly, 183, 421
Martin, Mrs. William T., 53
Mason, Samuel, 317, 357
Massey, James C., 221
Mayfield, Lucille: Byrnes, and Natchez Trace Association, 303, 305, 307–8; DAR national headquarters, 303; Natchez Trace Association, 296, 297, 298
Maynard, George, 298
McAliser, Hill, 322
McCain, William D., 277
McClure, James, 36
McDonnell, Carolyn C., 106
McGehee, Dan R.: Mexican diplomatic visit, 325; Natchez Trace Parkway politics, 306
McGill, Ralph, 351
McIlhenry, Carlotta Searles, 387
McKittrick family, 104

Meem, John Gaw: American architecture, 272; expectations becoming an obstacle, 283, 284; HABS advisory committee, 221

Melmont, 349

Melrose: ballet tableau, 140; early tours of homes, 100, 137; film and TV exposure, 17; foxhunt, 17; George and Ethel Kelly, 70, 93–97; "Great Punkah," 16, 112, 115; John Callon, 413; Natchez National Historical Park, 395, 413; pilgrimage in 1937, 177; place as feature of Natchez experience, 52; pre-Civil War architecture, 30; silent movie, 100; silverware pattern, 343, 358; *Slippy McGee* (movie), 359; splitting pilgrimage profits with homeowners, 169; state garden clubs convention in 1931, 103; tours of, 161–62, 415–16; year-round tours, 27

Memorial Hall: pre-Civil War architecture, 30; reserved for 1937 pilgrimage, 178

Menzies, William C., 367–70, 372–75, 377

Mercer, Anna Ellis, 229

Merrill, Jennie, 60, 122, 123

Merrill family, 349

Metcalf, Mary Louise: historic preservation, 157, 159; organizing first pilgrimage, 143; promotional brochures, 322; splitting pilgrimage profits with homeowners, 173, 174, 175, 176; working with Town to select buildings for HABS, 265

Metcalfe, Louise Learned, 116

Metcalfe, Zuleika Lyons, 86, 355–56

Metcalfe family, 349

Mexican Railway, 324

Mexico: Byrnes working with, 322–27; diplomatic visit to US, 325–27; Natchez Trace Parkway, 420; Natchez Trace project after WWII, 402

Mézières, Athanase de, 289

middle-class buildings, photos of, 380, 381

Miller, Alexander, 264

Miller, Joseph Balfour (Balfour): Copacabana Club, NYC, 398; income insufficient for home maintenance, 169; Katherine Miller, 82–83; Russie Butts, 178; splitting pilgrimage profits with homeowners, 173

Miller, Katherine Grafton: Alma Cassell Kellogg, 97; antebellum era tourism, 417; awards given to, 398; Charles Peterson, 280; clashes over heritage tourism, 339; commodification of Natchez, 425; controlling HABS in Mississippi, 213; death of, 413; entertaining celebrities, 354; erroneous history of Connelly's Tavern, 278; Ethel Kelly, 93; formation of PGC, 179, 341; Frances Johnston, 380, 383; guidebook, 22, 104, 112; HABS collection in Library of Congress, 280; historic preservation, 157; historic preservation as purpose, 79–84; Hope Farm (Villa) documentation, 278–79; invention of Spring Pilgrimage, 64; King's Tavern, 413; leading PGC, 393, 398–99; marketing built patrimony, 134; marketing Natchez as it should have been, 154–55, 156, 160–61; marketing tour, 143–57; meeting with Chatelain, 226; *Natchez and the Pilgrimage*, 105–6, 111; Natchez as "The Real South," 410–12, 417; *Natchez' First Ladies: Katherine Grafton Miller and the Pilgrimage* (Hammer), 98; *Natchez of Long Ago and the Pilgrimage*, 340, 341, 344; "Natchez - Where the Old South Still Lives" lecture, 144; NGC, 68; NGC lawsuits, 352; personalism in approach toward historic preservation, 282; persuading owners to open homes for tours, 137; photos of Hope Farm (Villa), 397, 398; PGC members giving private home tours, 353; PGC pilgrimages, 342, 347–54; photos, 340, 387, 397, 398, 399; photos in guidebook, 22, 112; pilgrimage expansion, 391; planner during early pilgrimages, 136, 137–38; portrait of, 426; resigning from NGC, 179, 347; restaurant for pilgrimage tourists, 160; saving Natchez, 394–95; selling Natchez history, 198; *So Red the Rose* Natchez Trace commemorative copies, 314; southern belle

myth, 22; Spanish Colonial period, 377; splitting NGC pilgrimage profits with homeowners, 345–46; splitting pilgrimage profits with homeowners, 168–69, 171–79; Spring Pilgrimage as lifelong career, 285; state garden clubs convention in 1931, 99, 100–101; working with Town to select buildings for HABS, 265
Miller, Mary Warren (Mimi), 229–30, 413
Miller, Rebecca, 349
Miller, Ronald: Historic Natchez Foundation, 413; preservation, 393
Minor, Stephen (Don Estevan), 92
minstrel shows, 103
Mission 66, 394, 405
Mississippi, the Magnolia State, 275
Mississippi Advertising Commission, 346–47
Mississippi Department of Archives and History: The Elms, 49; Forks of the Road slave market, 60; Hope Farm (Villa), 279; statewide preservation program, 395
Mississippi Federation of Garden Clubs. *See* Garden Clubs of Mississippi
Mississippi Fire Insurance Building, 225
Mississippi Highways, 320
Mississippi River: esplanade bluff, 24, 25; Great Flood of 1927, 35; as important geographical feature of Natchez, 34–36; planning of Natchez, 27–28; view of, 427
Mississippi State Gazette, 129
Mississippi State Mental Hospital, 225, 226
Mississippi Tourism Bureau, creation of, 18–19, 200
"Missy" distinguished service award, 398
Mistletoe: pre-Civil War architecture, 30; *This Too Is Natchez*, 125
Mitchell, Margaret: *Gone with the Wind*, 18, 23, 147, 342, 417; *Gone with the Wind* (movie), 360, 361–62, 363–65, 367–68, 377
Mobil Oil Company, 358
modern women: aspirational values, 78–79; emerging ideal of, 68; Garden Club of America, 76; merging with southern lady ideal, 77, 79, 401; NGC combining with nineteenth-century ideal, 68; Ruth Beltzhoover, 399–402; Theodora Marshall, 97
Monmouth: entrance gates as inspiration for Tara, 376; history of, 36, 37; nonparticipation in 1937 pilgrimage, 177; pictured on map, 14; splitting pilgrimage profits with homeowners, 170; Stark Young, 356; state garden clubs convention in 1931, 103; Tara design, 368, 369
Monteigne: Eleanor Roosevelt's visit to Natchez, 355; fountains, 136; Natchez Spring Pilgrimage of Antebellum Homes, 3; PGC 1937 pilgrimage, 349; restaurant for pilgrimage tourists, 160; state garden clubs convention in 1931, 103; William Kendall, 98
Montgomery sisters, 83
Monticello, 78, 216
Montieth, Laura, 73
monuments: Confederate, 73–75, 76; Natchez Trace, 74, 75; reasons for preservation, 424; seen through political lens, 10
Moore, Bessie Bailey, 126
Moore, Edith Wyatt: Alma Cassell Kellogg, 97; Arlington, 256; Belmont, 367; clashes over heritage tourism, 339; Connelly's Tavern as bonus for pilgrimage, 195; control of pilgrimage, 341; controlling HABS in Mississippi, 213; entertaining celebrities, 355; erroneous history of Connelly's Tavern, 278; "expert" knowledge about history, 391; Frances Johnston, 380, 383; Gilreath Hill House, 164–67; HABS collection in Library of Congress, 280; HABS focus on Spanish colonial buildings, 419; historic preservation as purpose, 79–80, 89–90; leading NGC after WWII, 406–9; Linden, 375; marketing built patrimony of Natchez, 134; memorializing Natchez Trace, 290; Natchez history, 198, 227, 228–34, 235; Natchez narrative archived in Library of Congress, 275; Natchez narrative embedded into Natchez Trace Parkway, 330; Natchez

Trace Association, 302; Natchez Trace location, 310; Natchez Trace Parkway, 298, 308; Natchez Trace Parkway driving guide, 317; *Natchez Under-the-Hill*, 90, 394; NGC 1937 pilgrimage, 349; personalism and HABS, 264–66, 418; personalism and historic preservation, 282; saving Natchez, 394–95; splitting pilgrimage profits with homeowners, 171–78; *So Red the Rose* (movie), 356; Spanish Colonial period, 228, 229–30, 232–34, 260–64, 265, 282–83, 377; Spanish heritage house tours, 103; *This Too Is Natchez*, 125; 311-313 Market Street, 258–61, 263–64; Women's Army Corps, 407; WPA Writers' Project, 343
Moore, Frank Jefferson, 89
Moore, Katherine, 275
Moore House, Yorktown, VA, 217
Moorish Revival style, 31, 105
Moritz, Hartman, 140
Moss, Margaret, 5
Mound Plantation, 276, 277, 331
Mounger, Mary, 87
Mount Locust Inn and Plantation, 333, 335, 336, 408, 409
Mount Repose, 30, 349
Mount Vernon, 10
Mount Vernon Ladies' Association: Ann Pamela Cunningham, 202; restoration of Mount Vernon, 75
Mount Vernon Memorial Highway (George Washington Memorial Parkway), 300
Múgica, Francisco José, 324, 325, 326, 327
Munson, Ona, 363
Murphy, Stan, 404
Murray, Elizabeth Dunbar, 140
Murrel, Mr., 357
Murrell, Mrs., 304
Murrell gang, 317
"My Old Kentucky Home," 102
Myrtle Bank, 349

N

Naef, Robert W., 421
Nájera, Francisco Castillo, 325
Naltes, Jose del Rosario, 260–61
narrative: commercialization of, 105, 420; components of, 51–60; evolving, 63–134; as important to historic preservation, 47–48; kitsch in Natchez, 388–91; linking African American and white people, 126–34; as marketing ploy, 344–45; Natchez post-WWII update, 402; NGC corrupting HABS objective-based mission, 223; "Old South" myth/ideal, 47–48, 98–111; performing, 28–29, 48–62; personalism in built patrimony, 75; in popular culture, 354–60; putting into print, 111–26; scientific or scholarly, challenged by consumerism, 203; variations making Natchez a historyland, 51
Nashville Automobile Club, 307
Natchez, MS: aerial view (1860), 24; arriving in, 32–48; branding and marketing, 342–43, 344–45; concentration of large numbers of historic buildings, 144; cotton mill (1910), 69; current status, 29–32; downtown (1940), 138; founding in 1716 as a French settlement, 25; Great Depression, 378–88; heritage *vs.* history, 5–6; historyland *vs.* illusion of authenticity, 13–19; home ownership and control of pilgrimage, 168–79, 345–46; homes reflecting Victorian English character and ideals, 29–30; land pirates, 17–18; Main Street (1925), 71; map, 14; motto of, 6; never the real antebellum South, 365; physical isolation, 285; residential scene (1938), 72; Sam Anzalone's service station (1930), 71; Spanish Rule responsible for urban design, 25; street scene (1938), 72; systemic racism, 13; view of bluffs, 39
Natchez and the Pilgrimage (Newell and Compton), 103, 104, 105–16
Natchez Association for the Preservation of African American Culture, 413
Natchez Chamber of Commerce, 157
Natchez Coca-Cola Bottling Company, 98
Natchez Convention Center, 36

Natchez Dance Hall Holocaust, 60
Natchez Democrat: Byrnes's Mexico City experiences, 323; Byrnes's op-ed, 320; Connelly's Tavern, 177, 190; Edith Wyatt Moore writing historical sketches of pilgrimage homes, 89; Ellicott Hill restoration, 168; Natchez Trace Parkway, 322; PGC members giving private home tours, 353; splitting pilgrimage profits with homeowners, 174, 175; state garden clubs convention in 1931, 99, 101; study on society and race, 378; Thomas Grafton, 82
Natchez Department Store (Famous & Price Store), 399, 400
Natchez Deputy City Tax Assessor, 97
Natchez' First Ladies: Katherine Grafton Miller and the Pilgrimage (Hammer), 98
Natchez Garden Center, 174–75
Natchez Garden Club (NGC): Alma Cassell Kellogg, 48, 97; "Battle of the Hoop Skirts," 345–54; Connelly's Tavern, 5, 240, 350; control of pilgrimage, 341; controlling Mississippi tourism and Natchez economy, 415; controlling Natchez historic preservation, 415; creation of Natchez as cultural tourist attraction, 14; Edith Wyatt Moore, 89, 406–10; Ethel Kelly, 96; experiences and characteristics of members, 66–79; formation of PGC, 178–79; fundraising and loans for first tour, 137; HABS and WPA Writers' Project, 201–2; HABS drawings used for promotion, 240, 247–48; Harriet Shields Dixon, 91; headquarters in Connelly's Tavern, 191, 192; introducing cultural tourism in 1932, 29; Katherine Miller, 83; marketing built patrimony of Natchez, 134; modern women's aspirational values, 78–79; narrative controlling perception of history, 201; narrative corrupting HABS objective-based mission, 223; Natchez Trace expanding influence of Natchez, 23; NPS underestimating influence of, 282; "Old Natchez on the Mississippi," 359, 360; pilgrimage in 1937, 349; political and economic involvement, 76; presenters as feature of Natchez experience, 54; "The Preservation Society of Ellicott Hill," 409; profit from early pilgrimages, 135; Roane Byrnes, 80; splitting pilgrimage profits with homeowners, 168–79; Spring Pilgrimage, 6, 26, 63–64; state garden clubs convention in 1931, 99, 100; suing PGC, 351–54; Theodora Marshall, 97; Town and Overstreet soliciting work from members, 281; transformation of Natchez, 391; Vivien Leigh, 361; waning of, 393; working with PGC, 19–20
Natchez Grand Hotel, 36
Natchez Historical Association, 389
Natchez Hotel, 142, 170–71
Natchez Indian Monument, 47, 48
Natchez Indians, 106, 317
Natchez Institute, 97
Natchez Junior College, 17
Natchez Light Rifles, 73
Natchez Museum of African American History and Culture: filling in gaps between slavery and MLK Jr., 60; Natchez Association for the Preservation of African American Culture, 413; site of, 44
Natchez National Historical Park: creation of, 395, 413; George Kelly's letters, 95
Natchez of Long Ago and the Pilgrimage (Miller), 143–44, 340, 341, 344
Natchez on the Mississippi (Kane), 23, 394
Natchez "On-Top-of-the-Hill," 38–39
"Natchez Pickaninnies," 150, 151
Natchez Pilgrimage Tours, 26–27, 57
Natchez Police Department, 157
Natchez Preservation Commission, 37
"Natchez Rose Jar," 343, 358
Natchez Spring Pilgrimage of Antebellum Homes: attendee numbers in 1932, 141–42; cultural tourism, 6, 11, 12–13; D'Evereux, 2; early business concerns, 157–62; early years of, 135–57; economic benefits in early 1930s, 162; economic benefits in

1970s, 413; entertainment as objective, 25–26; feuding over control of, 345–54; guidebooks, 103–22; house tours as multifaceted performance, 55–57; house tours conducted during daytime, 59; increasing numbers of tourists, 17–19; Katherine Miller, 82, 83–84; Linden, 13; Natchez Trace Parkway as institutionalized manifestation of, 335; overview of, 3; pilgrimages by NGC and PGC in 1937, 349; resumed after WWII, 393, 395; splitting NGC pilgrimage profits with homeowners, 168–79, 345–46; state garden clubs convention in 1931, 99, 100, 101, 103; tableaux, 16–17, 26, 55, 57–59, 140, 141, 360, 411

Natchez: Symbol of the Old South (Oliver), 103–4, 113, 116–24, 367

Natchez Times, 407

Natchez Trace: bandits, 111; conjured narrative of, 23; early interest in highway, 291–93; establishment of, 288–90; Fort Rosalie as terminus, 4; Gilreath Hill house, 164; land pirates, 17–18; memorializing, 32–33, 290–91, 311; monument, 74, 75; *The Natchez Trace* (movie), 394; "The Natchez Trace" (Swain), 290; *The Outlaw Years: The History of the Land Pirates of the Natchez Trace* (Coates), 17–18, 23, 338, 356–57; "Path of the Natchez Trace in the Country of the Natchez Tribes" (Moore), 317; road travel to Natchez, 108; slaves walked along to MS and LA, 44; view of, 110

Natchez Trace, The (movie), 394

"Natchez Trace, The" (Swain), 290

Natchez Trace Association (NTA): Alabama and Tennessee divisions, 297, 306; Alma Kellogg, 167; dormant during WWII, 402, 403; formation in 1916, 292–93; Natchez Trace Military Highway Association, 295–97; physical isolation of Natchez, 285; rights-of-way, 313–14; Roane Byrnes, 302–8

Natchez Trace Day, 314

Natchez Trace Parkway: changing geography of states, 415; complaints about proposed route, 319–20; conceptual design of, 311, 312–13; cultural resources, 335, 336, 338; determining original location, 309–11; driving guide, 317; economic development project, 170; economic significance, 316; evolution of, 334; funding, 318, 319, 321; funding for survey, 99; groundbreaking ceremony, 325; HABS documents used for, 274, 276, 277; historic architecture of Natchez, 395; kitsch, 388; maps, 15, 329; memorializing rather than restoring, 32–33, 290–91, 311; Mission 66, 394, 405; motorist experience, 337, 338; Mound Plantation, 276, 277; Natchez as "historyland," 36; NGC influencing, 202; political maneuvering, 419–20; post-WWII building activity, 402–6; promotional brochures, 286, 315–16, 317, 322; recreational purpose, 327–38, 388; Roane Byrnes, 80, 88, 89, 284, 391; view of, 328; WPA funding, 19

Natchez Train Station, 1900, 108

Natchez Under-the-Hill (Moore), 90, 394

Natchez "Under-the-Hill": bandits, 111; Connelly's Tavern Tap Room, 194, 195; described, 3–4; Great Depression photos of Natchez, 385; Mississippi River, 34, 35; *Natchez Under-the-Hill* (Moore), 90, 394; *The Outlaw Years: The History of the Land Pirates of the Natchez Trace* (Coates), 357; riverboat cruises, 413; riverfront complex, 38, 39; *This Too Is Natchez*, 124

Natchez Visitor Center, 27

Natchez Women's Club, 78

Natchez-Vidalia Bridge, 35–36

National Geographic magazine, 406

National Geographic Society, 3–4

National Highway, 292

National Historic Preservation Act of 1966, 395

National Hotel Disease, 36

National Park Service (NPS): administration of HABS, 219, 281; development of historic sites, 330–38; historic American architecture, 417–20; historic preservation as professional field, 202; misjudging conditions in 1934, 281; Mission 66, 405; mission including historic sites and monuments, 204–23; mission redefined to include recreation, 338, 420; Natchez Trace, 23; Natchez Trace Association, 297; Natchez Trace Parkway, 32–33, 327, 328; Natchez Trace Parkway broadened mission, 338; Natchez Trace Parkway rights-of-way deeds, 322; Natchez Trace Parkway survey and study, 308; national historical educational program, 210; parkway focus on history and natural scenery, 309; parkways built and managed by, 300

National Recovery Act of 1933, 295

National Register of Historic Places: Brumfield School, 60; Foster's Mound, 131

Nauvoo, IL, 47

Neibert, Joseph, 43

New Deal: built patrimony of Natchez, 6; photographing poverty in Natchez, 342

New Orleans, LA: The Cabildo, 237, 239; riverfront industry, 39

New York Times: Natchez and its preservation, 17; Natchez as "The Real South," 411; Natchez Pilgrimages, 162, 411–12; pilgrimages used for marketing, 351

Newell, Georgie Wilson: "Ballet Tableau," 59; *Natchez and the Pilgrimage*, 103, 104, 105–16

NGC. *See* Natchez Garden Club (NGC)

Nichols, Frederick Doveton, 268, 280

Nichols, William, 46

Noah Webster's Connecticut Home, 9

Nolen, John: conceptual design of Natchez Trace Parkway, 311, 312; "institutional vernacular" architecture, 333

Norman, Earl: Natchez antebellum grandeur photos, 383–84; photo of D'Evereux, 112; photographer, 104; slides for Miller's presentation, 144–45

Norman, Mrs. Earl, 349

Norwood, Ellie Earl, 226, 227

NPS. *See* National Park Service (NPS)

NTA. *See* Natchez Trace Association (NTA)

Nutt, Haller, 31

O

Oak Alley Plantation, 47

Oakland: Blair Sabol as a guide, 411; participation in 1937 pilgrimage, 177

Oakridge School, 97

Oaks, The (Boyd House), 235

Ogden, Florence Sillers, 304

"Old Agency," Jackson, MS, 32

Old American Town Hall, Greenfield Village, 8

"Old Black Joe," 102

Old Fort Rosalie: Gift Shop, 389–90; reconstruction, 344

Old French Fort, Pascagoula, MS, 277–78

Old Gaol, Colonial Williamsburg, VA, 9, 284

Old Mississippi Capitol, 235

"Old Natchez on the Mississippi" (travel movie), 343, 359–60

Old Rock House, St. Louis, MO, 275

Old San Antonio Road, 289

"Old South" myth/ideal: American fascination with, 102, 342; antebellum style as tangible expression of, 124; brand personalities, 388; created by old houses, 21–23; evoking atmosphere of, 98; evolution of, 63–64; *Gone with the Wind*, 377, 394; marketing of, 91; Miller's presentation based on, 144–57; Natchez antebellum architecture reinforcing, 47–48; new post-WWII buildings, 394; nostalgic sentimentality, 415; Stanton Hall as PGC clubhouse, 350

Old South toiletries, 343, 358

Old Spanish Market, 79

"Old Spanish Trail Highway Association," 292, 293

Old Sturbridge Village, MA, 64

Oliver, Nola Nance: *Natchez: Symbol of the Old South*, 103–4, 113, 116–24, 367; *This Too Is Natchez*, 104, 124–26

Olmsted, Frederick Law, 25

O'Neill, John P.: abdicating authority in HABS decisions to AIA, 223; HABS direct manager, 220–21; HABS district reorganization proposal, 419; HABS program management, 267–74; naïve about managers, 283; salary structure for HABS employees, 224

Ouachita (minstrel show), 103

Outlaw Years: The History of the Land Pirates of the Natchez Trace, The (Coates), 17–18, 23, 338, 356–57

Outline of European Architecture, An (Pevsner), 272

Overstreet, Noah Webster: Eudora Welty, 358; HABS district chief, 224, 225–26; HABS providing work during the Depression, 281; Natchez as state's historyland, 227; resuming private practice, 269, 270, 422; securing work in Natchez, 236

P

Paramount Pictures: attending pilgrimages, 135; *So Red the Rose*, 356, 357

Parish House. *See* 311-313 Market Street ("Priest House," "Spanish Priest's House," Parish House, James Andrews House)

parkways: built and managed by NPS, 300; differing from highways, 298; purposes of, 300–301

Parsonage, The, 349

"pastness," described, 66

"Path of the Natchez Trace in the Country of the Natchez Tribes" (Moore), 317

Path to the Choctaw Nation, 288

"Patio of the Oaks, The," 159–60

"Paving the Trace" (Elliott), 335

Pearls, George, 60, 122

Penny Day, 117

performances: component of narrative, 55–60; integral with place, 55. *See also* tableaux

Perkins, John, 122

Perrault, Katherine, 228

Perry, Shaw & Hepburn, 216–18, 221

Perry, William Graves: American architecture, 272; expectations becoming an obstacle, 283, 284; HABS proposal, 214–15

personalism: Charles Peterson, 212, 222; HABS documentation, 264–66; HABS falling prey to, 418–19; historic preservation, 75–76, 78, 282; professional narrative, 213; *vs.* professionalism, 203–23, 282

Peterson, Charles E. (Pete): arguing for HABS funding increase, 267; drawing as record and inspiration, 245; establishing HABS, 395; HABS archive, 218, 219, 361, 377; HABS falling prey to personalism, 418–19; HABS work, 423; importance of humble cabins, 332; new management model for HABS, 274–83; NPS and historic preservation, 210–21, 222, 223; "Old Parish House" addition, 408–9; preservation of rustic buildings, 331; Spanish Colonial period, 277, 408; Verne Chatelain, 212, 218, 222–23

PGC. *See* Pilgrimage Garden Club (PGC)

Pharr Mounds, 288

Phelps, Dawson: evaluating HABS archive, 275; Moore's history reports from local tradition, 282; Natchez Trace historian, 290; Natchez Trace location, 310–11; Natchez Trace Parkway, 308, 329

Pilgrimage Ball, 140

Pilgrimage Garden Club (PGC): achieving greater heights, 393; Alma Cassell Kellogg, 97; "Battle of the Hoop Skirts," 345–54; establishment and working with NGC, 19–20; founding of, 178–79, 341; home ownership providing control over pilgrimage, 417; Katherine Miller, 80, 398–99; King's Tavern and Longwood, 413; members giving private home tours, 353; Natchez Pilgrimage Tours, 413; Natchez Spring Pilgrimage of Antebellum Homes, 6, 7, 26–27; NGC lawsuits, 351–54; planning separate pilgrimage, 196; pilgrimage in 1937, 349; presenters as feature of Natchez experience, 54; second pilgrimage, 341, 342; Stanton Hall, 44, 349, 350

place: consciousness of and influences on, 61–62; component of narrative, 51, 52–53; integral with performance, 5
Platt, Joseph B., 365–68, 377
Pleasant Hill, 349
politics: HABS falling prey to, 418; local politics and HABS program, 222, 223; Mary Shields, 98; Natchez Trace Association, 303–7; segregation, 305
polka dancing at the Confederate Ball, 154, 155
Poole, Trebby, 140, 360
post office building, Natchez, 44
Postlethwaite, Mary Elizabeth, 131
Postelthwaite family, 349
Postwar Highway Act, 404
Potter, Amy, 54
Potter, David M., 415
poverty: Natchez African Americans, 116–18; Natchez Great Depression photos, 384–85, 387, 388; Natchez photos, 342, 343; pervasive in Natchez in early 1900s, 70–72; racial injustice, 379; shared condition, 60
presenters, as component of narrative, 53–55
"Preservation Society of Ellicott Hill, The," 409–10
Price, Virginia, 419
"Priest House." *See* 311-313 Market Street ("Priest House," "Spanish Priest's House," Parish House, James Andrews House)
Prince Among Slaves (Alford), 131
Pritchartt, Bessie Rose Grafton: NGC, 68; splitting pilgrimage profits with homeowners, 176
Propinquity, Natchez, MS: NGC 1937 pilgrimage, 349; poor condition of, 11
Pueblo culture, Santa Fe, NM, 10, 13
punkah features: Linden, 235; Melrose "Great Punkah," 16, 112, 115
Pyle, Ernie: decline of Natchez villas, 12, 414; Elms Court, 12; Eola Hotel, 36; Katherine Miller, 84; "The War of the Hoop Skirts," 416

Q
Qualey, Carlton, 208, 211
Quincy, IL: John Wood House, 44, 45; Mississippi River town, 47
Quitman, Eliza, 36
Quitman, John A., 36

R
racial relations: caste-class system, 378; denial of tensions by garden club women, 396; Mammy's Cupboard, 390; in Natchez, 344, 345; Natchez heritage experience, 58–61; postwar discrimination, 393. *See also* African Americans
racism: Great Depression photos of Natchez, 384–85, 388; *Natchez and the Pilgrimage*, 107; Natchez Trace Parkway politics, 305, 306; "Old Natchez on the Mississippi," 359, 360; poverty, 116–18, 379; systematic racism in Natchez, 13
Rahahman, Abduhl Ibrahim (Ibrahima), 86–87, 127–32, 356
railways: Mexican Railway, 324; Natchez Train Station, 1900, 108; passenger travel, 292
Raleigh News and Observer, 12
Raleigh Tavern, 9
Rankin, John, 306
Ratcliff, Harriet, 68
Ratcliff, Mrs. Ed, 304
Ravenna (Ravennaside): Anna Metcalfe Fleming and "Garden of Dreams" tableau, 58; Fleming-Byrnes family budget, 172; "Old Natchez on the Mississippi," 360; Richard Koch, 159, 179; Roane Byrnes, 85, 86; Stark Young, 187; state garden clubs convention in 1931, 103; Zuleika Lyons Metcalfe, 356
Reagan, Ronald, 395, 413
recreation: Natchez Trace Parkway including, 338; NPS mission to include, 420
Reed, Thomas J., 280
Register, Clarksdale, MS, 329
Register family, 349
restaurants: Carriage House, 354, 398, 412; Green Leaves, 416; Malt Shop,

421–22; Mammy's Cupboard, 22, 23, 344, 389, 390, 420; Pilgrimage attendees, 142, 157, 159–60; White's Restaurant, 142
Reynolds, Elizabeth, 279
Rhodes College (Southwestern Presbyterian University), 88
Rhythm Club Fire, 60
Richmond: Frances Johnston, 383; house tours, 103, 136; PGC 1937 pilgrimage, 349; Stark Young, 356; state garden club convention, 136; Theodora Marshall, 97
rights-of-way for parkways: difficulties after WWII, 403, 404–5; funding for, 327; negative reactions to, 301–2; NPS requirement, 302; states to provide, 313–14, 317–18, 319, 321–22
Robards, Rachel Donelson, 108, 109
Robber Bridegroom, The (Welty), 18, 23, 338, 358
Robbins, Tom, 404
Robert E. Lee statue, 424
Robinson, Blanche, 360
Robinson, Kathie, 360
Robinson, Mable, 87
Robinson, Mike, 55
Rockefeller, John D., Jr., 9, 216
Rocky Mountain Road, 319
Roosevelt, Eleanor: modern southern woman ideal, 401; visiting Natchez, 20, 343, 354–55
Roosevelt, Franklin: dismantling CWA, 266; historic sites and monuments transferred to NPS, 204, 205; Natchez Trace Parkway, 318, 406, 420; New Deal, 200
Rosalie: attic plan and roof details, 240; Federal style, 44; first-floor and plot plans, 238; floor plan as example for Tara, 375; HABS historical research, 231–32; measurement and documentation of, 18; Natchez Trace Parkway driving guide, 317; north elevation, 236; "Old Natchez on the Mississippi," 360; participation in 1937 pilgrimage, 177; photo of, 112, 113; section drawing, 239; Stark Young, 356; state garden clubs convention in 1931, 103; year-round tours, 27
Rose, Elodie, 82
Rose, Thomas: Katherine Miller, 82; pre-Civil War architect, 30; Stanton Hall, 43
Rose Hill Missionary Baptist Church, 59
Routhland, 125
Rowland, Dunbar, 296–97
Rural Home, GA, 361, 362
Ruskin, John, 29–30

S

Sabol, Blair, 411–12
Sachs, David, 422
San Francisco (plantation home), 47
Sanders, Robert J., 167–68
Santa Barbara, CA, 13
Santa Fe, NM, 10, 13
Santacruz, Carlos, 326
Saragossa: HABS historical research, 229–30, 231; Spanish heritage house tours, 103, 265
Sargent, Winthrop, 234
Savage, William, 259, 260, 264
Scott, Anne Firor: description of southern lady, 67, 68–69; southern belle/lady ideal, 364; women's history influenced by historic preservation, 21
Scott, Randolph, 356, 357
Second Presbyterian Church, 41
"Secret of the Wild Cherry Tree, The" (Byrnes), 87
segregation: housing for servants of attendees, 142; Natchez Trace Parkway politics, 305
Sellers, Horace W., 215
Selma Plantation, 30, 408, 409
Selznick, David O., 360, 361, 363, 364–65, 368
Sequoia National Park, 211
"Serenade, The" (Byrnes), 87
Shahn, Ben: Great Depression in Natchez, 383, 384–88; photos of Natchez, 7, 72; poverty in Natchez, 342, 343
Shamrock, Vicksburg, MS: HABS documentation, 240, 241; view of, 46
Shields, Ann, 138
Shields, Dunbar, 98

Shields, Mary Louise Kendall Goodrich: early house tours, 137; historic preservation as purpose, 79–80, 98; photo with daughters, 138
Shields family, 349
Shields Tavern, Colonial Williamsburg, VA, 9
Shils, Edward: heritage tourism, 20; monument preservation, 424; ownership as an expression of power, 415
Shyrock, Gideon, 46, 47
"Silent Sam" monument, 424
Silver, Jack W., 232
Simons, Albert: American architecture, 272; expectations becoming an obstacle, 283, 284; HABS advisory committee, 221
Sims, Alice, 93, 94
Skansen open-air museum, Sweden, 7, 9
"Skyfighter, The," 407
Skyline Drive, 205, 300
Slave Narrative Collection, 19
"Slave Trail," 290
slavery: Alice Sims and Jane Johnson, 93, 94, 360; creating Natchez villas, 395; Edith Wyatt Moore portraying slaves as happy, 90; Forks of the Road slave market, 60, 290; house tour narratives, 56; location of slave market, 44; Natchez heritage, 423; Slave Narrative Collection, 19; slave traders, 44, 289–90; slaves marched along Natchez Trace, 289–90; story of Ibrahima, 86–87, 127–32, 356
Slippy McGee (movie), 359
Sloan, Samuel, 31
Smith, Bessie, 33, 34
Smith, Ernest, 347, 348
Smith, Frazier, 419
Smith, J. Edwards, 41
Smith, John, 404
Smith, Ned, 323
Smith family, 349
Smithsonian Institution (US National Museum), 266
Snider, James B. (Billy), 346–47, 348, 349
So Red the Rose (movie), 356, 357
So Red the Rose (Young): antebellum era, 417; anti-heroes, 18; commercialization of Natchez narrative, 420; Eliza Quitman, 36; marketing of Connelly's Tavern, 187–89, 194; Natchez Trace commemorative copies, 314; Natchez Trace Parkway, 338; romantic Natchez narrative, 23; southern belle/lady ideal, 147; writing about Roane Byrnes's stories, 355–56
social status of participants: Natchez Spring Pilgrimage of Antebellum Homes, 26–27; presenters as feature of Natchez experience, 54
Society for the Colonization of Free People of Color of America, 128–29
Society for the Preservation of New England Antiquities, 202, 203
Society of Architectural Historians: historic preservation as professional field, 203; John Wood House, Quincy, IL, 44; *Journal of the Society of Architectural Historians*, 408; lack of oversight of HABS by architectural historians, 418
Sori (King of Futa Jalon), 87
South Atlantic Quarterly, 130
southern belle/lady ideal: Margaret Mitchell not an example of, 364; merging with modern woman ideal, 77, 79, 401; Miller presenting, 147–50, 155–57; myth of, 22
"Southern Colonial" period, 64
southern diaspora and returning to the South, 416
Southern Galaxy, 130
Southern Heritage on Display (Hoelscher), 48–50
Southwestern Presbyterian University (Rhodes College), 88
Spanish Colonial period: Airlie, 118; Charles Peterson, 277, 408; Connelly's Tavern, 350; Cottage Gardens, 121, 122; Edith Moore, 228, 229–30, 232–34, 260–64, 265, 282–83, 377; Gilreath Hill house, 163, 164; house tours, 103; Natchez narrative celebrating, 377; NGC fascination with, 282
"Spanish Priest's House." *See* 311-313 Market Street ("Priest House," "Spanish

Priest's House," Parish House, James Andrews House)
Spratling, William, 225
Spring Pilgrimage, original objective for, 64
Springfield, 108, 109
St. Louis, MO: Jefferson National Expansion Memorial, 221, 423; Old Rock House, 275; riverfront industry, 39
St. Louis Post Dispatch, 119
St. Mary Basilica: Confederate monument, 74; Gothic revival style, 112; "minor basilica" status, 40–41; pre-Civil War architecture, 30
St. Mary's Chapel, 229, 230
Stallone, Hugo, 126
Standard Life Building, 225
Stanton, Beatrice, 331
Stanton, Elizabeth Brandon: NGC lawsuit, 352; Windy Hill Manor, 331–32, 383
Stanton, Frederick, 43
Stanton, Maude, 331
Stanton, Robert, 331
Stanton, William, 241
Stanton College for Young Ladies, Natchez, MS, 44, 86
Stanton Hall: building cost, 3; celebrities entertained at, 399; Greek Revival style, 124; Katherine Miller, 80, 81; Mexican diplomatic visit, 325; Natchez Spring Pilgrimage of Antebellum Homes, 3; "Old South" narrative, 350; PGC clubhouse, 349, 350, 354; PGC expansion of, 398; place as feature of Natchez experience, 52; pre-Civil War architecture, 30; purchase and renovation, 341, 349, 350, 391; southern belle/lady ideal, 149; state garden clubs convention in 1931, 103; style and history of, 43–44; Thomas Rose, 82; year-round tours, 27
Starnes, Ellen, 157
State Garden Club of Mississippi. *See* Garden Clubs of Mississippi
Stennis, John, 403, 404, 405
Stephens, Hubert, 294, 298
Stevens, Jason R., 226
Stewart, Jennie Dixon, 130

Stietenroth, William, 168, 179, 192, 193
Stone, Alfred, 70
Stratford Hall, 216
suburban setting: Natchez as model for, 425; Natchez residences built in, 29, 30, 31, 424
Sullavan, Margaret, 356, 357
Summerset plantation, 317
Sunny Side, 103
Surget, Charlotte, 347
Sutton, Horace, 395–96
Swain, John: Natchez Trace location, 310; "The Natchez Trace," 290
"Swanee River," 102
Sweet Auburn, 125, 126
Sydnor, Charles S., 130

T

tableaux: allegorical, 58; ballet tableaux, 59, 140, 360; evening performances, 59; "Garden of Dreams" tableau, 58; "The Hunt" tableau, 140, 141, 360; Natchez Spring Pilgrimage, 16–17, 26; pilgrimage activity, 140; type of performance, 55, 57–59; wild after-parties, 411
Tallmedge, Thomas E., 221
tangible heritage: combining with intangible heritage, 28–29; personalism in built patrimony, 75
Tara: design for *Gone with the Wind*, 361–62, 364–72, 374–77
Taylor, Elizabeth, 20
Taylor, Marjorie, 360
Temple B'nai Israel: American Beaux Arts style, 40, 41; George Kelly, 96
"Temple of the Sun, The," 87
Tennessee, Natchez Trace associations, 298
Texada: HABS historical research, 229, 231; site of, 44
Texada Tavern, 125–26
This Too Is Natchez (Oliver), 104, 124–26
Thistle, Loxley, 367
Thompson, Jonathan, 257
311-313 Market Street ("Priest House," "Spanish Priest's House," Parish House, James Andrews House): addition for, 408, 409; current location, 259; floor

and site plans, 262; Frances Johnston, 383; HABS documentation, 258–64; incorrectly named, 419; preservation efforts, 80; relocation of, 407–8; Roane Byrnes, 80; south and north elevations, 261; west elevation, 263
"Thru the Ages" (Byrnes), 87
Time magazine, 353
Times-Picayune, New Orleans, LA: "cease-and-desist" order for PGC pilgrimage, 352–53; marketing for Natchez Pilgrimage, 160–61, 162
Tolson, Hillary A., 312, 404
Tomilson, William, 358
Toomer, Ashton, 319
tourism: heritage helping economy of Natchez, 395, 396; "Let's pretend" tourism, 13, 31–32, 102, 193, 265, 377, 415, 426; success as justification for means, 425; types of tourism in Natchez, 413–14
tourists: antebellum era, 417; house tour narratives suited to demographics, 56; increasing numbers of, 17–19. *See also* hotels and housing, Natchez; restaurants
Towers, The, 125
Town, A. Hays: erroneous history of Connelly's Tavern, 278; Eudora Welty, 358; Gilreath Hill House, 179–80, 181–83, 184; HABS and personalism, 264, 265–66, 418, 419; HABS collection in Library of Congress, 280; HABS district chief, 224–28, 230–31, 234–36, 238–64, 268–70; HABS providing work during the Depression, 281; legend created about his work in HABS, 422–23; "neotraditionalist" and "neo-Creole" architect, 395, 422; new building design preferred over old building restoration, 236
Trail of Tears, 290
Traveltalks (travel movies), 17
Treaty of Doak's Stand, 1820, 32
Treaty of San Lorenzo (Treaty of Madrid), 165
"Tree of Architecture, The," 270–71
Trinity Episcopal Church: Magnolia Hall (Henderson-Britton House), 410; pre-Civil War architecture, 30; splitting pilgrimage profits with homeowners, 174; style of, 40
Truett, Randle: Natchez Trace location, 310; Natchez Trace Parkway, 312, 420
Tulane University, 225
Tupelo battlefields, 395
Turner, Edward, 126
Tuscumbia Reporter, 306
Twin Oaks, 124, 126

U

UDC (United Daughters of the Confederacy), 73, 74
Ullman, Olivia, 68
Uncle Remus tales (Harris), 102
Uncle Wash, 117
"Under Many Flags" theme of first pilgrimage, 140
United Confederate Veterans, 73
United Daughters of the Confederacy (UDC), 73, 74
Universal Studios, 135
University of Louisiana, 225
University of Mississippi: Alma Carpenter, 48; Charles Byrnes, 88
University of Virginia, 77, 78
US Corps of Engineers, 35
US Farm Security Administration, 342, 343
US Highway 61: "Crossroads" sign, 33, 34; improvement of, 394; significance of, 33–34
US National Commission of UNESCO, 398
US National Museum (Smithsonian Institution), 266
US Postal Service, 289

V

van Altena, Edward, 145
Van Court House: east and west elevations, 252; first-floor plan, 248–49; HABS documentation, 248–53; interior details, 253; north elevation and exterior details, 249; second-floor plan, attic plan, and interior details, 251; south elevation, building section, and stair railing details, 250

Vasquez, Juan, 324
Venice Charter, 423
"vernacular" architecture: described, 301, 332–33, 335; Johnston's photographs, 380, 381
Vicksburg, MS, pilgrimage, 176
Vicksburg National Battlefield, 395
Vidal, Don Jose, 121, 122
Vidal, Donna, 122
Vidalia, LA, 35–36
Vidor, King, 356
Vint, Thomas C.: abdicating authority in HABS decisions to AIA, 223; extending HABS, 266; HABS chief administrator, 220, 221, 222; lack of oversight of HABS by architectural historians, 418–19; naïve about managers, 283; Natchez Trace location, 310, 311, 312; Natchez Trace Parkway funding, 319; Natchez Trace Parkway problems, 330; new management model for HABS, 274; purpose of parkways, 300; redefining NPS mission to include recreation, 338, 420; relocation of parkway headquarters, 328
Visiting Our Past: America's Historylands, 3–4
volunteer work, by Natchez women, 72

W

Wakefield: Albright and Ickes touring, 205; restoration of, 216
Waldrop, Jefferson Preston: capability as manager, 283; HABS district chief, 269–70, 272–73, 280, 422
Walker, Josephine Davis, 387
Walton, Jim: Natchez Trace Parkway, 420; reporting on Natchez Trace, 293–98
War Department historic sites and monuments, 204, 206
War of 1812: Battle of New Orleans, 289, 293, 297; Daughters of the War of 1812, 291, 293
Ware, Margaret, 399
Warner, W. Lloyd, 21
Warren, Robert Penn, 11
Washington, George: Cornwallis surrender at Yorktown, 217; Mount Vernon, 10; Treaty of San Lorenzo (Treaty of Madrid), 165
Washington Post: HABS project, 220; Peterson featured as leader of HABS, 423
Waterman, Thomas Tileston: assessing HABS documentation, 280; Connelly's Tavern, 190; Frances Johnston, 383; HABS assistant director, 268; Moore's history reports as local tradition, 282; rejecting Waldrop's work, 273
Waverly, 235
Webster Progress, 293
Weeks, Levi: Auburn, 118, 229; Concord, 92; pre–Civil War architect, 30
Weigle, Edith, 19
Weir, Harry E., 14
Welty, Eudora: *The Robber Bridegroom*, 18, 23, 338; *The Wide Net*, 358
West, Charles, 325, 327
Wheeler, Lyle R., 367–77
Wheeler family, 410
"Where the South Still Lives: Displaying Heritage in Natchez, Mississippi" (Hoelscher), 126–27
White, Gregory, 260
White, Hugh: cost of rights-of-way, 314; Natchez Trace Parkway groundbreaking, 287, 325; Natchez Trace Parkway politics, 306; supporting Natchez Trace Parkway, 318
White, Jane Surget, 256, 257
White, John, 58
White, John Hampton, 256, 257
White, Stanford, 256
White Horse Tavern, 317
White Pine Bureau, 215–16
White Pine Manufacturers of Idaho, 216
White's Restaurant, 142
Whittington, Homer, 126
Whittington, William M., 306
Wide Net, The (Welty), 358
Wilderness Road: Natchez Trace Association, 296; Pan-American parkway, 288
Wilkinson, James, 310
William H. Braden Elementary School, 421

William Johnson Home, 395, 413
Williams, Brown, 325
Wills, Frank, 243
Wilson, Edith Bolling, 143
Wilson, Richard, 159
Winchester, Josiah, 409
Windy Hill Manor: Frances Johnston, 382, 383; Stanton family, 331, 332; Stark Young, 356
Winston, E. T., 297, 298, 303
Winterthur, restoration of, 190
Wirth, Conrad, 405
women: described as southern lady, 67, 68–69; emerging modern woman ideal, 68; history of, influenced by historic preservation, 21; Katherine Miller on feminism, 412; volunteer work to change their fortunes, 72. *See also* modern women; southern belle/lady ideal
Women's Army Corps, 407
Wood, John, 44
Works Progress Administration (WPA): construction industry improvement, 269; Fort Marion National Monument, 209; Harry Hopkins, 208; Natchez Trace Parkway, 19; Natchez-Vidalia Bridge, 35; providing HABS funding, 267; Writers' Project and Historic American Buildings Survey (HABS), 19. *See also* WPA Writers' Project
World War II (WWII): change in Natchez, 344, 345; cultural tourism, 20; ending Pan-American parkway plan, 402; NGC and PGC both holding pilgrimages, 354; pilgrimages, 391
WPA. *See* Works Progress Administration (WPA)
WPA Writers' Project: Edith Wyatt Moore, 89–90, 164, 343; intimidating formerly enslaved persons, 90; *Mississippi, the Magnolia State*, 275; NGC influencing, 201–2; selecting historic buildings for HABS survey, 226, 227, 228; Slave Narrative Collection, 19
Wright Brothers' Bicycle Shop, Greenfield Village, 9
WWII. *See* World War II (WWII)

Y

Yancey, William L., 425
"Ye Olde Booke Shoppe," 97
Yetman, Norman, 90
Yorktown Colonial National Monument, 205
Young, Stark: Connelly's Tavern dedication, 314; marketing of Connelly's Tavern, 187–89, 194; *So Red the Rose* (movie), 356, 357; writing about Roane Byrnes's stories, 355–56. *See also So Red the Rose* (Young)

Z

Zimmer, Edward S.: "institutional vernacular" architecture, 333; Natchez Trace Parkway landscape design, 311, 312; nonhistoric nature of Natchez Trace Parkway, 330
Zion Chapel African Methodist Episcopal (A.M.E.) Church: African American performances, 59, 117, 126–27; Greek Revival Doric tetrastyle, 41; "Heaven Bound" folk drama, 17; profit from early pilgrimages, 135

ABOUT THE AUTHOR

Author photo by Hannah King

Paul Hardin Kapp is a professional and academic historic preservationist. He is associate professor of architecture at the School of Architecture and associate director of the Collaborative for Cultural Heritage and Policy, University of Illinois at Urbana-Champaign. He is author of *The Architecture of William Nichols: Building the Antebellum South in North Carolina, Alabama, and Mississippi*, published by University Press of Mississippi, and coeditor of *SynergiCity: Reinventing the Postindustrial City*. He is a National Endowment for the Humanities Fellow, a Senior Fulbright Scholar, a James Marston Fitch Mid-Career Fellow, and a Franklin Fellow, US Department of State.